The Beacon Book of
Quotations by Women

The Beacon Book of

QUOTATIONS by WOMEN

compiled by

Rosalie Maggio

Beacon Press · Boston

Beacon Press
25 Beacon Street
Boston, Massachusetts 02108-2892

Beacon Press books are published under the auspices of
the Unitarian Universalist Association of Congregations.

99 98 97 96 95 94   8 7 6 5 4 3 2

Text design by Gwen Frankfeldt

Typeset by Technologies 'N Typography

Permission to reprint was granted for poetry of five or
more lines: Excerpt from "Restricted," copyright ©
1974 by Eve Merriam, was reprinted by permission of
Marian Reiner for the author. The excerpt from "Three
Small Songs for the Muse," copyright © 1991 by
Kathleen Norris, was reprinted by permission of the
author. Excerpt from "Slow Down Rounding Curve,"
copyright © 1935 by Margaret Fishback, reprinted by
permission of Anthony F. Antolini. Excerpts from
"Lineage," copyright © 1942 by Margaret Walker,
reprinted by permission of the author.

Library of Congress Cataloging-in-Publication Data

The Beacon book of quotations by women / compiled
by Rosalie Maggio.
      p. cm.
   Includes indexes.
   ISBN 0-8070-6764-4 (cloth)
   ISBN 0-8070-6765-2 (paper)
      1. Quotations, English. 2. Women—Quotations.
I. Maggio, Rosalie. II. Title: Book of quotations by
women.
   PN6081.5.B43 1992
   082'.082—dc20   92-4697
                                            CIP

To DAVID

Liz, Katie, Matt

Special thanks to Liz Koskenmaki for her careful and tireless research; to Bonnie Z. Goldsmith, Mary Kaye Medinger, Michelle Edwards, Matt Koskenmaki, Sanford Berman, Diane Burns, Esther Lilley, Joyce Parr, Anne E. Patrick, Alexandra Robbin, and Heidi Eschenbacher for their help; to Susan Meigs for her meticulous copyediting; and to Susan Worst of Beacon Press, whose good-naturedness, support, and contributions have been invaluable.

Contents

Note to the Reader xi

Quotations 1

Name Index 365

Subject Index 387

Note to the Reader

User's guide

You can enter this collection of ideas, feelings, and brilliantly worked words through three doors. If you are looking for a quotation by a specific woman, use the biographical index in the back of the book. If you need a quotation on a specific subject, the narrow, alphabetically arranged topic headings and numerous cross-references will help you find what you need. You can also work from the subject index. If you are the third seeker, the browser, you need no further help. However, with you in mind, quotations have been arranged under topic headings to provide maximum reading enjoyment.

Quotations were selected for their memorability, their original use of language, their brevity, their ability to shatter conventional patterns of speech or thought, and their potential usefulness to readers needing quotations for speaking and writing. Although some quotations are included because they belong to the canon of the familiar, others bring you unfamiliar words by familiar women (and vice versa), while thousands of others appear for the first time in a collection of quotations.

The date that follows a book title is generally the date of first publication; in some cases this occurred years or even centuries after the quoted words were said or written. In many cases, more recent editions of the work are available. For consistency, spellings have been Americanized.

Sexist quotations

Given the grammatical "conventions" and social mores of their times, many women quoted here use language that is today considered sexist and inaccurate (for example, the pseudogeneric "he," "man," and "mankind"). Just as you may see "thee" or "thou" or "wouldst" in some of the quotations, so too you will see language that is archaic by today's inclusive standards.

Quotations with sexist language are reproduced here as they were originally written—out of respect for the writers, out of a feeling for reality that says "this is what was," and from a belief that one does not rewrite history or literature. Reinterpret, add to, discover lost pieces of, evaluate with new eyes—yes. Rewrite—no. However, I strongly urge anyone who uses quotations containing sexist language to adapt them so as not to perpetuate the sexism. This can be done in a number of ways.

- Put only part of the quotation in quotation marks, rewriting the rest. Agnes Repplier: "The vanity of man revolts from the serene indifference of the cat." Suggested adaptation: Agnes Repplier tells us that our vanity "revolts from the serene indifference of the cat." Jane Austen: "One man's way may be as good as another's, but we all like our own best." Suggested adaptation: When Jane Austen says that one person's way may be as good as another's she adds, "but we all like our own best."

- Use brackets or ellipsis dots to replace or omit sexist material. Vita Sackville-West: "Ambition, old as mankind, the immemorial weakness of the strong." Suggested adaptation: "Ambition, old as [creation], the immemorial weakness of the strong." Or: "Ambition . . . the immemorial weakness of the strong."

- In certain cases, you may want to use "[sic]" to indicate that the material was sexist in the original and to draw your audience's attention to the inaccuracy. Helen Rowland: "The dollar sign is the only sign in which the modern man appears to have any real faith." Suggested adaptation: "The dollar sign is the only sign in which the modern man [sic] appears to have any real faith."

• When a quotation is tightly woven with sexist words, credit the writer for the idea, omitting the quotation marks and rephrasing the words. Mary Renault: "In all men is evil sleeping; the good man is he who will not awaken it, in himself or in other men." Suggested adaptation: Mary Renault says that evil sleeps in all of us. The good among us will not awaken it, in ourselves or in others.

Your help wanted

Every effort has been made to reproduce quotations and references accurately and to locate the first appearance of a quotation whenever possible. Many quotable writers and speakers were not included in this volume, but, as Margaret Mitchell wrote, "tomorrow is another day." If you have corrections, additions, or suggestions for subsequent editions, I would appreciate hearing from you: Rosalie Maggio, Beacon Press, 25 Beacon Street, Boston, MA 02108-2892.

A

ABSENCE

Where you used to be, there is a hole in the world, which I find myself constantly walking around in the daytime, and falling into at night. I miss you like hell.

EDNA ST. VINCENT MILLAY, *Letters* (1952)

It takes time for the absent to assume their true shape in our thoughts.

COLETTE, *Sido* (1929)

Fond as we are of our loved ones, there comes at times during their absence an unexplained peace.

ANNE SHAW, *But Such Is Life* (1931)

The longest absence is less perilous to love than the terrible trials of incessant proximity.

OUIDA, *Wisdom, Wit and Pathos* (1884)

The heart may think it knows better: the senses know that absence blots people out. We have really no absent friends.

ELIZABETH BOWEN, *The Death of the Heart* (1938)

All along, one of my major complaints was his absence from home, and even worse, his absence when he *was* home.

SONIA JOHNSON, *From Housewife to Heretic* (1981)

See also Reunions.

ABSOLUTES

In this unbelievable universe in which we live there are no absolutes. Even parallel lines, reaching into infinity, meet somewhere yonder.

PEARL BUCK, *A Bridge for Passing* (1962)

I was seized again with a desperate longing for the absolute.

CARYL CHURCHILL, *Top Girls* (1984)

See also Dogma.

ACCEPTANCE

I accept the universe!

MARGARET FULLER, to Thomas Carlyle (1846)

Learning to live with what you're born with / is the process, / the involvement, / the making of a life.

DIANE WAKOSKI, "I Have Had to Learn to Live with My Face," *The Motorcycle Betrayal Poems* (1971)

If Fate should say, "Thy course is run," / It would not make me sad; / All that I wished to do is done, / All that I would have, had.

LAURENCE HOPE, "The Court of Pomegranates," *Stars of the Desert* (1903)

I love my past. I love my present. I'm not ashamed of what I've had, and I'm not sad because I have it no longer.

COLETTE, *The Last of Cheri* (1926)

There are people who live lives little different than the beasts, and I don't mean that badly. I mean that they accept whatever happens day to day without struggle or question or regret. To them things just are, like the earth and sky and seasons.

CELESTE DE BLASIS, *Wild Swan* (1984)

Everything in life that we really accept undergoes a change.

KATHERINE MANSFIELD (1920), *Journal of Katherine Mansfield* (1927)

See also Resignation.

ACCIDENTS

Don't go into Mr. McGregor's garden: your Father had an accident there; he was put in a pie by Mrs. McGregor.

BEATRIX POTTER, *The Tale of Peter Rabbit* (1901)

ACCOMPLISHMENT

Out of the strain of the Doing, / Into the peace of the Done.

JULIA LOUISE WOODRUFF, "Harvest Home," *Sunday at Home* (1910)

Accomplishments have no color.

LEONTYNE PRICE, in Brian Lanker, *I Dream a World* (1989)

I don't like the sound of all those lists he's making—it's like taking too many notes at school; you feel you've achieved something when you haven't.

DODIE SMITH, *I Capture the Castle* (1948)

See also Success.

ACTING

Acting is a form of confession.

TALLULAH BANKHEAD, *Tallulah* (1952)

Acting is standing up naked and turning around very slowly.

ROSALIND RUSSELL, *Life Is a Banquet* (1977)

I detest acting because it is sheer drudgery.

TALLULAH BANKHEAD, *Tallulah* (1952)

Without wonder and insight, acting is just a trade. With it, it becomes creation.

BETTE DAVIS, *The Lonely Life* (1962)

Fundamentally I feel that there is as much difference between the stage and the films as between a piano and a violin. Normally you can't become a virtuoso in both.

ETHEL BARRYMORE, in *New York Post* (1956)

The question actors most often get asked is how they can bear saying the same things over and over again night after night, but God knows the answer to *that* is, don't we all *anyway;* might as well get paid for it.

ELAINE DUNDY, *The Dud Avocado* (1958)

See also Actors, Films, Performance, Theater.

ACTIONS

What you will do matters. All you need is to do it.

JUDY GRAHN, *Another Mother Tongue: Gay Words, Gay Worlds* (1984)

If you could make a pudding wi' thinking o' the batter, it 'ud be easy getting dinner.

GEORGE ELIOT, *Adam Bede* (1859)

One never notices what has been done; one can only see what remains to be done.

MARIE CURIE, letter to her brother (1894)

We should do only those righteous actions which we cannot stop ourselves from doing.

SIMONE WEIL, *Gravity and Grace* (1947)

No good deed goes unpunished.

CLARE BOOTHE LUCE, in H. Faber, *The Book of Laws* (1980)

You ask me why I do not write something. . . . I think one's feelings waste themselves in words, they ought all to be distilled into actions and into actions which bring results.

FLORENCE NIGHTINGALE, in Cecil Woodham-Smith, *Florence Nightingale* (1951)

We have too many high sounding words, and too few actions that correspond with them.

ABIGAIL ADAMS, letter to John Adams (1774)

It is in vain to say human beings ought to be satisfied with tranquillity: they must have action; and they will make it if they cannot find it.

CHARLOTTE BRONTË, *Jane Eyre* (1847)

I've arrived at this outermost edge of my life by my own actions. Where I am is thoroughly unacceptable. Therefore, I must stop doing what I've been doing.

ALICE KOLLER, *An Unknown Woman* (1982)

I have long since come to believe that people never mean half of what they say, and that it is best to disregard their talk and judge only their actions.

DOROTHY DAY, *The Long Loneliness* (1952)

See also Behavior, Deeds.

ACTORS

An actor can remember his briefest notice well into senescence and long after he has forgotten his phone number and where he lives.

JEAN KERR, *Please Don't Eat the Daisies* (1957)

Every actor has a natural animosity toward every other actor, present or absent, living or dead.

LOUISE BROOKS, *Lulu in Hollywood* (1982)

I want only dead actors. That way there'll be no jealousy.

SIMONE SIGNORET, *Adieu, Volodya* (1986)

A painter paints, a musician plays, a writer writes—but a movie actor waits.

MARY ASTOR, *A Life on Film* (1967)

I have yet to see one completely unspoiled star, except for the animals—like Lassie.

EDITH HEAD, in *Saturday Evening Post* (1963)

We were worse name-droppers than people who dropped our names. Another actor was a "best friend," "know him very well," "died in my arms."

MARY ASTOR, *A Life on Film* (1967)

I do not regret one professional enemy I have made. Any actor who doesn't dare to make an enemy should get out of the business.

BETTE DAVIS, *The Lonely Life* (1962)

We're harmless megalomaniacs, fanatic in our devotion to a profession which rarely rewards us with a livelihood. Since we court public display we're the foes of privacy. The glass house is our favorite residence.

TALLULAH BANKHEAD, *Tallulah* (1952)

Without discipline and detachment, an actor is an emotional slob, spilling his insides out. This abandonment is having an unfortunate vogue. It is tasteless, formless, absurd. Without containment there is no art. All this vomiting and wheezing and bursting at the seams is no more great acting than the convulsions of raving maniacs.

BETTE DAVIS, *The Lonely Life* (1962)

For an actress to be a success she must have the face of Venus, the brains of Minerva, the grace of Terpsichore, the memory of Macaulay, the figure of Juno, and the hide of a rhinoceros.

ETHEL BARRYMORE, in George Jean Nathan, *The Theater in the Fifties* (1953)

Five stages in the life of an actor. . . . 1. Who's Mary Astor? 2. Get me Mary Astor. 3. Get me a Mary Astor type. 4. Get me a young Mary Astor. 5. Who's Mary Astor?

MARY ASTOR, *A Life on Film* (1967)

In those days [1940s], young stars, male and female, were all virgins until married, and if divorced, they returned magically to that condition.

SHELLEY WINTERS, *Shelley* (1980)

See also Acting, Hollywood.

ADDRESS

Nothing succeeds like address.

FRAN LEBOWITZ, *Metropolitan Life* (1978)

My address is like my shoes. It travels with me.

MOTHER JONES, in Linda Atkinson, *Mother Jones: The Most Dangerous Woman in America* (1978)

ADMIRATION

The modern world is not given to uncritical admiration. It expects its idols to have feet of clay and can be reasonably sure that press and camera will report their exact dimensions.

BARBARA WARD, in *Saturday Review* (1961)

You can't ever be really free if you admire somebody too much.

TOVE JANSSON, *Tales from Moominvalley* (1963)

See also Respect.

ADOLESCENCE

Adolescence is like cactus.

ANAïS NIN, *A Spy in the House of Love* (1954)

In no order of things is adolescence the time of the simple life.

JANET ERSKINE STUART, in Maud Monahan, *Life and Letters of Janet Erskine Stuart* (1922)

Show Miss Manners a grown-up who has happy memories of teenage years, with their endless round of merry-making and dancing the night away, and Miss Manners will show you a person who has either no heart or no memory.

JUDITH MARTIN, *Miss Manners' Guide to Rearing Perfect Children* (1984)

Adolescence is a twentieth-century invention most parents approach with dread and look back on with the relief of survivors.

FAYE MOSKOWITZ, *A Leak in the Heart* (1985)

With any child entering adolescence, one hunts for signs of health, is desperate for the smallest indication that the child's problems will never be important enough for a television movie.

DELIA EPHRON, *Funny Sauce* (1986)

The invention of the teenager was a mistake, in Miss Manners' opinion. . . . Once you identify a period of life in which people have few restrictions and, at the same time, few responsibilities—they get to stay out late but don't have to pay taxes—naturally, nobody wants to live any other way.

JUDITH MARTIN, *Miss Manners' Guide for the Turn-of-the-Millennium* (1989)

I did not write it [*Coming of Age in Samoa*] as a popular book, but only with the hope that it would be intelligible to those who might make the best use of its theme, that adolescence need not be the time of stress and strain which Western society made it; that growing up could be freer and easier and less complicated; and also that there were prices to pay for the very lack of complication I found in Samoa—less intensity, less individuality, less involvement with life.

MARGARET MEAD, *Coming of Age in Samoa* (1928)

We become adolescents when the words that adults exchange with one another become intelligible to us.

NATALIA GINZBURG, *The Little Virtues* (1962)

See also Childhood, Children, Youth.

ADULTERY

No adultery is bloodless.

NATALIA GINZBURG, *The City and the House* (1985)

That is what adultery is, a meanness and a stealing, a taking away from someone what should be theirs, a great selfishness, and surrounded and guarded by lies lest it should be found out. And out of this meanness and this selfishness and this lying flow love and joy and peace, beyond anything that can be imagined.

ROSE MACAULAY, *The Towers of Trebizond* (1956)

See also Infidelity.

ADULTHOOD

We thought we were running away from the grownups, and now we are the grownups.

MARGARET ATWOOD, *Cat's Eye* (1988)

If this was adulthood, the only improvement she could detect in her situation was that now she could eat dessert without eating her vegetables.

LISA ALTHER, *Kinflicks* (1975)

Another belief of mine: that everyone else my age is an adult, whereas I am merely in disguise.

MARGARET ATWOOD, *Cat's Eye* (1988)

When we were children, we used to think that when we were grown-up we would no longer be vulnerable. But to grow up is to accept vulnerability. . . . To be alive is to be vulnerable.

MADELEINE L'ENGLE, *Walking on Water: Reflections on Faith and Art* (1980)

Every human being on this earth is born with a tragedy, and it isn't original sin. He's born with the tragedy that he has to grow up. That he has to leave the nest, the security, and go out to do battle. He has to lose everything that is lovely and fight for a new loveliness of his own making, and it's a tragedy. A lot of people don't have the courage to do it.

HELEN HAYES, in Roy Newquist, *Showcase* (1966)

One of the signs of passing youth is the birth of a sense of fellowship with other human beings as we take our place among them.

VIRGINIA WOOLF, in *Times Literary Supplement* (1916)

To mature is in part to realize that while complete intimacy and omniscience and power cannot be had, self-transcendence, growth, and closeness to others are nevertheless within one's reach.

SISSELA BOK, *Secrets* (1983)

By the bye, as I must leave off being young, I find many Douceurs in being a sort of Chaperon for I am put on the Sofa near the fire and can drink as much wine as I like.

JANE AUSTEN, letter to her sister Cassandra (1813)

See also Age, Middle Age.

ADVENTURE

Send me out into another life. But get me back for supper.

FAITH POPCORN, *The Popcorn Report* (1991)

Nobody is ever met at the airport when beginning a new adventure. It's just not done.

ELIZABETH WARNOCK FERNEA, *A View of the Nile* (1970)

See also Travel.

ADVERSITY

If we had no winter, the spring would not be so pleasant: if we did not sometimes taste of adversity, prosperity would not be so welcome.

ANNE BRADSTREET, "Meditations Divine and Moral" (c. 1655), in John Harvard Ellis, *The Works of Anne Bradstreet in Prose and Verse* (1932)

It is not given to everyone to shine in adversity.

JANE AIKEN HODGE, *Marry in Haste* (1961)

See also Suffering, Trouble.

ADVERTISING

We grew up founding our dreams on the infinite promise of American advertising. I still believe that one can learn to play the piano by mail and that mud will give you a perfect complexion.

ZELDA FITZGERALD, *Save Me the Waltz* (1932)

All our advertising is propaganda, of course, but it has become so much a part of our life, is so pervasive, that we just don't know what it is propaganda *for*.

PAULINE KAEL, *I Lost It at the Movies* (1965)

Advertising today is not subliminal, but its subtle psychological effect is as devastating as any secret message flashed at high speeds to unsuspecting viewers.

LUCY KOMISAR, "The Image of Woman in Advertising," in Vivian Gornick and Barbara K. Moran, *Woman in Sexist Society* (1971)

The advertising media in this country continuously informs the American male of his need for indispensable signs of his virility.

FRANCES M. BEAL, "Double Jeopardy: To Be Black and Female," in Robin Morgan, *Sisterhood Is Powerful* (1970)

The advertising agency, as it stands today, is a peculiar manifestation of American business life of the twentieth century—glossy, brash, and insecure.

ILKA CHASE, *Past Imperfect* (1942)

ADVICE

It is very difficult to live among people you love and hold back from offering them advice.

ANNE TYLER, *Celestial Navigation* (1974)

Among the most disheartening and dangerous of . . . advisors, you will often find those closest to you, your dearest friends, members of your own family, perhaps, loving, anxious, and knowing nothing whatever.

MINNIE MADDERN FISKE, letter (1908), in Alexander Woollcott, *Mrs. Fiske* (1917)

The true secret of giving advice is, after you have honestly given it, to be perfectly indifferent whether it is taken or not, and never persist in trying to set people right.

HANNAH WHITALL SMITH (1902), in Logan Pearsall Smith, *Philadelphia Quaker* (1950)

Please give me some good advice in your next letter. I promise not to follow it.

EDNA ST. VINCENT MILLAY, *Letters* (1952)

I give myself sometimes admirable advice, but I am incapable of taking it.

LADY MARY WORTLEY MONTAGU (1739), in Robert Halsband, ed., *The Complete Letters of Lady Mary Wortley Montagu* (1965)

I am very handy with my advice and then when anybody appears to be following it, I get frantic.

FLANNERY O'CONNOR, in Sally Fitzgerald, ed., *The Habit of Being* (1979)

The strongest possible piece of advice I would give to any young woman is: Don't screw around, and don't smoke.

EDWINA CURRIE, in *Observer* (1988)

It is not advisable, James, to venture unsolicited opinions. You should spare yourself the embarrassing discovery of their exact value to your listener.

AYN RAND, *Atlas Shrugged* (1957)

AFRICA

Africa is less a wilderness than a repository of primary and fundamental values, and less a barbaric land than an unfamiliar voice.

BERYL MARKHAM, *West with the Night* (1942)

The breezes of the West African night were intimate and shy, licking the hair, sweeping through cotton dresses with unseemly intimacy, then disappearing into the utter blackness.

MAYA ANGELOU, *All God's Children Need Traveling Shoes* (1986)

In Africa people learn to serve each other. They live on credit balances of little favors that they give and may, one day, ask to have returned.

BERYL MARKHAM, *West with the Night* (1942)

We were Black Americans in West Africa, where for the first time in our lives the color of our skin was accepted as correct and normal.

MAYA ANGELOU, *All God's Children Need Traveling Shoes* (1986)

Africa is mystic; it is wild; it is a sweltering inferno; it is a photographer's paradise, a hunter's Valhalla, an escapist's Utopia. It is what you will, and it withstands all interpretations. It is the last vestige of a dead world or the cradle of a shiny new one. To a lot of people, as to myself, it is just "home." It is all these things but one thing—it is never dull.

BERYL MARKHAM, *West with the Night* (1942)

It is a cruel country; it takes your heart and grinds it into powdered stone—and no one minds.

ELSPETH HUXLEY, *The Flame Trees of Thika* (1959)

Africa is never the same to anyone who leaves it and returns again. It is not a land of change, but it is a land of moods and its moods are numberless. It is not fickle, but because it has mothered not only men, but races, and cradles not only cities, but civilizations—and seen them die, and seen new ones born again—Africa can be dispassionate, indifferent, warm, or cynical, replete with the weariness of too much wisdom.

BERYL MARKHAM, *West with the Night* (1942)

Writers brought up in Africa have many advantages—being at the center of a modern battlefield; part of a society in rapid, dramatic change. But in the long run it can also be a handicap: to wake up every morning with one's eyes on a fresh evidence of inhumanity; to be reminded twenty times a day of injustice, and always the same brand of it, can be limiting.

DORIS LESSING, *African Stories* (1965)

But the soul of Africa, its integrity, the slow inexorable pulse of its life, is its own and of such singular rhythm that no outsider, unless steeped from childhood in its endless, even beat, can ever hope to experience it, except only as a bystander might experience a Masai war dance knowing nothing of its music nor the meaning of its steps.

BERYL MARKHAM, *West with the Night* (1942)

AFRICAN AMERICANS

See Blacks.

AFTERLIFE

This World is not Conclusion. / A Sequel stands beyond— / Invisible, as Music— / But positive, as Sound.

EMILY DICKINSON (1862), *Poems, Third Series* (1896)

In health, in the bustle of living, it was easy to believe in heaven and a life to come. But when the blow fell, and those you loved passed into the great Silence, where you could not get at them, or they at you, then doubts, aching doubts took possession of one.

HENRY HANDEL RICHARDSON, *The Fortunes of Richard Mahoney: Ultima Thule* (1929)

Heaven is neither a place nor a time.

FLORENCE NIGHTINGALE, *Mysticism* (1873)

He [Christ] even restored the severed ear of the soldier who came to arrest Him—a fact that allows us to hope the resurrection will reflect a considerable attention to detail.

MARILYNNE ROBINSON, *Housekeeping* (1980)

I think the resurrection of the body, unless much improved in construction, a mistake.

EVELYN UNDERHILL, *The Letters of Evelyn Underhill* (1943)

What's so good about a heaven where, one of these days, you're going to get your embarrassing old body back?

MARSHA NORMAN, *The Fortune Teller* (1987)

I live now on borrowed time, waiting in the anteroom for the summons that will inevitably come. And then—I go on to the next thing, whatever it is. One doesn't luckily have to bother about that.

AGATHA CHRISTIE, *An Autobiography* (1977)

It's the possibility that when you're dead you might still go on hurting that bothers me.

KERI HULME, *The Bone People* (1983)

We were afraid of the dead because we never could tell when they might show up again.

JAMAICA KINCAID, *Annie John* (1983)

If there is whistling in the great beyond, I'll kill myself.

JEAN STAFFORD, *The Catherine Wheel* (1951)

See also Eternity, Immortality.

AGE

For years I wanted to be older, and now I am.

MARGARET ATWOOD, *Cat's Eye* (1988)

Age seldom arrives smoothly or quickly. It's more often a succession of jerks.

JEAN RHYS, in *Observer* (1975)

About the only thing that comes to us without effort is old age.

GLORIA PITZER, in *Reader's Digest* (1979)

The aging aren't only the old; the aging are all of us.

ALEXANDRA ROBBIN, *Aging: A New Look* (1982)

Do not deprive me of my age. I have earned it.

MAY SARTON, *The Poet and the Donkey* (1969)

I am luminous with age.

MERIDEL LE SUEUR, title poem, *Rites of Ancient Ripening* (1975)

Old age transfigures or fossilizes.

MARIE VON EBNER-ESCHENBACH, *Aphorisms* (1905)

Growing old is partly an inescapable process of accommodation and adjustment.

KÄTHE KOLLWITZ (1910), in Hans Kollwitz, ed., *The Diaries and Letters of Käthe Kollwitz* (1955)

We did not change as we grew older; we just became more clearly ourselves.

LYNN HALL, *Where Have All the Tigers Gone?* (1989)

Her grandmother, as she gets older, is not fading but rather becoming more concentrated.

PAULETTE BATES ALDEN, "Legacies," *Feeding the Eagles* (1988)

Let me advise thee not to talk of thyself as being *old*. There *is* something in Mind Cure, after all, and, if thee continually talks of thyself as being old, thee may perhaps bring on some of the infirmities of age. At least I would not risk it if I were thee.

HANNAH WHITALL SMITH (1907), in Logan Pearsall Smith, *Philadelphia Quaker* (1950)

Wisdom doesn't automatically come with old age. Nothing does—except wrinkles. It's true, some wines improve with age. But only if the grapes were good in the first place.

ABIGAIL VAN BUREN, syndicated column (1978)

There are no old people nowadays; they are either "wonderful for their age" or dead.

MARY PETTIBONE POOLE, *A Glass Eye at a Keyhole* (1938)

It is not mere chance that makes families speak of a child who is "extraordinary for his age" and also of an old man who is "extraordinary for his age"; the extraordinariness lies in their behaving like human beings when they are either not yet or no longer men.

SIMONE DE BEAUVOIR, *The Coming of Age* (1970)

She had finally reached the age where she was more afraid of getting old than dying.

JULIA PHILLIPS, *You'll Never Eat Lunch in This Town Again* (1991)

And indeed, it is old age, rather than death, that is to be contrasted with life. Old age is life's parody, whereas death transforms life into a destiny.

SIMONE DE BEAUVOIR, *The Coming of Age* (1970)

I've got everything I always had. Only it's six inches lower.

GYPSY ROSE LEE, in Barbara McDowell and Hana Umlauf, *Woman's Almanac* (1977)

After thirty, a body has a mind of its own.

BETTE MIDLER, in *Reader's Digest* (1982)

I have enjoyed greatly the second blooming that comes when you finish the life of the emotions and of personal relations; and suddenly find—at the age of fifty, say—that a whole new life has opened before you, filled with things you can

think about, study, or read about. . . . It is as if a fresh sap of ideas and thoughts was rising in you.

AGATHA CHRISTIE, *An Autobiography* (1977)

Though it sounds absurd, it is true to say I felt younger at sixty than I had felt at twenty.

ELLEN GLASGOW, *The Woman Within* (1954)

I have a problem about being nearly sixty: I keep waking up in the morning and thinking I'm thirty-one.

ELIZABETH JANEWAY, *Between Myth and Morning* (1974)

Being over seventy is like being engaged in a war. All our friends are going or gone and we survive amongst the dead and the dying as on a battlefield.

MURIEL SPARK, *Memento Mori* (1959)

In a dream you are never eighty.

ANNE SEXTON, "Old," *All My Pretty Ones* (1962)

It is so comic to hear one's self called old; even at ninety, I suppose!

ALICE JAMES, *Journal* (1889)

I have always felt that a woman has the right to treat the subject of her age with ambiguity until, perhaps, she passes into the realm of over ninety. Then it is better she be candid with herself and with the world.

HELENA RUBINSTEIN, *My Life for Beauty* (1966)

A woman who will tell her age will tell anything.

RITA MAE BROWN, *Southern Discomfort* (1982)

The great thing about getting older is that you don't lose all the other ages you've been.

MADELEINE L'ENGLE, in *New York Times* (1985)

When I am an old woman I shall wear purple.

JENNY JOSEPH, "Warning," in Sandra Martz, ed., *When I Am an Old Woman I Shall Wear Purple* (1987)

It's time for us old women to rip to shreds the veil of invisibility that has encased us. We have to fight the societal stereotype that keeps us on the periphery, outside the mainstream. We have experience to offer, judgment, wisdom, balance and charm.

MIRIAM REIBOLD, news item (1991)

Women may be the one group that grows more radical with age.

GLORIA STEINEM, *Outrageous Acts and Everyday Rebellions* (1983)

So much has been said and sung of beautiful young girls, why doesn't somebody wake up to the beauty of old women?

HARRIET BEECHER STOWE, *Uncle Tom's Cabin* (1852)

Time and trouble will tame an advanced young woman, but an advanced old woman is uncontrollable by any earthly force.

DOROTHY L. SAYERS, *Clouds of Witness* (1926)

The trouble was, she could not see the justice of her state. She was not old: she was a girl hidden behind a mask. Now that she had realized she was no longer young, she did not know how she should behave. She had become a stranger in her own life.

OLIVIA MANNING, *The Doves of Venus* (1955)

She was an old woman now, and her life had become memories.

LESLIE MARMON SILKO, "Lullaby," *Storyteller* (1981)

Being young is beautiful, but being old is comfortable.

MARIE VON EBNER-ESCHENBACH, *Aphorisms* (1905)

In youth we learn; in age we understand.

MARIE VON EBNER-ESCHENBACH, *Aphorisms* (1905)

The old creep out at the churchyard gate, while the young bound in at the front door.

ELIZABETH RUNDLE CHARLES, *Chronicles of the Schönberg-Cotta Family* (1863)

Paradoxical as it may seem, to believe in youth is to look backward; to look forward we must believe in age.

DOROTHY L. SAYERS, "Strong Meat" (1939)

We turn not older with years, but newer every day.

EMILY DICKINSON (1874), in Mabel Loomis Todd, *Letters of Emily Dickinson* (1894)

You stay young as long as you can learn, acquire new habits and suffer contradiction.

MARIE VON EBNER-ESCHENBACH, *Aphorisms* (1905)

'Tis a maxim with me to be young as long as one can: there is nothing can pay one for that invaluable ignorance which is the companion of youth; those sanguine groundless hopes, and that lively vanity, which make all the happiness of life. To my extreme mortification I grow wiser every day.

LADY MARY WORTLEY MONTAGU (1745), in Robert Halsband, ed., *The Complete Letters of Lady Mary Wortley Montagu* (1965)

I never feel age. . . . If you have creative work, you don't have age or time.

LOUISE NEVELSON (1980), in Alexandra Robbin, *Aging: A New Look* (1982)

It was formerly a terrifying view to me that I should one day be an old woman. I now find that Nature has provided pleasures for every state.

LADY MARY WORTLEY MONTAGU, letter (1747), in Octave Thanet, ed., *The Best Letters of Lady Mary Wortley Montagu* (1901)

I used to dread getting older because I thought I would not be able to do all the things I wanted to do, but now that I am older I find that I don't want to do them.

NANCY ASTOR, interview (1959), in Michèle Brown and Ann O'Connor, *Hammer and Tongues* (1986)

It is a mistake to regard age as a downhill grade toward dissolution. The reverse is true. As one grows older one climbs with surprising strides.

GEORGE SAND (1868), in Marie Jenny Howe, *The Intimate Journal of George Sand* (1929)

Old age is not an illness, it is a timeless ascent. As power diminishes, we grow toward the light.

MAY SARTON, in "The Family of Woman: Growing Toward the Light," *Ms.* (1982)

Of all the self-fulfilling prophecies in our culture, the assumption that aging means decline and poor health is probably the deadliest.

MARILYN FERGUSON, *The Aquarian Conspiracy* (1980)

The fear of aging, a commonplace neurosis, does not usually wait for age and spares neither sex.

COLETTE, *Journey for Myself* (1972)

Dread of one's own aging leads to fear and dislike of old people, and the fear feeds upon itself. In Western society this cycle of dread has been going on a long, long time.

ALEXANDRA ROBBIN, *Aging: A New Look* (1982)

I am enjoying to the full that period of reflection which is the happiest conclusion to a life of action.

WILLA CATHER, *Death Comes for the Archbishop* (1927)

The birds sing louder when you grow old.

ROSE CHERNIN, in Kim Chernin, *In My Mother's House* (1983)

How unnatural the imposed view, imposed by a puritanical ethos, that passionate love belongs only to the young, that people are dead from the neck down by the time they are forty, and that any deep feeling, any passion after that age, is either ludicrous or revolting!

MAY SARTON, *Journal of a Solitude* (1973)

Age puzzles me. I thought it was a quiet time. My seventies were interesting and fairly serene, but my eighties are passionate. I grow more intense as I age.

FLORIDA SCOTT-MAXWELL, *The Measure of My Days* (1968)

The crucial task of old age is balance: keeping just well enough, just brave enough, just gay and interested and starkly honest enough to remain a sentient human being.

FLORIDA SCOTT-MAXWELL, *The Measure of My Days* (1968)

It seems to me nowadays that the most important task for someone who is aging is to spread love and warmth wherever possible.

KÄTHE KOLLWITZ, letter (1916), in Hans Kollwitz, ed., *The Diaries and Letters of Käthe Kollwitz* (1955)

Ah well, perhaps one has to be very old before one learns how to be amused rather than shocked.

PEARL BUCK, *China, Past and Present* (1972)

I have never wanted to live to be old, so old I'd run out of friends or money.

MARGOT FONTEYN, in *Parade* (1991)

I'm at an age where my back goes out more than I do.

PHYLLIS DILLER, *The Joys of Aging and How to Avoid Them* (1981)

I've always thought that very few people grow old as admirably as academics. At least books never let them down.

MARGARET DRABBLE, *A Summer Bird-Cage* (1962)

It's wonderful to be married to an archaeologist—the older you get the more interested he is in you.

AGATHA CHRISTIE, quoting a never-identified woman (although the quote is always attributed to Christie), in Jeffrey Feinman, *The Mysterious World of Agatha Christie* (1975)

I'm in my anecdotage.

CLARE BOOTHE LUCE, in *Town and Country* (1981)

"I'm falling into disrepair," she told the children. "I've outlived myself."

ANNE TYLER, *Dinner at the Homesick Restaurant* (1982)

Every time I think that I'm getting old, and gradually going to the grave, something else happens.

LILLIAN CARTER, in *Ms.* (1976)

There is no such thing as old age, there is only sorrow.

EDITH WHARTON, "A First Word," *A Backward Glance* (1934)

Old age is a great trial, John. One has to be so damned *good!*

MAY SARTON, *Kinds of Love* (1970)

As in everything else, I find that age is not good for much, that one becomes deafer and less sensitive. Also, the higher up the mountain you climb, the less of a view you get. A mist closes in and cheats you of the hoped-for and expected opportunity to see far and wide.

KÄTHE KOLLWITZ, letter, in Hans Kollwitz, ed., *The Diaries and Letters of Käthe Kollwitz* (1955)

In all the world there are no people so piteous and forlorn as those who are forced to eat the bitter bread of dependency in their old age, and find how steep are the stairs of another man's house.

DOROTHY DIX, *Dorothy Dix, Her Book* (1926)

Science has salvaged scrap metal and even found vitamins and valuable oils in refuse, but old people are extravagantly wasted.

ANZIA YEZIERSKA, "One Thousand Pages of Research," *Commentary* (1963)

Society turns away from the aged worker as though he belonged to another species. That is why the whole question is buried in a conspiracy of silence. Old age exposes the failure of our entire civilization.

SIMONE DE BEAUVOIR, *The Coming of Age* (1970)

Never lose sight of the fact that old age needs so little but needs that little so much.

MARGARET WILLOUR, in *Reader's Digest* (1982)

Old age is like a plane flying through a storm. Once you're aboard there's nothing you can do.

GOLDA MEIR, quoted by Oriana Fallaci in *L'Europeo* (1973)

One keeps forgetting old age up to the very brink of the grave.

COLETTE, *My Mother's House* (1922)

The country of the aged is a land few people think very hard and seriously about before the time of life when they sense that they're *arriving* there. Somehow, throughout much of life, being old seems to be something that happens to other people.

MAGGIE SCARF, *Unfinished Business* (1980)

My age I will not once lament, / But sing, my time so near is spent.

ANNE BRADSTREET, "I Had Eight Birds" (1656), in Jeannine Hensley, *Works of Anne Bradstreet* (1967)

He moved, she noticed, frail as trailing smoke on soft autumn days, and she feared she would soon lose him, like smoke rising through the trees, not as a ripping flash of summer lightning, but softly one evening.

YVETTE NELSON, *We'll Come When It Rains* (1982)

See also Adolescence, Adulthood, Childhood, Middle Age, Retirement, Youth.

AIDS

Over and over, these men cry out against the weight of so many losses—not just a lover dead, but friends and friends of friends, dozens of them, until it seems that AIDS is all there is and all there ever will be.

JANE GROSS, in *New York Times* (1987)

Like the effects of industrial pollution and the new system of global financial markets, the AIDS crisis is evidence of a world in which nothing important is regional, local, limited; in which everything that can circulate does, and every problem is, or is destined to become, worldwide.

SUSAN SONTAG, *AIDS and Its Metaphors* (1989)

See also Illness.

ALARM

If you look at life one way, there is always cause for alarm.

ELIZABETH BOWEN, *The Death of the Heart* (1938)

Nervous alarms should always be communicated, that they may be dissipated.

CHARLOTTE BRONTË, *Shirley* (1849)

See also Fear.

ALCOHOL

Alcohol is a good preservative for everything but brains.

MARY PETTIBONE POOLE, *A Glass Eye at a Keyhole* (1938)

Alcohol is an allergy of the body and an obsession of the mind.

RITA MAE BROWN, *Starting From Scratch* (1988)

Employed as I had been employing it, liquor is a fixative of old patterns.

MARGARET HALSEY, *No Laughing Matter* (1977)

Maybe it picks you up a little bit, but it sure lets you down in a hurry.

BETTY FORD, with Chris Chase, *The Time of My Life* (1978)

Alcohol doesn't console, it doesn't fill up anyone's psychological gaps, all it replaces is the lack of God.

MARGUERITE DURAS, *Practicalities* (1987)

Alcohol flings back, almost illimitably, the boundaries of humor so that we can find uproarious things which our poor sober friends miss altogether. It is necessary, if the joke is really good and really should be shared, to repeat it time and again until finally it penetrates those solemn skulls.

JEAN STAFFORD, *Boston Adventure* (1944)

Alcoholism isn't a spectator sport. Eventually the whole family gets to play.

JOYCE REBETA-BURDITT, *The Cracker Factory* (1977)

See also Drink, Drug Abuse, Sobriety, Wine.

ALIENATION

Alienation produces eccentrics or revolutionaries.

JENNY HOLZER, *Truisms* (1977–1979)

Idealization of a group is a natural consequence of separation from the group; in other words, it is a by-product of alienation.

PAULA GUNN ALLEN, *The Sacred Hoop* (1986)

See also Outsiders.

ALONE

You come into the world alone and you go out of the world alone yet it seems to me you are more alone while living than even going and coming.

EMILY CARR, *Hundreds and Thousands* (1966)

Nobody, but nobody / Can make it out here alone.

MAYA ANGELOU, "Alone," *Oh Pray My Wings Are Gonna Fit Me Well* (1975)

To be alone is to be different, to be different is to be alone.

SUZANNE GORDON, *Lonely in America* (1976)

Anything we fully do is an alone journey.

NATALIE GOLDBERG, *Writing Down the Bones* (1986)

I want to be alone. . . . I just want to be alone.

GRETA GARBO, in William A. Drake, scriptwriter, *Grand Hotel* (1932)

I never said, "I want to be alone." I only said, "I want to be *let* alone." There is all the difference.

GRETA GARBO, in John Bainbridge, *Garbo* (1955)

And a Famous Film Star who is left alone is more alone than any other person has ever been in the whole Histry of the World, because of the contrast to our normal enviromint.

ANITA LOOS, *A Mouse Is Born* (1951)

Once you have lived with another it is a great torture to have to live alone.

CARSON MCCULLERS, *The Ballad of the Sad Café* (1953)

No matter how lonely you get or how many birth announcements you receive, the trick is not to get frightened. There's nothing wrong with being alone.

WENDY WASSERSTEIN, *Isn't It Romantic* (1983)

The Moon and Pleiades have set, / Midnight is nigh, / The time is passing, passing, yet / Alone I lie.

SAPPHO (6th century B.C.), in C. R. Haines, *Sappho: The Poems and Fragments* (1926)

Being alone and liking it is, for a woman, an act of treachery, an infidelity far more threatening than adultery.

MOLLY HASKELL, *Love and Other Infectious Diseases* (1990)

When you live alone, you can be sure that the person who squeezed the toothpaste tube in the middle wasn't committing a hostile act.

ELLEN GOODMAN, *Close to Home* (1979)

My kitchen linoleum is so black and shiny that I waltz while I wait for the kettle to boil. This pleasure is for the old who live alone. The others must vanish into their expected role.

FLORIDA SCOTT-MAXWELL, *The Measure of My Days* (1968)

See also Loneliness, Self-Sufficiency, Single, Solitude.

ALTRUISM

Every major horror of history was committed in the name of an altruistic motive. Has any act of selfishness ever equaled the carnage perpetrated by disciples of altruism?

AYN RAND, *The Fountainhead* (1943)

How wonderful it is that nobody need wait a single moment before starting to improve the world.

ANNE FRANK, *Diary of a Young Girl* (1952)

See also Unselfishness.

ALZHEIMER'S

Ann finds it hard to judge the placement of her chair. At one time she tried to sit on Noelle's lap. Neither one could solve the problem. In fact Noelle was content to serve as a chair.

JUDITH STOUGHTON, *One Woman's Pascal Journey* (1991)

See also Illness.

AMBITION

Mama exhorted her children at every opportunity to "jump at de sun." We might not land on the sun, but at least we would get off the ground.

ZORA NEALE HURSTON, *Dust Tracks on a Road* (1942)

I used to think I had ambition . . . but now I'm not so sure. It may have been only discontent. They're easily confused.

RACHEL FIELD, *All This and Heaven Too* (1939)

My passions were all gathered together like fingers that made a fist. Drive is considered aggression today; I knew it then as purpose.

BETTE DAVIS, *The Lonely Life* (1962)

To gain that which is worth having, it may be necessary to lose everything else.

BERNADETTE DEVLIN, *The Price of My Soul* (1969)

I always wanted to be somebody. If I made it, it's half because I was game enough to take a lot of punishment along the way and half because there were a lot of people who cared enough to help me.

ALTHEA GIBSON, *I Always Wanted to Be Somebody* (1958)

She had learned the self-deprecating ways of the woman who does not want to be thought hard and grasping, but her artifices could not always cover the nakedness of her need to excel.

FAITH SULLIVAN, *The Cape Ann* (1988)

Ambition, old as mankind, the immemorial weakness of the strong.

VITA SACKVILLE-WEST, *No Signposts in the Sea* (1961)

Ambition if it feeds at all, does so on the ambition of others.

SUSAN SONTAG, *The Benefactor* (1963)

AMBIVALENCE

Ambivalence is a wonderful tune to dance to. It has a rhythm all its own.

ERICA JONG, *Fear of Flying* (1973)

I happen to feel that the degree of a person's intelligence is directly reflected by the number of conflicting attitudes she can bring to bear on the same topic.

LISA ALTHER, *Kinflicks* (1975)

For the human soul is hospitable, and will entertain conflicting sentiments and contradictory opinions with much impartiality.

GEORGE ELIOT, *Romola* (1862)

At work, you think of the children you have left at home. At home, you think of the work you've left unfinished. Such a struggle is unleashed within yourself. Your heart is rent.

GOLDA MEIR, quoted by Oriana Fallaci in *L'Europeo* (1973)

See also Indecision, Paradox.

AMERICA

See United States.

ANCESTORS

We all grow up with the weight of history on us. Our ancestors dwell in the attics of our brains as they do in the spiraling chains of knowledge hidden in every cell of our bodies.

SHIRLEY ABBOTT, *Womenfolks: Growing Up Down South* (1983)

Ancestral habits of mind can be constricting; they also confer one's individuality.

BHARATI MUKHERJEE, in Janet Sternburg, ed., *The Writer on Her Work*, vol. 2 (1991)

Our mothers and grandmothers, some of them: moving to music not yet written.

ALICE WALKER, title essay (1974), *In Search of Our Mothers' Gardens* (1983)

See also Family, Grandparents, History, Roots.

ANCHORAGE

This city is made of stone, of blood, and fish.

JOY HARJO, "Anchorage," in Rayna Green, ed., *That's What She Said* (1984)

ANDROGYNY

Male and female represent the two sides of the great radical dualism. But, in fact, they are perpetually passing into one another. Fluid hardens to solid, solid rushes to fluid. There is no wholly masculine man, no purely feminine woman.

MARGARET FULLER, in *The Dial* (1843)

The term "androgyny" . . . defines a condition under which the characteristics of the sexes, and the human impulses expressed by men and women, are not rigidly assigned. Androgyny seeks to liberate the individual from the confines of the appropriate.

CAROLYN HEILBRUN, *Toward a Recognition of Androgyny* (1973)

What is most beautiful in virile men is something feminine; what is most beautiful in feminine women is something masculine.

SUSAN SONTAG, *Against Interpretation* (1966)

Androgyny suggests a spirit of reconciliation between the sexes.

CAROLYN HEILBRUN, *Toward a Recognition of Androgyny* (1973)

As to sex, the original pleasure, I cannot recommend too highly the advantages of androgyny.

JAN MORRIS, *Pleasures of a Tangled Life* (1989)

The word [androgyny] is misbegotten—conveying something like "John Travolta and Farrah Fawcett-Majors scotch-taped together."

MARY DALY, *Gyn/Ecology* (1978)

See also Gender, Sex Roles, Women and Men.

ANGER

Anger is a signal, and one worth listening to.

HARRIET LERNER, *The Dance of Anger* (1985)

Anger stirs and wakes in her; it opens its mouth, and like a hot-mouthed puppy, laps up the dredges of her shame. Anger is better. There is a sense of being in anger. A reality and presence. An awareness of worth.

TONI MORRISON, *The Bluest Eye* (1970)

I have a right to my anger, and I don't want anybody telling me I shouldn't be, that it's not nice to be, and that something's wrong with me because I get angry.

MAXINE WATERS, in Brian Lanker, *I Dream a World* (1989)

Anger as soon as fed is dead— / 'Tis starving makes it fat.

EMILY DICKINSON (1881), *Poems, Second Series* (1891)

When the habitually even-tempered suddenly fly into a passion, that explosion is apt to be more impressive than the outburst of the most violent amongst us.

MARGERY ALLINGHAM, *Death of a Ghost* (1934)

Through anger, the truth looks simple.

JANE McCABE, in Carolyn Heilbrun, *Writing a Woman's Life* (1988)

Anger makes us all stupid.

JOHANNA SPYRI, *Heidi* (1915)

Anger makes dull men witty, but it keeps them poor.

ELIZABETH I, in Francis Bacon, *Apophthegms* (1625)

See also Indignation, Outrage.

ANIMALS

Animals are such agreeable friends—they ask no questions, they pass no criticisms.

GEORGE ELIOT, "Mr. Gilfil's Love Story," *Scenes of Clerical Life* (1857)

Animals in different countries have different expressions just as the people in different countries differ in expression.

GERTRUDE STEIN, *Everybody's Autobiography* (1937)

Animals were once, for all of us, teachers. They instructed us in ways of being and perceiving that extended our imaginations, that were models for additional possibilities.

JOAN McINTYRE, *Mind in the Waters* (1974)

I am convinced that biology should be taught as a course in human-animal relationships—not as a study of dead bodies or caged victims.

DOROTHY RICHARDS, with HOPE SAWYER BUYUKMIHCI, *Beaversprite* (1977)

Birds and beasts have in fact our own nature, flattened a semi-tone.

LYDIA MARIA CHILD, *Letters from New York,* 2nd Series (1845)

The animals of the planet are in desperate peril. . . . Without free animal life I believe we will lose the spiritual equivalent of oxygen.

ALICE WALKER, *Living by the Word* (1988)

Since we humans have the better brain, isn't it our responsibility to protect our fellow creatures from, oddly enough, ourselves?

JOY ADAMSON, in Barbara McDowell and Hana Umlauf, *Woman's Almanac* (1977)

Animals give us their constant, unjaded faces and we burden them with our bodies and civilized ordeals.

GRETEL EHRLICH, *The Solace of Open Spaces* (1985)

But some animals, like some men, leave a trail of glory behind them. They give their spirit to the place where they have lived, and remain forever a part of the rocks and streams and the wind and sky.

MARGUERITE HENRY, *Brighty of the Grand Canyon* (1953)

My mother thought it would make us feel better to know animals had no souls and thus their deaths were not to be taken seriously. But it didn't help and when I think of some of the animals I have known, I wonder. The only really "soulful" eyes in the world belong to the dog or cat who sits on your lap or at your feet commiserating when you cry.

LIZ SMITH, *The Mother Book* (1978)

We call them dumb animals, and so they are, for they cannot tell us how they feel, but they do not suffer less because they have no words.

ANNA SEWELL, *Black Beauty* (1877)

You enter into a certain amount of madness when you marry a person with pets.

NORA EPHRON, *Heartburn* (1983)

It's funny how dogs and cats know the inside of folks better than other folks do, isn't it?

ELEANOR H. PORTER, *Pollyanna* (1912)

No animal should ever jump up on the dining-room furniture unless absolutely certain that he can hold his own in the conversation.

FRAN LEBOWITZ, *Social Studies* (1977)

The dog opened one eye, cocked it at me, and rolled it up before her lids closed. People should not feed moralistic animals. If they're so holy, where are their books?

ANNIE DILLARD, *The Writing Life* (1989)

Rabbits are a foolish people. They do not fight except with their own kind, nor use their paws except for feet, and appear to have no reason for existence but to furnish meals for meat-eaters. In flight they seem to rebound from the earth of their own elasticity, but keep a sober pace going to the spring. It is the young watercress that tempts them and the pleasures of society, for they seldom drink.

MARY AUSTIN, *The Land of Little Rain* (1904)

[The lion] began to contemplate me with a kind of quiet premeditation, like that of a slow-witted man fondling an unaccustomed thought.

BERYL MARKHAM, *West with the Night* (1942)

The giraffe, in their queer, inimitable, vegetative gracefulness, as if it were not a herd of animals but a family of rare, long-stemmed, speckled gigantic flowers slowly advancing.

ISAK DINESEN, *Out of Africa* (1937)

If you ever, ever, ever meet a grizzly bear, / You must never, never, never ask him *where* / He is going, / Or *what* he is doing; / For if you ever, ever dare / To stop a grizzly bear, / You will never meet *another* grizzly bear.

MARY AUSTIN, "Grizzly Bear," *The Children Sing in the Far West* (1928)

I startled a weasel who startled me, and we exchanged a long glance. . . . Our eyes locked, and someone threw away the key.

ANNIE DILLARD, *Teaching a Stone to Talk* (1982)

A beaver does not, as legend would have it, know which direction the tree will fall when he cuts it, but counts on alacrity to make up for lack of engineering expertise.

ANN ZWINGER, *Beyond the Aspen Grove* (1970)

I know animals more gallant than the African warthog, but none more courageous. He is the peasant of the plains—the drab and dowdy digger in the earth. He is the uncomely but intrepid defender of family, home, and bourgeois convention, and he will fight anything of any size that intrudes upon his smug existence. . . . His eyes are small and lightless and capable of but one expression—suspicion. What he does not understand, he suspects, and what he suspects, he fights.

BERYL MARKHAM, *West with the Night* (1942)

See also Birds, Cats, Dogs, Elephants, Gorillas, Horses, Wildlife, Wolves.

ANONYMOUS

I would venture to guess that Anon, who wrote so many poems without signing them, was often a woman.

VIRGINIA WOOLF, *A Room of One's Own* (1929)

Anonymous: Prolific female author. Has written hundreds of thousands of books, articles, poems, essays, memos, broadsides, and treatises. Under this name many women for centuries have written, published, or produced art, either deliberately to avoid the problems and punishments awaiting the woman artist or by default because their names were lost or forgotten.

CHERIS KRAMARAE AND PAULA A. TREICHLER, *A Feminist Dictionary* (1985)

ANSWERS

The only interesting answers are those which destroy the questions.

SUSAN SONTAG, in *Esquire* (1968)

Great evil has been done on earth by people who think they have all the answers.

RUBY PLENTY CHIEFS, in Lynn V. Andrews, *Crystal Woman* (1987)

What *is* the answer? . . . In that case, what is the question?

GERTRUDE STEIN, last words (1946)

See also Explanations, Questions.

ANTICIPATION

'Tain't worthwhile to wear a day all out before it comes.

SARAH ORNE JEWETT, *The Country of the Pointed Firs* (1896)

ANXIETY

I'm a firm believer in anxiety and the power of negative thinking.

GERTRUDE BERG, *Molly and Me* (1961)

If I knew what I was so anxious about, I wouldn't be so anxious.

MIGNON MCLAUGHLIN, *The Second Neurotic's Notebook* (1966)

Why is life speeded up so? Why are things so terribly, unbearably precious that you can't enjoy them but can only wait breathless in dread of their going?

ANNE MORROW LINDBERGH, *Hour of Gold, Hour of Lead* (1973)

Anxiety is love's greatest killer. It makes others feel as you might when a drowning man holds on to you. You want to save him, but you know he will strangle you with his panic.

ANAÏS NIN, *The Diary of Anaïs Nin*, vol. 4 (1944–1947)

See also Worry.

APATHY

Science may have found a cure for most evils; but it has found no remedy for the worst of them all—the apathy of human beings.

HELEN KELLER, *My Religion* (1927)

See also Indifference.

APPEARANCE

The tragedy of our time is that we are so eye centered, so appearance besotted.

JESSAMYN WEST, *Love Is Not What You Think* (1959)

In the short distance between the two houses he had somehow managed to acquire the ragged, spent look of a man who had crossed a continent on horseback.

LUCILLE KALLEN, *The Tanglewood Murder* (1980)

He looked home-made, as though his wife had self-consciously knitted or somehow contrived a husband when she sat alone at night.

EUDORA WELTY, "The Key," *A Curtain of Green* (1941)

The rehearsal had not been over for more than ten minutes and he could not have been standing there for more than six, but the look of exhaustion and reproach in his eyes suggested I had kept him waiting for days in some remote and shelterless mountain pass.

LUCILLE KALLEN, *The Tanglewood Murder* (1980)

With her skin deeply tanned by constant exposure to the sun, she had the shriveled appearance of a wind-dried shrimp.

LI ANG, *The Butcher's Wife* (1983)

Lots of women buy just as many wigs and makeup things as I do. They just don't wear them all at the same time.

DOLLY PARTON, in Barbara McDowell and Hana Umlauf, *Woman's Almanac* (1977)

You don't have to be dowdy to be a Christian.

TAMMY FAYE BAKKER, in *Newsweek* (1987)

Men seldom makes passes / At girls who wear glasses.

DOROTHY PARKER, "News Item," *Enough Rope* (1926)

My sort of looks are of the kind that bore me when I see them on other people.

MARGOT ASQUITH, *More or Less About Myself* (1934)

People on horses look better than they are. People in cars look worse than they are.

MARYA MANNES, *More in Anger* (1958)

Anybody who is anybody seems to be getting a lift—by plastic surgery these days. It's the new world wide craze that combines the satisfactions of psychoanalysis, massage, and a trip to the beauty salon.

EUGENIA SHEPPARD, in *New York Herald Tribune* (1958)

Women looked like great sea snails—the corded wood, babies, and laundry they carried were the whorls on their backs.

MAXINE HONG KINGSTON, *The Woman Warrior* (1976)

To superficial observers his chin had too vanishing an aspect, looking as if it were being gradually reabsorbed. And it did indeed cause him some difficulty about the fit of his satin stocks, for which chins were at that time useful.

GEORGE ELIOT, *Middlemarch* (1871)

Judge Taylor was on the bench, looking like a sleepy old shark, his pilot fish writing rapidly below in front of him.

HARPER LEE, *To Kill a Mockingbird* (1960)

General de Gaulle is very pituitary these days, to judge by his increased appearance at his recent, and important, press conference. . . . Time, weight, and, evidently, the General's glands are giving his visage a heavy, royal outline; he looks more like a man of dynasty than of destiny.

JANET FLANNER ("GENÊT"), *Paris Journal 1944–1965* (1965)

All God's children are not beautiful. Most of God's children are, in fact, barely presentable.

FRAN LEBOWITZ, Metropolitan Life (1978)

See also Beauty, Body, Clothes, Dress, Face.

APPEARANCES

The sweat of hard work is not to be displayed. It is much more graceful to appear favored by the gods.

MAXINE HONG KINGSTON, The Woman Warrior (1976)

[We] talked on about household forms and ceremonies, as if we all believed that our hostess had a regular servants' hall . . . instead of the one little charity-school maiden, whose short ruddy arms could never have been strong enough to carry the tray up-stairs, if she had not been assisted in private by her mistress, who now sat in state, pretending not to know what cakes were sent up; though she knew, and we knew, and she knew that we knew, and we knew that she knew that we knew, she had been busy all the morning making tea-bread and sponge cakes.

ELIZABETH GASKELL, *Cranford* (1853)

The majority cares little for ideals or integrity. What it craves is display.

EMMA GOLDMAN, "Minorities Versus Majorities," *Anarchism* (1910)

APPROVAL

Material things aside, we need no advice but approval.

COCO CHANEL, in Marcel Haedrich, *Coco Chanel: Her Life, Her Secrets* (1972)

I need no warrant for being, and no word of sanction upon my being. I am the warrant and the sanction.

AYN RAND, *Anthem* (1946)

Patrick Henry, Thomas Jefferson, and John Adams.

MOTHER JONES, replying to the judge who asked who had issued her a permit to speak on the streets, in Linda Atkinson, *Mother Jones: The Most Dangerous Woman in America* (1978)

ARCHITECTURE

Architecture should be working on improving the environment of people in their homes, in their places of work, and their places of recreation. It should be functional and pleasant, not just in the image of the architect's ego.

NORMA MERRICK SKLAREK, in Brian Lanker, *I Dream a World* (1989)

I realized that architecture was made for people who go about on their feet, that that is what architecture is made for.

GERTRUDE STEIN, "Raoul Dufy" (1946), in *Harper's Bazaar* (1949)

We have no sociology of architecture. Architects are unaccustomed to social analysis and mistrust it; sociologists have fatter fish to fry.

DENISE SCOTT BROWN, "Room at the Top" (1975), in Ellen Perry Berkeley and Matilda McQuaid, eds., *Architecture: A Place for Women* (1989)

See also Houses.

ARISTOCRACY

An aristocracy in a republic is like a chicken whose head has been cut off; it may run about in a lively way, but in fact it is dead.

NANCY MITFORD, *Noblesse Oblige* (1956)

The aristocrat, when he wants to, has very good manners. The Scottish upper classes, in particular, have that shell-shocked look that probably comes from banging their heads on low beams leaping to their feet whenever a woman comes into the room.

JILLY COOPER, *Class* (1979)

See also Class.

ARROGANCE

The scornful nostril and the high head gather not the odors that lie on the track of truth.

GEORGE ELIOT, *Felix Holt, the Radical* (1866)

I do not want Miss Mannin's feelings to be hurt by the fact that I have never heard of her. . . . At the moment I am debarred from the pleasure of putting her in her place by the fact that she has not got one.

EDITH SITWELL, in John Pearson, *Façades* (1978)

People in big empty places are likely to behave very much as the gods did on Olympus.

EDNA FERBER, *Giant* (1952)

See also Conceit, Egocentrism, Self-Importance, Vanity.

ART

Great art is cathartic; it is always moral.

JOYCE CAROL OATES, in Sandra M. Gilbert and Susan Gubar, eds., *The Norton Anthology of Literature by Women* (1985)

Art is the indispensable medium for the communication of a moral ideal.

AYN RAND, *The Romantic Manifesto* (1969)

The moral pleasure in art, as well as the moral service that art performs, consists in the intelligent gratification of consciousness.

SUSAN SONTAG, *Against Interpretation* (1966)

Many artists have said that when life itself becomes fully conscious, art as we know it will vanish. Art is only a stopgap, an imperfect effort to wrest meaning from an environment where nearly everyone is sleepwalking.

MARILYN FERGUSON, *The Aquarian Conspiracy* (1980)

What society requires from art . . . is that it function as an early warning system.

ELIZABETH JANEWAY, *Between Myth and Morning* (1974)

All art deals with the absurd and aims at the simple. Good art speaks truth, indeed *is* truth, perhaps the only truth.

IRIS MURDOCH, *The Black Prince* (1973)

Art is the objectification of feeling, and the subjectification of nature.

SUSANNE K. LANGER, *Mind* (1967)

Art must take reality by surprise.

FRANÇOISE SAGAN, in Malcolm Cowley, ed., *Writers at Work* (1958)

But art is so much more real than life. Some art is much more real than some life, I mean.

REBECCA WEST, *The Fountain Overflows* (1956)

While I recognize the necessity for a basis of observed reality . . . true art lies in a reality that is felt.

ODILON REDON, in R. J. Goldwater, ed., *Artists on Art* (1945)

Art doesn't come in measured quantities: it's got to be too much or it's not enough.

PAULINE KAEL (1965), in *Newsweek* (1991)

Real art has the capacity to make us nervous. By reducing the work of art to its content and then interpreting *that*, one tames the work of art. Interpretation makes art manageable, conformable.

SUSAN SONTAG, *Against Interpretation* (1966)

Art belongs to all times and to all countries; its special benefit is precisely to be still living when everything else seems dying; that is why Providence shields it from too personal or too general passions, and grants it a patient and persevering organization, durable sensibility, and the contemplative sense in which lies invincible faith.

GEORGE SAND (1863), in Raphaël Ledos de Beaufort, *Letters of George Sand* (1886)

Art is a kind of artificial memory and the pain which attends all serious art is a sense of that factitiousness.

IRIS MURDOCH, *The Black Prince* (1973)

Art is the only thing that can go on mattering once it has stopped hurting.

ELIZABETH BOWEN, *The Heat of the Day* (1949)

Art is not cozy and it is not mocked. Art tells the only truth that ultimately matters. It is the light by which human things can be mended. And after art there is, let me assure you all, nothing.

IRIS MURDOCH, *The Black Prince* (1973)

Art, it seems to me, should simplify. That, indeed, is very nearly the whole of the higher artistic process; finding what conventions of form and what detail one can do without and yet preserve the spirit of the whole—so that all that one has suppressed and cut away is there to the reader's consciousness as much as if it were in type on the page.

WILLA CATHER, "On the Art of Fiction" (1920)

A great work of Art demands a great thought, or a thought of beauty adequately expressed. Neither in Art nor literature more than in life can an ordinary thought be made interesting because well dressed.

MARGARET FULLER (1847), *At Home and Abroad* (1856)

The basic unit for contemporary art is not the idea, but the analysis of and extension of sensations.

SUSAN SONTAG, *Against Interpretation* (1966)

What was any art but an effort to make a sheath, a mold in which to imprison for a moment the shining, elusive element which is life itself,—life hurrying past us and running away, too strong to stop, too sweet to lose?

WILLA CATHER, *The Song of the Lark* (1915)

Art can only be truly Art by presenting an adequate outward symbol of some fact in the interior life.

MARGARET FULLER (1847), *At Home and Abroad* (1856)

Great art is the expression of a solution of the conflict between the demands of the world without and that within.

EDITH HAMILTON, *The Greek Way* (1930)

Art is an affirmation of life, a rebuttal of death. And here we blunder into paradox again, for during the creation of any form of art, which affirms the value and the holiness of life, the artist must die. To serve a work of art, great or small, is to die, to die to self.

MADELEINE L'ENGLE, *Walking on Water: Reflections on Faith and Art* (1980)

Art is the desire of a man to express himself, to record the reactions of his personality to the world he lives in.

AMY LOWELL, *Tendencies in Modern American Poetry* (1917)

I believe in art that conceals art.

RITA MAE BROWN, *Starting From Scratch* (1988)

Art is not for the cultivated taste. It is to cultivate taste.

NIKKI GIOVANNI, in *A Poetic Equation* (1974)

Art is the signature of civilizations.

BEVERLY SILLS, interview (1985)

The difference between writing a story and simply relating past events is that a story, in order to be acceptable, must have shape and meaning. It is the old idea that art is the bringing of order out of chaos.

KATHERINE PATERSON, *The Spying Heart* (1989)

If nothing will finally survive of life besides what artists report of it, we have no right to report what we know to be lies.

ALISON LURIE, *Real People* (1969)

Any authentic work of art must start an argument between the artist and his audience.

REBECCA WEST, *The Court and the Castle* (1957)

Masterpieces are not single and solitary births; they are the outcome of many years of thinking in common, of thinking by the body of the people, so that the experience of the mass is behind the single voice.

VIRGINIA WOOLF, *A Room of One's Own* (1929)

There is, in any art, a tendency to turn one's own preferences into a monomaniac theory.

PAULINE KAEL, *I Lost It at the Movies* (1965)

Genius can probably run on ahead and seek out new ways. But the good artists who follow after genius—and I count myself among these—have to restore the lost connection once more. A pure studio art is unfruitful and frail, for anything that does not form living roots—why should it exist at all?

KÄTHE KOLLWITZ (1916), in Hans Kollwitz, ed., *The Diaries and Letters of Käthe Kollwitz* (1955)

Religion and art spring from the same root and are close kin. Economics and art are strangers.

WILLA CATHER, *Willa Cather on Writing* (1949)

If it's bad art, it's bad religion, no matter how pious the subject.

MADELEINE L'ENGLE, *Walking on Water: Reflections on Faith and Art* (1980)

One thing living in Japan did for me was to make me feel that what is left out of a work of art is as important as, if not more important than, what is put in.

KATHERINE PATERSON, *The Spying Heart* (1989)

Most works of art, like most wines, ought to be consumed in the district of their fabrication.

REBECCA WEST, *Ending in Earnest* (1931)

Clay. It's rain, dead leaves, dust, all my dead ancestors. Stones that have been ground into sand. Mud. The whole cycle of life and death.

MARTINE VERMEULEN, on her pottery, in *New York Times* (1975)

"Organic" is a word I'll stick by. It means the work is an extension of your blood and body; it has the rhythm of nature. This is something artists don't talk about much and it's not even well understood: the fact that there exists a state of feeling and that when you reach it, when you hit it, you can't go wrong.

NELL BLAINE, in Eleanor Munro, *Originals: American Women Artists* (1979)

A work of art has an author and yet, when it is perfect, it has something which is essentially anonymous about it.

SIMONE WEIL, *Gravity and Grace* (1947)

Another unsettling element in modern art is that common symptom of immaturity, the dread of doing what has been done before.

EDITH WHARTON, *The Writing of Fiction* (1925)

Abstract art: a construction site for high fashion, for advertising, for furniture.

ADRIENNE MONNIER, *Les Gazettes d'Adrienne Monnier* (1939), in Richard McDougall, tr., *The Very Rich Hours of Adrienne Monnier* (1976)

Interpretation is the revenge of the intellect upon art.

SUSAN SONTAG, *Against Interpretation* (1966)

We should not have a tin cup out for something as important as the arts in this country, the richest in the world. Creative artists are always begging, but always being used when it's time to show us at our best.

LEONTYNE PRICE, in Brian Lanker, *I Dream a World* (1989)

See also Artists, Creation, Painting, Photography, Sculpture, Writing.

ARTISTS

No artist is ahead of his time. He *is* his time; it is just that others are behind the times.

MARTHA GRAHAM, in John Heilpern, "The Amazing Martha," *Observer* (1979)

The work of art which I do not make, none other will ever make it.

SIMONE WEIL, *The Notebooks of Simone Weil* (1951)

In art one is usually totally alone with oneself.

PAULA MODERSOHN-BECKER, in Gillian Perry, *Paula Modersohn-Becker: Her Life and Work* (1979)

The key is what is within the artist. The artist can only paint what she or he is about.

LEE KRASNER, in Eleanor Munro, *Originals: American Women Artists* (1979)

I think that one's art is a growth inside one. I do not think one can explain growth. It is silent and subtle. One does not keep digging up a plant to see how it grows.

EMILY CARR, *Hundreds and Thousands* (1966)

My painting is so biographical, if anyone can take the trouble to read it.

LEE KRASNER, in Eleanor Munro, *Originals: American Women Artists* (1979)

The artist is not separate from the work and therefore cannot judge it.

MADELEINE L'ENGLE, *Two-Part Invention* (1988)

No artist is pleased. . . . There is only a queer divine dissatisfaction, a blessed unrest that keeps us marching and makes us more alive than the others.

MARTHA GRAHAM, in Agnes de Mille, *Dance to the Piper* (1952)

The most demanding part of living a lifetime as an artist is the strict discipline of forcing oneself to work steadfastly along the nerve of one's own most intimate sensitivity.

ANNE TRUITT, in Annie Dillard, *The Writing Life* (1989)

When you make any kind of artwork, you have to serve it. You could easily call the artist a servant.

M. B. GOFFSTEIN, in *The Five Owls* (1991)

As long as critics have been around, they have insisted that the artist's life and art are inextricably linked.

CLAUDIA TATE, *Black Women Writers at Work* (1983)

Great artists are people who find the way to be themselves in their art. Any sort of pretension induces mediocrity in art and life alike.

MARGOT FONTEYN, *Margot Fonteyn: Autobiography* (1975)

Another real thing! I am not dead yet! I can still call forth a piece of soul and set it down in color, fixed forever.

KERI HULME, *The Bone People* (1983)

Every artist is an unhappy lover.

IRIS MURDOCH, *The Black Prince* (1973)

The independence of the artist is one of the great safeguards of the freedom of the human spirit.

C. V. WEDGWOOD, *Velvet Studies* (1946)

One day I found myself saying to myself . . . I can't live where I want to . . . I can't go where I want to . . . I can't do what I want to. I can't even say what I want to. I decided I was a very stupid fool not to at least paint as I wanted to and say what I wanted to when I painted, and that seemed to be the only thing I could do that didn't concern anybody but myself.

GEORGIA O'KEEFFE (1923), in Eleanor Munro, *Originals: American Women Artists* (1979)

The important thing is to keep producing. All artists have that quality. You have to be tenacious.

MARY FRANK, in Eleanor Munro, *Originals: American Women Artists* (1979)

Through poverty, godhunger, the family debacle, I kept a sense of worth. I could limn and paint like no-one else in this human-wounded land: I was worth the while of living. Now my skill is dead. I should be.

KERI HULME, *The Bone People* (1983)

One has to have a bit of neurosis to go on being an artist. A balanced human seldom produces art. It's that imbalance which impels us.

BEVERLY PEPPER, in Eleanor Munro, *Originals: American Women Artists* (1979)

The successful artist is one who, among other things, finds by luck, labor, instinct, or whatever a form and image to reflect in power (never in literal representation) the original sensory experiences that were received by the [child's] innocent mind. And by contrast, a failed or weak artist would then be one for whom, among other things, the way back is lost or confused or the reflecting image a counterfeit one or mechanically imitative.

ELEANOR MUNRO, *Originals: American Women Artists* (1979)

I believe that each work of art, whether it is a work of great genius, or something very small, comes to the artist and says, "Here I am. Enflesh me. Give birth to me."

MADELEINE L'ENGLE, *Walking on Water: Reflections on Faith and Art* (1980)

There is the falsely mystical view of art that assumes a kind of supernatural inspiration, a possession by universal forces unrelated to questions of power and privilege or the artist's relation to bread and blood. . . . The song is higher than the struggle, and the artist must choose between politics—here defined as earthbound factionalism, corrupt power struggles—

and art, which exists on some transcendent plane.

ADRIENNE RICH, title essay, *Blood, Bread, and Poetry* (1986)

Art is the only thing you cannot punch a button for. You must do it the old-fashioned way. Stay up and really burn the midnight oil. There are no compromises.

LEONTYNE PRICE, in Brian Lanker, *I Dream a World* (1989)

It is the nature of the artist to mind excessively what is said about him. Literature is strewn with the wreckage of men who have minded beyond reason the opinions of others.

VIRGINIA WOOLF, *A Room of One's Own* (1929)

After a little while I murmured to Picasso that I liked his portrait of Gertrude Stein. Yes, he said, everybody said that she does not look like it but that does not make any difference, she will, he said.

GERTRUDE STEIN, *The Autobiography of Alice B. Toklas* (1933)

Dead artists always bring out an older, richer crowd.

ELIZABETH SHAW, in *New York Times* (1976)

A painter is not intellectual when, having painted a nude woman, he leaves in our minds the idea that she is going to get dressed again right away.

ODILON REDON, in R. J. Goldwater, ed., *Artists on Art* (1945)

A primitive artist is an amateur whose work sells.

GRANDMA MOSES, in Otto Kallir, ed., *Grandma Moses: My Life's History* (1947)

If I didn't start painting, I would have raised chickens.

GRANDMA MOSES, in Otto Kallir, ed., *Grandma Moses: My Life's History* (1947)

During the Renaissance, women were not allowed to attend art school. Everyone asks, where are the great women painters of the Renaissance?

KAREN DeCROW, *Sexist Justice* (1974)

Our present-day artists do not transform, they deform. That gives pleasure to nobody. It changes everything, therefore it changes nothing.

ADRIENNE MONNIER, *Les Gazettes d'Adrienne Monnier* (1939), in Richard McDougall, tr., *The Very Rich Hours of Adrienne Monnier* (1976)

It seems likely that many of the young who don't wait for others to call them artists, but simply announce that they are, don't have the patience to make art.

PAULINE KAEL, *Kiss Kiss Bang Bang* (1968)

Very few people possess true artistic ability. It is therefore both unseemly and unproductive to irritate the situation by making an effort. If you have a burning, restless urge to write or paint, simply eat something sweet and the feeling will pass.

FRAN LEBOWITZ, *Metropolitan Life* (1978)

See also Dance, Poets, Singers, Writers.

ASIAN AMERICANS

born into the / skin of yellow women / we are born / into the armor of warriors.

KITTY TSUI, "Chinatown Talking Story," in Asian Women United of California, eds., *Making Waves: An Anthology of Writings By and About Asian American Women* (1989)

We are not afraid to rock the boat. Making waves. This is what Asian American women have done and will continue to do.

ASIAN WOMEN UNITED OF CALIFORNIA, eds., *Making Waves: An Anthology of Writings By and About Asian American Women* (1989)

As a first-generation "Asian American woman," for one thing, I knew there was no such thing as an "Asian American woman." Within this homogenizing labeling of an exotica, I knew there were entire racial/national/cultural/sexual-preferenced groups, many of whom find each other as alien as mainstream America apparently finds us.

SHIRLEY GEOK-LIN LIM, "A Dazzling Quilt," in Shirley Geok-lin Lim, Mayumi Tsutakawa, and Margarita Donnelly, eds., *The Forbidden Stitch: An Asian American Women's Anthology* (1989)

My race is a line that stretches across ocean and time to link me to the shrine where my grandmother was raised.

KESAYA E. NODA, "Growing Up Asian in America," in Asian Women United of California, eds., *Making Waves: An Anthology of Writings By and About Asian American Women* (1989)

See also Minorities.

ASSOCIATION

As every authoritarian regime knows, association can be a dangerous thing. From discussion it is only a few steps to action.

ANNE FIROR SCOTT, "The 'New Woman' in the New South," *South Atlantic Quarterly* (1962)

See also Meetings.

ATHLETES

It's really impossible for athletes to grow up. As long as you're playing, no one will let you. On the one hand, you're a child, still playing a game. And everybody around you acts like a kid, too. But on the other hand, you're a superhuman hero that everyone dreams of being. No wonder we have such a hard time understanding who we are.

BILLIE JEAN KING, *Billie Jean* (1982)

See also Sports.

ATTENTION

Attention is a tacit and continual compliment.

ANNE-SOPHIE SWETCHINE, *The Writings of Madame Swetchine* (1869)

We have to try to cure our faults by attention and not by will.

SIMONE WEIL, *Gravity and Grace* (1947)

Those who are unhappy have no need for anything in this world but people capable of giving them their attention.

SIMONE WEIL, *Waiting for God* (1950)

The authentic and pure values, truth, beauty, and goodness, in the activity of a human being are the result of one and the same act, a certain application of the full attention to the object. Teaching should have no aim but to prepare, by training the attention, for the possibility of such an act. All the other advantages of instruction are without interest.

SIMONE WEIL, *Gravity and Grace* (1947)

See also Listening, Publicity.

AUDIENCE

Audiences are always better pleased with a smart retort, some joke or epigram, than with any amount of reasoning.

CHARLOTTE PERKINS GILMAN, *The Living of Charlotte Perkins Gilman* (1935)

Believe me, nothing is so calculated to lose you audience sympathy as too many tears. Move your listeners all you can but let them do the crying.

ILKA CHASE, *Elephants Arrive at Half-Past Five* (1963)

I can never remember being afraid of an audience. If the audience could do better, they'd be up here on stage and I'd be out there watching them.

ETHEL MERMAN, in Barbara McDowell and Hana Umlauf, *Woman's Almanac* (1977)

In the theater, I've found that, in general, reaction and laughter come easier at an evening performance, when the audience is more inclined to forget its troubles. Matinee customers must enter the theater in a more matter-of-fact frame of mind, hanging on tightly before they let themselves go.

BEATRICE LILLIE, *Every Other Inch a Lady* (1972)

On the outskirts of every agony sits some observant fellow who points.

VIRGINIA WOOLF, *The Waves* (1931)

See also Performance.

AUTHORITY

Authority without wisdom is like a heavy axe without an edge: fitter to bruise than polish.

ANNE BRADSTREET, "Meditations Divine and Moral" (c. 1655), in John Harvard Ellis, *The Works of Anne Bradstreet in Prose and Verse* (1932)

It is just when opinions universally prevail and we have added lip service to their authority that we become sometimes most keenly conscious that we do not believe a word that we are saying.

VIRGINIA WOOLF, *The Common Reader* (1925)

I believe in a lively disrespect for most forms of authority.

RITA MAE BROWN, *Starting From Scratch* (1988)

See also Power.

AUTOBIOGRAPHY

All autobiography is self-indulgent.

DAPHNE DU MAURIER, *Myself When Young* (1977)

The urge to write one's autobiography, so I have been told, overtakes everyone sooner or later.

AGATHA CHRISTIE, *An Autobiography* (1977)

Autobiography at least saves a man or woman that the world is curious about from the publication of a string of mistakes called "Memoirs."

GEORGE ELIOT, letter (1876), in J. W. Cross, *George Eliot's Life as Related in Her Letters and Journals* (1884)

I'll be eighty this month. Age, if nothing else, entitles me to set the record straight before I dissolve. I've given my memoirs far more thought than any of my marriages. You can't divorce a book.

GLORIA SWANSON, in *New York Times* (1979)

To be sure, the ego is not always odious. Few books are more thrilling than certain confessions, but they must be honest, and the author must have something to confess.

SIMONE DE BEAUVOIR, *The Second Sex* (1949)

Thus, in a real sense, I am constantly writing autobiography, but I have to turn it into fiction in order to give it credibility.

KATHERINE PATERSON, *The Spying Heart* (1989)

Your life story would not make a good book. Do not even try.

FRAN LEBOWITZ, *Metropolitan Life* (1978)

See also Biography.

AUTUMN

Delicious autumn! My very soul is wedded to it, and if I were a bird I would fly about the earth seeking the successive autumns.

GEORGE ELIOT, letter (1840), in J. W. Cross, *George Eliot's Life as Related in Her Letters and Journals* (1884)

Autumn is a hound that shrills, my heart is for her gnawing. / The quarry goes to Autumn, let Spring die.

BABETTE DEUTSCH, "The Hound," *Banners* (1919)

All those golden autumn days the sky was full of wings. Wings beating low over the blue water of Silver Lake, wings beating high in the blue air far above it. Wings of geese, of brant, of ducks and pelicans and cranes and heron and swans and gulls, bearing them all away to green fields in the South.

LAURA INGALLS WILDER, *On the Shores of Silver Lake* (1939)

What of October, that ambiguous month, the month of tension, the unendurable month?

DORIS LESSING, *Martha Quest* (1952)

November is the most disagreeable month in the whole year.

LOUISA MAY ALCOTT, *Little Women* (1868)

On the steppes of Siberia, fall does not arrive with a great show of flaming leaves; it comes in with a great howling wind. . . . I thought that all the wolves of Siberia had gathered there at the mine to devour us.

ESTHER HAUTZIG, *The Endless Steppe* (1968)

AWARENESS

Some people are aware of everything that is going on everywhere at every moment in their lives.

ANNE TYLER, *Celestial Navigation* (1974)

It was as if I had worked for years on the wrong side of a tapestry, learning accurately all its lines and figures, yet always missing its color and sheen.

ANNA LOUISE STRONG, *I Change Worlds* (1935)

When you don't know when you have been spit on, it does not matter too much what else you think you know.

RUTH SHAYS, in John Langston Gwaltney, *Drylongso* (1980)

It's so easy to be wicked without knowing it, isn't it?

L. M. MONTGOMERY, *Anne of Green Gables* (1908)

It's exhilarating to be alive in a time of awakening consciousness; it can also be confusing, disorienting, and painful.

ADRIENNE RICH, "When We Dead Awaken: Writing as Re-Vision," *On Lies, Secrets, and Silence* (1978)

Eden is that old-fashioned House / We dwell in every day / Without suspecting our abode / Until we drive away.

EMILY DICKINSON (c. 1862–1886), *The Single Hound* (1914)

See also Knowledge, Self-Knowledge, Sensitivity.

B

BABIES

It sometimes happens, even in the best of families, that a baby is born. This is not necessarily cause for alarm. The important thing is to keep your wits about you and borrow some money.

ELINOR GOULDING SMITH, *The Complete Book of Absolutely Perfect Baby and Child Care* (1957)

Now the thing about having a baby—and I can't be the first person to have noticed this—is that thereafter you *have* it.

JEAN KERR, *Please Don't Eat the Daisies* (1957)

No animal is so inexhaustible as an excited infant.

AMY LESLIE, *Amy Leslie at the Fair* (1893)

Like a round loaf . . . , / I kneaded you, patted you, / greased you smooth, floured you.

JUDIT TÓTH, "To the Newborn," in Joanna Bankier and Deirdre Lashgari, eds., *Women Poets of the World* (1983)

Don't forget that compared to a grownup person every baby is a genius. Think of the capacity to learn! The freshness, the temperament, the will of a baby a few months old!

MAY SARTON, *Mrs. Stevens Hears the Mermaids Singing* (1965)

For years we have given scientific attention to the care and rearing of plants and animals, but we have allowed babies to be raised chiefly by tradition.

EDITH BELLE LOWRY, *False Modesty* (1912)

See also Childbirth, Children, Pregnancy.

BALLET

Ballet's image of perfection is fashioned amid a milieu of wracked bodies, fevered imaginations, Balkan intrigue, and sulfurous hatreds where anything is likely, and dancers know it.

SHANA ALEXANDER, *Nutcracker* (1985)

Ballet technique is arbitrary and very difficult. It never becomes easy; it becomes possible.

AGNES DE MILLE, *Dance to the Piper* (1952)

A toe shoe is as eccentric as the ballerina who wears it: their marriage is a commitment.

TONI BENTLEY, in *Smithsonian* (1984)

A brand-new pair of toe shoes presents itself to us as an enemy with a will of its own that must be tamed.

TONI BENTLEY, in *Smithsonian* (1984)

See also Artists, Dance.

BATH

There must be quite a few things a hot bath won't cure, but I don't know many of them.

SYLVIA PLATH, *The Bell Jar* (1963)

I can't think of any sorrow in the world that a hot bath wouldn't help, just a little bit.

SUSAN GLASPELL, *The Visioning* (1911)

BEAUTY

Beauty is everlasting / and dust is for a time.

MARIANNE MOORE, "In Distrust of Merits," *Collected Poems* (1951)

The beauty of the world . . . has two edges, one of laughter, one of anguish, cutting the heart asunder.

VIRGINIA WOOLF, *A Room of One's Own* (1929)

Beauty is altogether in the eye of the beholder.

MARGARET WOLFE HUNGERFORD, *Molly Bawn* (1878)

O, beauty, are you not enough? / Why am I crying after love?

SARA TEASDALE, "Spring Night," *Rivers to the Sea* (1915)

To die would have been beautiful. But I belong to those who do not die for the sake of beauty.

AGNES SMEDLEY, *Daughter of Earth* (1929)

You agree—I'm sure you agree, that beauty is the only thing worth living for.

AGATHA CHRISTIE, *The Moving Finger* (1942)

To seek after beauty as an end, is a wild goose chase, a will-o'-the-wisp, because it is to misunderstand the very nature of beauty, which is the normal condition of a thing being as it should be.

ADE BETHUNE, in Judith Stoughton, *Proud Donkey of Schaerbeek* (1988)

Was she so loved because her eyes were so beautiful or were her eyes so beautiful because she was so loved?

ANZIA YEZIERSKA, *Arrogant Beggar* (1927)

Oh who can tell the range of joy / Or set the bounds of beauty?

SARA TEASDALE, "A Winter Bluejay," *Rivers to the Sea* (1915)

Art should be Truth; and Truth unadorned, unsentimentalized, is Beauty.

ELIZABETH BORTON DE TREVIÑO, *I, Juan de Pareja* (1965)

All ugliness passes and beauty endures; except of the skin.

EDITH SITWELL, *Selected Letters* (1970)

All things are perceived in the light of charity, and hence under the aspect of beauty: for beauty is simply Reality seen with the eyes of love.

EVELYN UNDERHILL, *Mysticism* (1955)

A mode of conduct, a standard of courage, discipline, fortitude, and integrity can do a great deal to make a woman beautiful.

JACQUELINE BISSET, in *Los Angeles Times* (1974)

Perhaps all this modern ferment of what's known as "social conscience" or "civic responsibility" isn't a result of the sense of duty, but of the old, old craving for beauty.

DOROTHY CANFIELD FISHER, *The Bent Twig* (1915)

Think of all the beauty that's still left in and around you and be happy!

ANNE FRANK, *Diary of a Young Girl* (1952)

Beauty more than bitterness / Makes the heart break.

SARA TEASDALE, "Vignettes Overseas," *Rivers to the Sea* (1915)

I'm tired of all this nonsense about beauty being only skin-deep. That's deep enough. What do you want—an adorable pancreas?

JEAN KERR, *The Snake Has All the Lines* (1958)

See also Appearance.

BEGINNING

It is only the first step that is difficult.

MARIE DE VICHY-CHAMROND, MARQUISE DU DEFFAND, letter to d'Alembert (1763)

Nothing, of course, begins at the time you think it did.

LILLIAN HELLMAN, *An Unfinished Woman* (1969)

The world is round and the place which may seem like the end may also be only the beginning.

IVY BAKER PRIEST, in *Parade* (1958)

But the beginning of things, of a world especially, is necessarily vague, tangled, chaotic, and exceedingly disturbing.

KATE CHOPIN, *The Awakening* (1899)

In my end is my beginning—that's what people are always saying. But what does it mean?

AGATHA CHRISTIE, *Endless Night* (1968)

BEHAVIOR

Life with Mary was like being in a telephone booth with an open umbrella—no matter which way you turned, you got it in the eye.

JEAN KERR, *Mary, Mary* (1963)

I saw him riding in the Row, clinging to his horse like a string of onions.

MARGOT ASQUITH, *The Autobiography of Margot Asquith* (1923)

He used his hands as though they were feet.

RAE FOLEY, *The Hundredth Door* (1950)

[He drove] at a stately thirty miles an hour, triumphant but alert, eyes flicking left and right, like an Allied general entering a newly liberated town.

LUCILLE KALLEN, *Introducing C. B. Greenfield* (1979)

Mrs. Bennett was restored to her usual querulous serenity.

JANE AUSTEN, *Pride and Prejudice* (1813)

He's as finicky as the five-times-table, and about as lively.

MARY STEWART, *Nine Coaches Waiting* (1958)

Marcia was incredibly organized, obsessively neat. . . . I mean she folded her underwear like origami.

LINDA BARNES, "Lucky Penny," in Marilyn Wallace, ed., *Sisters in Crime* (1989)

"Ah," said Mrs. Peniston, shutting her lips with the snap of a purse closing against a beggar.

EDITH WHARTON, *The House of Mirth* (1905)

Her mouth dropped open to let this thought come in and nourish her brain.

AMY TAN, *The Kitchen God's Wife* (1991)

His tone was about as informative, and as welcoming, as a blank wall with broken glass on the top.

MARY STEWART, *This Rough Magic* (1964)

They were drinking ginger ale on her front porch and she kept rattling the ice in her glass, rattling her beads, rattling her bracelet like an impatient pony jingling its harness.

FLANNERY O'CONNOR, "The Displaced Person," *A Good Man Is Hard to Find* (1953)

When she raises her eyelids it's as if she were taking off all her clothes.

COLETTE, *Claudine and Annie* (1952)

Our humanity rests upon a series of learned behaviors, woven together into patterns that are infinitely fragile and never directly inherited.

MARGARET MEAD, *Male and Female* (1949)

See also Actions, Deeds.

BELGIUM

Life is long since asleep in Bruges; fantastic dreams alone breathe over tower and medieval house front, enchanting the eye, inspiring the soul and filling the mind with the great beauty of contemplation.

KATHERINE MANSFIELD, "A Truthful Adventure" (1910), *Something Childish* (1924)

See also Europe.

BELIEF

There are no atheists on turbulent airplanes.

ERICA JONG, *Fear of Flying* (1973)

You can make an audience see nearly anything, if you yourself believe in it.

MARY RENAULT, *The Mask of Apollo* (1966)

He was paralyzed with the impossibility of either belief or disbelief.

L. M. BOSTON, *A Stranger at Green Knowe* (1961)

I am always easy of belief when the creed pleases me.

CHARLOTTE BRONTË, *Shirley* (1849)

They were so strong in their beliefs that there came a time when it hardly mattered what exactly those beliefs were; they all fused into a single stubbornness.

LOUISE ERDRICH, *Love Medicine* (1984)

You're not free / until you've been made captive by / supreme belief.

MARIANNE MOORE, "Spenser's Ireland," *What Are Years?* (1941)

To believe in something not yet proved and to underwrite it with our lives; it is the only way we can leave the future open.

LILLIAN SMITH, *The Journey* (1954)

See also Credulity, Dogma, Faith, Philosophy, Superstition.

BETRAYAL

I saw this thing turn, like a flower, once picked, turning petals into bright knives in your hand. And it was so much desired, so lovely, that your fingers will not loosen, and you have only disbelief that this, of all you have ever known, should have the possibility of pain.

NADINE GORDIMER, *The Lying Days* (1953)

See also Infidelity, Treachery.

BIBLE

Though my father was poor and had nothing, the Torah, the poetry of prophets, was his daily bread.

ANZIA YEZIERSKA, *Red Ribbon on a White Horse* (1950)

Amid ancient lore the Word of God stands unique and pre-eminent. Wonderful in its construction, admirable in its adaptation, it contains truths that a child may comprehend, and mysteries into which angels desire to look.

FRANCES ELLEN WATKINS HARPER, "Christianity," *Poems on Miscellaneous Subjects* (1857)

In my opinion what distinguishes the Bible from the other books is its sense of time. Its first concern is to establish a calendar. Then it traces a genealogy. It imposes rhythms, it orders, it operates, it does not abandon the earth where its destiny must be fulfilled and whose own destiny must be fulfilled by it. Its history will be that of men and not of idle gods. The whole spirit must become incarnate and explore the possible.

ADRIENNE MONNIER, *Les Gazettes d'Adrienne Monnier* (1938), in Richard McDougall, tr., *The Very Rich Hours of Adrienne Monnier* (1976)

The consensus appears to be that as it is presented and practiced in our churches the gospel is NOT Good News for women.

ELAINE STORKEY, *What's Right with Feminism* (1985)

The Bible is used as a means of reinforcing . . . [women's] subordination to men through divine sanction.

LETTY RUSSELL, *The Liberating Word: A Guide to Nonsexist Interpretation of the Bible* (1976)

Kindly inform the Church of England they have loused up the most beautiful prose ever written, whoever told them to tinker with the Vulgate Latin? They'll burn for it, you mark my words.

HELENE HANFF, *84, Charing Cross Road* (1970)

BIOGRAPHY

The best biographies leave their readers with a sense of having all but entered into a second life and of having come to know another human being in some ways better than he knew himself.

MARY CABLE, in *New York Times* (1969)

In writing biography, fact and fiction shouldn't be mixed. And if they are, the fiction parts should be printed in red ink, the fact parts in black ink.

CATHERINE DRINKER BOWEN, in *Publishers Weekly* (1958)

Just how difficult it is to write biography can be reckoned by anybody who sits down and considers just how many people know the real truth about his or her love affairs.

REBECCA WEST, "The Art of Skepticism," *Vogue* (1952)

A woman's biography—with about eight famous historical exceptions—so often turns out to be the story of a man and the woman who helped his career.

CATHERINE DRINKER BOWEN, in Barbara Sicherman and Carol Hurd Green, eds., *Notable American Women: The Modern Period* (1980)

BIOLOGY

We are a sad lot, the cell biologists. Like the furtive collectors of stolen art, we are forced to be lonely admirers of spectacular architecture, exquisite symmetry, dramas of violence and death, nobility, self-sacrifice and, yes, rococo sex.

LORRAINE LEE CUDMORE, *The Center of Life* (1977)

Considering the very close genetic relationship that has been established by comparison of biochemical properties of blood proteins, protein structure and DNA, and immunological responses, the differences between a man and a chimpanzee are more astonishing than the resemblances.

ELAINE MORGAN, *The Aquatic Ape* (1982)

Man is the only mammal whose normal method of locomotion is to walk on two legs. A pattern of mammal behavior that emerges only once in the whole history of life on earth takes a great deal of explaining.

ELAINE MORGAN, *The Aquatic Ape* (1982)

BIRDS

I hope you love birds, too. It is economical. It saves going to Heaven.

EMILY DICKINSON, letter (1885), in Mabel Loomis Todd, *Letters of Emily Dickinson* (1894)

Few forms of life are so engaging as birds.

ELLEN GLASGOW, *Letters of Ellen Glasgow* (1958)

How pleasant the lives of the birds must be, / Living in love in a leafy tree!

MARY HOWITT, "Birds in Summer," *Ballads and Other Poems* (1847)

Did St. Francis really preach to the birds? Whatever for? If he really liked birds he would have done better to preach to the cats.

REBECCA WEST, *This Real Night* (1984)

Over increasingly large areas of the United States, spring now comes unheralded by the return of the birds, and the early mornings are strangely silent where once they were filled with the beauty of bird song.

RACHEL CARSON, *Silent Spring* (1962)

Shoot all the bluejays you want, if you can hit 'em, but remember it's a sin to kill a mockingbird. . . . Mockingbirds don't do one thing but make music for us to enjoy. They don't eat up people's gardens, don't nest in corncribs, they don't do one thing but sing their hearts out for us. That's why it's a sin to kill a mockingbird.

HARPER LEE, *To Kill a Mockingbird* (1960)

Healthy parakeets have the nervous energy of tennis players.

MIGNON MCLAUGHLIN, *The Second Neurotic's Notebook* (1966)

BIRTH

When I was born, I was so surprised I couldn't talk for a year and a half.

GRACIE ALLEN, *The Robert Burns Panatela Program* (1932)

I think of birth as the search for a larger apartment.

RITA MAE BROWN, *Starting From Scratch* (1988)

To be born is to start the journey towards death.

MADELEINE L'ENGLE, *Walking on Water: Reflections on Faith and Art* (1980)

I/woman give birth: / and this time to / myself.

ALMA VILLANUEVA, "I Sing to Myself," in *Third Chicano Literary Prize: Irvine 1976–1977* (1977)

See also Beginning, Childbirth.

BIRTH CONTROL

We want far better reasons for having children than not knowing how to prevent them.

DORA RUSSELL, Hypatia (1925)

Biological *possibility* and desire are not the same as biological *need*. Women have child-bearing equipment. For them to choose not to use the equipment is no more blocking what is instinctive than it is for a man who, muscles or no, chooses not to be a weightlifter.

BETTY ROLLIN, in *Look* (1971)

No woman can call herself free who does not own and control her body. No woman can call herself free until she can choose consciously whether she will or will not be a mother.

MARGARET H. SANGER, *Woman and the New Race* (1920)

BIRTHDAY

Happy birthday to you.

Patty S. Hill, song title (1893)

It is lovely, when I forget all birthdays, including my own, to find that somebody remembers me.

Ellen Glasgow, *Letters of Ellen Glasgow* (1958)

BITTERNESS

Bitterness hardly cares what food it eats.

Leslie Ford, *Invitation to Murder* (1954)

Bitterness had become a habit between them.

Edna O'Brien, "A Woman by the Seaside," *Mrs. Reinhardt* (1978)

Vinegar he poured on me all his life; I am well marinated; how can I be honey now?

Tillie Olsen, title story, *Tell Me a Riddle* (1956)

I have loved, and bitterness left me for that hour. But there are times when love itself is bitter.

Agnes Smedley, *Daughter of Earth* (1929)

See also Resentment.

BLACKS

For though I'm black, yet am I also fair / and in my mortal form, Thine doth appear.

Sor Juana Inés de la Cruz, "The Divine Narcissus" (c. 1690), in Irene Nicholson, *A Guide to Mexican Poetry* (1968)

We live surrounded by white images, and white in this world is synonymous with the good, light, beauty, success, so that, despite ourselves sometimes, we run after that whiteness and deny our darkness, which has been made into the symbol of all that is evil and inferior.

Paule Marshall, title story, *Reena* (1983)

never once / did she wanna / be white / to pass / dreamed only of bein darker.

Mary Hope Lee, "on not bein," in Cherríe Moraga and Gloria Anzaldúa, eds., *This Bridge Called My Back* (1983)

I am here and you will know that I am the best and will hear me. The color of my skin or the kink of my hair or the spread of my mouth has nothing to do with what you are listening to.

Leontyne Price, in *Time* (1985)

There is an incredible amount of magic and feistiness in black men that nobody has been able to wipe out. But everybody has tried.

Toni Morrison, in Dexter Fisher, *The Third Woman* (1980)

Any woman who has a great deal to offer the world is in trouble. And if she's a black woman, she's in deep trouble.

Hazel Scott, in Margo Jefferson, "Great (Hazel) Scott!" *Ms.* (1974)

No other group in America has so had their identity socialized out of existence as have black women. . . . When black people are talked about the focus tends to be on black *men;* and when women are talked about the focus tends to be on *white* women.

Bell Hooks, *Ain't I a Woman?* (1981)

And she had nothing to fall back on; not maleness, not whiteness, not ladyhood, not anything. And out of the profound desolation of her reality she may very well have invented herself.

Toni Morrison, "What the Black Women Think About Women's Lib," in *New York Times Magazine* (1971)

Let me state here and now that the black woman in America can justly be described as a "slave of a slave."

Frances M. Beal, "Double Jeopardy: To Be Black and Female," in Robin Morgan, *Sisterhood Is Powerful* (1970)

The colored woman of today occupies, one may say, a unique position in this country. In a period of itself transitional and unsettled, her status seems one of the least ascertainable and definitive of all the forces which make for our civilization. She is confronted by both a woman question and a race problem.

Anna Julia Cooper, *A Voice from the South* (1892)

Usually, when people talk about the "strength" of black women they are referring to the way in which they perceive black women coping with oppression. They ignore the reality that to be strong in the face of oppression is not the same as overcoming oppression, that endurance is not to be confused with transformation. . . . The tendency to romanticize the black female experience that began in the feminist movement was reflected in the culture as a whole.

BELL HOOKS, *Ain't I a Woman?* (1981)

On the road to equality there is no better place for blacks to detour around American values than in foregoing its example in the treatment of its women and the organization of its family life.

ELEANOR HOLMES NORTON, "For Sadie and Maude," in Robin Morgan, *Sisterhood Is Powerful* (1970)

Blacks concede that hurrawing, jibing, jiving, signifying, disrespecting, cursing, even outright insults might be acceptable under particular conditions, but aspersions cast against one's family call for immediate attack.

MAYA ANGELOU, *All God's Children Need Traveling Shoes* (1986)

Black people are the only segment in American society that is defined by its weakest elements. Every other segment is defined by its highest achievement. We have to turn that around.

JEWELL JACKSON MCCABE, in Brian Lanker, *I Dream a World* (1989)

It is not healthy when a nation lives within a nation, as colored Americans are living inside America. A nation cannot live confident of its tomorrow if its refugees are among its own citizens.

PEARL BUCK, *What America Means to Me* (1943)

Black people cannot and will not become integrated into American society on any terms but those of self-determination and autonomy.

GERDA LERNER, *Black Women in White America* (1972)

The drums of Africa still beat in my heart. They will not let me rest while there is a single Negro boy or girl without a chance to prove his worth.

MARY MCLEOD BETHUNE, in *Who, the Magazine About People* (1941)

Black ice is the smoothest naturally occurring ice there is, as if nature were condescending to art. . . . Black ice is an act of nature as elusive as grace, and far more rare. . . . I have never skated on black ice, but perhaps my children will. They'll know it, at least, when it appears: that the earth can stretch smooth and unbroken like grace, and they'll know as they know my voice that they were meant to have their share.

LORENE CARY, *Black Ice* (1991)

Anything I have ever learned of any consequence, I have learned from Black people. I have never been bored by *any* Black person, ever.

TONI MORRISON, in Roseann P. Bell, Bettye J. Parker, and Beverly Guy-Sheftall, *Sturdy Black Bridges* (1979)

The way I was taught, being black was a plus, always. Being a human being, being in America, and being black, all three were the greatest things that could happen to you. The combination was unbeatable.

LEONTYNE PRICE, in Brian Lanker, *I Dream a World* (1989)

BLACKS AND WHITES

White folks needs what black folks got just as much as black folks needs what white folks got, and we's all got to stay here mongst each other and git along, that's what.

MARGARET WALKER, *Jubilee* (1966)

Far as I'm concerned, friendship between black and white don't mean that much 'cause it usually ain't on a equal basis. . . . Maybe one day whites and blacks can be real friends, but right now the country ain't built that way.

MILDRED D. TAYLOR, *Roll of Thunder, Hear My Cry* (1976)

One very important difference between white people and black people is that white people think that you *are* your work. . . . Now, black people think that my work is just what I have to do to get what I want.

MAY ANNA MADISON, in *Drylongso* (1980)

It is not the destiny of black America to repeat white America's mistakes. But we will, if we mistake the trappings of success in a sick society for the signs of a meaningful life.

AUDRE LORDE, "Feminism and Black Liberation: The Great American Disease," *The Black Scholar* (1979)

See also Blacks, Racism, Whites.

BLAME

There's folks 'ud stand on their heads and then say the fault was i' their boots.

GEORGE ELIOT, *Adam Bede* (1859)

BODY

The body is a sacred garment.

MARTHA GRAHAM, *Blood Memory* (1991)

I believe that the physical is the geography of the being.

LOUISE NEVELSON, *Dawns + Dusks* (1976)

The body is shaped, disciplined, honored, and in time, trusted.

MARTHA GRAHAM, *Blood Memory* (1991)

The body has its own way of knowing, a knowing that has little to do with logic, and much to do with truth, little to do with control, and much to do with acceptance, little to do with division and analysis, and much to do with union.

MARILYN SEWELL, *Cries of the Spirit* (1991)

Over the years our bodies become walking autobiographies, telling friends and strangers alike of the minor and major stresses of our lives.

MARILYN FERGUSON, *The Aquarian Conspiracy* (1980)

We have so many words for states of mind, and so few for the states of the body.

JEANNE MOREAU, *New York Times* (1976)

The gesture is the thing truly expressive of the individual—as we think so will we act.

MARTHA GRAHAM, in John Heilpern, "The Amazing Martha," *Observer* (1979)

Movement never lies.

MARTHA GRAHAM, *Blood Memory* (1991)

Ro doesn't stand like Brent or Dad. His hands hang kind of stiffly from the shoulder joints, and when he moves, his palms are tucked tight against his thighs, his stomach sticks out like a slightly pregnant woman's. Each culture estab-lishes its own manly posture, different ways of claiming space.

BHARATI MUKHERJEE, *The Middleman and Other Stories* (1988)

At my age the bones are water in the morning until food is given them.

PEARL BUCK, *The Good Earth* (1931)

And how to paint your lovely hands, fluttering over the silks like two dark birds?

ELIZABETH BORTON DE TREVIÑO, *I, Juan de Pareja* (1965)

I had to face the facts, I was pear-shaped. I was a bit depressed because I hate pears.

CHARLOTTE BINGHAM, *Coronet Among the Weeds* (1963)

So the legs are a little short, the knees maybe knock a little but who listens?

GERTRUDE BERG, *Molly and Me* (1961)

See also Appearance, Beauty, Eyes, Face, Hair.

BOOKS

There is no Frigate like a Book / To take us Lands away.

EMILY DICKINSON (1873), in Mabel Loomis Todd, *Letters of Emily Dickinson* (1894)

Books . . . are like lobster shells, we surround ourselves with 'em, then we grow out of 'em and leave 'em behind, as evidence of our earlier stages of development.

DOROTHY L. SAYERS, *The Unpleasantness at the Bellona Club* (1928)

Books are the carriers of civilization. Without books, history is silent, literature dumb, science crippled, thought and speculation at a standstill.

BARBARA TUCHMAN, in *Authors' League Bulletin* (1979)

I think I was born with the impression that what happened in books was much more reasonable, and interesting, and *real*, in some ways, than what happened in life.

ANNE TYLER, in Janet Sternburg, ed., *The Writer on Her Work*, vol. 1 (1980)

The memory of having been read to is a solace one carries through adulthood. It can wash over a multitude of parental sins.

KATHLEEN ROCKWELL LAWRENCE, *The Boys I Didn't Kiss* (1990)

When I was about eight, I decided that the most wonderful thing, next to a human being, was a book.

MARGARET WALKER, in Brian Lanker, *I Dream a World* (1989)

I went to the library. They gave you books for nothing. You had to bring them back, but when you did, they let you take others.

BARBARA COHEN, *Gooseberries to Oranges* (1982)

It had been startling and disappointing to me to find out that story books had been written by *people,* that books were not natural wonders, coming up of themselves like grass.

EUDORA WELTY, *One Writer's Beginnings* (1984)

There are some books one needs maturity to enjoy just as there are books an adult can come upon too late to savor.

PHYLLIS McGINLEY, *The Province of the Heart* (1959)

Just the knowledge that a good book is awaiting one at the end of a long day makes that day happier.

KATHLEEN NORRIS, *Hands Full of Living* (1931)

Which is to say that I can easily do without people (there are days when I could easily do without myself), and that in the country of books where I dwell, the dead can count entirely as much as the living.

ADRIENNE MONNIER, in Richard McDougall, tr., *The Very Rich Hours of Adrienne Monnier* (1976)

The wonderful thing about books is that they allow us to enter imaginatively into someone else's life. And when we do that, we learn to sympathize with other people. But the real surprise is that we also learn truths about ourselves, about our own lives, that somehow we hadn't been able to see before.

KATHERINE PATERSON, in *The Horn Book* (1991)

If I read a book that impresses me, I have to take myself firmly in hand, before I mix with other people; otherwise they would think my mind rather queer.

ANNE FRANK, *Diary of a Young Girl* (1952)

Fitting people with books is about as difficult as fitting them with shoes.

SYLVIA BEACH, *Shakespeare and Company* (1956)

Let us secure not such books as people want, but books just above their wants, and they will reach up to take what is put out for them.

MARIA MITCHELL (1887), in Phebe Mitchell Kendall, ed., *Maria Mitchell, Life, Letters, and Journals* (1896)

He felt about books as doctors feel about medicines, or managers about plays—cynical but hopeful.

ROSE MACAULAY, *Crewe Train* (1926)

She is too fond of books, and it has turned her brain.

LOUISA MAY ALCOTT, *Work* (1873)

I suppose anyone who has ever written a travel book has had the experience of being accosted by a reader with blood in his eye and a lawsuit in his voice.

ILKA CHASE, *Elephants Arrive at Half-Past Five* (1963)

If we are told of some four-volume epic . . . we're apt to say "How interesting," but we never will read it unless we have both legs in traction.

MARTHA BAYLES, in *Wall Street Journal* (1984)

Leaving behind books is even more beautiful— there are far too many children.

MARGUERITE YOURCENAR, in *New York Times* (1980)

I do love secondhand books that open to the page some previous owner read oftenest.

HELENE HANFF, *84, Charing Cross Road* (1970)

This is a book lined with hard facts and stitched up with strong opinions.

SUZY MENKES, book review, *London Times* (1984)

I sat staring up at a shelf in my workroom from which thirty-one books identically dressed in neat dark green leather stared back at me with a sort of cold hostility like children who resent their parents. Don't stare at us like that! they said. Don't blame us if we didn't turn out to be the perfection you expected. We didn't ask to be brought into the world.

EDNA FERBER, *A Kind of Magic* (1963)

I can imagine now that a time will come, that it is almost upon us, when no one will love books. . . . It is no accident, I think, that books and nature (as we know it) may disappear simultaneously from human experience. There is no mind-body split.

ANDREA DWORKIN, "First Love," in Julia Wolf Mazow, ed., *The Woman Who Lost Her Names* (1980)

See also Borrowing, Prefaces, Publishing, Reading, Titles, Writing.

BORDERS

Living on borders and in margins, keeping intact one's shifting and multiple identity and integrity, is like trying to swim in a new element, an "alien" element.

GLORIA ANZALDÚA, *Borderlands/La Frontera: The New Mestiza* (1987)

I'm sick of seeing and touching / Both sides of things / Sick of being the damn bridge for everybody.

KATE RUSHIN, "The Bridge Poem," in Cherríe Moraga and Gloria Anzaldúa, eds., *This Bridge Called My Back* (1983)

It is hopeless to try to convert some borders into seams.

JANE JACOBS, *The Death and Life of Great American Cities* (1961)

The U.S.-Mexican border *es una herida abierta* where the Third World grates against the first and bleeds. And before a scab forms it hemorrhages again, the lifeblood of two worlds merging to form a third country—a border culture.

GLORIA ANZALDÚA, *Borderlands/La Frontera: The New Mestiza* (1987)

See also Immigrants, Refugees.

BOREDOM

She wanted something to happen—something, anything; she did not know what.

KATE CHOPIN, *The Awakening* (1899)

Every time I think I've touched bottom as far as boredom is concerned, new vistas of ennui open up.

MARGARET HALSEY, *No Laughing Matter* (1977)

One of the dreariest spots on life's road is the point of conviction that nothing will ever again happen to you.

FAITH BALDWIN, *The West Wind* (1962)

Monotony and repetition are characteristic of many parts of life, but these do not become sources of conscious discomfort until novelty and entertainment are built up as positive experiences.

MARY CATHERINE BATESON, *With a Daughter's Eye* (1984)

Ennui is the disease of hearts without feeling, and of minds without resources.

MARIE-JEANNE ROLAND (1793), in Lydia Maria Child, *Memoirs of Madame de Staël and of Madame Roland* (1847)

Bored people, unless they sleep a lot, are cruel.

RENATA ADLER, *Speedboat* (1976)

See also Bores, Dullness, Restlessness.

BORES

A bore is a person not interested in you.

MARY PETTIBONE POOLE, *A Glass Eye at a Keyhole* (1938)

A bore is a vacuum cleaner of society, sucking up everything and giving nothing. Bores are always eager to be seen talking to you.

ELSA MAXWELL, *How to Do It* (1957)

It is always your heaviest bore who is astonished at the tameness of modern celebrities: naturally; for a little of his company has reduced them to a state of flaccid fatigue.

GEORGE ELIOT, *Impressions of Theophrastus Such* (1879)

He's the kind of bore who's here today and here tomorrow.

BINNIE BARNES, in *The Wisdom of Women* (1971)

Under pressure, people admit to murder, setting fire to the village church or robbing a bank, but never to being bores.

ELSA MAXWELL, *How to Do It* (1957)

Tallulah [Bankhead] never bored anyone, and I consider that humanitarianism of a very high order indeed.

ANITA LOOS, in *New York Times* (1968)

See also Boredom.

BORROWING

Why is it that people who wouldn't dream of stealing anything else think it's perfectly all right to steal books?

HELENE HANFF, *84, Charing Cross Road* (1970)

They borrow books they will not buy, / They have no ethics or religions; / I wish some kind Burbankian guy / Would cross my books with homing pigeons.

CAROLYN WELLS, "Book Borrowers" (1900)

Everything they had was borrowed; they had nothing of their own at all.

MARY NORTON, *The Borrowers* (1952)

BRAIN

The softest, freest, most pliable and changeful living substance . . . the hardest and most iron-bound as well.

CHARLOTTE PERKINS GILMAN, *The Home: Its Work and Influence* (1904)

To repeat what others have said, requires education; to challenge it, requires brains.

MARY PETTIBONE POOLE, *A Glass Eye at a Keyhole* (1938)

He's very clever, but sometimes his brains go to his head.

MARGOT ASQUITH, *The Autobiography of Margot Asquith* (1923)

I feel like a baited bull and look a wreck, and as for my unfortunate brain well I saw it neatly described yesterday on an automatic thing in the tube: This machine is EMPTY till further notice.

JEAN RHYS, *Letters, 1931–1966* (1984)

The grim possibility is that she who "hides her brains" will, more than likely, end up with a mate who is only equal to a woman with "hidden brains" or none at all.

LORRAINE HANSBERRY, "In Defense of the Equality of Men," in The Norton Anthology of Literature by Women (1985)

See also Intelligence, Mind.

BREVITY

Brevity is the soul of lingerie.

DOROTHY PARKER (1916), in Marion Meade, *Dorothy Parker: What Fresh Hell Is This?* (1988)

BRIDGE

When the human passions are ebbing, bridge takes their place.

ANNE SHAW, *But Such Is Life* (1931)

See also Hobbies.

BROKEN HEART

There were many ways of breaking a heart. Stories were full of hearts being broken by love, but what really broke a heart was taking away its dream—whatever that dream might be.

PEARL BUCK, *The Patriot* (1939)

'Tis not love's going hurts my days, / But that it went in little ways.

EDNA ST. VINCENT MILLAY, "The Spring and the Fall," *The Harp-Weaver* (1923)

Pain / Rusts into beauty too. / I know full well that this is so: / I had a heartbreak long ago.

MARY CAROLYN DAVIES, "Rust," Youth Riding (1919)

A broken heart is what makes life so wonderful five years later, when you see the guy in an elevator and he is fat and smoking a cigar and saying long-time-no-see. If he hadn't broken your heart, you couldn't have that glorious feeling of relief!

PHYLLIS BATTELLE, in *Journal-American* (1962)

See also Heart, Love, Pain, Sorrow.

BULLIES

A bully is not reasonable—he is persuaded only by threats.

MARIE DE FRANCE (12th century), in Jeanette Beer, tr., *Medieval Fables of Marie de France* (1981)

The Argument from Intimidation is a confession of intellectual impotence.

AYN RAND, *The Virtue of Selfishness* (1964)

He could never see a belt without hitting below it.

MARGOT ASQUITH, on David Lloyd George, *The Autobiography of Margot Asquith* (1923)

BUREAUCRACY

Bureaucracy, the rule of no one, has become the modern form of despotism.

MARY MCCARTHY, in *New Yorker* (1958)

Batista wondered at the purpose of a bureaucracy which could not be subverted.

KAREN TEI YAMASHITA, *Through the Arc of the Rain Forest* (1990)

It never pays to deal with the flyweights of the world. They take far too much pleasure in thwarting you at every turn.

SUE GRAFTON, *"H" Is for Homicide* (1991)

What gets me is you work all your life like a dog, you pay into these government programs. But still, when you need help, the people that's paid to help you they act like it's coming out of their own pocket.

ARTIE CHANDLER, in Kathy Kahn, ed., *Hillbilly Women* (1973)

See also Government, Institutions.

BUSINESS

Business is other people's money.

DELPHINE DE GIRARDIN, *Marguerite* (1852)

Humans must breathe, but corporations must make money.

ALICE EMBREE, "Media Images I: Madison Avenue Brainwashing—the Facts," in *Sisterhood Is Powerful* (1970)

It's easy to make money. You put up the sign *Bank* and someone walks in and hands you his money. The façade is everything.

CHRISTINA STEAD, *House of All Nations* (1938)

Contrary to popular opinion, the hustle is not a new dance step—it is an old business procedure.

FRAN LEBOWITZ, in *Observer* (1979)

There are . . . other business societies—England, Holland, Belgium and France, for instance. But ours [the United States] is the only culture now extant in which business so completely dominates the national scene that sports, sex, death, philanthropy and Easter Sunday are money-making propositions.

MARGARET HALSEY, *The Folks at Home* (1952)

The trouble in corporate America is that too many people with too much power live in a box (their home), then travel the same road every day to another box (their office).

FAITH POPCORN, *The Popcorn Report* (1991)

Today's corporate family is headed by a "father" who finds the child he never had, the child he always wanted, at the office and guides him (sometimes her) up the ladder.

PAULA BERNSTEIN, *Family Ties, Corporate Bonds* (1985)

Many people called him a wizard of finance—which is not the same thing as a wizard of magic, though sometimes fairly similar.

DODIE SMITH, *One Hundred and One Dalmatians* (1956)

I ran the wrong kind of business, but I did it with integrity.

SYDNEY BIDDLE BARROWS, in Marian Christy, "'Mayflower Madam' Tells All," *Boston Globe* (1986)

Dear, never forget one little point: It's my business. You just work here.

ELIZABETH ARDEN, to her husband, in Alfred Lewis and Constance Woodworth, *Miss Elizabeth Arden* (1972)

See also Economics, Labor, Money, Profit, Work.

BUSYNESS

Too many people, too many demands, too much to do; competent, busy, hurrying people—It just isn't living at all.

ANNE MORROW LINDBERGH, *Bring Me a Unicorn* (1971)

Time is always wanting to me, and I cannot meet with a single day when I am not hurried along, driven to my wits'-end by urgent work, business to attend to, or some service to render.

GEORGE SAND (1863), in Raphaël Ledos de Beaufort, *Letters of George Sand* (1886)

Life comes in clusters, clusters of solitude, then a cluster when there is hardly time to breathe.

MAY SARTON, *Journal of a Solitude* (1973)

I am furious at all the letters to answer, when all I want to do is think and write poems. . . . I long for open time, with no obligations except toward the inner world and what is going on there.

MAY SARTON, *Journal of a Solitude* (1973)

Women never have an half-hour in all their lives (excepting before or after anybody is up in the house) that they can call their own, without fear of offending or of hurting someone. Why do people sit up so late, or, more rarely, get up so early? Not because the day is not long enough, but because they have "no time in the day to themselves."

FLORENCE NIGHTINGALE, *Cassandra* (1852)

See also Leisure, Time.

C

CALIFORNIA

California is a state peculiarly addicted to swift enthusiasms. It is a seed-bed of all manner of cults and theories, taken up, and dropped, with equal speed.

CHARLOTTE PERKINS GILMAN, *The Living of Charlotte Perkins Gilman* (1935)

Did California cause any of this? No, though it does seem to draw to it people with unusual inclinations.

JESSAMYN WEST, *The Life I Really Lived* (1979)

Californians are good at planning for the earthquake, while simultaneously denying it will happen.

SHEILA BALLANTYNE, "Letter to John Lennon," *Life on Earth* (1988)

Nobody can tell about this California climate. One minit its hot and the next minit its cold, so a person never knows what to hock.

ANITA LOOS, *A Mouse Is Born* (1951)

What was the use of my having come from Oakland it was not natural to have come from there yes write about it if I like or anything if I like but not there, there is no there there.

GERTRUDE STEIN, *Everybody's Autobiography* (1937)

CALM

I begin to think, that a calm is not desirable in any situation in life. . . . Man was made for action and for bustle too, I believe.

ABIGAIL ADAMS, letter to her sister, Mary Smith Cranch (1784)

They sicken of the calm, who knew the storm.

DOROTHY PARKER, "Fair Weather," *Sunset Gun* (1928)

See also Peace, Silence.

CALUMNY

Calumny is like counterfeit money; many people who would not coin it circulate it without qualms.

DIANE DE POITIERS, in G. H. Bushnell, *Diane de Poitiers and Her Books* (1927)

See also Gossip, Rumor.

CANDOR

A world of vested interests is not a world which welcomes the disruptive force of candor.

AGNES REPPLIER, *Under Dispute* (1924)

See also Honesty, Sincerity, Truth.

CAPITALISM

I came to condemn capitalism, not through any oppression endured by me personally, but through that very deification of efficiency which capitalism had taught me, for its own purposes.

ANNA LOUISE STRONG, *I Change Worlds* (1935)

I am going to fight capitalism even if it kills me. It is wrong that people like you should be comfortable and well fed while all around you people are starving.

SYLVIA PANKHURST, speech (1921)

Imperialism was born when the ruling class in capitalist production came up against national limits to its economic expansion.

HANNAH ARENDT, *Origins of Totalitarianism* (1951)

Capitalism and altruism are incompatible; they are philosophical opposites; they cannot co-exist in the same man or in the same society.

AYN RAND, *For the New Intellectual* (1961)

Capitalism with near-full employment was an impressive spectacle.

JOAN ROBINSON, in Rendigs Fels, ed., *The Second Crisis of Economic Theory* (1972)

See also Economics.

CATS

The vanity of man revolts from the serene indifference of the cat.

AGNES REPPLIER, *Americans and Others* (1912)

My cat does not talk as respectfully to me as I do to her.

COLETTE, *Prisons and Paradise* (1932)

I have just been given a very engaging Persian kitten, named after St. Philip Neri (who was very sound on cats) and his opinion is that *I* have been given to *him*.

EVELYN UNDERHILL, *The Letters of Evelyn Underhill* (1943)

Dogs come when they're called; cats take a message and get back to you.

MISSY DIZICK AND MARY BLY, *Dogs Are Better Than Cats* (1985)

Who can tell what just criticisms Murr the Cat may be passing on us beings of wider speculation?

GEORGE ELIOT, *Middlemarch* (1871)

Oh, the cats in this town have their secrets.

MARY VIRGINIA MICKA, "Small Things Tell Us," *Letter to My Landlady* (1986)

Mr. Cat knows that a whisker spied is not a whole mouse.

MARGUERITE HENRY, *San Domingo, the Medicine Hat Stallion* (1972)

Round, gray, plump-jowled like a grandmother, she washed, ate, and saw to it that she and her offspring went outside for calls of nature as regularly as any privy-bound housewife. With a recipe written in cat language, she could have baked cookies or fried a chicken.

JESSAMYN WEST, *The Life I Really Lived* (1979)

Oh cat; I'd say, or pray: Be-ooootiful cat! Delicious cat! Exquisite cat! Satiny cat! Cat like a soft owl, cat with paws like moths, jeweled cat, miraculous cat! Cat, cat, cat, cat.

DORIS LESSING, *Particularly Cats . . . and Rufus* (1967)

A black cat dropped soundlessly from a high wall, like a spoonful of dark treacle, and melted under a gate.

ELIZABETH LEMARCHAND, *Alibi for a Corpse* (1969)

If a fish is the movement of water embodied, given shape, then cat is a diagram and pattern of subtle air.

DORIS LESSING, *Particularly Cats . . . and Rufus* (1967)

Is it enough to know that one creature likes what you do and the way you do it and that that creature is your cat?

NAOMI THORNTON, in Sara Ruddick and Pamela Daniels, *Working It Out* (1977)

See also Animals.

CAUSES

It is often interesting, in retrospect, to consider the trifling causes that lead to great events. A chance encounter, a thoughtless remark—and the tortuous chain reaction of coincidence is set in motion, leading with devious inevitability to some resounding climax.

PATRICIA MOYES, *Down Among the Dead Men* (1961)

CAUTION

Everybody knows if you are too careful you are so occupied in being careful that you are sure to stumble over something.

GERTRUDE STEIN, *Everybody's Autobiography* (1937)

See also Fastidiousness.

CELEBRITIES

Celebrities used to be found in clusters, like oysters—and with much the same defensive mechanisms.

BARBARA WALTERS, *How to Talk with Practically Anybody About Practically Anything* (1970)

Go back to that wonderful Alan Jay Lerner song in *Camelot,* the one about "I wonder what the king is doing tonight." We really want to know what the king is up to. It must be something bred into us from peasantry.

LIZ SMITH, on celebrity journalism, in James Brady, "In Step with Liz Smith," *Parade* (1991)

Poring over fragments of other people's lives, peering into their bedrooms when they don't know we're there, we thrill to the glamour and the power of secret knowledge, partly detoxified but also heightened by being shared.

PATRICIA MEYER SPACKS, *Gossip* (1985)

See also Admiration, Fame, Glamour.

CENSORSHIP

The case against censoring anything is absolute: . . . nothing that could be censored can be so bad in its effects, *in the long run,* as censorship itself.

KATHARINE WHITEHORN, *Roundabout* (1962)

"Censorship" is a term pertaining only to governmental action. No private action is censorship. No private individual or agency can silence a man or suppress a publication; only the government can do so. The freedom of speech of private individuals includes the right not to agree, not to listen and not to finance one's own antagonists.

AYN RAND, *The Virtue of Selfishness* (1964)

It would be nice to think that a censor could allow a genuine work of artistic seriousness and ban a titillating piece of sadism, but it would take a miracle to make such a distinction stick.

KATHARINE WHITEHORN, *Roundabout* (1962)

The free expression of the hopes and aspirations of a people is the greatest and only safety in a sane society.

EMMA GOLDMAN, *Living My Life* (1931)

As a society in turmoil, we are going to see more, and more various, attempts to simulate order through repression; and art is a historical target for such efforts.

ADRIENNE RICH, in Richard Jones, *Poetry and Politics* (1985)

Crankish attacks on the freedom to read are common at present. When backed and coordinated by organized groups, they become sinister.

URSULA K. LE GUIN, *Dancing at the Edge of the World* (1989)

Censorship is the height of vanity.

MARTHA GRAHAM, *Blood Memory* (1991)

CERTAINTY

One certainty we all accept is the condition of being uncertain and insecure.

DORIS LESSING, *A Small Personal Voice* (1974)

The minute one utters a certainty, the opposite comes to mind.

MAY SARTON, *Mrs. Stevens Hears the Mermaids Singing* (1965)

See also Ambivalence, Exceptions, Security.

CHALLENGE

One sank into the ancient sin of anomie when challenges failed.

AMANDA CROSS, *Death in a Tenured Position* (1981)

Providence has hidden a charm in difficult undertakings which is appreciated only by those who dare to grapple with them.

ANNE-SOPHIE SWETCHINE, *The Writings of Madame Swetchine* (1869)

You must do the thing you think you cannot do.

ELEANOR ROOSEVELT, *You Learn by Living* (1960)

When people keep telling you that you can't do a thing, you kind of like to try it.

MARGARET CHASE SMITH, in *Time* (1964)

See also Opportunities.

CHANGE

Change is the constant, the signal for rebirth, the egg of the phoenix.

CHRISTINA BALDWIN, *One to One* (1977)

Autumn to winter, winter into spring, / Spring into summer, summer into fall,— / So rolls the changing year, and so we change; / Motion so swift, we know not that we move.

DINAH MULOCK CRAIK, "Immutable," *Mulock's Poems, New and Old* (1888)

With the only certainty in our daily existence being change, and a rate of change growing always faster in a kind of technological leapfrog game, speed helps people think they are keeping up.

GAIL SHEEHY, *Speed Is of the Essence* (1971)

We shall hardly notice in a year or two. / You can get accustomed to anything.

EDNA ST. VINCENT MILLAY, "Spring Song," *The Harp-Weaver* (1923)

It is wonderful how quickly you get used to things, even the most astonishing.

EDITH NESBITT, *Five Children and It* (1902)

A person can run for years but sooner or later he has to take a stand in the place which, for better or worse, he calls home, do what he can to change things there.

PAULE MARSHALL, *The Chosen Place, The Timeless People* (1969)

The difference between transformation by accident and transformation by a system is like the difference between lightning and a lamp. Both give illumination, but one is dangerous and unreliable, while the other is relatively safe, directed, available.

MARILYN FERGUSON, *The Aquarian Conspiracy* (1980)

It is not the conscious changes made in their lives by men and women—a new job, a new town, a divorce—which really shape them, like the chapter headings in a biography, but a long, slow mutation of emotion, hidden, all-penetrative; something by which they may be so taken up that the practical outward changes of their lives in the world, noted with surprise, scandal or envy by others, pass almost unnoticed by themselves. This gives a shifting quality to the whole surface of life; decisions made with reason and the tongue may never be made valid by the heart.

NADINE GORDIMER, *The Lying Days* (1953)

He acted too often without counting the cost, from some dazzling conception,—one could not

say from impulse, for impulses are from the heart. He liked to reorganize and change things for the sake of change, to make a fine gesture. He destroyed the old before he had clearly thought out the new.

WILLA CATHER, *Shadows on the Rock* (1931)

You must not change one thing, one pebble, one grain of sand, until you know what good and evil will follow on that act.

URSULA K. LE GUIN, *A Wizard of Earthsea* (1968)

But people themselves alter so much, that there is something new to be observed in them for ever.

JANE AUSTEN, *Pride and Prejudice* (1813)

People change and forget to tell each other.

LILLIAN HELLMAN, *Toys in the Attic* (1960)

The tragedy of life is that people do not change.

AGATHA CHRISTIE, *There Is a Tide* (1948)

It is only in romances that people undergo a sudden metamorphosis. In real life, even after the most terrible experiences, the main character remains exactly the same.

ISADORA DUNCAN, *My Life* (1942)

I am full of the sorrow that goes with changes in surroundings, those successive stages of annihilation that slowly lead to the great and final void.

ISABELLE EBERHARDT (1900), *The Passionate Nomad* (1988)

It's the most unhappy people who most fear change.

MIGNON MCLAUGHLIN, *The Second Neurotic's Notebook* (1966)

I'm doing well, especially since / I moved away from here.

JUDY GRAHN, *The Queen of Swords* (1987)

If one is going to change things, one has to make a fuss and catch the eye of the world.

ELIZABETH JANEWAY, in Barbaralee Diamonstein, *Open Secrets* (1972)

See also Growth, Social Change.

CHAOS

I have a great belief in the fact that whenever there is chaos, it creates wonderful thinking. I consider chaos a gift.

Septima Poinsette Clark, in Brian Lanker, *I Dream a World* (1989)

Chaos is not brought about by rebellion; it is brought about by the absence of political struggle.

Susan Sherman, "Women and Process," in Charlotte Bunch and Sandra Pollack, eds., *Learning Our Way* (1983)

The splendid discontent of God / With chaos, made the world.

Ella Wheeler Wilcox, "Discontent," *The Collected Poems* (1917)

See also Order.

CHARACTER

The best index to a person's character is (a) how he treats people who can't do him any good, and (b) how he treats people who can't fight back.

Abigail Van Buren, syndicated column (1974)

Character builds slowly, but it can be torn down with incredible swiftness.

Faith Baldwin, *Harvest of Hope* (1962)

Character cannot be developed in ease and quiet. Only through experience of trial and suffering can the soul be strengthened, vision cleared, ambition inspired, and success achieved.

Helen Keller, *Helen Keller's Journal* (1938)

It is not in the still calm of life, or the repose of a pacific station, that great characters are formed. . . . The habits of a vigorous mind are formed in contending with difficulties. All history will convince you of this, and that wisdom and penetration are the fruit of experience, not the lessons of retirement and leisure. Great necessities call out great virtues.

Abigail Adams, letter to her son, John Quincy Adams (1780)

People of character don't allow the environment to dictate their style.

Lucille Kallen, *The Tanglewood Murder* (1980)

The shell is America's most active contribution to the formation of character. A tough hide. Grow it early.

Anaïs Nin, *The Diary of Anaïs Nin,* vol. 4 (1944–1947)

The things people discard tell more about them than the things they keep.

Hilda Lawrence, *The Pavilion* (1946)

The two kinds of people on earth that I mean / Are the people who lift and the people who lean.

Ella Wheeler Wilcox, "To Lift or to Lean," *The Collected Poems* (1917)

There are only two kinds of people in the world that really count. One kind's wheat and the other kind's emeralds.

Edna Ferber, *So Big* (1924)

Why can't people be both flexible *and* efficient?

Margaret Drabble, *The Middle Ground* (1980)

Some people are molded by their admirations, others by their hostilities.

Elizabeth Bowen, *The Death of the Heart* (1938)

Mrs. Hopewell had no bad qualities of her own but she was able to use other people's in such a constructive way that she never felt the lack.

Flannery O'Connor, "Good Country People," *A Good Man Is Hard to Find* (1953)

He was a bit like a corkscrew. Twisted, cold and sharp.

Kate Cruise O'Brien, "A Just Desert," *A Gift Horse* (1978)

His movements were supremely deliberate and his pronouncements infinitely calculated; he moved through life like a man who found himself crossing a gorge on a high wire without a net.

Lucille Kallen, *Introducing C. B. Greenfield* (1979)

From a timid, shy girl I had become a woman of resolute character, who could no longer be frightened by the struggle with troubles.

Anna Dostoevsky (1871), in S. S. Koteliansky, tr., ed., *Dostoevsky Portrayed by His Wife, The Diary and Reminiscences of Mme. Dostoevsky* (1926)

See also Behavior, Essence, Fictional Characters, Human Differences, Identity, Personality, Temperament.

CHARISMA

There are some men who possess a quality which goes way beyond romantic or even sexual appeal, a quality which literally enslaves. It has very little to do with looks and nothing at all to do with youth, because there are some quite mature and unathletic specimens who have it. It's an expression in the eyes, or an aura of being in control, and responsible, or something easy and powerful in the stance, or who knows.

LUCILLE KALLEN, *Introducing C. B. Greenfield* (1979)

Lack of charisma can be fatal.

JENNY HOLZER, *Truisms* (1991)

See also Charm, Popularity.

CHARITY

Lots of people think they are charitable if they give away their old clothes and things they don't want.

MYRTLE REED, *Old Rose and Silver* (1909)

Pity and charity may be at root an attempt to propitiate the dark powers that have not touched us yet.

MARILYNNE ROBINSON, *Housekeeping* (1980)

The little entourage of friends and relatives whom she completely dominated was fond of saying, "Becky would give you the shirt off her back." And it was true. The only trouble was that she neglected to take it off first, and what you found on your back was not only Becky's shirt but Becky too.

MARGARET HALSEY, *No Laughing Matter* (1977)

A giver of the shirt from someone else's back.

RAE FOLEY, *Curtain Call* (1961)

For those who are not hungry, it is easy to palaver about the degradation of charity.

CHARLOTTE BRONTË, *Shirley* (1849)

You have no idea, sir, how difficult it is to be the victim of benevolence.

JANE AIKEN HODGE, *Marry in Haste* (1961)

To a haughty belly, kindness is hard to swallow and harder to digest.

ZORA NEALE HURSTON, *Moses: Man of the Mountain* (1939)

Charity degrades those who receive it and hardens those who dispense it.

GEORGE SAND, *Consuelo* (1842)

Charity is an ugly trick. It is a virtue grown by the rich on the graves of the poor. Unless it is accompanied by sincere revolt against the present social system, it is cheap moral swagger.

REBECCA WEST, in *The Clarion* (1912)

Private beneficence is totally inadequate to deal with the vast numbers of the city's disinherited.

JANE ADDAMS, *Twenty Years at Hull House* (1910)

Charity separates the rich from the poor; aid raises the needy and sets him on the same level with the rich. . . . Almsgiving tends to perpetuate poverty; aid does away with it once and for all.

EVA PERÓN, speech (1949)

There is an ordinary proverb for this: "Stinginess does not enrich; charity does not impoverish."

GLÜCKEL OF HAMELN, *The Life of Glückel of Hameln* (1646–1724), *Written by Herself* (1719)

The contents of his [Sitting Bull's] pockets were often emptied into the hands of small, ragged little boys, nor could he understand how so much wealth should go brushing by, unmindful of the poor.

ANNIE OAKLEY, in C. R. Cooper, *Annie Oakley: Woman at Arms* (1922)

See also Generosity, Giving, Virtue.

CHARM

People were not charmed with Eglantine because she herself was charming, but because she was charmed.

ADA LEVERSON, *Love at Second Sight* (1916)

I realized he would not make the first move to leave; it was instinctive with him to make a woman feel she was too important to be treated lightly—an instinct totally unrelated to the degree of his interest, but it had the effect of a pint of vodka, taken neat.

LUCILLE KALLEN, *Introducing C. B. Greenfield* (1979)

Charm is a cunning self-forgetfulness.

CHRISTINA STEAD, *House of All Nations* (1938)

There is entirely too much charm around, and something must be done to stop it.

DOROTHY PARKER, in *New Yorker* (1928)

See also Charisma.

CHAUVINISM

In men this blunder still you find, / All think their little set mankind.

HANNAH MORE, *Florio and His Friend* (1786)

When man, Apollo man, rockets into space, it isn't in order to find his brother, I'm quite sure of that. It's to confirm that he hasn't any brothers.

FRANÇOISE SAGAN, *Scars on the Soul* (1972)

We can never give up the belief that the good guys always win. And that we are the good guys.

FAITH POPCORN, *The Popcorn Report* (1991)

He was one of those staunch patriotic Britons who, having made a portion of a foreign country their own, strongly resent the original inhabitants of it.

AGATHA CHRISTIE, *The Mystery of the Blue Train* (1928)

It's his first exposure to Third World passion. He thought only Americans had informed political opinion—other people staged coups out of spite and misery. It's an unwelcome revelation to him that a reasonably educated and rational man like Ro would die for things that he, Brent, has never heard of and would rather laugh about.

BHARATI MUKHERJEE, *The Middleman and Other Stories* (1988)

See also Discrimination, Prejudice.

CHEERFULNESS

A happy woman is one who has no cares at all; a cheerful woman is one who has cares but doesn't let them get her down.

BEVERLY SILLS, interview (1975)

Cheerfulness, it would appear, is a matter which depends fully as much on the state of things within, as on the state of things without and around us.

CHARLOTTE BRONTË, *Shirley* (1849)

'Tis easy enough to be pleasant, / When life flows along like a song; / But the man worth while is the one who will smile / When everything goes dead wrong.

ELLA WHEELER WILCOX, "Worth While," *The Collected Poems* (1917)

See also Optimism.

CHILDBIRTH

The burning embers within me burst into flame / My body becomes a fire-lit torch. / Ho someone! Send for the mid-wife.

AMRITA PRITAM, "The Annunciation," in Joanna Bankier and Deirdre Lashgari, eds., *Women Poets of the World* (1983)

Good work, Mary. We all knew you had it in you.

DOROTHY PARKER, telegram sent (collect) after an ostentatious pregnancy, in Marion Meade, *Dorothy Parker: What Fresh Hell Is This?* (1988)

I'll bet you one thing, if the man had to have the first baby there wouldn't be but two in the family. Yes sir, let him have the first one and the woman the next one, and his time wouldn't come around no more.

JOSEPHINE RILEY MATTHEWS, in Brian Lanker, *I Dream a World* (1989)

If men had to have babies they would only ever have one each.

DIANA, PRINCESS OF WALES, in *Observer* (1984)

I lost everything in the post-natal depression.

ERMA BOMBECK, book title (1970)

See also Babies, Birth, Pregnancy.

CHILDHOOD

Childhood is the kingdom where nobody dies.

EDNA ST. VINCENT MILLAY, "Childhood Is the Kingdom Where Nobody Dies," *Wine From These Grapes* (1934)

The older I grow the more earnestly I feel that the few intense joys of childhood are the best that life has to give.

ELLEN GLASGOW, *Letters of Ellen Glasgow* (1958)

One of the luckiest things that can happen to you in life is, I think, to have a happy childhood.

AGATHA CHRISTIE, *An Autobiography* (1977)

Childhood has no forebodings; but then, it is soothed by no memories of outlived sorrow.

GEORGE ELIOT, *The Mill on the Floss* (1860)

The illusions of childhood are necessary experiences: a child should not be denied a balloon because an adult knows that sooner or later it will burst.

MARCELENE COX, in *Ladies' Home Journal* (1948)

Two things are terrible in childhood: helplessness (being in other people's power) and apprehension—the apprehension that something is being concealed from us because it was too bad to be told.

ELIZABETH BOWEN, *Collected Impressions* (1950)

To children childhood holds no particular advantage.

KATHLEEN NORRIS, *Hands Full of Living* (1931)

Adults are always telling young people, "These are the best years of your life." Are they? I don't know. Sometimes when adults say this to children I look into their faces. They look like someone on the top seat of the Ferris wheel who has had too much cotton candy and barbecue. They'd like to get off and be sick but everyone keeps telling them what a good time they're having.

ERMA BOMBECK, *At Wit's End* (1965)

Childhood is only the beautiful and happy time in contemplation and retrospect: to the child it is full of deep sorrows, the meaning of which is unknown.

GEORGE ELIOT, letter (1844), in J. W. Cross, *George Eliot's Life as Related in Her Letters and Journals* (1884)

Childhood is less clear to me than to many people: when it ended I turned my face away from it for no reason that I know about, certainly without the usual reason of unhappy memories. For many years that worried me, but then I discovered that the tales of former children are seldom to be trusted. Some people supply too many past victories or pleasures with which to comfort themselves, and other people cling to pains, real and imagined, to excuse what they have become.

LILLIAN HELLMAN, *Pentimento* (1973)

I never meet anyone nowadays who admits to having had a happy childhood.

JESSAMYN WEST, *The Life I Really Lived* (1979)

All the famous people had had an awful time. One of them had a drunken father. Another had a stammer. Another had to wash hundreds of dirty bottles. They had all had what was called a difficult childhood. Clearly you had to have one if you wanted to become famous.

JUDITH KERR, *When Hitler Stole Pink Rabbit* (1971)

The myth of childhood happiness flourishes so wildly not because it satisfies the needs of children but because it satisfies the needs of adults. In a culture of alienated people, the belief that everyone has at least one good period in life free of care and drudgery dies hard. And obviously you can't expect it in your old age. So it must be you've already had it.

SHULAMITH FIRESTONE, *The Dialectic of Sex* (1970)

Some veil between childhood and the present is necessary. If the veil is withdrawn, the artistic imagination sickens and dies, the prophet looks in the mirror with a disillusioned and cynical sneer, the scientist goes fishing.

MARGARET MEAD, *Male and Female* (1949)

I do not believe in a child world. It is a fantasy world. I believe the child should be taught from the very first that the whole world is his world, that adult and child share one world, that all generations are needed.

PEARL BUCK, *To My Daughters, With Love* (1967)

See also Adolescence, Children, Youth.

CHILDREN

But the hearts of small children are delicate organs. A cruel beginning in this world can twist them into curious shapes.

CARSON MCCULLERS, *The Ballad of the Sad Café* (1953)

That most sensitive, most delicate of instruments—the mind of a little child!

HENRY HANDEL RICHARDSON, *The Fortunes of Richard Mahoney: Ultima Thule* (1929)

Very young people are true but not resounding instruments.

ELIZABETH BOWEN, *The Death of the Heart* (1938)

The popular idea that a child forgets easily is not an accurate one. Many people go right through life in the grip of an idea which has been impressed on them in very tender years.

AGATHA CHRISTIE, *Murder in Mesopotamia* (1935)

Yes, the race of children possesses magically sagacious powers!

GAIL GODWIN, *Dream Children* (1976)

No one has yet fully realized the wealth of sympathy, kindness and generosity hidden in the soul of a child. The effort of every true education should be to unlock that treasure.

EMMA GOLDMAN, *Living My Life* (1931)

A Child of Happiness always seems like an old soul living in a new body, and her face is very serious until she smiles, and then the sun lights up the world. . . . Children of Happiness always look not quite the same as other children. They have strong, straight legs and walk with purpose. They laugh as do all children, and they play as do all children, they talk child talk as do all children, but they are different, they are blessed, they are special, they are sacred.

ANNE CAMERON, *Daughters of Copper Woman* (1981)

He is not like other children, not cruel, or savage. For this very reason he is called "strange." A child who is mature, in the sense that the heart is mature, is always, I have observed, called deficient.

DJUNA BARNES, *Nightwood* (1937)

When people ask me what qualifies me to be a writer for children, I say I was once a child. But I was not only a child, I was, better still, a weird little kid, and though I would never choose to give my own children this particular preparation for life, there are few things, apparently, more helpful to a writer than having once been a weird little kid.

KATHERINE PATERSON, *Gates of Excellence* (1981)

The character and history of each child may be a new and poetic experience to the parent, if he will let it.

MARGARET FULLER, *Summer on the Lakes* (1844)

There is a certain melancholy in having to tell oneself that one has said good-bye—unless of course one is a grandmother—to the age and the circumstances that enable one to observe young children closely and passionately.

COLETTE, *Paris From My Window* (1944)

What feeling is so nice as a child's hand in yours? So small, so soft and warm, like a kitten huddling in the shelter of your clasp.

MARJORIE HOLMES, *Love and Laughter* (1967)

Children are unaccountable little creatures.

KATHERINE MANSFIELD, "Sixpence" (1921), *Something Childish* (1924)

Children are rarely in the position to lend one a truly interesting sum of money. There are, however, exceptions, and such children are an excellent addition to any party.

FRAN LEBOWITZ, *Metropolitan Life* (1978)

Ask your child what he wants for dinner only if he's buying.

FRAN LEBOWITZ, *Social Studies* (1977)

One should, I think, always give children money, for they will spend it for themselves far more profitably than we can ever spend it for them.

ROSE MACAULAY, *A Casual Commentary* (1926)

Even when freshly washed and relieved of all obvious confections, children tend to be sticky.

FRAN LEBOWITZ, *Metropolitan Life* (1978)

Notoriously insensitive to subtle shifts in mood, children will persist in discussing the color of a recently sighted cement-mixer long after one's own interest in the topic has waned.

FRAN LEBOWITZ, *Metropolitan Life* (1978)

Never allow your child to call you by your first name. He hasn't known you long enough.

FRAN LEBOWITZ, *Social Studies* (1977)

Children make the most desirable opponents in Scrabble as they are both easy to beat and fun to cheat.

FRAN LEBOWITZ, *Metropolitan Life* (1978)

One of the things I've discovered in general about raising kids is that they really don't give a damn if you walked five miles to school.

PATTY DUKE, *Call Me Anna* (1987)

Parents of young children should realize that few people, and maybe no one, will find their children as enchanting as they do.

BARBARA WALTERS, *How to Talk With Practically Anybody About Practically Anything* (1970)

The real menace in dealing with a five-year-old is that in no time at all you begin to sound like a five-year-old.

JEAN KERR, *Please Don't Eat the Daisies* (1957)

One hour with a child is like a ten-mile run.

JOAN BENOIT SAMUELSON, in *New York Times* (1991)

I wasn't used to children and they were getting on my nerves. Worse, it appeared that I was a child, too. I hadn't known that before; I thought I was just short.

FLORENCE KING, on her first day in kindergarten, *Confessions of a Failed Southern Lady* (1985)

I was a very ancient twelve; my views at that age would have done credit to a Civil War veteran. I am much younger now than I was at twelve or anyway, less burdened. The weight of the centuries lies on children, I'm sure of it.

FLANNERY O'CONNOR, in Sally Fitzgerald, ed., *The Habit of Being* (1979)

We love those we feed, not vice versa; in caring for others we nourish our own self esteem. Children are dependent upon adults. It's a craven role for a child. It's very natural to want to bite the hand that feeds you.

JESSAMYN WEST, *The Life I Really Lived* (1979)

It is not a bad thing that children should occasionally, and politely, put parents in their place.

COLETTE, *My Mother's House* (1922)

There is such a rebound from parental influence that it generally seems that the child makes use of the directions given by the parent only to avoid the prescribed path.

MARGARET FULLER, in *The Dial* (1841)

Hedda was queasily phobic of children and, by extension, of short people in general. They were too condensed, like undiluted cans of soup—too intensely human and, therefore, too intensely not to be trusted. The mistakes in the basic ingredients—the stupidity, the cruelty—were overpoweringly present.

REBECCA GOLDSTEIN, *The Dark Sister* (1991)

Your sons weren't made to like you. That's what grandchildren are for.

JANE SMILEY, *Good Will* (1989)

As the youngsters grow attached to their teachers and classmates . . . they can finally say goodbye to their mothers without re-enacting the death scene from *Camille*.

SUE MITTENTHAL, in *New York Times* (1984)

It's clear that most American children suffer too much mother and too little father.

GLORIA STEINEM, in *New York Times* (1971)

Adorable children are considered to be the general property of the human race. (Rude children belong to their mothers.)

JUDITH MARTIN, *Miss Manners' Guide to Rearing Perfect Children* (1984)

In their sympathies, children feel nearer animals than adults.

JESSAMYN WEST, *The Life I Really Lived* (1979)

The finest inheritance you can give to a child is to allow it to make its own way, completely on its own feet.

ISADORA DUNCAN, *My Life* (1942)

At every step the child should be allowed to meet the real experiences of life; the thorns should never be plucked from his roses.

ELLEN KEY, *The Century of the Child* (1909)

Our children are not treated with sufficient respect as human beings, and yet from the moment they are born they have this right to respect. We keep them children for too long, their world separate from the real world of life.

PEARL BUCK, *My Several Worlds* (1954)

Perhaps I may record here my protest against the efforts, so often made, to shield children and young people from all that has to do with death and sorrow, to give them a good time at all hazards on the assumption that the ills of life will come soon enough. Young people themselves often resent this attitude on the part of their elders; they feel set aside and belittled as if they were denied the common human experiences.

JANE ADDAMS, *Twenty Years at Hull House* (1910)

In this era of affluence and of permissiveness, we have, in all but cultured areas, bred a nation of overprivileged youngsters, saturated with vitamins, television and plastic toys. But they are nurtured from infancy on a Dick-and-Jane literary and artistic level; and the cultural drought, as far as entertainment is concerned, sets in when they are between six and eight.

JUDITH CRIST, *The Private Eye, the Cowboy and the Very Naked Girl* (1968)

A child's attitude toward everything is an artist's attitude.

WILLA CATHER, *The Song of the Lark* (1915)

All children are artists, and it is an indictment of our culture that so many of them lose their creativity, their unfettered imaginations, as they grow older.

MADELEINE L'ENGLE, *Walking on Water: Reflections on Faith and Art* (1980)

I see the mind of the five-year-old as a volcano with two vents: destructiveness and creativeness.

SYLVIA ASHTON-WARNER, *Teacher* (1963)

Play is not for every hour of the day, or for any hour taken at random. There is a tide in the affairs of children. Civilization is cruel in sending them off to bed at the most stimulating time of dusk.

ALICE MEYNELL, *The Children* (1897)

Children are not born knowing the many opportunities that are theirs for the taking. Someone who does know must tell them.

RUTH HILL VIGUERS, in Joan Peterson, "Ruth Hill Viguers," *The Horn Book* (1991)

Children's talent to endure stems from their ignorance of alternatives.

MAYA ANGELOU, *I Know Why the Caged Bird Sings* (1970)

Everywhere, everywhere, children are the scorned people of the earth.

TONI MORRISON, in Charles Ruas, *Conversations with American Writers* (1984)

The children are always the chief victims of social chaos.

AGNES MEYER, *Out of These Roots* (1953)

So long as little children are allowed to suffer, there is no true love in this world.

ISADORA DUNCAN, "Memoirs," in *This Quarter* (1929)

The mother's battle for her child—with sickness, with poverty, with war, with all the forces of exploitation and callousness that cheapen human life—needs to become a common human battle, waged in love and in the passion for survival.

ADRIENNE RICH, *Of Woman Born* (1976)

We are willing to spend the least amount of money to keep a kid at home, more to put him in a foster home and the most to institutionalize him.

MARIAN WRIGHT EDELMAN, in Margie Casady, "Society's Pushed-Out Children," *Psychology Today* (1975)

If responsibility for the upbringing of children is to continue to be vested in the family, then the rights of children will be secured only when parents are able to make a living for their families with so little difficulty that they may give their best thought and energy to the child's development and the problem of helping it adjust itself to the complexities of the modern environment.

SUZANNE LAFOLLETTE, *Concerning Women* (1926)

Children cannot eat rhetoric and they cannot be sheltered by commissions. I don't want to see another commission that studies the needs of kids. We need to help them.

MARIAN WRIGHT EDELMAN, in Brian Lanker, *I Dream a World* (1989)

Oh dear, dark boy. There was such promise of happiness balanced there. But your mama never rocked you when you were a baby, you say, and your daddy died when you were seventeen. And all the rest of us can never make it up to you.

SONIA JOHNSON, *From Housewife to Heretic* (1981)

What its children become, that will the community become.

SUZANNE LAFOLLETTE, *Concerning Women* (1926)

If our American way of life fails the child, it fails us all.

PEARL BUCK, *The Child Who Never Grew* (1950)

When a species fails to care for its progeny, the species is doomed.

GEORGIA SAVAGE, interview (1991)

A child motivated by competitive ideals will grow into a man without conscience, shame, or true dignity.

GEORGE SAND (1837), in Marie Jenny Howe, *The Intimate Journal of George Sand* (1929)

There's a time when you have to explain to your children why they're born, and it's a marvelous thing if you know the reason by then.

HAZEL SCOTT, in Margo Jefferson, "Great (Hazel) Scott!" *Ms.* (1974)

When I am grappling with ideas which are radical enough to upset grown-ups, then I am likely to put these ideas into a story which will be marketed for children, because children understand what their parents have rejected and forgotten.

MADELEINE L'ENGLE, *Walking on Water: Reflections on Faith and Art* (1980)

[Children] use up the same part of my head as poetry does. To deal with children is a matter of terrific imaginative identification. And the children have to come first. It's no use putting off their evening meal for two months.

LIBBY HOUSTON, in Cheris Kramarae and Paula A. Treichler, *A Feminist Dictionary* (1985)

But children can't be a center of life and a reason for being. They can be a thousand things that are delightful, interesting, satisfying, but they can't be a wellspring to live from. Or they shouldn't be.

DORIS LESSING, "To Room Nineteen," *A Man and Two Women* (1963)

It seems to me that since I've had children, I've grown richer and deeper. They may have slowed down my writing for a while, but when I did write, I had more of a self to speak from.

ANNE TYLER, in Janet Sternburg, ed., *The Writer on Her Work*, vol. 1 (1980)

See also Adolescence, Babies, Childhood, Family, Generations, Grandparents, Parenting, Parents, Youth.

CHINA

Nothing and no one can destroy the Chinese people. They are relentless survivors. They are the oldest civilized people on earth. Their civilization passes through phases but its basic characteristics remain the same. They yield, they bend to the wind, but they never break.

PEARL BUCK, *China, Past and Present* (1972)

CHOCOLATE

Research tells us that fourteen out of any ten individuals like chocolate.

SANDRA BOYNTON, *Chocolate: The Consuming Passion* (1982)

Much serious thought has been devoted to the subject of chocolate: What does chocolate *mean?* Is the pursuit of chocolate a right or a privilege? Does the notion of chocolate preclude the concept of free will?

SANDRA BOYNTON, *Chocolate: The Consuming Passion* (1982)

As with most fine things, chocolate has its season. There is a simple memory aid that you can use to determine whether it is the correct time to order chocolate dishes: Any month whose name contains the letter a, e, or u is the proper time for chocolate.

SANDRA BOYNTON, *Chocolate: The Consuming Passion* (1982)

Cocoa. Damn miserable puny stuff, fit for kittens and unwashed boys. Did *Shakespeare* drink cocoa?

SHIRLEY JACKSON, *The Bird's Nest* (1954)

See also Food.

CHOICE

It is the ability to choose which makes us human.

MADELEINE L'ENGLE, *Walking on Water: Reflections on Faith and Art* (1980)

The strongest principle of growth lies in human choice.

GEORGE ELIOT, *Daniel Deronda* (1874)

We cannot freely and wisely choose the right way for ourselves unless we know both good and evil.

HELEN KELLER, *My Religion* (1927)

The ability to choose puts human beings in control of their actions. Implied in choice is that the action taken is best, and that all other options are overruled. We cannot knowingly choose what is not good for us. The ability to pursue a course, whether it is a popular one or not, is measured in courage. The greater the courage, the greater the possibility we will act for change. I build my characters around the dynamics of choice, courage, and change.

MILDRED PITTS WALTER, in *The Horn Book* (1991)

There are no signposts in the sea.

VITA SACKVILLE-WEST, *No Signposts in the Sea* (1961)

Long afterwards, she was to remember that moment when her life changed its direction. It was not predestined; she had a choice. Or it seemed that she had. To accept or refuse. To take one turning down the crossroads to the future or another. But this would be hindsight, and time always mocked truth.

EVELYN ANTHONY, *The Avenue of the Dead* (1982)

Bread sets free; but does not necessarily set free for good ends—that dear illusion of so many generous hearts. It sets a man free to choose: it often sets free for the bad, but man has a right to that choice and to that evil, without which he is no longer a man.

FRANÇOISE MALLET-JORIS, *A Letter to Myself* (1964)

See also Decision.

CHRIST

I am amazed by the sayings of Christ. They seem truer than anything I have ever read. And they certainly turn the world upside down.

KATHARINE BUTLER HATHAWAY, *The Journals and Letters of the Little Locksmith* (1946)

Where did your Christ come from? From God and a woman! Man had nothing to do with Him.

SOJOURNER TRUTH, speech (1851)

Jesus loves me—this I know, / For the Bible tells me so.

ANNA BARTLETT WARNER, "The Love of Jesus" (1858)

As we know, our own mother bore us only into pain and dying. But our true mother, Jesus, who is all love, bears us into joy and endless living.

JULIAN OF NORWICH, *Revelations of Divine Love* (1373)

I am not sure that Christ would have been very satisfied to foresee that He would be looked upon principally as a *redeemer* and nailed forever upon the cross by human ignorance. It seems to me that He above all desired to bring men a message of truth, that He wanted to heal them of their faults by making an appeal to all their energy; He shook them as much as He could, He did not seek to spare them the trouble.

ADRIENNE MONNIER, *Les Gazettes d'Adrienne Monnier* (1938), in Richard McDougall, tr., *The Very Rich Hours of Adrienne Monnier* (1976)

Jesus would be framed and in jail if he was living today.

CARSON MCCULLERS, *The Heart Is a Lonely Hunter* (1940)

See also Christianity, God.

CHRISTIANITY

The Christian tradition was passed on to me as a great rich mixture, a bouillabaisse of human imagination and wonder brewed from the richness of individual lives.

MARY CATHERINE BATESON, *With a Daughter's Eye* (1984)

Authentic Christianity never destroys what is good. It makes it grow, transfigures it and enriches itself from it.

CLAIRE HUCHET BISHOP, *France Alive* (1947)

It is a fact beyond question that there are two kinds of Christian experience, one of which is an experience of bondage, and the other an experience of liberty.

HANNAH WHITALL SMITH, *The Christian's Secret of a Happy Life* (1870)

Christian ideology has contributed no little to the oppression of woman.

SIMONE DE BEAUVOIR, *The Second Sex* (1949)

All through the ages, from the dissolution of antique capitalism to the latest crisis of modern capitalism, Christian institutions, whether Catholic, Calvinist or Methodist, have exercised a profound modifying and yet fostering influence upon commerce and the characters of those engaged in it. Christianity, which has ever sought to moderate the profit-seeking of the business man, has assisted him to develop finance and industry. It was the curious destiny of this greatest spiritual force in the Western world to prepare mankind for materialism and mechanization. Yet it has exerted ceaseless pressure on the

money-makers to consider the effects of their activities upon society and their own souls.

MIRIAM BEARD, *A History of Business* (1938)

See also Christ, Church, God, Religion, Spirituality, Theology.

CHRISTMAS

Welcome Christmas! heel and toe, / Come and fill us ere you go!

MARY MAPES DODGE, "Stocking Song on Christmas Eve," *Rhymes and Jingles* (1904)

God rest ye, merry gentlemen; let nothing you dismay, / For Jesus Christ, our Saviour, was born on Christmasday.

DINAH MULOCK CRAIK, "Christmas Carol," *Mulock's Poems, New and Old* (1888)

I do hope your Christmas has had a little touch of Eternity in among the rush and pitter patter and all. It always seems such a mixing of this world and the next—but that after all is the idea!

EVELYN UNDERHILL, *The Letters of Evelyn Underhill* (1943)

I can understand people simply fleeing the mountainous effort Christmas has become. . . . But there are always a few saving graces and finally they make up for all the bother and distress.

MAY SARTON, *Journal of a Solitude* (1973)

There is nothing sadder in this world than to awake Christmas morning and not be a child. . . . Time, self-pity, apathy, bitterness, and exhaustion can take the Christmas out of the child, but you cannot take the child out of Christmas.

ERMA BOMBECK, *I Lost Everything in the Post-Natal Depression* (1970)

Christmas won't be Christmas without any presents.

LOUISA MAY ALCOTT, *Little Women* (1868)

Our children await Christmas presents like politicians getting election returns; there's the Uncle Fred precinct and the Aunt Ruth district still to come in.

MARCELENE COX, in *Ladies' Home Journal* (1950)

No matter how many Christmas presents you give your child, there's always that terrible moment when he's opened the very last one. That's when he expects you to say, "Oh yes, I almost forgot," and take him out and show him the pony.

MIGNON McLAUGHLIN, *The Second Neurotic's Notebook* (1966)

For months they have lain in wait, dim shapes lurking in the forgotten corners of houses and factories all over the country and now they are upon us, sodden with alcohol, their massive bodies bulging with strange green protuberances, attacking us in our homes, at our friends' homes, at our offices—there is no escape, it is the hour of the fruitcake.

DEBORAH PAPIER, in *Insight* (1985)

Like everyone in his right mind, I feared Santa Claus.

ANNIE DILLARD, *Teaching a Stone to Talk* (1982)

Evidently Christmas was an unmitigated joy only for the people who inhabited department-store brochures and seasonal television specials. For everyone else the day seemed to be a trip across a mine field seeded with resurrected family feuds, exacerbated loneliness, emotional excess, and the inevitable disappointments that arise when expectations fall far short of reality.

JOYCE REBETA-BURDITT, *The Cracker Factory* (1977)

Christmas was a miserable time for a Jewish child in those days, and I still recall the feeling. . . . Decades later, I still feel left out at Christmas, but I sing the carols anyway. You might recognize me if you ever heard me. I'm the one who sings, "La-la, the la-la is born."

FAYE MOSKOWITZ, *A Leak in the Heart* (1985)

CHURCH

She say, Celie, tell the truth, have you ever found God in church? I never did. I just found a bunch of folks hoping for him to show. Any God I ever felt in church I brought in with me. And I think all the other folks did too. They come to church to *share* God, not find God.

ALICE WALKER, *The Color Purple* (1982)

Our Lord said, "Feed my sheep"; he did not say, "Count them."

DORA CHAPLIN, on undue emphasis on church attendance, *The Privilege of Teaching* (1962)

Everybody knows that really intimate conversation is only possible between two or three. As soon as there are six or seven, collective language begins to dominate. That is why it is a complete misinterpretation to apply to the Church the words "Wheresoever two or three are gathered together in my name, there am I in the midst of them." Christ did not say two hundred, or fifty, or ten. He said two or three.

SIMONE WEIL, "Spiritual Autobiography," *The Simone Weil Reader* (1977)

Most sermons sound to me like commercials—but I can't make out whether God is the Sponsor or the Product.

MIGNON McLAUGHLIN, *The Second Neurotic's Notebook* (1966)

The church belongs to its hierarchy, which is men in power. Those outside the hierarchy, and especially women, are at best only renters and at worst squatters in religious territory.

SONIA JOHNSON, *From Housewife to Heretic* (1981)

Again, as I had often met it in my own church, I was confronted with the Impurity of Women doctrine that seemed to preoccupy all clergymen.

HARPER LEE, *To Kill a Mockingbird* (1960)

The Bible and Church have been the greatest stumbling blocks in the way of women's emancipation.

ELIZABETH CADY STANTON, in *Free Thought Magazine* (1896)

Most churches on either side of the ocean see women as playing only a "supportive," if any, role in their congregations. Men preach, women listen. Men pray, women say Amen. Men study theology, women sew for the bazaar. Men make decisions, women make the tea.

ELAINE STORKEY, *What's Right With Feminism* (1985)

See also Christianity, God, Religion, Spirituality, Theology.

CIRCUS

The circus is perhaps the most vital of all spectacles. It is a place full of simple and powerful charms. Charms of childhood memories. Charms of the very form of the circus, of its odor, its clamor. Charms of the ritual that presides over the entrances and the stunts. These bodily acts, these attractions that are daughters of universal Attraction take place with great ceremony. What is so moving as the roll of the drum that precedes the most perilous moment of the number and the total silence that follows it? Shall we hesitate to think of the Elevation of the Mass? And what is so noble as the hand of the gymnast, who stands up absolutely straight after his stunt, with his palm open like the very symbol of work and its fulfillment?

ADRIENNE MONNIER, *Les Gazettes d'Adrienne Monnier* (1935), in Richard McDougall, tr., *The Very Rich Hours of Adrienne Monnier* (1976)

CITIES

In great cities where people of ability abound, there is always a feverish urge to keep ahead, to set the pace, to adopt each new fashion in thought and theory as well as in dress—or undress.

CHARLOTTE PERKINS GILMAN, *The Living of Charlotte Perkins Gilman* (1935)

In a few hours one could cover that incalculable distance; from the winter country and homely neighbors, to the city where the air trembled like a tuning-fork with unimaginable possibilities.

WILLA CATHER, *Lucy Gayheart* (1935)

No rural community, no suburban community, can ever possess the distinctive qualities that city dwellers have for centuries given to the world.

AGNES REPPLIER, "Town and Suburb," *Eight Decades* (1937)

To approach a city, or even a city neighborhood, as if it were a larger architectural problem, capable of being given order by converting it into a disciplined work of art, is to make the mistake of attempting to substitute art for life. The results of such profound confusion between art and life are neither life nor art. They are taxidermy.

JANE JACOBS, *The Death and Life of Great American Cities* (1961)

Great cities are not like towns, only larger. They are not like suburbs, only denser. They differ from towns and suburbs in basic ways, and one of these is that cities are, by definition, full of strangers.

JANE JACOBS, *The Death and Life of Great American Cities* (1961)

In our big cities there is nothing at all not made by ourselves except the air. We are our own context and live by picking each other's brains. There's no vital force. Electronic Man.

L. M. BOSTON, *A Stranger at Green Knowe* (1961)

Today barbarism has taken over many city streets, or people fear it has, which comes to much the same thing in the end.

JANE JACOBS, *The Death and Life of Great American Cities* (1961)

When we deal with cities we are dealing with life at its most complex and intense. Because this is so, there is a basic aesthetic limitation on what can be done with cities: A city cannot be a work of art.

JANE JACOBS, *The Death and Life of Great American Cities* (1961)

There is a strange depression that hangs over every little town that is no longer in the mainstream of life.

MARGARET CRAVEN, *Walk Gently This Good Earth* (1977)

CIVILIZATION

We are all born charming, fresh, and spontaneous and must be civilized before we are fit to participate in society.

JUDITH MARTIN, *Miss Manners' Guide to Excruciatingly Correct Behavior* (1982)

Whatever your color or creed may be, when you get too close to civilization, you can probably expect to be done in.

SHIRLEY ABBOTT, *Womenfolks: Growing Up Down South* (1983)

For the first time ever in the history of mankind, the wilderness is safer than "civilization."

FAITH POPCORN, *The Popcorn Report* (1991)

The age in which we live can only be characterized as one of barbarism. Our civilization is in the process not only of being militarized, but also being brutalized.

ALVA MYRDAL, in Barbara Shiels, *Women and the Nobel Prize* (1985)

The glossy surface of our civilization hides a real intellectual decadence.

SIMONE WEIL, "The Power of Words," *The Simone Weil Reader* (1977)

The whole world is nothing but a noise, as hot as the inside of a tiger's mouth. They call it civilization—that is a lie! But some day you may have to go out, someone will try to take you out, and you will not understand them or what they are saying, unless you understand nothing, absolutely nothing, then you will manage.

DJUNA BARNES, "Cassation," *Spillway* (1972)

The test of a civilization is in the way that it cares for its helpless members.

PEARL BUCK, *My Several Worlds* (1954)

Civilization is a perishable commodity.

HELEN MACINNES, *The Venetian Affair* (1963)

See also Society.

CLASS

Classism and greed are making insignificant all other kinds of isms.

RUBY DEE, in Brian Lanker, *I Dream a World* (1989)

It is impossible for one class to appreciate the wrongs of another.

ELIZABETH CADY STANTON, *The History of Woman Suffrage* (1881)

You who have read the history of nations, from Moses down to our last election, where have you ever seen one class looking after the interests of another?

ELIZABETH CADY STANTON, speech (1860)

I can assure you that the class system is alive and well and living in people's minds in England.

JILLY COOPER, *Class* (1979)

I classify Sao Paolo this way: The Governor's Palace is the living room. The mayor's office is the dining room and the city is the garden. And the favela is the back yard where they throw the garbage.

CAROLINA MARIA DE JESUS, *Child of the Dark, The Diary of Carolina Maria de Jesus* (1962)

Planning ahead is a measure of class. The rich and even the middle class plan for future generations, but the poor can plan ahead only a few weeks or days.

GLORIA STEINEM, *Outrageous Acts and Everyday Rebellions* (1983)

All new money is made through the shifting of social classes and the dispossession of old classes.

CHRISTINA STEAD, *House of All Nations* (1938)

The class struggle is precisely that which resolves the contradictions between two opposed classes by abolishing them at the same time that it constitutes and reveals them as classes.

MONIQUE WITTIG, "The Category of Sex" (1972), *The Straight Mind* (1992)

While he himself derived from the hardworking poor, he greatly mistrusted the ragtag and bobtail who lived in the shacks south of the junkyard, suspecting them of the criminality and moral decay to which he might sink, were he in their place.

FAITH SULLIVAN, *The Cape Ann* (1988)

See also Aristocracy, Middle Class.

CLEVERNESS

If all the good people were clever, / And all the clever people were good, / The world would be nicer than ever / We thought that it possibly could. / But somehow, 'tis seldom or never / The two hit it off as they should; / The good are so harsh to the clever, / The clever so rude to the good!

ELIZABETH WORDSWORTH, "The Clever and the Good," *St. Christopher and Other Poems* (1890)

See also Intelligence.

CLICHÉS

The clichés of a culture sometimes tell the deepest truths.

FAITH POPCORN, *The Popcorn Report* (1991)

It is strange how we rebel against a platitude until suddenly in a different lingo it looms up again as the only verity.

RUTH BENEDICT, in Margaret Mead, *An Anthropologist at Work: Writings of Ruth Benedict* (1959)

Your soul needs to be lonely so that its strangest elements can moil about, curl and growl and jump, fail and get triumphant, all inside you. Sociable people have the most trouble hearing their unconscious. They have trouble getting rid of clichés because clichés are sociable.

CAROL BLY, *The Passionate, Accurate Story* (1990)

See also Language, Words.

CLOTHES

Designer clothes worn by children are like snow-suits worn by adults. Few can carry it off successfully.

FRAN LEBOWITZ, *Social Studies* (1977)

While clothes with pictures and/or writing on them are not entirely an invention of the modern age, they are an unpleasant indication of the general state of things. . . . I mean, be realistic. If people don't want to listen to *you* what makes you think they want to hear from your sweater?

FRAN LEBOWITZ, *Metropolitan Life* (1978)

It is almost as stupid to let your clothes betray that you know you are ugly as to have them proclaim that you think you are beautiful.

EDITH WHARTON, *The House of Mirth* (1905)

Wet beige knee-highs hang in my hands like wilted skins.

CHRISTINA BALDWIN, *One to One* (1977)

See also Dress.

CODEPENDENCE

There are almost as many definitions of codependency as there are experiences that represent it . . . my definition of a codependent: A codependent person is one who has let another person's behavior affect him or her, and who is obsessed with controlling that person's behavior.

MELODIE BEATTIE, *Codependent No More* (1987)

It is easier to live through someone else than to become complete yourself.

BETTY FRIEDAN, *The Feminine Mystique* (1963)

Nora robbed herself for everyone; incapable of giving herself warning, she was continually turning about to find herself diminished. Wandering people the world over found her profitable in that she could be sold for a price forever, for she carried her betrayal money in her own pocket.

DJUNA BARNES, *Nightwood* (1937)

Is devotion to others a cover for the hungers and the needs of the self, of which one is ashamed? I was always ashamed to take. So I gave. It was not a virtue. It was a disguise.

ANAÏS NIN, *The Diary of Anaïs Nin,* vol. 4 (1944–1947)

I looked always outside of myself to see what I could make the world give me instead of looking within myself to see what was there.

BELLE LIVINGSTONE, *Belle of Bohemia* (1927)

We stay in the house so much because I am waiting for the telephone. I seem to be back in my teens, a period I thought I would never have to endure again: my life is spent hoping for things that only someone else can bring about.

ANNE TYLER, *Celestial Navigation* (1974)

COFFEE

Coffee was a food in that house, not a drink.

PATRICIA HAMPL, *A Romantic Education* (1981)

For a writer, it's more essential than food. Great American novel? Coming right up. We're talking second only to cocaine here, and hoarded as covetously.

JOAN FRANK, "Achieving Legal Liftoff," in *San Francisco Examiner Image* (1991)

There was a tiny range within which coffee was effective, short of which it was useless, and beyond which, fatal.

ANNIE DILLARD, *The Writing Life* (1989)

The coffee was so strong it snarled as it lurched out of the pot.

BETTY MacDONALD, *The Egg and I* (1945)

Never drink black coffee at lunch; it will keep you awake in the afternoon.

JILLY COOPER, *How to Survive from Nine to Five* (1970)

I found myself face to face with a long line of people resembling extras off the set of *Night of the Living Dead*: shuffling along, pale and twitching, empty cups in hand—murderous. Miserable. No matter that the air was rich with vapors of fresh-ground beans and warm muffins; no matter that the soft piped-in Vivaldi poured over us like steamed milk. These angry zombies were rushing to work, and their eyes flashed fair warning: *Don't mess with us. We haven't had our coffee.*

JOAN FRANK, "Achieving Legal Liftoff," in *San Francisco Examiner Image* (1991)

Coffee is not necessary to ministers of the reformed faith as to Catholic priests. The latter are not allowed to marry, and coffee is said to induce chastity.

CHARLOTTE-ELISABETH, DUCHESSE D'ORLÉANS, *Life and Letters of Charlotte Elizabeth* (1889)

COLD

The coldness had been admitted by none of the seven or eight people who, in degrees of elderly beauty, sat here full in the sun, at this sheltered edge of the lawn: they continued to master the coldness, or to deny it, as though with each it were some secret *malaise*.

ELIZABETH BOWEN, "Sunday Afternoon," *Ivy Gripped the Steps* (1946)

It's too cold to think warmly. Which gives me insight into the European. Where else would colonialism, slavery, capitalism come from except out of the icebox.

TONI CADE BAMBARA, "Broken Field Running," *The Sea Birds Are Still Alive* (1982)

See also Winter.

COLLECTING

The collector walks with blinders on; he sees nothing but the prize. In fact, the acquisitive instinct is incompatible with true appreciation of beauty.

ANNE MORROW LINDBERGH, *Gift From the Sea* (1955)

See also Hobbies.

COLORS

When I fell in love with black, it contained all color. It wasn't a negation of color. It was an acceptance. Because black encompasses all colors. Black is the most aristocratic color of all. The only aristocratic color. For me this is the ultimate. You can be quiet and it contains the whole thing. There is no color that will give you the feeling of totality. Of peace. Of greatness. Of quietness. Of excitement. I have *seen things* that were transformed into black, that took on just greatness.

LOUISE NEVELSON, *Dawns + Dusks* (1976)

Green is the fresh emblem of well-founded hopes. In blue the spirit can wander, but in green it can rest.

MARY WEBB, *The Spring of Joy* (1917)

Red has been praised for its nobility of the color of life. But the true color of life is not red. Red is the color of violence, or of life broken open, edited, and published.

ALICE MEYNELL, *The Color of Life* (1896)

Black was bestlooking. . . . Ebony was the best wood, the hardest wood; it was black. Virginia ham was the best ham. It was black on the outside. Tuxedos and tail coats were black and they were a man's finest, most expensive clothes. You had to use pepper to make most meats and vegetables fit to eat. The most flavorsome pepper was black. The best caviar was black. The rarest jewels were black: black opals, black pearls.

ANN PETRY, *The Narrows* (1953)

You think dark is just one color, but it ain't. There're five or six kinds of black. Some silky, some woolly. Some just empty. Some like fingers. And it don't stay still. It moves and changes from one kind of black to another. Saying something is pitch black is like saying something is green. What kind of green? Green like my bottles? Green like a grasshopper? Green like a cucumber, lettuce, or green like the sky is just before it breaks loose to storm? Well, night black is the same way. Might as well be a rainbow.

TONI MORRISON, *Song of Solomon* (1977)

COMEDIANS

The true art of the gods is the comic. The comic is a condescension of the divine to the world of man; it is the sublime vision, which cannot be studied, but must ever be celestially granted. In the comic the gods see their own being reflected as in a mirror, and while the tragic poet is bound by strict laws, they will allow the comic artist a freedom as unlimited as their own.

ISAK DINESEN, "Sorrow-Acre," *Winter's Tales* (1942)

Being a funny person does an awful lot of things to you. You feel that you mustn't get serious with people. They don't expect it from you, and they don't want to see it. You're not entitled to be serious, you're a clown, and they only want you to make them laugh.

FANNY BRICE, in Norman Katkov, *The Fabulous Fanny* (1952)

Comedy is very controlling—you are making people laugh. It is there in the phrase "*making people laugh.*" You feel completely in control when you hear a wave of laughter coming back at you that you have caused.

GILDA RADNER, *It's Always Something* (1989)

We never respect those who amuse us, however we may smile at their comic powers.

LADY MARGUERITE BLESSINGTON, *Desultory Thoughts and Reflections* (1839)

There is not one female comic who was beautiful as a little girl.

JOAN RIVERS, in Lydia Lane, "An Ugly Duckling Complex," *Los Angeles Times* (1974)

Comedians on the stage are invariably suicidal when they get home.

ELSA LANCHESTER, *Charles Laughton and I* (1938)

See also Humor.

COMFORT

I simply cannot understand the passion that some people have for making themselves thoroughly uncomfortable and then boasting about it afterwards.

PATRICIA MOYES, *Down Among the Dead Men* (1961)

One sits uncomfortably on a too comfortable cushion.

LILLIAN HELLMAN, *Scoundrel Time* (1976)

I love it—I love it, and who shall dare / To chide me for loving that old arm-chair?

ELIZA COOK, "The Old Arm-Chair," *The Poetical Works of Eliza Cook* (1848)

Comfort, however, easily merges into license.

MIRIAM BEARD, *A History of Business* (1938)

See also Consolation.

COMMITTEES

Any committee is only as good as the most knowledgeable, determined and vigorous person on it. There must be somebody who provides the flame.

LADY BIRD JOHNSON, *A White House Diary* (1970)

But the mind is an attribute of the individual. There is no such thing as a collective brain. There is no such thing as a collective thought. An agreement reached by a group of men is only a compromise or an average drawn upon many individual thoughts.

AYN RAND, *The Fountainhead* (1943)

See also Meetings.

COMMON SENSE

I'm not one o' those as can see the cat i' the dairy, an' wonder what she's come after.

GEORGE ELIOT, *Adam Bede* (1859)

If the cat has kittens in the oven, that don't make 'em biscuits.

ELISABETH OGILVIE, *The Summer of the Osprey* (1987)

Why are the umpires, the only two people on the field who aren't going to get grass stains on their knees, the only ones allowed to wear dark trousers?

KATHARINE WHITEHORN, *View From a Column* (1981)

One longs for a voice in the middle, and the mail often brings such balanced and refreshing views. In fact, the overwhelming majority of those who write me belong to this sensible persuasion— able to see a little right and a little wrong on both sides of many questions.

MILLICENT FENWICK, newsletter (1976)

COMMUNICATION

Once a human being has arrived on this earth, communication is the largest single factor determining what kinds of relationships he makes with others and what happens to him in the world about him.

VIRGINIA SATIR, *Peoplemaking* (1972)

Self-expression must pass into communication for its fulfillment.

PEARL BUCK, in Helen Hull, *The Writer's Book* (1950)

To be a bestseller is not necessarily a measure of quality, but it *is* a measure of communication.

BARBARA TUCHMAN, speech (1966)

My research suggests that men and women may speak different languages that they assume are the same, using similar words to encode disparate experiences of self and social relationships. Because these languages share an overlapping moral vocabulary, they contain a propensity for systematic mistranslation.

CAROL GILLIGAN, *In a Different Voice* (1982)

Good communication is stimulating as black coffee, and just as hard to sleep after.

ANNE MORROW LINDBERGH, *Gift From the Sea* (1955)

There can be too much communication between people.

ANN BEATTIE, "Weekend," *Secrets and Surprises* (1978)

See also Conversation, Letters, Speech, Talking, Telephone, Writing.

COMMUNISM

Such pipsqueaks as Nixon and McCarthy are trying to get us so frightened of Communism that we'll be afraid to turn out the lights at night.

HELEN GAHAGAN DOUGLAS, speech (1950)

Communists all seem to wear small caps, a look I consider better suited to tubes of toothpaste than to people.

FRAN LEBOWITZ, *Metropolitan Life* (1978)

COMPASSION

Spiritual energy brings compassion into the real world. With compassion, we see benevolently our own human condition and the condition of our fellow beings. We drop prejudice. We withhold judgment.

CHRISTINA BALDWIN, *Life's Companion, Journal Writing as a Spiritual Quest* (1990)

Here and there the lantern of compassion / can be shown to the fish, / where the fishhook is swallowed / or suffocation practiced.

NELLY SACHS, "Here and There the Lantern of Compassion," *O the Chimneys* (1967)

The love of our neighbor in all its fullness simply means being able to say to him, "What are you going through?"

SIMONE WEIL, *Waiting for God* (1950)

It is only the happy who are hard, Gilles. I think perhaps it is better for the world if—if one has a broken heart. One is quick to recognize it, elsewhere. And one has time to think about other people, if there is nothing left to hope for any more.

HELEN WADDELL, *Peter Abelard* (1933)

Even the little pigs grunt when the old boar suffers.

SELMA LAGERLÖF, *The General's Ring* (1928)

See also Charity, Empathy, Kindness, Service, Sympathy, Virtue.

COMPLACENCY

She had observed that it was from those who had never sailed stormy waters came the quickest and harshest judgments on bad seamanship in heavy seas.

SUSAN GLASPELL, *The Visioning* (1911)

If you think that you are where you are just because you worked hard, it is easy to become self-righteous and make classist moral judgments about others.

COLETTA REID AND CHARLOTTE BUNCH, *Class and Feminism* (1979)

Those who are happy and successful themselves are too apt to make light of the misfortunes of others.

ELIZABETH GASKELL, *North and South* (1854)

How easy to be amiable in the midst of happiness and success.

ANNE-SOPHIE SWETCHINE, *The Writings of Madame Swetchine* (1869)

Unhurt people are not much good in the world.

ENID STARKIE, in Joanna Richardson, *Enid Starkie* (1973)

The gain isn't counted to the recluse and inactive that, having nothing to measure themselves by and never being tested by failure, they simmer and soak perpetually in conscious complacency.

ALICE JAMES, *Journal* (1891)

See also Contentment.

COMPLAINING

Those who do not complain are never pitied.

JANE AUSTEN, *Pride and Prejudice* (1813)

To be reasonable one should never complain but when one hopes redress.

LADY MARY WORTLEY MONTAGU, letter to her husband (1712), in Octave Thanet, ed., *The Best Letters of Lady Mary Wortley Montagu* (1901)

COMPROMISE

There are two sides to every issue: one side is right and the other is wrong, but the middle is always evil.

AYN RAND, *Atlas Shrugged* (1957)

Don't compromise yourself. You are all you've got.

JANIS JOPLIN, in *Reader's Digest* (1973)

Compromise, if not the spice of life, is its solidity.

PHYLLIS McGINLEY, *The Province of the Heart* (1959)

CONCEALMENT

Show me one who boasts continually of his "openness," and I will show you one who conceals much.

MINNA THOMAS ANTRIM, *At the Sign of the Golden Calf* (1905)

But the gates of my happy childhood had clanged shut behind me; I had become adult enough to recognize the need to conceal unbearable emotions for the sake of others.

EVA FIGES, *Little Eden* (1978)

There is nothing that gives more assurance than a mask.

COLETTE, *My Apprenticeships* (1936)

See also Discretion, Hiding, Privacy, Secrets.

CONCEIT

Too much self-regard has never struck me as dignified: trying to twist over my shoulder to view my own behind.

MARGE PIERCY, *Braided Lives* (1982)

The affair between Margot Asquith and Margot Asquith will live as one of the prettiest love stories in all literature.

DOROTHY PARKER, in *New Yorker* (1927)

I've never any pity for conceited people, because I think they carry their comfort about with them.

GEORGE ELIOT, *The Mill on the Floss* (1860)

See also Arrogance, Egocentrism, Self-Importance, Vanity.

CONCEPTS

A concept is stronger than a fact.

CHARLOTTE PERKINS GILMAN, *Human Work* (1904)

See also Ideas, Theories, Thoughts.

CONCERN

Concern should drive us into action and not into a depression.

KAREN HORNEY, *Self-Analysis* (1942)

See also Worry.

CONCLUSION

I have come to the conclusion, after many years of sometimes sad experience, that you cannot come to any conclusion at all.

VITA SACKVILLE-WEST, *In Your Garden Again* (1953)

See also Decision.

CONDEMNATION

Someone has said that it requires less mental effort to condemn than to think.

EMMA GOLDMAN, title essay, *Anarchism* (1910)

See also Disapproval, Judgment.

CONFESSION

Most wrong-doing works, on the whole, less mischief than its useless confession.

EDITH WHARTON, *The Reef* (1912)

CONFIDENCE

I was thought to be "stuck up." I wasn't. I was just sure of myself. This is and always has been an unforgivable quality to the unsure.

BETTE DAVIS, *The Lonely Life* (1962)

I felt so young, so strong, so sure of God.

ELIZABETH BARRETT BROWNING, *Aurora Leigh* (1856)

If you think you can, you can. And if you think you can't, you're right.

MARY KAY ASH, in *New York Times* (1985)

If one burdens the future with one's worries, it cannot grow organically. I am filled with confidence, not that I shall succeed in worldly things, but that even when things go badly for me I shall still find life good and worth living.

ETTY HILLESUM, *An Interrupted Life: The Diaries of Etty Hillesum 1941–1943* (1983)

See also Self-Esteem.

CONFLICT

Conflict begins at the moment of birth.

JEAN BAKER MILLER, *Toward a New Psychology of Women* (1986)

People who fight fire with fire usually end up with ashes.

ABIGAIL VAN BUREN, syndicated column (1974)

I do not love strife, because I have always found that in the end each remains of the same opinion.

CATHERINE THE GREAT (c. 1770), in Katharine Anthony, *Catherine the Great* (1926)

The world is wide, and I will not waste my life in friction when it could be turned into momentum.

FRANCES WILLARD (1868), in Ray Strachey, *Frances Willard: Her Life and Work* (1912)

The moral absolute should be: if and when, in any dispute, one side *initiates* the use of physical force, *that side is wrong*—and no consideration or discussion of the issues is necessary or appropriate.

AYN RAND, in *The Objectivist* (1969)

For to be desperate is to discover strength. / We die of comfort and by conflict live.

MAY SARTON, "Take Anguish for Companion," *The Land of Silence* (1950–1953)

The children worked on each other like two indestructible pieces of sand-paper.

ELIZABETH BOWEN, "The Inherited Clock," *Ivy Gripped the Steps* (1946)

See also Quarreling, War.

CONFORMITY

Every society honors its live conformists and its dead troublemakers.

MIGNON McLAUGHLIN, *The Neurotic's Notebook* (1963)

For Miss Ogilvy had found as her life went on that in this world it is better to be one with the herd, that the world has no wish to understand those who cannot conform to its stereotyped pattern.

RADCLYFFE HALL, *Miss Ogilvy Finds Herself* (1926)

Honey, try harder to be like th rest—tu run with th rest—it's easier, an you'll be happier in th end—I guess.

HARRIETTE ARNOW, *The Dollmaker* (1954)

See also Conventionality, Conventions, Traditions.

CONFUSION

It is while trying to get everything straight in my head that I get confused.

MARY VIRGINIA MICKA, *Fiction, Oddly Enough* (1990)

CONGRESS

Congress—these, for the most part, illiterate hacks whose fancy vests are spotted with gravy, and whose speeches, hypocritical, unctuous, and slovenly, are spotted also with the gravy of political patronage.

MARY McCARTHY, *On the Contrary* (1961)

Congress seems drugged and inert most of the time.

SHIRLEY CHISHOLM, *Unbought and Unbossed* (1970)

I do strive to think well of my fellow man, but no amount of striving can give me confidence in the wisdom of a congressional vote.

AGNES REPPLIER, in Emma Repplier, *Agnes Repplier, A Memoir* (1957)

The inside operation of Congress—the deals, the compromises, the selling out, the co-opting, the unprincipled manipulating, the self-serving career-building—is a story of such monumental decadence that I believe if people find out about it they will demand an end to it.

BELLA ABZUG, *Bella!* (1972)

The Senate is the only show in the world where the cash customers have to sit in the balcony.

GRACIE ALLEN, *How to Become President* (1940)

We favor putting Congress on a commission basis. Pay them for results. If they do a good job and the country prospers, they get 10% of the extra take.

GRACIE ALLEN, *How to Become President* (1940)

See also Government, Politicians, Politics.

CONNECTIONS

Connections are made slowly, sometimes they grow underground.

MARGE PIERCY, "The Seven of Pentacles," *Circles on the Water* (1982)

Making mental connections is our most crucial learning tool, the essence of human intelligence: to forge links; to go beyond the given; to see patterns, relationship, context.

MARILYN FERGUSON, *The Aquarian Conspiracy* (1980)

CONSCIENCE

The one thing that doesn't abide by majority rule is a person's conscience.

HARPER LEE, *To Kill a Mockingbird* (1960)

Conscience is a treacherous thing, and mine behaves badly whenever there is a serious danger of being found out.

MARGARET LANE, *A Calabash of Diamonds* (1961)

I cannot and will not cut my conscience to fit this year's fashions, even though I long ago came to the conclusion that I was not a political person and could have no comfortable place in any political group.

LILLIAN HELLMAN, letter to the U.S. House of Representatives Committee on Un-American Activities (1952), in Lillian Hellman, *Scoundrel Time* (1976)

Altogether, his conscience pricked him a good deal; and when people's consciences prick them, sometimes they get angry with other people, which is very silly, and only makes matters worse.

DINAH MULOCK CRAIK, *The Adventures of a Brownie* (1872)

Well, I've got just as much conscience as any man in business can afford to keep,—just a little, you know, to swear by, as 'twere.

HARRIET BEECHER STOWE, *Uncle Tom's Cabin* (1852)

See also Judgment, Morality.

CONSOLATION

Let nothing disturb thee, / Nothing affright thee; / All things are passing; / God never changeth.

SAINT TERESA OF AVILA, "Bookmark," in Joanna Bankier and Deirdre Lashgari, eds., *Women Poets of the World* (1983)

All shall be well, and all shall be well, and all manner of thing shall be well.

JULIAN OF NORWICH, *Revelations of Divine Love* (1373)

Oh, no, I'm not brave. When a thing is certain, there's nothing to be brave about. All you can do is to find your consolation.

AGATHA CHRISTIE, *Endless Night* (1968)

Grass grows at last above all graves.

JULIA DORR, "Grass-Grown," *Poems* (1913)

He [Jesus] did not say, "You will never have a rough passage, you will never be over-strained, you will never feel uncomfortable," but he *did* say, "You will never be overcome."

JULIAN OF NORWICH, *Revelations of Divine Love* (1373)

No temple can still the personal griefs and strifes in the breasts of its visitors.

MARGARET FULLER, *Summer on the Lakes* (1844)

I can understand the things that afflict mankind, but I often marvel at those which console it.

ANNE-SOPHIE SWETCHINE, *The Writings of Madame Swetchine* (1869)

See also Comfort, Grief, Sorrow.

CONSUMERISM

America is a consumer culture, and when we change what we buy—and how we buy it—we'll change who we are.

FAITH POPCORN, *The Popcorn Report* (1991)

An honest man is one who knows that he can't consume more than he has produced.

AYN RAND, *Atlas Shrugged* (1957)

Great parts of our economy are directly dependent upon women having a weak self-concept. A multi-billion dollar fashion-cosmetic industry testifies to the validity of this approach. A woman who does not know who she is can be sold anything.

GABRIELLE BURTON, *I'm Running Away From Home But I'm Not Allowed to Cross the Street* (1972)

I'm not just buying a car—I'm buying a lifestyle!

LYNN JOHNSTON, *Pushing 40* (1988)

In department stores, so much kitchen equipment is bought indiscriminately by people who just come in for men's underwear.

JULIA CHILD, interview (1973)

One quarter of what you buy will turn out to be mistakes.

DELIA EPHRON, *Funny Sauce* (1986)

See also Materialism, Possessions.

CONTENTMENT

To be content with little is hard, to be content with much, impossible.

MARIE VON EBNER-ESCHENBACH, *Aphorisms* (1905)

See also Complacency, Happiness, Joy.

CONTROL

We are most deeply asleep at the switch when we fancy we control any switches at all.

ANNIE DILLARD, *Holy the Firm* (1977)

See also Force, Interference.

CONTROVERSY

I am not afraid the book will be controversial, I'm afraid it will not be controversial.

FLANNERY O'CONNOR, in Sally Fitzgerald, ed., *The Habit of Being* (1979)

CONVENTIONALITY

It saves trouble to be conventional, for you're not always explaining things.

MYRTLE REED, *Old Rose and Silver* (1909)

The truth was, she was becoming more and more uncomfortably conscious not only that the things she said, and a good many of the things she thought, had been taken down off a rack and put on, but that what she really felt was something else again.

DORIS LESSING, *The Summer Before the Dark* (1973)

It's terrible to allow conventional habits to gain a hold on a whole household; to eat, sleep and live by clock ticks.

ZELDA FITZGERALD, in Nancy Milford, *Zelda* (1970)

Outwardly she differed from the rest of the teaching staff in that she was still in a state of fluctuating development, whereas they had only too understandably not trusted themselves to change their minds, particularly on ethical questions, after the age of twenty.

MURIEL SPARK, *The Prime of Miss Jean Brodie* (1962)

If you are way ahead with your head you naturally are old-fashioned and regular in your daily life.

GERTRUDE STEIN, in John Malcolm Brinnin, *The Third Rose* (1959)

See also Normalcy, Ordinariness.

CONVENTIONS

Today's shocks are tomorrow's conventions.

CAROLYN HEILBRUN, *Toward a Recognition of Androgyny* (1973)

Human beings tend to regard the conventions of their own societies as natural, often as sacred.

MARY CATHERINE BATESON, *Composing a Life* (1989)

Convention was our safeguard: could one have stronger?

ELIZABETH BOWEN, "A Day in the Dark," in *Mademoiselle* (1957)

And so is the world put back by the death of every one who has to sacrifice the development of his or her peculiar gifts (which were meant, not for selfish gratification, but for the improvement of that world) to conventionality.

FLORENCE NIGHTINGALE, *Cassandra* (1852)

Grown people know that they do not always know the why of things, and even if they think they know, they do not know where and how they got the proof. Hence the irritation they show when children keep on demanding to know if a thing is so and how the grown folks got the proof of it. It is so troublesome because it is disturbing to the pigeonhole way of life.

ZORA NEALE HURSTON, *Dust Tracks on a Road* (1942)

See also Conformity, Traditions.

CONVERSATION

The real art of conversation is not only to say the right thing in the right place but to leave unsaid the wrong thing at the tempting moment.

DOROTHY NEVILL, *The Reminiscences of Lady Dorothy Nevill* (1907)

Ideal conversation must be an exchange of thought, and not, as many of those who worry most about their shortcomings believe, an eloquent exhibition of wit or oratory.

EMILY POST, *Etiquette* (1922)

A gossip is one who talks to you about others; a bore is one who talks to you about himself; a brilliant conversationalist is one who talks to you about yourself.

LISA KIRK, in *New York Journal-American* (1954)

Each person's life is lived as a series of conversations.

DEBORAH TANNEN, *You Just Don't Understand* (1990)

To talk easily with people, you must firmly believe that either you or they are interesting. And even then it's not easy.

MIGNON MCLAUGHLIN, *The Second Neurotic's Notebook* (1966)

Conversation's got to have some root in the past, or else you've got to explain every remark you make, an' it wears a person out.

SARAH ORNE JEWETT, *The Country of the Pointed Firs* (1896)

On the whole, and providing one is in good spirits and feeling reasonably bright, it is not hard to converse for a short space of time on subjects about which one knows little, and it is indeed often amusing to see how cunningly one can steer the conversational barque, hoisting and lowering her sails, tacking this way and that to avoid reefs, and finally racing feverishly for home with the outboard engine making a loud and cheerful noise.

VIRGINIA GRAHAM, *Say Please* (1949)

If one talks to more than four people, it is an audience; and one cannot really think or exchange thoughts with an audience.

ANNE MORROW LINDBERGH, *North to the Orient* (1935)

Too much brilliance has its disadvantages, and misplaced wit may raise a laugh, but often beheads a topic of profound interest.

MARGOT ASQUITH, *More or Less About Myself* (1934)

It is not restful, it is not *possible* to talk wholeheartedly to more than one person at a time. You can't really talk with a person unless you surrender to them, for the moment (all other talk is futile). You can't surrender to more than one person a moment.

ANNE MORROW LINDBERGH, *Bring Me a Unicorn* (1971)

Remember my unalterable maxim, where we love, we have always something to say.

LADY MARY WORTLEY MONTAGU (1755), in Octave Thanet, ed., *The Best Letters of Lady Mary Wortley Montagu* (1901)

One has to grow up with good talk in order to form the habit of it.

HELEN HAYES, *A Gift of Joy* (1965)

"My idea of good company, Mr. Elliot, is the company of clever, well-informed people, who have a great deal of conversation; that is what I call good company." "You are mistaken," said he gently, "that is not good company, that is the best."

JANE AUSTEN, *Persuasion* (1818)

The conversation whipped gaily around the table like rags in a high wind.

MARGARET HALSEY, *With Malice Toward Some* (1938)

She wanted to get away from herself, and conversation was the only means of escape that she knew.

EDITH WHARTON, *The House of Mirth* (1905)

She never lets ideas interrupt the easy flow of her conversation.

JEAN WEBSTER, *Daddy-Long-Legs* (1912)

Miss Bart had the gift of following an undercurrent of thought while she appeared to be sailing on the surface of conversation.

EDITH WHARTON, *The House of Mirth* (1905)

Miss Corby's rôle was jocularity: she always entered the conversation with a handspring.

EDITH WHARTON, *The House of Mirth* (1905)

Once someone like her gòt a leg in the conversation, she would be all over it.

FLANNERY O'CONNOR, "Revelation," *Everything That Rises Must Converge* (1965)

[Samuel] Johnson's conversation was by much too strong for a person accustomed to obsequiousness and flattery; it was *mustard in a young child's mouth!*

HESTER LYNCH PIOZZI (1781), in *Boswell's Life of Johnson* (1791)

Their civil discussions weren't interesting, and their interesting discussions weren't civil.

LISA ALTHER, *Kinflicks* (1975)

Polite conversation is rarely either.

FRAN LEBOWITZ, *Social Studies* (1977)

There is no such thing as conversation. It is an illusion. There are intersecting monologues, that is all.

REBECCA WEST, *There Is No Conversation* (1935)

See also Communication, Listening, Speech, Talking.

COOKING

Cooking is like love. It should be entered into with abandon or not at all.

HARRIET VAN HORNE, in *Vogue* (1956)

What I love about cooking is that after a hard day, there is something comforting about the fact that if you melt butter and add flour and then hot stock, *it will get thick!*

NORA EPHRON, *Heartburn* (1983)

Progress in civilization has been accompanied by progress in cookery.

FANNIE FARMER, *The Boston Cooking-School Cook Book* (1896)

Neither knowledge nor diligence can create a great chef. Of what use is conscientiousness as a substitute for inspiration?

COLETTE, *Prisons and Paradise* (1932)

Nothing stimulates the practiced cook's imagination like an egg.

IRMA S. ROMBAUER AND MARION ROMBAUER BECKER, *The Joy of Cooking* (1931)

I feel a recipe is only a theme, which an intelligent cook can play each time with a variation.

JEHANE BENOÎT, *Enjoying the Art of Canadian Cooking* (1974)

"Correct the seasoning"—how that time-tested direction stimulates the born cook!

IRMA S. ROMBAUER AND MARION ROMBAUER BECKER, *The Joy of Cooking* (1931)

Some people *pretend* to like capers, but the truth is that any dish that tastes good with capers in it tastes even better with capers not in it.

NORA EPHRON, *Heartburn* (1983)

Dried peas and beans, being rather on the dull side, much like dull people respond readily to the right contacts.

IRMA S. ROMBAUER AND MARION ROMBAUER BECKER, *The Joy of Cooking* (1931)

"May your rice never burn," is the New Year's greeting of the Chinese. "May it never be gummy," is ours.

IRMA S. ROMBAUER AND MARION ROMBAUER BECKER, *The Joy of Cooking* (1931)

Life is too short to stuff a mushroom.

SHIRLEY CONRAN, *Superwoman* (1975)

See also Eating, Food.

COUNTRY

The country washes to my door / Green miles on miles in soft uproar, / The thunder of the woods, and then / The backwash of green surf again.

KATHARINE TYNAN HINKSON, "The Old Love," in Burton E. Stevenson, *The Home Book of Modern Verse* (1925)

I suppose the pleasure of country life lies really in the eternally renewed evidences of the determination to live.

VITA SACKVILLE-WEST, *Country Notes* (1940)

This is a dream as old as America itself: give me a piece of land to call my own, a little town where everyone knows my name.

FAITH POPCORN, *The Popcorn Report* (1991)

Farmers are philosophical; they have learned that it is less wearing to shrug than to beat their breasts. But there is another angle to their attitude. Things happen rapidly in the country; something new always comes along to divert them and it isn't necessarily another calamity.

RUTH STOUT, *How to Have a Green Thumb Without an Aching Back* (1955)

See also Farmers, Land.

COURAGE

The only courage that matters is the kind that gets you from one moment to the next.

MIGNON MCLAUGHLIN, *The Second Neurotic's Notebook* (1966)

Courage is the ladder on which all the other virtues mount.

CLARE BOOTHE LUCE, in *Reader's Digest* (1979)

There are some women who seem to be born without fear, just as there are people who are born without the ability to feel pain. The painless ones go around putting their hands on hot stoves, freezing their feet to the point of gangrene, scalding the lining of their throats with boiling coffee, because there is no warning anguish. . . . Providence appears to protect such women, maybe out of astonishment.

MARGARET ATWOOD, "The Whirlpool Rapids," *Bluebeard's Egg* (1986)

The executioner is, I hear, very expert; and my neck is very slender.

ANNE BOLEYN (1536), in Willis John Abbot, *Notable Women in History* (1913)

Courage is the price that Life exacts for granting peace.

AMELIA EARHART, *Courage* (1927)

Life shrinks or expands in proportion to one's courage.

ANAÏS NIN, *The Diary of Anaïs Nin*, vol. 3 (1939–1944)

Anyone who has gumption knows what it is, and anyone who hasn't can never know what it is. So there is no need of defining it.

L. M. MONTGOMERY, *Anne of the Island* (1915)

I wanted you to see what real courage is, instead of getting the idea that courage is a man with a gun in his hand. It's when you know you're licked before you begin but you begin anyway and you see it through no matter what.

HARPER LEE, *To Kill a Mockingbird* (1960)

Courage! I have shown it for years; think you I shall lose it at the moment when my sufferings are to end?

MARIE ANTOINETTE, on the way to the guillotine (1793)

No coward soul is mine.

EMILY BRONTË, "No Coward Soul Is Mine" (1846)

For people sometimes believed that it was safer to live with complaints, was necessary to cooperate with grief, was all right to become an accomplice in self-ambush. . . . Took heart to flat out decide to be well and stride into the future sane and whole.

TONI CADE BAMBARA, *The Salt Eaters* (1980)

It takes far less courage to kill yourself than it takes to make yourself wake up one more time.

JUDITH ROSSNER, *Nine Months in the Life of an Old Maid* (1969)

Courage is as often the outcome of despair as of hope; in the one case we have nothing to lose, in the other everything to gain.

DIANE DE POITIERS, in Winifred Gordon, *A Book of Days* (1910)

Like a muscle, it is strengthened by use.

RUTH GORDON, in *L'Officiel* (1980)

Courage and clemency are equal virtues.

MARY DELARIVIER MANLEY, *The Royal Mischief* (1696)

There is plenty of courage among us for the abstract but not for the concrete.

HELEN KELLER, *Let Us Have Faith* (1940)

It's better to be a lion for a day than a sheep all your life.

ELIZABETH KENNY, in Victor Cohn, *Sister Kenny* (1976)

The truly fearless think of themselves as normal.

MARGARET ATWOOD, "The Whirlpool Rapids," *Bluebeard's Egg* (1986)

See also Adventure, Danger, Honor, Risk, Virtue.

CREATION

mitch had convinced sassafras that everything waz an art / so nothin in life cd be approached lightly / creation waz inherent in every thing anybody ever did right / that waz one of the mottos of the house.

NTOZAKE SHANGE, *Sassafras* (1976)

Creation is a better means of self-expression than possession; it is through creating, not possessing, that life is revealed.

VIDA D. SCUDDER, *The Privilege of Age* (1939)

The universe was not made in jest but in solemn incomprehensible earnest. By a power that is unfathomably secret, and holy, and fleet.

ANNIE DILLARD, *Pilgrim at Tinker Creek* (1974)

All things bright and beautiful, / All creatures great and small, / All things wise and wonderful, / The Lord God made them all.

MRS. CECIL FRANCES ALEXANDER, *All Things Bright and Beautiful* (1848)

Creations, whether they are children, poems, or organizations, take on a life of their own.

STARHAWK, *The Spiral Dance* (1979)

I beheld the wretch—the miserable monster whom I had created.

MARY SHELLEY, *Frankenstein* (1818)

See also Art, Creativity, Invention.

CREATIVITY

The process of writing, any form of creativity, is a power intensifying life.

RITA MAE BROWN, *Starting From Scratch* (1988)

When I can no longer create anything, I'll be done for.

COCO CHANEL, in Marcel Haedrich, *Coco Chanel: Her Life, Her Secrets* (1972)

I can always be distracted by love, but eventually I get horny for my creativity.

GILDA RADNER, *It's Always Something* (1989)

When we are writing, or painting, or composing, we are, during the time of creativity, freed from normal restrictions, and are opened to a wider world, where colors are brighter, sounds clearer, and people more wondrously complex than we normally realize.

MADELEINE L'ENGLE, *Walking on Water: Reflections on Faith and Art* (1980)

To fulfill a dream, to be allowed to sweat over lonely labor, to be given the chance to create, is the meat and potatoes of life. The money is the gravy. As everyone else, I love to dunk my crust in it. But alone, it is not a diet designed to keep body and soul together.

BETTE DAVIS, *The Lonely Life* (1962)

In this country we encourage "creativity" among the mediocre, but real bursting creativity appalls us. We put it down as undisciplined, as somehow "too much."

PAULINE KAEL (1965), in *Newsweek* (1991)

I do believe it is possible to create, even without ever writing a word or painting a picture, by simply molding one's inner life. And that too is a deed.

ETTY HILLESUM, *An Interrupted Life: The Diaries of Etty Hillesum 1941–1943* (1983)

Creativity is like a great receptive womb.

LYNN V. ANDREWS, Crystal Woman (1987)

Creativity comes from trust. Trust your instincts. And never hope more than you work.

RITA MAE BROWN, *Starting From Scratch* (1988)

It is the creative potential itself in human beings that is the image of God.

MARY DALY, *Beyond God the Father* (1973)

After each creative act one has to be sustained by one's strength of character, by a moral sense, by I don't know what, lest one tumble.

ETTY HILLESUM, *An Interrupted Life: The Diaries of Etty Hillesum 1941–1943* (1983)

I think most artists create out of despair . . . if labor pain is for physical birth, then there is a psychic pain and spiritual for creation. . . . The very nature of creation is not a performing glory on the outside, it's a painful, difficult search within.

LOUISE NEVELSON, Dawns + Dusks (1976)

Creative minds always have been known to survive any kind of bad training.

ANNA FREUD, speech (1968)

Living in a state of psychic unrest, in a Borderland, is what makes poets write and artists create.

GLORIA ANZALDÚA, *Borderlands/La Frontera: The New Mestiza* (1987)

One must also accept that one has "uncreative" moments. The more honestly one can accept that, the quicker these moments will pass. One must have the courage to call a halt, to feel empty and discouraged.

ETTY HILLESUM, *An Interrupted Life: The Diaries of Etty Hillesum 1941–1943* (1983)

Then and there I invented this rule for myself to be applied to every decision I might have to make in the future. I would sort out all the arguments and see which belonged to fear and which to creativeness, and other things being equal I would make the decision which had the larger number of creative reasons on its side. I think it must be a rule something like this that makes jonquils and crocuses come pushing through cold mud.

KATHARINE BUTLER HATHAWAY, *The Little Locksmith* (1942)

Under all the superficial praise of the "creative" is the desire to kill. It is the old war between the mystic and the nonmystic, a war to the death.

MAY SARTON, *Mrs. Stevens Hears the Mermaids Singing* (1965)

See also Art, Creation, Imagination.

CREDULITY

What one heart finds hard to believe, a hundred find easy.

NANCY WILLARD, *Things Invisible to See* (1984)

Credulity and the Want of Foresight, are Imperfections in the human Character, that no Politician can sufficiently guard against.

ABIGAIL ADAMS, letter to her husband, John Adams (1776)

A little credulity helps one on through life very smoothly.

ELIZABETH GASKELL, *Cranford* (1853)

See also Belief, Innocence.

CRIME

He'd forgotten just how addictive crime can be. Repeat offenders are motivated more by withdrawal symptoms than necessity.

SUE GRAFTON, *"H" Is for Homicide* (1991)

Crime is naught but misdirected energy.

EMMA GOLDMAN, title essay, *Anarchism* (1910)

There is hardly any deviancy, no matter how reprehensible in one context, which is not extolled as a virtue in another. There are no natural crimes, only legal ones.

FREDA ADLER, *Sisters in Crime* (1975)

See also Police, Vice.

CRISES

We don't get offered crises, they arrive.

ELIZABETH JANEWAY, *Cross Sections* (1982)

He was about as useful in a crisis as a sheep.

DOROTHY EDEN, *The Laughing Ghost* (1968)

See also Problems, Trouble.

CRITICISM

This book of essays . . . has all the depth and glitter of a worn dime.

DOROTHY PARKER, in *New Yorker* (1927)

Every word she writes is a lie, including *and* and *the.*

MARY MCCARTHY, televised remark about Lillian Hellman resulting in libel suit (1979)

This is not a novel to be tossed aside lightly. It should be thrown with great force.

DOROTHY PARKER, in Robert E. Drennan, *The Algonquin Wits* (1968)

There's less in this than meets the eye.

TALLULAH BANKHEAD (1922), *Tallulah* (1952)

The House Beautiful is the play lousy.

DOROTHY PARKER, in *New Yorker* (1933)

The central theme of the novel is that they were glad to see each other.

GERTRUDE STEIN, in John Malcolm Brinnin, *The Third Rose* (1959)

She ran the whole gamut of emotions, from A to B.

DOROTHY PARKER on Katharine Hepburn, play review (1933), in Robert E. Drennan, *The Algonquin Wits* (1968)

This play [John Drinkwater's *Abraham Lincoln*] holds the season's record, thus far, with a run of four evening performances and one matinee. By an odd coincidence, it ran just five performances too many.

DOROTHY PARKER, in *Vanity Fair* (1920)

Tonstant Weader fwowed up.

DOROTHY PARKER ("Constant Reader"), review of *The House at Pooh Corner*, in *New Yorker* (1928)

See also Books, Critics, Literature, Theater.

CRITICS

They never raised a statue to a critic.

MARTHA GRAHAM, in Agnes de Mille, *Dance to the Piper* (1952)

Too often do reviewers remind us of the mob of Astrologers, Chaldeans, and Soothsayers gathered before "the writing on the wall," and unable to read the characters or make known the interpretation.

CHARLOTTE BRONTË, biographical note (1850) to Emily Brontë's *Wuthering Heights* (1847)

If you think it so easy to be a critic, so difficult to be a poet or a painter or film experimenter, may I suggest you try both? You may discover why there are so few critics, so many poets.

PAULINE KAEL, *I Lost It at the Movies* (1965)

What tongue could speak but to an intelligent ear, and every noble work demands its critic. . . . The critic is not a base caviller, but the younger brother of genius. . . . The critic, then, should be

not merely a poet, nor merely a philosopher, not merely an observer, but tempered of all three.

MARGARET FULLER, in *The Dial* (1840)

See also Criticism.

CRUELTY

Cruelty is the only sin.

ELLEN GLASGOW, *The Woman Within* (1954)

A hurtful act is the transference to others of the degradation which we bear in ourselves.

SIMONE WEIL, *Gravity and Grace* (1947)

Unkindness almost always stands for the displeasure that one has in oneself.

ADRIENNE MONNIER, *Dernières Gazettes et Écrits divers* (1939), in Richard McDougall, tr., *The Very Rich Hours of Adrienne Monnier* (1976)

I think that the desire to be cruel and to hurt (with words because any other way might be dangerous to ourself) is part of human nature. Parties are battles (most parties), a conversation is a duel (often). Everybody's trying to hurt first, to get in the dig that will make him or her feel superior, feel triumph.

JEAN RHYS, *Letters, 1931–1966* (1984)

Cruelty is contagious in uncivilized communities.

HARRIET A. JACOBS, Incidents in the Life of a Slave Girl, Written by Herself (1861)

Experience has taught me that the only cruelties people condemn are those with which they do not happen to be familiar.

ELLEN GLASGOW, *Letters of Ellen Glasgow* (1958)

My doctrine is this, that if we see cruelty or wrong that we have the power to stop, and do nothing, we make ourselves sharers in the guilt.

ANNA SEWELL, *Black Beauty* (1877)

See also Evil, Vice.

CULTURE

Culture is both an intellectual phenomenon and a moral one.

RAISA M. GORBACHEV, *I Hope* (1991)

Most people are shaped to the form of their culture because of the enormous malleability of their original endowment. They are plastic to the molding force of the society into which they are born. It does not matter whether, with the Northwest Coast, it requires delusions of self-reference, or with our own civilization the amassing of possessions. In any case the great mass of individuals take quite readily the form that is presented to them.

RUTH BENEDICT, *Patterns of Culture* (1934)

Cultural constraints condition and limit our choices, shaping our characters with their imperatives.

JEANE J. KIRKPATRICK, speech (1981)

Culture is not a biologically transmitted complex.

RUTH BENEDICT, *Patterns of Culture* (1934)

The disintegration of a culture is a melancholy event.

SHIRLEY ABBOTT, *Womenfolks: Growing Up Down South* (1983)

Culture is an instrument wielded by professors to manufacture professors, who when their turn comes will manufacture professors.

SIMONE WEIL, *The Need for Roots* (1949)

Culture is what your butcher would have if he were a surgeon.

MARY PETTIBONE POOLE, *A Glass Eye at a Keyhole* (1938)

Mrs. Ballinger is one of the ladies who pursue Culture in bands, as though it were dangerous to meet alone.

EDITH WHARTON, title story, *Xingu* (1916)

See also Society.

CURIOSITY

Try curiosity.

DOROTHY PARKER, to a friend whose sick cat had to be put to sleep, in Robert E. Drennan, *The Algonquin Wits* (1968)

It doesn't do to be curious at Jamaica Inn, and I'll have you remember that.

DAPHNE DU MAURIER, *Jamaica Inn* (1935)

I think, at a child's birth, if a mother could ask a fairy godmother to endow it with the most useful gift, that gift should be curiosity.

ELEANOR ROOSEVELT, in *Reader's Digest* (1983)

Worlds can be found by a child and an adult bending down and looking together under the grass stems or at the skittering crabs in a tidal pool.

MARY CATHERINE BATESON, *With a Daughter's Eye* (1984)

See also Questions.

CYNICISM

Cynicism is an unpleasant way of saying the truth.

LILLIAN HELLMAN, *The Little Foxes* (1939)

Cynicism is more than a pose; it's also a handy time saver. By deflating your companion's enthusiasm, you can cut conversations in half.

LISA BIRNBACH, *The Official Preppy Handbook* (1980)

Cynical speech is characterized by a lengthening of vowel sounds in the syllable that is normally accented, i.e., "Woooonderful." Derivation of this attitude can be traced to the manufacture of the first synthetic fabrics. "That sweater's proooobably acryyyylic."

LISA BIRNBACH, *The Official Preppy Handbook* (1980)

A cynical young person is almost the saddest sight to see, because it means that he or she has gone from knowing nothing to believing in nothing.

MAYA ANGELOU, in Brian Lanker, *I Dream a World* (1989)

See also Pessimism.

D

DANCE

Dance is the hidden language of the soul.

MARTHA GRAHAM, in *New York Times* (1985)

The truest expression of a people is in its dances and its music.

AGNES DE MILLE, in *New York Times Magazine* (1975)

Dancing is just discovery, discovery, discovery.

MARTHA GRAHAM, in *New York Times* (1985)

Every dance is a kind of fever chart, a graph of the heart.

MARTHA GRAHAM, *Blood Memory* (1991)

I danced with a passion to spite the music.

GELSEY KIRKLAND, *Dancing on My Grave* (1986)

Think of the magic of that foot, comparatively small, upon which your whole weight rests. It's a miracle, and the dance . . . is a celebration of that miracle.

MARTHA GRAHAM, speech (1965)

The practice mirror is to be used for the correction of faults, not for a love affair, and the figure you watch should not become your dearest friend.

AGNES DE MILLE, in *Atlantic* (1960)

A good education is usually harmful to a dancer. A good calf is better than a good head.

AGNES DE MILLE, news item (1954)

Fine dancing, I believe, like virtue, must be its own reward. Those who are standing by are usually thinking of something very different.

JANE AUSTEN, *Emma* (1816)

We waltzed Lisztlessly.

KAREN ELIZABETH GORDON, *The Transitive Vampire* (1984)

See also Artists, Ballet.

DANGER

In danger there is great power.

AGNES WHISTLING ELK, in Lynn V. Andrews, *Crystal Woman* (1987)

There is nobody who is not dangerous for someone.

MARIE DE RABUTIN-CHANTAL, MARQUISE DE SÉVIGNÉ (c. 1680), *Letters of Madame de Sévigné to Her Daughter and Her Friends* (1811)

The more hidden the venom, the more dangerous it is.

MARGUERITE DE VALOIS (1594), *Memoirs* (1910)

To assess the damage is a dangerous act.

CHERRÍE MORAGA, "La Güera," in Cherríe Moraga and Gloria Anzaldúa, eds., *This Bridge Called My Back* (1983)

Avoiding danger is no safer in the long run than outright exposure. The fearful are caught as often as the bold.

HELEN KELLER, *Let Us Have Faith* (1940)

See also Courage, Risk.

DARKNESS

And I saw *darkness* for weeks. It never dawned on me that I could come out of it, but you heal. Nature heals you, and you do come out of it. All of a sudden I saw a crack of light . . . then all of a sudden I saw another crack of light. Then I saw *forms* in the light. And I recognized that there was no darkness, that in darkness there'll always be light.

LOUISE NEVELSON, *Dawns + Dusks* (1976)

I'm not frightened of the darkness outside. It's the darkness inside houses I don't like.

SHELAGH DELANEY, *A Taste of Honey* (1958)

See also Night.

DATA

Everything is data. But data isn't everything.

PAULINE BART, in Cheris Kramarae and Paula A. Treichler, *A Feminist Dictionary* (1985)

See also Facts, Information.

DAUGHTERS

Oh, my son's my son till he gets him a wife, / But my daughter's my daughter all her life.

DINAH MULOCK CRAIK, "Young and Old," *Mulock's Poems, New and Old* (1888)

But what mother and daughter understand each other, or even have the sympathy for each other's lack of understanding?

MAYA ANGELOU, *I Know Why the Caged Bird Sings* (1970)

Our mythology tells us so much about fathers and sons. . . . What do we know about mothers and daughters? . . . Our power is so oblique, so hidden, so ethereal a matter, that we rarely struggle with our daughters over actual kingdoms or corporate shares. On the other hand, our attractiveness dries as theirs blooms, our journey shortens just as theirs begins. We too must be afraid and awed and amazed that we cannot live forever and that our replacements are eager for their turn, indifferent to our wishes, ready to leave us behind.

ANNE ROIPHE, *Lovingkindness* (1987)

See also Family, Sisters.

DAWN

Dawn is the child / wet with birth.

CHARLOTTE DE CLUE, "Morning Song," in Rayna Green, ed., *That's What She Said* (1984)

Dawn and its excesses always reminded me of heaven, a place where I have always known I would not be comfortable.

MARILYNNE ROBINSON, *Housekeeping* (1980)

It was harder to drown at sunrise than in darkness.

EDITH WHARTON, *The House of Mirth* (1905)

Most people do not consider dawn to be an attractive experience—unless they are still up.

ELLEN GOODMAN, *Close to Home* (1979)

See also Morning.

DEAFNESS

Deafness has left me acutely aware of both the duplicity that language is capable of and the many expressions the body cannot hide.

TERRY GALLOWAY, in Marsha Saxton and Florence Howe, *With Wings* (1987)

The problems of deafness are deeper and more complex, if not more important, than the problems of blindness. Deafness is a much worse misfortune. For it means the loss of the most vital stimulus—the sound of the voice that brings language, sets thoughts astir and keeps us in the intellectual company of man.

HELEN KELLER, letter to Dr. J. Kerr Love (1910), in Brian Grant, ed., *The Quiet Ear* (1987)

I need to know what is being said. Always. Anywhere. Not just a word now and then.

ELEANORE DEVINE, "Brotherhood," *You're Standing in My Light* (1990)

The inability to hear is a nuisance; the inability to communicate is the tragedy.

LOU ANN WALKER, *A Loss for Words: The Story of Deafness in a Family* (1986)

See also Disabilities.

DEATH

Into the darkness they go, the wise and the lovely.

EDNA ST. VINCENT MILLAY, "Dirge Without Music," *The Buck in the Snow* (1928)

Watching a peaceful death of a human being reminds us of a falling star; one of the million lights in a vast sky that flares up for a brief moment only to disappear into the endless night forever.

ELISABETH KÜBLER-ROSS, *On Death and Dying* (1969)

Oh, write of me, not "Died in bitter pains," / But "Emigrated to another star!"

HELEN HUNT JACKSON, "Emigravit" (1875), in Edmund Clarence Stedman, *An American Anthology* (1906)

What we call death was to him only emigration.

AMELIA E. BARR, *All the Days of My Life* (1913)

When I am dead, my dearest, / Sing no sad songs for me; / Plant thou no roses at my head, / Nor shady cypress tree: / Be the green grass above me / With showers and dewdrops wet; / And if thou wilt, remember, / And if thou wilt, forget.

CHRISTINA ROSSETTI, "Song" (1848), *The Poetical Works of Christina Georgina Rossetti* (1906)

I would like to believe when I die that I have given myself away like a tree that sows seed every spring and never counts the loss, because it is not loss, it is adding to future life. It is the tree's way of being. Strongly rooted perhaps, but spilling out its treasure on the wind.

MAY SARTON, *Recovering: A Journal* (1978–1979)

Death still celebrates / the life in you.

NELLY SACHS, "Death Still Celebrates," *O the Chimneys* (1967)

For rain it hath a friendly sound / To one who's six feet under ground; / And scarce the friendly voice or face, / A grave is such a quiet place.

EDNA ST. VINCENT MILLAY, title poem, *Renascence* (1917)

Death is terrifying because it is so ordinary. It happens all the time.

SUSAN CHEEVER, *Home Before Dark* (1984)

Death in its way comes just as much of a surprise as birth.

EDNA O'BRIEN, "A Rose in the Heart," *Mrs. Reinhardt* (1978)

Why is it harder to think of his going to nothing than to think of his coming from nothing? One direction is just as dark as the other.

ANNE MORROW LINDBERGH, *Hour of Gold, Hour of Lead* (1973)

Down, down, down into the darkness of the grave / Gently they go, the beautiful, the tender, the kind; / Quietly they go, the intelligent, the witty, the brave. / I know. But I do not approve. And I am not resigned.

EDNA ST. VINCENT MILLAY, "Dirge Without Music," *The Buck in the Snow* (1928)

Death is an ill; 'tis thus the Gods decide: / For had death been a boon, the Gods had died.

SAPPHO (6th century B.C.), in C. R. Haines, *Sappho: The Poems and Fragments* (1926)

There is something disorderly about the death of a young person. In a universe disturbed by so much over which we have no control, an untimely tragedy rattles the teeth of our already shaken confidence. We want to domesticate death, fight it on our own turf, in familiar rooms with shades drawn evenly, top sheets turned back, and a circle of hushed voices closing in.

FAYE MOSKOWITZ, *A Leak in the Heart* (1985)

God have mercy, that such a young man should have to chew the black earth!

GLÜCKEL OF HAMELN, *The Life of Glückel of Hameln (1646–1724), Written by Herself* (1719)

So much do I love wandering, / So much I love the sea and sky, / That it will be a piteous thing / In one small grave to lie.

ZOË AKINS, "The Wanderer," in Burton E. Stevenson, *The Home Book of Modern Verse* (1925)

I shall die, but that is all that I shall do for Death; I am not on his pay-roll.

EDNA ST. VINCENT MILLAY, "Conscientious Objector," *Wine From These Grapes* (1934)

You do not die from being born, nor from having lived, nor from old age. You die from *something*. . . . There is no such thing as a natural death: nothing that happens to a man is ever natural, since his presence calls the world into question. All men must die: but for every man his death is an accident and, even if he knows it and consents to it, an unjustifiable violation.

SIMONE DE BEAUVOIR, *A Very Easy Death* (1966)

When I die people will say it is the best thing for me. It is because they know it is the worst. They want to avoid the feeling of pity. As though they were the people most concerned.

IVY COMPTON-BURNETT, *The Mighty and Their Fall* (1961)

There is no sound so terrible as a man's sorrow for his own death.

SUE GRAFTON, *"H" Is for Homicide* (1991)

I am not afraid of death, but would not want to die in some obscure or pointless way.

ISABELLE EBERHARDT (1901), *The Passionate Nomad* (1987)

I rebel against death, yet I know that it is how I respond to death's inevitability that is going to make me less or more fully alive.

MADELEINE L'ENGLE, *The Summer of the Great-Grandmother* (1974)

It is not *dying,* but *living,* that is a preparation for Death.

MARGOT ASQUITH, *More or Less About Myself* (1934)

By "coming to terms with life" I mean: the reality of death has become a definite part of my life; my life has, so to speak, been extended by death, by my looking death in the eye and accepting it, by accepting destruction as part of life and no longer wasting my energies on fear of death or the refusal to acknowledge its inevitability.

ETTY HILLESUM, *An Interrupted Life: The Diaries of Etty Hillesum 1941–1943* (1983)

An absolute condition of all successful living, whether for an individual or a nation, is the acceptance of death.

FREYA STARK, *The Journey's Echo* (1988)

If I knew for certain that I should die next week, I would still be able to sit at my desk all week and study with perfect equanimity, for I know now that life and death make a meaningful whole.

ETTY HILLESUM, *An Interrupted Life: The Diaries of Etty Hillesum 1941–1943* (1983)

You never realize death until you realize love.

KATHARINE BUTLER HATHAWAY, The Journals and Letters of the Little Locksmith (1946)

coming to the end of spring / my grandmother kicks off her shoes / steps out of her faltering body.

BETSY SHOLL, "Spring Fragments," *Rooms Overhead* (1986)

It'll be with me like it was with Uncle Ned's ole ox, I reckon; he kep' a-goin' an' a-goin' till he died a-standin' up, an' even then they had to push him over.

ALICE CALDWELL RICE, *Mrs. Wiggs of the Cabbage Patch* (1901)

I thought death would be a final leap out of the old tire swing into shimmering Bald Eagle Lake after a final push from long-dead Aunt Ethel, godmother and childhood pal.

JUDITH STOUGHTON, *One Woman's Pascal Journey* (1991)

He is not dead! he only left / A precious robe of clay behind, / To draw a robe of love and light / Around his disembodied mind.

FRANCES ELLEN WATKINS HARPER, "Obituary for J. Edwards Barnes," *National Anti-Slavery Standard* (1858)

And you walked over death / like a bird in snow.

NELLY SACHS, "Glowing Enigma III," *O the Chimneys* (1967)

All your lovely words are spoken. / Once the ivory box is broken, / Beats the golden bird no more.

EDNA ST. VINCENT MILLAY, "Elegy," *Second April* (1921)

I have faced Death. I have been caught in the wild weed tangles of her hair, seen the gleam of her jade eyes. I will go when it is time—no choice!—but now I *want* life.

KERI HULME, *The Bone People* (1983)

Just then, Death finished his prowling through the house on his padded feet and entered the room. He bowed to Mama in his way, and she made her manners and left us to act out our ceremonies over unimportant things.

ZORA NEALE HURSTON, *Dust Tracks on a Road* (1942)

Eternal death has worked like a warrior rat, with diabolical sense of duty, to gnaw my bottom. Everything is finished now.

AMA ATA AIDOO, "The Message" (1970), in Sandra M. Gilbert and Susan Gubar, eds., *The Norton Anthology of Literature by Women* (1985)

Death clutches me by the ear.

JOSEPHINE HERBST, chapter title, *Pity Is Not Enough* (1933)

Death is dancing me ragged.

LINDA HOGAN, "The Women Are Grieving," in Rayna Green, ed., *That's What She Said* (1984)

I know for sure / that at the end, / the playful stranger who appears / is not death / but love.

KATHLEEN NORRIS, "Three Small Songs for the Muse," in Marilyn Sewell, ed., *Cries of the Spirit* (1991)

This is the simplest of all thoughts, that Death must come when we call, although he is a god.

STEVIE SMITH, *Me Again* (1982)

University students are rarely able to cope with universals and death is the most embarrassing universal.

KATE CRUISE O'BRIEN, "Henry Died," *A Gift Horse* (1978)

The company you keep at death is, of all things, most dependent on chance.

KERI HULME, *The Bone People* (1983)

The timing of death, like the ending of a story, gives a changed meaning to what preceded it.

MARY CATHERINE BATESON, *With a Daughter's Eye* (1984)

There is nothing sadder than the cheerful letters of the dead, expressing hopes that were never fulfilled, ambitions that were never achieved, dreams cut off before they could come to fruition.

ELIZABETH PETERS, *Naked Once More* (1989)

How can they tell?

DOROTHY PARKER, on being told that President Coolidge was dead (1933), in J. Bryan III, *Merry Gentlemen (and One Lady)* (1985)

It costs me never a stab nor squirm / To tread by chance upon a worm. / "Aha, my little dear," I say, / "Your clan will pay me back one day."

DOROTHY PARKER, "Thought for a Sunshiny Morning," *Sunset Gun* (1928)

Listen, Fred, don't feel badly when I die, because I've been dead for a long time.

DOROTHY PARKER (1967), in Marion Meade, *Dorothy Parker: What Fresh Hell Is This?* (1988)

Heap not on this mound / Roses that she loved so well; / Why bewilder her with roses, / That she cannot see or smell?

EDNA ST. VINCENT MILLAY, "Epitaph," *Second April* (1921)

'Tis sweet to know that stocks will stand / When we with Daisies lie— / That Commerce will continue— / And Trades as briskly fly.

EMILY DICKINSON (1858), *Poems, Second Series* (1891)

Because I could not stop for Death— / He kindly stopped for me— / The Carriage held but just Ourselves— / And Immortality.

EMILY DICKINSON (1863), *Poems, First Series* (1890)

In the first moment when we come away from the presence of death, every other relation to the living is merged, to our feeling, in the great relation of a common nature and a common destiny.

GEORGE ELIOT, "The Lifted Veil" (1859)

Death . . . obliterates family resemblance as it does personality: there is no affinity between the living and the dead.

P. D. JAMES, *Death of an Expert Witness* (1977)

When I am dead and over me bright April / Shakes out her rain-drenched hair, / Though you should lean above me broken-hearted, / I shall not care.

SARA TEASDALE, "I Shall Not Care," *Collected Poems* (1937)

A beautiful death is for people who have lived like animals to die like angels.

MOTHER TERESA, in Kathryn Spinks, *For the Brotherhood of Man Under the Fatherhood of God* (1980)

The dead make rules, and I obey. / I too shall be dead some day.

MARY CAROLYN DAVIES, "The Dead Make Rules," in Burton E. Stevenson, *The Home Book of Modern Verse* (1925)

Death is a slave's freedom.

NIKKI GIOVANNI, speech at Martin Luther King, Jr.'s funeral (1968)

If there wasn't death I think you couldn't go on.

STEVIE SMITH, in *Observer* (1969)

Death? Why this fuss about death. Use your imagination, try to visualize a world *without* death!

CHARLOTTE PERKINS GILMAN, *The Living of Charlotte Perkins Gilman* (1935)

It's only another adventure, after all.

DOROTHY EDEN, *The Laughing Ghost* (1968)

I have only one curiosity left: death.

COCO CHANEL, in Marcel Haedrich, *Coco Chanel: Her Life, Her Secrets* (1972)

See also Dying, Euthanasia, Funerals, Grief, Mourning, Suicide.

DEBTS

The payment of debts is necessary for social order. The non-payment is quite equally necessary for social order. For centuries humanity has oscillated, serenely unaware, between these two contradictory necessities.

SIMONE WEIL (1937), *Selected Essays* (1962)

Man was lost if he went to a usurer, for the interest ran faster than a tiger upon him.

PEARL BUCK, *The First Wife* (1933)

I've often known people more shocked because you are not bankrupt than because you are.

MARGARET BAILLIE SAUNDERS, *A Shepherd of Kensington* (1907)

See also Economics, Money.

DECEPTION

The practice of deception was so constant with her that it got to be a kind of truth.

LOUISE ERDRICH, *Tracks* (1988)

See also Dishonesty.

DECISION

A peacefulness follows any decision, even the wrong one.

RITA MAE BROWN, *Sudden Death* (1983)

Once again she decided not to decide. She preferred being compelled into her decisions.

LISA ALTHER, *Kinflicks* (1975)

Like other potentates with a long habit of arbitrary authority, she covered her perplexity with a smart show of decision.

DOROTHY CANFIELD FISHER, *The Bent Twig* (1915)

If someone tells you he is going to make a "realistic decision," you immediately understand that he has resolved to do something bad.

MARY MCCARTHY, *On the Contrary* (1961)

See also Choice, Conclusion.

DEEDS

Our deeds determine us, as much as we determine our deeds.

GEORGE ELIOT, *Adam Bede* (1859)

One sad thing about this world is that the acts that take the most out of you are usually the ones that other people will never know about.

ANNE TYLER, *Celestial Navigation* (1974)

Our deeds still travel with us from afar, / And what we have been makes us what we are.

GEORGE ELIOT, *Middlemarch* (1871)

See also Actions, Behavior.

DEFEAT

Please understand that there is no one depressed in *this* house; we are not interested in the possibilities of defeat; they do not exist.

QUEEN VICTORIA, letter (1899)

In some circumstances, the refusal to be defeated is a refusal to be educated.

MARGARET HALSEY, *No Laughing Matter* (1977)

See also Failure.

DELAY

Delay breeds fear.

JESSAMYN WEST, *The Life I Really Lived* (1979)

See also Hesitation, Lateness.

DEMOCRACY

Democracy always makes for materialism, because the only kind of equality that you can guarantee to a whole people is, broadly speaking, physical.

KATHARINE FULLERTON GEROULD, *Modes and Morals* (1920)

Democracy cannot sustain itself amid a high degree of violence.

MARY RITTER BEARD (1950), in Nancy F. Cott, *A Woman Making History* (1991)

Democracy, like the human organism, carries within it the seed of its own destruction.

C. V. WEDGWOOD, *Velvet Studies* (1946)

Democracy is not an easy form of government, because it is never final; it is a living, changing organism, with a continuous shifting and adjusting of balance between individual freedom and general order.

ILKA CHASE, *Past Imperfect* (1942)

A democratic form of government, a democratic way of life, presupposes free public education over a long period; it presupposes also an education for personal responsibility that too often is neglected.

ELEANOR ROOSEVELT, "Let Us Have Faith in Democracy," in Department of Agriculture, *Land Policy Review* (1942)

Although most governments in the world are, as they always have been, autocracies of one kind or another, no idea holds greater sway in the mind of educated Americans than the belief that it is possible to democratize governments, anytime, anywhere, under any circumstances.

JEANE J. KIRKPATRICK, in *Commentary* (1979)

Small use it will be to save democracy for the race if we cannot save the race for democracy.

JEANNETTE RANKIN, in Hannah Josephson, *Jeannette Rankin: First Lady in Congress* (1947)

The capacity to combine commitment with skepticism is essential to democracy.

MARY CATHERINE BATESON, *Composing a Life* (1989)

In an autocracy, one person has his way; in an aristocracy a few people have their way; in a democracy no one has his way.

CELIA GREEN, *The Decline and Fall of Science* (1977)

In a true democracy everyone can be upper class and live in Connecticut.

LISA BIRNBACH, *The Official Preppy Handbook* (1980)

See also Government.

DEPRESSION

Sometimes one has simply to endure a period of depression for what it may hold of illumination if one can live through it, attentive to what it exposes or demands.

MAY SARTON, *Journal of a Solitude* (1973)

I was much too far out all my life / And not waving but drowning.

STEVIE SMITH, title poem, *Not Waving But Drowning* (1957)

Depression was a very active state really. Even if you appeared to an observer to be immobilized, your mind was in a frenzy of paralysis. You were unable to function, but were actively despising yourself for it.

LISA ALTHER, *Kinflicks* (1975)

Depression—that is what we all hate. We the afflicted. Whereas the relatives and shrinks, the tribal ring, they rather welcome it: you are quiet and you suffer.

KATE MILLETT, *The Loony-Bin Trip* (1990)

Like many people in personal turmoil, she rose late, didn't dress other than to cloak herself in her dressing gown, and she fell asleep easily throughout the day.

CAROL BLY, "Talk of Heroes," *Backbone* (1982)

People in delirium rise and sink, rise and sink, in and out of lucidity. The swaying, shuddering, thudding, flinging stops, and the furniture of life falls into place.

NADINE GORDIMER, *July's People* (1981)

He was in the grip of that most trying form of depression—the melancholy of enforced inaction.

PATRICIA MOYES, *Down Among the Dead Men* (1961)

If life is a bowl of cherries, what am I doing in the pits?

ERMA BOMBECK, book title (1971)

Noble deeds and hot baths are the best cures for depression.

DODIE SMITH, *I Capture the Castle* (1948)

See also Despair, Melancholy, Mental Illness.

DEPRIVATION

See Privation.

DESERT

The palpable sense of mystery in the desert air breeds fables, chiefly of lost treasure. . . . It is a question whether it is not better to be bitten by the little horned snake of the desert that goes sidewise and strikes without coiling, than by the tradition of a lost mine.

MARY AUSTIN, *The Land of Little Rain* (1904)

The Desert proclaiming itself, speaks gently . . . if you and the Desert have found each other, surely you will feel the drawing of your soul toward the eternal calm—the brooding peace that is there in the gray country.

IDAH MEACHAM STROBRIDGE, *In Miners' Mirage-Land* (1904)

For all the toll the desert takes of a man it gives compensations, deep breaths, deep sleep, and the communion of the stars.

MARY AUSTIN, *The Land of Little Rain* (1904)

A wind came up and ran along the rock base lifting the sand like the edge of a carpet.

OLIVIA MANNING, *The Danger Tree* (1977)

When your eye is so trained that it may discover the beauty that dwells in that vast, still corner of the world, and your ear is attuned to catch the music of the plains or the anthems sung in deep cañons by the winds; when your heart finds comradeship in the mountains and the great sand-seas, the sun and the stars, and the huge cloud-drifts that the Desert winds set a-rolling round the world—when all these reach your heart by way of your eye and your ear, then you shall find one of the alluring ways that belongs to the Desert.

IDAH MEACHAM STROBRIDGE, *In Miners' Mirage-Land* (1904)

The desert floras shame us with their cheerful adaptations to the seasonal limitations. Their whole duty is to flower and fruit, and they do it hardly, or with tropical luxuriance, as the rain admits. . . . One hopes the land may breed like qualities in her human offspring, not tritely to "try," but to do.

MARY AUSTIN, *The Land of Little Rain* (1904)

See also Nature.

DESERTION

But mayn't desertion be a brave thing? A fine thing? To desert a thing we've gone beyond—to have the courage to desert it and walk right off from the dead thing to the live thing—?

SUSAN GLASPELL, *The Visioning* (1911)

See also Parting, Renunciation.

DESIRE

Compared to my heart's desire / the sea is a drop.

ADÉLIA PRADO, "Denouement," in Ellen Watson, tr., *The Alphabet in the Park: Selected Poems of Adélia Prado* (1990)

There is only one big thing—desire. And before it, when it is big, all is little.

WILLA CATHER, *The Song of the Lark* (1915)

Life is made up of desires that seem big and vital one minute, and little and absurd the next. I guess we get what's best for us in the end.

ALICE CALDWELL RICE, *A Romance of Billy-Goat Hill* (1912)

In my experience, there is only one motivation, and that is desire. No reasons or principles contain it or stand against it.

JANE SMILEY, *Ordinary Love* (1989)

Our visions begin with our desires.

AUDRE LORDE, in Claudia Tate, ed., *Black Women Writers at Work* (1983)

This fire in me, it's not just the hunger of a woman for a man—it's the hunger of all my people back of me, from all ages, for light, for the life higher!

ANZIA YEZIERSKA, "Hunger," *Hungry Hearts* (1920)

But what was the desire of the flesh beside the desire of the mind?

HELEN WADDELL, *Peter Abelard* (1933)

You can have anything you want if you want it desperately enough. You must want it with an inner exuberance that erupts through the skin and joins the energy that created the world.

SHEILAH GRAHAM, *The Rest of the Story* (1964)

Our desire must be like a slow and stately ship, sailing across endless oceans, never in search of safe anchorage. Then suddenly, unexpectedly, it will find mooring for a moment.

ETTY HILLESUM, *An Interrupted Life: The Diaries of Etty Hillesum 1941–1943* (1983)

The more anybody wants a thing, the more they do think others want it.

MARY WEBB, *Precious Bane* (1924)

Desire can blind us to the hazards of our enterprises.

MARIE DE FRANCE (12th century), in Jeanette Beer, tr., *Medieval Fables of Marie de France* (1981)

Protect me from what I want.

JENNY HOLZER, *Truisms* (1977–1979)

See also Longing.

DESPAIR

I can't read or sleep. Without hope or youth or money I sit constantly wishing I were dead.

ZELDA FITZGERALD, letter to Scott Fitzgerald (1930), in Nancy Milford, *Zelda* (1970)

I'll have to, as you say, take a stand, do something toward shaking up that system. . . . Despair . . . is too easy an out.

PAULE MARSHALL, *The Chosen Place, The Timeless People* (1969)

See also Depression, Discouragement, Hope.

DESTINY

How rash to assert that man shapes his own destiny. All he can do is determine his inner responses.

ETTY HILLESUM, *An Interrupted Life: The Diaries of Etty Hillesum 1941–1943* (1983)

She felt again that small shiver that occurred to her when events hinted at a destiny being played out, of unseen forces intervening.

DOROTHY GILMAN, Mrs. Pollifax and the Whirling Dervish (1990)

See also Fate.

DESTROYERS

Those who cannot live fully often become destroyers of life.

ANAÏS NIN, *The Diary of Anaïs Nin*, vol. 4 (1944–1947)

Abel was a dog poisoner. It sometimes works out that way. A man wants to have some direct connection with life. If he can't bring life into being, he'll put an end to it. In that way he's not completely powerless. Some men can start it. Others can end it.

JESSAMYN WEST, *The Life I Really Lived* (1979)

See also Villains.

DETACHMENT

We are able to laugh when we achieve detachment, if only for a moment.

MAY SARTON, *Journal of a Solitude* (1973)

Attachment is a manufacturer of illusions and whoever wants reality ought to be detached.

SIMONE WEIL, *Gravity and Grace* (1947)

The work, once completed, does not need me. The work I'm working on needs my total concentration. The one that's finished doesn't belong to me anymore. It belongs to itself.

MAYA ANGELOU, in Claudia Tate, ed., *Black Women Writers at Work* (1983)

Only an indirect method is effective. We do nothing if we have not first drawn back.

SIMONE WEIL, *Gravity and Grace* (1947)

See also Objectivity.

DETERMINATION

"The doctor says I'm going blind," she told the children, but privately, she'd intended to do no such thing.

ANNE TYLER, *Dinner at the Homesick Restaurant* (1982)

If enough people think of a thing and work hard enough at it, I guess it's pretty nearly bound to happen, wind and weather permitting.

LAURA INGALLS WILDER, *On the Shores of Silver Lake* (1939)

I might have been born in a hovel, but I determined to travel with the wind and the stars.

JACQUELINE COCHRAN, *The Stars at Noon* (1954)

I am the initial Fish / rejected on the beach / but determined to live.

ETEL ADNAN, "The Beirut-Hell Express," in Joanna Bankier and Deirdre Lashgari, eds., *Women Poets of the World* (1983)

I would . . . be so exhausted by my determination that I had no strength left to do the actual work.

ETTY HILLESUM, *An Interrupted Life: The Diaries of Etty Hillesum 1941–1943* (1983)

See also Perseverance, Stubbornness.

DEVIL

Does the devil know he is a devil?

ELIZABETH MADOX ROBERTS, Black Is My Truelove's Hair (1938)

The devil never seems so busy as where the saints are.

ELIZABETH RUNDLE CHARLES, *Chronicles of the Schönberg-Cotta Family* (1863)

The devil's most devilish when respectable.

ELIZABETH BARRETT BROWNING, *Aurora Leigh* (1856)

What's devil to some is good to some others.

ELIZABETH MADOX ROBERTS, *Black Is My Truelove's Hair* (1938)

See also Evil, Sin, Villains.

DIARIES

Rather than calling this diary a record of my life, it's more accurate to regard it as the sum of all my tears.

DING LING, "Miss Sophia's Diary" (1927), in *I Myself Am a Woman: Selected Writings of Ding Ling* (1989)

Journal writing is a voyage to the interior.

CHRISTINA BALDWIN, *One to One* (1977)

Writing a journal means that facing your ocean you are afraid to swim across it, so you attempt to drink it drop by drop.

GEORGE SAND (1837), in Marie Jenny Howe, *The Intimate Journal of George Sand* (1929)

Recording happiness made it last longer, we felt, and recording sorrow dramatized it and took away its bitterness; and often we settled some problem which beset us even while we wrote about it.

DOROTHY DAY, *From Union Square to Rome* (1940)

My diaries were written primarily, I think, not to preserve the experience but to savor it, to make it even more real, more visible and palpable, than in actual life. For in our family an experience was not finished, not truly experienced, unless written down or shared with another.

ANNE MORROW LINDBERGH, *Bring Me a Unicorn* (1971)

What fun it is to generalize in the privacy of a note book. It is as I imagine waltzing on ice might be. A great delicious sweep in one direction, taking you your full strength, and then with no trouble at all, an equally delicious sweep in the opposite direction. My note book does not help me think, but it eases my crabbed heart.

FLORIDA SCOTT-MAXWELL, *The Measure of My Days* (1968)

I think that if I get into the habit of writing a bit about what happens, or rather doesn't happen, I may lose a little of the sense of isolation and desolation which abides with me. My circumstances allowing of nothing but the ejaculation of one-syllabled reflections, a written monologue by that most interesting being, myself, may have its yet to be discovered consolations.

ALICE JAMES, *Journal* (1889)

It's been a rare year, o paper soul, and against all the preceding bitterness and bile, this one shining scrawl . . . maybe I should fold you away to pull you out again in a decade, see whether the flowering that now seems promised, came; see whether it was untimely frostbit, or died without fruit, because you chart the real deeps of me. No: I hold you a pelorus, a flexing mirror, strange quarters for the wind of God.

KERI HULME, *The Bone People* (1983)

To one who has enjoyed the full life of any scene, of any hour, what thoughts can be recorded about it seem like the commas and semicolons in the paragraph—mere stops.

MARGARET FULLER, *Summer on the Lakes* (1844)

I get out this diary and read, as one always reads one's own writing, with a kind of guilty intensity.

VIRGINIA WOOLF, in Leonard Woolf, ed., *A Writer's Diary* (1954)

What is a diary as a rule? A document useful to the person who keeps it, dull to the contemporary who reads it, invaluable to the student, centuries afterwards, who treasures it!

ELLEN TERRY, *The Story of My Life* (1908)

See also Writing.

DICTATORS

There is an interesting resemblance in the speeches of dictators, no matter what country

they may hail from or what language they may speak.

EDNA FERBER, *A Kind of Magic* (1963)

See also Leaders, Tyranny.

DIET

If you have formed the habit of checking on every new diet that comes along, you will find that, mercifully, they all blur together, leaving you with only one definite piece of information: french-fried potatoes are out.

JEAN KERR, *Please Don't Eat the Daisies* (1957)

But if one doesn't have a character like Abraham Lincoln or Joan of Arc, a diet simply disintegrates into eating exactly what you want to eat, but with a bad conscience.

MARIA AUGUSTA TRAPP, *The Story of the Trapp Family Singers* (1949)

See also Food, Weight.

DIFFERENCES

Differences challenge assumptions.

ANNE WILSON SCHAEF, *Women's Reality* (1981)

There is no bleaker moment in the life of the city than that one which crosses the boundary lines between those who have not slept all night and those who are going to work. It was . . . as if two races of men and women lived on earth, the night people and the day people, never meeting face to face except at this moment.

ANAÏS NIN, *A Spy in the House of Love* (1954)

One half of the world cannot understand the pleasures of the other.

JANE AUSTEN, *Emma* (1816)

See also Human Differences.

DIRT

There are two types of dirt: the dark kind, attracted to light objects; and the light kind, attracted to dark objects.

ELY SLICK, in *Reader's Digest* (1982)

See also Housework.

DISABILITIES

Though people with disabilities have become more vocal in recent years, we still constitute a very small minority. Yet the Beautiful People—the slender, fair and perfect ones—form a minority that may be even smaller.

DEBRA KENT, in Marsha Saxton and Florence Howe, *With Wings* (1987)

See also Deafness.

DISAPPOINTMENT

My life is a perfect graveyard of buried hopes. That's a sentence I read in a book once, and I say it over to comfort myself whenever I'm disappointed in anything.

L. M. MONTGOMERY, *Anne of Green Gables* (1908)

See also Discouragement.

DISAPPROVAL

It was a pity he couldna be hatched o'er again, an' hatched different.

GEORGE ELIOT, *Adam Bede* (1859)

If we do not always see our own mistakes and omissions we can always see those of our neighbors.

KATHLEEN NORRIS, *Hands Full of Living* (1931)

Next to the joy of the egotist is the joy of the detractor.

AGNES REPPLIER, *Under Dispute* (1924)

He went to work on my character with the unstoppable fury of Oliver Cromwell putting dents in the church plate.

MARGARET HALSEY, *No Laughing Matter* (1977)

See also Condemnation, Nagging.

DISASTER

No one ever understood disaster until it came.

JOSEPHINE HERBST, *Nothing Is Sacred* (1928)

She suddenly felt quite safe. It was a very strange feeling, and she found it indescribably nice. But what was there to worry over? The disaster had come at last.

TOVE JANSSON, *Tales from Moominvalley* (1963)

I always thought it mattered, to know what is the worst possible thing that can happen to you, to know how you can avoid it, to not be drawn by the magic of the unspeakable.

AMY TAN, *The Joy Luck Club* (1989)

See also Tragedy.

DISCIPLINE

When you were quite a little boy somebody ought to have said "hush" just once.

MRS. PATRICK CAMPBELL, letter to George Bernard Shaw (1912)

See also Parenting.

DISCONTENT

Were there none who were discontented with what they have, the world would never reach anything better.

FLORENCE NIGHTINGALE, *Cassandra* (1852)

This struggle of people against their conditions, this is where you find the meaning in life.

ROSE CHERNIN, in Kim Chernin, *In My Mother's House* (1983)

Discontent and disorder were signs of energy and hope, not of despair.

C. V. WEDGWOOD, *The Great Rebellion: The King's War* (1958)

See also Restlessness, Unhappiness.

DISCOURAGEMENT

When we yield to discouragement it is usually because we give too much thought to the past and to the future.

ST. THERESE OF LISIEUX (c. 1890), in *Peacemaking* (1989)

Discouragement seizes us only when we can no longer count on chance.

GEORGE SAND, *Handsome Lawrence* (1872)

See also Despair, Disappointment, Melancholy.

DISCOVERY

Great inventors and discoverers seem to have made their discoveries and inventions as it were *by the way*, in the course of their everyday life.

ELIZABETH RUNDLE CHARLES, *Chronicles of the Schönberg-Cotta Family* (1863)

The poverty of our imagination is no measure of the world's resources. Our posterity will no doubt get fuel in ways that we are unable to devise for them.

GEORGE ELIOT, *Impressions of Theophrastus Such* (1879)

See also Innovation, Invention, Newness, Progress.

DISCRETION

Well, I aren't like a bird-clapper, forced to make a rattle when the wind blows on me. I can keep my own counsel when there's no good i' speaking.

GEORGE ELIOT, *Adam Bede* (1859)

There is such a thing as tempting the gods. Talking too much, too soon and with too much self-satisfaction has always seemed to me a sure way to court disaster. . . . The forces of retribution are always listening. They never sleep.

MEG GREENFIELD, in *Newsweek* (1991)

See also Concealment, Secrets.

DISCRIMINATION

We need every human gift and cannot afford to neglect any gift because of artificial barriers of sex or race or class or national origin.

MARGARET MEAD, *Male and Female* (1949)

Sometimes, I feel discriminated against, but it does not make me angry. It merely astonishes me. How *can* any deny themselves the pleasure of my company? It's beyond me.

ZORA NEALE HURSTON, "How It Feels to Be Colored Me" (1928), in Alice Walker, ed., *I Love Myself When I Am Laughing . . . And Then Again When I Am Looking Mean and Impressive* (1979)

Of my two "handicaps," being female put many more obstacles in my path than being black.

SHIRLEY CHISHOLM, *Unbought and Unbossed* (1970)

If threatened by law that either they welcome the outsiders into their midst or be punished for failure to do so, the insiders can make their system work so as to avoid either outcome entirely . . . saying that a person cannot be kept out doesn't ensure that that person can get in, and more important, stay in.

MARGARET HENNIG AND ANNE JARDIM, *The Managerial Woman* (1976)

As a society emphasizes and values some aspects of the total range of human potentials more than others, the valued aspects are associated closely with, and limited to, the dominant group's domain.

JEAN BAKER MILLER, *Toward a New Psychology of Women* (1986)

I can't change my sex. But you can change your policy.

HELEN KIRKPATRICK (1940), on being told a newspaper didn't have women on its foreign affairs staff, in Julia Edwards, *Women of the World: The Great Foreign Correspondents* (1988)

In the end, antiblack, antifemale, and all forms of discrimination are equivalent to the same thing—antihumanism.

SHIRLEY CHISHOLM, *Unbought and Unbossed* (1970)

The flour-merchant, the house-builder, and the postman charge us no less on account of our sex; but when we endeavor to earn money to pay all these, then, indeed, we find the difference.

LUCY STONE (1855), in Elizabeth Cady Stanton, *The History of Woman Suffrage* (1881)

It is interesting that many women do not recognize themselves as discriminated against; no better proof could be found of the totality of their conditioning.

KATE MILLETT, *Sexual Politics* (1969)

If they come for me in the morning, they will come for you at night.

ANGELA DAVIS, *If They Come for Me in the Morning* (1971)

See also Injustice, Prejudice.

DISHONESTY

There's a strong aroma of sawn lady about this.

JOSEPHINE TEY, *To Love and Be Wise* (1950)

She could carry off anything; and some people said that she did.

ADA LEVERSON, *Love at Second Sight* (1916)

Nothing he did was ever illegal—but as soon as he'd got on to it, you had to have a law about it, if you know what I mean.

AGATHA CHRISTIE, *Crooked House* (1949)

He was so crooked, you could have used his spine for a safety-pin.

DOROTHY L. SAYERS, *The Nine Tailors* (1934)

A certain percent of the population simply can't resist the urge to cheat.

SUE GRAFTON, *"H" Is for Homicide* (1991)

Do you know that the tendrils of graft and corruption have become mighty interlacing roots so that even men who would like to be honest are tripped and trapped by them.

AGNES SLIGH TURNBULL, *The Golden Journey* (1955)

See also Betrayal, Deception, Lying, Treachery.

DISTRUST

Set the foot down with distrust on the crust of the world—it is thin.

EDNA ST. VINCENT MILLAY, "Underground System," *Huntsman, What Quarry?* (1939)

But hers was one of those inconvenient natures which trust blindly or not at all: once worked on by a doubt or a suspicion, they are never able to shake themselves free of it again.

HENRY HANDEL RICHARDSON, *The Fortunes of Richard Mahoney: Australia Felix* (1917)

I wouldn't mind being your partner if there were two of me.

CHRISTINA STEAD, *House of All Nations* (1938)

What loneliness is more lonely than distrust?

GEORGE ELIOT, *Middlemarch* (1871)

See also Doubt, Misanthropy, Trust.

DIVINITY

Maybe the tragedy of the human race was that we had forgotten we were each Divine.

SHIRLEY MACLAINE, *Out on a Limb* (1983)

Divinity is in its omniscience and omnipotence like a wheel, a circle, a whole, that can neither be understood, nor divided, nor begun nor ended.

HILDEGARDE OF BINGEN, *Scivias* (1141–1150), in Gabriele Uhlein, ed., *Meditations with Hildegarde of Bingen* (1983)

See also God, Sacred, Spirituality.

DIVORCE

A divorce is like an amputation; you survive, but there's less of you.

MARGARET ATWOOD, in *Time* (1973)

Divorce is the psychological equivalent of a triple coronary by-pass. After such a monumental assault on the heart, it takes years to amend all the habits and attitudes that led up to it.

MARY KAY BLAKELY, in *Parade* (1987)

Being divorced is like being hit by a Mack truck—if you survive you start looking very carefully to the right and left.

JEAN KERR, *Mary, Mary* (1963)

Divorce is the one human tragedy that reduces everything to cash.

RITA MAE BROWN, *Sudden Death* (1983)

So many persons think divorce a panacea for every ill, find out, when they try it, that the remedy is worse than the disease.

DOROTHY DIX, *Dorothy Dix, Her Book* (1926)

However often marriage is dissolved, it remains indissoluble. Real divorce, the divorce of heart and nerve and fiber, does not exist, since there is no divorce from memory.

VIRGILIA PETERSON, *A Matter of Life and Death* (1961)

See also Broken Heart, Estrangement, Marriage.

DOCTORS

You know doctors. For every one thing they tell you, there are two things hidden under the tongue.

ROSE CHERNIN, in Kim Chernin, *In My Mother's House* (1983)

Doctors always think anybody doing something they aren't is a quack; also they think all patients are idiots.

FLANNERY O'CONNOR, in Sally Fitzgerald, ed., *The Habit of Being* (1979)

People coming away from a session with Dr. S. usually looked as if they had had fifty minutes on the anvil with an apprentice blacksmith.

MARGARET HALSEY, *No Laughing Matter* (1977)

Heart surgeons do not have the world's smallest egos: when you ask them to name the world's three leading practitioners, they never can remember the names of the other two.

SARA PARETSKY, "The Case of the Pietro Andromache," in Marilyn Wallace, ed., *Sisters in Crime* (1989)

A male gynecologist is like an auto mechanic who has never owned a car.

CARRIE SNOW, Comedy Celebration Day (1985)

Other books have been written by men physicians. . . . One would suppose in reading them that women possess but one class of physical organs, and that these are always diseased. Such teaching is pestiferous, and tends to cause and perpetuate the very evils it professes to remedy.

MARY ASHTON LIVERMORE, *What Shall We Do With Our Daughters?* (1883)

A physician can sometimes parry the scythe of death, but has no power over the sand in the hourglass.

HESTER LYNCH PIOZZI, letter to Fanny Burney (1781)

See also Hospital.

DOGMA

You can't teach an old dogma new tricks.

DOROTHY PARKER, in Robert E. Drennan, *The Algonquin Wits* (1968)

Creeds grow so thick along the way, / Their boughs hide God; I cannot pray.

LIZETTE WOODWORTH REESE, "Doubt," *Selected Poems* (1927)

Dogma can in no way limit a limitless God.

FLANNERY O'CONNOR, in Sally Fitzgerald, ed., *The Habit of Being* (1979)

The incidence of violent brand-loyalty to one's own current dogma has risen.

MARGE PIERCY, "The Grand Coolie Damn," in Robin Morgan, *Sisterhood Is Powerful* (1970)

See also Absolutes, Belief, Theology.

DOGS

I think dogs are the most amazing creatures; they give unconditional love. For me they are the role model for being alive.

GILDA RADNER, *It's Always Something* (1989)

Our dogs will love and admire the meanest of us, and feed our colossal vanity with their uncritical homage.

AGNES REPPLIER, *Under Dispute* (1923)

My little old dog: / A heart-beat at my feet.

EDITH WHARTON, "A Lyrical Epigram," *Artemis to Actaeon* (1909)

The dog is a creature that believes in order.

COLETTE, *Looking Backwards* (1941)

Dogs are wise. They crawl away into a quiet corner and lick their wounds and do not rejoin the world until they are whole once more.

AGATHA CHRISTIE, *The Moving Finger* (1942)

Fido and Rover are partaking of a mystery of which, further up on the table, Cézanne and Beethoven are participants also.

REBECCA WEST, *The Strange Necessity* (1928)

I am simply delighted that you have a Springer spaniel. That is the perfect final touch to our friendship. Do you know there is always a barrier between me and any man or woman who does not like dogs.

ELLEN GLASGOW, *Letters of Ellen Glasgow* (1958)

For Pastrasche was their alpha and omega; their treasury and granary; their store of gold and wand of wealth; their bread-winner and minister; their only friend and comforter. . . . Pastrasche was their dog.

LOUISE DE LA RAMÉE, *A Dog of Flanders* (1872)

Why, that dog is practically a Phi Beta Kappa. She can sit up and beg, and she can give her paw—I don't say she will but she can.

DOROTHY PARKER, "Toward the Dog Days," in *McCall's* (1928)

Like many other much-loved humans, they believed that they owned their dogs, instead of realizing that their dogs owned them.

DODIE SMITH, *One Hundred and One Dalmatians* (1956)

The only food he has ever stolen has been down on a coffee table. He claims that he genuinely believed it to be a table meant for dogs.

JEAN LITTLE, *Stars Come Out Within* (1990)

For though he had very little Latin beyond "Cave canem," he had, as a young dog, devoured Shakespeare (in a tasty leather binding).

DODIE SMITH, *One Hundred and One Dalmatians* (1956)

Many dogs can understand almost every word humans say, while humans seldom learn to recognize more than half a dozen barks, if that. And barks are only a small part of the dog language. A wagging tail can mean so many things. Humans know that it means a dog is pleased, but not what a dog is saying about his pleasedness. (Really, it is very clever of humans to understand a wagging tail at all, as they have no tails of their own.)

DODIE SMITH, *One Hundred and One Dalmatians* (1956)

A real dog, beloved and therefore pampered by his mistress, is a lamentable spectacle. He suffers from fatty degeneration of his moral being.

AGNES REPPLIER, *Under Dispute* (1923)

See also Animals.

DOMINATION

It is natural anywhere that people like their own kind, but it is not necessarily natural that their fondness for their own kind should lead them to the subjection of whole groups of other people not like them.

PEARL BUCK, *What America Means to Me* (1943)

Class supremacy, male supremacy, white supremacy—it's all the same game. If you're on top of someone, the society tells you that you are better. It gives you access to its privileges and security, and it works both to keep you on top and to keep you thinking that you deserve to be there.

COLETTA REID AND CHARLOTTE BUNCH, *Class and Feminism* (1979)

If one would discern the centers of dominance in any society, one need only look to its definitions of "virtue" and "vice" or "legal" and "criminal," for in the strength to set standards resides the strength to maintain control.

FREDA ADLER, *Sisters in Crime* (1975)

When a man curls his lip, when he uses ridicule, when he grows angry, you have touched a raw nerve in domination.

SHEILA ROWBOTHAM, *Woman's Consciousness, Man's World* (1973)

When an individual (or a group of individuals) is kept in a situation of inferiority, the fact is that he *is* inferior. But the significance of the verb *to be* must be rightly understood here; it is in bad faith to give it a static value when it really has the dynamic Hegelian sense of "to have become."

SIMONE DE BEAUVOIR, *The Second Sex* (1949)

Personal accomplishment is almost impossible in the human categories that are maintained collectively in an inferior situation.

SIMONE DE BEAUVOIR, *The Second Sex* (1949)

Tell a man what he may not sing and he is still half free; even all free, if he never wanted to sing it. But tell him what he must sing, take up his time with it so that his true voice cannot sound even in secret—there, I have seen is slavery.

MARY RENAULT, *The Praise Singer* (1978)

See also Oppression, Powerlessness.

DOUBT

I think there is no suffering greater than what is caused by the doubts of those who want to believe.

FLANNERY O'CONNOR, in Sally Fitzgerald, ed., *The Habit of Being* (1979)

Where so many hours have been spent in convincing myself that I am right, is there not some reason to fear I may be wrong?

JANE AUSTEN, *Sense and Sensibility* (1811)

See also Distrust.

DREAMS

Dreams are . . . illustrations from the book your soul is writing about you.

MARSHA NORMAN, *The Fortune Teller* (1987)

Dreams are the subtle Dower / That make us rich an Hour— / Then fling us poor / Out of the purple door.

EMILY DICKINSON (1876), *The Poems of Emily Dickinson* (1955)

Dreams the sources of action, the meeting and the end, / a resting-place among the flight of things.

MURIEL RUKEYSER, "Easter Eve 1945," *The Green Wave* (1948)

I've dreamt in my life dreams that have stayed with me ever after, and changed my ideas: they've gone through and through me, like wine through water, and altered the color of my mind.

EMILY BRONTË, *Wuthering Heights* (1847)

Dreams pass into the reality of action. From the action stems the dream again; and this interdependence produces the highest form of living.

ANAÏS NIN, *The Diary of Anaïs Nin,* vol. 4 (1944–1947)

Only the dreamer shall understand realities, though in truth his dreaming must be not out of proportion to his waking.

MARGARET FULLER, *Summer on the Lakes* (1844)

I believe that our dreams transport us through the underside of our days, and that if we wish to become acquainted with the dark side of what we are, the signposts are there, waiting for us to translate them.

GAIL GODWIN, *Dream Children* (1976)

our dreams draw blood from old sores.

NTOZAKE SHANGE, *spell # 7: geechee jibara quik magic trance manual for technologically stressed third world people* (1981)

When you dream, you dialogue with aspects of yourself that normally are not with you in the daytime and you discover that you know a great deal more than you thought you did.

TONI CADE BAMBARA, in Roseann P. Bell, Bettye J. Parker, and Beverly Guy-Sheftall, eds., *Sturdy Black Bridges* (1979)

Dreams say what they mean, but they don't say it in daytime language.

GAIL GODWIN, *Dream Children* (1976)

You know that there's a whole underground system that you call "dreams," having nothing better to call them, and that this system is not like roads or tunnels but more like a live body network, all coiling and stretching, unpredictable but finally familiar—where you are now, where you've always been.

ALICE MUNRO, *Friend of My Youth* (1990)

In forming a bridge between body and mind, dreams may be used as a springboard from which man can leap to new realms of experience lying outside his normal state of consciousness and enlarge his vision not only of himself, but also of the universe in which he lives.

ANN FARADAY, *Dream Power* (1972)

I was not looking for my dreams to interpret my life, but rather for my life to interpret my dreams.

SUSAN SONTAG, *The Benefactor* (1963)

When I dream / I am always ageless.

ELIZABETH COATSWORTH, *Personal Geography* (1976)

Saddle your dreams afore you ride 'em.

MARY WEBB, *Precious Bane* (1924)

Our dreams are never realized and as soon as we see them betrayed we realize that the intensest joys of our life have nothing to do with reality. No sooner do we see them betrayed than we are consumed with regret for the time when they glowed within us. And in this succession of hopes and regrets our life slips by.

NATALIA GINZBURG, *The Little Virtues* (1962)

It is in our idleness, in our dreams, that the submerged truth sometimes comes to the top.

VIRGINIA WOOLF, *A Room of One's Own* (1929)

Like all people who have nothing, I lived on dreams.

ANZIA YEZIERSKA, "The Miracle," *Hungry Hearts* (1920)

It's a risky thing to talk about one's most secret dreams a bit too early.

TOVE JANSSON, *Tales from Moominvalley* (1963)

Last night I dreamt I went to Manderley again.

DAPHNE DU MAURIER, *Rebecca* (1938)

See also Fantasy, Reverie, Visions.

DRESS

Their dress is very independent of fashion; as they observe, "What does it signify how we dress here at Cranford, where everybody knows us?" And if they go from home, their reason is equally cogent: "What does it signify how we dress here, where nobody knows us?"

ELIZABETH GASKELL, *Cranford* (1853)

From Memorial Day to Labor Day, you may wear white shoes. Not before and not after. As a command, the White Shoe Edict should be clear and simple enough. Do not violate it. In a society in which everything else has become relative, a matter of how it makes you feel, a question between you and your conscience, and an opportunity for you to be really you, this is an absolute.

JUDITH MARTIN, *Miss Manners' Guide for the Turn-of-the-Millennium* (1989)

It is the inalienable right of every man, woman, and child to wear khaki.

LISA BIRNBACH, *The Official Preppy Handbook* (1980)

Always underdress. The goal is not to look as if you made an effort for the particular event. If you can dress for a different party (i.e., wear black tie to a cocktail party, or tennis clothes for

lunch), so much the better. You give the impression of being much in demand.

LISA BIRNBACH, *The Official Preppy Handbook* (1980)

Preppy clothes are built to last, since they certainly won't go out of style.

LISA BIRNBACH, *The Official Preppy Handbook* (1980)

Wool, cotton, and the odd bits of silk and cashmere are the only acceptable materials for Prep clothes. They look better. They require professional maintenance. They are more expensive.

LISA BIRNBACH, *The Official Preppy Handbook* (1980)

Even if they've never been near a duck blind or gone beagling, Preppies are dressed for it.

LISA BIRNBACH, *The Official Preppy Handbook* (1980)

See also Appearance, Clothes.

DRINK

When I spoke of having *a* drink, it was a euphemism for having a whole flock of them.

MARGARET HALSEY, *No Laughing Matter* (1977)

Philip Toynbee had an unfortunate disposition to collapse under drink as though a sniper had picked him off.

JESSICA MITFORD, *The Face of Philip* (1984)

One more drink and I'd have been under the host.

DOROTHY PARKER (1930), in Howard Teichmann, *George S. Kaufman* (1972)

I was sitting before my third or fourth Jellybean—which is anisette, grain alcohol, a lit match, and a small, wet explosion in the brain.

LOUISE ERDRICH, "Scales," in Rayna Green, ed., *That's What She Said* (1984)

Do not allow your children to mix drinks. It is unseemly and they use too much vermouth.

FRAN LEBOWITZ, *Social Studies* (1977)

Now a double scotch is about the size of a small scotch before the war, and a single scotch is nothing more than a dirty glass.

LORA DUNDEE, in *Observer* (1960)

One reason I don't drink is that I want to know when I am having a good time.

Nancy Astor, in *Reader's Digest* (1960)

Even though a number of people have tried, no one has yet found a way to drink for a living.

Jean Kerr, *Poor Richard* (1963)

I acquired that drinker's face before I drank. Drink only confirmed it. The space for it existed in me.

Marguerite Duras, *The Lover* (1984)

If a man be discreet enough to take to hard drinking in his youth, before his general emptiness is ascertained, his friends invariably credit him with a host of shining qualities which, we are given to understand, lie balked and frustrated by his one unfortunate weakness.

Agnes Repplier, *Points of View* (1891)

Drinking isn't necessarily the same as wanting to die. But you can't drink without thinking you're killing yourself.

Marguerite Duras, *Practicalities* (1987)

What stops you killing yourself when you're intoxicated out of your mind is the thought that once you're dead you won't be able to drink any more.

Marguerite Duras, *Practicalities* (1987)

Why is it that one has to drink? / Why is it that one's hosts should think / It queer these days if guests prefer / A respite? Doesn't it occur / To anyone that no offense / Is meant by harmless abstinence?

Margaret Fishback, "Slow Down Rounding Curve," *I Take It Back* (1935)

See also Alcohol, Coffee, Tea, Wine.

DRIVERS

For a driver to be driven by somebody else is an ordeal, for there are only three types of drivers: the too fast, the timid and oneself.

Virginia Graham, *Say Please* (1949)

DRUG ABUSE

The only merciful thing about drug abuse is the speed with which it devastates you. Alcoholics can take decades to destroy themselves and everyone they touch. The drug addict can accomplish this in a year or two. Of course, suicide is even more efficient.

Rita Mae Brown, *Starting From Scratch* (1988)

Druggies don't keep their looks any longer than they keep their promises.

Liza Cody, "Lucky Dip," in Sara Paretsky, ed., *A Woman's Eye* (1991)

Of all the tyrannies which have usurped power over humanity, few have been able to enslave the mind and body as imperiously as drug addiction.

Freda Adler, *Sisters in Crime* (1975)

Just say no.

Nancy Reagan, slogan (1983)

See also Alcohol.

DUALISM

Spirit is the real and eternal; matter is the unreal and temporal.

Mary Baker Eddy, *Science and Health* (1875)

You are an indivisible entity of matter and consciousness. Renounce your consciousness and you become a brute. Renounce your body and you become a fake. Renounce the material world and you surrender it to evil.

Ayn Rand, *Atlas Shrugged* (1957)

DULLNESS

You could, without arousing a storm of protest, have described us as rather a dull couple.

Margaret Halsey, *No Laughing Matter* (1977)

Dullness is a kind of luxury.

Bharati Mukherjee, *Jasmine* (1989)

In all private quarrels the duller nature is triumphant by reason of dullness.

George Eliot, *Felix Holt, the Radical* (1866)

Let dullness have its due: and remember that if life and conversation are happily compared to a bowl of punch, there must be more water in it than spirit, acid, or sugar.

HESTER LYNCH PIOZZI (1817), in A. Hayward, ed., *Autobiography, Letters, and Literary Remains of Mrs. Piozzi (Thrale), vol. 2* (1861)

See also Boredom.

DUTY

I slept and dreamed that life was Beauty. / I woke—and found that life was Duty.

ELLEN STURGIS HOOPER, Beauty and Duty (1840)

We need to restore the full meaning of that old word, duty. It is the other side of rights.

PEARL BUCK, *To My Daughters, With Love* (1967)

Do your duty until it becomes your joy.

MARIE VON EBNER-ESCHENBACH, *Aphorisms* (1905)

The one predominant duty is to find one's work and do it.

CHARLOTTE PERKINS GILMAN, *The Living of Charlotte Perkins Gilman* (1935)

We cannot hope to scale great moral heights by ignoring petty obligations.

AGNES REPPLIER, *Americans and Others* (1912)

The boy stood on the burning deck, / Whence all but he had fled.

FELICIA HEMANS, "Casabianca," *Poetical Works* (1836)

One of the most destructive anti-concepts in the history of moral philosophy is the term "duty."

AYN RAND, *Philosophy: Who Needs It?* (1982)

Oh! Duty is an icy shadow.

AUGUSTA EVANS, *Beulah* (1859)

The worst of doing one's duty was that it apparently unfitted one for doing anything else.

EDITH WHARTON, *The Age of Innocence* (1920)

You are a member of the British royal family. We are *never* tired, and we all *love* hospitals.

QUEEN MARY, to her daughter, Queen Elizabeth II, in John Pearson, *The Selling of the Royal Family* (1986)

See also Responsibility.

DYING

My breath hovers over the river of God— / Softly I set my foot / On the path to my long home.

ELSE LASKER-SCHÜLER, "I Know That I Must Die Soon," in Nathan and Marynn Ausubel, *A Treasury of Jewish Poetry* (1957)

Dying was apparently a weaning process; all the attachments to familiar people and objects had to be undone.

LISA ALTHER, *Kinflicks* (1975)

But I'm gettin' ready to go. How am I doin' it? I'm layin' aside every weight and a sin that does so easily beset me and I'm gettin' light for the flight.

WILLIE MAE FORD SMITH, in Brian Lanker, *I Dream a World* (1989)

His grasp on life fanned shallow as poplar roots.

YVETTE NELSON, *We'll Come When It Rains* (1982)

Feelings are dulled these days, as though life is already going, slowly leaking out and ebbing away. Maybe it will make my dying that much easier . . . when I come to die, there will be little left to die. I'm already a ghost with set wings, stalking tombstone territory.

KERI HULME, *The Bone People* (1983)

Glad was the living—blessed be the dying. / Let the leaves fall.

HARRIET MONROE, "A Farewell," *You and I* (1914)

'Tis dying—I am doing—but / I'm not afraid to know.

EMILY DICKINSON (1863), *Poems, First Series* (1890)

I fall and burst beneath the sacred human tree. / Release my seed and let me fall.

MERIDEL LE SUEUR, title poem, *Rites of Ancient Ripening* (1975)

I think that the dying pray at the last not "please," but "thank you," as a guest thanks his host at the door. Falling from airplanes the people are crying thank you, thank you, all down the air; and the cold carriages draw up for them on the rocks.

ANNIE DILLARD, *Pilgrim at Tinker Creek* (1974)

Such hard work it is to die? Such hard work?

TILLIE OLSEN, title story, *Tell Me a Riddle* (1956)

The leaves move in the garden, the sky is pale, and I catch myself weeping. It is hard—it is hard to make a good death.

KATHERINE MANSFIELD (1920), *Journal of Katherine Mansfield* (1930)

The nearer she came to death, the more, by some perversity of nature, did she enjoy living.

ELLEN GLASGOW, *Barren Ground* (1925)

That is what they call being reconciled to die. They call it reconciled when pain has strummed a symphony of suffering back and forth across you, up and down, round and round you until each little fiber is worn tissue-thin with aching. And when you are lying beaten, and buffeted, battered and broken—pain goes out, joins hands with Death and comes back to dance, dance, dance, stamp, stamp, stamp down on you until you give up.

MARITA BONNER, "A Possible Triad on Black Notes" (1933), *Frye Street and Environs* (1987)

She had supposed that on her deathbed, she would have something final to tell her children when they gathered round. But nothing was final. She didn't have anything to tell them. She felt a kind of shyness; she felt inadequate.

ANNE TYLER, *Dinner at the Homesick Restaurant* (1982)

One had to listen very intently to catch the words that she labored to breathe out; words whose mystery made them as disturbing as those of an oracle. Her memories, her desires, her anxieties were floating somewhere outside time, turned into unreal and poignant dreams by her childlike voice and the imminence of death.

SIMONE DE BEAUVOIR, *A Very Easy Death* (1966)

I still grieve for the words unsaid. Something terrible happens when we stop the mouths of the dying before they are dead. A silence grows up between us then, profounder than the grave. If we force the dying to go speechless, the stone dropped into the well will fall forever before the answering splash is heard.

FAYE MOSKOWITZ, *A Leak in the Heart* (1985)

One cannot be honest even at the end of one's life, for no one is wholly alone. We are bound to those we love, or to those who love us, and to those who need us to be brave, or content, or even happy enough to allow them not to worry about us. So we must refrain from giving pain, as our last gift to our fellows.

FLORIDA SCOTT-MAXWELL, *The Measure of My Days* (1968)

She'd been preoccupied with death for several years now; but one aspect had never before crossed her mind: dying, you don't get to see how it all turns out.

ANNE TYLER, *Dinner at the Homesick Restaurant* (1982)

Dying nowadays is more gruesome in many ways, namely, more lonely, mechanical, and dehumanized; at times it is even difficult to determine technically when the time of death has occurred.

ELISABETH KÜBLER-ROSS, *On Death and Dying* (1969)

We look on those approaching the banks of a river all must cross, with ten times the interest they excited when dancing in the meadow.

HESTER LYNCH PIOZZI (1817), in A. Hayward, ed., *Autobiography, Letters, and Literary Remains of Mrs. Piozzi (Thrale)*, vol. 2 (1861)

Dying / Is an art, like everything else. / I do it exceptionally well.

SYLVIA PLATH, "Lady Lazarus," *Ariel* (1965)

I'm not afraid of life and I'm not afraid of death: Dying's the bore.

KATHERINE ANNE PORTER, in *New York Times* (1970)

The Heart asks Pleasure—first— / And then— Excuse from Pain— / And then—those little Anodynes / That deaden suffering— / And then—to go to sleep— / And then—if it should be / The will of its Inquisitor / The privilege to die.

EMILY DICKINSON (1862), *Poems, First Series* (1890)

Gracious dying is a huge, macabre and expensive joke on the American public.

JESSICA MITFORD, *The American Way of Death* (1963)

Is everybody happy? I want everybody to be happy. I know I'm happy.

ETHEL BARRYMORE, last words (1959)

See also Death, Grief, Mourning.

E

EARTH

How shall I / celebrate the planet / that, even now, carries me / in its fruited womb?

DIANE ACKERMAN, *The Planets* (1976)

If dead things love, if earth and water distinguish friends from enemies, I should like to possess their love. I should like the green earth not to feel my step as a heavy burden. I should like her to forgive that she for my sake is wounded by plow and harrow, and willingly to open for my dead body.

SELMA LAGERLÖF, *The Story of Gösta Berling* (1891)

We are earth of this earth, and we are bone of its bone. / This is a prayer I sing, for we have forgotten this and so / The earth is perishing.

BARBARA DEMING, "Spirit of Love," *We Are All Part of One Another* (1984)

Earth, old man of the planets, you suck at my foot / which wants to fly.

NELLY SACHS, "Earth, Old Man of the Planets, You Suck at My Foot," *O the Chimneys* (1967)

See also Environment, Land, Nature.

EATING

Eat breakfast like a king, lunch like a prince, and dinner like a pauper.

ADELLE DAVIS, *Let's Eat Right to Keep Fit* (1954)

Birth is beastly—and death—and digestion, if it comes to that. Sometimes when I think of what's happening inside me to a beautiful *suprème de sole,* with the caviar in boats, and the *croûtons* and the jolly little twists of potato and all the gadgets—I could cry. But there it is, don't you know.

DOROTHY L. SAYERS, *The Unpleasantness at the Bellona Club* (1928)

We are indeed much more than what we eat, but what we eat can nevertheless help us to be much more than what we are.

ADELLE DAVIS, *Let's Get Well* (1965)

The dinner table is the center for the teaching and practicing not just of table manners but of conversation, consideration, tolerance, family feeling, and just about all the other accomplishments of polite society except the minuet.

JUDITH MARTIN, *Miss Manners' Guide for the Turn-of-the-Millennium* (1989)

That's something I've noticed about food: whenever there's a crisis if you can get people to eating normally things get better.

MADELEINE L'ENGLE, *The Moon by Night* (1963)

The business of eating, which in common with a crisis or danger brings heterogeneous incompatibles comfortably together, was over and now suddenly we were all fallen apart.

NADINE GORDIMER, *The Lying Days* (1953)

They sat at a corner table in the little restaurant, eating with gusto and noise after the manner of simple-hearted people who like their neighbors to see and know their pleasures.

JEAN RHYS, *The Left Bank* (1927)

The waitress intoned the specialties of the day, "Chicken Cordon Bleu, Sole Amandine, Veal Marsala." She might have been a train conductor in a foreign country, calling out the strange names of the stations.

HILMA WOLITZER, *Hearts* (1980)

She could still taste the plump fine oysters from Zeeland that he had ordered for her last meal in the world, the dry sparkle of the vintage Rudesheimer which had cost him the fees of at least five visits to patients, and the ice cream richly sauced with crushed glazed chestnuts which she loved.

KATHRYN HULME, *The Nun's Story* (1956)

My grandmother, when she served dinner, was a virtuoso hanging on the edge of her own ecstatic performance. . . . She was a little power crazed: she had us and, by God, we were going to eat. . . . The futility of saying no was supreme, and no one ever tried it. How could a son-in-law, already weakened near the point of imbecility by the once, twice, thrice charge to the barricades of pork and mashed potato, be expected to gather his feeble wit long enough to ignore the final call of his old commander when she sounded the alarm: "Pie, Fred?"

PATRICIA HAMPL, *A Romantic Education* (1981)

See also Cooking, Diet, Food, Weight.

ECCENTRICITY

You can't break the mold and also be consoled for breaking it, old fool!

MAY SARTON, *Mrs. Stevens Hears the Mermaids Singing* (1965)

Crazy people who are judged to be harmless are allowed an enormous amount of freedom ordinary people are denied.

KATHERINE PATERSON, *Jacob Have I Loved* (1980)

You can always trust information given you by people who are crazy; they have an access to truth not available through regular channels.

SHEILA BALLANTYNE, *Norma Jean the Termite Queen* (1975)

It made me feel good. To know the nuts still have a chance to take over the world.

JUDITH GUEST, *Ordinary People* (1976)

See also Human Differences, Individuality, Uniqueness.

ECLECTICISM

I believe that we respond most and best to work in any art form (and to other experience as well) if we are pluralistic, flexible, relative in our judgments, if we are eclectic.

PAULINE KAEL, *I Lost It at the Movies* (1965)

ECONOMICS

Economics is not a science, in the sense that a policy can be repeatedly applied under similar conditions and will repeatedly produce similar results.

MILLICENT FENWICK, interview (1980)

I learned that economics was not an exact science and that the most erudite men would analyze the economic ills of the world and derive a totally different conclusion.

EDITH SUMMERSKILL, *A Woman's World* (1967)

Normality is a fiction of economic textbooks.

JOAN ROBINSON, in Rendigs Fels, ed., *The Second Crisis of Economic Theory* (1972)

The failures of national governments to force economic life to do their bidding suggest that nations are essentially irrelevant to promoting economic success.

JANE JACOBS, *Cities and the Wealth of Nations* (1984)

An economy may be in equilibrium from a short-period point of view and yet contain within itself incompatibilities that are soon going to knock it out of equilibrium.

JOAN ROBINSON, *Economic Philosophy* (1962)

What a country calls its vital economic interests are not the things which enable its citizens to live, but the things which enable it to make war; petrol is much more likely than wheat to be a cause of international conflict.

SIMONE WEIL, "The Power of Words" (c. 1940), *The Simone Weil Reader* (1977)

Only by transforming our own economy to one of peace can we make possible economic democracy in the Third World or our own country. The present economy generates wars to protect its profits and its short-term interests, while squandering the future. Unless we transform the economy, we cannot end war.

STARHAWK, *Truth or Dare* (1987)

Contrary to economists' beliefs, the informal sectors of the world's economies, in total, are predominant, and the institutionalized, monetized sectors grow out of them and rest upon them, rather than the reverse.

HAZEL HENDERSON, *The Politics of the Solar Age: Alternatives to Economics* (1981)

Capital is the result of saving, and not of spending. The spendthrift who wastes his substance in riotous living decreases the capital of the country, and therefore the excuse often made for extravagance, that it is good for trade, is based upon false notions respecting capital.

MILLICENT GARRETT FAWCETT, *Political Economy for Beginners* (1870)

Owning capital is not a productive activity.

JOAN ROBINSON, *An Essay on Marxian Economics* (1942)

Unequal distribution of income is an excessively uneconomic method of getting the necessary saving done.

JOAN ROBINSON, *An Essay on Marxian Economics* (1942)

A "mixed economy" is a society in the process of committing suicide.

AYN RAND, in *Los Angeles Times* (1962)

But with the slow menace of a glacier, depression came on. No one had any measure of its progress; no one had any plan for stopping it. Everyone tried to get out of its way.

FRANCES PERKINS, *People at Work* (1934)

The primary conflict, I think, is between people whose interests are with already well-established economic activities, and those whose interests are with the emergence of new economic activities.

JANE JACOBS, *The Economy of Cities* (1969)

Clothes, manners, and to a certain extent morals are the products of the economic life of the times.

MARY DAY WINN, *Adam's Rib* (1931)

Innovating economies expand and develop. Economies that do not add new kinds of goods and services, but continue only to repeat old work, do not expand much nor do they, by definition, develop.

JANE JACOBS, *The Economy of Cities* (1969)

Until economic freedom is attained for everybody, there can be no real freedom for anybody.

SUZANNE LaFOLLETTE, *Concerning Women* (1926)

If the present economic structure can change only by collapsing, then it had better collapse as soon as possible.

GERMAINE GREER, *The Female Eunuch* (1971)

See also Business, Capitalism, Debts, Money.

EDUCATION

Education is a private matter between the person and the world of knowledge and experience, and has little to do with school or college.

LILLIAN SMITH, in *Redbook* (1969)

The highest result of education is tolerance.

HELEN KELLER, *Optimism* (1903)

Education must have an end in view, for it is not an end in itself.

SYBIL MARSHALL, *An Experiment in Education* (1966)

To be able to be caught up into the world of thought—that is educated.

EDITH HAMILTON, in *Saturday Evening Post* (1958)

An educated man should know everything about something, and something about everything.

C. V. WEDGWOOD, speech (1963)

It is the function of a liberal university not to give right answers, but to ask right questions.

CYNTHIA OZICK, "Women and Creativity," *Motive* (1969)

Schooling, instead of encouraging the asking of questions, too often discourages it.

MADELEINE L'ENGLE, *Walking on Water: Reflections on Faith and Art* (1980)

It is in and through education that a culture, and polity, not only tries to perpetuate but enacts the kinds of thinking it welcomes, and discards and/or discredits the kinds it fears.

ELIZABETH KAMARCK MINNICK, *Transforming Knowledge* (1990)

Ignorance, arrogance, and racism have bloomed as Superior Knowledge in all too many universities.

ALICE WALKER, talk (1972), *In Search of Our Mothers' Gardens* (1983)

Most higher education is devoted to affirming the traditions and origins of an existing elite and transmitting them to new members.

MARY CATHERINE BATESON, *Composing a Life* (1989)

As educators, we live in a fool's paradise, or worse in a knave's, if we are unaware that when we are teaching *something* to anyone we are also teaching *everything* to that same anyone.

FLORENCE HOWE, *Myths of Coeducation: Selected Essays 1964–1983* (1984)

Men and women must be educated, in a great degree, by the opinions and manners of the society they live in. In every age there has been a stream of popular opinion that has carried all before it, and given a family character, as it were, to the century. It may then fairly be inferred, that, till society be differently constituted, much cannot be expected from education.

MARY WOLLSTONECRAFT, A Vindication of the Rights of Woman (1792)

To me education is a leading out of what is already there in the pupil's soul. To Miss Mackay it is a putting in of something that is not there, and that is not what I call education, I call it intrusion.

MURIEL SPARK, *The Prime of Miss Jean Brodie* (1962)

It is impossible to withhold education from the receptive mind, as it is impossible to force it upon the unreasoning.

AGNES REPPLIER, *Times and Tendencies* (1931)

Everywhere I go I'm asked if I think the university stifles writers. My opinion is that they don't stifle enough of them. There's many a bestseller that could have been prevented by a good teacher.

FLANNERY O'CONNOR, "The Nature and Aim of Fiction," in Sally and Robert Fitzgerald, eds., *Mystery and Manners* (1969)

It made me gladsome to be getting some education, it being like a big window opening.

MARY WEBB, *Precious Bane* (1924)

Education is a wonderful thing. If you couldn't sign your name you'd have to pay cash.

RITA MAE BROWN, *Starting From Scratch* (1988)

As I inched sluggishly along the treadmill of the Maycomb County school system, I could not help receiving the impression that I was being cheated out of something. Out of what I knew not, yet I did not believe that twelve years of unrelieved boredom was exactly what the state had in mind for me.

HARPER LEE, *To Kill a Mockingbird* (1960)

The first idea that the child must acquire in order to be actively disciplined is that of the difference between good and evil; and the task of the educator lies in seeing that the child does not confound good with immobility, and evil with activity.

MARIA MONTESSORI, *The Montessori Method* (1912)

Theories and goals of education don't matter a whit if you don't consider your students to be human beings.

LOU ANN WALKER, *A Loss for Words: The Story of Deafness in a Family* (1986)

We have what I would call educational genocide . . . when I see more black students in the laboratories than I see on the football field, I'll be happy.

JEWEL PLUMMER COBB, in Brian Lanker, *I Dream a World* (1989)

Both class and race survived education, and neither should. What is education then? If it doesn't help a human being to recognize that humanity is humanity, what is it for? So you can make a bigger salary than other people?

BEAH RICHARDS, in Brian Lanker, *I Dream a World* (1989)

The ladder was there, "from the gutter to the university," and for those stalwart enough to ascend it, the schools were a boon and a path out of poverty.

DIANE RAVITCH, *The Great School Wars* (1974)

At last I came to college. I rushed for it with the outstretched arms of youth's aching hunger to give and take of life's deepest, and highest, and I came against the solid wall of the well-fed, well-dressed world—the frigid whitewashed wall of cleanliness. . . . How I pinched, and scraped, and starved myself, to save enough to come to college! Every cent of the tuition fee I paid was drops of sweat and blood from underpaid laundry work. And what did I get for it? A crushed spirit, a broken heart, a stinging sense of poverty that I never felt before.

ANZIA YEZIERSKA, "Soap and Water," *Hungry Hearts* (1920)

Equalizing opportunity through universal higher education subjects the whole population to the intellectual mode natural only to a few. It violates the fundamental egalitarian principle of respect for the differences between people.

CAROLINE BIRD, *The Case Against College* (1975)

So far, we do not seem appalled at the prospect of exactly the same kind of education being applied to all the school children from the Atlantic to the Pacific, but there is an uneasiness in the air, a realization that the individual is growing less easy to find; an idea, perhaps, of what standardization might become when the units are not machines, but human beings.

EDITH HAMILTON, in Doris Fielding Reid, *Edith Hamilton* (1967)

I learned three important things in college—to use a library, to memorize quickly and visually, to drop asleep at any time given a horizontal surface and fifteen minutes. What I could not learn was to think creatively on schedule.

AGNES DE MILLE, *Dance to the Piper* (1952)

One might say that the American trend of education is to reduce the senses almost to nil.

ISADORA DUNCAN, *My Life* (1927)

Nowadays it seems that moral education is no longer considered necessary. Attention is wholly centered on intelligence, while the heart life is ignored.

GEORGE SAND (1837), in Marie Jenny Howe, *The Intimate Journal of George Sand* (1929)

Mistrust of godless higher education is a constant theme of the evangelicals. "You can educate yourself right out of a relationship with God."

TAMMY FAYE BAKKER, in *Observer* (1988)

If the study to which you apply yourself has a tendency to weaken your affections, and to destroy your taste for those simple pleasures in which no alloy can possibly mix, then that study is certainly unlawful, that is to say, not befitting the human mind.

MARY SHELLEY, *Frankenstein* (1818)

He who can't remember clearly his own childhood, is a poor educator.

MARIE VON EBNER-ESCHENBACH, *Aphorisms* (1905)

It's the educated barbarian who is the worst: he knows what to destroy.

HELEN MACINNES, *The Venetian Affair* (1963)

See also Knowledge, Learning, Teaching.

EGOCENTRISM

She invents dramas in which she always stars.

ANAÏS NIN, *The Diary of Anaïs Nin*, vol. 1 (1931–1934)

As subjects, we all live in suspense, from day to day, from hour to hour; in other words, we are the hero of our own story. We cannot believe that it is finished, that we are "finished," even though we may be so; we expect another chapter, another installment, tomorrow or next week.

MARY MCCARTHY, *On the Contrary* (1961)

There are characters which are continually creating collisions and nodes for themselves in dramas which nobody is prepared to act with them.

GEORGE ELIOT, *Middlemarch* (1871)

She had no tolerance for scenes which were not of her own making.

EDITH WHARTON, *The House of Mirth* (1905)

His sense of his desserts had grown. Now he was sure that what he desired, he deserved, and anyone who denied it merited punishment.

MARY RENAULT, *The Praise Singer* (1978)

The recognition of personal separateness—of others having their own concepts, different from his, because they see things from their position and condition as individuals and not from his own—is not ordinarily possible before a child is seven. Immaturity in adults reveals itself clearly in the retention of this infantile orientation.

MIRIAM LINDSTROM, *Children's Art* (1962)

Modern neurosis began with the discoveries of Copernicus. Science made man feel small by showing him that the earth was not the center of the universe.

MARY McCARTHY, *On the Contrary* (1961)

See also Arrogance, Chauvinism, Conceit, Self-Importance, Vanity.

ELECTIONS

An election is coming. Universal peace is declared, and the foxes have a sincere interest in prolonging the lives of the poultry.

GEORGE ELIOT, *Felix Holt, the Radical* (1866)

A platform is something a candidate stands for and the voters fall for.

GRACIE ALLEN, *How to Become President* (1940)

All the other candidates are making speeches about how much they have done for their country, which is ridiculous. I haven't done anything yet, and I think it's just common sense to send me to Washington and make me do my share.

GRACIE ALLEN, *How to Become President* (1940)

See also Politicians, Politics, Suffrage.

ELEGANCE

Elegance has a bad effect on my constitution.

LOUISA MAY ALCOTT, *Little Women* (1868)

The only real elegance is in the mind; if you've got that, the rest really comes from it.

DIANA VREELAND, in *Newsweek* (1962)

See also Fashion, Style.

ELEPHANTS

Nina felt as if she were being tracked down by a large placid resolute elephant.

ELIZABETH JANEWAY, *Leaving Home* (1953)

I had seen a herd of elephant traveling through dense native forest . . . pacing along as if they had an appointment at the end of the world.

ISAK DINESEN, *Out of Africa* (1937)

Once there was an elephant, / Who tried to use the telephant— / No! No! I mean an elephone / Who tried to use the telephone.

LAURA E. RICHARDS, "Eletelephony," *Tirra Lirra* (1890)

See also Animals.

EMOTIONS

He liked to observe emotions; they were like red lanterns strung along the dark unknown of another's personality, marking vulnerable points.

AYN RAND, *Atlas Shrugged* (1957)

I'm committed to the idea that one of the few things human beings have to offer is the richness of unconscious and conscious emotional responses to being alive. . . . The kind of esteem that's given to brightness/smartness obliterates average people or slow learners from participating fully in human life, particularly technical and intellectual life. But you cannot exclude any human being from emotional participation.

NTOZAKE SHANGE, in Claudia Tate, ed., *Black Women Writers at Work* (1983)

If facts are the seeds that later produce knowledge and wisdom, then the emotions and the impressions of the senses are the fertile soil in which the seeds must grow. . . . Once the emotions have been aroused—a sense of the beautiful, the excitement of the new and the unknown, a feeling of sympathy, pity, admiration or love—

then we wish for knowledge about the object of our emotional response.

RACHEL CARSON, *The Sense of Wonder* (1965)

A belief which does not spring from a conviction in the emotions is no belief at all.

EVELYN SCOTT, *Escapade* (1923)

For the decisions of our will are often so directly opposed to the decisions of our emotions, that, if we are in the habit of considering our emotions as the test, we shall be very apt to feel like hypocrites in declaring those things to be real which our will alone has decided.

HANNAH WHITALL SMITH, *The Christian's Secret of a Happy Life* (1870)

Unwonted circumstances may make us all rather unlike ourselves: there are conditions under which the most majestic person is obliged to sneeze, and our emotions are liable to be acted on in the same incongruous manner.

GEORGE ELIOT, *Middlemarch* (1871)

We are not, most of us, capable of exalted emotion, save rarely.

DOROTHY DAY, *From Union Square to Rome* (1940)

He . . . treats his emotions like mice that infest our basement or the rats in the garage, as vermin to be crushed in traps or poisoned with bait.

MARGE PIERCY, *Braided Lives* (1982)

When she fell in love it was with a perfect fury of accumulated dishonesty; she became instantly a dealer in second-hand and therefore incalculable emotions.

DJUNA BARNES, *Nightwood* (1937)

I hate people doing an emotional striptease. It's never genuine or they wouldn't drag outsiders in.

EVELYN ANTHONY, *The Avenue of the Dead* (1982)

He hated people who reeled off their thoughts and feelings to you, who took it for granted that you wanted to know all their inner mechanism. Reserve was always more interesting.

AGATHA CHRISTIE, *Sad Cypress* (1939)

Spilling your guts is just exactly as charming as it sounds.

FRAN LEBOWITZ, *Social Studies* (1977)

Anger and jealousy can no more bear to lose sight of their objects than love.

GEORGE ELIOT, *The Mill on the Floss* (1860)

He who is sorrowful can force himself to smile, but he who is glad cannot weep.

SELMA LAGERLÖF, *The Story of Gösta Berling* (1891)

Those who do not know how to weep with their whole heart don't know how to laugh either.

GOLDA MEIR, quoted by Oriana Fallaci in *L'Europeo* (1973)

See also Feelings.

EMPATHY

She did not talk to people as if they were strange hard shells she had to crack open to get inside. She talked as if she were already in the shell. In their very shell.

MARITA BONNER, "Nothing New" (1926), *Frye Street and Environs* (1987)

Unto a broken heart / No other one may go / Without the high prerogative / Itself hath suffered too.

EMILY DICKINSON (c. 1864), *The Poems of Emily Dickinson* (1955)

For the first time she had dimly realized that only the hopeless are starkly sincere and that only the unhappy can either give or take sympathy—even some of the bitter and dangerous voluptuousness of misery.

JEAN RHYS, *The Left Bank* (1927)

We want people to feel with us more than to act for us.

GEORGE ELIOT, letter (1856), in J. W. Cross, *George Eliot's Life as Related in Her Letters and Journals* (1884)

See also Compassion, Understanding.

END

The weariest nights, the longest days, sooner or later must perforce come to an end.

BARONESS ORCZY, *The Scarlet Pimpernel* (1905)

The adventure is over. Everything gets over, and nothing is ever enough. Except the part you carry with you.

E. L. KONIGSBURG, *From the Mixed-Up Files of Mrs. Basil E. Frankweiler* (1967)

The last time you're doing something—knowing you're doing it for the last—makes it even more alive than the first.

GLORIA NAYLOR, *Mama Day* (1988)

We begin to see that the completion of an important project has every right to be dignified by a natural grieving process. Something that required the best of us has ended. We will miss it.

ANNE WILSON SCHAEF, *Meditations for Women Who Do Too Much* (1990)

I have had enough.

GOLDA MEIR, upon resigning (1974)

That's all there is, there isn't any more.

ETHEL BARRYMORE, curtain call (1904)

Never think you've seen the last of anything.

EUDORA WELTY, *The Optimist's Daughter* (1968)

See also Farewells, Impermanence, Parting.

ENDURANCE

Patient endurance / Attaineth to all things.

SAINT TERESA OF AVILA, "Bookmark," in Joanna Bankier and Deirdre Lashgari, eds., *Women Poets of the World* (1983)

Folks differs, dearie. They differs a lot. Some can stand things that others can't. There's never no way of knowin' how much they can stand.

ANN PETRY, *The Street* (1946)

People have to learn sometimes not only how much the heart, but how much the head, can bear.

MARIA MITCHELL, diary (1853), in Phebe Mitchell Kendall, ed., *Maria Mitchell, Life, Letters, and Journals* (1896)

The thought that we are enduring the unendurable is one of the things that keep us going.

MOLLY HASKELL, *Love and Other Infectious Diseases* (1990)

Nothing great was ever done without much enduring.

ST. CATHERINE OF SIENA (c. 1370), *St. Catherine of Siena as Seen in Her Letters* (1911)

Some things persist by suffering change, others / Endure.

BABETTE DEUTSCH, "Homage to the Philosopher," in Nathan and Marynn Ausubel, *A Treasury of Jewish Poetry* (1957)

What is a ruin but Time easing itself of endurance?

DJUNA BARNES, *Nightwood* (1937)

See also Survival.

ENEMIES

People wish their enemies dead—but I do not; I say give them the gout, give them the stone!

LADY MARY WORTLEY MONTAGU (c. 1750), in Horace Walpole, letter (1778)

To have a good enemy, choose a friend: he knows where to strike.

DIANE DE POITIERS, in G. H. Bushnell, *Diane de Poitiers and Her Books* (1927)

Scratch a lover, and find a foe.

DOROTHY PARKER, "Ballade of a Great Weariness," *Enough Rope* (1926)

It is hard to fight an enemy who has outposts in your head.

SALLY KEMPTON, in *Esquire* (1970)

I don't have a warm personal enemy left. They've all died off. I miss them terribly because they helped define me.

CLARE BOOTHE LUCE, interview (1981)

I make enemies deliberately. They are the *sauce piquante* to my dish of life.

ELSA MAXWELL, in *New York Journal-American* (1963)

When my enemies stop hissing, I shall know I'm slipping.

MARIA CALLAS, *Maria Callas* (1981)

See also Opposition.

ENERGY

Energy is the power that drives every human being. It is not lost by exertion but maintained by it, for it is a faculty of the psyche.

GERMAINE GREER, *The Female Eunuch* (1971)

Life engenders life. Energy creates energy. It is by spending oneself that one becomes rich.

SARAH BERNHARDT, in Cornelia Otis Skinner, *Madame Sarah* (1966)

The human organism has only so much energy at its disposal. If you divert a great deal of it into any one channel, you can expect the others to collapse or atrophy. If you squander your vital energies on your emotional life, as you have been doing, plan to be physically and mentally bankrupt, as it were.

LISA ALTHER, *Kinflicks* (1975)

ENGLAND

England is an aquarium, not a nation.

RITA MAE BROWN, *Southern Discomfort* (1982)

I begin to suspect that England is the most melancholy country in the world.

NATALIA GINZBURG, *The Little Virtues* (1962)

England that little gray island in the clouds where governments don't fall overnight and children don't sell themselves in the street and my money is safe.

CARYL CHURCHILL, *Serious Money* (1987)

In this country, there are only two seasons, winter and winter.

SHELAGH DELANEY, *A Taste of Honey* (1958)

It was so cold I almost got married.

SHELLEY WINTERS, in *New York Times* (1956)

Those comfortably padded lunatic asylums which are known, euphemistically, as the stately homes of England.

VIRGINIA WOOLF, "Outlines: Lady Dorothy Nevill," *The Common Reader* (1925)

England is the only civilized country in the world where it is etiquette to fall on the food like a wolf the moment it is served. Elsewhere it is *comme il faut* to wait until everybody has helped himself to everything and until everything on everybody's plate is stone cold.

VIRGINIA GRAHAM, *Say Please* (1949)

I always felt that the boiled potato, not the Tudor rose, should be the national emblem.

ILKA CHASE, *Past Imperfect* (1942)

See also The English, Europe.

THE ENGLISH

It takes a great deal to produce ennui in an Englishman and if you do, he only takes it as convincing proof that you are well-bred.

MARGARET HALSEY, *With Malice Toward Some* (1938)

England is a country where people stay exactly as they are. The soul does not receive the slightest jolt.

NATALIA GINZBURG, *The Little Virtues* (1962)

The Englishwoman is so refined / She has no bosom and no behind.

STEVIE SMITH, "This Englishwoman," *A Good Time Was Had by All* (1937)

The trouble with most Englishwomen is that they *will* dress as if they had been a mouse in some previous incarnation.

EDITH SITWELL, "How to Wear Dramatic Clothes," in Elizabeth Salter and Allanah Harper, *Edith Sitwell: Fire of the Mind* (1976)

Contrary to popular belief, English women do not wear tweed nightgowns.

HERMIONE GINGOLD, in *Saturday Review* (1955)

Englishwomen's shoes look as if they had been made by someone who had often heard shoes described, but had never seen any.

MARGARET HALSEY, *With Malice Toward Some* (1938)

Listening to Britons dining out is like watching people play first-class tennis with imaginary balls.

MARGARET HALSEY, *With Malice Toward Some* (1938)

The English never smash in a face. They merely refrain from asking it to dinner.

MARGARET HALSEY, *With Malice Toward Some* (1938)

The English find ill-health not only interesting but respectable and often experience death in the effort to avoid a fuss.

PAMELA FRANKAU, *Pen to Paper* (1961)

She respected Americans: they were not like the English, who, under a surface of annoying moroseness of manner, were notoriously timid and easy to turn round your finger.

JEAN RHYS, *The Left Bank* (1927)

The English possess too many agreeable traits to permit them to be as much disliked as they think and hope they are.

AGNES REPPLIER, *Americans and Others* (1912)

See also England.

ENTHUSIASM

We is terrific.

DIANA ROSS, referring to the Supremes, in Mary Wilson, *Dreamgirl* (1986)

You will do foolish things, but do them with enthusiasm.

COLETTE, in *New York World-Telegram & Sun* (1961)

Latins are tenderly enthusiastic. In Brazil they throw flowers at you. In Argentina they throw themselves.

MARLENE DIETRICH, in *Newsweek* (1959)

Like simplicity and candor, and other much-commended qualities, enthusiasm is charming until we meet it face to face, and cannot escape from its charm.

AGNES REPPLIER, *Americans and Others* (1912)

A mediocre idea that generates enthusiasm will go further than a great idea that inspires no one.

MARY KAY ASH, *On People Management* (1984)

ENVIRONMENT

Something has gone unspeakably wrong . . . we human beings have made a terminal mess of this earth.

LISE WEIL, in Christina Thürmer-Rohr, *Vagabonding* (1991)

We have become as poisoned as the eagle's eggshell.

CHRYSTOS, "No Rock Scorns Me as Whore," in Cherríe Moraga and Gloria Anzaldúa, eds., *This Bridge Called My Back* (1983)

The maltreatment of the natural world and its impoverishment leads to the impoverishment of the human soul. It is related to the outburst of violence in human society. To save the natural world today means to save what is human in humanity.

RAISA M. GORBACHEV, *I Hope* (1991)

Only within the moment of time represented by the present century has one species—man—acquired significant power to alter the nature of his world.

RACHEL CARSON, *Silent Spring* (1962)

How can the spirit of the earth like the white man? That is why God will upset the world—because it is sore all over. Everywhere the white man has touched it, it is sore.

PRETTY SHIELD, in Frank Bird Linderman, *Pretty Shield, Medicine Woman of the Crows* (1932)

Man is a great blunderer going about in the woods, and there is no other except the bear that makes so much noise. . . . The cunningest hunter is hunted in turn, and what he leaves of his kill is meat for some other. That is the economy of nature, but with it all there is not sufficient account taken of the works of man. There is no scavenger that eats tin cans, and no wild thing leaves a like disfigurement on the forest floor.

MARY AUSTIN, *The Land of Little Rain* (1904)

Slowly the wasters and despoilers are impoverishing our land, our nature, and our beauty, so that there will not be one beach, one hill, one lane, one meadow, one forest free from the debris of man and the stigma of his improvidence.

MARYA MANNES, *More in Anger* (1958)

If I have learned nothing else in all these months in the woods, I have thoroughly learned to keep hands off the processes of nature.

LAURA LEE DAVIDSON, *A Winter of Content* (1922)

I had assumed that the Earth, the spirit of the Earth, noticed exceptions—those who wantonly damage it and those who do not. But the Earth is wise. It has given itself into the keeping of all, and all are therefore accountable.

ALICE WALKER, *Living by the Word* (1988)

[Man] thinks of himself as a creator instead of a user, and this delusion is robbing him, not only of his natural heritage, but perhaps of his future.

HELEN HOOVER, "The Waiting Hills," *The Long-Shadowed Forest* (1963)

For the first time in the history of the world, every human being is now subjected to contact with dangerous chemicals, from the moment of conception until death.

RACHEL CARSON, *Silent Spring* (1962)

The "control of nature" is a phrase conceived in arrogance, born of the Neanderthal age of biology and philosophy, when it was supposed that nature exists for the convenience of man.

RACHEL CARSON, *Silent Spring* (1962)

Every person who builds a second home on a pristine lake or in a secluded area of woods, or who invests in urban-sprawl development, is part of the same global pattern of encroachment that displaces wildlife and decreases the wild space our own species needs for its survival.

DEANE MORRISON, *Of Kinkajous, Capybaras, Seladangs, Horned-Beetles: And the Oddest and Most Wonderful Mammals, Insects, Birds, and Plants of Our World* (1991)

Those hills hold nothing now　Mostly leveled Without deer, without puma, without pheasant, without blue-bellied lizards, without quail, without ancient oaks　Lawns instead　Deeply disgusted by lawns　Stupid flat green crew cuts Nothing for anybody to eat.

CHRYSTOS, "No Rock Scorns Me as Whore," in Cherríe Moraga and Gloria Anzaldúa, eds., *This Bridge Called My Back* (1983)

As crude a weapon as the cave man's club, the chemical barrage has been hurled against the fabric of life—a fabric on the one hand delicate and destructible, on the other miraculously tough and resilient, and capable of striking back in unexpected ways.

RACHEL CARSON, *Silent Spring* (1962)

Today everyone can see the full extent of the past and present atrocities on this earth. No one can any longer claim she or he didn't know anything.

CHRISTINA THÜRMER-ROHR, *Vagabonding* (1991)

See also Earth, Land, Nature, Wilderness.

ENVY

An envious heart makes a treacherous ear.

ZORA NEALE HURSTON, *Their Eyes Were Watching God* (1937)

The happiness of others is never bearable for very long.

FRANÇOISE SAGAN, *A Reluctant Hero* (1985)

Spite is never lonely; envy always tags along.

MIGNON MCLAUGHLIN, *The Neurotic's Notebook* (1963)

See also Jealousy.

EQUALITY

I tasted the bread and wine of equality.

ANZIA YEZIERSKA, *Red Ribbon on a White Horse* (1950)

Who ever walked behind anyone to freedom? If we can't go hand in hand, I don't want to go.

HAZEL SCOTT, in Margo Jefferson, "Great (Hazel) Scott!" *Ms.* (1974)

We hold these truths to be self-evident: that all men and women are created equal.

"Declaration of Sentiments and Resolutions," The First Woman's Rights Convention (1848), in Elizabeth Cady Stanton, *The History of Woman Suffrage* (1881)

Men their rights and nothing more; women their rights and nothing less.

Susan B. Anthony and Elizabeth Cady Stanton, motto of newspaper, *The Revolution* (1868)

Feminism is the most revolutionary idea there has ever been. Equality for women demands a change in the human psyche more profound than anything Marx dreamed of. It means valuing parenthood as much as we value banking.

Polly Toynbee, in *Guardian* (1987)

'Tis woman's strongest vindication for speaking that *the world needs to hear her voice.* It would be subversive of every human interest that the cry of one-half the human family be stifled. . . . The world has had to limp along with the wobbling gait and one-sided hesitancy of a man with one eye. Suddenly the bandage is removed from the other eye and the whole body is filled with light. It sees a circle where before it saw a segment. The darkened eye restored, every member rejoices with it.

Anna Julia Cooper, *A Voice from the South* (1892)

Whatever advantages may have arisen, in the past, out of the existence of a specially favored and highly privileged aristocracy, it is clear to me that today no argument can stand that supports unequal opportunity or any intrinsic disqualification for sharing in the whole of life.

Margaret Mead, *Blackberry Winter* (1972)

An occupation that has no basis in sex-determined gifts can now recruit its ranks from twice as many potential artists.

Margaret Mead, *Sex and Temperament in Three Primitive Societies* (1935)

The woman's bill of rights is, unhappily, long overdue. It should have run along with the rights of man in the eighteenth century. Its drag as to time of official proclamation is a drag as to social vision. And even if equal rights were now written into the law of our land, it would be so inadequate today as a means to food, clothing and shelter for women at large that what they would still be enjoying would be equality in disaster rather than in realistic privilege.

Mary Ritter Beard (1937), in Nancy F. Cott, *A Woman Making History* (1991)

Equality . . . is the result of human organization. . . . We are not born equal.

Hannah Arendt, *Origins of Totalitarianism* (1951)

See also Discrimination, Gay, Human Differences, Justice, Racism, Sexism.

ERAS

The ages are but baubles hung upon / The thread of some strong lives—and one slight wrist / May lift a century above the dust.

Edith Wharton, "A Torchbearer," *Artemis to Actaeon* (1909)

Decades have a delusive edge to them. They are not, of course, really periods at all, except as any other ten years would be. But we, looking at them, are caught by the different name each bears, and give them different attributes, and tie labels on them, as if they were flowers in a border.

Rose Macaulay, *Told by an Idiot* (1923)

See also Time.

EROTICISM

American eroticism has always been of a different provenance and complexion than the European variety, an enjoyment both furtive and bland that is closer to a blushing cartoon than a sensual celebration.

Molly Haskell, *From Reverence to Rape* (1974)

We tend to think of the erotic as an easy, tantalizing sexual arousal. I speak of the erotic as the deepest life force, a force which moves us toward living in a fundamental way.

Audre Lorde, in Claudia Tate, ed., *Black Women Writers at Work* (1983)

See also Seduction, Sex.

ERROR

Who thinks it just to be judged by a single error?

BERYL MARKHAM, *West with the Night* (1942)

I was no pope—I could not boast infallibility.

CHARLOTTE BRONTË, *The Professor* (1846)

See also Mistakes.

ERUDITION

Erudition, like a bloodhound, is a charming thing when held firmly in leash, but it is not so attractive when turned loose upon a defenseless, unerudite public.

AGNES REPPLIER, *Points of View* (1891)

See also Knowledge.

ESSAYS

There is no room for the impurities of literature in an essay.

VIRGINIA WOOLF, "The Modern Essay," *The Common Reader* (1925)

An essay is a work of literary art which has a minimum of one anecdote and one universal idea.

CAROL BLY, *The Passionate, Accurate Story* (1990)

A good essay must have this permanent quality about it: it must draw its curtain round us, but it must be a curtain that shuts us in, not out.

VIRGINIA WOOLF, *The Common Reader* (1925)

See also Writing.

ESSENCE

Rose is a rose is a rose is a rose.

GERTRUDE STEIN, *Sacred Emily* (1913)

A snake will always be a snake, even if you put a chain around its neck and try to make it walk upright.

LISA ALTHER, *Kinflicks* (1975)

The Arabian horse will not plow well, nor can the plowhorse be rode to play the jereed.

MARGARET FULLER, *Summer on the Lakes* (1844)

You can't get tender shoots from a rotten bamboo stalk.

LI ANG, *The Butcher's Wife* (1983)

Wood may remain twenty years in the water, but it is still not a fish.

JANE YOLEN, *Sister Light, Sister Dark* (1988)

I think character never changes; the Acorn becomes an Oak, which is very little like an Acorn to be sure, but it never becomes an Ash.

HESTER LYNCH PIOZZI (1797), in Oswald G. Knapp, ed., *The Intimate Letters of Hester Piozzi and Penelope Pennington 1788–1821* (1914)

She was the same through and through. You could go on cutting slice after slice and you knew you would never light upon a plum or a cherry or even a piece of peel.

KATHERINE MANSFIELD (1918), Journal of Katherine Mansfield (1930)

With him for a sire and her for a dam, / What should I be but just what I am?

EDNA ST. VINCENT MILLAY, "The Singing-Woman From the Wood's Edge," *A Few Figs From Thistles* (1920)

My theory is that when we come on this earth, many of us are ready-made. Some of us—most of us—have genes that are ready for certain performances. Nature gives you these gifts. There's no denying that Caruso came with a voice, there's no denying that Beethoven came with music in his soul. Picasso was drawing like an angel in the crib. You're born with it.

LOUISE NEVELSON, *Dawns + Dusks* (1976)

One ship drives east and another drives west / With the selfsame winds that blow. / 'Tis the set of sails and not the gales / Which tells us the way to go.

ELLA WHEELER WILCOX, "Winds of Fate," *The Collected Poems* (1917)

Runners are poor walkers.

MARIE VON EBNER-ESCHENBACH, *Aphorisms* (1905)

Any one seed may be too old to sprout or inferior in some way, but it will never try to be something it isn't fitted to be. A man may study to be a surgeon when he should have been a shoemaker, a talented painter may spend his life trying to convince himself and his fellows that he is a lawyer, but a turnip seed will never attempt to grow into an ear of corn. If you plant a good turnip seed properly a turnip is what you will get every single time.

RUTH STOUT, *How to Have a Green Thumb Without an Aching Back* (1955)

I was raised the Chinese way: I was taught to desire nothing, to swallow other people's misery, to eat my own bitterness. And even though I taught my daughter the opposite, still she came out the same way! Maybe it is because she was born to me and she was born a girl. And I was born to my mother and I was born a girl. All of us are like stairs, one step after another, going up and down, but all going the same way.

AMY TAN, *The Joy Luck Club* (1989)

See also Character, Identity.

ESTRANGEMENT

My mother and father and I now lived in the intimacy of estrangement that exists between married couples who have nothing left in common but their incompatibility.

NADINE GORDIMER, *The Lying Days* (1953)

Sleep on, I sit and watch your tent in silence, / White as a sail upon this sandy sea, / And know the Desert's self is not more boundless / Than is the distance 'twixt yourself and me.

LAURENCE HOPE, title poem, *Stars of the Desert* (1903)

See also Divorce.

ETERNITY

Eternity is not something that begins after you are dead. It is going on all the time. We are in it now.

CHARLOTTE PERKINS GILMAN, in *The Forerunner* (1909)

Stars and blossoming fruit trees: Utter permanence and extreme fragility give an equal sense of eternity.

SIMONE WEIL, *Gravity and Grace* (1947)

See also Afterlife, Immortality.

ETHICS

To a thrifty theologian, bent on redemption with economy, there are few points of ethics too fine-spun for splitting.

ELLEN GLASGOW, *Barren Ground* (1925)

The stress laid on upward social mobility in the United States has tended to obscure the fact that there can be more than one kind of mobility and more than one direction in which it can go. There can be ethical mobility as well as financial, and it can go down as well as up.

MARGARET HALSEY, *No Laughing Matter* (1977)

It is no wonder we behave badly, we are literally ignorant of the laws of ethics, which is the simplest of sciences, the most necessary, the most continuously needed. The childish misconduct of our "revolted youth" is quite equaled by that of older people, and neither young nor old seem to have any understanding of the reasons why conduct is "good" or "bad."

CHARLOTTE PERKINS GILMAN, *The Living of Charlotte Perkins Gilman* (1935)

See also Evil, Morality, Sin.

ETIQUETTE

While we are at it, where is the salad knife? Evil people are forever putting lettuce wedges and other booby traps into salads, and then demanding that they be eaten with the unaided fork. Is it all that funny to watch people squirt salad dressing into their eyes?

JUDITH MARTIN, *Miss Manners' Guide for the Turn-of-the-Millennium* (1989)

When you see persons slip down on the ice, do not laugh at them. . . . It is more feminine on witnessing such a sight, to utter an involuntary scream than a shout of laughter.

ELIZA LESLIE, *Miss Leslie's Behavior Book: A Guide and Manual for Ladies* (1859)

Etiquette is what you are doing and saying when people are looking and listening. What you are thinking is your business.

VIRGINIA CARY HUDSON, *O Ye Jigs and Juleps* (1962)

In society it is etiquette for ladies to have the best chairs and get handed things. In the home the reverse is the case. That is why ladies are more sociable than gentlemen.

VIRGINIA GRAHAM, *Say Please* (1949)

See also Manners, Politeness, Rudeness.

EUPHEMISMS

There are new words now that excuse everybody. Give me the good old days of heroes and villains. The people you can bravo or hiss. There was a truth to them that all the slick credulity of today cannot touch.

BETTE DAVIS, *The Lonely Life* (1962)

The practice of hinting by single letters those expletives with which profane and violent persons are wont to garnish their discourse, strikes me as a proceeding which, however well meant, is weak and futile. I cannot tell what good it does—what feeling it spares—what horror it conceals.

CHARLOTTE BRONTË, editor's preface to new edition of Emily Brontë's *Wuthering Heights* (1847)

Excuse me, everybody, I have to go to the bathroom. I really have to telephone, but I'm too embarrassed to say so.

DOROTHY PARKER, in Robert E. Drennan, *The Algonquin Wits* (1968)

See also Words.

EUROPE

That is what is so marvelous about Europe; the people long ago learned that space and beauty and quiet refuges in a great city, where children may play and old people sit in the sun, are of far more value to the inhabitants than real estate taxes and contractors' greed.

ILKA CHASE, *Fresh From the Laundry* (1967)

See also Belgium, England, France, Holland, Ireland, Italy.

EUTHANASIA

Euthanasia is a long, smooth-sounding word, and it conceals its danger as long, smooth words do, but the danger is there, nevertheless.

PEARL BUCK, *The Child Who Never Grew* (1950)

The time is approaching when we shall consider it abhorrent to our civilization to allow a human being to die in prolonged agony which we should mercifully end in any other creature.

CHARLOTTE PERKINS GILMAN, *The Living of Charlotte Perkins Gilman* (1935)

See also Death.

EVASION

Fear not those who argue but those who dodge.

MARIE VON EBNER-ESCHENBACH, *Aphorisms* (1905)

See also Lying.

EVIL

There is evil everywhere under the sun.

AGATHA CHRISTIE, *Evil Under the Sun* (1940)

The arrogance of men, indeed, / comes full equipped with evil, / in promise and insistency, / the world, the flesh, the Devil.

SOR JUANA INÉS DE LA CRUZ (c. 1690), in Irene Nicholson, *A Guide to Mexican Poetry* (1968)

In all men is evil sleeping; the good man is he who will not awaken it, in himself or in other men.

MARY RENAULT, *The Praise Singer* (1978)

The evil of the world is made possible by nothing but the sanction you give it.

AYN RAND, *Atlas Shrugged* (1957)

The spread of evil is the symptom of a vacuum. Whenever evil wins, it is only by default: by the moral failure of those who evade the fact that there can be no compromise on basic principles.

AYN RAND, *Capitalism: The Unknown Ideal* (1966)

Evil is obvious only in retrospect.

GLORIA STEINEM, *Outrageous Acts and Everyday Rebellions* (1983)

There would be less evil on earth if evil could never be done in the name of good.

MARIE VON EBNER-ESCHENBACH, *Aphorisms* (1905)

We may draw good out of evil; we must not do evil, that good may come.

MARIA CHAPMAN, speech (1855)

There's too much tendency to attribute to God the evils that man does of his own free will.

AGATHA CHRISTIE, *The Moving Finger* (1942)

A towering intellect, grand in its achievements, and glorious in its possibilities, may, with the moral and spiritual faculties held in abeyance, be one of the most dangerous and mischievous forces in the world.

FRANCES ELLEN WATKINS HARPER, "A Factor in Human Progress," *African Methodist Episcopal Church Review* (1885)

It is bitter to lose a friend to evil, before one loses him to death.

MARY RENAULT, *The Praise Singer* (1978)

In any compromise between food and poison, it is only death that can win. In any compromise between good and evil, it is only evil that can profit.

AYN RAND, *Atlas Shrugged* (1957)

Evil when we are in its power is not felt as evil but as a necessity, or even a duty.

SIMONE WEIL, *Gravity and Grace* (1947)

It is right noble to fight with wickedness and wrong; the mistake is in supposing that spiritual evil can be overcome by physical means.

LYDIA MARIA CHILD, *Letters from New York*, 1st Series (1842)

And I believe that I will never be able to hate any human being for his so-called "wickedness," that I shall only hate the evil that is within me, though hate is perhaps putting it too strongly even then. In any case, we cannot be lax enough in what we demand of others and strict enough in what we demand of ourselves.

ETTY HILLESUM, *An Interrupted Life: The Diaries of Etty Hillesum 1941–1943* (1983)

We human beings cause monstrous conditions, but precisely because we cause them we soon learn to adapt ourselves to them. Only if we become such that we can no longer adapt ourselves, only if, deep inside, we rebel against every

kind of evil, will we be able to put a stop to it . . . while everything within us does not yet scream out in protest, so long will we find ways of adapting ourselves, and the horrors will continue.

ETTY HILLESUM, *An Interrupted Life: The Diaries of Etty Hillesum 1941–1943* (1983)

Imaginary evils are incurable.

MARIE VON EBNER-ESCHENBACH, Aphorisms (1905)

Between two evils, I always pick the one I never tried before.

MAE WEST, in *Klondike Annie* (1936)

See also Crime, Devil, Sin, Vice.

EXCELLENCE

The secret of joy in work is contained in one word—excellence. To know how to do something well is to enjoy it.

PEARL BUCK, *The Joy of Children* (1964)

The sad truth is that excellence makes people nervous.

SHANA ALEXANDER, *The Feminine Eye* (1970)

We only do well the things we like doing.

COLETTE, *Prisons and Paradise* (1932)

There's only one real sin, and that is to persuade oneself that the second-best is anything but the second-best.

DORIS LESSING, *Golden Notebook* (1962)

When we do the best that we can, we never know what miracle is wrought in our life, or in the life of another.

HELEN KELLER, *Out of the Dark* (1913)

See also Perfectionism.

EXCEPTIONS

There is always a *but* in this imperfect world.

ANNE BRONTË, *The Tenant of Wildfell Hall* (1848)

EXCESS

Something is always born of excess: great art was born of great terrors, great loneliness, great inhibitions, instabilities, and it always balances them.

ANAÏS NIN, *The Diary of Anaïs Nin*, vol. 4 (1944–1947)

I'm the foe of moderation, the champion of excess. If I may lift a line from a die-hard whose identity is lost in the shuffle, "I'd rather be strongly wrong than weakly right."

TALLULAH BANKHEAD, *Tallulah* (1952)

Modern life is given over to immoderation. Immoderation invades everything: actions and thought, public and private life.

SIMONE WEIL, *Gravity and Grace* (1947)

Perhaps too much of everything is as bad as too little.

EDNA FERBER, *Giant* (1952)

See also Extremism, Luxury.

EXPECTATIONS

Expectations are the most perilous form of dream, and when dreams do realize themselves it is in the waking world: the difference is subtly but often painfully felt.

ELIZABETH BOWEN, *The Death of the Heart* (1938)

No pleasure or success in life quite meets the capacity of our hearts. We take in our good things with enthusiasm, and think ourselves happy and satisfied; but afterward, when the froth and foam have subsided, we discover that the goblet is not more than half-filled with the golden liquid that was poured into it.

LOUISE IMOGEN GUINEY, *Goose-Quill Papers* (1885)

What is destructive is impatience, haste, expecting too much too fast.

MAY SARTON, *Journal of a Solitude* (1973)

Talk about the joys of the unexpected, can they compare with the joys of the expected, of finding everything delightfully and completely what you knew it was going to be?

ELIZABETH BIBESCO, *Balloons* (1922)

How extraordinary people are, that they get themselves into such situations where they go on doing what they dislike doing, and have no need

or obligation to do, simply because it seems to be expected.

MARGARET DRABBLE, *The Middle Ground* (1980)

Nothing is so good as it seems beforehand.

GEORGE ELIOT, *Silas Marner* (1861)

Expect nothing. Live frugally / On surprise.

ALICE WALKER, "Expect Nothing," *Revolutionary Petunias and Other Poems* (1971)

See also Anticipation, Hope, Unexpected.

EXPEDIENCE

That woman . . . would use the third-rising of a corpse for her ends.

DJUNA BARNES, *Nightwood* (1937)

Perhaps it is the expediency in the political eye that blinds it.

VIRGILIA PETERSON, *A Matter of Life and Death* (1961)

And lips say "God be pitiful," / Who ne'er said "God be praised."

ELIZABETH BARRETT BROWNING, "Cry of the Human," *Graham's American Magazine* (1842)

Wars come and wars go but the world does not change: it will always forget an indebtedness which it thinks it expedient not to remember.

RADCLYFFE HALL, *Miss Ogilvy Finds Herself* (1926)

I do not believe / our wants / have made our lies / holy.

AUDRE LORDE, "Between Ourselves," in Joanna Bankier and Deirdre Lashgari, eds., *Women Poets of the World* (1983)

EXPERIENCE

Experience is what you get looking for something else.

MARY PETTIBONE POOLE, *A Glass Eye at a Keyhole* (1938)

Experience is a good teacher, but she sends in terrific bills.

MINNA THOMAS ANTRIM, *Naked Truth and Veiled Illusions* (1902)

Experience isn't interesting till it begins to repeat itself—in fact, till it does that, it hardly *is* experience.

ELIZABETH BOWEN, *The Death of the Heart* (1938)

No one is so eager to gain new experience as he who doesn't know how to make use of the old ones.

MARIE VON EBNER-ESCHENBACH, *Aphorisms* (1905)

A rattlesnake that doesn't bite teaches you nothing.

JESSAMYN WEST, *The Life I Really Lived* (1979)

But there are roughly two sorts of informed people, aren't there? People who start off right by observing the pitfalls and mistakes and going round them, and the people who fall into them and get out and know they're there because of that. They both come to the same conclusions but they don't have quite the same point of view.

MARGERY ALLINGHAM, *Dancers in Mourning* (1937)

All writers, musicians, artists, choreographers/dancers, etc., work with the stuff of their experiences. It's the translation of it, the conversion of it, the shaping of it that makes for the drama.

TONI CADE BAMBARA, in Claudia Tate, ed., *Black Women Writers at Work* (1983)

I long to put the experience of fifty years at once into your young lives, to give you at once the key to that treasure chamber every gem of which has cost me tears and struggles and prayers, but you must work for these inward treasures yourselves.

HARRIET BEECHER STOWE, letter to her twin daughters (1861)

Over the airways, in movies, experiences have come to be dogmatized to certain kinds of experience at the cost of all others.

JOSEPHINE HERBST, *New Green World* (1954)

Conviction without experience makes for harshness.

FLANNERY O'CONNOR, in Sally Fitzgerald, ed., *The Habit of Being* (1979)

EXPLANATIONS

But let the wise be warned against too great readiness to explanation: it multiplies the sources of mistake, lengthening the sum for reckoners sure to go wrong.

GEORGE ELIOT, *Middlemarch* (1871)

I warned you / Don't ask for explanations / When you walk with me.

LAMI'A ABBAS AL-'IMARAH, "The Path of Silence," in Elizabeth Warnock Fernea, *Women and the Family in the Middle East* (1985)

Nothing annoys me more than having the most trivial action analyzed and explained.

ZELDA FITZGERALD, in Nancy Milford, *Zelda* (1970)

It is far easier to explain to a three-year-old how babies are made than to explain the processes whereby bread or sugar appear on the table.

DERVLA MURPHY, *Wheels Within Wheels* (1931)

See also Answers, Reason, Why.

EXTRAVAGANCE

Extravagance. The price of indulging yourself in your youth in the things you cannot afford is poverty and dependence in your old age.

DOROTHY DIX, *Dorothy Dix, Her Book* (1926)

We owe something to extravagance, for thrift and adventure seldom go hand in hand.

JENNIE JEROME CHURCHILL, "Extravagance," in *Pearson's* (1915)

See also Excess, Luxury, Self-Indulgence.

EXTREMISM

One cannot be too extreme in dealing with social ills; besides, the extreme thing is generally the true thing.

EMMA GOLDMAN, introduction, *Anarchism* (1910)

Every political good carried to the extreme must be productive of evil.

MARY WOLLSTONECRAFT, *The French Revolution* (1794)

See also Excess.

EYES

Look in the mirror. The face that pins you with its double gaze reveals a chastening secret. You are looking into a predator's eyes. Most predators have eyes set right on the front of their heads, so they can use binocular vision to sight and track their prey. . . . Prey, on the other hand, have eyes at the sides of their heads, because what they really need is peripheral vision, so they can tell when something is sneaking up behind them. Something like us.

DIANE ACKERMAN, *A Natural History of the Senses* (1990)

The eye is complicated. It mixes the colors [it sees] for you. . . . The painter must unmix them and lay them on again shade by shade, and then the eye of the beholder takes over and mixes them again.

ELIZABETH BORTON DE TREVIÑO, *I, Juan de Pareja* (1965)

She had always loved his eyes. They were completely clear and unflinching—the eyes of a boy who read adventure stories and had dedicated himself to live up to their code of courage and honor.

RUTH PRAWER JHABVALA, *Heat and Dust* (1975)

You need eyes like an archerfish, able to see what happens on two planes at once. One set for watching the hands [signing], and the other for watching whatever it is he mouths.

KERI HULME, *The Bone People* (1983)

See also Face.

F

FACE

Nature gives you the face you have when you are twenty. Life shapes the face you have at thirty. But it is up to you to earn the face you have at fifty.

Coco Chanel, in Marcel Haedrich, *Coco Chanel: Her Life, Her Secrets* (1972)

I have not learned happily / to live with my face.

Diane Wakoski, "I Have Had to Learn to Live with My Face," *The Motorcycle Betrayal Poems* (1971)

A face that has the marks of having lived intensely, that expresses some phase of life, some dominant quality or intellectual power, constitutes for me an interesting face. For this reason, the face of an older person, perhaps not beautiful in the strictest sense, is usually more appealing than the face of a younger person who has scarcely been touched by life.

Doris Ulmann, in Dale Warren, "Doris Ulmann: Photographer-in-Waiting," *The Bookman* (1930)

Her face worked and broke into strained, hardening lines, as if there had been a death—that too-explicit evidence of agony in the desire to communicate.

Eudora Welty, "The Key," *A Curtain of Green* (1941)

In every person's face, there is one place that seems to express them most accurately. With my grandmother you always looked at her mouth.

Mona Simpson, *Anywhere But Here* (1986)

Nothing ruins a face so fast as double-dealing. Your face telling one story to the world. Your heart yanking your face to pieces, trying to let the truth be known. One eyelid'll hang down lower than the other, one side of your mouth'll stay stiff while the other smiles. I know a dozen cases like that.

Jessamyn West, *The Life I Really Lived* (1979)

See also Body, Eyes, Smile.

FACTS

She always says, my lord, that facts are like cows. If you look them in the face hard enough they generally run away.

Dorothy L. Sayers, *Clouds of Witness* (1926)

If there's an opinion, facts will be found to support it.

Judy Sproles, in *Omni* (1979)

Fact explains nothing. On the contrary, it is fact that requires explanation.

Marilynne Robinson, *Housekeeping* (1980)

There's a world of difference between truth and facts. Facts can obscure the truth.

Maya Angelou, in Brian Lanker, *I Dream a World* (1989)

People who mistake facts for ideas are incomplete thinkers; they are gossips.

Cynthia Ozick, "We Are the Crazy Lady and Other Feisty Feminist Fables," in Francine Klagsbrun, ed., *The First Ms. Reader* (1972)

We must love all facts, not for their consequences, but because in each fact God is there present.

Simone Weil, *The Notebooks of Simone Weil* (1951)

In science, all facts, no matter how trivial or banal, enjoy democratic equality.

Mary McCarthy, *On the Contrary* (1961)

See also Data, Information, Knowledge.

FAILURE

A net in the depths, I return, / rising to the surface / without a single fish.

ROSARIO CASTELLANOS, "Useless Day," in Joanna Bankier and Deirdre Lashgari, eds., *Women Poets of the World* (1983)

Apparent failure may hold in its rough shell the germs of a success that will blossom in time, and bear fruit throughout eternity.

FRANCES ELLEN WATKINS HARPER, speech (1875)

People fail forward to success.

MARY KAY ASH, *On People Management* (1984)

In a total work, the failures have their not unimportant place.

MAY SARTON, *Mrs. Stevens Hears the Mermaids Singing* (1965)

Flops are a part of life's menu and I'm never a girl to miss out on any of the courses.

ROSALIND RUSSELL, in Barbara McDowell and Hana Umlauf, *Woman's Almanac* (1977)

If you have made mistakes, even serious ones, there is always another chance for you. What we call failure is not the falling down, but the staying down.

MARY PICKFORD, in *Reader's Digest* (1979)

Three failures denote uncommon strength. A weakling has not enough grit to fail thrice.

MINNA THOMAS ANTRIM, *At the Sign of the Golden Calf* (1905)

The sheer rebelliousness in giving ourselves permission to fail frees a childlike awareness and clarity. . . . When we give ourselves permission to fail, we at the same time give ourselves permission to excel.

ELOISE RISTAD, *A Soprano on Her Head* (1982)

Failure must be but a challenge to others.

AMELIA EARHART, *Last Flight* (1937)

Success is a public affair. Failure is a private funeral.

ROSALIND RUSSELL, *Life Is a Banquet* (1977)

When we can begin to take our failures non-seriously, it means we are ceasing to be afraid of them. It is of immense importance to learn to *laugh at ourselves.*

KATHERINE MANSFIELD (1922), *Journal of Katherine Mansfield* (1927).

Is it age, or was it always my nature, to take a bad time, block out the good times, until any success became an accident and failure seemed the only truth?

LILLIAN HELLMAN, *An Unfinished Woman* (1969)

Failure can get to be a rather comfortable old friend.

MIGNON MCLAUGHLIN, *The Second Neurotic's Notebook* (1966)

See also Defeat, Error, Mistakes.

FAITH

Faith is not *being sure.* It is *not being sure,* but betting with your last cent.

MARY JEAN IRION, *Yes, World* (1970)

If it can be verified, we don't need faith. . . . Faith is for that which lies on the *other* side of reason. Faith is what makes life bearable, with all its tragedies and ambiguities and sudden, startling joys.

MADELEINE L'ENGLE, *Walking on Water: Reflections on Faith and Art* (1980)

Who has seen the wind? / Neither you nor I; / But when the trees bow down their heads, / The wind is passing by.

CHRISTINA ROSSETTI, "Who Has Seen the Wind?" (1873), *The Poetical Works of Christina Georgina Rossetti* (1906)

It is the virtue of the storm, just as happiness is the virtue of the sunshine.

RUTH BENEDICT, in Margaret Mead, *An Anthropologist at Work: Writings of Ruth Benedict* (1959)

If there is a faith that can move mountains, it is faith in your own power.

MARIE VON EBNER-ESCHENBACH, *Aphorisms* (1905)

Kill the snake of doubt in your soul, crush the worms of fear in your heart and mountains will move out of your way.

KATE SEREDY, *The White Stag* (1937)

I feel no need for any other faith than my faith in human beings.

PEARL BUCK, *I Believe* (1939)

The prayer that reforms the sinner and heals the sick is an absolute faith that all things are possible to God.

MARY BAKER EDDY, *Science and Health* (1875)

It seems to me that in our time faith in God is the same thing as faith in good and the ultimate triumph of good over evil.

SVETLANA ALLILUYEVA, *Twenty Letters to a Friend* (1967)

Faith is not making religious-sounding noises in the daytime. It is asking your inmost self questions at night—and then getting up and going to work.

MARY JEAN IRION, *Yes, World* (1970)

Faith . . . is nothing at all tangible. It is simply believing God; and, like sight, it is nothing apart from its object. You might as well shut your eyes and look inside, and see whether you have sight, as to look inside to discover whether you have faith.

HANNAH WHITALL SMITH, *The Christian's Secret of a Happy Life* (1870)

Faith is not a series of gilt-edged propositions that you sit down to figure out, and if you follow all the logic and accept all the conclusions, then you have it. It is crumpling and throwing away everything, proposition by proposition, until nothing is left, and then writing a new proposition, your very own, to throw in the teeth of despair.

MARY JEAN IRION, *Yes, World* (1970)

Faith is the first factor in a life devoted to service. Without faith, nothing is possible. With it, nothing is impossible.

MARY MCLEOD BETHUNE, in Mary Alice Warner and Bayna Beilenson, *Women of Faith and Spirit* (1987)

"Faith" is a fine invention / When Gentlemen can *see*— / But *Microscopes* are prudent / In an Emergency.

EMILY DICKINSON (1860), *Poems, Second Series* (1891)

See also Belief, Trust.

FAITHFULNESS

My faithfulness is but fidelity / Since I am never faithful, but to you.

LAURENCE HOPE, "To Aziz: Song of Mahomed Akram," *Stars of the Desert* (1903)

Old love, old love, / How can I be true? / Shall I be faithless to myself / Or to you?

SARA TEASDALE, "New Love and Old," *Rivers to the Sea* (1915)

It is better to be unfaithful than faithful without wanting to be.

BRIGITTE BARDOT, in *Observer* (1968)

Monogamy is contrary to nature but necessary for the greater social good.

RITA MAE BROWN, *Starting From Scratch* (1988)

God has not called me to be successful; he has called me to be faithful.

MOTHER TERESA, in *New York Times* (1980)

And Ruth said, Entreat me not to leave thee, or to return from following after thee: for whither thou goest, I will go; and where thou lodgest, I will lodge; thy people shall be my people, and thy God, my God. Where thou diest, will I die, and there will I be buried: the Lord do so to me, and more also, if aught but death part thee and me.

RUTH, *Ruth I: 16, 17*

Oh! when thy heart and home were glad, / I freely shared thy joyous lot; / And now that heart is lone and sad, / Cease to entreat—I'll leave thee not.

FRANCES ELLEN WATKINS HARPER, "Ruth and Naomi," Poems on Miscellaneous Subjects (1857)

See also Loyalty, Virtue.

FAME

Fame is a fickle food / Upon a shifting plate.

EMILY DICKINSON (c. 1864), *The Single Hound* (1914)

Fame is a pearl many dive for and only a few bring up. Even when they do, it is not perfect, and they sigh for more, and lose better things in struggling for them.

LOUISA MAY ALCOTT, *Jo's Boys* (1886)

So this was fame at last! Nothing but a vast debt to be paid to the world in energy, blood, in time.

MAY SARTON, *Mrs. Stevens Hears the Mermaids Singing* (1965)

Fame always brings loneliness. Success is as ice cold and as lonely as the north pole.

VICKI BAUM, *Grand Hotel* (1929)

That's what fame is: solitude.

COCO CHANEL, in Marcel Haedrich, *Coco Chanel: Her Life, Her Secrets* (1972)

"What are you famous *for?*" "For nothing. I am just famous."

IRIS MURDOCH, *The Flight from the Enchanter* (1956)

The Press blew, the public stared, hands flew out like a million little fishes after bread.

ENID BAGNOLD, *National Velvet* (1935)

It takes very little fire to make a great deal of smoke nowadays, and notoriety is not real glory.

LOUISA MAY ALCOTT, *Jo's Boys* (1886)

There may be wonder in money, but, dear God, there is money in wonder.

ENID BAGNOLD, *National Velvet* (1935)

Americans respect talent only insofar as it leads to fame, and we reserve our most fervent admiration for famous people who destroy their lives as well as their talent. The fatal flaws of Elvis, Judy, and Marilyn register much higher on our national applause meter than their living achievements. In America, talent is merely a tool for becoming famous in life so you can become more famous in death—where all are equal.

FLORENCE KING, *Lump It or Leave It* (1990)

How dreary—to be—Somebody! / How public—like a Frog— / To tell one's name—the live-long June— / To an admiring Bog!

EMILY DICKINSON, (1861), *Poems, Second Series* (1891)

See also Celebrities.

FAMILIARITY

Fish are not the best authority on water.

JANE YOLEN, *Sister Light, Sister Dark* (1988)

You do not notice changes in what is always before you.

COLETTE, *My Apprenticeships* (1936)

Familiarity is a magician that is cruel to beauty but kind to ugliness.

OUIDA, *Wisdom, Wit and Pathos* (1884)

I like familiarity. In me it does not breed contempt. Only more familiarity.

GERTRUDE STEIN, in *Reader's Digest* (1935)

She was the crow of the reservation, she lived off our scraps, and she knew us best because the scraps told our story.

LOUISE ERDRICH, *Tracks* (1988)

See also Home.

FAMILY

The family—that dear octopus from whose tentacles we never quite escape, nor, in our inmost hearts, ever quite wish to.

DODIE SMITH, *Dear Octopus* (1938)

Family is just accident. . . . They don't mean to get on your nerves. They don't even mean to be your family, they just are.

MARSHA NORMAN, *'night, Mother* (1983)

Call it a clan, call it a network, call it a tribe, call it a family. Whatever you call it, whoever you are, you need one.

JANE HOWARD, *Families* (1978)

Families will not be broken. Curse and expel them, send their children wandering, drown them in floods and fires, and old women will make songs out of all these sorrows and sit in the porches and sing them on mild evenings.

MARILYNNE ROBINSON, *Housekeeping* (1980)

Our family never had any hard luck, because nothing seemed hard luck to it, nor was it ever disgraced for there was nothing which it would acknowledge as disgrace.

BOX-CAR BERTHA, *Sister of the Road* (1937)

If the Koran is the soul of Islam, then perhaps the institution of the Muslim family might be described as its body.

ELIZABETH WARNOCK FERNEA, *Women and the Family in the Middle East* (1985)

What families have in common the world around is that they are the place where people learn who they are and how to be that way.

JEAN ILLSLEY CLARKE, *Self-Esteem: A Family Affair* (1978)

Family jokes, though rightly cursed by strangers, are the bond that keeps most families alive.

STELLA BENSON, *Pipers and a Dancer* (1924)

Heirlooms we don't have in our family. But stories we've got.

ROSE CHERNIN, in Kim Chernin, *In My Mother's House* (1983)

Like all cultures, one of the family's first jobs is to persuade its members they're special, more wonderful than the neighboring barbarians. The persuasion consists of stories showing family members demonstrating admirable traits, which it claims are family traits. Attention to the stories' actual truth is never the family's most compelling consideration. Encouraging belief is. The family's survival depends on the shared sensibility of its members.

ELIZABETH STONE, *Black Sheep and Kissing Cousins* (1988)

Within our family there was no such thing as a person who did not matter. Second cousins thrice removed mattered. We knew—and thriftily made use of—everybody's middle name. We knew who was buried where. We all mattered, and the dead most of all.

SHIRLEY ABBOTT, *Womenfolks: Growing Up Down South* (1983)

In the traditional family structure of Persia . . . one simply cannot discard close relatives just because one does not like them; rather one has to accommodate them, make allowances and accept them, like misfortune.

SHUSHA GUPPY, *The Blindfold Horse: Memories of a Persian Childhood* (1988)

Healthy families are our greatest national resource.

DOLORES CURRAN, *Traits of a Healthy Family* (1983)

A group of closely related persons living under one roof; it is a convenience, often a necessity, sometimes a pleasure, sometimes the reverse; but who first exalted it as admirable, an almost religious ideal?

ROSE MACAULAY, *My World My Wilderness* (1950)

To my way of thinking, the American family started to decline when parents began to communicate with their children. When we began to "rap," "feed into one another," "let things hang out" that mother didn't know about and would rather not.

ERMA BOMBECK, *If Life Is a Bowl of Cherries, What Am I Doing in the Pits?* (1971)

The family as an institution is *both* oppressive and protective and, depending on the issue, is experienced sometimes one way, sometimes the other—often in some mix of the two—by most people who live in families.

LILLIAN BRESLOW RUBIN, *Worlds of Pain* (1976)

Personal hatred and family affection are not incompatible; they often flourish and grow strong together.

WILLA CATHER, *Lucy Gayheart* (1935)

Family life! The United Nations is child's play compared to the tugs and splits and need to understand and forgive in any family.

MAY SARTON, *Kinds of Love* (1970)

We do not discuss the members of our family to their faces.

IVY COMPTON-BURNETT, *A House and Its Head* (1935)

In families there are frequently matters of which no one speaks, nor even alludes. There are no words for these matters. As the binding skeleton beneath the flesh is never acknowledged by us and, when at last it defines itself, is after all an obscenity.

JOYCE CAROL OATES, *I Lock My Door Upon Myself* (1990)

One may have staunch friends in one's own family, but one seldom has admirers.

WILLA CATHER, *The Song of the Lark* (1915)

It was the old psychosomatic side-step. Everyone in my family dances it at every opportunity. You've given me a splitting headache! You've given me indigestion! You've given me crotch rot! You've given me auditory hallucinations! You've given me a heart attack! You've given me cancer!

ERICA JONG, *Fear of Flying* (1973)

The men in this family seemed like garden flowers, sweet and colorful and quick to fade. . . . The women, by contrast, were like weeds—there were so many of them, and they lasted on and on with a minimal flowering, able to subsist on altogether less in the way of space, nourishment and hope.

JUDITH GROSSMAN, *Her Own Terms* (1988)

In some families, *please* is described as the magic word. In our house, however, it was *sorry*.

MARGARET LAURENCE, *A Bird in the House* (1964)

I know that family life in America is a minefield, an economic trap for women, a study in disappointment for both sexes.

ANNE ROIPHE, *Lovingkindness* (1987)

The particular human chain we're part of is central to our individual identity. Even if we loathe our families, in order to know ourselves, we seem to need to know about them, just as prologue. Not to know is to live with some of the disorientation and anxiety of the amnesiac.

ELIZABETH STONE, *Black Sheep and Kissing Cousins* (1988)

Comparison is a death knell to sibling harmony.

ELIZABETH FISHEL, *Sisters: Love and Rivalry Inside the Family and Beyond* (1979)

Intimacy between step-children and step-parents is indeed proverbially difficult.

LADY MURASAKI, *The Tale of Genji* (c. 1008)

Families composed of rugged individualists have to do things obliquely.

FLORENCE KING, *Confessions of a Failed Southern Lady* (1985)

Nobody who has not been in the interior of a family can say what the difficulties of any individual of that family may be.

JANE AUSTEN, *Emma* (1816)

See also Ancestors, Childhood, Children, Daughters, Father, Grandparents, Husband, Mother, Parents, Relationships, Roots, Sisters, Sons, Uncles, Wife.

FANATICISM

Without fanaticism one cannot accomplish anything.

EVA PERÓN, in *Time* (1951)

FANTASY

If one is lucky, a solitary fantasy can totally transform one million realities.

MAYA ANGELOU, *The Heart of a Woman* (1981)

If you have enough fantasies, you're ready, in the event that something happens.

SHEILA BALLANTYNE, *Norma Jean the Termite Queen* (1975)

See also Dreams, Imagination, Reverie.

FAREWELLS

Mayo was anxious to leave and like so many enthusiasts seemed liable to turn a social escape into a jail break if anything threatened to hinder him.

MARGERY ALLINGHAM, *The Mind Readers* (1965)

Good-byes breed a sort of distaste for whomever you say good-bye to; this hurts, you feel, this must not happen again.

ELIZABETH BOWEN, *The House in Paris* (1935)

Nothing is so dear as what you're about to leave.

JESSAMYN WEST, *The Life I Really Lived* (1979)

Every arrival foretells a leave-taking: every birth a death. Yet each death and departure comes to us as a surprise, a sorrow never anticipated. Life is a long series of farewells; only the circumstances should surprise us.

JESSAMYN WEST, *The Life I Really Lived* (1979)

Every day I shall put my papers in order and every day I shall say farewell. And the real farewell, when it comes, will only be a small outward confirmation of what has been accomplished within me from day to day.

ETTY HILLESUM, *An Interrupted Life: The Diaries of Etty Hillesum 1941–1943* (1983)

See also End, Parting.

FARMERS

A farmer is dependent on too many things outside his control; it makes for modesty.

BHARATI MUKHERJEE, *Jasmine* (1989)

See also Country.

FASHION

I base most of my fashion taste on what doesn't itch.

GILDA RADNER, *It's Always Something* (1989)

Fashion is architecture: it is a matter of proportions.

COCO CHANEL, in Marcel Haedrich, *Coco Chanel: Her Life, Her Secrets* (1972)

To call a fashion wearable is the kiss of death. No new fashion worth its salt is ever wearable.

EUGENIA SHEPPARD, in *New York Herald Tribune* (1960)

Fashion is made to become unfashionable.

COCO CHANEL, in *Life* (1957)

See also Appearance, Clothes, Dress, Elegance, Trends.

FASTIDIOUSNESS

There is a great amount of poetry in unconscious fastidiousness.

MARIANNE MOORE, "Critics and Connoisseurs," *Selected Poems* (1935)

See also Caution.

FATE

Thus strangely are our souls constructed and by such slight ligaments are we bound to prosperity or ruin.

MARY SHELLEY, *Frankenstein* (1818)

Lives that flash in sunshine, and lives that are born in tears, receive their hue from circumstances.

HARRIET A. JACOBS, *Incidents in the Life of a Slave Girl, Written by Herself* (1861)

Oh, how unconstantly our fortune turns. / One hour in joy, the next with sorrow mourns.

MARY DELARIVIER MANLEY, *The Royal Mischief* (1696)

These great turning-days of life cast no shadow before, slip by unconsciously. Only a trifle, a little turn of the rudder, and the ship goes to heaven or hell.

REBECCA HARDING DAVIS, "Life in the Iron-Mills," in *Atlantic Monthly* (1861)

Resolved to take Fate by the throat and shake a living out of her.

LOUISA MAY ALCOTT, in Ednah Dow Cheney, ed., *Louisa May Alcott, Her Life, Letters, and Journals* (1890)

You strain like a hooked fish against this fate, then slowly weaken. Your silver scales dim.

SHEILA BALLANTYNE, "Letters to the Darkness," *Life on Earth* (1988)

Fate is not an eagle, it creeps like a rat.

ELIZABETH BOWEN, *The House in Paris* (1935)

See also Destiny, Free Will, Luck.

FATHER

No music is so pleasant to my ears as that word—father.

LYDIA MARIA CHILD, *Philothea* (1836)

The sound of his father's voice was a necessity. He longed for the sight of his stooped shoulders as he had never, in the sharpest of his hunger, longed for food.

MARJORIE KINNAN RAWLINGS, *The Yearling* (1938)

Old as she was, she still missed her daddy sometimes.

GLORIA NAYLOR, *Mama Day* (1988)

I wanted him to cherish and approve of me, not as he had when I was a child, but as the woman I was, who had her own mind and had made her own choices.

ADRIENNE RICH, "Split at the Root," *Blood, Bread, and Poetry* (1986)

It doesn't matter who my father was; it matters who I *remember* he was.

ANNE SEXTON, "All God's Children Need Radios," in *Ms.* (1973)

Josephine had had a moment of absolute terror at the cemetery, while the coffin was lowered, to think that she and Constantia had done this thing without asking his permission. What would father say when he found out? For he was bound to find out sooner or later. He always did. "Buried. You two girls had me *buried!*"

KATHERINE MANSFIELD, "The Daughters of the Late Colonel," *The Garden Party* (1922)

See also Parents.

FATIGUE

At last, deathly tiredness drained him of all apprehension; so might a man fall asleep half-an-hour before he was to be woken by a firing squad.

NADINE GORDIMER, *July's People* (1981)

I am worn to a raveling.

BEATRIX POTTER, *The Tailor of Gloucester* (1901)

See also Sleep.

FEAR

Fear has a smell, as / Love does.

MARGARET ATWOOD, *Surfacing* (1972)

Fear is a question: What are you afraid of, and why? Just as the seed of health is in illness, because illness contains information, our fears are a treasure house of self-knowledge if we explore them.

MARILYN FERGUSON, *The Aquarian Conspiracy* (1980)

When fear seizes, change what you are doing. You are doing something wrong.

JEAN CRAIGHEAD GEORGE, *Julie of the Wolves* (1972)

To fear is one thing. To let fear grab you by the tail and swing you around is another.

KATHERINE PATERSON, *Jacob Have I Loved* (1980)

My knees could have been stirred with a spoon.

MARGARET HALSEY, *With Malice Toward Some* (1938)

She was always the kid who had to back down the ladder of the high dive.

PAULETTE BATES ALDEN, "Ladies Luncheon," *Feeding the Eagles* (1988)

Proust has pointed out that the predisposition to love creates its own objects: is this not true of fear?

ELIZABETH BOWEN, *Collected Impressions* (1950)

Great self-destruction follows upon unfounded fear.

URSULA K. LE GUIN, *The Lathe of Heaven* (1971)

What difference do it make if the thing you scared of is real or not?

TONI MORRISON, *Song of Solomon* (1977)

A wild beast has no need to leap in order to promote fear.

COLETTE, *Cheri* (1930)

I think what weakens people most is fear of wasting their strength.

ETTY HILLESUM, *An Interrupted Life: The Diaries of Etty Hillesum 1941–1943* (1983)

It's like the smarter you are, the more things can scare you.

KATHERINE PATERSON, Bridge to Terabithia (1977)

The sight of a cage is only frightening to the bird that has once been caught.

RACHEL FIELD, *All This and Heaven Too* (1939)

That fear of missing out on things makes you miss out on everything. Keeps you from reality.

ETTY HILLESUM, *An Interrupted Life: The Diaries of Etty Hillesum 1941–1943* (1983)

Was there no one over thirty-five who had not some secret agony, some white-faced fear? Half one's life one walked carelessly, certain that some day one would have one's heart's desire: and for the rest of it, one either goes empty, or walks carrying a full cup, afraid of every step.

HELEN WADDELL, Peter Abelard (1933)

I have not ceased being fearful, but I have ceased to let fear control me. I have accepted fear as a part of life, specifically the fear of change, the fear of the unknown, and I have gone ahead despite the pounding in the heart that says: turn back, turn back, you'll die if you venture too far.

ERICA JONG, in Janet Sternburg, ed., The Writer on Her Work, vol. 1 (1980)

A man from hell is not afraid of hot ashes.

DOROTHY GILMAN, Incident at Badamyâ (1989)

See also Anxiety, Phobias, Superstition, Worry.

FEELINGS

Better to be without logic than without feeling.

CHARLOTTE BRONTË, The Professor (1846)

Our feelings are our most genuine paths to knowledge.

AUDRE LORDE, in Claudia Tate, ed., Black Women Writers at Work (1983)

Only that which is deeply felt can change us. Rational arguments alone cannot penetrate the layers of fear and conditioning that comprise our crippling belief system.

MARILYN FERGUSON, The Aquarian Conspiracy (1980)

Our society allows people to be absolutely neurotic and totally out of touch with their feelings and everyone else's feelings, and yet be very respectable.

NTOZAKE SHANGE, in Claudia Tate, ed., Black Women Writers at Work (1983)

It was one of those dangerous moments when speech is at once sincere and deceptive—when feeling, rising high above its average depth, leaves flood-marks which are never reached again.

GEORGE ELIOT, The Mill on the Floss (1860)

Men and women make sad mistakes about their own symptoms, taking their vague uneasy longings, sometimes for genius, sometimes for religion, and oftener still for a mighty love.

GEORGE ELIOT, Middlemarch (1871)

The truth is that we can overhaul our surroundings, renovate our environment, talk a new game, join a new club, far more easily than we can change the way we respond emotionally. It is easier to change behavior than feelings about that behavior.

ELLEN GOODMAN, Turning Points (1979)

An astonishing observation: it is precisely for feeling that one needs time, and not for thought. . . . Feeling is apparently more demanding than thought.

ANNA TSETSAEYVA (c. 1927), in Tillie Olsen, Silences (1978)

You cannot make yourself feel something you do not feel, but you can make yourself do right in spite of your feelings.

PEARL BUCK, To My Daughters, With Love (1967)

The best way of forgetting how you think you feel is to concentrate on what you know you know.

MARY STEWART, This Rough Magic (1964)

Why is it that people who cannot show feeling presume that that is a strength and not a weakness?

MAY SARTON, At Seventy: A Journal (1982)

People who cannot feel punish those who do.

MAY SARTON, Mrs. Stevens Hears the Mermaids Singing (1965)

Feelings are untidy.

ESTHER HAUTZIG, The Endless Steppe (1968)

To have felt too much is to end in feeling nothing.

DOROTHY THOMPSON, in Vincent Sheean, Dorothy and Red (1963)

See also Emotions.

FICTION

Fortunately, there is more to life than death. There is for one thing, fiction. A thousand thousand characters to be sent marching out into the world to divert time from its forward gallop to the terrible horizon.

FAY WELDON, *Down Among the Women* (1971)

Fiction reveals truths that reality obscures.

JESSAMYN WEST, in *Reader's Digest* (1973)

Fiction supplies the only philosophy that many readers know; it establishes their ethical, social, and material standards; it confirms them in their prejudices or opens their minds to a wider world.

DOROTHEA BRANDE, *Becoming a Writer* (1934)

"The proper stuff of fiction" does not exist; everything is the proper stuff of fiction, every feeling, every thought; every quality of brain and spirit is drawn upon; no perception comes amiss.

VIRGINIA WOOLF, "Modern Fiction," *The Common Reader* (1925)

Fiction is about everything human and we are made out of dust, and if you scorn getting yourself dusty, then you shouldn't write fiction. It isn't grand enough for you.

FLANNERY O'CONNOR, "The Nature and Aim of Fiction," in Sally and Robert Fitzgerald, eds., *Mystery and Manners* (1969)

Fiction is not a dream. Nor is it guesswork. It is imagining based on facts, and the facts must be accurate or the work of imagining will not stand up.

MARGARET CULKIN BANNING, in *The Writer* (1960)

Fiction is like a spider's web, attached ever so lightly perhaps, but still attached to life at all four corners.

VIRGINIA WOOLF, *A Room of One's Own* (1929)

Science fiction properly conceived, like all serious fiction, however funny, is a way of trying to describe what is in fact going on, what people actually do and feel, how people relate to everything else in this vast sack, this belly of the universe, this womb of things to be and tomb of things that were, this unending story.

URSULA K. LE GUIN, *Dancing at the Edge of the World* (1989)

The two worst sins of bad taste in fiction are pornography and sentimentality. One is too much sex and the other too much sentiment.

FLANNERY O'CONNOR, in Sally Fitzgerald, ed., *The Habit of Being* (1979)

See also Fictional Characters, Literature, Novels, Stories, Writers, Writing.

FICTIONAL CHARACTERS

Fictional characters, he had lately found, were generally more interesting dinner companions than flesh-and-blood ones.

MARTHA GRIMES, *The Old Silent* (1989)

I live with the people I create and it has always made my essential loneliness less keen.

CARSON MCCULLERS, *The Square Root of Wonderful* (1958)

To move among this bright, strange, often fabulous herd of beings, to summon them at my will, to fasten them on to paper like flies, that they may decorate it, this is the pleasure of writing.

ROSE MACAULAY, *Personal Pleasures* (1936)

I don't think I ever relinquish a person I have known, and surely not my fictional characters. I see them, I hear them, with a clarity that I would call hallucinatory if hallucination didn't mean something else. . . . A character whom we create can never die, any more than a friend can die, if you understand what I mean. . . . Through [my characters] I've lived many parallel lives.

MARGUERITE YOURCENAR, *With Open Eyes: Conversations With Matthieu Galey* (1980)

One of the strangest quirks of the human mind is its capacity for being moved to tears, laughter, anger, anxiety, joy by a "person" who exists nowhere except in imagination!

JANE FITZ-RANDOLPH, *How to Write for Children and Young Adults* (1980)

It is hard to make your adversaries real people unless you recognize yourself in them—in which case, if you don't watch out, they cease to be adversaries.

FLANNERY O'CONNOR, in Sally Fitzgerald, ed., *The Habit of Being* (1979)

I remember how surprised I was when my first novel was about to be published and I was informed that I could be sued for anything any one of my characters said. "But I often don't agree with what they say," I protested. The lawyer was not interested in the clear distinction I make between my own voice and the voices of my characters. Neither, I have found, are many of my readers.

JANE RULE, "Sexuality in Literature," *Outlander* (1981)

See also Fiction.

FILMS

People have been modeling their lives after films for years, but the medium is somehow unsuited to moral lessons, cautionary tales, or polemics of any kind.

RENATA ADLER, *A Year in the Dark* (1969)

If you're afraid of movies that excite your senses, you're afraid of movies.

PAULINE KAEL (1978), in *Newsweek* (1991)

I wouldn't say when you've seen one Western you've seen the lot; but when you've seen the lot you get the feeling you've seen one.

KATHARINE WHITEHORN, "Decoding the West," *Sunday Best* (1976)

Movies have been doing so much of the same thing—in slightly different ways—for so long that few of the possibilities of this great hybrid art have yet been explored.

PAULINE KAEL, *Going Steady* (1968)

Audiences will get just as tired of people wrestling on a bed as they did of Tom Mix kissing his horse.

MARY ASTOR, *A Life on Film* (1967)

The rich will always be with us. Especially on our movie screens.

KATHI MAIO, *Feminist in the Dark* (1988)

Me no Leica.

CAROLINE LEJEUNE, review of the film *I Am a Camera* (1955)

FIRE

The fire rose in two branched flames like the golden antlers of some enchanted stag.

KATHERINE MANSFIELD (1919), *Journal of Katherine Mansfield* (1927)

Nothing smelled so good or danced so well as a birch fire.

KATHERINE PATERSON, *Lyddie* (1991)

People who light fires on the slightest provocation are always the nicest. There's something comforting about fires.

JANE ENGLAND, in *New York Times* (1948)

Fire destroys that which feeds it.

SIMONE WEIL, *The Notebooks of Simone Weil* (1951)

FISHING

I really fished mainly because I wanted to be alone on the middle of the lake. . . . Sometimes a fish jumped nearby, as though it knew it was safe.

SUSAN ALLEN TOTH, *Blooming* (1978)

The curious thing about fishing is you never want to go home. If you catch something, you can't stop. If you don't catch anything, you hate to leave in case something might bite.

GLADYS TABER, in *Ladies' Home Journal* (1941)

The man who goes fishing gets something more than the fish he catches.

MARY ASTOR, *A Life on Film* (1967)

See also Hobbies.

FLATTERY

Flattery is praise without foundation.

ELIZA LESLIE, *Miss Leslie's Behavior Book: A Guide and Manual for Ladies* (1859)

The aim of flattery is to soothe and encourage us by assuring us of the truth of an opinion we have already formed about ourselves.

EDITH SITWELL, in Elizabeth Salter, *The Last Years of a Rebel* (1967)

Words really flattering are not those which we prepare but those which escape us unthinkingly.

NINON DE LENCLOS (c. 1660), *Letters* (1870)

It is happy for you that you possess the talent of flattering with delicacy. May I ask whether these pleasing attentions proceed from the impulse of the moment, or are the result of previous study?

JANE AUSTEN, *Pride and Prejudice* (1813)

See also Praise, Speech.

FLAWS

Your thorns are the best part of you.

MARIANNE MOORE, *Selected Poems* (1935)

For when one's outward lot is perfect, the sense of inward imperfection is the more pressing.

GEORGE ELIOT, letter (1872), in J. W. Cross, *George Eliot's Life as Related in Her Letters and Journals* (1884)

No honey for me, if it comes with a bee.

SAPPHO (6th century B.C.), in C. R. Haines, *Sappho: The Poems and Fragments* (1926)

You know, some people fall right through the hole in their lives. It's invisible, but they come to it after time, never knowing where.

LOUISE ERDRICH, *Love Medicine* (1984)

See also Character, Personality.

FLIRTATION

Flirtation is merely an expression of considered desire coupled with an admission of its impracticability.

MARYA MANNES, *But Will It Sell?* (1964)

See also Seduction.

FLOWERS

Flowers and plants are silent presences; they nourish every sense except the ear.

MAY SARTON, *Plant Dreaming Deep* (1958–1967)

People from a planet without flowers would think we must be mad with joy the whole time to have such things about us.

IRIS MURDOCH, *A Fairly Honorable Defeat* (1970)

Do you think amethysts can be the souls of good violets?

L. M. MONTGOMERY, *Anne of Green Gables* (1908)

I had not thought of violets of late, / The wild, shy kind that springs beneath your feet / In wistful April days.

ALICE DUNBAR-NELSON, "Violets," in *The Monthly Review* (1895)

We once had a lily here that bore *108* flowers on one stalk: it was photographed naturally for all the gardening papers. The bees came from miles and miles, and there were the most disgraceful Bacchanalian scenes: bees hardly able to find their way home.

EDITH SITWELL, *Selected Letters* (1970)

Forsythia is pure joy. There is not an ounce, not a glimmer of sadness or even *knowledge* in forsythia. Pure, undiluted, untouched joy.

ANNE MORROW LINDBERGH, *Bring Me a Unicorn* (1971)

Dandelions meet me wherever I am they overrun Germany's railway embankments dusty corners fields seize even well-trimmed gardens through hedges leaves like fine saws new flowers every day have the wind to carry them over rivers walled boundaries stick my fingers together when I try to fend them off.

SARAH KIRSCH, "Dandelions for Chains," in Joanna Bankier and Deirdre Lashgari, eds., *Women Poets of the World* (1983)

Arranging a bowl of flowers in the morning can give a sense of quiet in a crowded day—like writing a poem, or saying a prayer.

ANNE MORROW LINDBERGH, *Gift From the Sea* (1955)

I like to see flowers growing, but when they are gathered, they cease to please. I look on them as things rootless and perishable; their likeness to life makes me sad. I never offer flowers to those I love; I never wish to receive them from hands dear to me.

CHARLOTTE BRONTË, *Villette* (1853)

See also Gardening, Nature, Plants.

FLYING

This new sport is comparable to no other. It is, in my opinion, one of the most intoxicating forms of sport, and will, I am sure, become one of the most popular. Many of us will perish before then, but that prospect will not dismay the braver spirits. . . . It is so delicious to fly like a bird!

MARIE MARVINGT, in "The Sky Women," *Collier's* (1911)

Flying may not be all plain sailing, but the fun of it is worth the price.

AMELIA EARHART, *The Fun of It* (1932)

I feel about airplanes the way I feel about diets. It seems to me that they are wonderful things for other people to go on.

JEAN KERR, *The Snake Has All the Lines* (1958)

See also Travel.

FOOD

Food is an important part of a balanced diet.

FRAN LEBOWITZ, *Metropolitan Life* (1978)

Fake food—I mean those patented substances chemically flavored and mechanically bulked out to kill the appetite and deceive the gut—is unnatural, almost immoral, a bane to good eating and good cooking.

JULIA CHILD, *Julia Child and Company* (1978)

Another sad comestive truth is that the best foods are the products of infinite and wearying trouble. The trouble need not be taken by the consumer, but someone, ever since the Fall, has had to take it.

ROSE MACAULAY, *Personal Pleasures* (1936)

Cold soup is a very tricky thing and it is a rare hostess who can carry it off. More often than not the dinner guest is left with the impression that had he only come a little earlier he could have gotten it while it was still hot.

FRAN LEBOWITZ, *Metropolitan Life* (1978)

The soup, thin and dark and utterly savorless, tasted as if it had been drained out of the umbrella stand.

MARGARET HALSEY, *With Malice Toward Some* (1938)

An omelet so light we had to lay our knives across it and even then it struggled.

MARGARET HALSEY, *With Malice Toward Some* (1938)

Cheese that is required by law to append the word *food* to its title does not go well with red wine or fruit.

FRAN LEBOWITZ, *Metropolitan Life* (1978)

As for butter versus margarine, I trust cows more than chemists.

JOAN GUSSOW, in *New York Times* (1986)

To lift off the cover of a tomato-y mixture and let it bubble up mushroom and basil under my nose does a lot to counteract the many subtle efforts a part of me makes to punish myself for all those worst of my shortcomings—those I can neither name nor find a shape for. Terrible brown ghosts with sinews like bedsprings.

MARY VIRGINIA MICKA, *The Cazenovia Journal* (1986)

Tomatoes and oregano make it Italian; wine and tarragon make it French. Sour cream makes it Russian; lemon and cinnamon make it Greek. Soy sauce makes it Chinese; garlic makes it good.

ALICE MAY BROCK, *Alice's Restaurant Cookbook* (1969)

Your truffles must come to the table in their own stock. . . . And as you break open this jewel sprung from a poverty-stricken soil, imagine—if you have never visited it—the desolate kingdom where it rules.

COLETTE, *Prisons and Paradise* (1932)

[They] hunted mushrooms with Moravian cunning and passion.

PATRICIA HAMPL, *A Romantic Education* (1981)

While it is undeniably true that people love a surprise, it is equally true that they are seldom pleased to suddenly and without warning happen upon a series of prunes in what they took to be a normal loin of pork.

FRAN LEBOWITZ, *Metropolitan Life* (1978)

Roast Beef, Medium, is not only a food. It is a philosophy.

EDNA FERBER, *Roast Beef Medium* (1913)

Japanese food is very pretty and undoubtedly a suitable cuisine in Japan, which is largely populated by people of below average size. Hostesses hell-bent on serving such food to occidentals would be well advised to supplement it with something more substantial and to keep in mind that almost everybody likes french fries.

FRAN LEBOWITZ, *Metropolitan Life* (1978)

The effect of eating too much lettuce is "soporific."

BEATRIX POTTER, *Flopsy Bunnies* (1902)

Vegetables are interesting but lack a sense of purpose when unaccompanied by a good cut of meat.

FRAN LEBOWITZ, *Metropolitan Life* (1978)

Bread that must be sliced with an ax is bread that is too nourishing.

FRAN LEBOWITZ, *Metropolitan Life* (1978)

Fancy cream puffs so soon after breakfast. The very idea made one shudder. All the same, two minutes later Jose and Laura were licking their fingers with that absorbed inward look that only comes from whipped cream.

KATHERINE MANSFIELD, title story, *The Garden Party* (1922)

He said I was the most sensitive person he had ever seen—that I belonged to the hyper-hyper type and we *rarely* survive! Of course I was examined, and so was the éclair, and they found that the éclair contains *every*thing my system lacks. So I take three a day and I feel like a new woman.

RUTH DRAPER, "Doctors and Diets," *The Art of Ruth Draper* (1960)

Pistachio nuts, the red ones, cure any problem.

PAULA DANZIGER, *The Pistachio Prescription* (1978)

Food is the most primitive form of comfort.

SHEILAH GRAHAM, *A State of Heat* (1972)

Food for all is a necessity. Food should not be a merchandise, to be bought and sold as jewels are bought and sold by those who have the money to buy. Food is a human necessity, like water and air, and it should be available.

PEARL BUCK, *To My Daughters, With Love* (1967)

See also Chocolate, Cooking, Diet, Eating, Oysters.

FOOLS

People do not wish to appear foolish; to avoid the appearance of foolishness, they were willing to remain actually fools.

ALICE WALKER, in Janet Sternburg, ed., *The Writer on Her Work*, vol. 1 (1980)

Why is it that fools always have the instinct to hunt out the unpleasant secrets of life, and the hardiness to mention them?

EMILY EDEN, *The Semi-Attached Couple* (1928)

The fool shouts loudly, thinking to impress the world.

MARIE DE FRANCE (12th century), in Jeanette Beer, tr., *Medieval Fables of Marie de France* (1981)

To wish to act like angels while we are still in this world is nothing but folly.

ST. TERESA OF AVILA (1575), in Abbé Rodolphe Hoornaert, *St. Teresa in Her Writings* (1931)

It is in the nature of foolish reasonings to seem good to the foolish reasoner.

GEORGE ELIOT, *Impressions of Theophrastus Such* (1879)

When in doubt, make a fool of yourself. There is a microscopically thin line between being brilliantly creative and acting like the most gigantic idiot on earth. So what the hell, leap.

CYNTHIA HEIMEL, "Lower Manhattan Survival Tactics," in *Village Voice* (1983)

The first prerogative of an artist in any medium is to make a fool of himself.

PAULINE KAEL, *I Lost It at the Movies* (1965)

No one ever found wisdom without also being a fool. Writers, alas, have to be fools in public, while the rest of the human race can cover its tracks.

ERICA JONG, in Janet Sternburg, ed., *The Writer on Her Work,* vol. 1 (1980)

FORCE

How pure are those who have never forced anything open!

COLETTE, *La naissance du jour* (1928)

Now who is to decide between "Let it be" and "Force it"?

KATHERINE MANSFIELD (1914), *Journal of Katherine Mansfield* (1927)

You can't push a wave onto the shore any faster than the ocean brings it in.

SUSAN STRASBERG, *Bittersweet* (1980)

See also Domination, Violence.

FORESIGHT

Oh, if at every moment of our lives we could know the consequences of some of the utterings, thoughts and deeds that seem so trivial and unimportant at the time! And should we not conclude from such examples that there is no such thing in life as unimportant moments devoid of meaning for the future?

ISABELLE EBERHARDT (1901), *The Passionate Nomad* (1988)

It is seldom in life that one knows that a coming event is to be of crucial importance.

ANYA SETON, *The Turquoise* (1946)

In various and different circumstances certain objects and individuals are going to turn out to be vital. The wager of survival cannot, by its nature, reveal which, in advance of events.

NADINE GORDIMER, *July's People* (1981)

See also Preparedness.

FORGETTING

I shall go the way of the open sea, / To the lands I knew before you came, / And the cool clean breezes shall blow from me / The memory of your name.

LAURENCE HOPE, "The End," *Stars of the Desert* (1903)

See also Memory.

FORGIVENESS

Forgiveness is the act of admitting we are like other people.

CHRISTINA BALDWIN, *Life's Companion, Journal Writing as a Spiritual Quest* (1990)

If you haven't forgiven yourself something, how can you forgive others?

DOLORES HUERTA, in Barbara L. Baer, "Stopping Traffic: One Woman's Cause," *The Progressive* (1975)

If you understand something, you don't forgive it, you are the thing itself: forgiveness is for what you *don't* understand.

DORIS LESSING, "To Room Nineteen," *A Man and Two Women* (1963)

I realize that patriotism is not enough. I must have no hatred or bitterness towards anyone.

EDITH CAVELL, on the night before her execution (1915)

It is by forgiving that one is forgiven.

MOTHER TERESA, in Kathryn Spink, *For the Brotherhood of Man Under the Fatherhood of God* (1980)

I have resigned myself to the fact that Rick is always going to hate me because he has committed a grave offense against me, for which he will never forgive me.

SONIA JOHNSON, *From Housewife to Heretic* (1981)

If we forgive God for his crime against us, which is to have made us finite creatures, He will forgive our crime against him, which is that we are finite creatures.

SIMONE WEIL, *First and Last Notebooks* (1970)

Life had taught him that the unforgivable was usually the most easily forgiven.

P. D. JAMES, *Death of an Expert Witness* (1977)

I think one should forgive and remember. . . . If you forgive and forget in the usual sense, you're just driving what you remember into the subconscious; it stays there and festers. But to look, even regularly, upon what you remember and *know* you've forgiven is achievement.

FAITH BALDWIN, *The West Wind* (1962)

It makes you feel very virtuous when you forgive people, doesn't it?

L. M. MONTGOMERY, *Anne of Green Gables* (1908)

Forgiveness is the one unpardonable sin.

DOROTHY L. SAYERS, *The Five Red Herrings* (1931)

See also Mercy.

FRANCE

In France, cooking is a serious art form and a national sport.

JULIA CHILD, in *New York Times* (1986)

It may be the only country in the world where the rich are sometimes brilliant.

LILLIAN HELLMAN, *An Unfinished Woman* (1969)

See also Europe, Paris.

FREEDOM

Freedom breeds freedom. Nothing else does.

ANNE ROE, *The Making of a Scientist* (1952)

Freedom is fragile and must be protected. To sacrifice it, even as a temporary measure, is to betray it.

GERMAINE GREER, *The Female Eunuch* (1971)

There is nothing inevitable. The actions of the past operate at every instant and so, at every instant, does freedom.

NAN SHIN, *Diary of a Zen Nun* (1986)

Men would rather be starving and free than fed in bonds.

PEARL BUCK, *What America Means to Me* (1943)

None who have always been free can understand the terrible fascinating power of the hope of freedom to those who are not free.

PEARL BUCK, *What America Means to Me* (1943)

Freedom only for the supporters of the government—only for the members of one party, however numerous they may be—is no freedom at all. Freedom is always and exclusively for one who thinks differently. Not because of any fanatical concept of "justice" but because all that is instructive, wholesome and purifying in political freedom depends on this characteristic.

ROSA LUXEMBURG, *The Russian Revolution* (1916)

While any one is base, none can be entirely free and noble.

MARGARET FULLER, *Woman in the Nineteenth Century* (1845)

There are only two kinds of freedom in the world: the freedom of the rich and powerful, and the freedom of the artist and the monk who renounces possessions.

ANAÏS NIN, *The Diary of Anaïs Nin,* vol. 3 (1939–1944)

Only on the surface of things have I ever trod the beaten path. So long as I could keep from hurting anyone else, I have lived, as completely as it was possible, the life of my choice. I have been free. . . . I have done the work I wished to do for the sake of that work alone.

ELLEN GLASGOW, *The Woman Within* (1954)

As far as your self-control goes, as far goes your freedom.

MARIE VON EBNER-ESCHENBACH, *Aphorisms* (1905)

A nation has character only when it is free.

MADAME DE STAËL, *De la littérature* (1800)

When the freedom they wished for most was freedom from responsibility, then Athens ceased to be free and was never free again.

EDITH HAMILTON, *The Greek Way* (1930)

Total freedom is never what one imagines and, in fact, hardly exists. It comes as a shock in life to learn that we usually only exchange one set of restrictions for another. The second set, however, is self-chosen, and therefore easier to accept.

ANNE MORROW LINDBERGH, *Hour of Gold, Hour of Lead* (1973)

All at once the silence and the solitude were touched by wild music, thin as air, the faraway gabbling of geese flying at night. Presently I caught sight of them as they streamed across the face of the moon, the high, excited clamor of their voices tingling through the night, and suddenly I saw, in one of those rare moments of insight, what it means to be wild and free.

MARTHA REBEN, *A Sharing of Joy* (1963)

See also Independence, Liberation, Liberty, Self-Determination.

FREE WILL

He who believes in freedom of the will, has never loved and never hated.

MARIE VON EBNER-ESCHENBACH, *Aphorisms* (1905)

See also Fate.

FRIENDLINESS

I'm not against friendliness, she said, I'm not even against Americans.

GRACE PALEY, *Enormous Changes at the Last Minute* (1974)

You can't always be friendly. It's impossible, there isn't the time.

TOVE JANSSON, *Tales from Moominvalley* (1963)

See also Kindness.

FRIENDSHIP

It seems to me that trying to live without friends is like milking a bear to get cream for your morning coffee. It is a whole lot of trouble, and then not worth much after you get it.

ZORA NEALE HURSTON, *Dust Tracks on a Road* (1942)

Give me one friend, just one, who meets / The needs of all my varying moods.

ESTHER M. CLARK, "A Plea," *Verses by a Commonplace Person* (1906)

Each friend represents a world in us, a world possibly not born until they arrive, and it is only by this meeting that a new world is born.

ANAÏS NIN, *The Diary of Anaïs Nin,* vol. 2 (1934–1939)

I felt it shelter to speak to you.

EMILY DICKINSON, letter (1878), in Mabel Loomis Todd, *Letters of Emily Dickinson* (1894)

A friend can tell you things you don't want to tell yourself.

FRANCES WARD WELLER, *Boat Song* (1987)

In a world more and more polluted by the lying of politicians and the illusions of the media, I occasionally crave to hear and tell the truth. To borrow a beautiful phrase from Friedrich Nietzsche, I look upon my friend as "the beautiful enemy" who alone is able to offer me total candor. Friendship is by its very nature freer of deceit than any other relationship we can know because it is the bond least affected by striving for power, physical pleasure, or material profit, most liberated from any oath of duty or of constancy.

FRANCINE DU PLESSIX GRAY, in Adelaide Bry, *Friendship* (1979)

I always felt that the great high privilege, relief and comfort of friendship was that one had to explain nothing.

KATHERINE MANSFIELD, in Antony Alpers, *Katherine Mansfield* (1954)

Yes'm, old friends is always best, 'less you can catch a new one that's fit to make an old one out of.

SARAH ORNE JEWETT, *The Country of the Pointed Firs* (1896)

Even where the affections are not strongly moved by any superior excellence, the companions of our childhood always possess a certain power over our minds which hardly any later friend can obtain.

MARY SHELLEY, *Frankenstein* (1818)

She found to her surprise that an old friend is not always the person whom it is easiest to make a confidant of: there was the barrier of remembered communication under other circumstances—there was the dislike of being pitied and informed by one who had been long wont to allow her the superiority.

GEORGE ELIOT, *Middlemarch* (1871)

Only solitary men know the full joys of friendship. Others have their family; but to a solitary and an exile his friends are everything.

WILLA CATHER, *Shadows on the Rock* (1931)

Friendship with oneself is all-important, because without it one cannot be friends with anyone else in the world.

ELEANOR ROOSEVELT, in *Ladies' Home Journal* (1944)

There was a definite process by which one made people into friends, and it involved talking to them and listening to them for hours at a time.

REBECCA WEST, *The Thinking Reed* (1936)

Two may talk together under the same roof for many years, yet never really meet; and two others at first speech are old friends.

MARY CATHERWOOD, "Marianson," *Mackinac and Lake Stories* (1899)

Really, one has some friends, and when one comes to think about it, it is impossible to tell how one ever became friendly with them.

FRANÇOISE MALLET-JORIS, *A Letter to Myself* (1964)

Friendships begin with liking or gratitude— roots that can be pulled up.

GEORGE ELIOT, *Daniel Deronda* (1874)

It is wise to apply the oil of refined politeness to the mechanism of friendship.

COLETTE, *The Pure and the Impure* (1932)

You can keep your friends by not giving them away.

MARY PETTIBONE POOLE, *A Glass Eye at a Keyhole* (1938)

What I cannot love, I overlook. Is that real friendship?

ANAÏS NIN, *The Diary of Anaïs Nin*, vol. 5 (1947–1955)

Friendship, which is of its nature a delicate thing, fastidious, slow of growth, is easily checked, will hesitate, demur, recoil where love, good old blustering love, bowls ahead and blunders through every obstacle.

COLETTE, *My Apprenticeships* (1936)

Friendship is far more delicate than love. Quarrels and fretful complaints are attractive in the last, offensive in the first. And the very things which heap fuel on the fire of ardent passion, choke and extinguish sober and true regard. On the other hand, time, which is sure to *destroy* that love of which half certainly depends on *desire,* is as sure to increase a friendship founded on talents, warm with esteem, and ambitious of success for the object of it.

HESTER LYNCH PIOZZI (1820), in Oswald G. Knapp, ed., *The Intimate Letters of Hester Piozzi and Penelope Pennington 1788–1821* (1914)

Often intimacies between women go backwards, beginning with revelations and ending up in small talk without loss of esteem.

ELIZABETH BOWEN, The Death of the Heart (1938)

Writers seldom choose as friends those self-contained characters who are never in trouble, never unhappy or ill, never make mistakes, and always count their change when it is handed to them.

CATHERINE DRINKER BOWEN, in *Atlantic* (1957)

She didn't know how to be friends with more than one person at a time.

MARY CALHOUN, *Julie's Tree* (1988)

It is the steady and merciless increase of occupations, the augmented speed at which we are always trying to live, the crowding of each day with more work than it can profitably hold, which has cost us, among other good things, the undisturbed enjoyment of friends. Friendship takes time, and we have no time to give it.

AGNES REPPLIER, *In the Dozy Hours* (1894)

Business, you know, may bring money, but friendship hardly ever does.

JANE AUSTEN, *Emma* (1816)

The pleasures of intimacy in friendship depend far more on external circumstances than people of a sentimental turn of mind are willing to concede; and when constant companionship ceases to suit the convenience of both parties, the chances are that it will be dropped on the first favorable opportunity.

HESTER LYNCH PIOZZI (1783), in A. Hayward, ed., *Autobiography, Letters, and Literary Remains of Mrs. Piozzi (Thrale), vol. 1* (1861)

Friendship has no civil, and few emotional, rights in our society.

CHRISTINA BALDWIN, One to One (1977)

Oh dear—Oh dear—where are my people? With whom have I been happiest? With nobody in particular. It has all been mush of a mushness.

KATHERINE MANSFIELD (1918), Journal of Katherine Mansfield (1927)

True friendship is never serene.

MARIE DE RABUTIN-CHANTAL, MARQUISE DE SÉVIGNÉ (1671), Letters of Madame de Sévigné to Her Daughter and Her Friends (1811)

Though friendship is not quick to burn, / It is explosive stuff.

MAY SARTON, "Friendship: The Storms," A Grain of Mustard Seed (1971)

See also Intimacy, Lovers, Relationships, Togetherness.

FRUGALITY

Frugality without creativity is deprivation.

AMY DACYCZYN, "You Can Afford Your Dream," in Parade (1991)

See also Miserliness.

FUNCTION

Recognition of function always precedes recognition of being.

RITA MAE BROWN, Starting From Scratch (1988)

FUNERALS

Alas, poor Yorick! How surprised he would be to see how his counterpart of today is whisked off to a funeral parlor and is in short order sprayed, sliced, pierced, pickled, trussed, trimmed, creamed, waxed, painted, rouged and neatly dressed—transformed from a common corpse into a Beautiful Memory Picture.

JESSICA MITFORD, The American Way of Death (1963)

O death, where is thy sting? O grave, where is thy victory? Where, indeed. Many a badly stung survivor, faced with the aftermath of some relative's funeral, has ruefully concluded that the victory has been won hands down by a funeral establishment—in disastrously unequal battle.

JESSICA MITFORD, The American Way of Death (1963)

See also Death.

FUTILITY

It's but little good you'll do a-watering the last year's crop.

GEORGE ELIOT, Adam Bede (1859)

You can't make souffle rise twice.

ALICE ROOSEVELT LONGWORTH, in James T. Patterson, Mr. Republican (1972)

An ass may bray a good while before he shakes the stars down.

GEORGE ELIOT, Romola (1862)

See also Uselessness.

FUTURE

The future bears a great resemblance to the past, only more so.

FAITH POPCORN, The Popcorn Report (1991)

The future is made of the same stuff as the present.

SIMONE WEIL, On Science, Necessity, and the Love of God (1968)

The future was plump with promise.

MAYA ANGELOU, All God's Children Need Traveling Shoes (1986)

Our faith in the present dies out long before our faith in the future.

RUTH BENEDICT, in Margaret Mead, An Anthropologist at Work: Writings of Ruth Benedict (1959)

The wave of the future is coming and there is no stopping it.

ANNE MORROW LINDBERGH, The Wave of the Future (1940)

We grow in time to trust the future for our answers.

RUTH BENEDICT, in Margaret Mead, An Anthropologist at Work: Writings of Ruth Benedict (1959)

You can trust a crystal ball about as far as you can throw it.

<small>FAITH POPCORN</small>, *The Popcorn Report* (1991)

We all want to leave our children the Garden of Eden and we wind up giving them hardscrabble.

<small>RITA MAE BROWN</small>, *Southern Discomfort* (1982)

Children of yesterday, heirs of tomorrow, / What are you weaving? Labor and sorrow? / Look to your looms again; faster and faster / Fly the great shuttles prepared by the Master. / Life's in the loom! Room for it, room!

<small>MARY ARTEMISIA LATHBURY</small>, "Song of Hope," *Poems of Mary Artemisia Lathbury* (1915)

If we can recognize that change and uncertainty are basic principles, we can greet the future and the transformation we are undergoing with the understanding that *we do not know enough to be pessimistic.*

<small>HAZEL HENDERSON</small>, *The Politics of the Solar Age* (1981)

See also Past, Present, Time, Tomorrow.

G

GAIETY

There is nothing more tedious than a constant round of gaiety.

MARGERY SHARP, *The Rescuers* (1959)

See also Parties.

GARDENING

Gardening has compensations out of all proportion to its goals. It is creation in the pure sense.

PHYLLIS MCGINLEY, *The Province of the Heart* (1959)

Gardening is not a rational act.

MARGARET ATWOOD, "Unearthing Suite," *Bluebeard's Egg* (1986)

Gardening is an exercise in optimism. Sometimes, it is the triumph of hope over experience.

MARINA SCHINZ, *Visions of Paradise* (1985)

The trouble with gardening is that it does not remain an avocation. It becomes an obsession.

PHYLLIS MCGINLEY, *The Province of the Heart* (1959)

Working in the garden . . . gives me a profound feeling of inner peace. Nothing here is in a hurry. There is no rush toward accomplishment, no blowing of trumpets. Here is the great mystery of life and growth. Everything is changing, growing, aiming at something, but silently, unboastfully, taking its time.

RUTH STOUT, *How to Have a Green Thumb Without an Aching Back* (1955)

I think this is what hooks one on gardening: it is the closest one can come to being present at the Creation.

PHYLLIS THEROUX, in *Reader's Digest* (1979)

We have descended into the garden and caught three hundred slugs. How I love the mixture of the beautiful and the squalid in gardening. It makes it so lifelike.

EVELYN UNDERHILL, *The Letters of Evelyn Underhill* (1943)

Walter would not tolerate an unhealthy or badly grown plant and if he saw anything that wasn't looking happy he pulled it up. Often I would go out and find a row of sick looking plants laid out like a lot of dead rats.

MARGERY FISH, *We Made a Garden* (1956)

Firmness in all aspects is a most important quality when gardening, not only in planting but in pruning, dividing and tying up. Plants are like babies, they know when an amateur is handling them.

MARGERY FISH, *We Made a Garden* (1956)

Nature soon takes over if the gardener is absent.

PENELOPE HOBHOUSE, *The Country Gardener* (1989)

I wanted no one lifting a finger in that garden unless he loved doing it. What if Fred had hired a man to dig those trenches and it had turned out that he didn't love to dig? Who could eat that kind of asparagus?

RUTH STOUT, *How to Have a Green Thumb Without an Aching Back* (1955)

To create a garden is to search for a better world. In our effort to improve on nature, we are guided by a vision of paradise. Whether the result is a horticultural masterpiece or only a modest vegetable patch, it is based on the expectation of a glorious future. This hope for the future is at the heart of all gardening.

MARINA SCHINZ, *Visions of Paradise* (1985)

See also Gardens.

GARDENS

Gardens are the result of a collaboration between art and nature.

PENELOPE HOBHOUSE, *Garden Style* (1988)

O the green things growing, the green things growing, / The faint sweet smell of the green things growing!

DINAH MULOCK CRAIK, "Green Things Growing," *Mulock's Poems, New and Old* (1888)

I love spring anywhere, but if I could choose I would always greet it in a garden.

RUTH STOUT, *How to Have a Green Thumb Without an Aching Back* (1955)

The kiss of sun for pardon, / The song of the birds for mirth, / One is nearer God's Heart in a garden / Than anywhere else on earth.

DOROTHY GURNEY, "God's Garden," *Poems* (1913)

Every flower holds the whole mystery in its short cycle, and in the garden we are never far away from death, the fertilizing, good, *creative* death.

MAY SARTON, *Journal of a Solitude* (1973)

A garden is to be enjoyed, and should satisfy the mind and not only the eye of the beholder. Sounds such as the rustle of bamboo and the dripping of water, scents and sensations such as grass or gravel or stone underfoot, appeal to the emotions and play a part in the total impression.

PENELOPE HOBHOUSE, *The Country Gardener* (1989)

You mustn't rely on your flowers to make your garden attractive. A good bone structure must come first, with an intelligent use of evergreen plants so that the garden is always clothed, no matter what time of year. Flowers are an added delight, but a good garden is the garden you enjoy looking at even in the depths of winter.

MARGERY FISH, *We Made a Garden* (1956)

The eighteenth-century view of the garden was that it should lead the observer to the enjoyment of the aesthetic sentiments of regularity and order, proportion, color and utility, and, furthermore, be capable of arousing feelings of grandeur, gaiety, sadness, wildness, domesticity, surprise and secrecy.

PENELOPE HOBHOUSE, *The Country Gardener* (1989)

Weather means more when you have a garden. There's nothing like listening to a shower and thinking how it is soaking in and around your lettuce and green beans.

MARCELENE COX, in *Ladies' Home Journal* (1944)

I am weary of swords and courts and kings. Let us go into the garden and watch the minister's bees.

MARY JOHNSTON, *To Have and to Hold* (1900)

If "heartache" sounds exaggerated then surely you have never gone to your garden one rare morning in June to find that the frost, without any perceptible motive, any hope of personal gain, has quietly killed your strawberry blossoms, tomatoes, lima and green beans, corn, squash, cucumbers. A brilliant sun is now smiling at this disaster with an insensitive cheerfulness as out of place as a funny story would be if someone you loved had just died.

RUTH STOUT, *How to Have a Green Thumb Without an Aching Back* (1955)

See also Gardening, Plants.

GAY

Gay culture is far from "marginal," being rather "intersectional," the conduits between unlike beings.

JUDY GRAHN, *Another Mother Tongue: Gay Words, Gay Worlds* (1984)

They are a very extensive minority who have suffered discrimination and who have the same right to participation in the promise and fruits of society as every other individual.

BELLA ABZUG, press conference (1975)

The tribal attitude said, and continues to say, that Gay people are especially empowered because we are able to identify with both sexes and can see into more than one world at once, having the capacity to see from more than one point of view at a time. And that is also an Indian way of seeing.

JUDY GRAHN, *Another Mother Tongue: Gay Words, Gay Worlds* (1984)

No government has the right to tell its citizens when or whom to love. The only queer people are those who don't love anybody.

RITA MAE BROWN, news item (1982)

The walls of the closet are guarded by the dogs of terror, and the inside of the closet is a house of mirrors.

JUDY GRAHN, *Another Mother Tongue: Gay Words, Gay Worlds* (1984)

Within any society men and women develop differently and have, each, a subculture of their own that is overbalanced in the importance it places on particular jobs, attitudes, amount of aggressiveness, roles it plays, amounts of expressed physicality and tenderness, and that has different understandings of children, of the universe, of the sciences or different access to parts of the economy, the healing arts, transportation services, and so on. One of the major homosexual/shamanic functions in any society is to *cross over* between these two essentially different worlds and reveal them to each other.

JUDY GRAHN, *Another Mother Tongue: Gay Words, Gay Worlds* (1984)

If you removed all of the homosexuals and homosexual influence from what is generally regarded as American culture, you would be pretty much left with *Let's Make a Deal*.

FRAN LEBOWITZ, in Leigh W. Rutledge, *Unnatural Quotations: A Compendium of Quotations by, for, or About Gay People* (1988)

See also Lesbians.

GENDER

To me gender is not physical at all, but is altogether insubstantial. It is soul, perhaps, it is talent, it is taste, it is environment, it is how one feels, it is light and shade, it is inner music.

JAN MORRIS, *Conundrum* (1974)

See also Androgyny, Sex Roles.

GENERATIONS

Every generation must go further than the last or what's the use in it?

MERIDEL LE SUEUR, *Salute to Spring* (1940)

They're grown up and moved to Minneapolis. Every generation goes someplace bigger.

FAITH SULLIVAN, *The Cape Ann* (1988)

The dead might as well try to speak to the living as the old to the young.

WILLA CATHER, *One of Ours* (1922)

As long as any adult thinks that he, like the parents and teachers of old, can become introspective, invoking his own youth to understand the youth before him, he is lost.

MARGARET MEAD, *Culture and Commitment* (1970)

You are all a lost generation.

GERTRUDE STEIN, in Ernest Hemingway, *The Sun Also Rises* (1926)

It was this hotel keeper who said what it is said I said that the war generation was a lost generation. And he said it this way. He said that every man becomes civilized between the ages of eighteen and twenty-five. If he does not go through a civilizing experience at that time in his life he will not be a civilized man. And men who went to the war at eighteen missed the period of civilizing, and they could never be civilized. They were a lost generation.

GERTRUDE STEIN, *Everybody's Autobiography* (1937)

I happen to feel that total separation between parents and [adult] children is one of the great tragedies of our culture. Both generations really need the sustenance the other has to give and both are impoverished when the relationship does not continue.

ADELAIDE BRY, *Friendship* (1979)

And we are a people without tears. The things that moved our parents do not move us at all.

NATALIA GINZBURG, *The Little Virtues* (1962)

See also Ancestors, Children, Parents.

GENEROSITY

We'd all like a reputation for generosity and we'd all like to buy it cheap.

MIGNON MCLAUGHLIN, *The Neurotic's Notebook* (1963)

See also Charity, Giving, Kindness, Virtue.

GENIUS

It takes a lot of time to be a genius, you have to sit around so much doing nothing, really doing nothing.

GERTRUDE STEIN, *Everybody's Autobiography* (1937)

You cannot create genius. All you can do is nurture it.

NINETTE DE VALOIS, in *Time* (1960)

No one can arrive from being talented alone. God gives talent, work transforms talent into genius.

ANNA PAVLOVA, in A. H. Franks, ed., *Pavlova: A Biography* (1956)

Genius will live and thrive without training, but it does not the less reward the watering pot and pruning knife.

MARGARET FULLER, in Thomas Wentworth Higginson, *Life of Margaret Fuller Ossoli* (1884)

The life of great geniuses is nothing but a sublime storm.

GEORGE SAND, in *French Wit and Wisdom* (1950)

Genius . . . arises in the natural, aboriginal concern for the conscious unity of all phenomena.

MARY AUSTIN, *Earth Horizon* (1932)

It takes people a long time to learn the difference between talent and genius, especially ambitious young men and women.

LOUISA MAY ALCOTT, *Little Women* (1868)

There are some people that you cannot change, you must either swallow them whole, or leave them alone. . . . You can do something with talent, but nothing with genius.

MARGOT ASQUITH, *More or Less About Myself* (1934)

Since when was genius found respectable?

ELIZABETH BARRETT BROWNING, *Aurora Leigh* (1856)

See also Intelligence, Precocity, Talent.

GHETTO

And one day you find yourself entangled—enmeshed—pinioned in the seaweed of a Black Ghetto. . . . Milling around like live fish in a basket. Those at the bottom crushed into a sort of stupid apathy by the weight of those on top. Those on top leaping, leaping; leaping to scale the sides; to get out.

MARITA BONNER, "On Being Young—A Woman—and Colored" (1925), *Frye Street and Environs* (1987)

See also Poverty.

GIVING

The fragrance always remains in the hand that gives the rose.

HEDA BEJAR, in *Peacemaking: Day by Day,* vol. 2 (1989)

A cheerful giver does not count the cost of what he gives. His heart is set on pleasing and cheering him to whom the gift is given.

JULIAN OF NORWICH, *Revelations of Divine Love* (1373)

Blessed are those who can give without remembering, and take without forgetting.

ELIZABETH BIBESCO, *Balloons* (1922)

We are rich only through what we give, and poor only through what we refuse.

ANNE-SOPHIE SWETCHINE, *The Writings of Madame Swetchine* (1869)

If my hands are fully occupied in holding on to something, I can neither give nor receive.

DOROTHEE SÖLLE, in Mary Alice Warner and Bayna Beilenson, *Women of Faith and Spirit* (1987)

But you cannot give to people what they are incapable of receiving.

AGATHA CHRISTIE, *Funerals Are Fatal* (1953)

There is only one real deprivation, I decided this morning, and that is not to be able to give one's gifts to those one loves most.

MAY SARTON, *Journal of a Solitude* (1973)

It may be more blessed to give than to receive, but there is more grace in receiving than giving. When you receive, whom do you love and praise? The giver. When you give, the same holds true.

JESSAMYN WEST, *The Woman Said Yes: Encounters With Life and Death* (1976)

Nothing is more pleasing and engaging than the sense of having conferred benefits. Not even the gratification of receiving them.

ELLIS PETERS, *The Hermit of Eyton Forest* (1987)

See also Charity, Generosity, Philanthropy, Receiving, Sacrifice, Sharing.

GLADNESS

"Oh, I'm so glad," exulted Pollyanna.

ELEANOR H. PORTER, *Pollyanna* (1912)

The game was to just find something about everything to be glad about—no matter what 'twas. . . . You see, when you're hunting for the glad things, you sort of forget the other kind.

ELEANOR H. PORTER, *Pollyanna* (1912)

See also Contentment, Happiness, Joy.

GLAMOUR

Well, there are always those who cannot distinguish between glitter and glamour . . . the glamour of Isadora Duncan came from her great, torn, bewildered, foolhardy soul.

DOROTHY PARKER, in *New Yorker* (1928)

See also Celebrities, Elegance, Fame.

GOALS

I want a busy life, a just mind and a timely death.

ZORA NEALE HURSTON, *Dust Tracks on a Road* (1942)

Goals too clearly defined can become blinkers.

MARY CATHERINE BATESON, *Composing a Life* (1989)

See also Ambition, Journeys, Means, Purpose.

GOD

Earth's crammed with heaven, / And every common bush afire with God.

ELIZABETH BARRETT BROWNING, *Aurora Leigh* (1856)

It is easier to gaze into the sun, than into the face of the mystery of God. Such is its beauty and its radiance.

HILDEGARDE OF BINGEN, *Scivias* (1141–1150), in Gabriele Uhlein, ed., *Meditations With Hildegarde of Bingen* (1983)

God, I can push the grass apart / And lay my finger on Thy heart!

EDNA ST. VINCENT MILLAY, title poem, *Renascence* (1917)

Nearer, my God, to Thee, / Nearer to Thee.

SARAH FLOWER ADAMS, *Nearer My God to Thee* (1876)

Until I am essentially united with God, I can never have full rest or real happiness.

JULIAN OF NORWICH, *Revelations of Divine Love* (1373)

Home is the definition of God.

EMILY DICKINSON (1879), in Mabel Loomis Todd, *Letters of Emily Dickinson* (1894)

How much did I hear of religion as a child? Very little, and yet my heart leaped when I heard the name of God. I do believe every soul has a tendency toward God.

DOROTHY DAY, *The Long Loneliness* (1952)

I cannot walk an inch / without trying to walk to God.

ANNE SEXTON, "Not So. Not So," *The Awful Rowing Toward God* (1975)

Destiny doesn't exist. It's God we need, and fast.

ADÉLIA PRADO, "Dysrhythmia," in Ellen Watson, tr., *The Alphabet in the Park: Selected Poems of Adélia Prado* (1990)

God is not indifferent to your need. / You have a thousand prayers, / but God has one.

ANNE SEXTON, "Not So. Not So," *The Awful Rowing Toward God* (1975)

Sickness, sin, and death, being inharmonious, do not originate in God nor belong to His government.

MARY BAKER EDDY, *Science and Health* (1875)

Gd is a Gd of Lovingkindness.

ANNE ROIPHE, *Lovingkindness* (1987)

The soul is kissed by God in its innermost regions.

HILDEGARDE OF BINGEN, *Scivias* (1141–1150), in Gabriele Uhlein, ed., *Meditations With Hildegarde of Bingen* (1983)

For god is nothing other than the eternally creative source of our relational power, our common strength, a god whose movement is to empower, bringing us into our own together, a god whose name in history is love.

CARTER HEYWARD, *Our Passion for Justice* (1984)

i found god in myself / & i loved her / i loved her fiercely.

NTOZAKE SHANGE, *For Colored Girls Who Have Considered Suicide/When the Rainbow Is Enuf* (1975)

Metaphors for God drawn from human experience can easily be literalized. While we are immediately aware that the personal God is not really a rock or a mother eagle, it is easy enough to imagine that God is really a king or a father.

SANDRA M. SCHNEIDERS, *Women and the Word* (1986)

As truly as God is our Father, so truly is God our Mother.

JULIAN OF NORWICH, *Revelations of Divine Love* (1373)

She makes everything possible.

HELEN REDDY, in Barbara McDowell and Hana Umlauf, *Woman's Almanac* (1977)

No matter how entrenched in the imagination of the average Christian the image of a male God might be, theological tradition has never assigned sex to God.

SANDRA M. SCHNEIDERS, *Women and the Word* (1986)

If God is male, then the male is God. The divine patriarch castrates women as long as he is allowed to live on in the human imagination.

MARY DALY, *Beyond God the Father* (1973)

God is inside you and inside everybody else. You come into the world with God. But only them that search for it inside find it. And sometimes it just manifest itself even if you not looking, or don't know what you looking for. Trouble do it

for most folks, I think. . . . Yeah, It. God ain't a he or a she, but a It.

ALICE WALKER, *The Color Purple* (1982)

The gender of God, God's presumed masculinity, has functioned as the ultimate religious legitimization of the unjust social structures which victimize women.

SANDRA M. SCHNEIDERS, *Women and the Word* (1986)

Ain't no way to read the bible and not think God white, she say. Then she sigh. When I found out I thought God was white, and a man, I lost interest.

ALICE WALKER, *The Color Purple* (1982)

In the native world, major gods come in trios, duos, and groups. It is the habit of non-natives to discover the supreme being, the one and only head god, a habit lent to them by monotheism.

PAULA GUNN ALLEN, *Grandmothers of the Light* (1991)

God's been going deaf. . . . Here God used to raineth bread from clouds, smite the Phillipines, sling fire down on red-light districts where people got stabbed. He even appeared in person every once in a while. God used to pay attention, is what I'm saying.

LOUISE ERDRICH, *Love Medicine* (1984)

I'll bet when you get down on them rusty knees and get to worrying God, He just goes in his privy-house and slams the door. That's what he thinking about *you* and *your* prayers.

ZORA NEALE HURSTON, *Seraph on the Suwanee* (1948)

It isn't that I believe God is dead, but God is so silent, has been for so long, and is so hidden, I take it as a sign I must watch in other places or simply tend my small fires until the end.

MARY VIRGINIA MICKA, *The Cazenovia Journal* (1986)

I'd begun to think you were a bit like God—you make things happen but you don't exist.

CARYL CHURCHILL, *Serious Money* (1987)

It is madness to wear ladies' . . . hats to church; we should all be wearing crash helmets. Ushers should issue life preservers and signal flares; they should lash us to our pews. For the sleeping God may wake someday and take offense, or the waking God may draw us out to where we can never return.

ANNIE DILLARD, *Teaching a Stone to Talk* (1982)

I read the book of Job last night—I don't think God comes well out of it.

VIRGINIA WOOLF, *The Letters of Virginia Woolf: Vol. II, 1912–1922* (1975)

The popular protest is that anything God does is right! He could never be so vulnerable as to be lonely and need someone to slap Him on the shoulder, tweak His ear, or buy Him a beer.

GWENDOLYN BROOKS, in Claudia Tate, ed., *Black Women Writers at Work* (1983)

Sophia wished that Florence would not talk about the Almighty as if his real name was Godfrey, and God was just Florence's nickname for him.

NANCY MITFORD, *Pigeon Pie* (1940)

There is nothing like despair to make one throw oneself upon the gods.

MARY RENAULT, *The Praise Singer* (1978)

New gods arise when they are needed.

JOSEPHINE JOHNSON, in Lorraine Anderson, ed., *Sisters of the Earth* (1991)

Of two men who have no experience of God, he who denies him is perhaps nearer to him than the other.

SIMONE WEIL, *Gravity and Grace* (1947)

Just as a circle embraces all that is within it, so does the God-head embrace all. No one has the power to divide this circle, to surpass it, or to limit it.

HILDEGARDE OF BINGEN, *Scivias* (1141–1150), in Gabriele Uhlein, ed., *Meditations With Hildegarde of Bingen* (1983)

Listen, God love everything you love—and a mess of stuff you don't. But more than anything else, God love admiration. . . . I think it pisses God off if you walk by the color purple in a field somewhere and don't notice it.

ALICE WALKER, *The Color Purple* (1982)

Why indeed must "God" be a noun? Why not a verb—the most active and dynamic of all?

MARY DALY, *Beyond God the Father* (1973)

See also Christ, Devil, Divinity, Religion, Sacred, Spirituality, Theology.

GOLD

Gold has no name, it licks the hand of anyone who has it: good dog!

CHRISTINA STEAD, *House of All Nations* (1938)

When people are collecting gold they aren't doing business. . . . Gold is constipation: even bankruptcy is more fluid. Gold isn't wealth: positions in markets are wealth.

CHRISTINA STEAD, *House of All Nations* (1938)

See also Money, Wealth.

GOOD

I did and still do find a serious error in the emphasis of spiritual masters and hagiographers of all faiths on self-denial and austerity as an end in itself, instead of a means. L'art pour l'art. We must do the good because it is good, not because it is difficult.

ADE BETHUNE, in Judith Stoughton, *Proud Donkey of Schaerbeek* (1988)

There is a haphazard sort of doing good, which is nothing but temperamental pleasure-seeking.

FANNY LEWALD, *Gefühltes und Gedachtes* (1900)

Too much of a good thing can be wonderful.

MAE WEST, in Diane Arbus, "Mae West: Emotion in Motion," *Show* (1965)

When I'm good I'm very good, but when I'm bad I'm better.

MAE WEST, in *I'm No Angel* (1933)

See also Goodness.

GOODNESS

The first condition of human goodness is something to love; the second, something to reverence.

GEORGE ELIOT, "Janet's Repentance," *Scenes of Clerical Life* (1857)

We can be wise from goodness and good from wisdom.

MARIE VON EBNER-ESCHENBACH, *Aphorisms* (1905)

She tended to be impatient with that sort of intellectual who, for all his brilliance, has never been able to arrive at the simple conclusion that to be reasonably happy you have to be reasonably good.

CAROLYN KIZER, "A Slight Mechanical Failure," in Howard Moss, ed., *The Poet's Story* (1973)

See also Good, Morality, Saints, Virtue.

GORILLAS

A gorilla is a stupendous creature, very up and coming. He seems to belong to the dawn of his time, the origin, not the end, the elemental stuff packed with compressed vitality from whom everything is still to come.

L. M. BOSTON, *A Stranger at Green Knowe* (1961)

If we don't exterminate the gorillas before we exterminate ourselves, the gorilla will have his chance. He's one of the really great ones of the earth, and he's not specialized, he's versatile. It's the versatile who survive.

L. M. BOSTON, *A Stranger at Green Knowe* (1961)

See also Animals.

GOSSIP

Gossip is a sort of smoke that comes from the dirty tobacco-pipes of those who diffuse it; it proves nothing but the bad taste of the smoker.

GEORGE ELIOT, *Daniel Deronda* (1874)

You're shocked, Mr. Burton, at hearing what our gossiping little town thinks. I can tell you this—they always think the worst!

AGATHA CHRISTIE, *The Moving Finger* (1942)

It is almost impossible to throw dirt on someone without getting a little on yourself.

ABIGAIL VAN BUREN, syndicated column (1991)

Show me someone who never gossips, and I'll show you someone who isn't interested in people.

BARBARA WALTERS, *How to Talk With Practically Anybody About Practically Anything* (1970)

Never . . . use the word *gossip* in a pejorative sense. It's the very stuff of biography and has to be woven in. To suggest that the personal life is not an essential element in the creative life is absurd.

JOAN PEYSER, in *Publishers Weekly* (1987)

Gossip is just news running ahead of itself in a red satin dress.

LIZ SMITH, in *Dallas Times-Herald* (1978)

If you haven't anything nice to say about anyone, come and sit by me.

ALICE ROOSEVELT LONGWORTH, motto embroidered on sofa cushion, in Michael Teague, *Mrs. L.: Conversations with Alice Roosevelt Longworth* (1981)

Gossip, even when it avoids the sexual, bears around it a faint flavor of the erotic.

PATRICIA MEYER SPACKS, *Gossip* (1985)

Some men kiss and do not tell, some kiss and tell; but George Moore told and did not kiss.

SUSAN MITCHELL, in Oliver St. John Gogarty, *As I Was Going Down Sackville Street* (1937)

See also Calumny, Rumor, Talking, "They."

GOVERNMENT

There is no such thing as a good government.

EMMA GOLDMAN, in Katherine Anne Porter, *The Never-Ending Wrong* (1977)

We must have government, but we must watch them like a hawk.

MILLICENT FENWICK, in *Reader's Digest* (1983)

A government is not legitimate merely because it exists.

JEANE J. KIRKPATRICK, in *Time* (1985)

We've got to bring the government up to date. It's insane to try to live under the same governmental structures set up nearly two hundred years ago.

BELLA ABZUG, *Bella!* (1972)

This used to be a government of checks and balances. Now it's all checks and no balances.

GRACIE ALLEN, *How to Become President* (1940)

The stakes . . . are too high for government to be a spectator sport.

BARBARA JORDAN, speech (1977)

There is only one institution that can arrogate to itself the power legally to trade by means of rubber checks: the government. And it is the only institution that can mortgage your future without your knowledge or consent: government securities (and paper money) are promissory notes on future tax receipts, i.e., on your future production.

AYN RAND, *Philosophy: Who Needs It?* (1982)

The business of government should be business-like.

DORCAS HARDY, in *Christian Science Monitor* (1987)

Ah! that Senate is a world of ice and darkness! It votes the destruction of peoples as the simplest and wisest thing; for its members themselves are moribund.

GEORGE SAND (1863), in Raphaël Ledos de Beaufort, *Letters of George Sand* (1886)

There is hardly a facet of life that is now free of some sort of federal action.

MILLICENT FENWICK, *Speaking Up* (1982)

Everyone in America seems to be joining an organization of some kind, and in Congress one hears from them all.

MILLICENT FENWICK, newsletter (1975)

The advance planning and sense stimuli employed to capture a $10 million cigarette or soap market are nothing compared to the brainwashing and propaganda blitzes used to ensure control of the largest cash market in the world: the Executive Branch of the United States Government.

PHYLLIS SCHLAFLY, *A Choice Not an Echo* (1964)

Everyone else is represented in Washington by a rich and powerful lobby, it seems. But there is no lobby for the people.

SHIRLEY CHISHOLM, *Unbought and Unbossed* (1970)

The only people who should be in government are those who care more about people than they do about power.

MILLICENT FENWICK, interview (1980)

There is something that governments care far more for than human life, and that is the security of property.

EMMELINE PANKHURST, *My Own Story* (1914)

Till I see money spent on the betterment of man instead of on his idleness and destruction, I shall not believe in any perfect form of government.

MARGOT ASQUITH, *More or Less About Myself* (1934)

If there is one thing the past years have taught us, it is the importance of a keen and high sense of honor in those who handle our governmental affairs.

MILLICENT FENWICK, *New York Times* (1976)

In Britain the government has to come down in front of Parliament every day to explain its actions, but here the President never answers directly to Congress.

BELLA ABZUG, *Bella!* (1972)

For a considerable price, it [government] relieves us of responsibilities, performing acts that would be as unsavory for most of us as butchering our own beef. As our agent, the government can bomb and tax. As our agent, it can relieve us of the responsibilities once borne face to face by the community: caring for the young, the war-wounded, the aged, the handicapped. It extends our impersonal benevolence to the world's needy, relieving our collective conscience without uncomfortable first-hand involvement. It takes our power, our responsibility, *our consciousness*.

MARILYN FERGUSON, *The Aquarian Conspiracy* (1980)

It is not that the U.S. government is an entirely comic matter; but to deal in power, ambition, and the people driven by both, a fine madness and sense of humor are handy things to have.

BARBARA HOWAR, *Laughing All the Way* (1973)

See also Congress, Leaders, Politicians, Politics.

GRACE

Grace fills empty spaces, but it can only enter where there is a void to receive it, and it is grace itself which makes this void.

SIMONE WEIL, *Gravity and Grace* (1947)

See also Mercy.

GRACIOUSNESS

It's a rare thing, graciousness. The shape of it can be acquired, but not, I think, the substance.

GERTRUDE SCHWEITZER, *Shadows on the Left Bank* (1973)

See also Kindness, Tact.

GRANDPARENTS

I suddenly realized that through no act of my own I had become biologically related to a new human being.

MARGARET MEAD, *Blackberry Winter* (1972)

My grandmothers were strong. / Why am I not as they?

MARGARET WALKER, "Lineage," *For My People* (1942)

Helped grandma with the weekend shopping. She was dead fierce in the grocer's; she watched the scales like a hawk watching a fieldmouse. Then she pounced and accused the shop assistant of giving her underweight bacon. The shop assistant was dead scared of her and put another slice on.

SUE TOWNSEND, *The Secret Diary of Adrian Mole Aged 13-3/4* (1982)

Grandma was a kind of first-aid station, or a Red Cross nurse, who took up where the battle ended, accepting us and our little sobbing sins, gathering the whole of us into her lap, restoring us to health and confidence by her amazing faith in life and in a mortal's strength to meet it.

LILLIAN SMITH, in Tillie Olsen, Mother to Daughter, Daughter to Mother (1984)

I cultivate / Being Uppity / It's something / My Gramom taught me.

KATE RUSHIN, "Family Tree," in Patricia Bell-Scott et al., eds., *Double Stitch* (1991)

I'm a flower, Poa, a flower opening and reaching for the sun. You are the sun, grandma, you are the sun in my life.

KITTY TSUI, "Poa Poa Is Living Breathing Light," in Elly Bulkin, ed., *Lesbian Fiction* (1981)

My grandmothers are full of memories / Smelling of soap and onions and wet clay / With veins rolling roughly over quick hands / They have many clean words to say.

MARGARET WALKER, "Lineage," *For My People* (1942)

Hindered characters / seldom have mothers— / in Irish stories— / but they all have grandmothers.

MARIANNE MOORE, "Spenser's Ireland," *What Are Years?* (1941)

As I do not live in an age when rustling black skirts billow about me, and I do not carry an ebony stick to strike the floor in sharp rebuke, as this is denied me, I rap out a sentence in my note book and feel better. If a grandmother wants to put her foot down, the only safe place to do it in these days is in a note book.

FLORIDA SCOTT-MAXWELL, *The Measure of My Days* (1968)

Why do grandparents and grandchildren get along so well? They have the same enemy—the mother.

CLAUDETTE COLBERT, in *Time* (1981)

The closest friends I have made all through life have been people who also grew up close to a loved and loving grandmother or grandfather.

MARGARET MEAD, *Blackberry Winter* (1972)

I loved their home. Everything smelled older, worn but safe; the food aroma had baked itself into the furniture.

SUSAN STRASBERG, *Bittersweet* (1980)

See also Family.

GRATITUDE

It was easier to do a friendly thing than it was to stay and be thanked for it.

Louisa May Alcott, *Little Women* (1868)

We have all known ingratitude, ungrateful we have never been.

Diane de Poitiers, in Winifred Gordon, *A Book of Days* (1910)

See also Receiving.

GREED

We're all born brave, trusting, and greedy, and most of us remain greedy.

Mignon McLaughlin, *The Second Neurotic's Notebook* (1966)

I did not have three thousand pairs of shoes, I had one thousand and sixty.

Imelda Marcos, news item (1987)

Greed probably figures in my intellectual life as well, as I attempt to absorb a massive amount of information with consequent mental indigestion.

Etty Hillesum, *An Interrupted Life: The Diaries of Etty Hillesum 1941–1943* (1983)

See also Selfishness.

GRIEF

My bowl is full of grief / and the wind is up.

Meridel Le Sueur, "Let the Bird of Earth Fly!" *Rites of Ancient Ripening* (1975)

Grief can't be shared. Everyone carries it alone, his own burden, his own way.

Anne Morrow Lindbergh, *Dearly Beloved* (1962)

My dear mother, sisters and brothers comforted me, but their comfort only increased my sorrow and poured more oil on the fire, so that the flames grew ever higher.

Glückel of Hameln, *The Life of Glückel of Hameln (1646–1724), Written by Herself* (1719)

Since every death diminishes us a little, we grieve—not so much for the death as for ourselves.

Lynn Caine, *Widow* (1974)

The sun has set in your life; it is getting cold. The hundreds of people around you cannot console you for the loss of the one.

Maria Augusta Trapp, *The Story of the Trapp Family Singers* (1949)

How cold to the living hour grief could make you!

Eudora Welty, "Music from Spain," *The Golden Apples* (1949)

The Bustle in a House / The Morning after Death / Is solemnest of industries / Enacted upon earth— / The Sweeping up the Heart / And putting Love away / We shall not want to use again / Until Eternity.

Emily Dickinson (1866), *Poems, First Series* (1890)

Have you ever thought, when something dreadful happens, "a moment ago things were not like this; let it be *then,* not *now,* anything but *now*"? And you try and try to remake *then,* but you know you can't. So you try to hold the moment quite still and not let it move on and show itself.

Mary Stewart, *Nine Coaches Waiting* (1958)

After great pain, a formal feeling comes— / . . . / This is the Hour of Lead— / Remembered, if outlived, / As Freezing persons, recollect the Snow— / First—Chill—then Stupor—then the letting go—.

Emily Dickinson (1862), *Further Poems of Emily Dickinson* (1929)

There is no aristocracy of grief. Grief is a great leveler.

Anne Morrow Lindbergh, *Hour of Gold, Hour of Lead* (1973)

A woman who could bend to grief, / But would not bow to shame.

Frances Ellen Watkins Harper, "Vashti," *The New National Era* (1870)

I tell you, hopeless grief is passionless.

Elizabeth Barrett Browning, "Grief," *Poems* (1844)

I measure every Grief I meet / With narrow, probing Eyes— / I wonder if It weighs like Mine— / Or has an Easier size.

Emily Dickinson (1862), *Poems, Third Series* (1896)

Grief may be joy misunderstood; / Only the Good discerns the good.

ELIZABETH BARRETT BROWNING, "De Profundis," *Last Poems* (1862)

See also Loss, Mourning, Sorrow, Suffering.

GROWTH

Growth itself contains the germ of happiness.

PEARL BUCK, *To My Daughters, With Love* (1967)

We are not unlike a particularly hardy crustacean. . . . With each passage from one stage of human growth to the next we, too, must shed a protective structure. We are left exposed and vulnerable—but also yeasty and embryonic again, capable of stretching in ways we hadn't known before. These sheddings may take several years or more. Coming out of each passage, though, we enter a longer and more stable period in which we can expect relative tranquillity and a sense of equilibrium regained.

GAIL SHEEHY, *Passages* (1976)

We do not grow absolutely, chronologically. We grow sometimes in one dimension, and not in another, unevenly. We grow partially. We are relative. We are mature in one realm, childish in another. The past, present, and future mingle and pull us backward, forward, or fix us in the present. We are made up of layers, cells, constellations.

ANAÏS NIN, *The Diary of Anaïs Nin*, vol. 4 (1944–1947)

Our consciousness rarely registers the beginning of a growth within us any more than without us: there have been many circulations of the sap before we detect the smallest sign of the bud.

GEORGE ELIOT, *Silas Marner* (1861)

But buds will be roses, and kittens, cats,—more's the pity!

LOUISA MAY ALCOTT, *Little Women* (1868)

See also Adulthood, Change, Maturity.

GUESTS

It is a widespread and firm belief among guests that their departure is always a matter of distress to their hosts, and that in order to indicate that they have been pleasantly entertained, they must demonstrate an extreme unwillingness to allow the entertainment to conclude. This is not necessarily true.

JUDITH MARTIN, *Miss Manners' Guide for the Turn-of-the-Millennium* (1989)

Emily was feeling the elation of conscientious hosts when they can temporarily escape a ubiquitous houseguest.

CAROL BLY, "Talk of Heroes," *Backbone* (1982)

My father used to say, / "Superior people never make long visits."

MARIANNE MOORE, "Silence," *Black Earth* (1921)

GUILT

I believe in guilt. There's not enough guilt around these days for my taste.

JOY WILLIAMS, in Janet Sternburg, ed., *The Writer on Her Work*, vol. 2 (1991)

Guilt is an emotion that has periodically served me well.

BARBARA E. MRAZ, in Barbara Mraz, ed., *Sacred Strands* (1991)

We all want to be guilty, because guilt is power.

ALISON LURIE, *Love and Friendship* (1962)

Guilt is the one burden human beings can't bear alone.

ANAÏS NIN, *A Spy in the House of Love* (1954)

Ah! it is well for the unfortunate to be resigned, but for the guilty there is no peace.

MARY SHELLEY, *Frankenstein* (1818)

Guilt is a rope that wears thin.

AYN RAND, *Atlas Shrugged* (1957)

H

HABIT

Habit has a kind of poetry.

SIMONE DE BEAUVOIR, *The Coming of Age* (1970)

Curious things, habits. People themselves never knew they had them.

AGATHA CHRISTIE, title story, *Witness for the Prosecution* (1924)

Rigid, the skeleton of habit alone upholds the human frame.

VIRGINIA WOOLF, *Mrs. Dalloway* (1925)

Old habits are strong and jealous.

DOROTHEA BRANDE, *Becoming a Writer* (1934)

Looking back at a repetition of empty days, one sees that monuments have sprung up. Habit is not mere subjugation, it is a tender tie: when one remembers habit it seems to have been happiness.

ELIZABETH BOWEN, *The Death of the Heart* (1938)

Small habits well pursued betimes / May reach the dignity of crimes.

HANNAH MORE, *Florio and His Friend* (1786)

We each have a litany of holiday rituals and everyday habits that we hold on to, and we often greet radical innovation with the enthusiasm of a baby meeting a new sitter. We defend against it and—not always, but often enough—reject it. Slowly we adjust, but only if we have to.

ELLEN GOODMAN, *Turning Points* (1979)

Everything was leveled, there were no extremes of joy or sorrow any more but only habit, routine, ancient family names and rites and customs, slow careful old people moving cautiously around furniture that had sat in the same positions for fifty years.

ANNE TYLER, *Searching for Caleb* (1975)

See also Traditions.

HAIR

Ethel patted her hair and looked very sneery.

DAISY ASHFORD (aged 9), *The Young Visiters* (1919)

[Long hair] is considered bohemian, which may be why I grew it, but I keep it long because I love the way it feels, part cloak, part fan, part mane, part security blanket.

MARGE PIERCY, *Braided Lives* (1982)

See also Appearance, Body.

HAPPINESS

Happiness is nothing but everyday living seen through a veil.

ZORA NEALE HURSTON, *Moses: Man of the Mountain* (1939)

Happiness lies in the consciousness we have of it.

GEORGE SAND, *Handsome Lawrence* (1872)

Happiness is not a possession to be prized, it is a quality of thought, a state of mind.

DAPHNE DU MAURIER, *Rebecca* (1938)

That is happiness; to be dissolved into something complete and great.

WILLA CATHER, *My Antonia* (1918)

Happiness is that state of consciousness which proceeds from the achievement of one's values.

AYN RAND, *Atlas Shrugged* (1957)

Many persons have a wrong idea of what constitutes real happiness. It is not obtained through self-gratification, but through fidelity to a worthy purpose.

HELEN KELLER, *Helen Keller's Journal 1936–1937* (1938)

There is only one happiness in life, to love and be loved.

GEORGE SAND, letter (1862)

When a small child . . . I thought that success spelled happiness. I was wrong, happiness is like a butterfly which appears and delights us for one brief moment, but soon flits away.

ANNA PAVLOVA, in A. H. Franks, ed., Pavlova: A Biography (1956)

Happiness hangs by a hair.

MARY O'HARA, *Thunderhead* (1943)

Happiness is excitement that has found a settling down place, but there is always a little corner that keeps flapping around.

E. L. KONIGSBURG, *From the Mixed-Up Files of Mrs. Basil E. Frankweiler* (1967)

Happiness for the average person may be said to flow largely from common sense—adapting oneself to circumstances—*and* a sense of humor.

BEATRICE LILLIE, *Every Other Inch a Lady* (1972)

Happiness is to take up the struggle in the midst of the raging storm and not to pluck the lute in the moonlight or recite poetry among the blossoms.

DING LING, "Thoughts on March 8" (1942), in *I Myself Am a Woman: Selected Writings of Ding Ling* (1989)

Happiness puts on as many shapes as discontent, and there is nothing odder than the satisfactions of one's neighbor.

PHYLLIS MCGINLEY, *The Province of the Heart* (1959)

Happiness, to some elation; / Is, to others, mere stagnation.

AMY LOWELL, "Happiness," *Sword Blades and Poppy Seeds* (1914)

When one door of happiness closes another opens; but often we look so long at the closed door that we do not see the one which has been opened for us.

HELEN KELLER, *We Bereaved* (1929)

It may be that true happiness lies in the conviction that one has irremediably lost happiness. Then we can begin to move through life without hope or fear, capable of finally enjoying all the small pleasures, which are the most lasting.

MARIA-LUISA BOMBAL, "The Tree," in Zoila Nelken and Rosalie Torres-Rioseco, eds., *Short Stories of Latin America* (1963)

Recurrence is sure. What the mind suffered last week, or last year, it does not suffer now; but it will suffer again next week or next year. Happiness is not a matter of events; it depends upon the tides of the mind.

ALICE MEYNELL, *Prose and Poetry* (1947)

If you haven't been happy very young, you can still be happy later on, but it's much harder. You need more luck.

SIMONE DE BEAUVOIR, in *Observer* (1975)

New happiness too must be learned to bear.

MARIE VON EBNER-ESCHENBACH, *Aphorisms* (1905)

See also Contentment, Joy, Pleasure.

HATE

It was hate at first sight, clean, pure and strong as grain alcohol.

ELIZABETH PETERS, *Naked Once More* (1989)

I tell you, there is such a thing as creative hate!

WILLA CATHER, *The Song of the Lark* (1915)

I know that you cannot hate other people without hating yourself.

OPRAH WINFREY, in Brian Lanker, *I Dream a World* (1989)

Didn't you ever notice how it's always people who wish they had somethin' or had done somethin' that hate the hardest?

GRACE METALIOUS, *Peyton Place* (1956)

In hatred as in love, we grow like the thing we brood upon. What we loathe, we graft into our very soul.

MARY RENAULT, *The Mask of Apollo* (1966)

Now when you hates you shrinks up inside and gets littler and you squeezes your heart tight and you stays so mad with peoples you feels sick all the time like you needs the doctor.

MARGARET WALKER, *Jubilee* (1966)

God . . . cannot occupy the human soul at the same time that it is occupied by hatred.

ANN FAIRBAIRN, *Five Smooth Stones* (1966)

They say that oppression engenders hate. They are heard on all sides crying hate hate.

MONIQUE WITTIG, *Les Guérillères* (1969)

None do we hate so heartily as those who try to use us, unless it may be those whom we try in vain to use.

MINNA THOMAS ANTRIM, *At the Sign of the Golden Calf* (1905)

Misery generates hate.

CHARLOTTE BRONTË, *Shirley* (1849)

Only ways you can keep folks hating is to keep them apart and separated from each other.

MARGARET WALKER, *Jubilee* (1966)

I don't hate anyone. I dislike. But my dislike is the equivalent of anyone else's hate.

ELSA MAXWELL, in *Time* (1963)

One should hate very little, because it's extremely fatiguing. One should despise much, forgive often and never forget. Pardon does not bring with it forgetfulness; at least not for me.

SARAH BERNHARDT, in Cornelia Otis Skinner, *Madame Sarah* (1966)

I really can't hate more than five or ten years. Wouldn't it be terrible to be always burdened with those primary emotions you had at one time?

HAN SUYIN, in *New York Times* (1985)

To be loved is to be fortunate, but to be hated is to achieve distinction.

MINNA THOMAS ANTRIM, *Naked Truth and Veiled Illusions* (1902)

Love commingled with hate is more powerful than love. Or hate.

JOYCE CAROL OATES, *On Boxing* (1987)

Hate doesn't last. Love does.

AGATHA CHRISTIE, *The Moving Finger* (1942)

See also Misanthropy.

HEALTH

Thousands upon thousands of persons have studied disease. Almost no one has studied health.

ADELLE DAVIS, *Let's Eat Right to Keep Fit* (1954)

Health is not simply the absence of sickness.

HANNAH GREEN, *I Never Promised You a Rose Garden* (1964)

Health is not a condition of matter, but of Mind.

MARY BAKER EDDY, *Science and Health* (1875)

As I see it, every day you do one of two things: build health or produce disease in yourself.

ADELLE DAVIS, *Let's Eat Right to Keep Fit* (1954)

I got well by talking. Death could not get a word in edgewise, grew discouraged, and traveled on.

LOUISE ERDRICH, *Tracks* (1988)

It is strange indeed that the more we learn about how to build health, the less healthy Americans become.

ADELLE DAVIS, *Let's Have Healthy Children* (1951)

See also Illness.

HEART

My heart is like a singing bird.

CHRISTINA ROSSETTI, "A Birthday" (1861), *The Poetical Works of Christina Georgina Rossetti* (1906)

Nobody has ever measured, even poets, how much a heart can hold.

ZELDA FITZGERALD, in Nancy Milford, *Zelda* (1970)

The heart outstrips the clumsy senses, and sees—perhaps for an instant, perhaps for long periods of bliss—an undistorted and more veritable world.

EVELYN UNDERHILL, *Mysticism* (1955)

The logic of the heart is absurd.

JULIE DE LESPINASSE, letter (1774)

We are adhering to life now with our last muscle—the heart.

DJUNA BARNES, *Nightwood* (1937)

The human heart, at whatever age, opens only to the heart that opens in return.

MARIA EDGEWORTH, *Letters to Literary Ladies* (1814)

Always there remain portions of our heart into which no one is able to enter, invite them as we may.

MARY DIXON THAYER, "Things to Live By," *Sonnets* (1933)

I am all for people having their heart in the right place; but the right place for a heart is not inside the head.

KATHARINE WHITEHORN, *Roundabout* (1962)

Pity me that the heart is slow to learn / What the swift mind beholds at every turn.

EDNA ST. VINCENT MILLAY, "Pity Me Not," *The Harp-Weaver* (1923)

Many think they have a kind heart who have only weak nerves.

MARIE VON EBNER-ESCHENBACH, *Aphorisms* (1905)

See also Broken Heart, Love.

HERESY

The heresy of one age becomes the orthodoxy of the next.

HELEN KELLER, *Optimism* (1903)

HEROES

Heroes take journeys, confront dragons, and discover the treasure of their true selves.

CAROL PEARSON, *The Hero Within* (1986)

There are stars whose radiance is visible on earth though they have long been extinct. There are people whose brilliance continues to light the world though they are no longer among the living. These lights are particularly bright when the night is dark.

HANNAH SENESH (1940), *Hannah Senesh: Her Life and Diary* (1966)

Even in the darkest of times we have the right to expect some illumination, and that such illumination may come less from theories and concepts than from the uncertain, flickering, and often weak light that some men and women, in their lives and work, will kindle under almost all circumstances and shed over the time-span that was given them on earth.

HANNAH ARENDT, *Men in Dark Times* (1968)

To be a hero, one must give an order to oneself.

SIMONE WEIL, *The Notebooks of Simone Weil* (1951)

We agreed that great men and women should be forced to live as long as possible. The reverence they enjoyed was a life sentence, which they could neither revoke nor modify.

MAYA ANGELOU, *All God's Children Need Traveling Shoes* (1986)

The selective winnowing of time leaves only a few recognizable individuals behind for the historian to light on. Thus the historian who finds the human being more interesting than what the human being has done must inevitably endow the comparatively few individuals he can identify with too great an importance in relation to their time. Even so, I prefer this overestimate to the opposite method which treats developments as though they were the massive anonymous waves of an unhuman sea or pulverizes the fallible surviving records of human life into the gray dust of statistics.

C. V. WEDGWOOD, *Velvet Studies* (1946)

When folk tell me of this great man and that great man, I think to myself. Who was stinted of joy for his glory? How many old folk and children did his coach wheels go over? What bridal lacked his song, and what mourner his tears, that he found time to climb so high?

MARY WEBB, *Precious Bane* (1924)

No man is a hero to his valet.

ANNE-MARIE BIGOT DE CORNUEL, in Mademoiselle
Aissé, *Lettres* (1728)

See also Saints.

HESITATION

He who hesitates is last.

MAE WEST, in Joseph Weintraub, ed., *The Wit and
Wisdom of Mae West* (1967)

See also Delay.

HIDING

Hiding leads nowhere except to more hiding.

MARGARET A. ROBINSON, *A Woman of Her Tribe*
(1990)

Let us not fear the hidden. Or each other.

MURIEL RUKEYSER, "Letter to the Front," *Beast in
View* (1944)

What I have found is, anything one keeps hidden
should now and then be hidden somewhere else.

ELIZABETH BOWEN, *The Death of the Heart* (1938)

I wonder why we are always sort of ashamed of
our best parts and try to hide them. We don't
mind ridicule of our "sillinesses" but of our "so-
bers."

EMILY CARR, *Hundreds and Thousands* (1966)

See also Concealment, Secrets.

HISTORIANS

Every historian discloses a new horizon.

GEORGE SAND (1871), in Raphaël Ledos de Beaufort,
Letters of George Sand (1886)

What his imagination is to the poet, facts are to
the historian. His exercise of judgment comes in
their selection, his art in their arrangement.

BARBARA TUCHMAN, in *New York Times Book Review*
(1964)

A nation does not create the historians it deserves; the historians are far more likely to create
the nation.

C. V. WEDGWOOD, *Velvet Studies* (1946)

See also History.

HISTORY

History moves in contradictory waves, not in
straight lines.

LOIS BECK AND NIKKI KEDDIE, *Women in the Muslim
World* (1978)

How is one to say exactly where history begins
or ends? It is all slow oscillations, curves, and
waves which take so long to reveal themselves
. . . like watching a tree grow.

GRETEL EHRLICH, *Heart Mountain* (1988)

History, in spite of the occasional protest of historians, will always be used in a general way as
a collection of political and moral precedents.

C. V. WEDGWOOD, *Velvet Studies* (1946)

History is a stern judge.

SVETLANA ALLILUYEVA, *Twenty Letters to a Friend*
(1967)

The perpetual stream of human nature is formed
into ever-changing shallows, eddies, falls and
pools by the land over which it passes. Perhaps
the only real value of history lies in considering
this endlessly varied play between the essence
and the accidents.

MARY RENAULT, *The Mask of Apollo* (1966)

History is an illogical record. It hinges on nothing. It is a story that changes and has accidents
and recovers with scars.

GRETEL EHRLICH, *Heart Mountain* (1988)

Written history is, in fact, nothing of the kind; it
is the fragmentary record of the often inexplica-
ble actions of innumerable bewildered human
beings, set down and interpreted according to
their own limitations by other human beings,
equally bewildered. The tribunal of history
judges about as fairly as an average bench of
magistrates; which is exactly what it is.

C. V. WEDGWOOD, *Velvet Studies* (1946)

The unrecorded past is none other than our old friend, the tree in the primeval forest which fell without being heard.

BARBARA TUCHMAN, in *New York Times* (1964)

I learned a history not then written in books but one passed from generation to generation on the steps of moonlit porches and beside dying fires in one-room houses, a history of great-grandparents and of slavery and of the days following slavery; of those who lived still not free, yet who would not let their spirits be enslaved.

MILDRED D. TAYLOR, *Roll of Thunder, Hear My Cry* (1976)

The history of every country begins in the heart of a man or a woman.

WILLA CATHER, *O Pioneers!* (1913)

If we do not know our own history, we are doomed to live it as though it were our private fate.

HANNAH ARENDT, in Carolyn Heilbrun, *Writing a Woman's Life* (1988)

If every nation gets the government it deserves, every generation writes the history which corresponds with its view of the world.

ELIZABETH JANEWAY, *Between Myth and Morning* (1974)

Somewhere about the eighteenth century, history tacitly replaced religion as the school of public morals.

C. V. WEDGWOOD, *Velvet Studies* (1946)

History is not truth versus falsehoods, but a mixture of both, a mélange of tendencies, reactions, dreams, errors, and power plays. What's important is what we make of it; its moral use. By writing history, we can widen readers' thinking and deepen their sympathies in every direction. Perhaps history should show us not how to control the world, but how to enlarge, deepen, and discipline ourselves.

GRETEL EHRLICH, *Heart Mountain* (1988)

Within the limits of the modern nation, history tends to repeat itself by a process of almost deliberate imitation. We know what to expect of ourselves and, by expecting, do it.

C. V. WEDGWOOD, *Velvet Studies* (1946)

My own varying estimates of the facts themselves, as the years passed, showed me too clearly how much of history must always rest in the eye of the beholder; our deductions are so often different it is impossible they should always be right.

C. V. WEDGWOOD, *Velvet Studies* (1946)

Once a president gets to the White House, the only audience that is left that really matters is history.

DORIS KEARNS GOODWIN, in *New York Times* (1985)

Historical research of the truly scholastic kind is not connected with human beings at all. It is a pure study, like higher mathematics.

C. V. WEDGWOOD, *Velvet Studies* (1946)

History as a discipline can be characterized as having a collective forgetfulness about women.

CLARICE STASZ STOLL, *Female and Male* (1974)

The volumes which record the history of the human race are filled with the deeds and the words of great men . . . [but] The Twentieth Century Woman . . . questions the completeness of the story.

MARY RITTER BEARD, "The Twentieth-Century Woman Looking Around and Backward," *Young Oxford* (1900)

See also Ancestors, Historians, Past.

HOBBIES

A hobby a day keeps the doldrums away.

PHYLLIS McGINLEY, *A Pocketful of Wry* (1940)

See also Bridge, Collecting, Fishing, Gardening.

HOLIDAY

See Vacation.

HOLINESS

Every day is a god, each day is a god, and holiness holds forth in time.

ANNIE DILLARD, *Holy the Firm* (1977)

Holy persons draw to themselves all that is earthly.

HILDEGARDE OF BINGEN, *Scivias* (1141–1150), in Gabriele Uhlein, ed., *Meditations with Hildegarde of Bingen* (1983)

Holiness consists in doing the will of God with a smile.

MOTHER TERESA, in Billy Graham, *The Secret of Happiness* (1955)

Who can order the Holy? It is like a rain forest, dripping, lush, fecund, wild. We enter its abundance at our peril, for here we are called to the wholeness for which we long, but which requires all we are and can hope to be.

MARILYN SEWELL, *Cries of the Spirit* (1991)

See also God, Religion, Ritual, Sacred, Saints, Spirituality, Theology.

HOLLAND

There is not a richer or more carefully tilled garden spot in the whole world than this leaky, springy little country.

MARY MAPES DODGE, *Hans Brinker* (1865)

The entire country is a kind of saturated sponge.

MARY MAPES DODGE, *Hans Brinker* (1865)

See also Europe.

HOLLYWOOD

No one has a closest friend in Hollywood.

SHEILAH GRAHAM, *The Rest of the Story* (1964)

With a mental equipment which allows me to tell the difference between hot and cold, I stand out in this community like a modern-day Cicero.

ANITA LOOS, *No Mother to Guide Her* (1961)

To survive there, you need the ambition of a Latin-American revolutionary, the ego of a grand opera tenor, and the physical stamina of a cow pony.

BILLIE BURKE, with Cameron Shipp, *With a Feather on My Nose* (1949)

The convictions of Hollywood and television are made of boiled money.

LILLIAN HELLMAN, *An Unfinished Woman* (1969)

Hollywood money isn't money. It's congealed snow, melts in your hand, and there you are.

DOROTHY PARKER, in Malcolm Cowley, ed., *Writers at Work* (1958)

See also Actors, California, Celebrities.

HOLOCAUST

The stench of human wreckage in which the Nazi regime finally sank down to defeat has been the most shocking fact of modern times.

JANET FLANNER ("Genêt"), *Paris Journal 1944–1965* (1965)

O the chimneys / On the ingeniously devised habitations of death / When Israel's body drifted as smoke / Through the air.

NELLY SACHS, title poem, O the Chimneys (1967)

World, do not ask those snatched from death / where they are going, / they are always going to their graves.

NELLY SACHS, "World, Do Not Ask Those Snatched from Death," *O the Chimneys* (1967)

HOME

"Home" is any four walls that enclose the right person.

HELEN ROWLAND, *Reflections of a Bachelor Girl* (1909)

Home. It's being new and old all rolled into one. Measuring your new against old friends, old ways, old places. Knowing that as long as the old survives, you can keep changing as much as you want without the nightmare of waking up to a total stranger.

GLORIA NAYLOR, *Mama Day* (1988)

The ideal of happiness has always taken material form in the house, whether cottage or castle; it stands for permanence and separation from the world.

SIMONE DE BEAUVOIR, *The Second Sex* (1949)

A house is no home unless it contain food and fire for the mind as well as for the body.

MARGARET FULLER, *Woman in the Nineteenth Century* (1845)

One's own surroundings means so much to one, when one is feeling miserable.

EDITH SITWELL, *Selected Letters* (1970)

I don't know exactly why the notion of home-ownership has such a grasp on the American imagination. Perhaps as descendants of landless immigrants we turn our plots into symbols of stability.

ELLEN GOODMAN, *Close to Home* (1979)

My prairie people are my home / Bird I return flying to their breasts.

MERIDEL LE SUEUR, "Offer Me Refuge," *Rites of Ancient Ripening* (1975)

See also Familiarity, Houses, Places, Roots.

HOMELESSNESS

People who are homeless are not social inadequates. They are people without homes.

SHEILA MCKECHNIE, in *Christian Science Monitor* (1985)

From my family I have learned the secrets / of never having a home.

LINDA HOGAN, "Heritage," in Rayna Green, ed., *That's What She Said* (1984)

/ but for the homeless all ways wither / like cut flowers.

NELLY SACHS, "World, Do Not Ask Those Snatched from Death," *O the Chimneys* (1967)

See also Poverty.

HONESTY

He is only honest who is not discovered.

SUSANNAH CENTLIVRE, *The Artifice* (1722)

I liked the store detective who said he'd seen a lot of people who were so confused that they'd stolen things, but never one so confused that they'd paid twice.

BARONESS PHILLIPS, in *The Sunday Telegraph* (1977)

Honesty has come to mean the privilege of insulting you to your face without expecting redress.

JUDITH MARTIN, *Common Courtesy* (1985)

It's important to our friends to believe that we are unreservedly frank with them, and important to friendship that we are not.

MIGNON MCLAUGHLIN, *The Neurotic's Notebook* (1963)

See also Candor, Dishonesty, Sincerity, Truth, Virtue.

HONOR

Honor wears different coats to different eyes.

BARBARA TUCHMAN, *The Guns of August* (1962)

See also Courage, Reputation, Virtue.

HOPE

"Hope" is the thing with feathers— / That perches in the soul— / And sings the tune without the words— / And never stops—at all.

EMILY DICKINSON (1861), *Poems, Second Series* (1891)

Hope is the feeling you have that the feeling you have isn't permanent.

JEAN KERR, *Finishing Touches* (1973)

There never was night that had no morn.

DINAH MULOCK CRAIK, "The Golden Gate," *Mulock's Poems, New and Old* (1888)

The longest day must have its close—the gloomiest night will wear on to a morning. An eternal, inexorable lapse of moments is ever hurrying the day of the evil to an eternal night, and the night of the just to an eternal day.

HARRIET BEECHER STOWE, *Uncle Tom's Cabin* (1852)

Music played in the resurrection ashes.

NELLY SACHS, "Night of Nights," *O the Chimneys* (1967)

There is hope for all of us. Well, anyway, if you don't die you live through it, day in, day out.

MARY BECKETT, *A Belfast Woman: Stories* (1980)

Rage for the world as it is / but for what it may be / more love now than last year.

MURIEL RUKEYSER, "This Place in the Ways," *The Green Wave* (1948)

Hope is a very unruly emotion.

GLORIA STEINEM, *Outrageous Acts and Everyday Rebellions* (1983)

We all hope for a—must I say the word—recipe, we all believe, however much we know we shouldn't, that maybe somebody's got that recipe and can show us how not to be sick, suffer and die.

NAN SHIN, *Diary of a Zen Nun* (1986)

Take hope from the heart of man and you make him a beast of prey.

OUIDA, *Wisdom, Wit and Pathos* (1884)

When hope is taken away from a people moral degeneration follows swiftly after.

PEARL BUCK, in *New York Times* (1941)

To eat bread without hope is still slowly to starve to death.

PEARL BUCK, *To My Daughters, With Love* (1967)

Hope is a strange invention— / A Patent of the Heart— / In unremitting action / Yet never wearing out.

EMILY DICKINSON (1877), in Mabel Loomis Todd, *Letters of Emily Dickinson* (1894)

Whenever hope and illusion become the source of the will to live, all knowledge of reality becomes highly threatening, since at any time a new piece of information might remove the grounds for this hope. This is exactly the case now. When life is motivated by hope for improvement, denial of reality is necessarily renewed and fortified.

CHRISTINA THÜRMER-ROHR, *Vagabonding* (1991)

See also Expectations, Faith, Optimism.

HORSES

When Allah created the horse, he said to the wind, "I will that a creature proceed from thee.

Condense thyself." And the wind condensed itself, and the result was the horse.

MARGUERITE HENRY, *King of the Wind* (1948)

I'd kiss his glossy neck, stroke his mane and say "Darling, darling!" for he was a staid horse who allowed intimacies.

JEAN RHYS, *Smile Please: An Unfinished Autobiography* (1979)

I do feel that horses have faces—and feelings too.

ALANNA KNIGHT, *Lament for Lost Lovers* (1973)

I still subscribe to the minority view that all horses are offensive weapons and not to be trusted a yard.

M. M. KAYE, *The Sun in the Morning* (1990)

See also Animals.

HOSPITAL

It may seem a strange principle to enunciate as the very first requirement in a Hospital that it should do the sick no harm.

FLORENCE NIGHTINGALE, *Notes on Hospitals* (1859)

Hospitals, like airports and supermarkets, only pretend to be open nights and weekends.

MOLLY HASKELL, *Love and Other Infectious Diseases* (1990)

One of the most difficult things to contend with in a hospital is the assumption on the part of the staff that because you have lost your gall bladder you have also lost your mind.

JEAN KERR, *Please Don't Eat the Daisies* (1957)

The ultimate indignity is to be given a bedpan by a stranger who calls you by your first name.

MAGGIE KUHN, in *Observer* (1978)

In hospitals there was no time off for good behavior.

JOSEPHINE TEY, *The Daughter of Time* (1951)

See also Doctors, Illness, Medication, Nurses.

HOUSES

A house can have integrity, just like a person.

AYN RAND, *The Fountainhead* (1943)

A house that does not have one worn, comfy chair in it is soulless.

MAY SARTON, *Journal of a Solitude* (1973)

The house, while sound in wind and limb, was described as being of "no character." We didn't think then that it had anything but character, rather sinister perhaps, but definitely character.

MARGERY FISH, *We Made a Garden* (1956)

It was a Victorian parlor maid's nightmare, marked by the kind of decor involving the word "throw." Throw pillows, throw covers, throw cloths. . . . Next to throw, the operative word was "occasional." Occasional tables, occasional chairs, occasional lamps; footstools, hassocks, stacked trays, wheeled teacarts, and enough card tables to start a gambling den.

FLORENCE KING, *Confessions of a Failed Southern Lady* (1985)

Old houses, I thought, do not belong to people, ever, not really, people belong to them.

GLADYS TABER, *Stillmeadow Daybook* (1955)

A man builds a house in England with the expectation of living in it and leaving it to his children; while we shed our houses in America as easily as a snail does his shell.

HARRIET BEECHER STOWE, in Cathrene P. Gilbertson, *Harriet Beecher Stowe* (1937)

When you dwell in a house you mislike, you will look out of a window a deal more than those that are content with their dwelling.

MARY WEBB, *Precious Bane* (1924)

A house is not a home.

POLLY ADLER, on her life as a madam, book title (1953)

See also Home, Housework, Rooms, Walls.

HOUSEWORK

Housekeeping ain't no joke.

LOUISA MAY ALCOTT, *Little Women* (1868)

Of all hateful occupations, housekeeping is to my mind the most hateful.

HANNAH WHITALL SMITH (1902), in Logan Pearsall Smith, *Philadelphia Quaker* (1950)

Few tasks are more like the torture of Sisyphus than housework, with its endless repetition: the clean becomes soiled, the soiled is made clean, over and over, day after day.

SIMONE DE BEAUVOIR, *The Second Sex* (1949)

Invisible, repetitive, exhausting, unproductive, uncreative—these are the adjectives which most perfectly capture the nature of housework.

ANGELA DAVIS, *Women, Race and Class* (1981)

Housework's the hardest work in the world. That's why men won't do it.

EDNA FERBER, *So Big* (1924)

Upstairs she lay awake and planned a new, heroic role for herself. She would expiate all her sins by sinking into domesticity. . . . She would put her lily hand down into sewerages and save him the trouble of lifting up the ooze and hairs and gray slime that resulted from their daily lives.

EDNA O'BRIEN, *Girls in Their Married Bliss* (1964)

The important thing about women today is, as they get older, they still keep house. It's one reason they don't die, but men die when they retire. Women just polish the teacups.

MARGARET MEAD, in Elizabeth Fishel, *Sisters: Love and Rivalry Inside the Family and Beyond* (1979)

A woman's work, from the time she gets up to the time she goes to bed, is as hard as a day at war, worse than a man's working day. . . . To men, women's work was like the rain-bringing clouds, or the rain itself. The task involved was carried out every day as regularly as sleep. So men were happy—men in the Middle Ages, men at the time of the Revolution, and men in 1986: everything in the garden was lovely.

MARGUERITE DURAS, *Practicalities* (1987)

I buried a lot of my ironing in the back yard.

PHYLLIS DILLER, in Barbara McDowell and Hana Umlauf, *Woman's Almanac* (1977)

I would rather lie on a sofa than sweep beneath it.

SHIRLEY CONRAN, *Superwoman* (1975)

Have you ever taken anything out of the clothes basket because it had become, relatively, the cleaner thing?

KATHARINE WHITEHORN, in *Observer* (1964)

Cleaning your house while your kids are still growing / Is like shoveling the walk before it stops snowing.

PHYLLIS DILLER, *Phyllis Diller's Housekeeping Hints* (1966)

No laborer in the world is expected to work for room, board, and love—except the housewife.

LETTY COTTIN POGREBIN, *How to Make It in a Man's World* (1970)

The labor of women in the house, certainly, enables men to produce more wealth than they otherwise could; and in this way women are economic factors in society. But so are horses.

CHARLOTTE PERKINS GILMAN, *Women and Economics* (1900)

The unwaged condition of housework has been the most powerful weapon in reinforcing the common assumption that *housework is not work,* thus preventing women from struggling against it, except in the privatized kitchen-bedroom quarrel that all society agrees to ridicule, thereby further reducing the protagonist of a struggle. We are seen as nagging bitches, not workers in struggle.

SILVIA FEDERICI, "Wages Against Housework" (1975), in Evelyn Shapiro and Barry M. Shapiro, *The Women Say/The Men Say* (1979)

No longer will we [women] agree to protect the hearth at the price of extinguishing the fire within ourselves.

CELIA GILBERT, in Sara Ruddick and Pamela Daniels, *Working It Out* (1977)

At the worst, a house unkept cannot be so distressing as a life unlived.

ROSE MACAULAY, *A Casual Commentary* (1926)

See also Dirt, Work.

HUMAN DIFFERENCES

I love *different* folks.

ELEANOR H. PORTER, *Pollyanna* (1912)

The fact that we are human beings is infinitely more important than all the peculiarities that distinguish human beings from one another.

SIMONE DE BEAUVOIR, *The Second Sex* (1949)

There is nothing I should care more to do, if it were possible, than to rouse the imagination of men and women to a vision of human claims in those races of their fellow-men who most differ from them in customs and beliefs.

GEORGE ELIOT, letter to Harriet Beecher Stowe (1876), in J. W. Cross, *George Eliot's Life as Related in Her Letters and Journals* (1884)

When those closest to us respond to events differently than we do, when they seem to see the same scene as part of a different play, when they say things that we could not imagine saying in the same circumstances, the ground on which we stand seems to tremble and our footing is suddenly unsure.

DEBORAH TANNEN, *You Just Don't Understand* (1990)

Instead of being presented with stereotypes by age, sex, color, class, or religion, children must have the opportunity to learn that within each range, some people are loathsome and some are delightful.

MARGARET MEAD, *Twentieth Century Faith: Hope and Survival* (1972)

Deviance is whatever is condemned by the community. Most societies try to get rid of their deviants. Most cultures have burned and beaten their homosexuals and others who deviate from the sexual common. The queer are the mirror reflecting the heterosexual tribe's fear: being different, being other and therefore lesser, therefore sub-human, in-human, non-human.

GLORIA ANZALDÚA, *Borderlands/La Frontera: The New Mestiza* (1987)

There's a difference between exotic and foreign, isn't there? Exotic means you know how to use your foreignness, or you make yourself a little foreign in order to appear exotic. Real foreign is a little scary, believe me.

BHARATI MUKHERJEE, *The Middleman and Other Stories* (1988)

But it is not really difference the oppressor fears so much as similarity.

CHERRÍE MORAGA, "La Guëra," in Cherríe Moraga and Gloria Anzaldúa, eds., *This Bridge Called My Back* (1983)

Like and equal are two entirely different things.

MADELEINE L'ENGLE, *A Wrinkle in Time* (1962)

See also Character, Class, Differences, Eccentricity, Human Nature, Minorities, Oppression, Sexism.

HUMAN FAMILY

I am an uncompromising pacifist. . . . I have no sense of nationalism, only a cosmic consciousness of belonging to the human family.

ROSIKA SCHWIMMER, citizenship court hearing (1928)

Remember that you are all people and that all people are you.

JOY HARJO, "Remember," in Rayna Green, ed., *That's What She Said* (1984)

Today, as never before, the fates of men are so intimately linked to one another that a disaster for one is a disaster for everybody.

NATALIA GINZBURG, *The Little Virtues* (1962)

We are all bound up together in one great bundle of humanity, and society cannot trample on the weakest and feeblest of its members without receiving the curse in its own soul.

FRANCES ELLEN WATKINS HARPER, speech (1866)

We must stand together; if we don't, there will be no victory for any one of us.

MOTHER JONES, in Linda Atkinson, *Mother Jones: The Most Dangerous Woman in America* (1978)

If you're going to care about the fall of the sparrow you can't pick and choose who's going to be the sparrow. It's everybody.

MADELEINE L'ENGLE, *The Arm of the Starfish* (1965)

But only those who have aims and ambitions for the benefit, not of the individual, but of humankind as a whole can persevere to the end.

DING LING, "Thoughts on March 8" (1942), *I Myself Am a Woman: Selected Writings of Ding Ling* (1989)

We have to face the fact that either all of us are going to die together or we are going to learn to live together and if we are to live together we have to talk.

ELEANOR ROOSEVELT, in *New York Times* (1960)

When you make a world tolerable for yourself, you make a world tolerable for others.

ANAÏS NIN, *The Diary of Anaïs Nin,* vol. 5 (1947–1955)

Each person born into this world has a right to everything he needs. His right, however, is bound up with that of every other creature and gives him no license to grab everything he can without allowing a share for others.

DOROTHY RICHARDS, with HOPE SAWYER BUYUKMIHCI, *Beaversprite* (1977)

He had the uneasy manner of a man who is not among his own kind, and who has not seen enough of the world to feel that all people are in some sense his own kind.

WILLA CATHER, *The Song of the Lark* (1915)

Humanity finds itself in the midst of the world. In the midst of all other creatures humanity is the most significant and yet the most dependent upon the others.

HILDEGARDE OF BINGEN, *Scivias* (1141–1150), in Gabriele Uhlein, ed., *Meditations with Hildegarde of Bingen* (1983)

We humans are herd animals of the monkey tribe, not natural individuals as lions are. Our individuality is partial and restless; the stream of consciousness that we call "I" is made of shifting elements that flow from our group and back to our group again. Always we seek to be ourselves and the herd together, not One against the herd.

ANNA LOUISE STRONG, *I Change Worlds* (1935)

If the whole human race lay in one grave, the epitaph on its headstone might well be: "It seemed a good idea at the time."

REBECCA WEST, in *New York Times* (1977)

See also Civilization, Interdependence, Society.

HUMAN NATURE

I liked human beings, but I did not love human nature.

ELLEN GLASGOW, *The Woman Within* (1954)

Poor human nature, what horrible crimes have been committed in thy name!

EMMA GOLDMAN, title essay, *Anarchism* (1910)

Everybody in Maycomb, it seemed, had a streak: a Drinking Streak, a Gambling Streak, a Mean Streak, a Funny Streak.

HARPER LEE, *To Kill a Mockingbird* (1960)

It is human nature to stand in the middle of a thing.

MARIANNE MOORE, "A Grave," *Collected Poems* (1951)

Humans can learn to like anything, that's why we are such a successful species. . . . You can drop humans anywhere and they'll thrive—only the rat does as well.

JEANNETTE DESOR, in *Smithsonian* (1986)

See also Differences, Human Differences, Life, "Natural."

HUMILITY

Humility is attentive patience.

SIMONE WEIL, *First and Last Notebooks* (1970)

Humility has its origin in an awareness of unworthiness, and sometimes too in a dazzled awareness of saintliness.

COLETTE, *Belles saisons* (1955)

Compassion directed to oneself is humility.

SIMONE WEIL, *First and Last Notebooks* (1970)

In the intellectual order, the virtue of humility is nothing more nor less than the power of attention.

SIMONE WEIL, *Gravity and Grace* (1947)

Though God hath raised me high, yet this I count the glory of my crown: that I have reigned with your loves.

ELIZABETH I, *The Golden Speech* (1601)

Humility is not my forte, and whenever I dwell for any length of time on my own shortcomings, they gradually begin to seem mild, harmless, rather engaging little things, not at all like the staring defects in other people's characters.

MARGARET HALSEY, *With Malice Toward Some* (1938)

The woman had a humble, cringing manner. Of course, she had discovered that, having neither money nor virtue, she had better be humble if she knew what was good for her.

JEAN RHYS, *After Leaving Mr. Mackenzie* (1930)

I have often wished I had time to cultivate modesty. . . . But I am too busy thinking about myself.

EDITH SITWELL, in *Observer* (1950)

Humility is no substitute for a good personality.

FRAN LEBOWITZ, *Metropolitan Life* (1978)

See also Virtue.

HUMOR

Humor brings insight and tolerance.

AGNES REPPLIER, *In Pursuit of Laughter* (1936)

Humor comes from self-confidence. There's an aggressive element to wit.

RITA MAE BROWN, *Starting From Scratch* (1988)

The essence of humor is that it should be unexpected, that it should embody an element of surprise, that it should startle us out of that reasonable gravity which, after all, must be our habitual frame of mind.

AGNES REPPLIER, *Americans and Others* (1912)

Humor to me, Heaven help me, takes in many things. There must be courage; there must be no awe. There must be criticism, for humor, to my mind, is encapsulated in criticism. There must be a disciplined eye and a wild mind. There must be a magnificent disregard of your reader, for if he cannot follow you, there is nothing you can do about it.

DOROTHY PARKER, introduction to S. J. Perelman, *The Most of S. J. Perelman* (1953)

How fatally the entire want of humor cripples the mind.

ALICE JAMES, *Journal* (1889)

Total absence of humor renders life impossible.

COLETTE, *Chance Acquaintances* (1952)

Humor is the first of the gifts to perish in a foreign tongue.

VIRGINIA WOOLF, *The Common Reader* (1925)

It is a difficult thing to like anybody's else ideas of being funny.

GERTRUDE STEIN, *Everybody's Autobiography* (1937)

A difference of taste in jokes is a great strain on the affections.

GEORGE ELIOT, *Daniel Deronda* (1874)

It's dreadful when two people's senses of humor are antagonistic. I don't believe there's any bridging that gulf!

JEAN WEBSTER, *Daddy-Long-Legs* (1912)

There's a hell of a distance between wisecracking and wit. Wit has truth in it; wisecracking is simply calisthenics with words.

DOROTHY PARKER, in Malcolm Cowley, ed., *Writers at Work* (1958)

The announcement that you are going to tell a good story (and the chuckle that precedes it) is always a dangerous opening.

MARGOT ASQUITH, *More or Less About Myself* (1934)

I sometimes think humor and satire are more effective techniques for expressing social statements than direct comment.

KRISTIN HUNTER, in Claudia Tate, *Black Women Writers at Work* (1983)

Exaggeration is the cheapest form of humor.

ELIZABETH PETERS, *Naked Once More* (1989)

Humor distorts nothing, and only false gods are laughed off their earthly pedestals.

AGNES REPPLIER, *Points of View* (1891)

Though her capacity for emotion was dead, some diabolical sense of humor had sprung up like fireweed from the ruins. She could laugh at everything now, but it was ironic laughter.

ELLEN GLASGOW, *Barren Ground* (1925)

She chuckled now and again at a joke, but it was the amused grim chuckle of a person who looks up to discover that they have coincided with the needs of nature in a bird.

DJUNA BARNES, *Nightwood* (1937)

We are not amused!

QUEEN VICTORIA, in *Notebooks of a Spinster Lady* (1900)

See also Comedians, Irony, Laughter, Satire, Wit.

HUNGER

Work went on monotonously, and our constant hunger was wrenching: rice powder and bran, which I sometimes roasted in an attempt to give it some flavor, had torn my insides to shreds. One morning I didn't have the strength to get up, and no one came to see what had happened to me. Everyone was so used to having people just disappear.

MOLYDA SZYMUSIAK, *The Stones Cry Out: A Cambodian Childhood 1975–1980* (1984)

Hungry people cannot be good at learning or producing anything, except perhaps violence.

PEARL BAILEY, *Pearl's Kitchen* (1973)

What good is school when you're hungry?

LEILA ABOUZEID, "Divorce," in Elizabeth Warnock Fernea, *Women and the Family in the Middle East* (1985)

Hunger steals the memory.

LOUISE ERDRICH, *Tracks* (1988)

Hunger also changes the world—when eating can't be a habit, then neither can seeing.

MAXINE HONG KINGSTON, *The Woman Warrior* (1976)

A man with money to pay for a meal can talk about hunger without demeaning himself. But for a man with no money hunger is a disgrace.

VICKI BAUM, *Martin's Summer* (1931)

When we are not physically starving, we have the luxury to realize psychic and emotional starvation.

CHERRÍE MORAGA, "La Güera," in Cherríe Moraga and Gloria Anzaldúa, eds., *This Bridge Called My Back* (1983)

The feeding of those that are hungry is a form of contemplation.

Simone Weil, *The Notebooks of Simone Weil* (1951)

See also Poverty, Privation.

HUSBAND

Husbands are like fires. They go out when unattended.

Zsa Zsa Gabor, in *Newsweek* (1960)

One thing she has noticed about married women, and that is how many of them have to go about creating their husbands. They have to start ascribing preferences, opinions, dictatorial ways. Oh, yes, they say, my husband is very particular. He won't touch turnips. He won't eat fried meat. (Or he will only eat fried meat.) He likes me to wear blue (brown) all the time. He can't stand organ music. He hates to see a woman go out bareheaded. He would kill me if I took one puff of tobacco. This way, bewildered, sidelong-looking men are made over, made into husbands, heads of households.

Alice Munro, *Friend of My Youth* (1990)

The *divine right* of husbands, like the divine right of kings, may, it is hoped, in this enlightened age, be contested without danger.

Mary Wollstonecraft, *A Vindication of the Rights of Women* (1792)

I never married because there was no need. I have three pets at home which answer the same purpose as a husband. I have a dog which growls every morning, a parrot which swears all afternoon and a cat that comes home late at night.

Marie Corelli, in Judy Allen, *Picking on Men* (1985)

It's a matter of opinion.

Hermione Gingold, when asked if her husband was still living, *How to Grow Old Disgracefully* (1988)

You mean apart from my own?

Zsa Zsa Gabor, when asked how many husbands she had had, in K. Edwards, *I Wish I'd Said That* (1976)

See also Family, Lovers, Marriage, Wife.

HYPOCRISY

Hypocrisy, the lie, is the true sister of evil, intolerance and cruelty.

Raisa M. Gorbachev, *I Hope* (1991)

One face to the world, another at home makes for misery.

Amy Vanderbilt, *New Complete Book of Etiquette* (1963)

The prohibition law, written for weaklings and derelicts, has divided the nation, like Gaul, into three parts—wets, drys, and hypocrites.

Florence Sabin, speech (1931)

See also Deception, Dishonesty.

I

ICEBERGS

Are you aware an iceberg takes repose / With you, and when it wakes may pasture on your snows?

ELIZABETH BISHOP, "The Imaginary Iceberg," *North and South* (1955)

The iceberg cuts its facets from within / Like jewelry from a grave.

ELIZABETH BISHOP, "The Imaginary Iceberg," *North and South* (1955)

IDEALISM

But she had told them nothing, given them the stone of her abstract, colorless idealism while they sat there, open-mouthed for sentimental bread.

ELIZABETH BOWEN, "Daffodils," *Early Stories* (1951)

IDEAS

Beware of people carrying ideas. Beware of ideas carrying people.

BARBARA GRIZZUTI HARRISON, *Foreign Bodies* (1984)

One can live in the shadow of an idea without grasping it.

ELIZABETH BOWEN, *The Heat of the Day* (1949)

Ideas move rapidly when their time comes.

CAROLYN HEILBRUN, *Toward a Recognition of Androgyny* (1973)

General notions are generally wrong.

LADY MARY WORTLEY MONTAGU, letter to future husband (1710), in Octave Thanet, ed., *The Best Letters of Lady Mary Wortley Montagu* (1901)

I had never been as resigned to ready-made ideas as I was to ready-made clothes, perhaps because although I couldn't sew, I could think.

JANE RULE, *Lesbian Images* (1975)

These people who are always briskly doing something and as busy as waltzing mice, they have little, sharp, staccato ideas, such as: "I see where I can make an annual cut of $3.47 in my meat budget." But they have no slow, big ideas.

BRENDA UELAND, *If You Want to Write* (1938)

Like an enormous walnut in feeble, jittery squirrel hands, an idea, bigger and closer than any idea he had ever known, had been revolving in his mind for several days.

PATRICIA HIGHSMITH, *Strangers on a Train* (1950)

He arrived at ideas the slow way, never skating over the clear, hard ice of logic, nor soaring on the slipstreams of imagination, but slogging, plodding along on the heavy ground of existence.

URSULA K. LE GUIN, *The Lathe of Heaven* (1971)

The idea was fragrant with possibilities.

JEAN FERRIS, *Invincible Summer* (1987)

A man with big ideas is a hard neighbor to live with.

MARIE VON EBNER-ESCHENBACH, *Aphorisms* (1905)

We are so placid that the smallest tremor of objection to anything at all is taken as a full-scale revolution. Should any soul speak up in favor of the obvious, it is taken as a symptom of the influence of the left, the right, the pink, the black, the dangerous. An idea for its own sake—especially an obvious idea—has no respectability.

CYNTHIA OZICK, "Women and Creativity," *Motive* (1969)

If you have one good idea, people will lend you twenty.

MARIE VON EBNER-ESCHENBACH, *Aphorisms* (1905)

And now let me ask you, my friend, whether you do not think, that many of our disappointments and much of our unhappiness arise from our forming false notions of things and persons.

ABIGAIL ADAMS, letter to Mrs. H. Lincoln (1761)

A writer didn't need "an" idea for a book; she needed at least forty. And "get" was the wrong word, implying that you received an idea as you would a gift. You didn't get ideas. You smelled them out, tracked them down, wrestled them into submission; you pursued them with forks and hope, and if you were lucky enough to catch one you impaled it, with the forks, before the sneaky little devil could get away.

ELIZABETH PETERS, *Naked Once More* (1989)

Now some people when they sit down to write and nothing special comes, no good ideas, are so frightened that they drink a lot of strong coffee to hurry them up, or smoke packages of cigarettes, or take drugs or get drunk. They do not know that ideas come slowly, and that the more clear, tranquil and unstimulated you are, the slower the ideas come, but the better they are.

BRENDA UELAND, *If You Want to Write* (1938)

See also Concepts, Theories, Thoughts.

IDENTITY

I am aware of myself as a four-hundred-year-old woman, born in the captivity of a colonial, pre-industrial oral culture and living now as a contemporary New Yorker.

BHARATI MUKHERJEE, in Janet Sternburg, ed., *The Writer on Her Work*, vol. 2 (1991)

There is no place on earth, no day or night, no hour or minute, when one is not a Jew or a woman.

ANDREA DWORKIN, "First Love," in Julia Wolf Mazow, ed., *The Woman Who Lost Her Names* (1980)

Split at the root, neither Gentile nor Jew, / Yankee nor Rebel.

ADRIENNE RICH, "Readings of History," *Snapshots of a Daughter-in-Law* (1967)

I was like a cat always climbing the wrong tree.

CARSON MCCULLERS, *Clock Without Hands* (1961)

A strong sense of identity gives man an idea he can do no wrong; too little accomplishes the same.

DJUNA BARNES, *Nightwood* (1937)

See also Character, Essence, Self.

IDLENESS

We owe most of our great inventions and most of the achievements of genius to idleness—either enforced or voluntary. The human mind prefers to be spoon-fed with the thoughts of others, but deprived of such nourishment it will, reluctantly, begin to think for itself—and such thinking, remember, is original thinking and may have valuable results.

AGATHA CHRISTIE, *The Moving Finger* (1942)

See also Indolence, Leisure.

IGNORANCE

The most violent element in society is ignorance.

EMMA GOLDMAN, title essay, *Anarchism* (1910)

Only ignorance! only *ignorance!* how can you talk about *only* ignorance? Don't you know that it is the worst thing in the world, next to wickedness? And which does the most mischief Heaven only knows. If people can say, "Oh! I did not know, I did not mean any harm," they think it is all right.

ANNA SEWELL, *Black Beauty* (1877)

The bliss that comes from ignorance should seldom be encouraged for it is likely to do one out of a more satisfying bliss.

RUTH STOUT, *How to Have a Green Thumb Without an Aching Back* (1955)

Too many of our countrymen rejoice in stupidity, look upon ignorance as a badge of honor. They condemn everything they don't understand.

TALLULAH BANKHEAD, *Tallulah* (1952)

Nowadays a man can belong to so-called cultured circles without, on the one hand, having any sort of conception about human destiny or, on the other hand, being aware, for example, that all the constellations are not visible at all seasons of the year.

SIMONE WEIL, *The Need for Roots* (1949)

Ignorance gives one a large range of probabilities.

GEORGE ELIOT, *Daniel Deronda* (1874)

ILLNESS

Everyone who is born holds dual citizenship, in the kingdom of the well and in the kingdom of the sick. Although we all prefer to use only the good passport, sooner or later each of us is obliged, at least for a spell, to identify ourselves as citizens of that other place.

SUSAN SONTAG, *Illness as Metaphor* (1978)

The sick soon come to understand that they live in a different world from that of the well and that the two cannot communicate.

JESSAMYN WEST, *The Woman Said Yes: Encounters With Life and Death* (1976)

Diseases have no eyes. They pick with a dizzy finger anyone, just anyone.

SANDRA CISNEROS, *The House on Mango Street* (1989)

Being a sick man is like being a log caught in a stream, Gilles. All the straws gather around it.

HELEN WADDELL, *Peter Abelard* (1933)

Severe illness isolates those in close contact with it, because it inevitably narrows the focus of concern. To a certain extent this can lead to healing, but not if the circle of concern is so tight that it cannot be broken into, or out of.

MADELEINE L'ENGLE, *Two-Part Invention* (1988)

Disease is an experience of so-called mortal mind. It is fear made manifest on the body.

MARY BAKER EDDY, *Science and Health* (1875)

Illness and accidents were mysterious manifestations of the war of the spirits, fought on the battleground of the body.

JEAN AUEL, *Clan of the Cave Bear* (1980)

No man needs curing of his individual sickness; his universal malady is what he should look to.

DJUNA BARNES, *Nightwood* (1937)

The disease is painless; it's the cure that hurts.

KATHARINE WHITEHORN, in *Observer* (1966)

The goal is to live a full, productive life even with all that ambiguity. No matter what happens, whether the cancer never flares up again or whether you die, the important thing is that the days that you have had you will have *lived*.

GILDA RADNER, *It's Always Something* (1989)

Ever since I have been ill, I have longed and longed for some palpable disease, no matter how conventionally dreadful a label it might have, but I was always driven back to stagger alone under the monstrous mass of subjective sensations, which that sympathetic being "the medical man" had no higher inspiration than to assure me I was personally responsible for, washing his hands of me with graceful complacency under my very nose. Dr. Torrey was the only man who did not assume because I was a victim to many pains, that I was, of necessity, an arrested mental development, too.

ALICE JAMES, *Journal* (1891)

I have never been anywhere but sick. In a sense sickness is a place, more instructive than a long trip to Europe, and it's always a place where there's no company, where nobody can follow. Sickness before death is a very appropriate thing and I think those who don't have it miss one of God's mercies.

FLANNERY O'CONNOR, in Sally Fitzgerald, ed., *The Habit of Being* (1979)

How impossible it is for strong healthy people to understand the way in which bodily *malaise* and suffering eats at the root of one's life! The philosophy that is true—the religion that is strength to the healthy—is constantly emptiness to one when the head is distracted and every sensation is oppressive.

GEORGE ELIOT, letter (1863), in J. W. Cross, *George Eliot's Life as Related in Her Letters and Journals* (1884)

Now I am beginning to live a little, and feel less like a sick oyster at low tide.

LOUISA MAY ALCOTT, in Ednah Dow Cheney, ed., *Louisa May Alcott, Her Life, Letters, and Journals* (1890)

There are no sick people in North Oxford. They are either dead or alive. It's sometimes difficult to tell the difference, that's all.

BARBARA PYM, *Crampton Hodnet* (1985)

"Dear! Everybody is ill now, I think," said Mrs. Hale, with a little of the jealousy which one invalid is apt to feel of another.

ELIZABETH GASKELL, *North and South* (1854)

See also AIDS, Alzheimer's, Doctors, Health, Hospital, Medication, Mental Illness, Nurses, Pain.

ILLUSION

Illusions are art, for the feeling person, and it is by art that we live, if we do.

ELIZABETH BOWEN, *The Death of the Heart* (1938)

One illusion is as good as another.

ZELDA FITZGERALD, letter to Scott Fitzgerald (1930), in Nancy Milford, *Zelda* (1970)

Some of my best friends are illusions. Been sustaining me for years.

SHEILA BALLANTYNE, *Norma Jean the Termite Queen* (1975)

It is only that my illusion is more real to me than reality. And so do we often build our world on an error, and cry out that the universe is falling to pieces, if any one but lift a finger to replace the error by truth.

MARY ANTIN, *The Promised Land* (1912)

It's far harder to kill a phantom than a reality.

VIRGINIA WOOLF, "Professions for Women," *The Death of the Moth* (1942)

And if you ever do a survey, you'll find that people prefer illusion to reality, ten to one. Twenty, even.

JUDITH GUEST, *Ordinary People* (1976)

See also Fantasy, Imagination.

IMAGES

An image is a stop the mind makes between uncertainties.

DJUNA BARNES, *Nightwood* (1937)

An image is a bridge between evoked emotion and conscious knowledge; words are the cables that hold up the bridge. Images are more direct, more immediate than words, and closer to the unconscious. Picture language precedes thinking in words; the metaphorical mind precedes analytical consciousness.

GLORIA ANZALDÚA, *Borderlands/La Frontera: The New Mestiza* (1987)

She never wanted these pictures called up on some future hot, dry day in some other place. She squinted, closed her eyes even, 'less the pictures cling to her eyes, store in the brain, to roll out later and crush her future with the weight of this place and its troubles.

TONI CADE BAMBARA, "The Organizer's Wife," *The Sea Birds Are Still Alive* (1982)

See also Photography.

IMAGINATION

Imagination and fiction make up more than three quarters of our real life.

SIMONE WEIL, *Gravity and Grace* (1947)

So you see the imagination needs moodling,— long, inefficient, happy idling, dawdling and puttering.

BRENDA UELAND, *If You Want to Write* (1938)

My imagination longs to dash ahead and plan developments; but I have noticed that when things happen in one's imaginings, they never happen in one's life, so I am curbing myself.

DODIE SMITH, *I Capture the Castle* (1948)

Indigo, I don't want to hear another word about it, do you understand me. I'm not setting the table with my Sunday china for fifteen dolls who got their period today.

NTOZAKE SHANGE, *Sassafrass, Cypress & Indigo* (1982)

See also Creativity, Fantasy, Illusion.

IMMIGRANTS

I do not know the speech / Of this cool land, / I cannot keep its pace.

ELSE LASKER-SCHÜLER, "Homesickness," *Hebrew Ballads and Other Poems* (1980)

I'm one of the millions of immigrant children, children of loneliness, wandering between worlds that are at once too old and too new to live in.

ANZIA YEZIERSKA, title story, *Children of Loneliness* (1923)

I'm very lonely now, Mary, / For the poor make no new friends.

LADY DUFFERIN, "Lament of the Irish Emigrant" (1894)

As one of the dumb, voiceless ones I speak. One of the millions of immigrants beating, beating out their hearts at your gates for a breath of understanding.

ANZIA YEZIERSKA, "America and I," *Children of Loneliness* (1923)

A characteristic thing about the aspiring immigrant is the fact that he is not content to progress alone. Solitary success is imperfect success in his eyes. He must take his family with him as he rises.

MARY ANTIN, *The Promised Land* (1912)

In spite of everything, we never gave up. The more we were despised, the harder we worked. We always had hope that some day things would be better. If not for us, then for our children.

YOSHIKO UCHIDA, *A Jar of Dreams* (1981)

My literary agenda begins by acknowledging that America has transformed *me*. It does not end until I show how I (and the hundreds of thousands like me) have transformed America.

BHARATI MUKHERJEE, in Janet Sternburg, ed., *The Writer on Her Work*, vol. 2 (1991)

The United States, which has been called the home of the persecuted and the dispossessed, has been since its founding an asylum for emotional orphans. For over three hundred years, refugees from political oppression, religious persecution, famine, poverty, and a rigid class system which limited educational and economic opportunities have been leaving their native villages and cities and coming to the United States in search of freedom and a better life.

EILEEN SIMPSON, *Orphans: Real and Imaginary* (1990)

See also Borders, Refugees.

IMMORTALITY

Millions long for immortality who do not know what to do with themselves on a rainy Sunday afternoon.

SUSAN ERTZ, *Anger in the Sky* (1943)

One of the strange things about living in the world is that it is only now and then one is quite sure one is going to live forever and ever and ever.

FRANCES HODGSON BURNETT, *The Secret Garden* (1911)

I think immortality is the passing of a soul through many lives or experiences, and such as are truly lived, used, and learned, help on to the next, each growing richer, happier and higher, carrying with it only the real memories of what has gone before.

LOUISA MAY ALCOTT, in Ednah Dow Cheney, ed., *Louisa May Alcott, Her Life, Letters, and Journals* (1890)

If we really believed that those who are gone from us were as truly alive as ourselves, we could not invest the subject with such awful depth of gloom as we do. If we would imbue our children with distinct faith in immortality, we should never speak of people as dead, but as passed into another world. We should speak of the body as a cast-off garment, which the wearer had outgrown; consecrated indeed by the beloved being that used it for a season, but of no value within itself.

LYDIA MARIA CHILD, *Letters from New York*, 2nd Series (1845)

The outrage was on the scale of God. My younger brother was immortal and they hadn't noticed. Immortality had been concealed in my brother's body while he was alive, and we hadn't noticed that it dwelt there. Now my brother's body was dead, and immortality with it. . . .

And the error, the outrage, filled the whole universe.

MARGUERITE DURAS, *The Lover* (1984)

See also Afterlife.

IMPATIENCE

I have been devoured all my life by an incurable and burning impatience: and to this day find all oratory, biography, operas, films, plays, books, and persons, too long.

MARGOT ASQUITH, *More or Less About Myself* (1934)

IMPERMANENCE

Faith, Sir, we are here today, and gone tomorrow.

APHRA BEHN, *The Lucky Chance* (1686)

The hardest thing for me is the sense of impermanence. All passes; nothing returns.

ELLEN GLASGOW, *Letters of Ellen Glasgow* (1958)

See also Death, End.

IMPOSSIBLE

He was by this time in that state of exaltation in which the impossible looks quite natural and commonplace.

OUIDA, "The Nürnberg Stove," in H. W. Mabie, *Famous Stories Every Child Should Know* (1907)

INADEQUACY

Let's face it—who ever is adequate? We all create situations each other can't live up to, then break our hearts at them because they don't.

ELIZABETH BOWEN, *The Death of the Heart* (1938)

And knew he was one of the ones who yearned / for something his heart wasn't big enough / to handle.

JOY HARJO, "New Orleans," in Rayna Green, ed., *That's What She Said* (1984)

She posed as being more indolent than she felt, for fear of finding herself less able than she could wish.

ELIZABETH BOWEN, *The Death of the Heart* (1938)

Here we are sitting in a shower of gold and nothing to hold up but a pitchfork!

CHRISTINA STEAD, *House of All Nations* (1938)

See also Ineptitude, Limitations.

INDECISION

I know not what to do; my mind is divided.

SAPPHO, in Henry Thornton Wharton, *Sappho* (1895)

Then again, maybe I won't.

JUDY BLUME, book title (1971)

Never mind.

GILDA RADNER (as "Emily Litella"), *It's Always Something* (1989)

See also Ambivalence, Doubt.

INDEPENDENCE

Impatience is the mark of independence, / not of bondage.

MARIANNE MOORE, "Marriage," *Collected Poems* (1951)

It is easy to be independent when you've got money. But to be independent when you haven't got a thing—that's the Lord's test.

MAHALIA JACKSON, *Movin' On Up* (1966)

See also Self-Sufficiency.

INDIA

India always changes people, and I have been no exception.

RUTH PRAWER JHABVALA, *Heat and Dust* (1975)

INDIFFERENCE

Indifference is the invincible giant of the world.

OUIDA, *Wisdom, Wit and Pathos* (1884)

The accomplice to the crime of corruption is frequently our own indifference.

BESS MYERSON, in Claire Safran, "Impeachment?" *Redbook* (1974)

I want to make people feel intensely alive. I'd rather have them against me than indifferent.

MARTHA GRAHAM, in Barbara McDowell and Hana Umlauf, *Woman's Almanac* (1977)

People never write calmly but when they write indifferently.

LADY MARY WORTLEY MONTAGU, letter (1709), in Octave Thanet, ed., *The Best Letters of Lady Mary Wortley Montagu* (1901)

My dear, I don't give a damn.

MARGARET MITCHELL, *Gone With the Wind* (1936)

As I grow older and older, / And totter towards the tomb, / I find that I care less and less / Who goes to bed with whom.

DOROTHY L. SAYERS, "That's Why I Never Read Modern Novels," in Janet Hitchman, *Such a Strange Lady* (1975)

See also Apathy.

INDIGNATION

I was so obsessed and consumed with my grievances that I could not get away from myself and think things out in the light. I was in the grip of that blinding, destructive, terrible thing—righteous indignation.

ANZIA YEZIERSKA, "Soap and Water," *Hungry Hearts* (1920)

See also Anger, Outrage.

INDIVIDUALITY

The individual—stupendous and beautiful paradox—is at once infinitesimal dust and the cause of all things.

C. V. WEDGWOOD, *Velvet Studies* (1946)

The boughs of no two trees ever have the same arrangement. Nature always produces *individuals;* She never produces *classes.*

LYDIA MARIA CHILD, *Letters from New York,* 2nd Series (1845)

Nature never repeats herself, and the possibilities of one human soul will never be found in another.

ELIZABETH CADY STANTON, "Solitude of Self" (1892)

One cup poured into another makes different waters; tears shed by one eye would blind if wept into another's eye. The breast we strike in joy is not the breast we strike in pain; any man's smile would be consternation on another's mouth.

DJUNA BARNES, *Nightwood* (1937)

To have one's individuality completely ignored is like being pushed quite out of life. Like being blown out as one blows out a light.

EVELYN SCOTT, *Escapade* (1923)

A child develops individuality long before he develops taste.

ERMA BOMBECK, *If Life Is a Bowl of Cherries, What Am I Doing in the Pits?* (1971)

The thing that makes you exceptional, if you are at all, is inevitably that which must also make you lonely.

LORRAINE HANSBERRY, in Robert Nemiroff, ed., *To Be Young, Gifted and Black* (1969)

I happen to believe that most people—and this is where I differ from many of my contemporaries, or at least as they express themselves—I think that virtually every human being is dramatically interesting. Not only is he dramatically interesting, he is a creature of stature whoever he is.

LORRAINE HANSBERRY, in Robert Nemiroff, ed., *To Be Young, Gifted and Black* (1969)

Every heart is the other heart. Every soul is the other soul. Every face is the other face. The individual is the one illusion.

MARGUERITE YOUNG, *Miss MacIntosh, My Darling* (1965)

I'm a ragged individualist.

JANE ACE, in Goodman Ace, *The Fine Art of Hypochondria* (1966)

See also Character, Self, Stereotypes, Uniqueness.

INDOLENCE

To will the impossible is usually a sin of indolence.

FANNY LEWALD, *Gefühltes und Gedachtes* (1900)

See also Idleness.

INEPTITUDE

The adversary she found herself forced to fight was not worth matching or beating; it was not a superior ability which she would have found honor in challenging; it was ineptitude.

AYN RAND, *Atlas Shrugged* (1957)

See also Inadequacy.

INFIDELITY

People who are so dreadfully devoted to their wives are so apt, from mere habit, to get devoted to other people's wives as well.

JANE WELSH CARLYLE, on her faithless husband (c. 1860), in Michèle Brown and Ann O'Connor, *Hammer and Tongues* (1986)

When something like this happens, you suddenly have no sense of reality at all. You have lost a piece of your past. The infidelity itself is small potatoes compared to the low-level brain damage that results when a whole chunk of your life turns out to have been completely different from what you thought it was. It becomes impossible to look back at anything that's happened . . . without wondering what was really going on.

NORA EPHRON, *Heartburn* (1983)

See also Adultery, Betrayal.

INFLUENCE

Everybody is influenced by somebody or something. If there's an original, who is the original?

ERNESTINE ANDERSON, in Brian Lanker, *I Dream a World* (1989)

One life stamps and influences another, which in turn stamps and influences another, on and on, until the soul of human experience breathes on in generations we'll never even meet.

MARY KAY BLAKELY, *Wake Me When It's Over* (1988)

It is easier to influence strong than weak characters in life.

MARGOT ASQUITH, *More or Less About Myself* (1934)

See also Inspiration.

INFORMATION

Everybody gets so much information all day long that they lose their common sense.

GERTRUDE STEIN, "Reflection on the Atomic Bomb" (1946), in R. A. Goldwin, ed., *Readings in World Politics* (1959)

See also Data, Facts, Knowledge.

INJUSTICE

I have come to believe that the one thing people cannot bear is a sense of injustice. Poverty, cold, even hunger, are more bearable than injustice.

MILLICENT FENWICK, interview (1980)

Injustice boils in men's hearts as does steel in its caldron, ready to pour forth, white hot, in the fullness of time.

MOTHER JONES, in Linda Atkinson, *Mother Jones: The Most Dangerous Woman in America* (1978)

An unrectified case of injustice has a terrible way of lingering, restlessly, in the social atmosphere like an unfinished question.

MARY MCCARTHY, *On the Contrary* (1961)

I don't have general views about anything, except social injustice.

MARGUERITE DURAS, *Practicalities* (1987)

One had better die fighting against injustice than to die like a dog or a rat in a trap.

IDA B. WELLS (1892), in Alfreda M. Duster, ed., *The Autobiography of Ida B. Wells* (1970)

It would have cost me more trouble to escape from injustice, than it does to submit to it.

MARIE-JEANNE ROLAND (1793), in Lydia Maria Child, *Memoirs of Madame de Staël and of Madame Roland* (1847)

If I did half of the things this sorry President [Nixon] did, they would put me under the jail and send every key to the moon. They have the little punishments for the big men and the heavy chastisement for the poor.

RUTH SHAYS, in John Langston Gwaltney, *Drylongso* (1980)

The golf links lie so near the mill / That almost every day / The laboring children can look out / And see the men at play.

SARAH N. CLEGHORN, "The Golf Links Lie So Near the Mill," *Portraits and Protests* (1917)

People so reasonable, so devoted, so strongly loving and hard working should have been exempt, one feels, from the vagaries of a malicious fate.

JANET LEWIS, *The Wife of Martin Guerre* (1941)

A man may be outlawed for the sake of a fish net he has never seen.

SELMA LAGERLÖF, *The Outlaws* (1907)

When one has been threatened with a great injustice, one accepts a smaller as a favor.

JANE WELSH CARLYLE, *Journal* (1855)

See also Discrimination, Intolerance, Justice, Oppression.

INNER LIFE

In the life of each of us, I said to myself, there is a place remote and islanded, and given to endless regret or secret happiness.

SARAH ORNE JEWETT, *The Country of the Pointed Firs* (1896)

I soon realized that no journey carries one far unless, as it extends into the world around us, it goes an equal distance into the world within.

LILLIAN SMITH, *The Journey* (1954)

If we go down into ourselves we find that we possess exactly what we desire.

SIMONE WEIL, *Gravity and Grace* (1947)

Inside myself is a place where I live all alone and that's where you renew your springs that never dry up.

PEARL BUCK, in *New York Post* (1959)

After all it is those who have a deep and real inner life who are best able to deal with the "irritating details of outer life."

EVELYN UNDERHILL, *The Letters of Evelyn Underhill* (1943)

My life is increasingly an inner one and the outer setting matters less and less.

ETTY HILLESUM, *An Interrupted Life: The Diaries of Etty Hillesum 1941–1943* (1983)

Some peoples' lives are affected by what happens to their person or their property; but for others fate is what happens to their feelings and their thoughts—that and nothing more.

WILLA CATHER, Lucy Gayheart (1935)

I swear that each of us keeps, battened down inside himself, a sort of lunatic giant—impossible socially, but full-scale—and that it's the knockings and batterings we sometimes hear in each other that keeps our intercourse from utter banality.

ELIZABETH BOWEN, *The Death of the Heart* (1938)

Suddenly many movements are going on within me, many things are happening, there is an almost unbearable sense of sprouting, of bursting encasements, of moving kernels, expanding flesh.

MERIDEL LE SUEUR, *Salute to Spring* (1940)

And now that I don't want to own anything any more and am free, now I suddenly own everything, now my inner riches are immeasurable.

ETTY HILLESUM, *An Interrupted Life: The Diaries of Etty Hillesum 1941–1943* (1983)

Might we not say to the confused voices which sometimes arise from the depths of our being: "Ladies, be so kind as to speak only four at a time"?

ANNE-SOPHIE SWETCHINE, The Writings of Madame Swetchine (1869)

See also Emotions, Feelings, Self, Soul, Spirituality, Wholeness.

INNOCENCE

What I call innocence is the spirit's unself-conscious state at any moment of pure devotion to any object. It is at once a receptiveness and total concentration.

ANNIE DILLARD, *Pilgrim at Tinker Creek* (1974)

To be innocent is to bear the weight of the entire universe. It is to throw away the counterweight.

SIMONE WEIL, *Gravity and Grace* (1947)

Innocence is impossible when people have never had the choice of becoming corrupt by dominating others.

SHEILA ROWBOTHAM, *Woman's Consciousness, Man's World* (1973)

Innocence ends when one is stripped of the delusion that one likes oneself.

JOAN DIDION, *On Self Respect* (1961)

What hope is there for innocence if it is not recognized?

SIMONE WEIL, *Gravity and Grace* (1947)

It's innocence when it charms us, ignorance when it doesn't.

MIGNON McLAUGHLIN, *The Second Neurotic's Notebook* (1966)

I am ill at ease with people whose lives are an open book.

IVY COMPTON-BURNETT, *More Women Than Men* (1933)

It's some damned innocent. Some little head so full of wool it doesn't know it's bleating.

MARGERY ALLINGHAM, *The Mind Readers* (1965)

See also Purity.

INNOVATION

At first people refuse to believe that a strange new thing can be done, then they begin to hope it can be done, then they see it can be done—then it is done and all the world wonders why it was not done centuries ago.

FRANCES HODGSON BURNETT, *The Secret Garden* (1911)

Innovators are inevitably controversial.

EVA LE GALLIENNE, *The Mystic in the Theater: Eleanora Duse* (1965)

There was never a place for her [Isadora Duncan] in the ranks of the terrible, slow army of the cautious. She ran ahead, where there were no paths.

DOROTHY PARKER, in *New Yorker* (1928)

Pioneers may be picturesque figures, but they are often rather lonely ones.

NANCY ASTOR, *My Two Countries* (1923)

See also Change, Discovery, Invention, Progress.

INSANITY

See Mental Illness.

INSECTS

In the South Pacific, because of their size, mosquitoes are required to file flight plans.

ERMA BOMBECK, *When You Look Like Your Passport Photo, It's Time to Go Home* (1991)

Seventeen times he had been attacked by those vicious insects, those aberrations of nature, and his neck, arms, and ankles were battlefields where small red bumps marked the final filling stations of dead but satisfied mosquitoes.

LUCILLE KALLEN, *The Tanglewood Murder* (1980)

Flies are the price we pay for summer.

ANN ZWINGER, *Beyond the Aspen Grove* (1970)

INSENSITIVITY

One can suffer a convulsion of one's entire nature, and, unless it makes some noise, no one notices. It's not just that we are incurious; we completely lack any sense of each other's existences.

ELIZABETH BOWEN, *The Death of the Heart* (1938)

If the people have no bread, let them eat cake.

MARIE ANTOINETTE, attributed (1770)

See also Complacency.

INSOMNIA

To wake in the night: be wide awake in an instant, with all your faculties on edge: to wake, and be under compulsion to set in, night for night, at the same point, knowing from grim experience, that the demons awaiting you have each to be grappled with in turn, no single one of them left unthrown, before you can win through to the peace that is utter exhaustion.

HENRY HANDEL RICHARDSON, *The Fortunes of Richard Mahoney: Ultima Thule* (1929)

Sleeplessness is a desert without vegetation or inhabitants.

JESSAMYN WEST, *The Woman Said Yes: Encounters With Life and Death* (1976)

See also Sleep.

INSPIRATION

The most beautiful thing in the world is, precisely, the conjunction of learning and inspiration.

WANDA LANDOWSKA, in Denise Resout, ed., *Landowska on Music* (1964)

I could never tell where inspiration begins and impulse leaves off. I suppose the answer is in the outcome. If your hunch proves a good one, you were inspired; if it proves bad, you are guilty of yielding to thoughtless impulse.

BERYL MARKHAM, *West With the Night* (1942)

There are two ways of spreading light: to be / The candle or the mirror that reflects it.

EDITH WHARTON, "Vesalius in Zante," *Artemis to Actaeon* (1909)

See also Influence.

INSTINCT

It is only by following your deepest instinct that you can lead a rich life and if you let your fear of consequence prevent you from following your deepest instinct, then your life will be safe, expedient and thin.

KATHARINE BUTLER HATHAWAY, *The Journals and Letters of the Little Locksmith* (1946)

The point is that one's got an *instinct* to live. One doesn't live because one's *reason* assents to living. People who, as we say, "would be better dead" don't want to die! People who apparently have everything to live for just let themselves fade out of life because they haven't got the energy to fight.

AGATHA CHRISTIE, *Sad Cypress* (1939)

I believe that we are always attracted to what we need most, an instinct leading us towards the persons who are to open new vistas in our lives and fill them with new knowledge.

HELENE ISWOLSKY, *Light Before Dusk* (1942)

See also Intuition.

INSTITUTIONS

Individuals learn faster than institutions and it is always the dinosaur's brain that is the last to get the new messages!

HAZEL HENDERSON, *The Politics of the Solar Age* (1981)

See also Bureaucracy.

INTELLECTUALS

It's no surprise to me that intellectuals commit suicide, go mad or die from drink. We feel things more than other people. We know the world is rotten and that chins are ruined by spots.

SUE TOWNSEND, *The Secret Diary of Adrian Mole Aged 13-3/4* (1982)

I don't want people running around saying Gwen Brooks's work is intellectual. That makes people think instantly about obscurity. It shouldn't have to mean that, but it often seems to.

GWENDOLYN BROOKS, in Claudia Tate, ed., Black Women Writers at Work (1983)

But, of course only morons would ever think or speak of themselves as intellectuals. That's why they all look so sad.

ELLEN GLASGOW, *Letters of Ellen Glasgow* (1958)

Ben was an intellectual, and intellectuals, say what you like, seemed to last longer than anyone else.

MURIEL SPARK, "The Fathers' Daughters" (1961)

See also Genius, Intelligence.

INTELLIGENCE

The naked intellect is an extraordinarily inaccurate instrument.

MADELEINE L'ENGLE, *A Wind in the Door* (1973)

For there is nothing more misleading than sagacity if it happens to get on a wrong scent.

GEORGE ELIOT, *The Mill on the Floss* (1860)

The collective intelligence of any group of people who are thinking as a "herd" rather than individually is no higher than the intelligence of the stupidest members.

MARY DAY WINN, *Adam's Rib* (1931)

People who cannot recognize a palpable absurdity are very much in the way of civilization.

AGNES REPPLIER, *In Pursuit of Laughter* (1936)

Maybe people have become so stupid as a result of having too many machines   The company we keep.

CHRYSTOS, "No Rock Scorns Me as Whore," in Cherríe Moraga and Gloria Anzaldúa, eds., *This Bridge Called My Back* (1983)

In our society to admit inferiority is to be a fool, and to admit superiority is to be an outcast. Those who are in reality superior in intelligence can be accepted by their fellows only if they pretend they are not.

MARYA MANNES, *More in Anger* (1958)

Had I been in anything inferior to him, he would not have hated me so thoroughly, but I knew all that he knew, and, what was worse, he suspected that I kept the padlock of silence on mental wealth in which he was no sharer.

CHARLOTTE BRONTË, *The Professor* (1846)

It is not true that a man's intellectual power is, like the strength of a timber beam, to be measured by its weakest point.

GEORGE ELIOT, *Impressions of Theophrastus Such* (1879)

See also Cleverness, Genius, Intellectuals.

INTENSITY

Sometimes I would almost rather have people take away years of my life than take away a moment.

PEARL BAILEY, *Talking to Myself* (1971)

My candle burns at both ends; / It will not last the night; / But ah, my foes, and oh, my friends— / It gives a lovely light!

EDNA ST. VINCENT MILLAY, "First Fig," *A Few Figs From Thistles* (1920)

See also Passion.

INTERDEPENDENCE

The crocodile doesn't harm the bird that cleans his teeth for him. He eats the others but not that one.

LINDA HOGAN, *Mean Spirit* (1990)

Breath is life, and the intermingling of breaths is the purpose of good living. This is in essence the great principle on which all productive living must rest, for relationships among all the beings of the universe must be fulfilled; in this way each individual life may also be fulfilled.

PAULA GUNN ALLEN, *The Sacred Hoop* (1986)

In reality, all communication that debilitates females also debilitates males, for if any system diminishes a part of the species, it diminishes all of it.

BOBBYE D. SORRELS, *The Nonsexist Communicator* (1983)

See also Human Family, Wholeness.

INTERESTING

It has all been very interesting.

LADY MARY WORTLEY MONTAGU, last words (1762)

Generally speaking anybody is more interesting doing nothing than doing something.

GERTRUDE STEIN, *Everybody's Autobiography* (1937)

It is completely unimportant. That is why it is so interesting.

AGATHA CHRISTIE, *The Murder of Roger Ackroyd* (1926)

INTERFERENCE

Those who make some other person their job . . . are dangerous.

DOROTHY L. SAYERS, *Gaudy Night* (1935)

I am one of those people who are blessed, or cursed, with a nature which has to interfere. If I see a thing that needs doing I do it.

MARGERY ALLINGHAM, *Death of a Ghost* (1934)

There are plenty of people, in Avonlea and out of it, who can attend closely to their neighbors' business by dint of neglecting their own; but Mrs. Rachel Lynde was one of those capable creatures who can manage their own concerns and those of other folks into the bargain.

L. M. MONTGOMERY, *Anne of Green Gables* (1908)

There were too many ears that listened for others besides themselves, and too many tongues that wagged to those they shouldn't.

MILDRED D. TAYLOR, *Roll of Thunder, Hear My Cry* (1976)

I always distrust people who know so much about what God wants them to do to their fellows.

SUSAN B. ANTHONY, in National American Woman Suffrage Association's *Proceedings* (1896)

More children suffer from interference than from non-interference.

AGATHA CHRISTIE, *Crooked House* (1949)

See also Codependence, Control.

INTERRUPTION

Interruption is a form of contempt.

LUCILLE KALLEN, *Introducing C. B. Greenfield* (1979)

See also Conversation, Listening.

INTIMACY

Intimacy is a difficult art.

VIRGINIA WOOLF, "Geraldine and Jane," *The Second Common Reader* (1932)

We commonly confuse *closeness* with *sameness* and view intimacy as the merging of two separate "I's" into one worldview.

HARRIET LERNER, *Dance of Intimacy* (1989)

See also Friendship, Love, Lovers, Marriage, Relationships, Togetherness.

INTOLERANCE

The last refuge of intolerance is in not tolerating the intolerant.

GEORGE ELIOT, letter (1857), in J. W. Cross, *George Eliot's Life as Related in Her Letters and Journals* (1884)

Traditional Anglo-Saxon intolerance is a local and temporal culture-trait like any other. . . We have failed to understand the relativity of cultural habits, and we remain debarred from much profit and enjoyment in our human relations with people of different standards, and untrustworthy in our dealings with them.

RUTH BENEDICT, *Patterns of Culture* (1934)

See also Prejudice.

INTROVERSION

Introversion, at least if extreme, is a sign of mental and spiritual immaturity.

PEARL BUCK, in Helen Hull, *The Writer's Book* (1950)

See also Inner Life.

INTUITION

Intuition is a suspension of logic due to impatience.

RITA MAE BROWN, *Southern Discomfort* (1982)

Intuition is a spiritual faculty and does not explain, but simply points the way.

FLORENCE SCOVEL SHINN, in Mary Alice Warner and Bayna Beilenson, eds., *Women of Faith and Spirit* (1987)

Trusting our intuition often saves us from disaster.

ANNE WILSON SCHAEF, *Meditations for Women Who Do Too Much* (1990)

I don't believe in intuition. When you get sudden flashes of perception, it is just the brain working faster than usual. But you've been getting ready to know it for a long time, and when it comes, you feel you've known it always.

KATHERINE ANNE PORTER, in George Plimpton, ed., *The Writer's Chapbook* (1989)

Enoch never nagged his blood to tell him a thing until it was ready.

FLANNERY O'CONNOR, *Wise Blood* (1949)

One of the many sad results of the Industrial Revolution was that we came to depend more than ever on the intellect, and to ignore the intuition with its symbolic thinking.

MADELEINE L'ENGLE, *Walking on Water: Reflections on Faith and Art* (1980)

See also Instinct.

INVENTION

I don't think necessity is the mother of invention—invention, in my opinion, arises directly from idleness, possibly also from laziness. To save oneself trouble.

AGATHA CHRISTIE, *An Autobiography* (1977)

See also Creation, Discovery, Innovation.

IOWA

You are brilliant and subtle if you come from Iowa and really strange and you live as you live and you are always very well taken care of if you come from Iowa.

GERTRUDE STEIN, *Everybody's Autobiography* (1937)

IRELAND

I am troubled; I'm dissatisfied, I'm Irish.

MARIANNE MOORE, "Spenser's Ireland," *What Are Years?* (1941)

Our Irish blunders are never blunders of the heart.

MARIA EDGEWORTH, *Essay on Irish Bulls* (1787)

Among the best traitors Ireland has ever had, Mother Church ranks at the very top, a massive obstacle in the path to equality and freedom.

BERNADETTE DEVLIN, *The Price of My Soul* (1969)

Not in vain is Ireland pouring itself all over the earth. . . . The Irish, with their glowing hearts and reverent credulity, are needed in this cold age of intellect and skepticism.

LYDIA MARIA CHILD, *Letters from New York*, 1st Series (1842)

It is really astonishing of what various and comprehensive powers this neglected language [Irish] is possessed. In the pathetic it breathes the most beautiful and affecting simplicity; and in the bolder species of composition it is distinguished by a freedom of expression, a sublime dignity, and rapid energy, which it is scarcely possible for any translation fully to convey.

CHARLOTTE BROOKE, *Reliques of Irish Poetry* (1789)

In some parts of Ireland the sleep which knows no waking is always followed by a wake which knows no sleeping.

MARY WILSON LITTLE, *A Paragrapher's Reveries* (1904)

See also Europe.

IRONY

Pleasure in irony, either in your own life or in what you read, is an ego trip. "I know what others do not."

JESSAMYN WEST, *The Life I Really Lived* (1979)

Irony is an indispensable ingredient of the critical vision; it is the safest antidote to sentimental decay.

ELLEN GLASGOW, *A Certain Measure* (1943)

See also Humor, Satire.

IRRATIONALITY

The irrational haunts the metaphysical.

ANNIE DILLARD, *The Writing Life* (1989)

The human animal varies from class to class, culture to culture. In one way we are consistent: We are irrational.

RITA MAE BROWN, *Starting From Scratch* (1988)

See also Rationality.

ISRAEL

Let me tell you something we Israelis have against Moses. He took us forty years through the desert in order to bring us to the one spot in the Middle East that has no oil!

GOLDA MEIR, in *New York Times* (1973)

ITALY

Italy is a country which is willing to submit itself to the worst governments. It is, as we know, a country ruled by disorder, cynicism, incompetence and confusion. Nevertheless we are aware of intelligence circulating in the streets like a vivid bloodstream.

NATALIA GINZBURG, *The Little Virtues* (1962)

Sometimes one feels that Italians should be with a capital and sometimes with a small letter, one can feel like that about almost anything.

GERTRUDE STEIN, "Poetry and Grammar," in Patricia Meyerowitz, ed., *Gertrude Stein, Writings and Lectures 1909–1945* (1974)

See also Europe, Rome, Venice.

J

JAPAN

One must learn, if one is to see the beauty in Japan, to like an extraordinarily restrained and delicate loveliness.

MIRIAM BEARD, *Realism in Romantic Japan* (1930)

JEALOUSY

Jealousy is all the fun you *think* they had.

ERICA JONG, *How to Save Your Own Life* (1977)

Jealousy is the most dreadfully involuntary of all sins.

IRIS MURDOCH, *The Black Prince* (1973)

Her jealousy never slept.

MARY SHELLEY, "The Mortal Immortal" (1833)

Jealousy is like a hot pepper. Use it mildly, and you add spice to the relationship. Use too much of it and it can burn.

AYALA M. PINES, *Romantic Jealousy* (1992)

Jealousy is never satisfied with anything short of an omniscience that would detect the subtlest fold of the heart.

GEORGE ELIOT, *The Mill on the Floss* (1860)

Jealousy, he thought, was as physical as fear; the same dryness of the mouth, the thudding heart, the restlessness which destroyed appetite and peace.

P. D. JAMES, *Death of an Expert Witness* (1977)

Jealousy is no more than feeling alone against smiling enemies.

ELIZABETH BOWEN, *The House in Paris* (1935)

There are two dogs who stand guard in your stomach. Their names in English are jealousy and fear. One guardian dog is jealously fearful, the other fearfully jealous. They are medicine to protect you.

AGNES WHISTLING ELK, in Lynn V. Andrews, *Medicine Woman* (1981)

To jealousy, nothing is more frightful than laughter.

FRANÇOISE SAGAN, *La Chamade* (1965)

Some . . . have imagined that by arousing a baseless suspicion in the mind of the beloved we can revive a waning devotion. But this experiment is very dangerous. Those who recommend it are confident that so long as resentment is groundless one need only suffer it in silence and all will soon be well. I have observed however that this is by no means the case.

LADY MURASAKI, *The Tale of Genji* (c. 1008)

The jealousy of the dead is lasting!

JEAN GARRIGUE, "The Snowfall," in Howard Moss, ed., *The Poet's Story* (1973)

See also Envy.

JEWS

To be a Jew is a destiny.

VICKI BAUM, *And Life Goes On* (1931)

Jews are the intensive form of any nationality whose language and customs they adopt.

EMMA LAZARUS, *Epistles to the Hebrews* (1882)

A people . . . wise-hearted with the sorrows of every land.

JESSIE SAMPTER, *Book of the Nations* (1917)

The nations which have received and in any way dealt fairly and mercifully with the Jew have prospered, and the nations that have tortured and oppressed him have written out their own curse.

OLIVE SCHREINER, *A Letter on the Jew* (1906)

To be a Jew in the twentieth century / Is to be offered a gift. If you refuse, / Wishing to be invisible, you choose / Death of the spirit, the stone insanity.

MURIEL RUKEYSER, "Letter to the Front," *Beast in View* (1944)

The usual attitude of Christians towards Jews is—I hardly know whether to say more impious or more stupid, when viewed in the light of their professed principles. . . . They hardly know Christ was a Jew. And I find men, educated, supposing that Christ spoke Greek. To my feeling, this deadness to the history which has prepared half our world for us, this inability to find interest in any form of life that is not clad in the same coat-tails and flounces as our own, lies very close to the worst kind of irreligion.

GEORGE ELIOT, letter to Harriet Beecher Stowe (1876), in J. W. Cross, *George Eliot's Life as Related in Her Letters and Journals* (1884)

The Jews are the victims of the strongest of collective suggestions. The truth is that they are neither better nor worse than others, but what comes from them is underlined, exaggerated, made responsible for all evil. They seem to have perpetually to fulfill the function of the scapegoat.

ADRIENNE MONNIER, *Les Gazettes d'Adrienne Monnier* (1938), in Richard McDougall, tr., *The Very Rich Hours of Adrienne Monnier* (1976)

The old truth is confirmed: "What *one* Christian does is his own responsibility, what *one* Jew does is thrown back at all Jews."

ANNE FRANK, *Diary of a Young Girl* (1952)

We Jews are alike. We have the same intensities, the sensitiveness, poetry, bitterness, sorrow, the same humor, the same memories. The memories are not those we can bring forth from our minds: they are centuries old and are written in our features, in the cells of our brains.

LEAH MORTON, *I Am a Woman—and a Jew* (1926)

You feel oppressed by your Judaism only as long as you do not take pride in it.

BERTHA PAPPENHEIM, in *Blätter d. jüd. Frauenbundes* (1936)

The Jewish heart has always starved unless it was fed through the Jewish intellect.

HENRIETTA SZOLD, in Mary Alice Warner and Bayna Beilenson, *Women of Faith and Spirit* (1987)

There is never a Jewish community without its scholars, but where Jews may not be both intellectuals and Jews, they prefer to remain Jews.

MARY ANTIN, *The Promised Land* (1912)

The Jews have produced only three originative geniuses: Christ, Spinoza, and myself.

GERTRUDE STEIN, in James R. Mellow, *Charmed Circle* (1974)

Pessimism is a luxury that a Jew can never allow himself.

GOLDA MEIR, in *Observer* (1974)

Poverty becomes a Jew like a red ribbon on a white horse.

ANZIA YEZIERSKA, *Red Ribbon on a White Horse* (1950)

The alchemy of home life went far to turn the dross of the Ghetto into gold.

LADY KATIE MAGNUS, *Jewish Portraits* (1905)

See also Holocaust, Israel, Minorities, Religion, Spirituality.

JOURNALISM

Journalism—an ability to meet the challenge of filling space.

REBECCA WEST, in *New York Herald Tribune* (1956)

You should always believe all you read in the newspapers, as this makes them more interesting.

ROSE MACAULAY, *A Casual Commentary* (1926)

I suppose you know where this country would be, where the *world* would be, if everyone who got depressed by the papers stopped reading them.

SUE KAUFMAN, *Diary of a Mad Housewife* (1967)

It is grievous to read the papers in most respects, I agree. More and more I skim the headlines only, for one can be sure what is carried beneath them quite automatically, if one has long been a reader of the press journalism.

MARY RITTER BEARD (1948), in Nancy F. Cott, *A Woman Making History* (1991)

What bothers me about the journalistic tendency to reduce unmanageable reality to self-contained, movielike little dramas is not just that we falsify when we do this. It is also that we really miss the good story.

MEG GREENFIELD, in *Newsweek* (1991)

The world is full of happy people, but no one ever hears of them. You have to fight and make a scandal to get into the papers.

GENE STRATTON-PORTER, *A Girl of the Limberlost* (1909)

Mother . . . considered a press conference on a par with a visit to a cage of cobras.

MARGARET TRUMAN, *Bess W. Truman* (1986)

Dead news like dead love has no phoenix in its ashes.

ENID BAGNOLD, *National Velvet* (1935)

See also Magazines, Writing.

JOURNEYS

Ah, I like the look of packing crates! A household in preparation for a journey! . . . Something full of the flow of life, do you understand? Movement, progress.

LORRAINE HANSBERRY, *A Raisin in the Sun* (1959)

A person needs at intervals to separate himself from family and companions and go to new places. He must go without his familiars in order to be open to influences, to change.

KATHARINE BUTLER HATHAWAY, *The Journals and Letters of the Little Locksmith* (1946)

It's not good to take sentimental journeys. You see the differences instead of the samenesses.

MARY ASTOR, *A Life on Film* (1967)

It is good to have an end to journey towards; but it is the journey that matters in the end.

URSULA K. LE GUIN, *The Left Hand of Darkness* (1969)

I am one of those who never knows the direction of my journey until I have almost arrived.

ANNA LOUISE STRONG, *I Change Worlds* (1935)

We all ended up somewhere with our various uncertain lives flapping about us in tatters and our pockets full of foreign coins.

KAREN ELIZABETH GORDON, *The Transitive Vampire* (1984)

See also Adventure, Travel.

JOY

O world, I cannot hold thee close enough!

EDNA ST. VINCENT MILLAY, "God's World," *Renascence* (1917)

Surely the strange beauty of the world must somewhere rest on pure joy!

LOUISE BOGAN, in Ruth Limmer, ed., *What the Woman Lived* (1973)

Townfolk know pleasures, country people joys.

MINNA THOMAS ANTRIM, *At the Sign of the Golden Calf* (1905)

People need joy quite as much as clothing. Some of them need it far more.

MARGARET COLLIER GRAHAM, *Gifts and Givers* (1906)

The sharing of joy, whether physical, emotional, psychic or intellectual, forms a bridge between the sharers which can be the basis for understanding much of what is not shared between them, and lessens the threat of their difference.

AUDRE LORDE, *Uses of the Erotic* (1978)

Birds sing after a storm; why shouldn't people feel as free to delight in whatever remains to them?

ROSE KENNEDY, *Times to Remember* (1974)

If all the people who have been hurt by the war were to exclude joy from their lives, it would almost be as if they had died. Men without joy seem like corpses.

KÄTHE KOLLWITZ (1918), in Hans Kollwitz, ed., *The Diaries and Letters of Käthe Kollwitz* (1955)

The unendurable is the beginning of the curve of joy.

DJUNA BARNES, *Nightwood* (1937)

See also Contentment, Happiness, Pleasure.

JUDGMENT

That would be a good thing for them to cut on my tombstone: Wherever she went, including here, it was against her better judgment.

DOROTHY PARKER, "But the One on the Right," in *New Yorker* (1929)

A mistake in judgment isn't fatal, but too much anxiety about judgment is.

PAULINE KAEL, *I Lost It at the Movies* (1965)

See also Taste.

JUSTICE

The wheels of justice . . . they're square wheels.

BARBARA CORCORAN, *The Hideaway* (1987)

Justice and judgment lie often a world apart.

EMMELINE PANKHURST, *My Own Story* (1914)

One must always be ready to change sides with justice, that fugitive from the winning camp.

SIMONE WEIL, in Peter Viereck, *The Unadjusted Man* (1956)

Justice consists in seeing that no harm is done to men. Whenever a man cries inwardly: "Why am I being hurt?" harm is being done to him. He is often mistaken when he tries to define the harm, and why and by whom it is being inflicted on him. But the cry itself is infallible.

SIMONE WEIL, "Human Personality," *The Simone Weil Reader* (1977)

I decided as usual that justice lay in the middle—that is to say nowhere.

ANTONIA FRASER, *Quiet As a Nun* (1977)

When it comes to the cause of justice, I take no prisoners and I don't believe in compromising.

MARY FRANCES BERRY, in Brian Lanker, *I Dream a World* (1989)

Ain't I hurt enough without you having to hurt me yet with charity? You want to give me hush money to swallow down unrightness that burns my flesh? I want justice.

ANZIA YEZIERSKA, "The Lost Beautifulness," *Hungry Hearts* (1920)

I never promised you a rose garden. I never promised you perfect justice.

HANNAH GREEN, *I Never Promised You a Rose Garden* (1964)

Justice is / reason enough for anything ugly. It balances the beauty in the world.

DIANE WAKOSKI, "Justice Is Reason Enough," in Paris Leary and Robert Kelly, *A Controversy of Poets* (1965)

When a just cause reaches its flood tide . . . whatever stands in the way must fall before its overwhelming power.

CARRIE CHAPMAN CATT, speech (1911)

If my cup won't hold but a pint, and yours holds a quart, wouldn't you be mean not to let me have my little half-measure full?

SOJOURNER TRUTH, speech (1851)

Someone / will take the ball / from the hands that play / the game of terror.

NELLY SACHS, "Someone," *O the Chimneys* (1967)

There is always a time to make right / what is wrong.

SUSAN GRIFFIN, "I Like to Think of Harriet Tubman," *Like the Iris of an Eye* (1976)

See also Equality, Injustice, Rights.

K

KINDNESS

To be civilized is to be incapable of giving unnecessary offense, it is to have some quality of consideration for all who cross our path.

AGNES REPPLIER, *Americans and Others* (1912)

My feeling is that there is nothing in life but refraining from hurting others, and comforting those that are sad.

OLIVE SCHREINER, *The Letters of Olive Schreiner, 1876–1920* (1976)

If you stop to be kind, you must swerve often from your path.

MARY WEBB, *Precious Bane* (1924)

When kindness has left people, even for a few moments, we become afraid of them, as if their reason had left them.

WILLA CATHER, *My Mortal Enemy* (1926)

The king has been very good to me. He promoted me from a simple maid to be a marchioness. Then he raised me to be a queen. Now he will raise me to be a martyr.

ANNE BOLEYN (1536), in Willis John Abbot, *Notable Women in History* (1913)

See also Compassion, Friendliness, Generosity, Goodness, Graciousness, Virtue.

KNOWLEDGE

We have a hunger of the mind which asks for knowledge of all around us, and the more we gain, the more is our desire; the more we see, the more are we capable of seeing.

MARIA MITCHELL (1878), in Phebe Mitchell Kendall, ed., *Maria Mitchell, Life, Letters, and Journals* (1896)

Knowledge of what you love somehow comes to you; you don't have to read nor analyze nor study. If you love a thing enough, knowledge of it seeps into you, with particulars more real than any chart can furnish.

JESSAMYN WEST, *The Friendly Persuasion* (1940)

It is important to use all knowledge ethically, humanely, and lovingly.

CAROL PEARSON, *The Hero Within* (1986)

It is not only by the questions we have answered that progress may be measured, but also by those we are still asking. The passionate controversies of one era are viewed as sterile preoccupations by another, for knowledge alters what we seek as well as what we find.

FREDA ADLER, *Sisters in Crime* (1975)

But need alone is not enough to set power free: there must be knowledge.

URSULA K. LE GUIN, *A Wizard of Earthsea* (1968)

Nobody knows enough, but many too much.

MARIE VON EBNER-ESCHENBACH, *Aphorisms* (1905)

I am never afraid of what I know.

ANNA SEWELL, *Black Beauty* (1877)

She knows what she sees. She has her eyes in the right place.

JOHANNA SPYRI, *Heidi* (1915)

Now peculiar scraps of knowledge were stuck to him like lint from all his jobs.

ANNE TYLER, *Searching for Caleb* (1975)

He that knew all that ever learning writ, / Knew only this—that he knew nothing yet.

APHRA BEHN, *The Emperor of the Moon* (1687)

You don't have to lay an egg to know if it tastes good.

PAULINE KAEL, *I Lost It at the Movies* (1965)

See also Common Sense, Curiosity, Data, Facts, Information, Learning, Teaching, Understanding.

L

LABOR

The other man's money is *capital;* getting it is *labor.*

MARY PETTIBONE POOLE, *A Glass Eye at a Keyhole* (1938)

One should not be assigned one's identity in society by the job slot one happens to fill. If we truly believe in the dignity of labor, any task can be performed with equal pride because none can demean the basic dignity of a human being.

JUDITH MARTIN, *Common Courtesy* (1985)

The trade agreement has become a rather distinct feature of the American labor movement. . . . It is based on the idea that labor shall accept the capitalist system of production and make terms of peace with it.

MARY RITTER BEARD, *A Short History of the American Labor Movement* (1920)

On their side the workers had only the Constitution. The other side had bayonets.

MOTHER JONES, in Linda Atkinson, *Mother Jones: The Most Dangerous Woman in America* (1978)

See also Business, Work.

LADIES

I have defined Ladies as people who did not do things themselves.

GWEN RAVERAT, *Period Piece* (1952)

She was a perfect lady—just set in her seat and stared.

EUDORA WELTY, "Lily Daw and the Three Ladies," *A Curtain of Green* (1941)

The Word *Lady*: Most Often Used to Describe Someone You Wouldn't Want to Talk to for Even Five Minutes.

FRAN LEBOWITZ, *Metropolitan Life* (1978)

See also Women.

LAND

It has been proved that the land can exist without the country—and be better for it; it has not been proved . . . that the country can exist without the land.

ALICE WALKER, *Living by the Word* (1988)

I think nobody owns land until their dead are in it.

JOAN DIDION, *Run River* (1961)

To the land, she had given her mind and heart with the abandonment that she had found disastrous in any human relation.

ELLEN GLASGOW, *Barren Ground* (1925)

The truth is I've got the land on my back, an' it's drivin' me. Land is a hard driver.

ELLEN GLASGOW, *Barren Ground* (1925)

See also Earth, Nature.

LANGUAGE

Language helps form the limits of our reality.

DALE SPENDER, *Man Made Language* (1980)

The basic agreement between human beings, indeed what makes them human and makes them social, is language.

MONIQUE WITTIG, "On the Social Contract," *The Straight Mind* (1992)

Only where there is language is there world.

ADRIENNE RICH, "The Demon Lover," *Leaflets* (1969)

Words, volumes of words, all signed, were the eloquent metaphor of my life. It was the language born of hands that was my beginning.

RUTH SIDRANSKY, *In Silence* (1990)

Language screens reality as a filter on a camera lens screens light waves.

CASEY MILLER AND KATE SWIFT, *Words and Women* (1976)

Language is neither innocent nor neutral. Linguistic habits condition our view of the world and hinder social change.

CARMEN MARTÍNEZ TEN, in *España 91* (1991)

Language is not neutral. It is not merely a vehicle which carries ideas. It is itself a shaper of ideas.

DALE SPENDER, *Man Made Language* (1980)

Language, as symbol, determines much of the nature and quality of our experience.

SONIA JOHNSON, *The Ship That Sailed Into the Living Room* (1991)

Language casts sheaves of reality upon the social body, stamping it and violently shaping it.

MONIQUE WITTIG, "The Mark of Gender," *The Straight Mind* (1992)

Language makes culture, and we make a rotten culture when we abuse words.

CYNTHIA OZICK, "We Are the Crazy Lady and Other Feisty Feminist Fables," in Francine Klagsbrun, ed., *The First Ms. Reader* (1972)

Every language reflects the prejudices of the society in which it evolved.

CASEY MILLER AND KATE SWIFT, *The Handbook of Nonsexist Writing* (1980)

Language is the road map of a culture. It tells you where its people come from and where they are going.

RITA MAE BROWN, *Starting From Scratch* (1988)

Language conveys a certain power. It is one of the instruments of domination. It is carefully guarded by the superior people because it is one of the means through which they conserve their supremacy.

SHEILA ROWBOTHAM, *Woman's Consciousness, Man's World* (1973)

Language exerts hidden power, like the moon on the tides.

RITA MAE BROWN, *Starting From Scratch* (1988)

This monopoly over language is one of the means by which males have ensured their own primacy, and consequently have ensured the invisibility or "other" nature of females.

DALE SPENDER, *Man Made Language* (1980)

"When you say Man," said Oedipus, "you include women / too. Everyone knows that." She said, "That's what / you think."

MURIEL RUKEYSER, "Myth," *Breaking Open* (1973)

I believe the deeply rooted semantic confusion between "man" as a male and "man" as a species has been fed back into and vitiated a great deal of the speculation that goes on about the origins, development, and nature of the human race.

ELAINE MORGAN, *The Descent of Woman* (1972)

What has been termed "correct" English is nothing other than the blatant legitimation of the white middle-class code.

DALE SPENDER, *Man Made Language* (1980)

Conventional English usage, including the generic use of masculine-gender words, often obscures the actions, the contributions, and sometimes the very presence of women. Turning our backs on that insight is an option, of course, but it is an option like teaching children that the world is flat.

CASEY MILLER AND KATE SWIFT, *The Handbook of Nonsexist Writing* (1980)

In many patriarchies, language, as well as cultural tradition, reserve the human condition for the male. With the Indo-European languages this is a nearly inescapable habit of mind, for despite all the customary pretense that "man" and "humanity" are terms which apply equally to both sexes, the fact is hardly obscured that in practice, general application favors the male far more often than the female as referent, or even sole referent, for such designations.

KATE MILLETT, *Sexual Politics* (1969)

Just as the development of computer science has necessitated an expanded technical vocabulary, so too do social changes require transformations in traditional language usage.

FRANCINE WATTMAN FRANK AND PAULA A. TREICHLER, *Language, Gender, and Professional Writing* (1989)

Our native language is like a second skin, so much a part of us we resist the idea that it is constantly changing, constantly being renewed.

CASEY MILLER AND KATE SWIFT, *The Handbook of Nonsexist Writing* (1980)

Few would suggest that sexual or racial inequality exists because of language use. Nor would many argue that banishing sexist and racist labeling would in itself result in a just society. At the same time, it is clear that language not only reflects social structures but, more important, sometimes serves to perpetuate existing differences in power; thus a serious concern with linguistic usage is fully warranted.

FRANCINE WATTMAN FRANK AND PAULA A. TREICHLER, *Language, Gender, and Professional Writing* (1989)

The dictionary is . . . only a rough draft.

MONIQUE WITTIG AND SANDE ZEIG, *Lesbian Peoples* (1976)

You and I come by road or rail, but economists travel on infrastructure.

MARGARET THATCHER, in *Observer* (1985)

She calls a spade a delving instrument.

RITA MAE BROWN, *Southern Discomfort* (1982)

She spoke academese, a language that springs like Athene from an intellectual brow, and she spoke it with a nonregional, "good" accent.

MAY SARTON, *The Small Room* (1961)

I'm bilingual. I speak English and I speak educationese.

SHIRLEY M. HUFSTEDLER, in *Newsweek* (1980)

A great many people think that polysyllables are a sign of intelligence.

BARBARA WALTERS, *How to Talk With Practically Anybody About Practically Anything* (1970)

I might not know how to use thirty-four words where three would do, but that does not mean I don't know what I'm talking about.

RUTH SHAYS, in John Langston Gwaltney, *Drylongso* (1980)

Whatever its function, / *Like*'s not a conjunction.

MARGARET FISHBACK, "The Purist to Her Love," *I Take It Back* (1935)

We defend ourselves with descriptions and tame the world by generalizing.

IRIS MURDOCH, *The Black Prince* (1973)

A candidate for office can have no greater advantage than muddled syntax; no greater liability than a command of language.

MARYA MANNES, *More in Anger* (1958)

English is weak in describing emotional states or intensities of interpersonal relationships.

RITA MAE BROWN, *Starting From Scratch* (1988)

I try to write each piece in the language of the piece, so that I'm not using the same language from piece to piece. I may be using ten or twenty languages. That multiplicity of language and the use of words is African in tradition. And black writers have definitely taken that up and taken it in. It's like speaking in tongues. It may sound like gibberish to somebody, but you know it's a tongue of some kind. Black people have this. We have the ability as a race to speak in tongues, to dream in tongues, to love in tongues.

ALEXIS DE VEAUX, in Claudia Tate, ed., *Black Women Writers at Work* (1983)

Language is decanted and shared. If only one person is left alive speaking a language—the case with some American Indian languages—the language is dead. Language takes two and their multiples.

RITA MAE BROWN, *Starting From Scratch* (1988)

See also Clichés, Words, Writing.

LATENESS

Five minutes! Zounds! I have been five minutes too late all my lifetime!

HANNAH COWLEY, *The Belle's Stratagem* (1780)

Ah, "All things come to those who wait." / They come, but often come too late.

LADY MARY M. CURRIE, *Tout Vient à Qui Sait Attendre* (1890)

Now that Fate / Has brought me what so long, I so desired, / It is too late, / I am too tired.

LAURENCE HOPE, "To Aziz," *Stars of the Desert* (1903)

If something anticipated arrives too late it finds us numb, wrung out from waiting, and we feel— nothing at all. The best things arrive on time.

DOROTHY GILMAN, *A New Kind of Country* (1978)

I suppose we are all the same, we human beings. We always learn too late.

MADELEINE BRENT, *Merlin's Keep* (1977)

One doesn't recognize in one's life the really important moments—not until it's too late.

AGATHA CHRISTIE, *Endless Night* (1968)

But for most of us the space between "dreaming on things to come" and "it is too late, it is all over" is too tiny to enter.

IRIS MURDOCH, *The Black Prince* (1973)

By the time a person has achieved years adequate for choosing a direction, the die is cast and the moment has long since passed which determined the future.

ZELDA FITZGERALD, *Save Me the Waltz* (1932)

See also Delay, Time, Timeliness.

LAUGHTER

Laughter is by definition healthy.

DORIS LESSING, *The Summer Before the Dark* (1973)

He who laughs, lasts!

MARY PETTIBONE POOLE, *A Glass Eye at a Keyhole* (1938)

Love cannot exorcise the gifts of hate. / Hate cannot exorcise what has no weight, / But laughter we can never over-rate.

MAY SARTON, "An Intruder," *A Grain of Mustard Seed* (1971)

We cannot really love anybody with whom we never laugh.

AGNES REPPLIER, *Americans and Others* (1912)

Laugh and the world laughs with you, snore and you sleep alone.

MRS. PATRICK CAMPBELL, letter to George Bernard Shaw (1912)

There is always a secret irritation about a laugh into which we cannot join.

AGNES REPPLIER, *Points of View* (1891)

It was the kind of laughter that caught like briars in her chest and felt very much like pain.

KATHERINE PATERSON, *Lyddie* (1991)

Hostility is expressed in a number of ways. One is laughter.

KATE MILLETT, *Sexual Politics* (1969)

See also Humor, Smile.

LAW

For many persons, law appears to be black magic—an obscure domain that can be fathomed only by the professional initiated into its mysteries.

SUSAN C. ROSS, *The Rights of Women* (1973)

Law to her was all Greek and turkey tracks.

JESSAMYN WEST, *The Friendly Persuasion* (1940)

[Law] is one part justice to nine parts expediency. Who needs it.

LUCILLE KALLEN, *Introducing C. B. Greenfield* (1979)

If you love the law and you love good sausage, don't watch either of them being made.

BETTY TALMADGE, in *The Reader* (1977)

Laws are felt only when the individual comes into conflict with them.

SUZANNE LaFOLLETTE, *Concerning Women* (1926)

Law is a reflection and a source of prejudice. It both enforces and suggests forms of bias.

DIANE B. SCHULDER, "Does the Law Oppress Women?" in Robin Morgan, *Sisterhood Is Powerful* (1970)

Woman throughout the ages has been mistress to the law, as man has been its master.

FREDA ADLER, *Sisters in Crime* (1975)

Every form of bigotry can be found in ample supply in the legal system of our country.

FLORYNCE KENNEDY, "Institutionalized Oppression vs. the Female," in Robin Morgan, *Sisterhood Is Powerful* (1970)

If you got the sayso you want to keep it, whether you are right or wrong. That's why they have to keep changing the laws—so they don't unbenefit any of these big white men.

RUTH SHAYS, in John Langston Gwaltney, *Drylongso* (1980)

Gerry's friends, you see, had no confidence in the United States judicial system. They did not seem comfortable in the courtroom, and this increased their unreliability in the eyes of judge and jury. If you trust the authorities, they trust you better back, it seems.

LOUISE ERDRICH, *Love Medicine* (1984)

Petty laws breed great crimes.

OUIDA, *Wisdom, Wit and Pathos* (1884)

That is what is so bizarre about the American legal system. Where else in the world would stealing from a phone booth be considered more serious than polluting the earth?

LAURA NADER, in Karen DeCrow, *Sexist Justice* (1974)

Life and death do not wait for legal action.

DAPHNE DU MAURIER, *My Cousin Rachel* (1952)

The contempt for law and the contempt for the human consequences of lawbreaking go from the bottom to the top of American society.

MARGARET MEAD, in Claire Safran, "Impeachment?" *Redbook* (1974)

See also Justice, Lawyers, Litigation.

LAWYERS

Lawyers are . . . operators of the toll bridge which anyone in search of justice must pass.

JANE BRYANT QUINN, in *Newsweek* (1978)

A lawyer's relationship to justice and wisdom . . . is on a par with a piano tuner's relationship to a concert. He neither composes the music, nor interprets it—he merely keeps the machinery running.

LUCILLE KALLEN, *Introducing C. B. Greenfield* (1979)

You want the unvarnished and ungarnished truth, and I'm no hand for that. I'm a lawyer.

MARY ROBERTS RINEHART, *The Man in Lower Ten* (1909)

Never, never, never, on cross-examination ask a witness a question you don't already know the answer to, was a tenet I absorbed with my baby-food. Do it, and you'll often get an answer you don't want.

HARPER LEE, *To Kill a Mockingbird* (1960)

See also Law.

LEADERS

It is high time that we had lights that are not incendiary torches.

GEORGE SAND (1863), in Raphaël Ledos de Beaufort, *Letters of George Sand* (1886)

A leader who doesn't hesitate before he sends his nation into battle is not fit to be a leader.

GOLDA MEIR, in Israel and Mary Shenker, eds., *As Good as Golda* (1970)

Would the world ever be run by anything better than personal passion, and the scoring off each other of amoral schoolboys?

KATE O'BRIEN, *That Lady* (1946)

You take people as far as they will go, not as far as you would like them to go.

JEANNETTE RANKIN, in Hannah Geffen Josephson, *Jeannette Rankin: First Lady in Congress* (1974)

Reformers must expect to be disowned by those who are only too happy to enjoy what has been won for them.

DORIS LESSING, *Golden Notebook* (1962)

The speed of the leader is the speed of the gang.

MARY KAY ASH, *On People Management* (1984)

See also Dictators, Government, Politicians.

LEARNING

One can learn, at least. One can go on learning until the day one is cut off.

FAY WELDON, *Down Among the Women* (1971)

The joy of learning is as indispensable in study as breathing is in running. Where it is lacking there are no real students, but only poor caricatures of apprentices who, at the end of their apprenticeship, will not even have a trade.

SIMONE WEIL, "Reflections on the Right Use of School Studies," *The Simone Weil Reader* (1977)

The world of learning is so broad, and the human soul is so limited in power! We reach forth and strain every nerve, but we seize only a bit of the curtain that hides the infinite from us.

MARIA MITCHELL, diary (1854), in Phebe Mitchell Kendall, ed., *Maria Mitchell, Life, Letters, and Journals* (1896)

The excitement of learning separates youth from old age. As long as you're learning you're not old.

ROSALYN S. YALOW, in Barbara Shiels, *Women and the Nobel Prize* (1985)

That's the way things come clear. All of a sudden. And then you realize how obvious they've been all along.

MADELEINE L'ENGLE, *The Arm of the Starfish* (1965)

That is what learning is. You suddenly understand something you've understood all your life, but in a new way.

DORIS LESSING, *The Four-Gated City* (1969)

I think you should learn, of course, and some days you must learn a great deal. But you should also have days when you allow what is already in you to swell up inside of you until it touches everything. And you can feel it inside you. If you never take time out to let that happen, then you just accumulate facts, and they begin to rattle around inside of you. You can make noise with them, but never really feel anything with them. It's hollow.

E. L. KONIGSBURG, *From the Mixed-Up Files of Mrs. Basil E. Frankweiler* (1967)

There are some things you learn best in calm, and some in storm.

WILLA CATHER, *The Song of the Lark* (1915)

Now, there are two ways to approach a subject that frightens you and makes you feel stupid: you can embrace it with humility and an open mind, or you can ridicule it mercilessly.

JUDITH STONE, *Light Elements: Essays in Science From Gravity to Levity* (1991)

Too much rigidity on the part of teachers should be followed by a brisk spirit of insubordination on the part of the taught.

AGNES REPPLIER, *Points of View* (1891)

Music lessons—or lessons in anything—can be dangerous to us, for the weekly guilt can become addictive. We can come to believe that we deserve scorn, and that we really can profit from being told repeatedly how to do it, from being given "right " answers. Gradually we lose our child-like enthusiasm for music or tennis or roller-skating or tightrope walking and substitute an intense yearning to do it "right" for the teacher.

ELOISE RISTAD, *A Soprano on Her Head* (1982)

See also Education, Research, Teaching, Understanding.

LEGENDS

Facts are fine, fer as they go . . . but they're like water bugs skittering atop the water. Legends, now—they go deep down and bring up the heart of a story.

MARGUERITE HENRY, *Misty of Chincoteague* (1947)

These are the stories that never, never die, that are carried like seed into a new country, are told to you and me and make in us new and lasting strengths.

MERIDEL LE SUEUR, *Nancy Hanks of Wilderness Road* (1949)

But, like all very handsome men who die tragically, he left not so much a character behind him as a legend. Youth and death shed a halo through which it is difficult to see a real face.

VIRGINIA WOOLF, "A Sketch of the Past" (1940), *Moments of Being* (1976)

See also Heroes, Myth, Stories.

LEISURE

Leisure and the cultivation of human capacities are inextricably interdependent.

MARGARET MEAD, in *Redbook* (1963)

It is in his pleasure that a man really lives; it is from his leisure that he constructs the true fabric of self.

AGNES REPPLIER, *Essays in Idleness* (1893)

People who know how to employ themselves, always find leisure moments, while those who do nothing are forever in a hurry.

MARIE-JEANNE ROLAND (1792), in Lydia Maria Child, *Memoirs of Madame de Staël and of Madame Roland* (1847)

The multi-billion-dollar entertainment and leisure industries notwithstanding, Americans have not learned how to use large amounts of leisure in noncompulsive, personally satisfying ways.

JANET SALTZMAN CHAFETZ, *Masculine/Feminine or Human?* (1974)

See also Busyness, Idleness, Retirement, Vacation.

LESBIANS

The suppressed lesbian I had been carrying in me since adolescence began to stretch her limbs.

ADRIENNE RICH, "Split at the Root," *Blood, Bread, and Poetry* (1986)

The Lesbian is one of the least known members of our culture. Less is known about her—and less accurately—than about the Newfoundland dog.

SIDNEY ABBOTT AND BARBARA LOVE, *Sappho Was a Right-On Woman* (1972)

Once a woman is known as a Lesbian, both she and society often feel that no other fact about

her can rival the sexual identification. . . . No matter what a Lesbian achieves, her sexuality will remain her *primary* identity.

SIDNEY ABBOTT AND BARBARA LOVE, *Sappho Was a Right-On Woman* (1972)

If Lesbians were purple, none would be admitted to respected places. But if all Lesbians suddenly turned purple today, society would be surprised at the number of purple people in high places.

SIDNEY ABBOTT AND BARBARA LOVE, *Sappho Was a Right-On Woman* (1972)

I was so excited to be able to say that I was a lesbian that I would shake hands with strangers on the street and say, "Hi! I'm Sally Gearhart and I'm a lesbian." Once, appearing on a panel program, I began, "I'm Sally Lesbian and I'm a gearhart!" I realized then that I had put too much of my identity into being lesbian.

SALLY GEARHART, in Leigh W. Rutledge, *Unnatural Quotations: A Compendium of Quotations by, for, or about Gay People* (1988)

Historically, this culture has come to identify lesbians as women who over time, engage in a range and variety of sexual-emotional relationships with women. I, for one, identify a woman as a lesbian who says she is.

CHERYL CLARKE, "Lesbianism: An Act of Resistance," in Cherríe Moraga and Gloria Anzaldúa, eds., *This Bridge Called My Back* (1983)

For a woman to be a lesbian in a male-supremacist, capitalist, misogynist, racist, homophobic, imperialist culture, such as that of North America, is an act of resistance.

CHERYL CLARKE, "Lesbianism: An Act of Resistance," in Cherríe Moraga and Gloria Anzaldúa, eds., *This Bridge Called My Back* (1983)

Our very strength as lesbians lies in the fact that we are outside of patriarchy; our existence challenges its life.

CHARLOTTE BUNCH, "Not for Lesbians Only," *Quest* (1975)

Of course it is extremely difficult to like oneself in a culture which thinks you are a disease.

CHRYSTOS, "I Don't Understand Those Who Have Turned Away From Me," in Cherríe Moraga and Gloria Anzaldúa, eds., *This Bridge Called My Back* (1983)

A Lesbian who consents to guilt for her sexual preference is her own worst oppressor. She accepts and internalizes prejudices and uses them against herself.

SIDNEY ABBOTT AND BARBARA LOVE, *Sappho Was a Right-On Woman* (1972)

See also Gay.

LETTERS

A letter always seemed to me like immortality because it is the mind alone without corporeal friend.

EMILY DICKINSON (1867), in Mabel Loomis Todd, *Letters of Emily Dickinson* (1894)

Why is it that you can sometimes feel the reality of people more keenly through a letter than face to face?

ANNE MORROW LINDBERGH, *Bring Me a Unicorn* (1971)

The one good thing about not seeing you is that I can write you letters.

SVETLANA ALLILUYEVA, *Twenty Letters to a Friend* (1967)

All letters, methinks, should be as free and easy as one's discourse, not studied as an oration, nor made up of hard words like a charm.

DOROTHY OSBORNE, letter to her husband (1653)

It is well enough, when one is talking to a friend, to lodge in an odd word by way of counsel now and then; but there is something mighty irksome in its staring upon one in a letter, where one ought to see only kind words and friendly remembrances.

MARY LAMB, in *The Letters of Charles and Mary Lamb* (1912)

It takes two to write a letter as much as it takes two to make a quarrel.

ELIZABETH DREW, *The Literature of Gossip* (1964)

Why it should be such an effort to write to the people one loves I can't imagine. It's none at all to write to those who don't really count.

KATHERINE MANSFIELD (1922), *Journal of Katherine Mansfield* (1927)

A letter is a barrier, a reprieve, a charm against the world, an almost infallible method of acting at a distance.

IRIS MURDOCH, *The Black Prince* (1973)

The best letters of our time are precisely those that can never be published.

VIRGINIA WOOLF, "Modern Letters," *The Captain's Death Bed* (1950)

I for one appreciate a good form letter, having worked on Capitol Hill and learned seven dozen cordial ways to say nothing.

CARRIE JOHNSON, in *New York Times* (1984)

See also Writing.

LIBERATION

It's as if we think liberation a fixed quantity, that there is only so much to go around. That an individual or community is liberated at the expense of another. When we view liberation as a scarce resource, something only a precious few of us can have, we stifle our potential, our creativity, our genius for living, learning and growing.

ANDREA CANAAN, "Brownness," in Cherríe Moraga and Gloria Anzaldúa, eds., *This Bridge Called My Back* (1983)

See also Freedom.

LIBERTY

O Liberty! O Liberty! How many crimes are committed in thy name!

MARIE-JEANNE ROLAND (1793), on her way to the guillotine, in Alphonse de Lamartine, *Histoire des Girondins* (1847)

If we do not die for liberty, we shall soon have nothing left to do but weep for her.

MARIE-JEANNE ROLAND (1791), in Lydia Maria Child, *Memoirs of Madame de Staël and of Madame Roland* (1847)

There was one of two things I had a *right* to, liberty, or death; if I could not have one, I would have the other; for no man should take me alive.

HARRIET TUBMAN, in Sarah H. Bradford, *Harriet, the Moses of Her People* (1869)

Liberty is not less a blessing, because oppression has so long darkened the mind that it can not appreciate it.

LUCRETIA MOTT, speech (1849), in Elizabeth Cady Stanton, *The History of Woman Suffrage* (1881)

When liberty is taken away by force it can be restored by force. When it is relinquished voluntarily by default it can never be recovered.

DOROTHY THOMPSON, "What Price Liberty?" in *Ladies' Home Journal* (1958)

Liberty, as it is conceived by current opinion, has nothing inherent about it; it is a sort of gift or trust bestowed on the individual by the state pending *good behavior*.

MARY MCCARTHY, lecture (1952)

See also Freedom.

LIFE

Life is a frail moth flying / Caught in the web of the years that pass.

SARA TEASDALE, "Come," *Rivers to the Sea* (1915)

Life is like a great jazz riff. You sense the end the very moment you were wanting it to go on forever.

SHEILA BALLANTYNE, title story, *Life on Earth* (1988)

Life itself is a party; you join after it's started and you leave before it's finished.

ELSA MAXWELL, *How to Do It* (1957)

Life is an illusion.

MATA HARI, as she prepared to meet firing squad (1917), in Barbara McDowell and Hana Umlauf, *Woman's Almanac* (1977)

Life is a tragic mystery. We are pierced and driven by laws we only half understand, we find that the lesson we learn again and again is that of accepting heroic helplessness.

FLORIDA SCOTT-MAXWELL, *The Measure of My Days* (1968)

Could anything be absurder than a man? The animal who knows everything about himself—except why he was born and the meaning of his unique life?

STORM JAMESON, *Before the Crossing* (1947)

It began in mystery, and it will end in mystery, but what a savage and beautiful country lies in between.

DIANE ACKERMAN, *A Natural History of the Senses* (1990)

Life seems to be a choice between two wrong answers.

SHARYN MCCRUMB, *If Ever I Return, Pretty Peggy-O* (1990)

Life is painful, nasty and short . . . in my case it has only been painful and nasty.

DJUNA BARNES, in Hank O'Neal, *Life Is Painful, Nasty and Short . . .* (1991)

Life offstage has sometimes been a wilderness of unpredictables in an unchoreographed world.

MARGOT FONTEYN, *Margot Fonteyn: Autobiography* (1976)

All [life] is pattern . . . but we can't always see the pattern when we're part of it.

BELVA PLAIN, *Crescent City* (1984)

Life is either a daring adventure or nothing. To keep our faces toward change and behave like free spirits in the presence of fate is strength undefeatable.

HELEN KELLER, *Let Us Have Faith* (1940)

Life forms illogical patterns. It is haphazard and full of beauties which I try to catch as they fly by, for who knows whether any of them will ever return?

MARGOT FONTEYN, *Margot Fonteyn: Autobiography* (1976)

It's not true that life is one damn thing after another—it's one damn thing over and over.

EDNA ST. VINCENT MILLAY, in Allan Ross Macdougall, *Letters of Edna St. Vincent Millay* (1952)

Life is something to do when you can't get to sleep.

FRAN LEBOWITZ, in *Observer* (1979)

It has begun to occur to me that life is a stage I'm going through.

ELLEN GOODMAN, *Close to Home* (1979)

And life goes on forever like the gnawing of a mouse.

EDNA ST. VINCENT MILLAY, "Ashes of Life," *Renascence* (1917)

Life, the permission to know death.

DJUNA BARNES, *Nightwood* (1937)

You are dipped up from the great river of consciousness, and death only pours you back.

DOROTHY CANFIELD FISHER, *The Bent Twig* (1915)

Life does not accommodate you, it shatters you. It is meant to, and it couldn't do it better. Every seed destroys its container or else there would be no fruition.

FLORIDA SCOTT-MAXWELL, *The Measure of My Days* (1968)

But how meager one's life becomes when it is reduced to its basic facts. . . . And the last, most complete, reduction is on one's tombstone: a name, two dates.

HELEN MACINNES, *The Venetian Affair* (1963)

That it will never come again / Is what makes life so sweet.

EMILY DICKINSON (c. 1864), *Bolts of Melody* (1945)

Sometimes it seemed to him that his life was delicate as a dandelion. One little puff from any direction, and it was blown to bits.

KATHERINE PATERSON, *Bridge to Terabithia* (1977)

Life cannot be captured in a few axioms. And that is just what I keep trying to do. But it won't work, for life is full of endless nuances and cannot be captured in just a few formulae.

ETTY HILLESUM, *An Interrupted Life: The Diaries of Etty Hillesum 1941–1943* (1983)

Life is better than death, I believe, if only because it is less boring, and because it has fresh peaches in it.

ALICE WALKER, "Only Justice Can Stop a Curse," In Search of Our Mothers' Gardens (1983)

I took one Draught of Life— / I'll tell you what I paid— / Precisely an existence— / The market price, they said.

EMILY DICKINSON (c. 1864), *Further Poems of Emily Dickinson* (1929)

When I can look Life in the eyes, / Grown calm and very coldly wise, / Life will have given me the Truth, / And taken in exchange—my youth.

SARA TEASDALE, "Wisdom," *Dark of the Moon* (1926)

Life after life after life goes by / without poetry, / without seemliness, / without love.

DENISE LEVERTOV, "The Mutes," *The Sorrow Dance* (1967)

If I can stop one Heart from breaking, / I shall not live in vain / If I can ease one Life the Aching / Or cool one pain / Or help one fainting Robin / Unto his Nest again / I shall not live in vain.

EMILY DICKINSON (1864), *Poems, First Series* (1890)

Except for our higher order of minds we are like the little moles under the earth carrying out blindly the work of digging, thinking our own dark passage-ways constitute all there is to the world.

BESS STREETER ALDRICH, *Spring Came on Forever* (1935)

It was not . . . that she was unaware of the frayed and ragged edges of life. She would merely iron them out with a firm hand and neatly hem them down.

P. D. JAMES, *Death of an Expert Witness* (1977)

There must be more to life than just eating and getting bigger.

TRINA PAULUS, *Hope for the Flowers* (1972)

I am one of those people who just can't help getting a kick out of life—even when it's a kick in the teeth.

POLLY ADLER, *A House Is Not a Home* (1953)

I postpone death by living, by suffering, by error, by risking, by giving, by losing.

ANAÏS NIN, *The Diary of Anaïs Nin*, vol. 1 (1931–1934)

Love and life cannot help but marry and stay married with an exhausting violence of fidelity.

KATE O'BRIEN, *Mary Lavelle* (1936)

You make what seems a simple choice: choose a man or a job or a neighborhood—and what you have chosen is not a man or a job or a neighborhood, but a life.

JESSAMYN WEST, *The Life I Really Lived* (1979)

Dying is a short horse and soon curried. Living is a horse of another color and bigger.

JESSAMYN WEST, *The Woman Said Yes: Encounters With Life and Death* (1976)

To live fully, outwardly and inwardly, not to ignore external reality for the sake of the inner life, or the reverse—that's quite a task.

ETTY HILLESUM, *An Interrupted Life: The Diaries of Etty Hillesum 1941–1943* (1983)

The years seem to rush by now, and I think of death as a fast approaching end of a journey—double and treble reasons for loving as well as working while it is day.

GEORGE ELIOT, letter (1861), in J. W. Cross, *George Eliot's Life as Related in Her Letters and Journals* (1884)

I don't want to get to the end of my life and find that I lived just the length of it. I want to have lived the width of it as well.

DIANE ACKERMAN, in *Newsweek* (1986)

I have always had a dread of becoming a passenger in life.

PRINCESS MARGRETHE OF DENMARK, in *Life* (1968)

I was merely a disinterested spectator at the Banquet of Life.

ELAINE DUNDY, *The Dud Avocado* (1958)

People do not live nowadays—they get about ten percent out of life.

ISADORA DUNCAN, "Memoirs," in *This Quarter* (1929)

They are committing murder who merely live.

MAY SARTON, "Summary," *Inner Landscape* (1936–1938)

I had not loved enough. I'd been busy, busy, so busy, preparing for life, while life floated by me, quiet and swift as a regatta.

LORENE CARY, *Black Ice* (1991)

Her life was like running on a treadmill or riding on a stationary bike; it was aerobic, it was healthy, but she wasn't going anywhere.

JULIA PHILLIPS, *You'll Never Eat Lunch in This Town Again* (1991)

Men for the sake of getting a living forget to live.

MARGARET FULLER, *Summer on the Lakes* (1844)

It seems to me you can be awfully happy in this life if you stand aside and watch and mind your own business, and let other people do as they like about damaging themselves and one another. You go on kidding yourself that you're impartial and tolerant and all that, then all of a sudden you realize you're dead, and you've never been alive at all.

MARY STEWART, *This Rough Magic* (1964)

Life was meant to be lived, and curiosity must be kept alive. One must never, for whatever reason, turn his back on life.

ELEANOR ROOSEVELT, *Autobiography of Eleanor Roosevelt* (1961)

It's only when we truly know and understand that we have a limited time on earth—and that we have no way of knowing when our time is up—that we will begin to live each day to the fullest, as if it was the only one we had.

ELISABETH KÜBLER-ROSS, in *Parade* (1991)

Not everyone's life is what they make it. Some people's life is what other people make it.

ALICE WALKER, *You Can't Keep a Good Woman Down* (1981)

It is so hard for us little human beings to accept this deal that we get. It's really crazy, isn't it? We get to live, then we have to die. What we put into every moment is all we have. . . . What spirit human beings have! It *is* a pretty cheesy deal—all the pleasures of life, and then death.

GILDA RADNER, *It's Always Something* (1989)

I like living. I have sometimes been wildly, despairingly, acutely miserable, racked with sorrow, but through it all I still know quite certainly that just to *be* alive is a grand thing.

AGATHA CHRISTIE, *An Autobiography* (1977)

Notwithstanding the poverty of my outside experience, I have always had a significance for myself, and every chance to stumble along my straight and narrow little path, and to worship at the feet of my Deity, and what more can a human soul ask for?

ALICE JAMES (1892), in Leon Edel, ed., *The Diary of Alice James* (1964)

I asked myself the question, "What do you want of your life?" and I realized with a start of recognition and terror, "Exactly what I have—but to be commensurate, to handle it all better."

MAY SARTON, *Journal of a Solitude* (1973)

I began to have an idea of my life, not as the slow shaping of achievement to fit my preconceived purposes, but as the gradual discovery and growth of a purpose which I did not know.

JOANNA FIELD, *A Life of One's Own* (1934)

You took what you wanted from life, if you could get it, and you did without the rest.

ZELDA FITZGERALD, *Save Me the Waltz* (1932)

The life . . . that she had complained against, had murmured at, had raged at and defied—none the less she had loved it so, joyed in it so, both in good days and evil, that not one day had there been when 'twould not have seemed hard to give it back to God, nor one grief that she could have forgone without regret.

SIGRID UNDSET, *Kristin Lavransdatter: The Cross* (1922)

I look back on my life like a good day's work, it was done and I am satisfied with it.

GRANDMA MOSES, in Otto Kallir, ed., *Grandma Moses: My Life's History* (1947)

I was, being human, born alone; / I am, being woman, hard beset; / I live by squeezing from a stone / The little nourishment I get. / In masks outrageous and austere / The years go by in single file; / But none has merited my fear, / And none has quite escaped my smile.

ELINOR WYLIE, "Let No Charitable Hope," *Black Armour* (1923)

How we spend our days is, of course, how we spend our lives.

ANNIE DILLARD, *The Writing Life* (1989)

You don't get to choose how you're going to die. Or when. You can only decide how you're going to live. Now.

JOAN BAEZ, *Daybreak* (1968)

If you wish to live, you must first attend your own funeral.

KATHERINE MANSFIELD, in Antony Alpers, *Katherine Mansfield* (1954)

When you consider something like death, after which (there being no news flash to the contrary)

we may well go out like a candle flame, then it probably doesn't matter if we try too hard, are awkward sometimes, care for one another too deeply, are excessively curious about nature, are too open to experience, enjoy a nonstop expense of the senses in an effort to know life intimately and lovingly.

DIANE ACKERMAN, *A Natural History of the Senses* (1990)

Children, you must remember something. A man without ambition is dead. A man with ambition but no love is dead. A man with ambition and love for his blessings here on earth is ever so alive. Having been alive, it won't be hard in the end to lie down and rest.

PEARL BAILEY, *Talking to Myself* (1971)

Your life feels different on you, once you greet death and understand your heart's position. You wear your life like a garment from the mission bundle sale ever after—lightly because you realize you never paid nothing for it, cherishing because you know you won't ever come by such a bargain again.

LOUISE ERDRICH, *Love Medicine* (1984)

And there is no living creature, though the whims of eons had put its eyes on boggling stalks and clamped it in a carapace, diminished it to a pinpoint and given it a taste for mud and stuck it down a well or hid it under a stone, but that creature will live on if it can.

MARILYNNE ROBINSON, *Housekeeping* (1980)

Naked were we born and naked must we depart. . . No matter what you may lose, be patient for nothing belongs; it is only lent.

GLÜCKEL OF HAMELN, *The Life of Glückel of Hameln (1646–1724), Written by Herself* (1719)

[Ade Bethune's] life itself stands as her major work of art, her great design, lovingly worked out over the years.

JUDITH STOUGHTON, *Proud Donkey of Schaerbeek* (1988)

There is something all life has in common, and when I know what it is I shall know myself.

JEAN CRAIGHEAD GEORGE, *The Summer of the Falcon* (1962)

Sacredness of human life! The world has never believed it! It has been with life that we settled our quarrels, won wives, gold and land, defended ideas, imposed religions. We have held that a death toll was a necessary part of every human achievement, whether sport, war, or industry. A moment's rage over the horror of it, and we have sunk into indifference.

IDA TARBELL, *New Ideals in Business* (1914)

Life must go on, / I forget just why.

EDNA ST. VINCENT MILLAY, "Lament" (1921), *Collected Poems* (1956)

That's the way the system works. Sometimes you get the bear, sometimes the bear gets you.

SUE GRAFTON, *"H" Is for Homicide* (1991)

It's always something.

GILDA RADNER (as "Roseanne Roseannadanna"), *It's Always Something* (1989)

See also Human Nature.

LIFESTYLE

Alternative Lifestyles, the emotional fly-drive packages of our times, come equipped with a set of clothes, a choice of authors, a limited menu of sports and a discount coupon book of clichés.

ELLEN GOODMAN, *Close to Home* (1979)

Like everything else, Preppiness begins in the home.

LISA BIRNBACH, *The Official Preppy Handbook* (1980)

LIMITATIONS

There is only one woman I know of who could never be a symphony conductor, and that's the Venus de Milo.

MARGARET HILLIS, in *New York Times* (1979)

I think knowing what you can *not* do is more important than knowing what you can do. In fact, that's good taste.

LUCILLE BALL, in Eleanor Harris, *The Real Story of Lucille Ball* (1954)

See also Inadequacy, Weakness.

LISTENING

Blessed are they who listen when no one is left to speak.

LINDA HOGAN, "Blessing," *Calling Myself Home* (1978)

The only listening that counts is that of the talker who alternately absorbs and expresses ideas.

AGNES REPPLIER, *Compromises* (1904)

It seemed rather incongruous that in a society of supersophisticated communication, we often suffer from a shortage of listeners.

ERMA BOMBECK, *If Life Is a Bowl of Cherries, What Am I Doing in the Pits?* (1971)

I looked for a sounding-board and I found none. / The hearts that I called out to, remained stone.

HENRIETTE ROLAND-HOLST, "I Looked for a Sounding-Board," in Joanna Bankier and Deirdre Lashgari, eds., *Women Poets of the World* (1983)

[He] stood listening in that peculiar state of tension which everyone feels when they call and are not answered.

MARY O'HARA, *Thunderhead* (1943)

No one really listens to anyone else, and if you try it for a while you'll see why.

MIGNON MCLAUGHLIN, *The Second Neurotic's Notebook* (1966)

The opposite of talking isn't listening. The opposite of talking is waiting.

FRAN LEBOWITZ, *Social Studies* (1977)

See also Attention, Conversation, Interruption, Talking.

LITERATURE

The test of literature is, I suppose, whether we ourselves live more intensely for the reading of it.

ELIZABETH DREW, *The Modern Novel* (1926)

The body of literature, with its limits and edges, exists outside some people and inside others. Only after the writer lets literature shape her can she perhaps shape literature.

ANNIE DILLARD, *The Writing Life* (1989)

Of course the illusion of art is to make one believe that great literature is very close to life, but exactly the opposite is true. Life is amorphous, literature is formal.

FRANÇOISE SAGAN, in Malcolm Cowley, ed., *Writers at Work* (1958)

Literature is my Utopia. Here I am not disenfranchised. No barrier of the senses shuts me out from the sweet, gracious discourse of my book friends. They talk to me without embarrassment or awkwardness.

HELEN KELLER, *The Story of My Life* (1902)

When literature becomes deliberately indifferent to the opposition of good and evil it betrays its function and forfeits all claim to excellence.

SIMONE WEIL, *On Science, Necessity, and the Love of God* (1968)

Don't ask to live in tranquil times. Literature doesn't grow there.

RITA MAE BROWN, *Starting From Scratch* (1988)

The secret of literature, which conventional people don't guess, is that writers are forever looking for the *surprising revelation*—not for reinforcement of collective wisdom.

CAROL BLY, *The Passionate, Accurate Story* (1990)

Perversity is the muse of modern literature.

SUSAN SONTAG, *Against Interpretation* (1966)

The poet gives us his essence, but prose takes the mold of the body and mind entire.

VIRGINIA WOOLF, "Reading," *The Captain's Death Bed* (1950)

The borderline between prose and poetry is one of those fog-shrouded literary minefields where the wary explorer gets blown to bits before ever seeing anything clearly. It is full of barbed wire and the stumps of dead opinions.

URSULA K. LE GUIN, *Dancing at the Edge of the World* (1989)

Exciting literature after supper is not the best digestive.

CHARLOTTE PERKINS GILMAN, *The Living of Charlotte Perkins Gilman* (1935)

I believe all literature started as gossip.

RITA MAE BROWN, *Starting From Scratch* (1988)

Besides Shakespeare and me, who do you think there is?

GERTRUDE STEIN, to someone who knew little about literature, in James R. Mellow, *Charmed Circle* (1974)

See also Books, Essays, Novels, Poetry, Stories, Writing.

LITIGATION

In the strange heat all litigation brings to bear on things, the very process of litigation fosters the most profound misunderstandings in the world.

RENATA ADLER, *Reckless Disregard* (1986)

See also Law.

LOGIC

If the world were a logical place, men would ride side-saddle.

RITA MAE BROWN, *Sudden Death* (1983)

Nothing is as depressing as absolute logic. Look at the maze of French politics perpetrated by a logical people.

RAE FOLEY, *The Hundredth Door* (1950)

See also Rationality, Reason.

LONDON

London, how could one ever be tired of it?

MARGARET DRABBLE, *The Middle Ground* (1980)

Wonderful, mysterious, grand, clever old London, who keeps the Ritz Hotel front-door closed on Sundays and the side-door open!

LADY NORAH BENTINCK, *My Wanderings and Memories* (1921)

The London streets are paths of loveliness; the very omnibuses look like colored archangels, their laps filled full of little trustful souls.

EVELYN UNDERHILL, *Mysticism* (1955)

See also England, Europe.

LONELINESS

I've been so lonely for long periods of my life that if a rat walked in I would have welcomed it.

LOUISE NEVELSON, *Dawns + Dusks* (1976)

Loneliness and the feeling of being unwanted is the most terrible poverty.

MOTHER TERESA, in *Time* (1975)

We have all known the long loneliness and we have learned that the only solution is love and that love comes with community.

DOROTHY DAY, *The Long Loneliness* (1952)

Loneliness is never more cruel than when it is felt in close propinquity with someone who has ceased to communicate.

GERMAINE GREER, *The Female Eunuch* (1971)

I have known no loneliness like this, / Locked in your arms and bent beneath your kiss.

BABETTE DEUTSCH, "Solitude," *Banners* (1919)

Life may be brimming over with experiences, but somewhere, deep inside, all of us carry a vast and fruitful loneliness wherever we go. And sometimes the most important thing in a whole day is the rest we take between two deep breaths, or the turning inwards in prayer for five short minutes.

ETTY HILLESUM, *An Interrupted Life: The Diaries of Etty Hillesum 1941–1943* (1983)

Solitude is one thing and loneliness is another.

MAY SARTON, I Knew a Phoenix (1959)

At any moment solitude may put on the face of loneliness.

MAY SARTON, *Plant Dreaming Deep* (1958–1967)

Loneliness is the poverty of self; solitude is the richness of self.

MAY SARTON, *Mrs. Stevens Hears the Mermaids Singing* (1965)

But she knew that she had encountered one of the more devastating kinds of loneliness in existence: that of being in close contact with someone to whom she was a nonperson, and who thereby rendered her invisible and of no consequence.

DOROTHY GILMAN, *Mrs. Pollifax and the Whirling Dervish* (1990)

And I was to find out then, as I found out so many times, over and over again, that women especially are social beings, who are not content with just husband and family, but must have a community, a group, an exchange with others. A child is not enough. A husband and children, no matter how busy one may be kept by them, are not enough. Young and old, even in the busiest years of our lives, we women especially are victims of the long loneliness.

DOROTHY DAY, *The Long Loneliness* (1952)

See also Alone, Solitude.

LONGING

It seems to me we can never give up longing and wishing while we are thoroughly alive. There are certain things we feel to be beautiful and good, and we *must* hunger after them.

GEORGE ELIOT, *The Mill on the Floss* (1860)

The act of longing for something will always be more intense than the requiting of it.

GAIL GODWIN, *Dream Children* (1976)

Of one thing alone I am very sure: it is a law of our nature that the memory of longing should survive the more fugitive memory of fulfillment.

ELLEN GLASGOW, *The Woman Within* (1954)

The force behind the movement of time is a mourning that will not be comforted. That is why the first event is known to have been an expulsion, and the last is hoped to be a reconciliation and return. So memory pulls us forward, so prophecy is only brilliant memory—there will be a garden where all of us as one child will sleep in our mother Eve, hooped in her ribs and staved by her spine.

MARILYNNE ROBINSON, *Housekeeping* (1980)

See also Desire, Hope.

LOS ANGELES

Visitors to Los Angeles, then and now, were put out because the residents of Los Angeles had the inhospitable idea of building a city comfortable to live in, rather than a monument to astonish the eye of jaded travelers.

JESSAMYN WEST, *Hide and Seek* (1973)

In a foreign country people don't expect you to be just like them, but in Los Angeles, which is infiltrating the world, they don't consider that you might be different because they don't recognize any values except their own. And soon there may not be any others.

PAULINE KAEL, *I Lost It at the Movies* (1965)

See also California, Hollywood.

LOSS

The longed-for ships / Come empty home or founder on the deep, / And eyes first lose their tears and then their sleep.

EDITH WHARTON, "Non Dolet!" *Artemis to Actaeon* (1909)

For the first time, I was pierced by the little panic and tristesse occasioned by small things passing irrevocably from view.

FAITH SULLIVAN, *The Cape Ann* (1988)

I still miss those I loved who are no longer with me but I find I am grateful for having loved them. The gratitude has finally conquered the loss.

RITA MAE BROWN, *Starting From Scratch* (1988)

It is better to be drunk with loss and to beat the ground, than to let the deeper things gradually escape.

IVY COMPTON-BURNETT (1969), in Hilary Spurling, *Ivy* (1984)

I cannot say what loves have come and gone; / I only know that summer sang in me / A little while, that in me sings no more.

EDNA ST. VINCENT MILLAY, "What My Lips Have Kissed, and Where, and Why" (1923)

When I am dead and opened, you shall find "Calais" lying in my heart.

MARY I, in Raphael Holinshed, *Chronicles* (1577)

First I lost weight, then I lost my voice, and now I've lost Onassis.

MARIA CALLAS, in Barbara McDowell and Hana Umlauf, *Woman's Almanac* (1977)

See also Grief, Mourning, Privation, Suffering.

LOVE

How do I love thee? Let me count the ways. / I love thee to the depth and breadth and height / My soul can reach.

ELIZABETH BARRETT BROWNING, *Sonnets From the Portuguese* (1850)

Love—is anterior to Life— / Posterior—to Death.

EMILY DICKINSON (1864), *Poems, Third Series* (1896)

I love thee with a love I seemed to lose / With my lost saints,—I love thee with the breath, / Smiles, tears, of all my life!—and, if God choose, / I shall but love thee better after death.

ELIZABETH BARRETT BROWNING, *Sonnets From the Portuguese* (1850)

Love—bittersweet, irrepressible— / loosens my limbs and I tremble.

SAPPHO, "To Atthis" (6th century B.C.), in Willis Barnstone, *Sappho* (1965)

Whatever our souls are made of, his and mine are the same.

EMILY BRONTË, *Wuthering Heights* (1847)

My love for you is the sole image / Of God a human is allowed.

ELSE LASKER-SCHÜLER, "To My Child" (1920), *Hebrew Ballads and Other Poems* (1980)

Let us now bask under the spreading trees said Bernard in a passionate tone. Oh yes lets said Ethel and she opened her dainty parasole and sank down upon the long grass. She closed her eyes but was far from asleep.

DAISY ASHFORD (aged 9), *The Young Visiters* (1919)

If I had never met him I would have dreamed him into being.

ANZIA YEZIERSKA, *Red Ribbon on a White Horse* (1950)

Pale hands I loved beside the Shalimar, / Where are you now? Who lies beneath your spell?

LAURENCE HOPE, "Pale Hands I Loved," *Songs from the Garden of Kama* (1901)

Bernard placed one arm tightly round her. When will you marry me Ethel he uttered you must be my wife it has come to that I love you so intensely that if you say no I shall perforce dash my body to the brink of yon muddy river he panted wildly. O don't do that implored Ethel breathing rather hard.

DAISY ASHFORD (aged 9), *The Young Visiters* (1919)

In short I will part with anything for you but you.

LADY MARY WORTLEY MONTAGU, letter to her future husband (1712), in Octave Thanet, ed., *The Best Letters of Lady Mary Wortley Montagu* (1901)

The memories of long love gather like drifting snow, poignant as the mandarin ducks who float side by side in sleep.

LADY MURASAKI, *The Tale of Genji* (c. 1008)

Love is the only thing that keeps me sane.

SUE TOWNSEND, *The Secret Diary of Adrian Mole Aged 13-3/4* (1982)

Love, I find is like singing. Everybody can do enough to satisfy themselves, though it may not impress the neighbors as being very much.

ZORA NEALE HURSTON, Dust Tracks on a Road (1942)

Love is a context, not a behavior.

MARILYN FERGUSON, *The Aquarian Conspiracy* (1980)

In real love you want the other person's good. In romantic love you want the other person.

MARGARET ANDERSON, *The Fiery Fountains* (1969)

Love is a choice—not simply, or necessarily, a rational choice, but rather a willingness to be present to others without pretense or guile.

CARTER HEYWARD, *Our Passion for Justice* (1984)

Love is the vital essence that pervades and permeates, from the center to the circumference, the graduating circles of all thought and action. Love is the talisman of human weal and woe— the open sesame to every soul.

ELIZABETH CADY STANTON, speech (1860)

Love has the quality of informing almost everything—even one's work.

SYLVIA ASHTON-WARNER, *Myself* (1967)

The story of a love is not important—what is important is that one is capable of love. It is perhaps the only glimpse we are permitted of eternity.

HELEN HAYES, in *Guideposts* (1960)

If it is your time love will track you down like a cruise missile. If you say "No! I don't want it right now," that's when you'll get it for sure. Love will make a way out of no way. Love is an exploding cigar which we willingly smoke.

LYNDA BARRY, *Big Ideas* (1983)

Intense love is often akin to intense suffering.

FRANCES ELLEN WATKINS HARPER, "The Two Offers," in *Anglo-African Magazine* (1859)

Love me in full being.

ELIZABETH BARRETT BROWNING, "A Man's Requirements," *Love Poems* (1909)

We love because it's the only true adventure.

NIKKI GIOVANNI, in *Reader's Digest* (1982)

Whoever has loved knows all that life contains of sorrow and of joy.

GEORGE SAND, in *French Wit and Wisdom* (1950)

To care passionately for another human creature brings always more sorrow than joy; but all the same, Elinor, one would not be without that experience.

AGATHA CHRISTIE, *Sad Cypress* (1939)

The verb "to love" in Persian is "to have a friend." "I love you" translated literally is "I have you as a friend," and "I don't like you" simply means "I don't have you as a friend."

SHUSHA GUPPY, *The Blindfold Horse: Memories of a Persian Childhood* (1988)

I love you no matter what you do, but do you have to do so much of it?

JEAN ILLSLEY CLARKE, chapter title, *Self-Esteem: A Family Affair* (1978)

Whoso loves believes the impossible.

ELIZABETH BARRETT BROWNING, *Aurora Leigh* (1856)

Great loves too must be endured.

COCO CHANEL, in Marcel Haedrich, *Coco Chanel: Her Life, Her Secrets* (1972)

Love doesn't just sit there, like a stone, it has to be made, like bread; re-made all the time, made new.

URSULA K. LE GUIN, *The Lathe of Heaven* (1971)

To love deeply in one direction makes us more loving in all others.

ANNE-SOPHIE SWETCHINE, *The Writings of Madame Swetchine* (1869)

I was in love with the whole world and all that lived in its rainy arms.

LOUISE ERDRICH, *Love Medicine* (1984)

Never, never have I been loved as I love others!

MADAME DE STAËL (1786), in Lydia Maria Child, *Memoirs of Madame de Staël and of Madame Roland* (1847)

No one has ever loved anyone the way everyone wants to be loved.

MIGNON MCLAUGHLIN, *The Neurotic's Notebook* (1963)

I have found the paradox that if I love until it hurts, then there is no hurt, but only more love.

MOTHER TERESA, in Daphne Rae, *Love Until It Hurts* (1981)

I'm glad it cannot happen twice, the fever of first love.

DAPHNE DU MAURIER, *Rebecca* (1938)

It was the kind of desperate, headlong, adolescent calf love that he should have experienced years ago and got over.

AGATHA CHRISTIE, *Remembered Death* (1945)

She's got most of the symptoms—is twittery and cross, doesn't eat, lies awake, and mopes in corners.

LOUISA MAY ALCOTT, *Little Women* (1868)

A man when he is making up to anybody can be cordial and gallant and full of little attentions and altogether charming. But when a man is really in love he can't help looking like a sheep.

AGATHA CHRISTIE, *The Mystery of the Blue Train* (1928)

Indeed, the sole criticism of him was that he prolonged beyond the point of decency, his look of nuptial rapture and the vagueness which rendered him, in conversation, slightly stupid.

JEAN STAFFORD, *Boston Adventure* (1944)

Love is like the measles. The older you get it, the worse the attack.

MARY ROBERTS RINEHART, *The Man in Lower Ten* (1909)

We don't believe in rheumatism and true love until after the first attack.

MARIE VON EBNER-ESCHENBACH, *Aphorisms* (1905)

Everyone wants Love to follow them / down their road; / where is it that Love wants to go?

JUDY GRAHN, *The Queen of Swords* (1987)

Love, from its very nature, must be transitory.

MARY WOLLSTONECRAFT, *A Vindication of the Rights of Woman* (1833)

To love without criticism is to be betrayed.

DJUNA BARNES, *Nightwood* (1937)

We love what we should scorn if we were wiser.

MARIE DE FRANCE (12th century), in Jeanette Beer, tr., *Medieval Fables of Marie de France* (1981)

Love is not enough. It must be the foundation, the cornerstone—but not the complete structure. It is much too pliable, too yielding.

BETTE DAVIS, *The Lonely Life* (1962)

Love's a thin diet, nor will keep out cold.

APHRA BEHN, *The Lucky Chance* (1686)

Love is not all: it is not meat nor drink / Nor slumber nor a roof against the rain; / Nor yet a floating spar to men that sink.

EDNA ST. VINCENT MILLAY, *Fatal Interview* (1931)

The fate of love is that it always seems too little or too much.

AMELIA E. BARR, *The Bell of Bowling Green* (1904)

Love so seldom means happiness.

MARGERY ALLINGHAM, *Death of a Ghost* (1934)

Love, love love—all the wretched cant of it, masking egotism, lust, masochism, fantasy under a mythology of sentimental postures, a welter of self-induced miseries and joys, blinding and masking the essential personalities in the frozen gestures of courtship, in the kissing and the dating and the desire, the compliments and the quarrels which vivify its barrenness.

GERMAINE GREER, *The Female Eunuch* (1971)

Love says, mine. Love says, I could eat you up. Love says, stay as you are, be my own private thing, don't you dare have ideas I don't share. Love has just got to gobble the other, bones and all, crunch. I don't want to do that. I sure don't want it done to me!

MARGE PIERCY, *Braided Lives* (1982)

I dream that love without tyranny is possible.

ANDREA DWORKIN, "First Love," in Julia Wolf Mazow, ed., *The Woman Who Lost Her Names* (1980)

The more you love someone the more he wants from you and the less you have to give since you've already given him your love.

NIKKI GIOVANNI, *Gemini* (1971)

I'd always rather be with people who loved me too little rather than with people who loved me too much.

KATHERINE MANSFIELD (1919), *Journal of Katherine Mansfield* (1927)

Whoever said love conquers all was a fool. Because almost everything conquers love—or tries to.

EDNA FERBER, *Giant* (1952)

When success comes in the door, it seems, love often goes out the window.

JOYCE BROTHERS, *The Brothers System for Liberated Love and Marriage* (1972)

Love never dies of starvation, but often of indigestion.

NINON DE LENCLOS (c. 1660), *Letters* (1870)

Love will not always linger longest / With those who hold it in too clenched a fist.

ALICE DUER MILLER, *Forsaking All Others* (1931)

How do you know love is gone? If you said that you would be there at seven and you get there by nine, and he or she has not called the police yet—it's gone.

MARLENE DIETRICH, *Marlene Dietrich's ABC* (1962)

After all, my erstwhile dear, / My no longer cherished, / Need we say it was not love, / Just because it perished?

EDNA ST. VINCENT MILLAY, "Passer Mortuus Est," *Second April* (1921)

Love, for both of them, had ceased to be a journey, an adventure, an essay of hope. It had become an infection, a ritual, a drama with a bloody last act, and they could both foresee the final carnage.

MARGARET DRABBLE, *The Middle Ground* (1980)

Love was a terrible thing. You poisoned it and stabbed at it and knocked it down into the mud—well down—and it got up and staggered on, bleeding and muddy and awful. Like—like Rasputin.

JEAN RHYS, *Quartet* (1928)

Grumbling is the death of love.

MARLENE DIETRICH, *Marlene Dietrich's ABC* (1962)

The tragedy is not that love doesn't last. The tragedy is the love that lasts.

SHIRLEY HAZZARD, *The Transit of Venus* (1980)

If only one could tell true love from false love as one can tell mushrooms from toadstools.

KATHERINE MANSFIELD (1917), *Journal of Katherine Mansfield* (1930)

For the little while when we was lovers I breathed the air from the high places where love comes from, and I can't no more come down.

ANZIA YEZIERSKA, "Where Lovers Dream," *Hungry Hearts* (1920)

My life will be sour grapes and ashes without you.

DAISY ASHFORD (aged 9), *The Young Visiters* (1919)

If I'm not loved when I love, the lack can't be repaired by any action of mine or repented by the person who doesn't love me.

ALICE KOLLER, *An Unknown Woman* (1982)

A woman has got to love a bad man once or twice in her life, to be thankful for a good one.

MARJORIE KINNAN RAWLINGS, *The Yearling* (1938)

If you never want to see a man again, say, "I love you. I want to marry you. I want to have children"—they leave skid marks.

RITA RUDNER, in *New York Times* (1985)

My boyfriend and I broke up. He wanted to get married, and I didn't want him to.

RITA RUDNER, in *Ms.* (1984)

You need someone to love you while you're looking for someone to love.

SHELAGH DELANEY, *A Taste of Honey* (1958)

Most of us love from our need to love not because we find someone deserving.

NIKKI GIOVANNI, "The Women Gather," *The Women and the Men* (1975)

Love is the image of ourself until ourself destroys us.

JEAN GARRIGUE, "The Snowfall," in Howard Moss, ed., *The Poet's Story* (1973)

Every love's the love before / In a duller dress.

DOROTHY PARKER, "Summary," *Death and Taxes* (1931)

How absurd and delicious it is to be in love with somebody younger than yourself. Everybody should try it.

BARBARA PYM, *A Very Private Eye* (1984)

The human need for love and sex is made to bear the burden of all our bodily starvation for contact and sensation, all our creative starvation, all our need for social contact, and even our need to find meaning in our lives.

DEIRDRE ENGLISH AND BARBARA EHRENREICH, in Evelyn Shapiro and Barry M. Shapiro, *The Women Say/The Men Say* (1979)

Perhaps loving something is the only starting place there is for making your life your own.

ALICE KOLLER, *An Unknown Woman* (1982)

Love opens the doors into everything, as far as I can see, including and perhaps most of all, the door into one's own secret, and often terrible and frightening, real self.

MAY SARTON, *Mrs. Stevens Hears the Mermaids Singing* (1965)

Till it has loved, no man or woman can become itself.

EMILY DICKINSON, letter (1879), in Mabel Loomis Todd, *Letters of Emily Dickinson* (1894)

I don't want to live—I want to love first, and live incidentally.

ZELDA FITZGERALD, in Nancy Milford, *Zelda* (1970)

There is always something left to love. And if you ain't learned that, you ain't learned nothing.

LORRAINE HANSBERRY, *A Raisin in the Sun* (1959)

The surest way of winning love is to look as if you didn't need it.

ELLEN GLASGOW, *Barren Ground* (1925)

You see I thought love got easier over the years so it didn't hurt so bad when it hurt, or feel so good when it felt good. I thought it smoothed out and old people hardly noticed it. I thought it curled up and died, I guess. Now I saw it rear up like a whip and lash.

LOUISE ERDRICH, *Love Medicine* (1984)

Liszt said to me to-day that God alone deserves to be loved. It may be true, but when one has loved a man it is very difficult to love God. It is so different.

GEORGE SAND (1834), in Marie Jenny Howe, *The Intimate Journal of George Sand* (1929)

I do not think reading the mystics would hurt you myself. You say you must avoid books which deal with "feelings"—but the mystics don't deal with *feelings* but with *love* which is a very different thing. You have too many "feelings," but not nearly enough love.

EVELYN UNDERHILL, *The Letters of Evelyn Underhill* (1943)

There is a net of love by which you can catch souls.

MOTHER TERESA, in Kathryn Spinks, *For the Brotherhood of Man Under the Fatherhood of God* (1980)

It is not a matter of thinking a great deal but of loving a great deal, so do whatever arouses you most to love.

ST. TERESA OF AVILA, *The Interior Castle* (1575)

See also Broken Heart, Desire, Heart, Intimacy, Lovers, Passion, Peace and Love, Sex, Virtue.

LOVERS

The absolute yearning of one human body for another particular one and its indifference to substitutes is one of life's major mysteries.

IRIS MURDOCH, *The Black Prince* (1973)

In a great romance, each person basically plays a part that the other really likes.

ELIZABETH ASHLEY, in *San Francisco Chronicle* (1982)

To be together is for us to be at once as free as in solitude, as gay as in company. We talk, I believe, all day long: to talk to each other is but a more animated and an audible thinking.

CHARLOTTE BRONTË, *Jane Eyre* (1847)

It is the way of lovers to think that none can bless or succor their love but their own selves. And there is a touch of truth in it, maybe more than a touch.

MARY WEBB, *Precious Bane* (1924)

There is probably nothing like living together for blinding people to each other.

IVY COMPTON-BURNETT, *Mother and Son* (1955)

It is better to know as little as possible of the defects of the person with whom you are to pass your life.

JANE AUSTEN, *Pride and Prejudice* (1813)

Sometimes idiosyncrasies which used to be irritating become endearing, part of the complexity of a partner who has become woven deep into our own selves.

MADELEINE L'ENGLE, *Two-Part Invention* (1988)

Secretly, we wish anyone we love will think exactly the way we do.

KIM CHERNIN, *In My Mother's House* (1983)

This was life, that two people, no matter how carefully chosen, could not be everything to each other.

DORIS LESSING, "To Room Nineteen," *A Man and Two Women* (1963)

No partner in a love relationship (whether homo- or heterosexual) should feel that he has to give up an essential part of himself to make it viable.

MAY SARTON, *Journal of a Solitude* (1973)

So each will have two lives, a doubled state; / Each in himself will live, and in his mate.

LOUISE LABÉ, "Sonnet XVIII" (c. 1545), in Joanna Bankier and Deirdre Lashgari, eds., *Women Poets of the World* (1983)

There will be a time you bury me / Or I bury you in the garden.

TOMIOKA TAEKO, "Living Together," in Joanna Bankier and Deirdre Lashgari, eds., *Women Poets of the World* (1983)

See also Friendship, Love, Marriage, Relationships.

LOYALTY

I am come amongst you, as you see, at this time, not for my recreation and disport, but being resolved, in the midst and heat of the battle, to live or die amongst you all; to lay down for my God, and for my kingdom, and my people, my honor and my blood, even in the dust.

ELIZABETH I, speech to the troops at Tilbury (1588)

She's the kind of woman who'd go through hell, high water, or a paper shredder for a pal.

KATHI MAIO, *Feminist in the Dark* (1988)

Loyal? As loyal as anyone who plays second fiddle ever is.

WILLA CATHER, *Lucy Gayheart* (1935)

See also Faithfulness.

LUCK

Luck is not chance— / It's Toil— / Fortune's expensive smile / Is earned.

EMILY DICKINSON (1875), *The Poems of Emily Dickinson* (1955)

How can you say luck and chance are the same thing? Chance is the first step you take, luck is what comes afterwards.

AMY TAN, *The Kitchen God's Wife* (1991)

People always call it luck when you've acted more sensibly than they have.

ANNE TYLER, *Celestial Navigation* (1974)

To a brave man, good and bad luck are like his right and left hand. He uses both.

ST. CATHERINE OF SIENA (c. 1370), *St. Catherine of Siena as Seen in Her Letters* (1911)

You is born lucky, and it's better to be born lucky than born rich, cause if you is lucky you can git rich, but if you is born rich and you ain't lucky you is liables to lose all you got.

MARGARET WALKER, *Jubilee* (1966)

Fortune is proverbially called changeful, yet her caprice often takes the form of repeating again and again a similar stroke of luck in the same quarter.

CHARLOTTE BRONTË, *Shirley* (1849)

See also Fate.

LUXURY

Luxury that baneful poison has unstrung and enfeebled her [America's] sons. . . The Benevo-lent wish of general good is swallowed up by a Narrow selfish Spirit, by a spirit of oppression and extortion.

ABIGAIL ADAMS, letter to John Adams (1779)

Luxuries unfit us for returning to hardships easily endured before.

MARY MAPES DODGE, *Hans Brinker* (1865)

In a socialist country you can get rich by providing necessities, while in a capitalist country you can get rich by providing luxuries.

NORA EPHRON, *Heartburn* (1983)

A private railroad car is not an acquired taste. One takes to it at once.

ELEANOR ROBSON BELMONT, *The Fabric of Memory* (1957)

See also Excess, Extravagance, Rich, Wealth.

LYING

Lying is done with words and also with silence.

ADRIENNE RICH, *On Lies, Secrets, and Silence* (1978)

I am in perfect health, and hear it said I look better than ever I did in my life, which is one of those lies one is always glad to hear.

LADY MARY WORTLEY MONTAGU, letter (1747), in Octave Thanet, ed., *The Best Letters of Lady Mary Wortley Montagu* (1901)

Never to lie is to have no lock to your door.

ELIZABETH BOWEN, *The House in Paris* (1935)

See also Deception, Dishonesty, Evasion, Flattery.

M

MAGAZINES

Magazines all too frequently lead to books and should be regarded by the prudent as the heavy petting of literature.

FRAN LEBOWITZ, *Metropolitan Life* (1974)

See also Journalism.

MAGIC

Faced with unmeasurables, people steer their way by magic.

DENISE SCOTT BROWN, "Room at the Top" (1975), in Ellen Perry Berkeley and Matilda McQuaid, eds., *Architecture: A Place for Women* (1989)

Magic is the craft of shaping, the craft of the wise, exhilarating, dangerous—the ultimate adventure. The power of magic should not be underestimated. It works, often in ways that are unexpected and difficult to control.

STARHAWK, *The Spiral Dance* (1979)

I am sure there is Magic in everything, only we have not sense enough to get hold of it and make it do things for us.

FRANCES HODGSON BURNETT, *The Secret Garden* (1911)

Where there is a woman there is magic.

NTOZAKE SHANGE, *Sassafrass, Cypress & Indigo* (1982)

See also Mystery.

MANNERS

The idea that people can behave naturally, without resorting to an artificial code tacitly agreed upon by their society, is as silly as the idea that they can communicate by a spoken language without commonly accepted semantic and grammatical rules.

JUDITH MARTIN, *Common Courtesy* (1985)

The challenge of manners is not so much to be nice to someone whose favor and/or person you covet (although more people need to be reminded of that necessity than one would suppose) as to be exposed to the bad manners of others without imitating them.

JUDITH MARTIN, *Miss Manners' Guide for the Turn-of-the-Millennium* (1989)

Good manners have much to do with the emotions. To make them ring true, one must feel them, not merely exhibit them.

AMY VANDERBILT, *New Complete Book of Etiquette* (1963)

Like language, a code of manners can be used with more or less skill, for laudable or for evil purposes, to express a great variety of ideas and emotions. In itself, it carries no moral value, but ignorance in use of this tool is not a sign of virtue.

JUDITH MARTIN, *Common Courtesy* (1985)

It is bad manners to contradict a guest. You must never insult people in your own house—always go to theirs.

MYRTLE REED, *The Book of Clever Beasts* (1904)

See also Etiquette, Politeness, Rudeness.

MARRIAGE

Reader, I married him.

CHARLOTTE BRONTË, *Jane Eyre* (1847)

Nothing in life is as good as the marriage of true minds between man and woman. As good? It is life itself.

PEARL BUCK, *To My Daughters, With Love* (1967)

There is nothing more lovely in life than the union of two people whose love for one another has grown through the years from the small acorn of passion to a great rooted tree. Surviving all vicissitudes, and rich with its manifold branches, every leaf holding its own significance.

VITA SACKVILLE-WEST, *No Signposts in the Sea* (1961)

A successful marriage requires falling in love many times, always with the same person.

MIGNON MCLAUGHLIN, *The Second Neurotic's Notebook* (1966)

It takes a long time to be really married. One marries many times at many levels within a marriage. If you have more marriages than you have divorces within the marriage, you're lucky and you stick it out.

RUBY DEE, in Brian Lanker, *I Dream a World* (1989)

One advantage of marriage, it seems to me, is that when you fall out of love with him, or he falls out of love with you, it keeps you together until you maybe fall in again.

JUDITH VIORST, in *Redbook* (1975)

I suspect that in every good marriage there are times when love seems to be over.

MADELEINE L'ENGLE, *Two-Part Invention* (1988)

A good marriage is one which allows for change and growth in the individuals and in the way they express their love.

PEARL BUCK, *To My Daughters, With Love* (1967)

If kissing and being engaged were this inflammatory, marriage must burn clear to the bone. I wondered how flesh and blood could endure the ecstasy. How did married couples manage to look so calm and unexcited?

JESSAMYN WEST, *The Life I Really Lived* (1979)

The sign of a good marriage is that everything is debatable and challenged; nothing is turned into law or policy. The rules, if any, are known only to the two players, who seek no public trophies.

CAROLYN HEILBRUN, *Writing a Woman's Life* (1988)

One doesn't have to get anywhere in a marriage. It's not a public conveyance.

IRIS MURDOCH, *A Severed Head* (1961)

A revolutionary marriage . . . [is] one in which both partners have work at the center of their lives and must find a delicate balance that can support both together and each individually.

CAROLYN HEILBRUN, *Writing a Woman's Life* (1988)

Were marriage no more than a convenient screen for sexuality, some less cumbersome and costly protection must have been found by this time to replace it. One concludes therefore that people do not marry to cohabit; they cohabit to marry.

VIRGILIA PETERSON, *A Matter of Life and Death* (1961)

A long-term marriage has to move beyond chemistry to compatibility, to friendship, to companionship. It is certainly not that passion disappears, but that it is conjoined with other ways of love.

MADELEINE L'ENGLE, *Two-Part Invention* (1988)

The very fact that we make such a to-do over golden weddings indicates our amazement at human endurance. The celebration is more in the nature of a reward for stamina.

ILKA CHASE, *Free Admission* (1948)

With children no longer the universally accepted reason for marriage, marriages are going to have to exist on their own merits.

ELEANOR HOLMES NORTON, "For Sadie and Maude," in Robin Morgan, *Sisterhood Is Powerful* (1970)

A simple enough pleasure, surely, to have breakfast alone with one's husband, but how seldom married people in the midst of life achieve it.

ANNE MORROW LINDBERGH, *Gift From the Sea* (1955)

The deep, deep peace of the double-bed after the hurly-burly of the chaise longue.

MRS. PATRICK CAMPBELL, on her recent marriage, in Alexander Woollcott, *While Rome Burns* (1934)

Personally I know nothing about sex because I've always been married.

ZSA ZSA GABOR, in *Observer* (1987)

It is not an accident that most men start thinking of getting married as soon as they get their first job. This is not only because now they can afford it, but because having somebody at home who takes care of you is the only condition not to go crazy after a day spent on an assembly line or at a desk.

SILVIA FEDERICI, "Wages Against Housework" (1975), in Evelyn Shapiro and Barry M. Shapiro, *The Women Say/The Men Say* (1979)

I cannot abide the Mr. and Mrs. Noah attitude towards marriage; the animals went in two by two, forever stuck together with glue.

VITA SACKVILLE-WEST, *No Signposts in the Sea* (1961)

Evidently, whatever else marriage might prevent, it was not a remedy for isolation of spirit.

ELLEN GLASGOW, *Barren Ground* (1925)

It is true that I never should have married, but I didn't want to live without a man. Brought up to respect the conventions, love had to end in marriage. I'm afraid it did.

BETTE DAVIS, *The Lonely Life* (1962)

If you want to sacrifice the admiration of many men for the criticism of one, go ahead, get married.

KATHARINE HOUGHTON HEPBURN, to daughter Katharine (1928), in Anne Edwards, *A Remarkable Woman* (1985)

If the right man does not come along, there are many fates far worse. One is to have the wrong man come along.

LETITIA BALDRIGE, *Of Diamonds and Diplomats* (1968)

Love the quest; marriage the conquest; divorce the inquest.

HELEN ROWLAND, *Reflections of a Bachelor Girl* (1909)

When two people marry they become in the eyes of the law one person, and that one person is the husband!

SHANA ALEXANDER, *State-by-State Guide to Women's Legal Rights* (1975)

To a man, marriage means giving up four out of five of the chiffonier drawers; to a woman, giving up four out of five of her opinions.

HELEN ROWLAND, *Reflections of a Bachelor Girl* (1909)

As so often happens in marriage, roles that had begun almost playfully, to give line and shape to our lives, had hardened like suits of armor and taken us prisoner.

MOLLY HASKELL, *Love and Other Infectious Diseases* (1990)

Being married was like having a hippopotamus sitting on my face, Mrs. Brown. No matter how hard I pushed or which way I turned, I couldn't get up. I couldn't even breathe. . . . Hippopotamuses aren't all bad. They are what they are. But I wasn't meant to have one sitting on my face.

FAITH SULLIVAN, *The Cape Ann* (1988)

All that is good and commendable now existing would continue to exist if all marriage laws were repealed tomorrow. . . . I have an inalienable constitutional and natural right to love whom I may, to love as long or as short a period as I can, to change that love every day if I please!

VICTORIA CLAFIN WOODHULL (1871), in Germaine Greer, *The Female Eunuch* (1971)

Any one must see at a glance that if men and women marry those whom they do not love, they must love those whom they do not marry.

HARRIET MARTINEAU, *Society in America* (1837)

You know that the urge for revenge is a fact of marital life.

JANE SMILEY, *Good Will* (1989)

Happiness in marriage is entirely a matter of chance.

JANE AUSTEN, *Pride and Prejudice* (1813)

There is one thing I can't get in my head— / Why *do* people marry the people they wed?

CAROLYN WELLS, "The Mystery," in Carolyn Wells, ed., *The World's Best Humor* (1923)

See also Intimacy, Love, Lovers, Relationships, Togetherness, Weddings.

MARXISM

To be a Marxist does not mean that one becomes a Communist party member. There are as many varieties of Marxists as there are of Protestants.

HELEN FOSTER SNOW, *Women in Modern China* (1967)

[Marx's] most explosive and indeed most original contribution to the cause of revolution was that he interpreted the compelling needs of mass poverty in political terms as an uprising, not for the sake of bread or wealth, but for the sake of freedom as well.

HANNAH ARENDT, *On Revolution* (1963)

MATERIALISM

Destitution and excessive luxury develop apparently the same ideals, the same marauding attitude towards mankind, the intensity of struggle for material goods,—surely showing how perfect is the meeting of extremes.

ALICE JAMES, *Journal* (1889)

See also Consumerism, Possessions.

MATHEMATICS

I see a certain order in the universe and math is one way of making it visible.

MAY SARTON, *As We Are Now* (1973)

Although I am not stupid, the mathematical side of my brain is like dumb notes upon a damaged piano.

MARGOT ASQUITH, *More or Less About Myself* (1934)

Stand firm in your refusal to remain conscious during algebra. In real life, I assure you, there is no such thing as algebra.

FRAN LEBOWITZ, *Social Studies* (1977)

MEANS

Methods and means cannot be separated from the ultimate aim.

EMMA GOLDMAN, *My Further Disillusionment in Russia* (1924)

There are many trails up the mountain, but in time they all reach the top.

ANYA SETON, *The Turquoise* (1946)

It is not *what* I do, it is the *way* I do it, that will get me in the end.

ANNE WILSON SCHAEF, *Meditations for Women Who Do Too Much* (1990)

See also Goals, Journeys.

MEDICATION

Medication without explanation is obscene.

TONI CADE BAMBARA, "Christmas Eve at Johnson's Drugs N Goods," *The Sea Birds Are Still Alive* (1982)

She said they [injections of morphine] didn't kill the pain but locked her up inside it.

SHIRLEY ABBOTT, *Womenfolks: Growing Up Down South* (1983)

See also Illness.

MEDIOCRITY

The only sin is mediocrity.

MARTHA GRAHAM, in *New York Times* (1985)

Over and over again mediocrity is promoted because real worth isn't to be found.

KATHLEEN NORRIS, *Hands Full of Living* (1931)

Mediocrity is safe.

NIKKI GIOVANNI, in Claudia Tate, ed., *Black Women Writers at Work* (1983)

Most of the men or women who have contributed to our civilization or our culture have been vilified in their day. . . . As we denounce the rebellious, the nonconformists, so we reward mediocrity so long as it mirrors herd standards.

TALLULAH BANKHEAD, *Tallulah* (1952)

We cling to a bourgeois mediocrity which would make it appear we are all Americans, made in the image and likeness of George Washington, all of a pattern, all prospering if we are good, and going down in the world if we are bad.

DOROTHY DAY, *The Long Loneliness* (1952)

Do you know the hallmark of the second-rater? It's resentment of another man's achievement.

AYN RAND, *Atlas Shrugged* (1957)

What depresses me is the inevitable way the second rate forges ahead and the deserving is left behind.

ELLEN GLASGOW, *Letters of Ellen Glasgow* (1958)

"Mediocrity" does not mean an average intelligence; it means an average intelligence that resents and envies its betters.

AYN RAND, *The New Left: The Anti-Industrial Revolution* (1971)

I shouldn't mind it if I saw the admirable sweep on to success, or immortality, but always it seems to be the ordinary, the vulgar, and the average, or the lower average, that triumphs.

ELLEN GLASGOW, *Letters of Ellen Glasgow* (1958)

A person may be totally unimaginative and have the social vision of a mole, and we still call him a decent man.

MARGARET HALSEY, *No Laughing Matter* (1977)

A list of our authors who have made themselves most beloved and, therefore, most comfortable financially, shows that it is our national joy to mistake for the first-rate, the fecund rate.

DOROTHY PARKER, in *New Yorker* (1929)

See also Conformity, Conventionality.

MEETINGS

Meetings . . . are rather like cocktail parties. You don't want to go, but you're cross not to be asked.

JILLY COOPER, *How to Survive from Nine to Five* (1970)

Meetings that do not come off keep a character of their own. They stay as they were projected.

ELIZABETH BOWEN, *The House in Paris* (1935)

The length of a meeting rises with the square of the number of people present.

EILEEN SHANAHAN, in Harold Faber, *New York Times Magazine* (1968)

Committee meetings are always held at inconvenient times and usually take place in dark, dusty rooms the temperatures of which are unsuited to the human body.

VIRGINIA GRAHAM, *Say Please* (1949)

See also Association, Committees.

MELANCHOLY

Gaiety is forgetfulness of the self, melancholy is memory of the self: in that state the soul feels all the power of its roots, nothing distracts it from its profound homeland and the look that it casts upon the outer world is gently dismayed.

ADRIENNE MONNIER, *Les Gazettes d'Adrienne Monnier* (1942), in Richard McDougall, tr., *The Very Rich Hours of Adrienne Monnier* (1976)

He is as melancholy as an unbraced drum.

SUSANNAH CENTLIVRE, *The Wonder!* (1714)

I was not always free from melancholy; but even melancholy had its charms.

MARIE-JEANNE ROLAND (1791), in Lydia Maria Child, *Memoirs of Madame de Staël and of Madame Roland* (1847)

See also Depression, Unhappiness.

MEMORY

Memory is the diary we all carry about with us.

MARY H. WALDRIP, in *Reader's Digest* (1979)

Memories are like corks left out of bottles. They swell. They no longer fit.

HARRIET DOERR, *Stones for Ibarra* (1978)

Here, in memory, we live *and* die.

PATRICIA HAMPL, *A Romantic Education* (1981)

It is memory that provides the heart with impetus, fuels the brain, and propels the corn plant from seed to fruit.

JOY HARJO, conference (1991)

Recollection . . . is not something that I can summon up, it simply comes and I am the servant of it.

EDNA O'BRIEN, in *New York Times* (1984)

The charm, one might say the genius, of memory is that it is choosy, chancy and temperamental; it rejects the edifying cathedral and indelibly photographs the small boy outside, chewing a hunk of melon in the dust.

ELIZABETH BOWEN, in *Vogue* (1955)

I can never remember things I didn't understand in the first place.

AMY TAN, *The Joy Luck Club* (1989)

Memory is a magnet. It will pull to it and hold only material nature has designed it to attract.

JESSAMYN WEST, *The Life I Really Lived* (1979)

I can understand that memory must be selective, else it would choke on the glut of experience. What I cannot understand is why it selects what it does.

VIRGILIA PETERSON, *A Matter of Life and Death* (1961)

I think, myself, that one's memories represent those moments which, insignificant as they may seem, nevertheless represent the inner self and oneself as most really oneself.

AGATHA CHRISTIE, *An Autobiography* (1977)

How we remember, what we remember, and why we remember form the most personal map of our individuality.

CHRISTINA BALDWIN, *One to One* (1977)

As to memory, it is known that this frail faculty naturally lets drop the facts which are less flattering to our self-love—when it does not retain them carefully as subjects not to be approached, marshy spots with a warning flag over them.

GEORGE ELIOT, *Impressions of Theophrastus Such* (1879)

My memory is a card shark, reshuffling the deck to hide what I fear to know, unable to keep from fingering the ace at the bottom of the deck when I'm doing nothing more than playing Fish in the daylight with children.

LORENE CARY, *Black Ice* (1991)

Memories stretch and pull around me— / Bark drying on a new canoe.

MARY TALLMOUNTAIN, "Ts'eekkaayah," in Rayna Green, ed., *That's What She Said* (1984)

Some memories are realities, and are better than anything that can ever happen to one again.

WILLA CATHER, *My Antonia* (1918)

Sometimes what we call "memory" and what we call "imagination" are not so easily distinguished.

LESLIE MARMON SILKO, *Storyteller* (1981)

What a strange thing is memory, and hope; one looks backward, the other forward. The one is of today, the other is of tomorrow. Memory is history recorded in our brain, memory is a painter, it paints pictures of the past and of the day.

GRANDMA MOSES, in Otto Kallir, ed., *Grandma Moses: My Life's History* (1947)

Just remember enough never to be vulnerable again: total forgetting could be as self-destructive as complete remembering.

HELEN MACINNES, *The Venetian Affair* (1963)

There can be no harm / In just remembering— that is all.

KATHERINE MANSFIELD, "The Arabian Shawl," *Poems* (1930)

In memory each of us is an artist: each of us creates.

PATRICIA HAMPL, *A Romantic Education* (1981)

A person without a memory is either a child or an amnesiac. A country without a memory is neither a child nor an amnesiac, but neither is it a country.

MARY ASTOR, *A Life on Film* (1967)

Looking repeatedly into the past, you do not necessarily become fascinated with your own life, but rather with the phenomenon of memory.

PATRICIA HAMPL, *A Romantic Education* (1981)

My memory is certainly in my hands. I can remember things only if I have a pencil and I can write with it and I can play with it. I think your hand concentrates for you. I don't know why it should be so.

REBECCA WEST, in George Plimpton, ed., *The Writer's Chapbook* (1989)

And isn't it funny, she thought, that it takes two generations to kill off a man? . . . First him, and then his memory.

SHIRLEY ANN GRAU, *The Keepers of the House* (1964)

I fear / the place I have / in the memory of others. / They remind me of things / I myself have forgot.

Tove Ditlevsen, "Self Portrait 4," in Joanna Bankier and Deirdre Lashgari, eds., *Women Poets of the World* (1983)

Proust's tea cake has nothing on one hour in a college dorm.

Gloria Steinem, *Outrageous Acts and Everyday Rebellions* (1983)

See also Forgetting, Past, Remembrance.

MEN

The only time a woman really succeeds in changing a man is when he's a baby.

Natalie Wood, in Bob Chieger, *Was It Good for You, Too?* (1983)

"Boyfriends" weren't friends at all; they were prizes, escorts, symbols of achievement, fascinating strangers, the Other.

Susan Allen Toth, *Blooming* (1978)

It's not the men in my life that counts, it's the life in my men.

Mae West, in *I'm No Angel* (1933)

I always did like a man in uniform. And that one fits you grand. Why don't you come up sometime and see me?

Mae West, in *Diamond Lil* (1932)

A man in the house is worth two in the street.

Mae West, in *Belle of the Nineties* (1934)

There are men I could spend eternity with. But not this life.

Kathleen Norris, "Blue Mountain," *The Middle of the World* (1981)

There are far too many men in politics and not enough elsewhere.

Hermione Gingold, *How to Grow Old Disgracefully* (1988)

What's with you men? Would hair stop growing on your chest if you asked directions somewhere?

Erma Bombeck, *When You Look Like Your Passport Photo, It's Time to Go Home* (1991)

I want to know why, if men rule the world, they don't stop wearing neckties.

Linda Ellerbee, *Move On* (1991)

Men often marry their mothers.

Edna Ferber, *Saratoga Trunk* (1941)

A fox is a wolf who sends flowers.

Ruth Weston, in *New York Post* (1955)

Men weren't really the enemy—they were fellow victims suffering from an outmoded masculine mystique that made them feel unnecessarily inadequate when there were no bears to kill.

Betty Friedan, in *Christian Science Monitor* (1974)

See also Father, Husband, Sons, Uncles, Women and Men.

MENTAL ILLNESS

Mystical state, madness, how it frightens people. How utterly crazy *they* become, remote, rude, peculiar, cruel, taunting, farouche as wild beasts who have smelled danger, the unthinkable.

Kate Millett, *The Loony-Bin Trip* (1990)

Madness is always fascinating, for it reveals the ungluing we all secretly fear: the mind taking off from the body, the possibility that the magnet that attaches us to a context in the world can lose its grip.

Molly Haskell, *Love and Other Infectious Diseases* (1990)

Insanity is doing the same thing over and over again, but expecting different results.

Rita Mae Brown, *Sudden Death* (1983)

If only no one had told them I was mad. Then I wouldn't be.

Kate Millett, *The Loony-Bin Trip* (1990)

See also Depression, Illness, Psychiatry.

MERCY

We hand folks over to God's mercy, and show none ourselves.

GEORGE ELIOT, *Adam Bede* (1859)

See also Compassion, Forgiveness, Grace, Kindness, Virtue.

MIDDLE AGE

Shall I not bless the middle years? / Not I for youth repine.

SARAH N. CLEGHORN, "Contented at Forty," *Portraits and Protests* (1917)

For is it not possible that middle age can be looked upon as a period of second flowering, second growth, even a kind of second adolescence? It is true that society in general does not help one accept this interpretation of the second half of life.

ANNE MORROW LINDBERGH, *Gift From the Sea* (1955)

We in middle age require adventure.

AMANDA CROSS, *Sweet Death, Kind Death* (1984)

Few women, I fear, have had such reason as I have to think the long sad years of youth were worth living for the sake of middle age.

GEORGE ELIOT, journal (1857), in J. W. Cross, *George Eliot's Life as Related in Her Letters and Journals* (1884)

These years are still the years of my prime. It is important to recognize the years of one's prime, always remember that. . . . One's prime is elusive.

MURIEL SPARK, *The Prime of Miss Jean Brodie* (1962)

The middle-aged, who have lived through their strongest emotions, but are yet in the time when memory is still half passionate and not merely contemplative, should surely be a sort of natural priesthood, whom life has disciplined and consecrated to be the refuge and rescue of early stumblers and victims of self-despair.

GEORGE ELIOT, *The Mill on the Floss* (1860)

Perhaps middle age is, or should be, a period of shedding shells; the shell of ambition, the shell of material accumulations and possessions, the shell of the ego.

ANNE MORROW LINDBERGH, *Gift From the Sea* (1955)

The middle years, caught between children and parents, free of neither: the past stretches back too densely, it is too thickly populated, the future has not yet thinned out.

MARGARET DRABBLE, *The Middle Ground* (1980)

In middle age we are apt to reach the horrifying conclusion that all sorrow, all pain, all passionate regret and loss and bitter disillusionment are self-made.

KATHLEEN NORRIS, *Hands Full of Living* (1931)

We Americans, with our terrific emphasis on youth, action, and material success, certainly tend to belittle the afternoon of life and even to pretend it never comes. We push the clock back and try to prolong the morning, over-reaching and over-straining ourselves in the unnatural effort. . . . In our breathless attempts we often miss the flowering that waits for afternoon.

ANNE MORROW LINDBERGH, *Gift From the Sea* (1955)

Shipwreck in youth is sorrowful enough, but one looks for storms at the spring equinox. Yet it is the September equinox that drowns.

HELEN WADDELL, *Peter Abelard* (1933)

I am a woman of a certain age / becoming invisible. / I walk the street unseen.

SUZANNE LABERGE, "The Metaphysics of Menopause," in Dena Taylor and Amber Coverdale Sumrall, *Women of the Fourteenth Moon* (1991)

The really frightening thing about middle age is the knowledge that you'll grow out of it.

DORIS DAY, in A. E. Hotchner, *Doris Day: Her Own Story* (1976)

See also Age.

MIDDLE CLASS

The last boat to the middle class was leaving and we'd better get on it.

ELLEN GOODMAN, *Close to Home* (1979)

The upper classes are merely a nation's past; the middle class is its future.

AYN RAND, in *The Ayn Rand Letter* (1971)

See also Class.

MILITARISM

Militarism is the most energy-intensive, entropic activity of humans, since it converts stored energy and materials directly into waste and destruction without any useful intervening fulfillment of basic human needs. Ironically, the net effect of military, as opposed to civilian, expenditures is to increase unemployment *and* inflation.

HAZEL HENDERSON, *The Politics of the Solar Age* (1981)

I am not being facetious when I say that the real enemies in this country are the Pentagon and its pals in big business.

BELLA ABZUG, *Bella!* (1972)

"Readiness," far from assuring peace, has at all times and in all countries been instrumental in precipitating armed conflicts.

EMMA GOLDMAN, *Living My Life* (1931)

No one can claim to be Christian who gives money for the building of warships and arsenals.

BELVA LOCKWOOD, speech (1886)

The contention that a standing army and navy is the best security of peace is about as logical as the claim that the most peaceful citizen is he who goes about heavily armed.

EMMA GOLDMAN, "Patriotism," *Anarchism* (1910)

Militarism . . . is one of the chief bulwarks of capitalism, and the day that militarism is undermined, capitalism will fail.

HELEN KELLER, *The Story of My Life* (1902)

Nothing so comforts the military mind as the maxim of a great but dead general.

BARBARA TUCHMAN, *The Guns of August* (1962)

Dead battles, like dead generals, hold the military mind in their dead grip.

BARBARA TUCHMAN, *The Guns of August* (1962)

See also Nuclear Weapons, War.

MIND

You know the mind *is* an astonishing, long-living, erotic thing.

GRACE PALEY, *Enormous Changes at the Last Minute* (1974)

The mind has no sex.

GEORGE SAND (1863), in Raphaël Ledos de Beaufort, *Letters of George Sand* (1886)

A closed mind is a dying mind.

EDNA FERBER, radio broadcast (1947)

Some minds remain open long enough for the truth not only to enter but to pass on through by way of a ready exit without pausing anywhere along the route.

ELIZABETH KENNY, with Martha Ostenso, *And They Shall Walk* (1943)

She rode her mind like a bitted horse.

STORM JAMESON, *The Clash* (1922)

His mind was an intricate, multigeared machine, or perhaps some little animal with skittery paws.

ANNE TYLER, *Searching for Caleb* (1975)

Her mind traveled crooked streets and aimless goat paths, arriving sometimes at profundity, other times at the revelations of a three-year-old.

TONI MORRISON, *Song of Solomon* (1977)

Such a cultivated mind doesn't really attract me. . . . No, no, the mind I love must still have wild places, a tangled orchard where dark damsons drop in the heavy grass, an overgrown little wood, the chance of a snake or two (real snakes), a pool that nobody's fathomed the depth of—and paths threaded with those little flowers planted by the mind.

KATHERINE MANSFIELD (1920), *Journal of Katherine Mansfield* (1927)

All I can say about my mind is that, like a fire carefully laid by a good housemaid, it is one that any match will light.

MARGOT ASQUITH, *More or Less About Myself* (1934)

No point in asking Greenfield what he was up to; he had pulled up his mental drawbridge and there was no way over the moat.

LUCILLE KALLEN, *The Tanglewood Murder* (1980)

You're a perfect child, a stubborn child! Your mind's in pigtails, like your hair.

MARY ROBERTS RINEHART, *Affinities and Other Stories* (1920)

The mind's cross-indexing puts the best librarian to shame.

SHARON BEGLEY, in *Newsweek* (1986)

His mind is furnished as hotels are, with everything for occasional and transient use.

GEORGE ELIOT, *Impressions of Theophrastus Such* (1879)

He has a brilliant mind until he makes it up.

MARGOT ASQUITH, *The Autobiography of Margot Asquith* (1923)

A ruffled mind makes a restless pillow.

CHARLOTTE BRONTË, *The Professor* (1846)

I was an excellent student until ten, and then my mind began to wander.

GRACE PALEY, in Harriet Shapiro, "Art Is on the Side of the Underdog," *Ms.* (1974)

Like water which can clearly mirror the sky and the trees only so long as its surface is undisturbed, the mind can only reflect the true image of the Self when it is tranquil and wholly relaxed.

INDRA DEVI, *Renewing Your Life Through Yoga* (1963)

It's as if tendencies that seem most deeply rooted in our minds, most private and singular, have come in as spores on the prevailing wind, looking for any likely place to land, any welcome.

ALICE MUNRO, *Friend of My Youth* (1990)

The mind is like a richly woven tapestry in which the colors are distilled from the experiences of the senses, and the design drawn from the convolutions of the intellect.

CARSON MCCULLERS, *Reflections in a Golden Eye* (1941)

The mind can store an estimated 100 trillion bits of information—compared with which a computer's mere billions are virtually amnesiac.

SHARON BEGLEY, in *Newsweek* (1986)

See also Brain, Intelligence, Thinking, Thoughts.

MINDSET

No man ever looks at the world with pristine eyes. He sees it edited by a definite set of customs and institutions and ways of thinking.

RUTH BENEDICT, *Patterns of Culture* (1934)

Creatures of a very particular making, we need to know the cultural blinders that narrow our world view as well as the psychological blinders that narrow our view of our personal experience.

CHRISTINA BALDWIN, *One to One* (1977)

We live what we know. If we believe the universe and ourselves to be mechanical, we will live mechanically. On the other hand, if we know that we are part of an open universe, and that our minds are a matrix of reality, we will live more creatively and powerfully.

MARILYN FERGUSON, *The Aquarian Conspiracy* (1980)

The transcendental point of view, the habit of thought bred by communion with earth and sky, had refined the grain while it had roughened the husk.

ELLEN GLASGOW, *Barren Ground* (1925)

The temper of mind that sees tragedy in life has not for its opposite the temper that sees joy. The opposite pole to the tragic view of life is the sordid view.

EDITH HAMILTON, *The Greek Way* (1930)

To work in the world lovingly means that we are defining what we will be *for*, rather than reacting to what we are against.

CHRISTINA BALDWIN, *Life's Companion, Journal Writing as a Spiritual Quest* (1990)

See also Perception, Philosophy.

MINORITIES

Every effort for progress, for enlightenment, for science, for religious, political, and economic liberty, emanates from the minority, and not from the mass.

EMMA GOLDMAN, "Minorities Versus Majorities," *Anarchism* (1910)

Being a minority in both caste and class, we moved about anyway on the hem of life, struggling to consolidate our weaknesses and hang on, or to creep singly up into the major folds of the garment.

TONI MORRISON, *The Bluest Eye* (1970)

I am visible—see this Indian face—yet I am invisible. I both blind them with my beak nose and am their blind spot. But I exist, we exist. They'd like to think I have melted in the pot. But I haven't, we haven't.

GLORIA ANZALDÚA, *Borderlands/La Frontera: The New Mestiza* (1987)

It is the curse of minorities in this power-worshipping world that either from fear or from an uncertain policy of expedience they distrust their own standards and hesitate to give voice to their deeper convictions, submitting supinely to estimates and characterizations of themselves as handed down by a not unprejudiced dominant majority.

ANNA JULIA COOPER, *A Voice from the South* (1892)

If the majority culture know so little about us, it must be *our* problem, they seem to be telling us; the burden of teaching is on us.

MITSUYE YAMADA, "Asian Pacific American Women and Feminism," in Cherríe Moraga and Gloria Anzaldúa, eds., *This Bridge Called My Back* (1983)

MIRACLES

It was a miracle; it was all a miracle: and one ought to have known, from the sufferings of saints, that miracles are horror.

NADINE GORDIMER, *July's People* (1981)

See also Magic, Wonder.

MISANTHROPY

As is the case of many misanthropes, his disdain for people led him into a profession designed to serve them.

TONI MORRISON, *The Bluest Eye* (1970)

I do not want people to be very agreeable, as it saves me the trouble of liking them a great deal.

JANE AUSTEN, letter to her sister Cassandra (1798)

See also Distrust, Hate.

MISCHIEF

Between frivolity and intentional mischief there is little difference, none in the results.

ILKA CHASE, *I Love Miss Tilli Bean* (1946)

I can sometimes resist temptation, but never mischief.

JOYCE REBETA-BURDITT, *The Cracker Factory* (1977)

See also Gaiety.

MISERLINESS

Miserliness is a capital quality to run in families; it's the safe side for madness to dip on.

GEORGE ELIOT, *Middlemarch* (1871)

She was tight as the paper on the wall.

MIGNON EBERHART, *Escape the Night* (1944)

Meanness inherits a set of silverware and keeps it in the bank. Economy uses it only on important occasions, for fear of loss. Thrift sets the table with it every night for pure pleasure, but counts the butter spreaders before they are put away.

PHYLLIS MCGINLEY, *Sixpence in Her Shoe* (1964)

See also Frugality.

MISERY

If you feel depressed you shouldn't go out on the street because it will show on your face and you'll give it to others. Misery is a communicable disease.

MARTHA GRAHAM, in John Heilpern, "The Amazing Martha," *Observer* (1979)

Take away the miseries and you take away some folks' reason for living. Their conversation piece anyway.

TONI CADE BAMBARA, *The Salt Eaters* (1980)

Real misery cuts off all paths to itself.

IRIS MURDOCH, *The Black Prince* (1973)

It is human misery and not pleasure which contains the secret of the divine wisdom.

SIMONE WEIL, *Gravity and Grace* (1947)

See also Grief, Sorrow, Unhappiness.

MISTAKES

Every great mistake has a halfway moment, a split second when it can be recalled and perhaps remedied.

PEARL BUCK, *What America Means to Me* (1943)

See also Error, Sin.

MODERATION

I have changed my ministers, but I have not changed my measures; I am still for moderation and will govern by it.

QUEEN ANNE, speech (1711)

MONDAY

I should think you could be gladder on Monday mornin' than any other day in the week, because 'twould be a whole *week* before you'd have another one!

ELEANOR H. PORTER, *Pollyanna* (1912)

MONEY

Money is the barometer of a society's virtue.

AYN RAND, *Atlas Shrugged* (1957)

In America, money takes the place of God.

ANZIA YEZIERSKA, *Red Ribbon on a White Horse* (1950)

The dollar sign is the only sign in which the modern man appears to have any real faith.

HELEN ROWLAND, *Reflections of a Bachelor Girl* (1909)

More and more I am certain that the only difference between man and animals is that men can count and animals cannot and if they count they mostly do count money.

GERTRUDE STEIN, *Everybody's Autobiography* (1937)

Money speaks sense in a language all nations understand.

APHRA BEHN, *The Rover* (1677)

The war [World War II], which destroyed so much of everything, was also constructive, in a way. It established clearly the cold, and finally unhypocritical fact that the most important thing on earth to men today is money.

JANET FLANNER ("Genêt"), *Paris Journal 1944–1965* (1965)

What I have here is a complete indictment of our present-day society, our whole world. What's wrong with it is money, honey, money.

MARGARET WALKER, in Claudia Tate, ed., Black Women Writers at Work (1983)

Money is everything in the world to some people and more than the next to other poor souls.

AUGUSTA EVANS, *Beulah* (1859)

I believe only in money, not in love or tenderness. Love and tenderness meant only pain and suffering and defeat. I would not let it ruin me as it ruined others! I would speak only with money, hard money.

AGNES SMEDLEY, *Daughter of Earth* (1929)

People who think money can do anything may very well be suspected of doing anything for money.

MARY PETTIBONE POOLE, *A Glass Eye at a Keyhole* (1938)

He . . . knew now, more than ever, that money was everything, the wall that stood between all he loathed and all he wanted.

WILLA CATHER, *Youth and the Bright Medusa* (1920)

No one would remember the Good Samaritan if he'd only had good intentions. He had money as well.

MARGARET THATCHER, in *London Times* (1986)

Americans want action for their money. They are fascinated by its self-reproducing qualities.

PAULA NELSON, *The Joy of Money* (1975)

Some people think they are worth a lot of money just because they have it.

FANNIE HURST (1952), in Joseph L. Baron, *A Treasury of Jewish Quotations* (1956)

Money is always dull, except when you haven't got any, and then it's terrifying.

SHEILA BISHOP, *The House With Two Faces* (1960)

I must say I hate money but it's the lack of it I hate most.

KATHERINE MANSFIELD, in Antony Alpers, *Katherine Mansfield* (1954)

Indeed, I thought, slipping the silver into my purse, it is remarkable, remembering the bitterness of those days, what a change of temper a fixed income will bring about.

VIRGINIA WOOLF, *A Room of One's Own* (1929)

There are many to whom money has no personal appeal, but who can be tempted by the power it confers.

AGATHA CHRISTIE, *Crooked House* (1949)

I have a prejudice against people with money. I have known so many, and none have escaped the corruption of power. In this I am a purist. I love people motivated by love and not by power. If you have money and power, and are motivated by love, you give it all away.

ANAÏS NIN, *The Diary of Anaïs Nin*, vol. 4 (1944–1947)

Being moderate with oneself and generous with others; this is what is meant by having a just relationship with money, by being free as far as money is concerned.

NATALIA GINZBURG, *The Little Virtues* (1962)

I make money using my brains and lose money listening to my heart. But in the long run my books balance pretty well.

KATE SEREDY, *The Singing Tree* (1939)

There are a handful of people whom money won't spoil, and we all count ourselves among them.

MIGNON MCLAUGHLIN, *The Second Neurotic's Notebook* (1966)

So you think that money is the root of all evil? Have you ever asked what is the root of money?

AYN RAND, *Atlas Shrugged* (1957)

The best way to attract money, she had discovered, was to give the appearance of having it.

GAIL SHEEHY, *Hustling* (1973)

It is true that money attracts; but much money repels.

CYNTHIA OZICK, *Trust* (1966)

Money demands that you sell, not your weakness to men's stupidity, but your talent to their reason.

AYN RAND, *Atlas Shrugged* (1957)

Need of money, dear.

DOROTHY PARKER, when asked what was the source of most of her work, in Malcolm Cowley, ed., *Writers at Work* (1958)

Money dignifies what is frivolous if unpaid for.

VIRGINIA WOOLF, *A Room of One's Own* (1929)

The two most beautiful words in the English language are "check enclosed."

DOROTHY PARKER, in *New York Herald Tribune* (1932)

I want to ask thee a solemn question. Did thee ever one single time have thy Bank book balance and thy own check book balance agree exactly?

HANNAH WHITALL SMITH, letter to her sister (1885), in Logan Pearsall Smith, *Philadelphia Quaker* (1950)

Gone today, here tomorrow.

CATHERINE CROOK DE CAMP, on retirement savings, *The Money Tree* (1972)

Money can be translated into the beauty of living, a support in misfortune, an education, or future security. It also can be translated into a source of bitterness.

SYLVIA PORTER, *Sylvia Porter's Money Book* (1975)

Where there is money, there is fighting.

MARIAN ANDERSON, in Kosti Vehanen, *Marian Anderson, a Portrait* (1941)

Money is only money, beans tonight and steak tomorrow. So long as you can look yourself in the eye.

MERIDEL LE SUEUR, *Crusaders* (1955)

As a cousin of mine once said about money, money is always there but the pockets change; it is not in the same pockets after a change, and that is all there is to say about money.

GERTRUDE STEIN, in C. P. Curtis, Jr. and Ferris Greenlet, *The Practical Cogitator* (1945)

As soon as you bring up money, I notice, conversation gets sociological, then political, then moral.

JANE SMILEY, *Good Will* (1989)

Money creates taste.

JENNY HOLZER, *Truisms* (1991)

Those who never think of money need a great deal of it.

AGATHA CHRISTIE, "The Second Gong," *Witness for the Prosecution* (1924)

The only way not to think about money is to have a great deal of it.

EDITH WHARTON, *The House of Mirth* (1905)

Money's queer. It goes where it's wanted.

AGATHA CHRISTIE, *Endless Night* (1968)

You don't seem to realize that a poor person who is unhappy is in a better position than a rich person who is unhappy. Because the poor person has hope. He thinks money would help.

JEAN KERR, *Poor Richard* (1963)

In my book, anyone pretending he has no interest in money is either a fool or a knave.

LESLIE FORD, *Invitation to Murder* (1954)

Friends and good manners will carry you where money won't go.

MARGARET WALKER, *Jubilee* (1966)

Does anybody who gave up smoking to save a pound a week *have* a pound at the end of the week? Not on your life.

KATHARINE WHITEHORN, *Roundabout* (1962)

See also Business, Gold, Profit, Rich, Taxes, Wealth.

MONOTONY

I feel monotony and death to be almost the same.

CHARLOTTE BRONTË, *Shirley* (1849)

See also Boredom.

MOON

The moon / waning or waxing / a sliver set / like a cradle / a thin suggestion, / the lit edge / of porcelain.

YVETTE NELSON, *We'll Come When It Rains* (1982)

Moon, worn thin to the width of a quill, / In the dawn clouds flying, / How good to go, light into light, and still / Giving light, dying.

SARA TEASDALE, "Moon's Ending," *Strange Victory* (1933)

Stars veil their beauty soon / Beside the glorious moon, / When her full silver light / Doth make the whole earth bright.

SAPPHO (6th century B.C.), in C. R. Haines, *Sappho: The Poems and Fragments* (1926)

You Moon! Have you done something wrong in heaven, / That God has hidden your face?

JEAN INGELOW, "Seven Times One," *Songs of Seven* (1885)

I consulted the moon / like a crystal ball.

DIANE ACKERMAN, *The Planets* (1976)

The moon develops the imagination, as chemicals develop photographic images.

SHEILA BALLANTYNE, *Norma Jean the Termite Queen* (1975)

See also Sky, Stars.

MORALITY

A straight line is the shortest in morals as in geometry.

RACHEL [ELIZABETH FELIX], in Joseph L. Baron, *A Treasury of Jewish Quotations* (1956)

No morals are better than bad ones.

MINNA THOMAS ANTRIM, *At the Sign of the Golden Calf* (1905)

Morality is observance of the laws of wholesome living. . . . In matters of morals we can hold certain assumptions: that there are some things better or worse in human affairs; that we ought to discover the better ways; that human beings are of great worth; that good should be done and evil avoided.

ANGELA M. RAIMO, in *Christopher News Notes* (1991)

A moral choice in its basic terms appears to be a choice that favors survival: a choice made in favor of life.

URSULA K. LE GUIN, *Dancing at the Edge of the World* (1989)

Is it really so difficult to tell a good action from a bad one? I think one usually knows right away or a moment afterward, in a horrid flash of regret.

MARY MCCARTHY, *On the Contrary* (1961)

The morals of to-day are the immorals of yesterday, the creeds of tomorrow.

MINNA THOMAS ANTRIM, *At the Sign of the Golden Calf* (1905)

The more immoral we become in big ways, the more puritanical we become in little ways.

FLORENCE KING, *Lump It or Leave It* (1990)

Life itself, however, flows and is sequential and punishes those who try to compartmentalize it. Thus if, for any reason whatsoever, moral standards are conspicuously and unprecedentedly breached in one area of society, such as the political, it will follow as the night the day that those standards will start collapsing all down the line—in sports, entertainment, education, the armed forces, business and government.

MARGARET HALSEY, *No Laughing Matter* (1977)

Perhaps the straight and narrow path would be wider if more people used it.

KAY INGRAM, in *Saturday Evening Post* (1950)

Your morals are like roads through the Alps. They make these hairpin turns all the time.

ERICA JONG, *Fear of Flying* (1973)

It is a depressing fact that Americans tend to confuse morality and art (to the detriment of both) and that, among the educated, morality tends to mean social consciousness.

PAULINE KAEL, *I Lost It at the Movies* (1965)

Conventionality is not morality. Self-righteousness is not religion. To attack the first is not to assail the last.

CHARLOTTE BRONTË, *Jane Eyre* (1847)

Morality is not tied to divine bookkeeping. God and humanity are not business partners checking out each other's claims.

CHRISTINA THÜRMER-ROHR, *Vagabonding* (1991)

You are so afraid of losing your moral sense that you are not willing to take it through anything more dangerous than a mud-puddle.

GERTRUDE STEIN, "Q.E.D." (1903), *Fernhurst, Q.E.D., and Other Early Writings* (1971)

People want to be amused, not preached at, you know. Morals don't sell nowadays.

LOUISA MAY ALCOTT, *Little Women* (1868)

Whoever gives the common people food to eat is a good person whoever lets the common people starve is a bad person.

HUALING NIEH, *Mulberry and Peach* (1981)

See also Conscience, Ethics, Good, Principles, Taboos, Virtue.

MORNING

Morning has broken / Like the first morning. / Blackbird has spoken / Like the first bird.

ELEANOR FARJEON, "A Morning Song (for the First Day of Spring)," *Children's Bells* (1957)

There is no doubt that running away on a fresh, blue morning can be exhilarating.

JEAN RHYS, *The Left Bank* (1927)

I have always felt that the moment when first you wake up in the morning is the most wonderful of the twenty-four hours. No matter how weary or dreary you may feel, you possess the certainty that . . . absolutely anything may happen. And the fact that it practically always *doesn't*, matters not one jot. The possibility is always there.

MONICA BALDWIN, *I Leap Over the Wall* (1950)

The average, healthy, well-adjusted adult gets up at seven-thirty in the morning feeling just plain terrible.

JEAN KERR, *Please Don't Eat the Daisies* (1957)

To have a reason to get up in the morning, it is necessary to possess a guiding principle. A belief of some kind. A bumper sticker if you will.

JUDITH GUEST, *Ordinary People* (1976)

Statistically speaking, the Cheerful Early Riser is rejected more completely than a member of any other subculture, save those with boot odor.

ELLEN GOODMAN, *Close to Home* (1979)

See also Dawn.

MOTHER

My mother is a poem I'll never be able to write / though everything I write is a poem to my mother.

SHARON DOUBIAGO, in Tillie Olsen, *Mother to Daughter, Daughter to Mother* (1984)

No song or poem will bear my mother's name. Yet so many of the stories that I write, that we all write, are my mother's stories.

ALICE WALKER, title essay (1974), *In Search of Our Mothers' Gardens* (1983)

My mother, religious-negro, proud of / having waded through a storm, is very obviously, / a sturdy Black bridge that I / crossed over, on.

CAROLYN M. RODGERS, "It Is Deep (Don't never forget the bridge that you crossed over on)," in Roseann P. Bell, Bettye J. Parker, and Beverly Guy-Sheftall, *Sturdy Black Bridges* (1979)

I cannot forget my mother. Though not as sturdy as others, she is my bridge. When I needed to get across, she steadied herself long enough for me to run across safely.

RENITA WEEMS, "'Hush, Mama's Gotta Go Bye-Bye,'" in Patricia Bell-Scott et al., eds., *Double Stitch* (1991)

My mother is a woman who speaks with her life as much as with her tongue.

KESAYA E. NODA, "Growing Up Asian in America," in Asian Women United of California, eds., *Making Waves: An Anthology of Writings By and About Asian American Women* (1989)

To my first Love, my Mother, on whose knee / I learnt love-lore that is not troublesome.

CHRISTINA ROSSETTI, "To My First Love, My Mother," in Mildred P. Harrington and Josephine H. Thomas, *Our Holidays in Poetry* (1929)

I learned your walk, talk, gestures and nurturing laughter. At that time, Mama, had you swung from bars, I would, to this day, be hopelessly, imitatively, hung up.

SDIANE BOGUS, "Mom de Plume" (1977), in Patricia Bell-Scott et al., eds., *Double Stitch* (1991)

My mother wasn't what the world would call a good woman. She never said she was. And many people, including the police, said she was a bad woman. But she never agreed with them, and she had a way of lifting up her head when she talked back to them that made me know she was right.

BOX-CAR BERTHA, *Sister of the Road* (1937)

She knew how to make virtues out of necessities.

AUDRE LORDE, *Zami: A New Spelling of My Name* (1983)

Who ran to help me when I fell, / And would some pretty story tell, / Or kiss the place to make it well? / My Mother.

ANN TAYLOR, "My Mother," *Original Poems for Infant Minds* (1804)

Were my smile not submerged in my countenance, / I should suspend it over her grave.

ELSE LASKER-SCHÜLER, "My Mother" (1925), *Hebrew Ballads and Other Poems* (1980)

A mother is not a person to lean on but a person to make leaning unnecessary.

DOROTHY CANFIELD FISHER, *Her Son's Wife* (1926)

You never get over being a child, long as you have a mother to go to.

SARAH ORNE JEWETT, *The Country of the Pointed Firs* (1896)

A woman *is* her mother. / That's the main thing.

ANNE SEXTON, "Housewife" (1962), in Sandra M. Gilbert and Susan Gubar, eds., *The Norton Anthology of Literature by Women* (1985)

i am not you anymore / i am my own collection of / gifts and errors.

SAUNDRA SHARP, "Double Exposure," in Patricia Bell-Scott et al., eds., *Double Stitch* (1991)

Out of the corner of one eye, I could see my mother. Out of the corner of the other eye, I could see her shadow on the wall, cast there by the lamplight. It was a big and solid shadow, and it looked so much like my mother that I became frightened. For I could not be sure whether for the rest of my life I would be able to tell when it was really my mother and when it was really her shadow standing between me and the rest of the world.

JAMAICA KINCAID, *Annie John* (1983)

She was the archetypal selfless mother: living only for her children, sheltering them from the consequences of their actions—and in the end doing them irreparable harm.

MARCIA MULLER, "Benny's Space," in Sara Paretsky, ed., *A Woman's Eye* (1991)

On one thing professionals and amateurs agree: mothers can't win.

MARGARET DRABBLE, *The Middle Ground* (1980)

Oh! mothers aren't fair—I mean it's not fair of nature to weigh us down with them and yet expect us to be our own true selves. The handicap's too great. All those months, when the same blood's running through two sets of veins—there's no getting away from that, ever after. Take yours. As I say, does she need to open her mouth? Not she! She's only got to let it hang at the corners, and you reek, you drip with guilt.

HENRY HANDEL RICHARDSON, *Two Hanged Women* (1934)

My mother phones daily to ask, "Did you just try to reach me?" When I reply, "No," she adds, "So, if you're not too busy, call me while I'm still alive," and hangs up.

ERMA BOMBECK, *The 1992 Erma Bombeck Calendar* (1992)

Blaming mother is just a negative way of clinging to her still.

NANCY FRIDAY, *My Mother/My Self* (1977)

I fear, as any daughter would, losing myself back into the mother.

KIM CHERNIN, *In My Mother's House* (1983)

At that moment, I missed my mother more than I had ever imagined possible and wanted only to live somewhere quiet and beautiful with her alone, but also at that moment I wanted only to see her lying dead, all withered and in a coffin at my feet.

JAMAICA KINCAID, *Annie John* (1983)

No matter how old a mother is, she watches her middle-aged children for signs of improvement.

FLORIDA SCOTT-MAXWELL, *The Measure of My Days* (1968)

Whenever I'm with my mother, I feel as though I have to spend the whole time avoiding land mines.

AMY TAN, *The Kitchen God's Wife* (1991)

Now that I am in my forties, she tells me I'm beautiful; now that I am in my forties, she sends me presents and we have the long, personal and even remarkably honest phone calls I always wanted so intensely I forbade myself to imagine them. How strange. Perhaps Shaw was correct and if we lived to be several hundred years old, we would finally work it all out. I am deeply grateful. With my poems, I finally won even my mother. The longest wooing of my life.

MARGE PIERCY, *Braided Lives* (1982)

She never outgrows the burden of love, and to the end she carries the weight of hope for those she bore. Oddly, very oddly, she is forever surprised and even faintly wronged that her sons and daughters are just people, for many mothers hope and half expect that their newborn child will make the world better, will somehow be a redeemer. Perhaps they are right, and they can believe that the rare quality they glimpsed in the child is active in the burdened adult.

FLORIDA SCOTT-MAXWELL, *The Measure of My Days* (1968)

When my mother had to get dinner for eight she'd just make enough for sixteen and only serve half.

GRACIE ALLEN, in Liz Smith, *The Mother Book* (1978)

One of my children wrote in a third-grade piece on how her mother spent her time . . . "one-half time on home, one-half time on outside things, one-half time writing."

CHARLOTTE MONTGOMERY, in *Good Housekeeping* (1959)

She said that if I listened to her, later I would know what she knew: where true words came from, always from up high, above everything else. And if I didn't listen to her, she said my ear would bend too easily to other people, all saying words that had no lasting meaning, because they came from the bottom of their hearts, where their own desires lived, a place where I could not belong.

AMY TAN, *The Joy Luck Club* (1989)

And it came to me, and I knew what I had to have before my soul would rest. I wanted to belong—to belong to my mother. And in re-turn—I wanted my mother to belong to me.

GLORIA VANDERBILT, *Once Upon a Time* (1985)

My life now is only mine.

TOBY TALBOT, on her mother's death, in Tillie Olsen, *Mother to Daughter, Daughter to Mother* (1984)

Lennie, suffering not alone for her who was dying, but for that in her which never lived (for that which in him might never live). From him too, unspoken words: *good-bye Mother who taught me to mother myself.*

TILLIE OLSEN, title story, *Tell Me a Riddle* (1956)

I acknowledge the cold truth of her death for perhaps the first time. She is truly gone, forever out of reach, and I have become my own judge.

SHEILA BALLANTYNE, *Imaginary Crimes* (1982)

The woman who bore me is no longer alive, but I seem to be her daughter in increasingly pro-found ways.

JOHNNETTA B. COLE, in Patricia Bell-Scott et al., eds., *Double Stitch* (1991)

My mother was dead for five years before I knew that I had loved her very much.

LILLIAN HELLMAN, *An Unfinished Woman* (1969)

Time is the only comforter for the loss of a mother.

JANE WELSH CARLYLE, letter to Thomas Carlyle on the death of his mother (1853)

See also Parents.

MOTIVES

Too great a preoccupation with motives (espe-cially one's own motives) is liable to lead to too little concern for consequences.

KATHARINE WHITEHORN, *Roundabout* (1962)

We must not inquire too curiously into mo-tives. . . They are apt to become feeble in the utterance: the aroma is mixed with the grosser air. We must keep the germinating grain away from the light.

GEORGE ELIOT, *Middlemarch* (1871)

What makes life dreary is the want of motive.

GEORGE ELIOT, *Daniel Deronda* (1874)

See also Purpose.

MOUNTAINS

If you grow up where a snow mountain lifts its proud crown on the home horizon, in some strange way it becomes a member of the family.

MARGARET CRAVEN, *Walk Gently This Good Earth* (1977)

The mountains were getting ready for winter, too. They were very sly about it and tried to look summery and casual but I could tell by their contours that they had slipped on an extra layer of snow—that the misty scarf blowing about that one's head would soon be lying whitely around her neck.

BETTY MACDONALD, *The Egg and I* (1945)

When you are a child of the mountains yourself, you really belong to them. You need them. They become the faithful guardians of your life. If you cannot dwell on their lofty heights all your life, if you are in trouble, you want at least to look at them.

MARIA AUGUSTA TRAPP, *The Story of the Trapp Family Singers* (1949)

My help is in the mountain / Where I take myself to heal / The earthly wounds / That people give to me.

NANCY WOOD, "My Help Is in the Mountain," *Hollering Sun* (1972)

There came without warning a flowing into me of that which I have come to associate with the gods. I went to the open door and looked up at the mountains with something akin to awe. It forced me out into the open where I could look up to the sacred high places on which humans do not dwell. Then it left me—perhaps to return to those sacred places.

EDITH WARNER, in Peggy Pond Church, *The House at Otowi Bridge* (1959)

You never conquer a mountain. You stand on the summit a few moments; then the wind blows your footprints away.

ARLENE BLUM, *Annapurna* (1980)

All mountain streets have streams to thread them, or deep grooves where a stream might run. You would do well to avoid that range uncomforted by singing floods. You will find it forsaken of most things but beauty and madness and death and God.

MARY AUSTIN, *The Land of Little Rain* (1904)

To rise above treeline is to go above thought, and after, the descent back into birdsong, bog orchids, willows, and firs is to sink into the preliterate parts of ourselves.

GRETEL EHRLICH, in William Kittredge, ed., *Montana Spaces* (1988)

The low-lying mountains sleep at the edge of the world.

HARRIET MONROE, "The Blue Ridge," *The Difference and Other Poems* (1924)

MOURNING

The distance that the dead have gone / Does not at first appear— / Their coming back seems possible / For many an ardent year.

EMILY DICKINSON, *Poems, Third Series* (1896)

Mourning is not forgetting. . . . It is an undoing. Every minute tie has to be untied and something permanent and valuable recovered and assimilated from the dust.

MARGERY ALLINGHAM, *The Tiger in the Smoke* (1952)

One must go through periods of numbness that are harder to bear than grief.

ANNE MORROW LINDBERGH, *Hour of Gold, Hour of Lead* (1973)

The grass is waking in the ground, / Soon it will rise and blow in waves— / How can it have the heart to sway / Over the graves, / New graves?

SARA TEASDALE, "Spring in War-Time," *Rivers to the Sea* (1915)

These talkings and comfortings lasted two or three weeks; after that no one knew me. . . . After the first thirty days of mourning, no brother, no sister, no relative came to ask: "How are you? and how are things?"

GLÜCKEL OF HAMELN, *The Life of Glückel of Hameln (1646–1724), Written by Herself* (1719)

The time at length arrives, when grief is rather an indulgence than a necessity and the smile that plays upon the lips, although it may be deemed a sacrilege, is not banished.

MARY SHELLEY, *Frankenstein* (1818)

In coming to terms with the newly dead, I seem to have agitated the spirits of the long dead. They were stirring uneasily in their graves, demanding to be mourned as I had not mourned them when they were buried. I was plunged into retroactive grief for my father, and could no longer deny, though I still tried, the loss I'd suffered at the death of my mother. . . . Was it possible . . . that one could mourn over losses that had occurred more than half a century earlier?

EILEEN SIMPSON, *Orphans: Real and Imaginary* (1990)

We met . . . Dr. Hall in such very deep mourning that either his mother, his wife, or himself must be dead.

JANE AUSTEN, letter to her sister Cassandra (1799)

See also Death, Grief, Loss, Pain, Sorrow.

MOVEMENTS

Social movements are frequently characterized by gaps between the lives of the theorists who lead the movements and those of the followers who try to practice the theorists' ideas.

ARLENE ROSSEN CARDOZO, *Sequencing* (1986)

Unity in a movement situation is overrated. If you were the Establishment, which would you rather see coming in the door, five hundred mice or one lion?

FLORYNCE KENNEDY, in Gloria Steinem, *Outrageous Acts and Everyday Rebellions* (1983)

It takes six simpletons and one zealot to start a movement.

ANZIA YEZIERSKA, "One Thousand Pages of Research," *Commentary* (1963)

See also Protest, Revolution, Social Change.

MUSIC

Music has been my playmate, my lover, and my crying towel.

BUFFY SAINTE-MARIE, in *Ms.* (1975)

Music my rampart, and my only one.

EDNA ST. VINCENT MILLAY, "On Hearing a Symphony of Beethoven," *The Buck in the Snow* (1928)

Music relates sound and time and so pictures the ultimate edges of human communications.

IRIS MURDOCH, *The Black Prince* (1973)

Words are wearisome and worn, while the arabesques of music are forever new.

COLETTE, *My Apprenticeships* (1936)

While I listened, music was to my soul what the atmosphere is to my body; it was the breath of my inward life. I felt, more deeply than ever, that music is the highest symbol of the infinite and holy. . . . With renewed force I felt what I have often said, that the secret of creation lay in music. "A *voice* to light gave being." Sound led the stars into their places.

LYDIA MARIA CHILD, *Letters from New York,* 2nd Series (1845)

Music revives the recollections it would appease.

MADAME DE STAËL, *Corinne* (1807)

The music sounded flat—it had the kind of depth that comes from bitterness, not wonder.

GRETEL EHRLICH, *Heart Mountain* (1988)

What good is music? None . . . and that is the point. To the world and its states and armies and factories and Leaders, music says, "You are irrelevant"; and, arrogant and gentle as a god, to the suffering man it says only, "Listen." For being saved is not the point. Music saves nothing. Merciful, uncaring, it denies and breaks down all the shelters, the houses men build for themselves, that they may see the sky.

URSULA K. LE GUIN, "An die Musik," *Western Humanities Review* (1961)

Like the brushing of swallows' wings against the willows—sweet, sweet music!

LOUISE CRANE, *The Magic Spear and Other Stories of China's Famous Heroes* (1938)

I am always thirsting for beautiful, beautiful, beautiful music. I wish I could make it. Perhaps there isn't any music on earth like what I picture to myself.

OLIVE SCHREINER, *The Letters of Olive Schreiner, 1876–1920* (1976)

I think I should have no other mortal wants, if I could always have plenty of music. It seems to infuse strength into my limbs and ideas into my brain. Life seems to go on without effort, when I am filled with music.

GEORGE ELIOT, The Mill on the Floss (1860)

No one really understood music unless he was a scientist, her father had declared, and not just a scientist, either, oh, no, only the real ones, the theoreticians, whose language was mathematics.

PEARL BUCK, *The Goddess Abides* (1972)

It had never occurred to me before that music and thinking are so much alike. In fact you could say music is another way of thinking, or maybe thinking is another kind of music.

URSULA K. LE GUIN, *Very Far Away From Anywhere Else* (1976)

Writing more and more to the sound of music, writing more and more like music. Sitting in my studio tonight, playing record after record, music a stimulant of the highest order, far more potent than wine.

ANAÏS NIN, *The Diary of Anaïs Nin,* vol. 2 (1934–1939)

Rhythm is one of the principal translators between dream and reality. Rhythm might be described as, to the world of sound, what light is to the world of sight. It shapes and gives new meaning. Rhythm was described by Schopen-hauer as melody deprived of its pitch.

EDITH SITWELL, *Taken Care Of* (1965)

Seated one day at the organ, / I was weary and ill at ease, / And my fingers wandered idly / Over the noisy keys. / But I struck one chord of music / Like the sound of a great Amen.

ADELAIDE A. PROCTOR, "A Lost Chord," *Legends and Lyrics* (1858)

I never practice; I always play.

WANDA LANDOWSKA, in *Time* (1952)

A piano is full of suppressed desires, recalci-trance, inhibition, conflict.

ANITA T. SULLIVAN, *The Seventh Dragon* (1985)

Jean turned the piano into a human voice, wak-ing them out of sodden sleep. Just listening was living. Life filtered through tired bodies, bent backs. Heads lifted. Fear and worry fled from their eyes. For an instant, they breathed in a fullness of life denied them in life.

ANZIA YEZIERSKA, *Arrogant Beggar* (1927)

Chamber music—a conversation between friends.

CATHERINE DRINKER BOWEN, *Friends and Fiddlers* (1934)

To Jack (my husband), his violin is comfort and relaxation. To his inky wife, it's time to put her head down the waste disposal unit again.

MAUREEN LIPMAN, *How Was It for You?* (1985)

Miss Beevor had made her playing at once much better and much worse, by giving her resolute fingers greater power to express her misunder-standing of sound.

REBECCA WEST, *The Fountain Overflows* (1956)

Miss Eckhart worshiped her metronome. She kept it, like the most precious secret in the teach-ing of music, in a wall safe.

EUDORA WELTY, "June Recital," *The Golden Apples* (1949)

I wish the Government would put a tax on pi-anos for the incompetent.

EDITH SITWELL, *Selected Letters* (1970)

How pleasant it is to be ignorant! Not to know exactly who Mozart was, to ignore his origin, his influence, the details of his technique! To just let him lead one by the hand.

MARIA-LUISA BOMBAL, "The Tree," in Zoila Nelken and Rosalie Torres-Rioseco, eds., *Short Stories of Latin America* (1963)

I want Bach's Toccata and Fugue in D played at my funeral. If it isn't I shall jolly well want to know why.

SYBIL THORNDIKE, in *English Digest* (1965)

I find that I never lose Bach. I don't know why I have always loved him so. Except that he is so pure, so relentless and incorruptible, like a prin-ciple of geometry.

EDNA ST. VINCENT MILLAY (1920), in Allan Ross Macdougall, *Letters of Edna St. Vincent Millay* (1952)

The one Bach piece I learnt made me feel I was being repeatedly hit on the head with a tea-spoon.

DODIE SMITH, *I Capture the Castle* (1948)

There are some composers—at the head of whom stands Beethoven—who not only do not know when to stop but appear to stop many times before they actually do.

VIRGINIA GRAHAM, *Say Please* (1949)

If morning-glories had come out of the horn in-stead of those sounds, Josie would not have felt a more astonished delight. She was pierced with pleasure.

EUDORA WELTY, "The Winds," *The Wide Net* (1943)

I stole everything I ever heard, but mostly I stole from the horns.

ELLA FITZGERALD, in Barbara McDowell and Hana Umlauf, *Woman's Almanac* (1977)

Anybody singing the blues is in a deep pit yelling for help.

MAHALIA JACKSON, *Movin' On Up* (1966)

Nobody can teach you how to sing the blues, you have to feel the blues.

ERNESTINE ANDERSON, in Brian Lanker, *I Dream a World* (1989)

Blues are the songs of despair, but gospel songs are the songs of hope.

MAHALIA JACKSON, *Movin' On Up* (1966)

All riddles are blues, / And all blues are sad, / And I'm only mentioning / Some blues I've had.

MAYA ANGELOU, "A Good Woman Feeling Bad," *Shaker, Why Don't You Sing?* (1983)

The blues records of each decade explain something about the philosophical basis of our lives as black people. . . . Blues is a basis of historical continuity for black people. It is a ritualized way of talking about ourselves and passing it on.

SHERLEY ANNE WILLIAMS, in Claudia Tate, ed., *Black Women Writers at Work* (1983)

Audiences like their blues singers to be miserable.

JANIS JOPLIN, in Barbara McDowell and Hana Umlauf, *Woman's Almanac* (1977)

Jazz exemplifies artistic activity that is at once individual and communal, performance that is both repetitive and innovative, each participant sometimes providing background support and sometimes flying free.

MARY CATHERINE BATESON, *Composing a Life* (1989)

An opera begins long before the curtain goes up and ends long after it has come down. It starts in my imagination, it becomes my life, and it stays part of my life long after I've left the opera house.

MARIA CALLAS, *Maria Callas* (1981)

The Hawaiian people have been from time immemorial lovers of poetry and music, and have been apt in improvising historic poems, songs of love, and chants of worship, so that praises of the living or wails over the dead were with them but the natural expression of their feelings.

LYDIA KAMEKEHA LILIUOKALANI, *Hawaii's Story* (1898)

Only dead people need loud music, you know.

ALICE WALKER, *Temple of My Familiar* (1989)

See also Singing, Song.

MYSTERY

No object is mysterious. The mystery is your eye.

ELIZABETH BOWEN, *The House in Paris* (1936)

See also Magic.

MYSTICISM

There is a hard clear rationality about Quakers—and, indeed, all mysticism, which, once experienced, makes other ways appear indirect, childish, and crude.

JESSAMYN WEST, *The Quaker Reader* (1962)

The worst danger of the mystic is a quest of spiritual privilege leading to aloofness from the common lot.

VIDA D. SCUDDER, *The Privilege of Age* (1939)

See also Shamans, Spirituality, Visions.

MYTH

The test of a true myth is that each time you return to it, new insights and interpretations arise.

STARHAWK, *The Spiral Dance* (1989)

Myths are early science, the result of men's first trying to explain what they saw around them.

EDITH HAMILTON, *Mythology* (1942)

Myth is someone else's religion.

CAROLINE LLEWELLYN, *The Lady of the Labyrinth* (1990)

See also Legends.

N

NAGGING

Nagging is the repetition of unpalatable truths.

EDITH SUMMERSKILL, speech (1960)

See also Disapproval.

NAMES

I am the one whose love / overcomes you, already with you / when you think to call my name.

JANE KENYON, "Briefly It Enters, and Briefly Speaks," *The Boat of Quiet Hours* (1986)

say / who I am. Set / our two fires climbing.

MARY VIRGINIA MICKA, "Greeting," *All Rounds Returning* (1986)

The "t" is silent, as in Harlow.

MARGOT ASQUITH, on her name being mispronounced by Jean Harlow, in T. S. Matthews, *Great Tom* (1974)

Both legally and familiarly, as well as in my books, I now have only one name, which is my own.

COLETTE, *La Naissance du jour* (1928)

It would have saved trouble had I remained Perkins from the first, this changing of women's names is a nuisance we are now happily outgrowing.

CHARLOTTE PERKINS GILMAN, *The Living of Charlotte Perkins Gilman* (1935)

Hoary idea, in any case, expecting a woman to surrender her name to her husband's in exchange for his. Why? Would any man submerge his identity and heritage to the woman he wed?

MARYA MANNES, *Out of My Time* (1968)

See also Naming.

NAMING

The name we give to something shapes our attitude toward it.

KATHERINE PATERSON, *Gates of Excellence* (1981)

I understand why one wants to know the names of what he loves. . . . Naming is a kind of possessing, of caressing and fondling.

JESSAMYN WEST, *Hide and Seek* (1973)

From antiquity, people have recognized the connection between naming and power.

CASEY MILLER AND KATE SWIFT, *Words and Women* (1976)

What we name must answer to us; we can shape it if not control it.

STARHAWK, *Dreaming the Dark* (1982)

Nature is intricately and infinitely connected. The minute I name something and begin to regard it as a separate entity, I break this unbreakable unity. So that which makes it possible for us to seek truths about the universe and about ourselves has within itself the guarantee that we will never be able to find the Truth. Our knowledge must be forever fragmented, because that is the nature of systematic knowledge.

KATHERINE PATERSON, *Gates of Excellence* (1981)

Human names for natural things are superfluous. Nature herself does not name them. The important thing is to *know* this flower, look at its color until the blueness becomes as real as a keynote of music.

SALLY CARRIGHAR, *Home to the Wilderness* (1973)

See also Names.

NATIVE AMERICANS

An odd thing occurs in the minds of Americans when Indian civilization is mentioned: little or nothing.

PAULA GUNN ALLEN, *The Sacred Hoop* (1986)

She realized that white people rarely concerned themselves with Indian matters, that Indians were the shadow people, living almost invisibly on the fringes around them, and that this shadowy world allowed for a strange kind of freedom.

LINDA HOGAN, *Mean Spirit* (1990)

America does not seem to remember that it derived its wealth, its values, its food, much of its medicine, and a large part of its "dream" from Native America.

PAULA GUNN ALLEN, *The Sacred Hoop* (1986)

Being Indian is an attitude, a state of mind, a way of being in harmony with all things and all beings. It is allowing the heart to be the distributor of energy on this planet: to allow feelings and sensitivities to determine where energy goes; bringing aliveness up from the Earth and down from the Sky, putting it in and giving it out from the heart.

BROOKE MEDICINE EAGLE, in Joan Halifax, *Shamanic Voices: A Survey of Visionary Narratives* (1979)

For the American Indian, the ability of all creatures to share in the process of ongoing creation makes all things sacred.

PAULA GUNN ALLEN, *The Sacred Hoop* (1986)

My sacred beliefs have been made pencils, names of cities, gas stations / My knee is wounded so badly that I limp constantly / Anger is my crutch / I hold myself upright with it.

CHRYSTOS, "I Walk in the History of My People," in Cherríe Moraga and Gloria Anzaldúa, eds., *This Bridge Called My Back* (1983)

Indians think it is important to remember, while Americans believe it is important to forget.

PAULA GUNN ALLEN, *The Sacred Hoop* (1986)

They liked to romanticize the earlier days when they believed the Indians lived in a simple way and wore more colorful clothing than the complicated Indians who lived alongside them in the modern world. They believed the Indians used to have power. In the older, better times, that is, before the people had lost their land and their sacred places on earth to the very people who wished the Indians were as they had been in the past.

LINDA HOGAN, *Mean Spirit* (1990)

Our tribe unraveled like a coarse rope, frayed at either end as the old and new among us were taken.

LOUISE ERDRICH, *Tracks* (1988)

We are the land. To the best of my understanding, that is the fundamental idea that permeates American Indian life.

PAULA GUNN ALLEN, *The Sacred Hoop* (1986)

There is also the paradox that the dominating culture imbues the Indian past with great meaning and significance; it is valued more because it is seen as part of the past. And it is the romantic past, not the present, that holds meaning and spiritual significance for so many members of the dominating culture. It has seemed so strange to me that the larger culture, with its own absence of spirit and lack of attachment for the land, respects these very things about Indian traditions, without adopting those respected ways themselves.

LINDA HOGAN, "The Sacred Seed of the Medicine Tree," *Northern Lights* (1990)

They seemed to have none of the European's desire to "master" nature, to arrange and re-create. They spent their ingenuity in the other direction; in accommodating themselves to the scene in which they found themselves. . . . It was as if the great country were asleep, and they wished to carry on their lives without awakening it.

WILLA CATHER, *Death Comes for the Archbishop* (1927)

It is impossible to come into contact with Native American spirituality and not be struck with the immensity of the gratitude expressed.

ANNE WILSON SCHAEF, *Meditations for Women Who Do Too Much* (1990)

When I look back on reservation life it seems that I spent a great deal of time attending the funerals of my relatives or friends of my family. . . . Death was so common on the reservation that I did not understand the implications of the high death rate until after I moved away and was surprised to learn that I've seen more dead bodies than my friends will probably ever see in their lifetime.

BARBARA CAMERON, in Cherríe Moraga and Gloria Anzaldúa, eds., *This Bridge Called My Back* (1983)

By the time I was done with the car it looked worse than any typical Indian car that has been driven all its life on reservation roads, which they always say are like government promises—full of holes.

LOUISE ERDRICH, *Love Medicine* (1984)

See also Minorities.

"NATURAL"

Often, when the "natural" is invoked, we are left in the dark as to whether it is meant as an explanation, a recommendation, a claim for determinism, or simply a desperate appeal, as if the "natural" were some sort of metaphysical glue that could hold our claims or values together.

CHRISTINE PIERCE, "Natural Law Language and Women," in Vivian Gornick and Barbara K. Moran, *Woman in Sexist Society* (1971)

The "natural" is not necessarily a "human" value.

SHULAMITH FIRESTONE, *The Dialectic of Sex* (1970)

Many "natural" events—like early death, disease, hardship—are neither desirable nor necessary.

PHYLLIS CHESLER, *Women and Madness* (1972)

See also Human Nature.

NATURE

Nature has been for me, for as long as I can remember, a source of solace, inspiration, adventure, and delight; a home, a teacher, a companion.

LORRAINE ANDERSON, in Lorraine Anderson, ed., *Sisters of the Earth* (1991)

The love of nature is a passion for those in whom it once lodges. It can never be quenched.

It cannot change. It is a furious, burning, physical greed, as well as a state of mystical exaltation. It will have its own.

MARY WEBB, *The House in Dormer Forest* (1920)

All my life through, the new sights of Nature made me rejoice like a child.

MARIE CURIE, *Pierre Curie* (1923)

The natural world is dynamic. From the expanding universe to the hair on a baby's head, nothing is the same from now to the next moment.

HELEN HOOVER, "The Waiting Hills," *The Long-Shadowed Forest* (1963)

The power that makes grass grow, fruit ripen, and guides the bird in flight is in us all.

ANZIA YEZIERSKA, *Red Ribbon on a White Horse* (1950)

Meanings, moods, the whole scale of our inner experience, finds in nature the "correspondences" through which we may know our boundless selves.

KATHLEEN RAINE, *Selected Poems* (1988)

Nature is the common, universal language, understood by all.

KATHLEEN RAINE, *Selected Poems* (1988)

i keep hearing / tree talk / water words / and i keep knowing what they mean.

LUCILLE CLIFTON, "Breaklight," *An Ordinary Woman* (1974)

Those who dwell, as scientists or laymen, among the beauties and mysteries of the earth are never alone or weary of life. . . . Those who contemplate the beauty of the earth find reserves of strength that will endure as long as life lasts.

RACHEL CARSON, *The Sense of Wonder* (1965)

There is nothing in nature that can't be taken as a sign of both mortality and invigoration.

GRETEL EHRLICH, *The Solace of Open Spaces* (1985)

There is no shame when one is foolish with a tree   No bird ever called me crazy   No rock scorns me as a whore   The earth means exactly what it says.

CHRYSTOS, "No Rock Scorns Me as Whore," in Cherríe Moraga and Gloria Anzaldúa, eds., *This Bridge Called My Back* (1983)

Teach the legal rights of trees, the nobility of hills; respect the beauty of singularity, the value of solitude.

JOSEPHINE JOHNSON, in Lorraine Anderson, ed., *Sisters of the Earth* (1991)

That is the charm of woods, anyway. Things live and breathe quietly and out of sight. You can sense it, but you don't know what or even if it isn't the wood itself, more alive than it seems.

L. M. BOSTON, *A Stranger at Green Knowe* (1961)

There are dangers in sentimentalizing nature. Most sentimental ideas imply, at bottom, a deep if unacknowledged disrespect. It is no accident that we Americans, probably the world's champion sentimentalizers about nature, are at one and the same time probably the world's most voracious and disrespectful destroyers of wild and rural countryside.

JANE JACOBS, *The Death and Life of Great American Cities* (1961)

We have for too long accepted a traditional way of looking at nature, at nature's creatures, which has blinded us to their incredible essence, and which has made us incomparably lonely. It is our loneliness as much as our greed which can destroy us.

JOAN MCINTYRE, *Mind in the Waters* (1974)

Nature operates by profusion. Think of the nearly infinite number of seeds that fall to earth, only a fraction of which take root to become trees; of those five thousand or so drones that exist solely to ensure the fertilization of one queen bee; of the millions of sperm competing so fiercely to fertilize one egg.

GABRIELE LUSSER RICO, *Writing the Natural Way* (1973)

Nature is just enough; but men and women must comprehend and accept her suggestions.

ANTOINETTE BROWN BLACKWELL, *The Sexes Throughout Nature* (1875)

I have stopped sleeping inside. A house is too small, too confining. I want the whole world, and the stars too.

SUE HUBBELL, *A Country Year* (1986)

Yesterday I sat in a field of violets for a long time perfectly still, until I really sank into it—into the rhythm of the place, I mean—then when I got up to go home I couldn't walk quickly or evenly because I was still in time with the field.

ANNE MORROW LINDBERGH, *Bring Me a Unicorn* (1971)

Valleys are the sunken places of the earth, cañons are scored out by the glacier plows of God.

MARY AUSTIN, *The Land of Little Rain* (1904)

The land around San Juan Capistrano is the pocket where the Creator keeps all his treasures. Anything will grow there.

FRANCES MARION, *Westward the Dream* (1948)

Now, nature, as I am only too well aware, has her enthusiasts, but on the whole, I am not to be counted among them. To put it rather bluntly, I am not the type who wants to go back to the land—I am the type who wants to go back to the hotel.

FRAN LEBOWITZ, *Social Studies* (1977)

See also Animals, Country, Desert, Earth, Flowers, Gardening, Land, Plants, Trees, Wilderness, Wildlife.

NECESSITY

Necessity is God's veil.

SIMONE WEIL, *Gravity and Grace* (1947)

Necessity does the work of courage.

GEORGE ELIOT, *Romola* (1862)

The contradictions the mind comes up against, these are the only realities, the criterion of the real. There is no contradiction in what is imaginary. Contradiction is the test of necessity.

SIMONE WEIL, *Gravity and Grace* (1947)

See also Need.

NEED

It is inevitable when one has a great need of something one finds it. What you need you attract like a lover.

GERTRUDE STEIN, in Elizabeth Sprigge, *Gertrude Stein: Her Life and Her Work* (1957)

God forgives those who invent what they need.

LILLIAN HELLMAN, *The Little Foxes* (1939)

There wasn't enough for Indigo in the world she'd been born to, so she made up what she needed. What she thought the black people needed.

NTOZAKE SHANGE, *Sassafrass, Cypress & Indigo* (1982)

In my life's chain of events nothing was accidental. Everything happened according to an inner need.

HANNAH SENESH (1943), *Hannah Senesh: Her Life and Diary* (1966)

See also Necessity.

THE NETHERLANDS
See Holland.

NEWNESS

We tend to think things are new because we've just discovered them.

MADELEINE L'ENGLE, *A Wind in the Door* (1973)

New things are always ugly.

WILLA CATHER, in Phyllis C. Robinson, *Willa* (1983)

In trying to make something new, half the undertaking lies in discovering whether it can be done. Once it has been established that it can, duplication is inevitable.

HELEN GAHAGAN DOUGLAS, *A Full Life* (1982)

The road was new to me, as roads always are, going back.

SARAH ORNE JEWETT, *The Country of the Pointed Firs* (1896)

See also Discovery, Unknown.

NEWSPAPERS
See Journalism.

NEW YORK

No place has delicatessen like New York.

JUDY BLUME, *Are You There, God? It's Me, Margaret* (1970)

New York is like a disco, but without the music.

ELAINE STRITCH, in *Observer* (1980)

The world is grand, awfully big and astonishingly beautiful, frequently thrilling. But I love New York.

DOROTHY KILGALLEN, *Girl Around the World* (1936)

I miss the animal buoyancy of New York, the animal vitality. I did not mind that it had no meaning and no depth.

ANAÏS NIN, *The Diary of Anaïs Nin*, vol. 2 (1934–1939)

Situated on an island, which I think it will one day cover, it rises like Venice, from the sea, and like the fairest of cities in the days of her glory, receives into its lap tribute of all the riches of the earth.

FRANCES TROLLOPE, *Domestic Manners of the Americans* (1832)

There's something hypocritical about a city that keeps half of its population underground half of the time; you can start believing that there's much more space than there really is—to live, to work.

GLORIA NAYLOR, *Mama Day* (1988)

It is often said that New York is a city for only the very rich and the very poor. It is less often said that New York is also, at least for those of us who came there from somewhere else, a city for only the very young.

JOAN DIDION, *Slouching Towards Bethlehem* (1968)

A car is useless in New York, essential everywhere else. The same with good manners.

MIGNON MCLAUGHLIN, *The Second Neurotic's Notebook* (1966)

NIGHT

Now the day is over, / Night is drawing nigh. / Shadows of the evening / Steal across the sky.

Sabine Baring-Gould, "Now the Day Is Over," in Tasha Tudor, *First Prayers* (1952)

Night is the first skin around me.

Roberta Hill Whiteman, "The Recognition," *Star Quilt* (1984)

The night will slip away / Like sorrow or a tune.

Eleanor Farjeon, "The Night Will Never Stay," *Gypsy and Ginger* (1920)

Well, this is the end of a perfect day, / Near the end of a journey, too.

Carrie Jacobs Bond, *A Perfect Day* (1910)

The dead of midnight is the noon of thought.

Anna Letitia Barbauld, "A Summer's Evening Meditation," *Poems* (1792)

For the night was not impartial. No, the night loved some more than others, served some more than others.

Eudora Welty, "Moon Lake," *The Golden Apples* (1949)

In the evening your vision widens / looks out beyond midnight— / . . . / We are in a sickroom. / But the night belongs to the angels.

Nelly Sachs, "In the Evening Your Vision Widens," *O the Chimneys* (1967)

It was the sort of night when you think you could lie in the snow until morning and never get cold.

Faith Sullivan, *The Cape Ann* (1988)

It was one of those nights when the air is blood temperature and it's impossible to tell where you leave off and it begins.

Elaine Dundy, *The Dud Avocado* (1958)

See also Darkness, Sleep, Sunset.

NORMALCY

As we do at such times, I turned on my automatic pilot and went through the motions of normalcy on the outside, so that I could concen-

trate all my powers on surviving the near-mortal wound inside.

Sonia Johnson, *From Housewife to Heretic* (1981)

She always says she dislikes the abnormal. . . . She says the normal is so much more simply complicated and interesting.

Gertrude Stein, *The Autobiography of Alice B. Toklas* (1933)

Normal day, let me be aware of the treasure you are. Let me learn from you, love you, bless you before you depart. Let me not pass you by in quest of some rare and perfect tomorrow. Let me hold you while I may, for it may not always be so. One day I shall dig my nails into the earth, or bury my face in the pillow, or stretch myself taut, or raise my hands to the sky and want, more than all the world, your return.

Mary Jean Irion, *Yes, World* (1970)

See also Conventionality, Ordinariness.

NOSTALGIA

It is better to remember our love as it was in the springtime.

Bess Streeter Aldrich, *Spring Came on Forever* (1935)

A mark was on him from the day's delight, so that all his life, when April was a thin green and the flavor of rain was on his tongue, an old wound would throb and a nostalgia would fill him for something he could not quite remember.

Marjorie Kinnan Rawlings, *The Yearling* (1938)

See also Memory, Remembrance, Sentimentality.

NOVELS

The novel is an art form and when you use it for anything other than art, you pervert it.

Flannery O'Connor, in Sally Fitzgerald, ed., *The Habit of Being* (1979)

Surely the novel should be a form of art—but art was not enough. It must contain not only the perfection of art, but the imperfection of nature.

Ellen Glasgow, *The Woman Within* (1954)

The story is a piece of work. The novel is a way of life.

TONI CADE BAMBARA, in Janet Sternburg, ed., *The Writer on Her Work,* vol. 1 (1980)

A great novel is a kind of conversion experience. We come away from it changed.

KATHERINE PATERSON, *Gates of Excellence* (1981)

For me, the novel is experience illumined by imagination.

ELLEN GLASGOW, 1933 preface, *Barren Ground* (1925)

Each sentence must have, at its heart, a little spark of fire, and this, whatever the risk, the novelist must pluck with his own hands from the blaze.

VIRGINIA WOOLF, *The Common Reader* (1925)

I don't think you should write something as long as a novel around anything that is not of the gravest concern to you and everybody else and for me this is always the conflict between an attraction for the Holy and the disbelief in it that we breathe in with the air of the times.

FLANNERY O'CONNOR, in Sally Fitzgerald, ed., *The Habit of Being* (1979)

In any work that is truly creative, I believe, the writer cannot be omniscient in advance about the effects that he proposes to produce. The suspense of a novel is not only in the reader, but in the novelist, who is intensely curious about what will happen to the hero.

MARY McCARTHY, *On the Contrary* (1961)

A novelist's chief desire is to be as unconscious as possible. He has to induce in himself a state of perpetual lethargy. He wants life to proceed with the utmost quiet and regularity. He wants to see the same faces, to read the same books, to do the same things day after day, month after month, while he is writing, so that nothing may break the illusion in which he is living—so that nothing may disturb or disquiet the mysterious nosings about, feelings around, darts, dashes, and sudden discoveries of that very shy and illusive spirit, the imagination.

VIRGINIA WOOLF, "Professions for Women," *The Death of the Moth* (1942)

The novelist, afraid his ideas may be foolish, slyly puts them in the mouth of some other fool, and reserves the right to disavow them.

DIANE JOHNSON, in *New York Times Book Review* (1979)

One should be able to return to the first sentence of a novel and find the resonances of the entire work.

GLORIA NAYLOR, in *New York Times* (1985)

See also Fiction, Fictional Characters, Literature, Writing.

NUCLEAR WEAPONS

It is ironical that in an age when we have prided ourselves on our progress in the intelligent care and teaching of children we have at the same time put them at the mercy of new and most terrible weapons of destruction.

PEARL BUCK, *What America Means to Me* (1943)

See also Militarism, War.

NUDISTS

Nudists are fond of saying that when you come right down to it everyone is alike, and, again, that when you come right down to it everyone is different.

DIANE ARBUS, "Notes on the Nudist Camp," *Magazine Work* (1984)

NUMBERS

See Quantity.

NURSERY RHYMES

Twinkle, twinkle, little star; / How I wonder what you are! / Up above the world so high, / Like a diamond in the sky.

JANE TAYLOR, "Twinkle, Twinkle, Little Star" (1806)

"Will you walk into my parlor?" said the Spider to the Fly; / "'Tis the prettiest little parlor that ever you did spy."

MARY HOWITT, "The Spider and the Fly," *Ballads and Other Poems* (1847)

Mary had a little lamb, / Its fleece was white as snow; / And everywhere that Mary went / The lamb was sure to go.

SARA JOSEPHA HALE, "Mary's Little Lamb," *Poems for Our Children* (1830)

NURSES

Nursing was regarded as simply an extension of the unpaid services performed by the housewife—a characteristic attitude that haunts the profession to this day.

GERDA LERNER, "The Lady and the Mill Girl: Changes in the Status of Women in the Age of Jackson," *Midcontinent American Studies Journal* (1969)

No *man,* not even a doctor, ever gives any other definition of what a nurse should be than this—

"devoted and obedient." This definition would do just as well for a porter. It might even do for a horse. It would not do for a policeman.

FLORENCE NIGHTINGALE, *Notes on Nursing* (1860)

A good nurse is of more importance than a physician.

HANNAH FARNHAM LEE, *The Log Cabin* (1844)

Nurses—nurses, you'm all the same. Full of cheerfulness over other people's troubles.

AGATHA CHRISTIE, *Sad Cypress* (1939)

See also Hospital.

O

OBJECTIVITY

I make no pretensions to "objectivity," a fraudulent concept in an era of industrialized and politicized science in which intellectual mercenaries too often serve power and greed, the ambitions of competing nation-states, or the requirements of commerce.

HAZEL HENDERSON, *The Politics of the Solar Age* (1981)

See also Detachment.

OBVIOUS

The hardest thing to explain is the glaringly evident which everybody had decided not to see.

AYN RAND, *The Fountainhead* (1943)

OFFENSIVENESS

If a person begins by telling you, "Do not be offended at what I am going to say," prepare yourself for something that she knows will certainly offend you.

ELIZA LESLIE, *Miss Leslie's Behavior Book: A Guide and Manual for Ladies* (1859)

Unhappily the habit of being offensive "without meaning it" leads usually to a way of making amends which the injured person cannot but regard as being amiable without meaning it.

GEORGE ELIOT, *Impressions of Theophrastus Such* (1879)

You can say the nastiest things about yourself without offending anyone.

PHYLLIS DILLER, in Barbara McDowell and Hana Umlauf, *Woman's Almanac* (1977)

See also Rudeness.

OPPORTUNITIES

Nothing is so often irretrievably missed as a daily opportunity.

MARIE VON EBNER-ESCHENBACH, *Aphorisms* (1905)

One can present people with opportunities. One cannot make them equal to them.

ROSAMOND LEHMANN, *The Ballad and the Source* (1945)

See also Challenges.

OPPOSITION

To oppose something is to maintain it.

URSULA K. LE GUIN, *The Left Hand of Darkness* (1969)

Opposition may become sweet to a man when he has christened it persecution.

GEORGE ELIOT, "Janet's Repentance," *Scenes of Clerical Life* (1857)

Elinor agreed with it all, for she did not think he deserved the compliment of rational opposition.

JANE AUSTEN, *Sense and Sensibility* (1811)

I always cheer up immensely if an attack is particularly wounding because I think, well, if they attack one personally, it means they have not a single political argument left.

MARGARET THATCHER, *London Daily Telegraph* (1986)

I have spent many years of my life in opposition, and I rather like the role.

ELEANOR ROOSEVELT, letter to Bernard Baruch (1952)

See also Conflict, Enemies.

OPPRESSION

All oppression creates a state of war.

SIMONE DE BEAUVOIR, *The Second Sex* (1949)

Where a system of oppression has become institutionalized it is unnecessary for individuals to be oppressive.

FLORYNCE KENNEDY, "Institutionalized Oppression vs. the Female," in Robin Morgan, *Sisterhood Is Powerful* (1970)

We first crush people to the earth, and then claim the right of trampling on them forever, because they are prostrate.

LYDIA MARIA CHILD, *An Appeal on Behalf of That Class of Americans Called Africans* (1833)

In order to perpetuate itself, every oppression must corrupt or distort those various sources of power within the culture of the oppressed that can provide energy for change.

AUDRE LORDE, *Uses of the Erotic* (1978)

If you're going to hold someone down you're going to have to hold onto the other end of the chain. You are confined by your own system of repression.

TONI MORRISON, in Brian Lanker, *I Dream a World* (1989)

It is precisely because certain groups have no representation in a number of recognized political structures that their position tends to be so stable, their oppression so continuous.

KATE MILLETT, *Sexual Politics* (1969)

The history of an oppressed people is hidden in the lies and the agreed-upon myth of its conquerors.

MERIDEL LE SUEUR, *Crusaders* (1955)

Now I say that with cruelty and oppression it is everybody's business to interfere when they see it.

ANNA SEWELL, *Black Beauty* (1877)

The revolt against any oppression usually goes to an opposite extreme for a time.

TENNESSEE CLAFLIN, in *Woodhull and Claflin's Weekly* (1871)

In order to create an alternative an oppressed group must at once shatter the self-reflecting world which encircles it and, at the same time, project its own image onto history.

SHEILA ROWBOTHAM, *Woman's Consciousness, Man's World* (1973)

Oppressed people are frequently very oppressive when first liberated. And why wouldn't they be? They know best two positions. Somebody's foot on their neck or their foot on somebody's neck.

FLORYNCE KENNEDY, "Institutionalized Oppression vs. the Female," in Robin Morgan, *Sisterhood Is Powerful* (1970)

The oppressed without hope are mysteriously quiet. When the conception of change is beyond the limits of the possible, there are no words to articulate discontent so it is sometimes held not to exist. This mistaken belief arises because we can only grasp silence in the moment in which it is breaking.

SHEILA ROWBOTHAM, *Woman's Consciousness, Man's World* (1973)

Obviously the most oppressed of any oppressed group will be its women.

LORRAINE HANSBERRY, interview (1959)

In this country, lesbianism is a poverty—as is being brown, as is being a woman, as is being just plain poor. The danger lies in ranking the oppressions.

CHERRÍE MORAGA, "La Güera," in Cherríe Moraga and Gloria Anzaldúa, eds., *This Bridge Called My Back* (1983)

It is critical for both more privileged and relatively more oppressed groups to listen to each other's pain without playing the who-is-more-oppressed game.

CAROL PEARSON, *The Hero Within* (1986)

All of us would do well to stop fighting each other for our space at the bottom, because there ain't no more room.

CHERYL CLARKE, "Lesbianism: An Act of Resistance," in Cherríe Moraga and Gloria Anzaldúa, eds., *This Bridge Called My Back* (1983)

These my two hands / quick to slap my face / before others could slap it.

GLORIA ANZALDÚA, "The Woman Who Lived Forever," in Cherríe Moraga and Gloria Anzaldúa, eds., *This Bridge Called My Back* (1983)

See also Discrimination, Domination, Minorities, Revolution, Tyranny.

OPTIMISM

An optimist is the human personification of spring.

SUSAN J. BISSONETTE, in *Reader's Digest* (1979)

Some folks are natural born kickers. They can always find a way to turn disaster into butter.

KATHERINE PATERSON, *Lyddie* (1991)

The optimism of a healthy mind is indefatigable.

MARGERY ALLINGHAM, *Death of a Ghost* (1934)

Rose-colored spectacles the hopeful wear.

SOR JUANA INÉS DE LA CRUZ (c. 1690), in Irene Nicholson, *A Guide to Mexican Poetry* (1968)

I do not believe that true optimism can come about except through tragedy.

MADELEINE L'ENGLE, *Two-Part Invention* (1988)

Am I like the optimist who, while falling ten stories from a building, says at each story, "I'm all right so far"?

GRETEL EHRLICH, *Heart Mountain* (1988)

See also Cheerfulness, Gladness, Hope.

ORDER

Order is the shape upon which beauty depends.

PEARL BUCK, *To My Daughters, With Love* (1967)

A place for everything and everything in its place.

ISABELLA MARY BEETON, *The Book of Household Management* (1861)

A life lived in chaos is an impossibility for the artist. No matter how unstructured may seem the painter's garret in Paris or the poet's pad in Greenwich Village, the artist must have some kind of order or he will produce a very small

body of work. To create a *work* of art, great or small, is *work,* hard work, and work requires discipline and order.

MADELEINE L'ENGLE, *Walking on Water: Reflections on Faith and Art* (1980)

Tidied all my papers. Tore up and ruthlessly destroyed much. This is always a great satisfaction.

KATHERINE MANSFIELD (1922), *Journal of Katherine Mansfield* (1927)

A schedule defends from chaos and whim. It is a net for catching days. It is a scaffolding on which a worker can stand and labor with both hands at sections of time. A schedule is a mock-up of reason and order—willed, faked, and so brought into being.

ANNIE DILLARD, *The Writing Life* (1989)

And what would happen to my illusion that I am a force for order in the home if I wasn't married to the only man north of the Tiber who is even untidier than I am?

KATHARINE WHITEHORN, *Sunday Best* (1976)

See also Chaos, Shape.

ORDINARINESS

Ordinary is a word that has no meaning.

ROBIN MORGAN, "The Pedestrian Woman," *Lady of the Beasts* (1975)

See also Conventionality, Normalcy.

ORPHANS

Psychic orphanhood is not new. . . . For hundreds of years, the word "orphan" had been vividly associated with massive asylums and the pale, undersized inmates in institutional garb incarcerated within their walls. It was necessary for these associations to fade, as fade they did with the sharp decline in the number of orphans, before the word could be used as a simile: I felt *like* an orphan.

EILEEN SIMPSON, *Orphans: Real and Imaginary* (1990)

If you cannot trust your father and mother to love you and accept you and protect you, then you are an orphan, although your parents are upstairs asleep in their bed.

ELIZABETH FEUER, *Paper Doll* (1990)

OUTRAGE

Outrage, combining as it does shock, anger, reproach, and helplessness, is perhaps the most unmanageable, the most demoralizing of all the emotions.

MARGERY ALLINGHAM, *Death of a Ghost* (1934)

See also Anger.

OUTSIDERS

Be nobody's darling; / Be an outcast. / Qualified to live / Among your dead.

ALICE WALKER, "Be Nobody's Darling," *Revolutionary Petunias and Other Poems* (1971)

He was an outsider who lived by his ability to manipulate the inside.

JOAN DIDION, *A Book of Common Prayer* (1977)

When you are a member of an out-group, and you challenge others with whom you share this outsider position to examine some aspect of their lives that distorts differences between you, then there can be a great deal of pain.

AUDRE LORDE, in Claudia Tate, ed., *Black Women Writers at Work* (1983)

The world was one of great contrasts, she thought, and if the richest part of it was to be fenced off so that people like herself could only look at it with no expectation of ever being able to get inside it, then it would be better to have been born blind so you couldn't see it, born deaf so you couldn't hear it, born with no sense of touch so you couldn't feel it. Better still, born with no brain so that you would be completely unaware of anything, so that you would never know there were places that were filled with sunlight and good food and where children were safe.

ANN PETRY, *The Street* (1946)

Do you know what it's like to feel *wrong* twenty-four hours a day? Do you know what it's like to be disapproved of, not only for what you do and say and think but for what you *are*?

JOYCE REBETA-BURDITT, *The Cracker Factory* (1977)

You can tell by looking at most people that the world remains a stone to them and a closed door.

MERIDEL LE SUEUR, *Salute to Spring* (1940)

See also Alienation, Minorities, Strangers.

OYSTERS

An oyster leads a dreadful but exciting life. Indeed, his chance to live at all is slim, and if he should survive the arrows of his own outrageous fortune and in the two weeks of his carefree youth find a clean smooth place to fix on, the years afterwards are full of stress, passion, and danger.

M. F. K. FISHER, *Consider the Oyster* (1941)

If you don't love life you can't enjoy an oyster; there is a shock of freshness to it and intimations of the ages of man, some piercing intuition of the sea and all its weeds and breezes. [They] shiver you for a split second.

ELEANOR CLARK, *The Oysters of Locmariaquer* (1964)

Almost any normal oyster never knows from one year to the next whether he is he or she, and may start at any moment, after the first year, to lay eggs where before he spent his sexual energies in being exceptionally masculine.

M. F. K. FISHER, *Consider the Oyster* (1941)

On the other hand, a flaccid, moping, debauched mollusk, tired from too much love and loose-nerved from general world conditions, can be a shameful thing served raw upon the shell.

M. F. K. FISHER, *Consider the Oyster* (1941)

See also Food.

P

PACIFISM

Pacifism simply is not a matter of calm looking on; it is work, hard work.

KÄTHE KOLLWITZ, letter (1944), in Hans Kollwitz, ed., *The Diaries and Letters of Käthe Kollwitz* (1955)

The quietly pacifist peaceful / always die / to make room for men / who shout.

ALICE WALKER, "The QPP," *Revolutionary Petunias and Other Poems* (1971)

See also Peace.

PAIN

My soul is a broken field / plowed by pain.

SARA TEASDALE, "The Broken Field," *Collected Poems* (1937)

Pain—has an Element of Blank— / It cannot recollect / When it began—or if there were / A time when it was not.

EMILY DICKINSON (1862), *Poems, First Series* (1890)

I could not recall how much time had passed for somehow or other pain is timeless, absolute. It has removed itself from space. It always has been and always will be for it exists independent of relations. I feel it as myself, and when it ceases I will cease.

EVELYN SCOTT, *Escapade* (1923)

There was no reality to pain when it left one, though while it held one fast all other realities faded.

RACHEL FIELD, *All This and Heaven Too* (1939)

In the country of pain we are each alone.

MAY SARTON, "The Country of Pain," *Halfway to Silence* (1980)

Once you get beyond the crust of the first pang it is all the same and you can easily bear it. It is just the transition from painlessness to pain that is so terrible.

ANNE MORROW LINDBERGH, *Bring Me a Unicorn* (1971)

There are hurts so deep that one cannot reach them or heal them with words.

KATE SEREDY, *The Singing Tree* (1939)

One does not die from pain unless one chooses to.

WAKAKO YAMAUCHI, "Makapuu Bay," in Asian Women United of California, eds., *Making Waves: An Anthology of Writings By and About Asian American Women* (1989)

Even pain / Pricks to livelier living.

AMY LOWELL, "Happiness," *Sword Blades and Poppy Seeds* (1914)

Sometimes pain was a crutch to hold on to when the only alternative was nothing at all.

SYLVIE SOMMERFIELD, *Bittersweet* (1991)

It's odd that you can get so anesthetized by your own pain or your own problem that you don't quite fully share the hell of someone close to you.

LADY BIRD JOHNSON, *A White House Diary* (1970)

There is much pain that is quite noiseless; and vibrations that make human agonies are often a mere whisper in the roar of hurrying existence.

GEORGE ELIOT, *Felix Holt, the Radical* (1866)

Both Grace and I "took on" when in pain. We were Irish. We didn't wait for the wake to wail. We wailed while we were still hurting, not leaving all the work for others after we were past helping.

JESSAMYN WEST, *The Woman Said Yes: Encounters with Life and Death* (1976)

See also Sorrow, Suffering.

PAINTING

I paint from the top down. First the sky, then the mountains, then the hills, then the houses, then the cattle, and then the people.

GRANDMA MOSES, in Otto Kallir, ed., *Grandma Moses: My Life's History* (1947)

Certainly we have bad paintings. We have only the "greatest" bad paintings.

FRANÇOISE CACHIN, Director of the Musée d'Orsay in Paris, in *Time* (1986)

A painting is like a man. If you can live without it, then there isn't much point in having it.

LILA ACHESON WALLACE, in *Time* (1981)

See also Art, Artists.

PARADOX

I learned to make my mind large, as the universe is large, so that there is room for paradoxes.

MAXINE HONG KINGSTON, *The Woman Warrior* (1976)

The world of science lives fairly comfortably with paradox. We know that light is a wave, and also that light is a particle. The discoveries made in the infinitely small world of particle physics indicate randomness and chance, and I do not find it any more difficult to live with the paradox of a universe of randomness and chance and a universe of pattern and purpose than I do with light as a wave and light as a particle. Living with contradiction is nothing new to the human being.

MADELEINE L'ENGLE, *Two-Part Invention* (1988)

I have learned since that sometimes the things we want most are impossible for us. You may long to come home, yet wander forever.

NADINE GORDIMER, *The Lying Days* (1953)

And she saw now that the strong impulses which had once wrecked her happiness were the forces that had enabled her to rebuild her life out of the ruins.

ELLEN GLASGOW, *Barren Ground* (1925)

It was to her faults that she turned to save herself now.

MADELEINE L'ENGLE, *A Wrinkle in Time* (1962)

To light a candle is to cast a shadow.

URSULA K. LE GUIN, *A Wizard of Earthsea* (1968)

PARENTING

An atmosphere of trust, love, and humor can nourish extraordinary human capacity. One key is authenticity: parents acting as people, not as roles.

MARILYN FERGUSON, *The Aquarian Conspiracy* (1980)

There are so many disciplines in being a parent besides the obvious ones like getting up in the night and putting up with the noise during the day. And almost the hardest of all is learning to be a well of affection and not a fountain, to show them we love them, not when *we* feel like it, but when they do.

NAN FAIRBROTHER, *An English Year* (1954)

Bringing up children is not a real occupation, because children come up just the same, brought or not.

GERMAINE GREER, *The Female Eunuch* (1971)

The best way to raise a child is to LAY OFF.

SHULAMITH FIRESTONE, *The Dialectic of Sex* (1970)

See also Children, Discipline, Generations, Parents.

PARENTS

Are anybody's parents typical?

MADELEINE L'ENGLE, *Two-Part Invention* (1988)

Parenthood: That state of being better chaperoned than you were before marriage.

MARCELENE COX, in *Ladies' Home Journal* (1944)

Parents learn a lot from their children about coping with life.

MURIEL SPARK, *The Comforters* (1957)

If you have never been hated by your child, you have never been a parent.

BETTE DAVIS, *The Lonely Life* (1962)

When she had been a child, children were expected to defer to their parents in everything, to wait on them and help around the house and so on; but when she became a parent and was ready to enjoy her turn at being deferred to, the winds of fashion in child rearing had changed, and parents were expected to defer to their children in hopes of not squelching their imagination and creativity. She had missed out all the way around.

LISA ALTHER, *Kinflicks* (1975)

Not being one to calculate or look ahead, I had not stopped to think, when boys started paying attention to me, that the cup might be dashed from my lips, though experience should have taught me that dashing cups from lips was the way Victorian parents got most of their exercise.

MARGARET HALSEY, *No Laughing Matter* (1977)

Over the years I have learned that motherhood is much like an austere religious order, the joining of which obligates one to relinquish all claims to personal possessions.

NANCY STAHL, *If It's Raining This Must Be the Weekend* (1979)

Being a housewife and a mother is the biggest job in the world, but if it doesn't interest you, don't do it. It didn't interest me, so I didn't do it. Anyway, I would have made a terrible parent. The first time my child didn't do what I wanted, I'd kill him.

KATHARINE HEPBURN, in Liz Smith, *The Mother Book* (1978)

Most of us become parents long before we have stopped being children.

MIGNON MCLAUGHLIN, *The Second Neurotic's Notebook* (1966)

We all of us wanted babies—but did we want children?

EDA J. LESHAN, *How to Survive Parenthood* (1965)

They [my parents] shared decisions and the making of all policy, both in their business and in the family. . . . They spoke all through my childhood with one unfragmentable and unappealable voice.

AUDRE LORDE, *Zami: A New Spelling of My Name* (1983)

Parents have become so convinced that educators know what is best for children that they forget that they themselves are really the experts.

MARIAN WRIGHT EDELMAN, in Margie Casady, "Society's Pushed-Out Children," *Psychology Today* (1975)

Before we can leave our parents, they stuff our heads like the suitcases which they jam-pack with homemade underwear.

MAXINE HONG KINGSTON, *The Woman Warrior* (1976)

One reason you are stricken when your parents die is that the audience you've been aiming at all your life—shocking it, pleasing it—has suddenly left the theater.

KATHARINE WHITEHORN, in *Observer* (1983)

When parents die, all of the partings of the past are reevoked with the realization that this time they will not return.

MARY CATHERINE BATESON, *With a Daughter's Eye* (1984)

We are never done with thinking about our parents, I suppose, and come to know them better long after they are dead than we ever did when they were alive.

MAY SARTON, *At Seventy: A Journal* (1982)

The debt of gratitude we owe our mother and father goes forward, not backward. What we owe our parents is the bill presented to us by our children.

NANCY FRIDAY, *My Mother/My Self* (1977)

If you harbor ill-will toward your parents, I think you have disowned part of yourself.

ADELAIDE BRY, *Friendship* (1979)

"You almost died," a nurse told her. But that was nonsense. Of course she wouldn't have died; she had children. When you have children, you're obligated to live.

ANNE TYLER, *Dinner at the Homesick Restaurant* (1982)

I discovered when I had a child of my own that I had become a biased observer of small children. Instead of looking at them with affectionate but nonpartisan eyes, I saw each of them as older or younger, bigger or smaller, more or less graceful, intelligent, or skilled than my own child.

MARGARET MEAD, *Blackberry Winter* (1972)

See also Children, Family, Father, Generations, Mother, Parenting.

PARIS

People come to Paris, to the capital, to give their lives a sense of belonging, of an almost mythical participation in society.

MARGUERITE DURAS, *Practicalities* (1987)

The perfect classroom is Paris.

LETITIA BALDRIGE, *Of Diamonds and Diplomats* (1968)

The Left Bank called me and even now it does not cease to call me and to keep me. I cannot imagine that I could ever leave it, any more than an organ can leave the place that is assigned to it in the body.

ADRIENNE MONNIER, in Richard McDougall, tr., *The Very Rich Hours of Adrienne Monnier* (1976)

Trade is art, and art's philosophy, / In Paris.

ELIZABETH BARRETT BROWNING, *Aurora Leigh* (1856)

Food is still what Parisians buy if they can. It is a nervous means of getting satisfaction, a holdover from the lean years of the Occupation.

JANET FLANNER ("Genêt"), *Paris Journal 1944–1965* (1965)

If I were to choose one single thing that would restore Paris to the senses, it would be that strangely sweet, unhealthy smell of the Métro, so very unlike the dank cold or the stuffy heat of subways in New York.

MAY SARTON, *I Knew a Phoenix* (1959)

See also France.

PARTIES

One cannot have too large a party.

JANE AUSTEN, *Emma* (1816)

A balanced guest list of mixed elements is to a successful party what the seasoning is to a culinary triumph.

LETITIA BALDRIGE, *Of Diamonds and Diplomats* (1968)

For some unexplained reason, it's always the other end of the table that's wild and raucous, with screaming laughter and a fella who plays "Holiday for Strings" on water glasses.

ERMA BOMBECK, *I Lost Everything in the Post-Natal Depression* (1970)

I misremember who first was cruel enough to nurture the cocktail party into life. But perhaps it would be not too much to say, in fact it would be not enough to say, that it was not worth the trouble.

DOROTHY PARKER, in *Esquire* (1964)

Cocktail parties . . . are usually not parties at all but mass ceremonials designed to clear up at one great stroke a wealth of obligations.

PHYLLIS McGINLEY, *Sixpence in Her Shoe* (1964)

The fact is, the cocktail party has much in its favor. Going to one is a good way of indicating that you're still alive and about, if such is the case, and that you're glad other people are, without having to spend an entire evening proving it.

PEG BRACKEN, *I Try to Behave Myself* (1963)

See also Gaiety, Guests.

PARTING

Parting is all we know of heaven, / And all we need of hell.

EMILY DICKINSON, *Poems, Third Series* (1896)

In every parting there is an image of death.

GEORGE ELIOT, "The Sad Fortunes of the Rev. Amos Barton," *Scenes of Clerical Life* (1857)

Every time one leaves anywhere, something precious, which ought not to be killed, is left to die.

KATHERINE MANSFIELD (1922), *Journal of Katherine Mansfield* (1927)

If you must leave a place that you have lived in and loved and where all your yesterdays are buried deep—leave it any way except a slow way, leave it the fastest way you can. Never turn back and never believe that an hour you remember is a better hour because it is dead.

BERYL MARKHAM, *West With the Night* (1942)

Time manages the most painful partings for us. One has only to set the date, buy the ticket, and let the earth, sun, and moon make their passages through the sky, until inexorable time carries us with it to the moment of parting.

JILL KER CONWAY, *The Road from Coorain* (1989)

It is never any good dwelling on goodbyes. It is not the being together that it prolongs, it is the parting.

ELIZABETH BIBESCO, *The Fir and the Palm* (1924)

It was typical of him that he lacked the taste to make a final exit. He spent too long at his farewells, chatting in the doorway, letting in the cold.

ANNE TYLER, *Dinner at the Homesick Restaurant* (1982)

You have delighted us long enough.

JANE AUSTEN, *Pride and Prejudice* (1813)

See also Desertion, Farewells.

PASSION

Passion is our ground, our island—do others exist?

EUDORA WELTY, "Circe," *The Bride of the Innisfallen* (1955)

Passion is more important than justice.

CARSON MCCULLERS, *Clock Without Hands* (1961)

The capacity for passion is both cruel and divine.

GEORGE SAND (1834), *Intimate Journal* (1929)

There's plenty of fire in the coldest flint!

RACHEL FIELD, *All This and Heaven Too* (1939)

The worst sin—perhaps the only sin—passion can commit, is to be joyless.

DOROTHY L. SAYERS, *Gaudy Night* (1935)

Jump out the window if you are the object of passion. Flee it if you feel it. . . . Passion goes, boredom remains.

COCO CHANEL, in *McCall's* (1965)

It is the soul's duty to be loyal to its own desires. It must abandon itself to its master passion.

REBECCA WEST, in Alfred Leslie Rowse, *Glimpses of the Great* (1985)

A continual atmosphere of hectic passion is very trying if you haven't got any of your own.

DOROTHY L. SAYERS, *The Unpleasantness at the Bellona Club* (1928)

See also Desire, Intensity, Longing, Love.

PAST

I cannot sing the old songs, / Or dream those dreams again.

CHARLOTTE ALINGTON BARNARD, "I Cannot Sing the Old Songs" (1860)

A long past vividly remembered is like a heavy garment that clings to your limbs when you would run.

MARY ANTIN, *The Promised Land* (1912)

The farther behind I leave the past, the closer I am to forging my own character.

ISABELLE EBERHARDT (1900), *The Passionate Nomad* (1988)

I am never free of the past. I have made it crystal clear that I believe the past is part of the present which becomes part of the future.

LEE KRASNER, in Eleanor Munro, *Originals: American Women Artists* (1979)

All normal human beings are interested in their past. Only when the interest becomes an obsession, overshadowing present and future conduct, is it a danger. In much the same way healthy nations are interested in their history, but a morbid preoccupation with past glories is a sign that something is wrong with the constitution of the State.

C. V. WEDGWOOD, *Velvet Studies* (1946)

We are tomorrow's past.

MARY WEBB, *Precious Bane* (1924)

The destruction of the past is perhaps the greatest of all crimes.

SIMONE WEIL, *The Need for Roots* (1949)

It is not that I belong to the past, but that the past belongs to me.

Mary Antin, *The Promised Land* (1912)

Sometimes a person has to go back, really back—to have a sense, an understanding of all that's gone to make them—before they can go forward.

Paule Marshall, *The Chosen Place, The Timeless People* (1969)

There are moments in history when brooding tragedy and its dark shadows can be lightened by recalling great moments of the past.

Indira Gandhi, letter (1971)

But there is, I have learned, no permanent escape from the past. It may be an unrecognized law of our nature that we should be drawn back, inevitably, to the place where we have suffered most.

Ellen Glasgow, *The Woman Within* (1954)

Each had his past shut in him like the leaves of a book known to him by heart; and his friends could only read the title.

Virginia Woolf, *Jacob's Room* (1922)

We cannot live in the past, nor can we re-create it. Yet as we unravel the past, the future also unfolds before us, as though they are mirrors without which neither can be seen or happen.

Judy Grahn, *Another Mother Tongue: Gay Words, Gay Worlds* (1984)

While to live in the past and think of what was good and beautiful about it amounts to a sort of *seasoning* of the present, the perennial wait for tomorrow is bound to result in chronic discontent that poisons one's entire outlook.

Isabelle Eberhardt (1900), *The Passionate Nomad* (1988)

We are pushed forward by the social forces, reluctant and stumbling, our faces over our shoulders, clutching at every relic of the past as we are forced along; still adoring whatever is behind us. We insist upon worshipping "the God of our fathers." Why not the God of our children? Does eternity only stretch one way?

Charlotte Perkins Gilman, *The Home: Its Work and Influence* (1904)

You cannot see the past that did not happen any more than you can foresee the future.

Madeleine L'Engle, *The Arm of the Starfish* (1965)

The only thing I regret about my past life is the length of it. If I had my past life over again I'd make all the same mistakes—only sooner.

Tallulah Bankhead, in *The Times* (1981)

See also Future, History, Nostalgia, Present, Remembrance, Time.

PATHOS

The pathos of life is worse than the tragedy.

Ellen Glasgow, *Barren Ground* (1925)

It's not the tragedies that kill us, it's the messes.

Dorothy Parker, in Malcolm Cowley, ed., *Writers at Work* (1958)

See also Pity, Tragedy.

PATIENCE

Patience is bitter, but its fruit is sweet.

Lida Clarkson, "Brush Studies," in *Ladies' Home Journal* (1884)

What is so certain of victory as patience?

Selma Lagerlöf, *The Story of Gösta Berling* (1891)

I am extraordinarily patient, provided I get my own way in the end.

Margaret Thatcher, in *Observer* (1989)

He was resigned and on the whole patient, like a man with a very old illness.

Margery Allingham, *The Mind Readers* (1965)

Patience! Patience! Patience is the invention of dullards and sluggards. In a well-regulated world there should be no need of such a thing as patience.

Grace King, *Balcony Stories* (1893)

See also Endurance, Perseverance, Virtue.

PATRIOTISM

American patriotism is generally something that amuses Europeans, I suppose because children look idiotic saluting the flag and because the constitution contains so many cracks through which the lawyers may creep.

KATHARINE WHITEHORN, *Roundabout* (1962)

You can't prove you're an American by waving Old Glory.

HELEN GAHAGAN DOUGLAS, *A Full Life* (1982)

That kind of patriotism which consists in hating all other nations.

ELIZABETH GASKELL, *Sylvia's Lovers* (1863)

The development of the national spirit in its present form leads into blind alleys. Some condition *must* be found which preserves the life of the nation, but rules out the fatal rivalry among nations.

KÄTHE KOLLWITZ, letter (1917), in Hans Kollwitz, ed., *The Diaries and Letters of Käthe Kollwitz* (1955)

A patriot is one who wrestles for the / soul of her country / as she wrestles for her own being.

ADRIENNE RICH, *An Atlas of the Difficult World: Poems 1988–1991* (1991)

I'm a universal patriot, if you could understand me rightly: my country is the world.

CHARLOTTE BRONTË, The Professor (1846)

See also Chauvinism.

PATRONIZING

A patronizing disposition always has its meaner side.

GEORGE ELIOT, *Adam Bede* (1859)

Don't Preach. Don't Patronize.

Slogan of the woman-run Americanization Committee that helped immigrants adjust to American life, in *Woman Citizen* (1917)

PEACE

Peace is not a passive but an active condition, not a negation but an affirmation. It is a gesture as strong as war.

MARY ROBERTS RINEHART (1918), in Julia Edwards, *Women of the World: The Great Foreign Correspondents* (1988)

They have not wanted *Peace* at all; they have wanted to be spared war—as though the absence of war was the same as peace.

DOROTHY THOMPSON, *On the Record* (1958)

The struggle to maintain peace is immeasurably more difficult than any military operation.

ANNE O'HARE MCCORMICK, in Julia Edwards, *Women of the World: The Great Foreign Correspondents* (1988)

Everyone speaks of peace; no one knows what peace is. We know at best a poisoned peace. No one has lived on an earth without weapons, without war and the threat of war on a large and small scale.

CHRISTINA THÜRMER-ROHR, *Vagabonding* (1991)

It isn't enough to talk about peace. One must believe in it. And it isn't enough to believe in it. One must work at it.

ELEANOR ROOSEVELT, radio broadcast (1951)

Peace is achieved one person at a time, through a series of friendships.

FATMA REDA, in *Minnesota Women's Press* (1991)

You cannot shake hands with a clenched fist.

INDIRA GANDHI, press conference (1971)

Peace is not won by those who fiercely guard their differences but by those who with open minds and hearts seek out connections.

KATHERINE PATERSON, *The Spying Heart* (1989)

It seems to me that there are two great enemies of peace—fear and selfishness.

KATHERINE PATERSON, in *The Horn Book* (1991)

Ultimately, we have just one moral duty: to reclaim large areas of peace in ourselves, more and more peace, and to reflect it toward others. And the more peace there is in us, the more peace there will be in our troubled world.

ETTY HILLESUM, *An Interrupted Life: The Diaries of Etty Hillesum 1941–1943* (1983)

Acquire inner peace and a multitude will find their salvation near you.

CATHERINE DE HUECK DOHERTY, Poustinia (1975)

Whatever peace I know rests in the natural world, in feeling myself a part of it, even in a small way.

MAY SARTON, *Journal of a Solitude* (1973)

Peace is when time doesn't matter as it passes by.

MARIA SCHELL, in *Time* (1958)

There is no such thing as inner peace. There is only nervousness or death.

FRAN LEBOWITZ, *Metropolitan Life* (1978)

See also Calm, Human Family, Pacifism, Peace and Love, War.

PEACE AND LOVE

Love is not a doctrine. Peace is not an international agreement. Love and Peace are beings who live as possibilities in us.

MARY CAROLINE RICHARDS, *Centering: In Pottery, Poetry, and Person* (1964)

Peace and love are always alive in us, but we are not always alive to peace and love.

JULIAN OF NORWICH, *Revelations of Divine Love* (1373)

See also Love, Peace.

PERCEPTION

Nothing that God ever made is the same thing to more than one person.

ZORA NEALE HURSTON, *Dust Tracks on a Road* (1942)

To the person in the bell jar, blank and stopped as a dead baby, the world itself is the bad dream.

SYLVIA PLATH, *The Bell Jar* (1963)

What one reads, or rather all that comes to us, is surely only of interest and value in proportion as we find ourselves therein,—form given to what was vague, what slumbered stirred to life.

ALICE JAMES, *Journal* (1889)

I often see through things right to the apparition itself.

GRACE PALEY, *Enormous Changes at the Last Minute* (1974)

I am firm. You are obstinate. He is a pig-headed fool.

KATHARINE WHITEHORN, in *Observer* (1974)

Someone will always tell you what you want to hear.

DELIA EPHRON, *Funny Sauce* (1986)

See also Mindset, Tact.

PERFECTIONISM

Striving for excellence motivates you; striving for perfection is demoralizing.

HARRIET BRAIKER, *The Type E Woman* (1986)

See also Excellence.

PERFORMANCE

Does the real thing ever have the perfection of a stage performance?

AGATHA CHRISTIE, *Crooked House* (1949)

It is in performance that the sudden panic hits, that we beg for release from our destiny and at the same time court the very experience that terrifies us. . . . A well-meaning friend says, "There's nothing to get nervous about," and it almost helps, because the desire to strangle distracts us for the moment.

ELOISE RISTAD, *A Soprano on Her Head* (1982)

Once you get on stage, everything is right. I feel the most beautiful, complete, fulfilled. I think that's why, in the case of noncompromising career women, parts of our personal lives don't work out. One person can't give you the feeling that thousands of people give you.

LEONTYNE PRICE, in Brian Lanker, *I Dream a World* (1989)

When you perform . . . you are out of yourself—larger and more potent, more beautiful. You are for minutes heroic. This is power. This is glory on earth. And it is yours, nightly.

AGNES DE MILLE, in *New York Times* (1963)

Every now and then, when you're on the stage, you hear the best sound a player can hear. It is a sound you can't get in movies or in television. It is the sound of a wonderful, deep silence that means you've hit them where they live.

SHELLEY WINTERS, in *Theatre Arts* (1956)

When it's all over and the ON THE AIR signs go off there isn't a more lost feeling in the world. The wonderful, exciting, even glamorous, studio is now just a room dirty with coffee cartons and cigarette butts.

GERTRUDE BERG, *Molly and Me* (1961)

See also Acting, Audience, Singing, Theater.

PERSEVERANCE

Diamonds are only chunks of coal, / That stuck to their jobs, you see.

MINNIE RICHARD SMITH, "Stick to Your Job," in Christian F. Kleinknecht, *Poor Richard's Anthology of Thoughts on Success* (1947)

The great thing and the hard thing is to stick to things when you have outlived the first interest, and not yet got the second which comes with a sort of mastery.

JANET ERSKINE STUART, in Maud Monahan, *Life and Letters of Janet Erskine Stuart* (1922)

See also Determination, Patience, Stubbornness.

PERSONALITY

She had to confess to inexperience: her personality was still too much for her, like a punt pole.

ELIZABETH BOWEN, *Friends and Relations* (1931)

She [Ethel Waters] is one of the strangest bundles of people that I have ever met. You can just see the different folks wrapped up in her if you associate with her long. Just like watching an open fire—the color and shape of her personality is never the same twice.

ZORA NEALE HURSTON, *Dust Tracks on a Road* (1942)

See also Behavior, Character, Temperament.

PESSIMISM

It doesn't pay well to fight for what we believe in.

LILLIAN HELLMAN, *Watch on the Rhine* (1941)

Dwelling on the negative simply contributes to its power.

SHIRLEY MACLAINE, *Out on a Limb* (1983)

How happy are the pessimists! What joy is theirs when they have proved there is no joy.

MARIE VON EBNER-ESCHENBACH, *Aphorisms* (1905)

See also Cynicism, Despair.

PHILANTHROPY

All philanthropy . . . is only a savory fumigation burning at the mouth of a sewer.

ELLEN KEY, *The Century of the Child* (1909)

The results of philanthropy are always beyond calculation.

MIRIAM BEARD, *A History of Business* (1938)

See also Charity, Giving.

PHILOSOPHY

A philosophy is characterized more by the formulation of its problems than by its solution of them.

SUSANNE K. LANGER, *Philosophy in a New Key* (1942)

As a human being, you have no choice about the fact that you need a philosophy. Your only choice is whether you define your philosophy by a conscious, rational, disciplined process of thought and scrupulously logical deliberation— or let your subconscious accumulate a junk heap of unwarranted conclusions, false generalizations, undefined contradictions, undigested slogans, unidentified wishes, doubts and fears, thrown together by chance, but integrated by your subconscious into a kind of mongrel philosophy and fused into a single, solid weight: *self-doubt*, like a ball and chain in the place where your mind's wings should have grown.

AYN RAND, *Philosophy: Who Needs It?* (1982)

There is no monster more destructive than the inventive mind that has outstripped philosophy.

ELLEN GLASGOW, *Letters of Ellen Glasgow* (1958)

I have a simple philosophy. Fill what's empty. Empty what's full. Scratch where it itches.

ALICE ROOSEVELT LONGWORTH, in Peter Russell and Leonard Ross, *The Best* (1974)

I make the most of all that comes, / And the least of all that goes.

SARA TEASDALE, "The Philosopher," *Collected Poems* (1937)

Some people talk of morality, and some of religion, but give me a little snug property.

MARIA EDGEWORTH, *The Absentee* (1804)

I am open to conviction on all points except dinner and debts. I hold that the one must be eaten and the other paid. Those are my only prejudices.

GEORGE ELIOT, letter (1857), in J. W. Cross, *George Eliot's Life as Related in Her Letters and Journals* (1884)

See also Belief, Mindset, Morality, Principles.

PHOBIAS

I have three phobias which, could I mute them, would make my life as slick as a sonnet, but as dull as ditch water: I hate to go to bed, I hate to get up, and I hate to be alone.

TALLULAH BANKHEAD, *Tallulah* (1952)

See also Fear.

PHOTOGRAPHY

Photography can never grow up if it imitates some other medium. It has to walk alone; it has to be itself.

BERENICE ABBOTT, "It Has to Walk Alone," in *Infinity* (1951)

A photograph is not only an image (as a painting is an image), an interpretation of the real; it is also a trace, something directly stenciled off the real, like a footprint or a death mask.

SUSAN SONTAG, *On Photography* (1977)

A photograph is a secret about a secret. The more it tells you the less you know.

DIANE ARBUS, in Doon Arbus, ed., *Diane Arbus: An Aperture Monograph* (1972)

Instead of just recording reality, photographs have become the norm for the way things appear to us, thereby changing the very idea of reality and of realism.

SUSAN SONTAG, *On Photography* (1977)

Life is not significant details, illuminated by a flash, fixed forever. Photographs are.

SUSAN SONTAG, *On Photography* (1977)

The camera makes everyone a tourist in other people's reality, and eventually in one's own.

SUSAN SONTAG, in *New York Review of Books* (1974)

While there is perhaps a province in which the photograph can tell us nothing more than what we see with our own eyes, there is another in which it proves to us how little our eyes permit us to see.

DOROTHEA LANGE (1950), in Milton Meltzer, *Dorothea Lange: Life Through the Camera* (1985)

My best pictures are always taken when I succeed in establishing a bond of sympathy with my sitter. When there is the slightest suggestion of antagonism, then my best efforts are of no avail.

DORIS ULMANN, in Dale Warren, "Doris Ulmann: Photographer-in-Waiting," *The Bookman* (1930)

I have always taken pictures the way people keep journals and diaries. It's a way of ordering my reactions to the world, of placing my ideas and feelings in a concrete form outside myself, of breaking my isolation.

DIANA MICHENER, in Sara Ruddick and Pamela Daniels, *Working It Out* (1977)

I really believe there are things nobody would see if I didn't photograph them.

DIANE ARBUS, in Doon Arbus, ed., *Diane Arbus: An Aperture Monograph* (1972)

We have become a nation of Kodachrome, Nikon, Instamatic addicts. But we haven't yet developed a clear idea of the ethics of picture-taking. . . . Where do we get the right to bring other people home in a canister? Where did we lose the right to control our image?

ELLEN GOODMAN, *Close to Home* (1979)

My mother is not smiling; Chinese do not smile for photographs. Their faces command relatives in foreign lands—"Send money"—and posterity forever—"Put food in front of the picture."

MAXINE HONG KINGSTON, *The Woman Warrior* (1976)

Very few people, thank God, look like the pictures of them which are published in the papers and the weekly magazines.

ILKA CHASE, *Free Admission* (1948)

See also Art, Images.

PITY

Pity is a corroding thing.

MARTHA GRAHAM, in Robin Stringer, *Daily Telegraph* (1979)

Pity is the least of the emotions.

TALLULAH BANKHEAD, *Tallulah* (1952)

I seem to be the only person in the world who doesn't mind being pitied. If you love me, pity me. The human state is pitiable: born to die, capable of so much, accomplishing so little; killing instead of creating, destroying instead of building, hating instead of loving. Pitiful, pitiful.

JESSAMYN WEST, *Hide and Seek* (1973)

More helpful than all wisdom is one draft of simple human pity that will not forsake us.

GEORGE ELIOT, *The Mill on the Floss* (1860)

See also Compassion, Kindness, Pathos, Self-Pity, Sympathy.

PLACES

How hard it is to escape from places. However carefully one goes they hold you—you leave little bits of yourself fluttering on the fences—little rags and shreds of your very life.

KATHERINE MANSFIELD, in Leslie Moore, *Katherine Mansfield: The Memories of L. M.* (1971)

You have to pick the places you don't walk away from.

JOAN DIDION, *A Book of Common Prayer* (1977)

One does not love a place the less for having suffered in it unless it has all been suffering, nothing but suffering.

JANE AUSTEN, *Persuasion* (1818)

I have before seen other countries, in the same manner, give themselves to you when you are about to leave them.

ISAK DINESEN, *Out of Africa* (1937)

Old Magic, Old Ways, the Old Ones themselves often seem powerless in a new place.

ANNE CAMERON, *Daughters of Copper Woman* (1981)

Setting . . . is accident. Either a building is part of a place, or it is not. Once that kinship is there, time will only make it stronger.

WILLA CATHER, *Death Comes for the Archbishop* (1927)

See also Home, Roots, Travel.

PLAGIARISM

Some persons are so constituted that the very excellence of an idea seems to them a convincing reason that it must be, if not solely, yet especially theirs. It fits in so beautifully with their general wisdom, it lies implicitly in so many of their manifested opinions, that if they have not yet expressed it (because of preoccupation), it is clearly a part of their indigenous produce, and is proved by their immediate eloquent promulgation of it to belong more naturally and appropriately to them than to the person who seemed first to have alighted on it, and who sinks in their all-originating consciousness to that low kind of entity, a second cause.

GEORGE ELIOT, *Impressions of Theophrastus Such* (1879)

PLANETS

The Planets / are nine dice rolling in the dark.

DIANE ACKERMAN, *The Planets* (1976)

PLANTS

Once a century, all of a certain kind of bamboo flower on the same day. Whether they are in Malaysia or in a greenhouse in Minnesota makes no difference, nor does the age or size of the plant. They flower. Some current of an inner language passes between them, through space and separation, in ways we cannot explain in our language. They are all, somehow, one plant, each with a share of communal knowledge.

LINDA HOGAN, in Lorraine Anderson, ed., *Sisters of the Earth* (1991)

There is no question that plants have [all] kinds of sensitivities. They do a lot of responding to their environment. They can do almost anything you can think of. But just because they sit there, anybody walking down the road considers them just a plastic area to look at, [as if] they're not really alive.

BARBARA MCCLINTOCK, in Evelyn Fox Keller, *A Feeling for the Organism* (1983)

See also Flowers, Gardening, Gardens, Nature, Trees.

PLEASURE

Few pleasures there are indeed without an aftertouch of pain, but that is the preservation which keeps them sweet.

HELEN KELLER, *Helen Keller's Journal* (1938)

A fool bolts pleasure, then complains of moral indigestion.

MINNA THOMAS ANTRIM, *Naked Truth and Veiled Illusions* (1902)

It isn't the great big pleasures that count the most; it's making a great deal out of the little ones.

JEAN WEBSTER, *Daddy-Long-Legs* (1912)

See also Joy.

POETRY

The words loved me and I loved them in return.

SONIA SANCHEZ, *Under a Soprano Sky* (1987)

There is no architect / Can build as the muse can; / . . . / She lays her beams in music, / In music every one.

SUSAN GLASPELL, *Alison's House* (1930)

Poetry is life distilled.

GWENDOLYN BROOKS, in Brian Lanker, *I Dream a World* (1989)

Poetry is an act of distillation. It takes contingency samples, is selective. It telescopes time. It focuses what most often floods past us in a polite blur.

DIANE ACKERMAN, in Janet Sternburg, ed., *The Writer on Her Work,* vol. 2 (1991)

Poetry is, indeed, the deification of reality.

EDITH SITWELL, *The Outcasts* (1962)

Poems come from incomplete knowledge.

DIANE WAKOSKI, "With Words," *The Motorcycle Betrayal Poems* (1971)

This chain of enigmas / hung on the neck of night.

NELLY SACHS, "This Chain of Enigmas," *O the Chimneys* (1967)

Poetry is a string of words that parades without a permit.

LINDA HOGAN, in Janet Sternburg, ed., *The Writer on Her Work,* vol. 2 (1991)

The poet speaks to all men of that other life of theirs that they have smothered and forgotten.

EDITH SITWELL, "Rhyme and Reason," in Elizabeth Salter and Allanah Harper, *Edith Sitwell: Fire of the Mind* (1976)

Poems reveal secrets when they are analyzed. The poet's pleasure in finding ingenious ways to enclose her secrets should be matched by the reader's pleasure in unlocking and revealing these secrets.

DIANE WAKOSKI, in *Writer's Digest* (1991)

It seems to me that this is the true test for poetry:—that it should go beneath experience, as prose can never do, and awaken an apprehension of things we have never, and can never, know in the actuality.

ELLEN GLASGOW, *Letters of Ellen Glasgow* (1958)

For poetry exists to break through to below the level of reason where the angels and monsters that the amenities keep in the cellar may come out to dance, to rove and roar, growling and singing, to bring life back to the enclosed rooms where too often we are only "living and partly living."

May Sarton, "On Growth and Change," *Sarton Selected* (1991)

A poem records emotions and moods that lie beyond normal language, that can only be patched together and hinted at metaphorically.

Diane Ackerman, in Janet Sternburg, ed., *The Writer on Her Work,* vol. 2 (1991)

If I read a book and it makes my whole body so cold no fire can ever warm me, I know *that* is poetry. If I feel physically as if the top of my head were taken off, I know *that* is poetry. These are the only ways I know it. Is there any other way?

Emily Dickinson (1870), in Martha Dickinson Bianchi, *The Life and Letters of Emily Dickinson* (1924)

Any time is the time to make a poem.

Gertrude Stein, *Everybody's Autobiography* (1937)

Poetry does not necessarily have to be beautiful to stick in the depths of our memory.

Colette, *The Blue Lantern* (1949)

I, too, dislike it: there are things that are important beyond all this fiddle. / Reading it, however, with a perfect contempt for it, one discovers in it after all, a place for the genuine.

Marianne Moore, "Poetry," *Selected Poems* (1935)

It is as unseeing to ask what is the *use* of poetry as it would be to ask what is the use of religion.

Edith Sitwell, *The Outcasts* (1962)

Poetry has a way of teaching one what one needs to know . . . if one is honest.

May Sarton, *Mrs. Stevens Hears the Mermaids Singing* (1965)

What was the function of poetry if not to improve the petty, cautious minds of evasive children?

Bharati Mukherjee, *The Middleman and Other Stories* (1988)

Poetry is the most mistaught subject in any school because we teach poetry by form and not by content.

Nikki Giovanni, in Claudia Tate, ed., *Black Women Writers at Work* (1983)

If food is poetry, is not poetry also food?

Joyce Carol Oates, "Writers' Hunger: Food as Metaphor," in *New York Times* (1986)

To write about the monstrous sense of alienation the poet feels in this culture of polarized hatreds is a way of staying sane. With the poem, I reach out to an audience equally at odds with official policy, and I celebrate our mutual humanness in an inhuman world.

Maxine Kumin, "A Way of Staying Sane," in Marilyn Sewell, ed., *Cries of the Spirit* (1991)

For me a true poem is on the way when I begin to be haunted, when it seems as if I were being asked an inescapable question by an angel with whom I must wrestle to get at the answer.

May Sarton, "Revision as Creation," *Sarton Selected* (1991)

Your poems will happen when no one is there.

May Sarton, "A Last Word," *A Grain of Mustard Seed* (1971)

Try making a poem as if it were a table, clear and solid, standing there outside you.

May Sarton, *Mrs. Stevens Hears the Mermaids Singing* (1965)

The beautiful feeling after writing a poem is on the whole better even than after sex, and that's saying a lot.

Anne Sexton, in Howard Moss, ed., *The Poet's Story* (1974)

I tell poets that when a line just floats into your head, don't pay attention 'cause it probably has floated into somebody else's head.

Gwendolyn Brooks, in Brian Lanker, *I Dream a World* (1989)

Poetry is a dangerous profession between conflict and resolution, between feeling and thought, between becoming and being, between the ultra-personal and the universal—and these balances are shifting all the time.

MAY SARTON, "On Growth and Change," *Sarton Selected* (1991)

Of all the art forms, poetry is the most economical . . . the one which can most easily be done between shifts at the plant, in the hospital pantry, on the crowded subway, and on scraps of surplus paper. . . Poetry has become the major voice of poor, working-class, and Third World women. A room of one's own may be a necessity for writing prose, but so are reams of paper, a working typewriter, and plenty of time.

AUDRE LORDE, *Age, Race, Class and Sexuality* (1980)

We have let rhetoric do the job of poetry.

CHERRÍE MORAGA, "La Guera," in Cherríe Moraga and Gloria Anzaldúa, eds., *This Bridge Called My Back* (1983)

This poem isn't for you / but for me / after all.

JOY HARJO, "Your Phone Call at Eight A.M.," in Rayna Green, ed., *That's What She Said* (1984)

Poem me no poems.

ROSE MACAULAY, in *Poetry Review* (1963)

Making verses is almost as common as taking snuff, and God can tell what miserable stuff people carry about in their pockets, and offer to all their acquaintances, and you know one cannot refuse reading and taking a pinch.

LADY MARY WORTLEY MONTAGU, letter (1747), in Octave Thanet, ed., *The Best Letters of Lady Mary Wortley Montagu* (1901)

The fear of poetry is an indication that we are cut off from our own reality.

MURIEL RUKEYSER, *The Life of Poetry* (1949)

See also Literature, Poets, Verse, Writing.

POETS

To me the Muses truly gave / An envied and a happy lot: / E'en when I lie within the grave, / I cannot, shall not, be forgot.

SAPPHO (6th century B.C.), in C. R. Haines, *Sappho: The Poems and Fragments* (1926)

The people must grant a hearing to the best poets they have else they will never have better.

HARRIET MONROE, in Hope Stoddard, "Harriet Monroe," *Famous American Women* (1970)

It is the gift of all poets to find the commonplace astonishing, and the astonishing quite natural.

MARGERY SHARP, *The Rescuers* (1959)

A poet perceives and gives whole-hearted expression to that which our sensibilities, not less lively but less musicianly, keep stored inside.

COLETTE, *Paris From My Window* (1944)

He who draws noble delights from the sentiments of poetry is a true poet, though he has never written a line in all his life.

GEORGE SAND, *The Haunted Pool* (1851)

Women have always been poor, not for two hundred years merely, but from the beginning of time. . . . Women, then, have not had a dog's chance of writing poetry. That is why I have laid so much stress on money and a room of one's own.

VIRGINIA WOOLF, *A Room of One's Own* (1929)

The fact is that I have lived with the belief that power, any kind of power, was the one thing forbidden to poets. . . . Power requires that the inner person never be unmasked. No, we poets have to go naked. And since this is so, it is better that we stay private people; a naked public person would be rather ridiculous, what?

MAY SARTON, *Mrs. Stevens Hears the Mermaids Singing* (1965)

A poet *never* feels useful.

MAY SARTON, *Mrs. Stevens Hears the Mermaids Singing* (1965)

A poet will even face death when he sees his people oppressed.

CAROLINA MARIA DE JESUS, *Child of the Dark, The Diary of Carolina Maria de Jesus* (1962)

I notice that many great poets emerge from motherless childhoods. They are either early orphans or their mothers are not mentioned at all. It is not so amazing that many of these same artists turned out to be hounded by depression, drugs, and insanity, but did being motherless also drive them to creativity?

LIZ SMITH, *The Mother Book* (1978)

People wish to be poets more than they wish to write poetry, and that's a mistake. One should wish to celebrate more than one wishes to be celebrated.

LUCILLE CLIFTON, in *Poets & Writers Magazine* (1992)

And I'll stay off Verlaine too; he was always chasing Rimbauds.

DOROTHY PARKER, "The Little Hours," *The Portable Dorothy Parker* (1944)

See also Artists, Poetry, Writers.

POLICE

There's really no such thing as an "ex-cop" or a cop who's "off-duty" or "retired." Once trained, once indoctrinated, a cop is always alert, assessing reality in terms of its potential for illegal acts.

SUE GRAFTON, *"H" Is for Homicide* (1991)

See also Crime.

POLITENESS

Civility costs nothing, and buys everything.

LADY MARY WORTLEY MONTAGU, letter (1756), in Robert Halsband, ed., *The Complete Letters of Lady Mary Wortley Montagu* (1965)

I come from people who have always been polite enough to feel that nothing has ever happened to them.

PATRICIA HAMPL, *A Romantic Education* (1981)

There is a politeness so terrible, that rage beside it is balm.

MINNA THOMAS ANTRIM, *At the Sign of the Golden Calf* (1905)

See also Etiquette, Manners, Rudeness, Tact.

POLITICAL PARTIES

Party politics is now a real farce.

GEORGE SAND (1875), in Raphaël Ledos de Beaufort, *Letters of George Sand* (1886)

At every political convention all matters of right, of justice, of the eternal verities themselves, are swallowed up in the one all-important question, "Will it bring party success?"

SUSAN B. ANTHONY AND IDA HUSTED HARPER, eds., *The History of Woman Suffrage,* vol. IV (1902)

[A political party] tends to stifle honesty and individuality. It substitutes numerical strength for sound reasoning, power for justice, organized machinery for the labor of conversion; the machine takes the place of the mind.

TERESA BILLINGTON-GREIG (1911), in Cheris Kramarae and Paula A. Treichler, *A Feminist Dictionary* (1985)

See also Politicians, Politics.

POLITICIANS

There are no such things as good politicians and bad politicians. There are only politicians, which is to say, they all have personal axes to grind, and all too rarely are they honed for the public good.

BARBARA HOWAR, *Laughing All the Way* (1973)

A politician is a fellow who will lay down your life for his country.

TEXAS GUINAN, nightclub act (c. 1920)

He had grown up in a country run by politicians who sent the pilots to man the bombers to kill the babies to make the world safe for children to grow up in.

URSULA K. LE GUIN, *The Lathe of Heaven* (1971)

Politicians are the source of all disillusionment.

SHIRLEY ABBOTT, *Womenfolks: Growing Up Down South* (1983)

There is little place in the political scheme of things for an independent, creative personality, for a fighter. Anyone who takes that role must pay a price.

SHIRLEY CHISHOLM, *Unbought and Unbossed* (1970)

Convictions no doubt have to be modified or expanded to meet changing conditions but . . . to be a reliable political leader sooner or later your anchors must hold fast where other men's drag.

MARGOT ASQUITH, *More or Less About Myself* (1934)

Brains, integrity, and force may be all very well, but what you need today is Charm. Go ahead and work on your old economic programs if you want to, I'll develop my radio personality.

GRACIE ALLEN, *How to Become President* (1940)

I must say acting was good training for the political life which lay ahead for us.

NANCY REAGAN, *Nancy* (1980)

He had the misleading air of open-hearted simplicity that people have come to demand of their politicians.

RAE FOLEY, *The Hundredth Door* (1950)

What troubles me is not that movie stars run for office, but that they find it easy to get elected. It should be difficult. It should be difficult for millionaires, too.

SHANA ALEXANDER, in *Life* (1966)

I was cooking breakfast this morning for my kids, and I thought, "He's just like a Teflon frying pan: Nothing sticks to him."

PATRICIA SCHROEDER, on Ronald Reagan, in *Boston Globe* (1984)

I would feel sorry for her if she did.

PAT NIXON, on whether she would want daughter Tricia to marry a politician, in Barbara McDowell and Hana Umlauf, *Woman's Almanac* (1977)

A politician ought to be born a foundling and remain a bachelor.

LADY BIRD JOHNSON, in *Time* (1975)

I'm the candidate who forgot to take off her hat before she threw it in the ring.

GRACIE ALLEN, *How to Become President* (1940)

See also Government, Leaders, Political Parties, Politics.

POLITICS

Politics are usually the executive expression of human immaturity.

VERA BRITTAIN, *The Rebel Passion* (1964)

Truthfulness has never been counted among the political virtues, and lies have always been regarded as justifiable tools in political dealings.

HANNAH ARENDT, *Crises of the Republic* (1972)

Policy and politics generally go contrary to principle.

FLANNERY O'CONNOR, in Sally Fitzgerald, ed., *The Habit of Being* (1979)

From politics, it was an easy step to silence.

JANE AUSTEN, *Northanger Abbey* (1818)

International politics, by and large, are a depressing study.

C. V. WEDGWOOD, *Velvet Studies* (1946)

I was well on the way to forming my present attitude toward politics as it is practiced in the United States: it is a beautiful fraud that has been imposed on the people for years, whose practitioners exchange gilded promises for the most valuable thing their victims own, their votes.

SHIRLEY CHISHOLM, *Unbought and Unbossed* (1970)

I believe that everything is political, and as such it should concern all of us. Authors who claim they don't deal with politics in their work are being naive, because even that is a political stance.

ELENA PONIATOWSKA, in Marie-Lise Gazarian-Gautiez, *Interviews With Latin American Writers* (1989)

The personal is political.

SLOGAN, women's movement (1970s)

There aren't many idealists in politics.

EVELYN ANTHONY, *The Avenue of the Dead* (1982)

The political arena leaves one no alternative, one must either be a dunce or a rogue.

EMMA GOLDMAN, title essay, *Anarchism* (1910)

What can the people think when, thanks to disclosure, the slimy trail from the contribution to the vote can be so easily traced?

MILLICENT FENWICK, in *Washington Post* (1976)

Haven't you ever noticed how highways always get beautiful near the state capital?

SHIRLEY ANN GRAU, *The Wind Shifting West* (1973)

If you're going to play the game properly, you'd better know every rule.

BARBARA JORDAN, in Charles L. Saunders, "Barbara Jordan," *Ebony* (1975)

A theme is always necessary, a plain, simple, unadorned theme to confuse the ignorant.

LILLIAN HELLMAN, *Scoundrel Time* (1976)

Our political scene is more volatile and given to sudden switches and memory lapses bordering on soap-opera-type amnesia (epidemic, total and terminal) than any other I know of. We are fickle and we are insatiable in our appetite for new news, new issues, new biases, new clichés. . . . It's not just (as another cliché, lifted from Andy Warhol, has it) that individuals all seem to get their fifteen minutes of celebrity in this country; everything gets only fifteen minutes.

MEG GREENFIELD, in *Newsweek* (1991)

Women are young at politics, but they are old at suffering; soon they will learn that through politics they can prevent some kinds of suffering.

NANCY ASTOR, *My Two Countries* (1923)

Never lose your temper with the Press or the public is a major rule of political life.

CHRISTABEL PANKHURST, *Unshackled* (1959)

See also Democracy, Elections, Government, Political Parties, Politicians, Suffrage.

POLLS

If Rosa Parks had taken a poll before she sat down in the bus in Montgomery, she'd still be standing.

MARY FRANCES BERRY, in Brian Lanker, *I Dream a World* (1989)

See also Public Opinion.

POPULARITY

Being popular is important. Otherwise people might not like you.

MIMI POND, *The Valley Girl's Guide to Life* (1982)

See also Charisma, Charm.

PORNOGRAPHY

Pornography is the undiluted essence of anti-female propaganda.

SUSAN BROWNMILLER, *Against Our Will: Men, Women and Rape* (1975)

For many feminists, pornography is the theory and rape is the practice.

CHERIS KRAMARAE AND PAULA A. TREICHLER, *A Feminist Dictionary* (1985)

Pornography is a direct denial of the power of the erotic, for it represents the suppression of true feeling. Pornography emphasizes sensation without feeling.

AUDRE LORDE, *Uses of the Erotic* (1978)

What pornographic literature does is precisely to drive a wedge between one's existence as a full human being and one's existence as a sexual being—while in ordinary life one hopes to prevent such a wedge from being driven.

SUSAN SONTAG, in Douglas A. Hughes, ed., *Perspectives on Pornography* (1970)

Pornography is not about sex. It's about an imbalance of male-female power that allows and even requires sex to be used as a form of aggression. . . . But until we finally untangle sexuality and aggression, there will be more pornography and less erotica. There will be little murders in our beds—and very little love.

GLORIA STEINEM, *Outrageous Acts and Everyday Rebellions* (1983)

We are unalterably opposed to the presentation of the female body being stripped, bound, raped, tortured, mutilated and murdered in the name of commercial entertainment and free speech.

SUSAN BROWNMILLER, *Against Our Will: Men, Women and Rape* (1975)

POSSESSIONS

He greatly valued his possessions, chiefly because they were his, and derived genuine pleasure from contemplating a painting, a statuette, a rare lace curtain—no matter what—after he had bought it and placed it among his household gods.

KATE CHOPIN, *The Awakening* (1899)

The pleasure of possession, whether we possess trinkets or offspring—or possibly books, or chessmen, or postage stamps—lies in showing these things to friends who are experiencing no immediate urge to look at them.

AGNES REPPLIER, *Times and Tendencies* (1931)

Only in a house where one has learnt to be lonely does one have this solicitude for *things*. One's relation to them, the daily seeing or touching, begins to become love, and to lay one open to pain.

ELIZABETH BOWEN, *The Death of the Heart* (1938)

It matters less to venerate things than to live with them on terms of good friendship.

ADRIENNE MONNIER, *Dernières Gazettes et Écrits divers* (1938), in Richard McDougall, tr., *The Very Rich Hours of Adrienne Monnier* (1976)

Lost things, she felt certain, had a life of their own. They came back to their families like stray dogs.

NANCY WILLARD, *Things Invisible to See* (1984)

One attacks those who possess things that one does not possess. The attack is all the more savage because the one who attacks is destitute and the one who is attacked is well provided. The one who attacks always considers himself to be in the position of legitimate offense.

ADRIENNE MONNIER, *Les Gazettes d'Adrienne Monnier* (1938), in Richard McDougall, tr., *The Very Rich Hours of Adrienne Monnier* (1976)

We possess nothing in the world—a mere chance can strip us of everything—except the power to say "I."

SIMONE WEIL, *Gravity and Grace* (1947)

Spoiled. That's all it's about—can't live without this, can't live without that. You can live without anything you weren't born with, and you can make it through on even half of that.

GLORIA NAYLOR, *Mama Day* (1988)

See also Consumerism, Materialism.

POUTING

I believe she keeps on being queenly in her own room, with the door shut.

EDITH WHARTON, *The House of Mirth* (1905)

One should know the value of Life better than to *pout* any part of it away.

HESTER LYNCH PIOZZI (1789), in Oswald G. Knapp, *The Intimate Letters of Hester Piozzi and Penelope Pennington 1788–1821* (1914)

POVERTY

That's the definition of poverty. The less choice you have, the poorer you are.

CARRIE SAXON PERRY, in Brian Lanker, I Dream a World (1989)

There is something about poverty that smells like death. Dead dreams dropping off the heart like leaves in a dry season and rotting around the feet; impulses smothered too long in the fetid air of underground caves.

ZORA NEALE HURSTON, *Dust Tracks on a Road* (1942)

Poverty made me feel weak, as if I were coming down with an awful, debilitating, communicable disease—the disease of being without money. Instead of going to the hospital, you went to the poor farm. The difference was, you never got well at the poor farm.

FAITH SULLIVAN, *The Cape Ann* (1988)

Abstractions hardened into the concrete: even death is a purchase. One of Bam's senior partners could afford his at the cost of a private plane—in which he crashed. July's old mother (was she not perhaps his grandmother?) would crawl, as Maureen was watching her now, coming home with wood, and grass for her brooms on her head, bent lower and lower towards the earth until finally she sank to it—the only death she could afford.

NADINE GORDIMER, *July's People* (1981)

We live in the richest country in the world. There's plenty and to spare for no man, woman, or child to be in want. And in addition to this our country was founded on what should have been a great, true principle—the freedom, equality, and rights of each individual. Huh! And what has come of that start? There are corporations worth billions of dollars—and hundreds of thousands of people who don't get to eat.

CARSON MCCULLERS, *The Heart Is a Lonely Hunter* (1940)

I don't believe that it's true that the poor will always be with us. I think that kind of pious fatalism is just an excuse for keeping things the way they are.

MARGARET CULKIN BANNING, *The Quality of Mercy* (1963)

We always come back to the same vicious circle—an extreme degree of material or intellectual poverty does away with the means of alleviating it.

SIMONE DE BEAUVOIR, *The Coming of Age* (1970)

Poor people who had escaped from poverty as I had, feared it, hated it and fled from it all their lives. Those born rich could afford to be touched by it.

ANZIA YEZIERSKA, *Red Ribbon on a White Horse* (1950)

For those who have lived on the edge of poverty all their lives, the semblance of poverty affected by the affluent is both incomprehensible and insulting.

LILLIAN BRESLOW RUBIN, *Worlds of Pain* (1976)

But even if there were no Communists, the wealthy white western minority of the world could not hope to prosper if most of the rest of mankind were foundering in hopeless poverty. Islands of plenty in a vast ocean of misery have never been a good recipe for commercial success.

BARBARA WARD, in Richard Thruelsen and John Kobler, *Adventures of the Mind* (1959)

See also Ghetto, Homelessness, Hunger.

POWER

You see what power is—holding someone else's fear in your hand and showing it to them!

AMY TAN, *The Kitchen God's Wife* (1991)

Power in the hands of particular groups and classes serves like a prism to refract reality through their own perspective.

SHEILA ROWBOTHAM, *Woman's Consciousness, Man's World* (1973)

Abuse of power comes as no surprise.

JENNY HOLZER, *Truisms* (1977–1979)

I am more and more convinced that man is a dangerous creature; and that power, whether vested in many or a few, is ever grasping, and, like the grave, cries "Give, give."

ABIGAIL ADAMS, letter to her husband, John Adams (1775)

Power should not be concentrated in the hands of so few, and powerlessness in the hands of so many.

MAGGIE KUHN, in *Ms.* (1975)

"Must power always be for destruction?" said Anna. "That has so far been largely the experience."

SYBILLE BEDFORD, *A Favorite of the Gods* (1963)

Bodies in power tend to stay in power, unless external forces disturb them.

CATHARINE STIMPSON, "The Power to Name," in E. J. Sherman and E. Beck, eds., *The Prism of Sex* (1979)

Power can be taken, but not given. The process of the taking is empowerment in itself.

GLORIA STEINEM, *Outrageous Acts and Everyday Rebellions* (1983)

Power, however it has evolved, whatever its origins, will not be given up without a struggle.

SHULAMITH FIRESTONE, *The Dialectic of Sex* (1970)

But I have noticed this about ambitious men, or men in power—they fear even the slightest and least likely threat to it.

MARY STEWART, *The Crystal Cave* (1970)

Providence is always on the side of the big battalions.

MARIE DE RABUTIN-CHANTAL, MARQUISE DE SÉVIGNÉ, letter to her daughter (c. 1675), *Letters of Madame de Sévigné to Her Daughter and Her Friends* (1811)

In this world, all power rests upon force.

MARIE VON EBNER-ESCHENBACH, *Aphorisms* (1905)

Most power is illusionary and perceptual. You have to create an environment in which people perceive you as having some power.

CARRIE SAXON PERRY, in Brian Lanker, *I Dream a World* (1989)

Power . . . is not an end in itself, but is an instrument that must be used toward an end.

JEANE J. KIRKPATRICK, speech (1981)

To get power over is to defile. To possess is to defile.

SIMONE WEIL, *First and Last Notebooks* (1970)

I do not wish them [women] to have power over men; but over themselves.

MARY WOLLSTONECRAFT, *A Vindication of the Rights of Women* (1792)

The less powerful group usually knows the powerful one much better than vice versa—blacks have had to understand whites in order to survive, women have had to know men—yet the powerful group can afford to regard the less powerful one as a mystery.

GLORIA STEINEM, *Outrageous Acts and Everyday Rebellions* (1983)

Ironically, women who acquire power are more likely to be criticized for it than are the men who have always had it.

CAROLYN HEILBRUN, *Writing a Woman's Life* (1988)

Power travels in the bloodlines, handed out before birth.

LOUISE ERDRICH, *Tracks* (1988)

Power is the test. Some, once they have it, are content to buy the show of liking, and punish those who withhold it; then you have a despot. But some keep a true eye for how they seem to others, and care about it, which holds them back from much mischief.

MARY RENAULT, *The Praise Singer* (1978)

Surely a king who loves pleasure is less dangerous than one who loves glory.

NANCY MITFORD, *The Water Beetle* (1962)

Being physically close to extreme power causes one to experience a giddiness, an intoxication.

MAYA ANGELOU, *All God's Children Need Traveling Shoes* (1986)

Our sources and uses of power set our boundaries, give form to our relationships, even determine how much we let ourselves liberate and express aspects of the self. More than party reg-

istration, more than our purported philosophy or ideology, personal power defines our politics.

MARILYN FERGUSON, *The Aquarian Conspiracy* (1980)

See also Authority, Domination, Oppression, Powerlessness.

POWERLESSNESS

At times it is strangely sedative to know the extent of your own powerlessness.

ERICA JONG, *Fear of Flying* (1973)

See also Domination, Vulnerability.

PRAISE

It gives me no joy to be praised at the expense of a better artist, by someone who does not know the difference or who thinks me too vain to be aware of it myself.

MARY RENAULT, *The Mask of Apollo* (1966)

Praise out of season, or tactlessly bestowed, can freeze the heart as much as blame.

PEARL BUCK, *To My Daughters, With Love* (1967)

See also Flattery.

PRAYER

Prayer oneth the soul to God.

JULIAN OF NORWICH, *Revelations of Divine Love* (1373)

Prayer is more than meditation. In meditation the source of strength is one's self. When one prays he goes to a source of strength greater than his own.

MADAME CHIANG KAI-SHEK, *I Confess My Faith* (1943)

Absolutely unmixed attention is prayer.

SIMONE WEIL, *Gravity and Grace* (1947)

He prayed as he breathed, forming no words and making no specific requests, only holding in his heart, like broken birds in cupped hands, all those people who were in stress or grief.

ELLIS PETERS, *A Morbid Taste for Bones* (1977)

A desire to kneel down sometimes pulses through my body, or rather it is as if my body had been meant and made for the act of kneeling. Sometimes, in moments of deep gratitude, kneeling down becomes an overwhelming urge, head deeply bowed, hands before my face.

ETTY HILLESUM, *An Interrupted Life: The Diaries of Etty Hillesum 1941–1943* (1983)

Prayer does not use any artificial energy, it doesn't burn up any fossil fuel, it doesn't pollute.

MARGARET MEAD, in Mary Alice Warner and Bayna Beilenson, Women of Faith and Spirit (1987)

True prayer is not asking God for love; it is learning to love, and to include all mankind in one affection.

MARY BAKER EDDY, *No and Yes* (1909)

This morning I stood on the river bank to pray. I knew then that the ancient ones were wise to pray for peace and beauty and not for specific gifts except fertility which is continued life. And I saw that if one has even a small degree of the ability to take into and unto himself the peace and beauty the gods surround him with, it is not necessary to ask for more.

EDITH WARNER, in Peggy Pond Church, *The House at Otowi Bridge* (1959)

Pray inwardly, even if you do not enjoy it. It does good, though you feel nothing. Yes, even though you think you are doing nothing.

JULIAN OF NORWICH, *Revelations of Divine Love* (1373)

She makes long, long prayers, they say—so long that she has been found in the morning fainting on the cold floor of the convent church. . . . They all say she will have a very high place in heaven; but it seems to me, unless there is a very great difference between the highest and lowest places in heaven, it is a great deal of trouble to take.

ELIZABETH RUNDLE CHARLES, *Chronicles of the Schönberg-Cotta Family* (1863)

Oh, I wish that God had not given me what I prayed for! It was not so good as I thought.

JOHANNA SPYRI, *Heidi* (1915)

Of Course—I prayed— / And did God Care?

EMILY DICKINSON (1862), *Further Poems of Emily Dickinson* (1929)

If prayers worked, Hitler would have been stopped at the border of Poland by angels with swords of fire.

NANCY WILLARD, *Things Invisible to See* (1984)

See also Spirituality.

PRECOCITY

For precocity some great price is always demanded sooner or later in life.

MARGARET FULLER, in Thomas Wentworth Higginson, *Life of Margaret Fuller Ossoli* (1884)

See also Genius, Intelligence, Talent.

PREFACES

I ought to have put this in the preface, but I never read prefaces, and it is not much good writing things just for people to skip. I wonder other authors have never thought of this.

EDITH NESBITT, *The Bastable Children* (1928)

See also Books.

PREGNANCY

When I had almost reached my term, I looked like a rat dragging a stolen egg.

COLETTE, *The Evening Star* (1946)

I was slowly taking on the dimensions of a chest of drawers.

MARIA AUGUSTA TRAPP, *The Story of the Trapp Family Singers* (1949)

Getting company inside one's skin.

MAGGIE SCARF, *Unfinished Business* (1980)

There were, in the beginning, seven children, each rising out of my great-grandmother's darkness every twelve or thirteen months like little full moons, following, even in birth, the quirky Jewish calendar. . . . My great-grandmother conceived and bore them, I am told, with bemused passivity, as tolerant as the moon must be of her own swellings and thinnings and equally unconscious.

HARRIET ROSENSTEIN, "The Fraychie Story," in *Ms.* (1974)

Lie in the sun with the child in your flesh shining like a jewel. Dream and sing, pagan, wise in your vitals. Stand still like a fat budding tree, like a stalk of corn athrob and aglisten in the heat. Lie like a mare panting with the dancing feet of colts against her sides. Sleep at night as the spring earth. Walk heavily as a wheat stalk at its full time bending towards the earth waiting for the reaper. Let your life swell downward so you become like a vase, a vessel. Let the unknown child knock and knock against you and rise like a dolphin within.

MERIDEL LE SUEUR, *Salute to Spring* (1940)

If pregnancy were a book, they would cut the last two chapters.

NORA EPHRON, *Heartburn* (1983)

If men could get pregnant, abortion would be a sacrament.

FLORYNCE KENNEDY, in Gloria Steinem, "The Verbal Karate of Florynce Kennedy," *Ms.* (1973)

See also Childbirth.

PREJUDICE

Every bigot was once a child free of prejudice.

SISTER MARY DE LOURDES, in *Reader's Digest* (1983)

Prejudices, it is well known, are most difficult to eradicate from the heart whose soil has never been loosened or fertilized by education; they grow there, firm as weeds among stones.

CHARLOTTE BRONTË, *Jane Eyre* (1847)

Prejudices such as sexism and the deeply related homophobia, racism, and classism are not just personal problems, sets of peculiar and troubling beliefs. Exclusions and devaluations of whole groups of people on the scale and of the range, tenacity, and depth of racism and sexism and classism are systemic and shape the world within which we all struggle to live and find meaning.

ELIZABETH KAMARCK MINNICK, *Transforming Knowledge* (1990)

Sometimes, it's like a hair across your cheek. You can't see it, you can't find it with your fingers, but you keep brushing at it because the feel of it is irritating.

MARIAN ANDERSON, in *Ladies' Home Journal* (1960)

Whenever someone speaks with prejudice against a group—Catholics, Jews, Italians, Negroes—someone else usually comes up with a classic line of defense: "Look at Einstein!" "Look at Carver!" "Look at Toscanini!" So, of course, Catholics (or Jews, or Italians, or Negroes) must be all right. They mean well, these defenders. But their approach is wrong. It is even bad. What a minority group wants is not the right to have geniuses among them but the right to have fools and scoundrels without being condemned as a group.

AGNES ELIZABETH BENEDICT, *Progress to Freedom* (1942)

Given the ethnic and racial hierarchies of American life, there are those who dish it out and those who have to take it. Some get to dish it out without ever having to take it, some take it from those above and dish it out to those below, and some find themselves in the position of always having to take it. Such a position is, psychologically and emotionally speaking, almost unbearable. Rage and despair accumulate with no place to go.

ELIZABETH STONE, *Black Sheep and Kissing Cousins* (1988)

You understand / That personally I feel / Indeed, I'd just as soon shake hands / Why, lots of them are just as / Why / As you and I.

EVE MERRIAM, "Restricted," *Jewish Life* (1947)

See also Chauvinism, Discrimination, Injustice, Race, Racism, Sexism.

PREPAREDNESS

She had the loaded handbag of someone who camps out and seldom goes home, or who imagines life must be full of emergencies.

MAVIS GALLANT, *A Fairly Good Time* (1970)

I always knew I would turn a corner and run into this day, but I ain't prepared for it nohow.

LOUISE MERIWETHER, *Daddy Was a Number Runner* (1970)

See also Foresight.

PRESENT

The present is the point of power.

KATE GREEN, *Night Angel* (1989)

No time like the present.

MARY DELARIVIER MANLEY, *The Lost Lover* (1696)

The present was his; he would arrange the past to suit it.

NADINE GORDIMER, *July's People* (1981)

If you let yourself be absorbed completely, if you surrender completely to the moments as they pass, you live more richly those moments.

ANNE MORROW LINDBERGH, *Bring Me a Unicorn* (1971)

I take a sun bath and listen to the hours, formulating, and disintegrating under the pines, and smell the resiny hardihood of the high noon hours. The world is lost in a blue haze of distances, and the immediate sleeps in a thin and finite sun.

ZELDA FITZGERALD, in Nancy Milford, *Zelda* (1970)

I have learned to live each day as it comes, and not to borrow trouble by dreading tomorrow. It is the dark menace of the future that makes cowards of us.

DOROTHY DIX, *Dorothy Dix: Her Book* (1926)

She seems to have had the ability to stand firmly on the rock of her past while living completely and unregretfully in the present.

MADELEINE L'ENGLE, *The Summer of the Great-Grandmother* (1974)

To live exhilaratingly in and for the moment is deadly serious work, fun of the most exhausting sort.

BARBARA GRIZZUTI HARRISON, *Off Center* (1980)

I want now to be of today. It is painful to be conscious of two worlds. The Wandering Jew in me seeks forgetfulness.

MARY ANTIN, *The Promised Land* (1912)

There is something about the present which we would not exchange, though we were offered a choice of all past ages to live in.

VIRGINIA WOOLF, *The Common Reader* (1925)

To those leaning on the sustaining infinite, today is big with blessings.

MARY BAKER EDDY, *Science and Health* (1875)

Every age, / Through being beheld too close, is ill-discerned / By those who have not lived past it.

ELIZABETH BARRETT BROWNING, *Aurora Leigh* (1856)

The future has become uninhabitable. Such hopelessness can arise, I think, only from an inability to face the present, to live in the present, to live as a responsible being among other beings in this sacred world here and now, which is all we have, and all we need, to found our hope upon.

URSULA K. LE GUIN, *Dancing at the Edge of the World* (1989)

See also Future, Past.

PRIDE

Pride is a tricky, glorious, double-edged feeling.

ADRIENNE RICH, "If Not With Others, How?" *Blood, Bread, and Poetry* (1986)

Supreme pride is supreme / renunciation. I did not want / to be the dead star / that absorbs borrowed light to revive itself.

ROSARIO CASTELLANOS, "Foreign Woman," in Joanna Bankier and Deirdre Lashgari, eds., *Women Poets of the World* (1983)

Wounded vanity knows when it is mortally hurt; and limps off the field, piteous, all disguises thrown away. But pride carries its banner to the last; and fast as it is driven from one field unfurls it in another.

HELEN HUNT JACKSON, *Ramona* (1884)

See also Self-Esteem.

PRINCIPLES

Whenever two good people argue over principles, they are both right.

MARIE VON EBNER-ESCHENBACH, *Aphorisms* (1905)

There is nothing as dangerous as an unembodied principle: no matter what blood flows, the principle comes first. The First Amendment absolutists operate precisely on unembodied principle.

ANDREA DWORKIN, *Letters From a War Zone* (1988)

See also Conscience, Morality, Values.

PRISON

You have put me in here a cub, but I will come out roaring like a lion, and I will make all hell howl!

CARRY NATION (1901), in Carleton Beals, *Cyclone Carry* (1962)

I always slept in my clothes, for I never knew what might happen. Not even my incarceration in a damp underground dungeon will make me give up the fight in which I am engaged for liberty and for the rights of the working people. To be shut from the sunlight is not pleasant but . . . I shall stand firm. To be in prison is no disgrace.

MOTHER JONES, in Linda Atkinson, *Mother Jones: The Most Dangerous Woman in America* (1978)

I lost all consciousness of any cause. I had no sense of being a radical, making a protest against a government, carrying on a nonviolent revolution. . . . I lost all feeling of my own identity. I reflected on the desolation of poverty, of destitution, of sickness and sin. That I would be free after thirty days meant nothing to me. I would never be free again.

DOROTHY DAY, *The Long Loneliness* (1952)

Jails and prisons are designed to break human beings, to convert the population into specimens in a zoo—obedient to our keepers, but dangerous to each other.

ANGELA DAVIS, *An Autobiography* (1974)

The character and mentality of the keepers may be of more importance in understanding prisons than the character and mentality of the kept.

JESSICA MITFORD, *Kind and Usual Punishment* (1973)

It was better to be in a jail where you could bang the walls than in a jail you could not see.

CARSON MCCULLERS, *The Member of the Wedding* (1946)

PRIVACY

The human animal needs a privacy seldom mentioned, freedom from intrusion. He needs a little privacy quite as much as he wants understanding or vitamins or exercise or praise.

PHYLLIS MCGINLEY, "A Lost Privilege," *The Province of the Heart* (1959)

Everyone old enough to have a secret is entitled to have some place to keep it.

JUDITH MARTIN, *Miss Manners' Guide to Rearing Perfect Children* (1984)

See also Rooms, Secrets, Solitude.

PRIVATION

Privation is the source of appetite.

SOR JUANA INÉS DE LA CRUZ (1691), in Margaret Sayers Peden, tr., *A Woman of Genius: The Intellectual Autobiography of Sor Juana Inés de la Cruz* (1982)

I drank at every vine. / The last was like the first. / I came upon no wine / So wonderful as thirst.

EDNA ST. VINCENT MILLAY, "Feast," *The Harp-Weaver* (1923)

All sorts of spiritual gifts come through privations, if they are accepted.

JANET ERSKINE STUART, in Maud Monahan, *Life and Letters of Janet Erskine Stuart* (1922)

See also Frugality, Hunger, Poverty, Suffering.

PRIVILEGE

Privilege is the greatest enemy of right.

MARIE VON EBNER-ESCHENBACH, *Aphorisms* (1905)

PROBLEMS

When one's own problems are unsolvable and all best efforts frustrated, it is lifesaving to listen to other people's problems.

SUZANNE MASSIE, *Journey* (1975)

Problems, unfortunately, can be addicting. Like it or not, we take a certain amount of pride in the very problems that distress us.

ELOISE RISTAD, *A Soprano on Her Head* (1982)

See also Crises, Trouble.

PROFIT

No mass appeal. Ergo no profit. Ergo no use. The current World Credo.

LUCILLE KALLEN, *The Tanglewood Murder* (1980)

The suppression of civil liberties is to many less a matter of horror than the curtailment of the freedom to profit.

MARYA MANNES, *But Will It Sell?* (1964)

A hobby is, of course, an abomination, as are all consuming interests and passions that do not lead directly to large, personal gain.

FRAN LEBOWITZ, *Metropolitan Life* (1978)

What most people don't seem to realize is that there is just as much money to be made out of the wreckage of a civilization as from the up-building of one.

MARGARET MITCHELL, *Gone With the Wind* (1936)

Society cares for the individual only in so far as he is profitable.

SIMONE DE BEAUVOIR, *The Coming of Age* (1970)

See also Business, Money, Surplus.

PROGRESS

Progress—progress is the dirtiest word in the language—who ever told us— / And made us believe it—that to take a step forward was necessarily, was always / A good idea?

EDNA ST. VINCENT MILLAY, untitled poem, *Make Bright the Arrows* (1940)

People tend to think that life really does progress for everyone eventually, that people progress, but actually only *some* people progress. The rest of the people don't.

ALICE WALKER, in Claudia Tate, ed., *Black Women Writers at Work* (1983)

"Progress" affects few. Only revolution can affect many.

ALICE WALKER, in Janet Sternburg, ed., *The Writer on Her Work,* vol. 1 (1980)

There have always been a large class of thinkers who deny that the world makes any progress. They say we move in a circle; that evils are never conquered, but only change their forms.

LYDIA MARIA CHILD, *Letters from New York,* 2nd Series (1845)

Perhaps all human progress stems from the tension between two basic drives: to have just what everyone else has and to have what no one has.

JUDITH STONE, *Light Elements: Essays in Science From Gravity to Levity* (1991)

If a man has lived in a tradition which tells him that nothing can be done about his human condition, to believe that progress is possible may well be the greatest revolution of all.

BARBARA WARD, lecture (1961)

Why do progress and beauty have to be so opposed?

ANNE MORROW LINDBERGH, *Hour of Gold, Hour of Lead* (1973)

See also Change, Innovations, Social Change.

PROSPERITY

Prosperity is like perfume, it often makes the head ache.

MARGARET CAVENDISH, DUCHESS OF NEWCASTLE, *Female Orations* (1662)

See also Success.

PROSTITUTION

Whether our reformers admit it or not, the economic and social inferiority of woman is responsible for prostitution.

EMMA GOLDMAN, "The Traffic in Women," *Anarchism* (1910)

The pimp who peddles good clean stuff is nevertheless engaged in prostitution.

PAULINE KAEL, *I Lost It at the Movies* (1965)

Well, there's a Book that says we're all sinners and I at least chose a sin that's made quite a few people happier than they were before they met me.

SALLY STANFORD, *The Lady of the House* (1966)

I've made so many movies playing a hooker that they don't pay me in the regular way any more. They leave it on the dresser.

SHIRLEY MacLAINE, *Out on a Limb* (1983)

PROTEST

If I cannot air this pain and alter it, I will surely die of it. That's the beginning of social protest.

AUDRE LORDE, in Claudia Tate, ed., *Black Women Writers at Work* (1983)

The human race / Has climbed on protest.

ELLA WHEELER WILCOX, "Protest," *Poems of Problems* (1914)

See also Movements, Revolution, Social Change.

PSYCHIATRY

Freud is the father of psychoanalysis. It had no mother.

GERMAINE GREER, *The Female Eunuch* (1971)

All the art of analysis consists in saying a truth only when the other person is ready for it, has been prepared for it by an organic process of gradation and evolution.

ANAÏS NIN, *The Diary of Anaïs Nin*, vol. 1 (1931–1934)

Analysts keep having to pick away at the scab that the patient tries to form between himself and the analyst to cover over his wounds. [The analyst] keeps the surface raw, so that the wound will heal properly.

JANET MALCOLM, *Psychoanalysis: The Impossible Profession* (1981)

Fortunately, analysis is not the only way to resolve inner conflicts. Life itself still remains a very effective therapist.

KAREN HORNEY, *Our Inner Conflicts* (1945)

When mental sickness increases until it reaches the danger point, do not exhaust yourself by efforts to trace back to original causes. Better accept them as inevitable and save your strength to fight against the effects.

GEORGE SAND (1837), in Marie Jenny Howe, *The Intimate Journal of George Sand* (1929)

"You seem to be reacting to your boyfriend as if he were your father," your shrink may say stonily (unless she is a strict Freudian, in which case she'll shut up and wait until you think of it yourself, a process that usually takes ten years. This is why strict Freudians have such lovely summer houses).

CYNTHIA HEIMEL, *Sex Tips for Girls* (1983)

I'm devoting my life to being a psychiatric patient. It's a vocation, like being a nun, only a lot more expensive.

JOYCE REBETA-BURDITT, *The Cracker Factory* (1977)

Psychology which explains everything / explains nothing / and we are still in doubt.

MARIANNE MOORE, "Marriage," *Selected Poems* (1935)

See also Mental Illness.

THE PUBLIC

Since there is no such entity as "the public," since the public is merely a number of individuals, any claimed or implied conflict of "the public interest" with private interests means that the interests of some men are to be sacrificed to the interests and wishes of others. Since the concept is so conveniently undefinable, its use rests only on any given gang's ability to proclaim that "The public, *c'est moi*"—and to maintain the claim at the point of a gun.

AYN RAND, *The Virtue of Selfishness* (1964)

Great bodies of people are never responsible for what they do.

VIRGINIA WOOLF, *A Room of One's Own* (1929)

People on the whole are very simple-minded in whatever country one finds them. They are so simple as to take literally, more often than not, the things their leaders tell them.

PEARL BUCK, *What America Means to Me* (1943)

The public is more easily swayed by persons than by principles.

RACHEL FIELD, *All This and Heaven Too* (1939)

Only when human sorrows are turned into a toy with glaring colors will baby people become interested—for a while at least. The people are a very fickle baby that must have new toys every day.

EMMA GOLDMAN, "The Traffic in Women," *Anarchism* (1910)

See also Public Opinion.

PUBLICITY

I don't care what is written about me so long as it isn't true.

KATHARINE HEPBURN, news item (1954)

You've got to win in sports—that's talent—but you've also got to learn how to remind everybody how you did win, and how often. That comes with experience.

BILLIE JEAN KING, *Billie Jean* (1982)

We must try to find ways to starve the terrorist and the hijacker of the oxygen of publicity on which they depend.

MARGARET THATCHER, in *The Times* (1985)

See also Attention.

PUBLIC OPINION

The world is not run by thought, nor by imagination, but by opinion.

ELIZABETH DREW, *The Modern Novel* (1926)

In America, public opinion is the leader.

FRANCES PERKINS, *People at Work* (1934)

I've seen public opinion shift like a wind and put out the very fire it lighted.

RACHEL FIELD, *All This and Heaven Too* (1939)

No written law has ever been more binding than unwritten custom supported by popular opinion.

CARRIE CHAPMAN CATT, speech (1900)

Thea was still under the belief that public opinion could be placated; that if you clucked often enough, the hens would mistake you for one of themselves.

WILLA CATHER, *The Song of the Lark* (1915)

See also Polls.

PUBLISHING

The share of the sympathetic publisher in the author's success—the true success so different from the ephemeral—is apt to be overlooked in these blatant days, so it is just as well that some of us should keep it in mind.

ELLEN GLASGOW, *Letters of Ellen Glasgow* (1958)

So, either you run your publishing business far away, where your writer can't get at it, or you publish right alongside of him—and have much more fun—and much more expense.

SYLVIA BEACH, on working with James Joyce, *Shakespeare and Company* (1956)

Publishers, theatrical managers, and critics ask not for the quality inherent in creative art, but will it meet with a good sale, will it suit the palate of the people? Alas, this palate is like a dumping ground; it relishes anything that needs no mental mastication.

EMMA GOLDMAN, "Minorities Versus Majorities," *Anarchism* (1910)

I don't believe in publishers. . . . I consider they're too grabby altogether. They love to keep the Sabbath and everything else they can lay their hands on.

AMANDA MCKITTRICK ROS, letter (1910)

The publishing business is an amoral industry.

CAROL EHRLICH, "The Woman Book Industry," in Joan Huber, ed., *Changing Women in a Changing Society* (1973)

See also Books, Magazines, Writing.

PURITY

Purity strikes me as the most mysterious of the virtues and the more I think about it the less I know about it.

FLANNERY O'CONNOR, in Sally Fitzgerald, ed., *The Habit of Being* (1979)

Purity is the ability to contemplate defilement.

SIMONE WEIL, *Gravity and Grace* (1947)

See also Innocence, Virtue.

PURPOSE

Nothing contributes so much to tranquilize the mind as a steady purpose—a point on which the soul may fix its intellectual eye.

MARY SHELLEY, *Frankenstein* (1818)

I am in the world / to change the world.

MURIEL RUKEYSER, "Käthe Kollwitz," *The Speed of Darkness* (1968)

See also Function, Goals, Motives.

Q

QUANTITY

The lure of quantity is the most dangerous of all.

SIMONE WEIL, *First and Last Notebooks* (1970)

Counting is the religion of this generation it is its hope and its salvation.

GERTRUDE STEIN, *Everybody's Autobiography* (1937)

Every true American likes to think in terms of thousands and millions. The word "million" is probably the most pleasure-giving vocable in the language.

AGNES REPPLIER, *Times and Tendencies* (1931)

One cannot lay a foundation by scattering stones, nor is a reputation for good work to be got by strewing volumes about the world.

ELLEN GLASGOW, *Letters of Ellen Glasgow* (1958)

Those who create are rare; those who cannot are numerous. Therefore, the latter are stronger.

COCO CHANEL, in *This Week* (1961)

See also Size, Surplus.

QUARRELING

They buried the hatchet, but in a shallow, well-marked grave.

DOROTHY WALWORTH, in *The Reader's Digest Dictionary of Quotations* (1968)

I don't even remember what Mother and I quarreled about: it is a continual quarrel that began when I reached puberty.

MARGE PIERCY, *Braided Lives* (1982)

In time they quarreled, of course, and about an abstraction,—as young people often do, as mature people almost never do.

WILLA CATHER, "Coming, Aphrodite!" *Youth and the Bright Medusa* (1920)

It was completely fruitless to quarrel with the world, whereas the quarrel with oneself was occasionally fruitful, and always, she had to admit, interesting.

MAY SARTON, *Mrs. Stevens Hears the Mermaids Singing* (1965)

For forty-seven years they had been married. How deep back the stubborn, gnarled roots of the quarrel reached, no one could say—but only now, when tending to the needs of others no longer shackled them together, the roots swelled up visible, split the earth between them, and the tearing shook even to the children, long since grown.

TILLIE OLSEN, title story, *Tell Me a Riddle* (1956)

Never go to bed mad. Stay up and fight.

PHYLLIS DILLER, *Phyllis Diller's Housekeeping Hints* (1966)

See also Conflict.

QUESTIONS

If we would have new knowledge, we must get a whole world of new questions.

SUSANNE K. LANGER, *Philosophy in a New Key* (1942)

Bromidic though it may sound, some questions *don't* have answers, which is a terribly difficult lesson to learn.

KATHARINE GRAHAM, in Jane Howard, "The Power That Didn't Corrupt," *Ms.* (1974)

Once you start asking questions, innocence is gone.

MARY ASTOR, *A Life on Film* (1967)

Asking questions in therapy would be so helpful if anyone ever answered them accurately. But no one ever does.

VIRGINIA MAE AXLINE, *Dibs: In Search of Self* (1965)

Hypothetical questions get hypothetical answers.

JOAN BAEZ, *Daybreak* (1968)

See also Answers, Curiosity, Why.

QUILTS

My focus on silence is to be understood as an intrinsic part of the body's search for meaning amongst the noisy assaults of everyday life. . . . What quilts have brought to the viewing of art generally is this intervening layer of silence, of collected thought and concerted attention.

RADKA DONNELL, *Quilts as Women's Art: A Quilt Poetic* (1990)

knotted with love / the quilts sing on.

TERESA PALMA ACOSTA, "My Mother Pieced Quilts," in Joanna Bankier and Deirdre Lashgari, eds., *Women Poets of the World* (1983)

What my mother teaches me are the essential lessons of the quilt: that people and actions do move in multiple directions at once.

ELSA BARKLEY BROWN, "African-American Women's Quilting," in *SIGNS* (1989)

QUOTATIONS

The most disheartening tendency common among readers is to tear out one sentence from a work, as a criterion of the writer's ideas or personality.

EMMA GOLDMAN, introduction, *Anarchism* (1910)

Sometimes it seems the only accomplishment my education ever bestowed on me, the ability to think in quotations.

MARGARET DRABBLE, *A Summer Bird-Cage* (1962)

I love them because it is a joy to find thoughts one might have, beautifully expressed with much authority by someone recognizedly wiser than oneself.

MARLENE DIETRICH, *Marlene Dietrich's ABC* (1962)

The next best thing to being clever is being able to quote some one who is.

MARY PETTIBONE POOLE, *A Glass Eye at a Keyhole* (1938)

I always have a quotation for everything—it saves original thinking.

DOROTHY L. SAYERS, *Have His Carcase* (1932)

R

RACE

Race, what is that? Race is a competition, somebody winning and somebody losing. . . . Blood doesn't run in races! Come on!

BEAH RICHARDS, in Brian Lanker, *I Dream a World* (1989)

Light came to me when I realized that I did not have to consider any racial group as a whole. God made them duck by duck and that was the only way I could see them.

ZORA NEALE HURSTON, *Dust Tracks on a Road* (1942)

What a child does not know and does not want to know of race and color and class, he learns soon enough as he grows to see each man flipped inexorably into some predestined groove like a penny or a sovereign in a banker's rack.

BERYL MARKHAM, *West With the Night* (1942)

There will be strange ebbs and flows in the tide of race feelings.

AMY LEVY, *Reuben Sachs* (1888)

No matter what learned scientists may say, race is, politically speaking, not the beginning of humanity but its end, not the origin of peoples but their decay, not the natural birth of man but his unnatural death.

HANNAH ARENDT, *Origins of Totalitarianism* (1951)

See also Racism.

RACISM

Racism is so universal in this country, so widespread and deep-seated, that it is invisible because it is so normal.

SHIRLEY CHISHOLM, *Unbought and Unbossed* (1970)

Racism is so extreme and so pervasive in our American society that no black individual lives in an atmosphere of freedom.

MARGARET WALKER, in Janet Sternburg, ed., *The Writer on Her Work,* vol. 1 (1980)

O we are all racist we are all sexist some of us only some of us are the targets of racism of sexism of homophobia of class denigration but we all all breathe in racism with the dust in the streets with the words we read and we struggle those of us who struggle we struggle endlessly endlessly to think and be and act differently from all that.

ROSARIO MORALES, "We're All in the Same Boat," in Cherríe Moraga and Gloria Anzaldúa, eds., *This Bridge Called My Back* (1983)

Race prejudice is not only a shadow over the colored—it is a shadow over all of us, and the shadow is darkest over those who feel it least and allow its evil effects to go on.

PEARL BUCK, *What America Means to Me* (1943)

Racism is used *both* to create false differences among us *and* to mask very significant ones.

MIRTHA QUINTANALES, "I Paid Very Hard for My Immigrant Ignorance," in Cherríe Moraga and Gloria Anzaldúa, eds., *This Bridge Called My Back* (1983)

When a white man in Africa by accident looks into the eyes of a native and sees the human being (which it is his chief preoccupation to avoid), his sense of guilt, which he denies, fumes up in resentment and he brings down the whip.

DORIS LESSING, *The Grass Is Singing* (1950)

The main barrier between East and West today is that the white man is not willing to give up his superiority and the colored man is no longer willing to endure his inferiority.

PEARL BUCK, *What America Means to Me* (1943)

In the last few years, race relations in America have entered upon a period of intensified craziness wherein fear of being *called* a racist has so thoroughly overwhelmed fear of *being* a racist that we are in danger of losing sight of the distinction.

FLORENCE KING, *Lump It or Leave It* (1990)

Can you imagine if this country were not so afflicted with racism? Can you imagine what it would be like if the vitality, humor, and resilience of the black American were infused throughout this country?

MAYA ANGELOU, in Brian Lanker, *I Dream a World* (1989)

See also Blacks and Whites.

RAIN

Surround of rainbows / Listen / The rain comes upon us / Restore us.

MERIDEL LE SUEUR, "Surround of Rainbows," *Rites of Ancient Ripening* (1975)

It's raining fish-hooks and hammer handles!

LAURA INGALLS WILDER, *On the Banks of Plum Creek* (1937)

In the country they say, "We'll come when it rains." When the soft rains come soaking through the day and into the night, they go visiting, they sit around the kitchen table in a dry place and talk of children and crops.

YVETTE NELSON, *We'll Come When It Rains* (1982)

See also Weather.

RAPE

Perhaps it is the only crime in which the victim becomes the accused.

FREDA ADLER, *Sisters in Crime* (1975)

No zoologist, as far as I know, has ever observed that animals rape in their natural habitat, the wild.

SUSAN BROWNMILLER, *Against Our Will: Men, Women and Rape* (1975)

Rapists perform for sexist males the same function that the Ku Klux Klan performed for racist whites; they keep women in their "place" through fear.

JO-ANN EVANS GARDNER (1972), in Karen DeCrow, *Sexist Justice* (1974)

See also Violence.

RATIONALITY

A rational process is a *moral* process.

AYN RAND, *Atlas Shrugged* (1957)

See also Irrationality, Logic, Reason.

READING

No entertainment is so cheap as reading, nor any pleasure so lasting.

LADY MARY WORTLEY MONTAGU, letter (1753), in Octave Thanet, ed., *The Best Letters of Lady Mary Wortley Montagu* (1901)

The greatest gift is a passion for reading. It is cheap, it consoles, it distracts, it excites, it gives you knowledge of the world and experience of a wide kind. It is a moral illumination.

ELIZABETH HARDWICK, in George Plimpton, ed., *The Writer's Chapbook* (1989)

I learned from the age of two or three that any room in our house, at any time of day, was there to read in, or to be read to.

EUDORA WELTY, *One Writer's Beginnings* (1984)

When I only begin to read, I forget I'm on this world. It lifts me on wings with high thoughts.

ANZIA YEZIERSKA, "Wings," *Hungry Hearts* (1920)

I easily sink into mere absorption of what other minds have done, and should like a whole life for that alone.

GEORGE ELIOT, letter (1872), in J. W. Cross, *George Eliot's Life as Related in Her Letters and Journals* (1884)

I have sometimes dreamt, at least, that when the Day of Judgment dawns and the great conquerors and lawyers and statesmen come to receive their rewards—their crowns, their laurels, their names carved indelibly upon imperishable marble—the Almighty will turn to Peter and will say, not without a certain envy when He sees us coming with our books under our arms, "Look, these need no reward. We have nothing to give them here. They have loved reading."

VIRGINIA WOOLF, "How Should One Read a Book?" *The Second Common Reader* (1932)

Ever since I was first read to, then started reading to myself, there has never been a line read that I didn't *hear*. As my eyes followed the sentence, a voice was saying it silently to me. It isn't my mother's voice, or the voice of any person I can identify, certainly not my own. It is human, but inward, and it is inwardly that I listen to it. It is to me the voice of the story or the poem itself.

EUDORA WELTY, *One Writer's Beginnings* (1984)

The pleasure of all reading is doubled when one lives with another who shares the same books.

KATHERINE MANSFIELD, letter (1928)

I have only ever read one book in my life, and that is *White Fang*. It's so frightfully good I've never bothered to read another.

NANCY MITFORD, *The Pursuit of Love* (1945)

See also Books, Literature.

REAL

Generally, by the time you are Real, most of your hair has been loved off, and your eyes drop out, and you get loose in the joints and very shabby. But these things don't matter at all, because once you are Real, you can't be ugly, except to people who don't understand.

MARGERY WILLIAMS, *The Velveteen Rabbit* (1927)

The longer you wear pearls, the realer they become.

COLETTE, *Cheri* (1930)

The real thing creates its own poetry.

ANZIA YEZIERSKA, *Red Ribbon on a White Horse* (1950)

Nothing became real for her until she had had time to live it over again. An actual occurrence was nothing but the blankness of a shock, then the knowledge that something had happened; afterwards one could creep back and look into one's mind and find new things in it, clear and solid. It was like waiting outside the hen-house

until the hen came off the nest and then going in to look for the egg.

ELIZABETH BOWEN, "Coming Home," *Early Stories* (1951)

The Real is the sole foundation of the Ideal.

GRACE AGUILAR, *Amete and Yafeh* (1850)

See also Reality, Truth.

REALITY

What we call reality is an agreement that people have arrived at to make life more livable.

LOUISE NEVELSON, *Dawns + Dusks* (1976)

Fluidity and discontinuity are central to the reality in which we live.

MARY CATHERINE BATESON, *Composing a Life* (1989)

A test of what is real is that it is hard and rough. Joys are found in it, not pleasure. What is pleasant belongs to dreams.

SIMONE WEIL, *Gravity and Grace* (1947)

The dream is real, my friends. The failure to realize it is the only unreality.

TONI CADE BAMBARA, *The Salt Eaters* (1980)

My nightmares have become news stories.

JENNY HOLZER, *Truisms* (1991)

Reality, like God and History, tends to direct people to wherever they want to go.

PAULINE KAEL, *I Lost It at the Movies* (1965)

The people who say you are not facing reality actually mean that you are not facing *their idea* of reality. Reality is above all else a variable, and nobody is qualified to say that he or she knows exactly what it is. As a matter of fact, with a firm enough commitment, you can sometimes create a reality which did not exist before.

MARGARET HALSEY, *No Laughing Matter* (1977)

We live in a fantasy world, a world of illusion. The great task in life is to find reality.

IRIS MURDOCH, in Rachel Billington, "Profile: Iris Murdoch," *London Times* (1983)

My greatest enemy is reality. I have fought it successfully for thirty years.

MARGARET ANDERSON, *My Thirty Years' War* (1930)

He knew that in so far as one denies what is, one is possessed by what is not, the compulsions, the fantasies, the terrors that flock to fill the void.

URSULA K. LE GUIN, *The Lathe of Heaven* (1971)

The world comes second hand—fifth hand—to us and the illusion that it is fresh because it is shown as a picture of an actual place or is given as a "true account" by some reporter who claims to have been "there" divides man into incalculable parts without any true center.

JOSEPHINE HERBST, *New Green World* (1954)

Colors seen by candle-light / Will not look the same by day.

ELIZABETH BARRETT BROWNING, "The Lady's 'Yes,'" *Poems* (1844)

Dismounted from her dream, she could not find footing again on solid ground. Her realities repelled her.

MARY O'HARA, *Thunderhead* (1943)

See also Real, Truth.

REASON

The sign of an intelligent people is their ability to control emotions by the application of reason.

MARYA MANNES, *More in Anger* (1958)

I'll not listen to reason. . . . Reason always means what someone else has got to say.

ELIZABETH GASKELL, *Cranford* (1853)

There was always a real reason for everything— why spoons tarnished, and jam furred, and people declined into God, or drink, or card games.

EDNA O'BRIEN, "A Woman by the Seaside," *Mrs. Reinhardt* (1978)

See also Explanations, Logic, Rationality.

RECEIVING

Giving is not at all interesting; but receiving is, there is no doubt about it, delightful.

ROSE MACAULAY, *A Casual Commentary* (1926)

See also Giving, Gratitude.

REFUGEES

Therefore the sudden violent dispossession accompanying a refugee flight is much more than the loss of a permanent home and a traditional occupation, or than the parting from close friends and familiar places. It is also the death of the person one has become in a particular context, and every refugee must be his or her own midwife at the painful process of rebirth.

DERVLA MURPHY, *Tibetan Foothold* (1966)

See also Borders, Immigrants.

REFUSAL

You start by saying no to requests. Then if you have to go to yes, OK. But if you start with yes, you can't go to no.

MILDRED PERLMAN, in *New York Times* (1975)

REGRET

I have made it a rule of my life never to regret and never to look back. Regret is an appalling waste of energy . . . you can't build on it; it's only good for wallowing in.

KATHERINE MANSFIELD, *Bliss* (1920)

The bitterest tears shed over graves are for words left unsaid and deeds left undone.

HARRIET BEECHER STOWE, *Little Foxes* (1871)

This is the bitterest of all,—to wear the yoke of our own wrong-doing.

GEORGE ELIOT, *Daniel Deronda* (1874)

But that was the best time of my life, and only now that it has gone from me forever—only now do I realize it.

NATALIA GINZBURG, *The Little Virtues* (1962)

Regrets are as personal as fingerprints.

MARGARET CULKIN BANNING, in *Reader's Digest* (1958)

See also Remorse.

REJECTION

From this haunting feeling of being not wanted, which remained a recurrent haunt through life, I found two ways of escape, both of which in changing form also persisted. One was the invention of gods, the other was personal efficiency in work.

ANNA LOUISE STRONG, *I Change Worlds* (1935)

I think all great innovations are built on rejections.

LOUISE NEVELSON, *Dawns + Dusks* (1976)

RELATIONSHIPS

We had a lot in common, I loved him and he loved him.

SHELLEY WINTERS (1952), in Susan Strasberg, *Bittersweet* (1980)

Can I ever know you / Or you know me?

SARA TEASDALE, "The Mystery," *Flame and Shadow* (1920)

Do we really know anybody? Who does not wear one face to hide another?

FRANCES MARION, *Westward the Dream* (1948)

When you hug someone, you learn something else about them. An important something else.

E. L. KONIGSBURG, *From the Mixed-Up Files of Mrs. Basil E. Frankweiler* (1967)

Union is only possible to those who are units. To be fit for relations in time, souls, whether of Man or Woman, must be able to do without them in the spirit.

MARGARET FULLER, "The Great Lawsuit," in *The Dial* (1843)

Intimate relationships cannot substitute for a life plan. But to have any meaning or viability at all, a life plan must include intimate relationships.

HARRIET LERNER, *Dance of Intimacy* (1989)

She felt the natural ties of affinity rather than the conventional blind ties of the blood.

NADINE GORDIMER, "La Vie Boheme," *Face to Face* (1949)

I have noticed before that there is a category of acquaintanceship that is not friendship or business or romance, but speculation, fascination.

JANE SMILEY, *Good Will* (1989)

All tragedies deal with fated meetings; how else could there be a play? Fate deals its stroke; sor-

row is purged, or turned to rejoicing; there is death, or triumph; there has been a meeting, and a change. No one will ever make a tragedy—and that is as well, for one could not bear it—whose grief is that the principals never met.

MARY RENAULT, *The Mask of Apollo* (1966)

Underground issues from one relationship or context invariably fuel our fires in another.

HARRIET LERNER, *The Dance of Anger* (1985)

Ah, the relationships we get into just to get out of the ones we are not brave enough to say are over.

JULIA PHILLIPS, *You'll Never Eat Lunch in This Town Again* (1991)

The long-term accommodation that protects marriage and other such relationships is . . . forgetfulness.

ALICE WALKER, *You Can't Keep a Good Woman Down* (1981)

Relationships that do not end peacefully, do not end at all.

MERRIT MALLOY, in Merrit Malloy and Shauna Sorensen, *The Quotable Quote Book* (1990)

See also Friendship, Intimacy, Lovers, Marriage, Togetherness.

RELIGION

Religion is love; in no case is it logic.

BEATRICE POTTER WEBB, *My Apprenticeship* (1926)

Religion is a temper, not a pursuit.

HARRIET MARTINEAU, *Society in America* (1837)

And what is religion, you might ask. It's a technology of living.

TONI CADE BAMBARA, *The Salt Eaters* (1980)

Religion controls inner space; inner space controls outer space.

ZSUZSANNA E. BUDAPEST, "Self-Blessing Ritual," in Carol P. Christ and Judith Plaskow, *Womanspirit Rising* (1979)

Workers need poetry more than bread. They need that their life should be a poem. They need some light from eternity. Religion alone can be the source of such poetry.

SIMONE WEIL, *Gravity and Grace* (1947)

To this day I do not know whether the power which has inspired my works is something related to religion, or is indeed religion itself.

KÄTHE KOLLWITZ, letter, in Hans Kollwitz, ed., *The Diaries and Letters of Käthe Kollwitz* (1955)

Extreme happiness invites religion almost as much as extreme misery.

DODIE SMITH, *I Capture the Castle* (1948)

What is your religion? I mean—not what you know about religion but the belief that helps you most?

GEORGE ELIOT, *Middlemarch* (1871)

In fact, to this very day, common sense in religion is rare, and we are too often trying to be heroic instead of just ordinarily good and kind.

DOROTHY DAY (1958) in William D. Miller, *Dorothy Day: A Biography* (1982)

Religion, to be a factor in experience, must be pleasurable.

MARY AUSTIN, *Earth Horizon* (1932)

There is no religion without love, and people may talk as much as they like about their religion, but if it does not teach them to be good and kind to man and beast, it is all a sham.

ANNA SEWELL, *Black Beauty* (1877)

On this earth there are many roads to heaven; and each traveler supposes his own to be the best. But they must all unite in one road at the last. It is only Omniscience that can decide. And it will then be found that no sect is excluded because of its faith.

ELIZA LESLIE, *Miss Leslie's Behavior Book: A Guide and Manual for Ladies* (1859)

I would no more quarrel with a man because of his religion than I would because of his art.

MARY BAKER EDDY, *Miscellaneous Writings 1883–1896* (1897)

How strange that some people cannot believe in both the Book of Nature and the Book of God.

MARIA MITCHELL (1874), in Phebe Mitchell Kendall, ed., Maria Mitchell, Life, Letters, and Journals (1896)

Science and religion, religion and science, put it as I may, they are two sides of the same glass, through which we see darkly until these two, focusing together, reveal the truth.

PEARL BUCK, *A Bridge for Passing* (1962)

The devil makes a great deal of the religion we see.

ELIZABETH RUNDLE CHARLES, *Chronicles of the Schönberg-Cotta Family* (1863)

It must in candor be said that his religion sat upon him lightly.

ILKA CHASE, *I Love Miss Tilli Bean* (1946)

Parsons always seem to be specially horrified about things like sunbathing and naked bodies. They don't mind poverty and misery and cruelty to animals nearly so much.

SUSAN ERTZ, *The Story of Julian* (1931)

"There is no doubt, I suppose," retorted our grandmother, "about heaven repaying you; but there seems to be a good deal of doubt whether it will be in current coin."

ELIZABETH RUNDLE CHARLES, *Chronicles of the Schönberg-Cotta Family* (1863)

The spirit of religious totalitarianism is abroad in the world; it is in the very air we breathe today in this land. Everywhere are those who claim to have a corner on righteousness, on direct access to God. . . . The bigots of the world are having a heyday.

SONIA JOHNSON, *From Housewife to Heretic* (1981)

Religion supports and perpetuates the social organization it reflects.

RIANE EISLER, *The Chalice and the Blade* (1987)

All outward forms of religion are almost useless, and are the causes of endless strife. . . . Believe there is a great power silently working all things for good, behave yourself and never mind the rest.

BEATRIX POTTER, in Leslie Linder, transcriber, *Journals 1881–1897* (1966)

It may be that religion is dead, and if it is, we had better know it and set ourselves to try to discover other sources of moral strength before it is too late.

PEARL BUCK, What America Means to Me (1943)

And what a flurry of preparation for the Passover feast! What a chopping of fish and a simmering of soup and a baking of *tsimmes* and a roasting of capon and an assembling of *taigloch!* Grandma was in her element, humming Russian tunes, a beaming earth mother with her sleeves rolled up and her eyes shining. I did love Passover. And Grandma's observance of it was devout, but it was the domestic, the kitchen side of religion.

EDITH KONECKY, Allegra Maud Goldman (1976)

See also Christianity, God, Judaism, Mysticism, Spirituality, Theology.

REMEDIES

Desperate ills need desperate remedies.

AGATHA CHRISTIE, The Mystery of the Blue Train (1928)

REMEMBRANCE

Remember me when I am gone away, / Gone far away into the silent land.

CHRISTINA ROSSETTI, "Remember" (1849), Goblin Market (1862)

O may I join the choir invisible / Of those immortal dead who live again / In minds made better by their presence.

GEORGE ELIOT, "O May I Join the Choir Invisible," The Legend of Jubal and Other Poems, Old and New (1867)

Someone, I tell you / will remember us. / We are oppressed by / fears of oblivion.

SAPPHO, "Someone, I Tell You" (6th century B.C.), in Willis Barnstone, Sappho (1965)

Better by far you should forget and smile / Than that you should remember and be sad.

CHRISTINA ROSSETTI, "Remember" (1849), Goblin Market (1862)

Nothing is more consuming, or more illogical, than the desire for remembrance.

ELLEN GLASGOW, The Woman Within (1954)

See also Memory, Nostalgia.

REMORSE

Remorse is the poison of life.

CHARLOTTE BRONTË, Jane Eyre (1847)

See also Regret.

RENUNCIATION

Renunciation is submission to time.

SIMONE WEIL, The Notebooks of Simone Weil (1951)

We only possess what we renounce; what we do not renounce escapes from us.

SIMONE WEIL, Gravity and Grace (1947)

REPUTATION

Until you've lost your reputation, you never realize what a burden it was or what freedom really is.

MARGARET MITCHELL, Gone With the Wind (1936)

Good repute is water carried in a sieve. / Only if you can grasp the wind in your fist / or hold an elephant chained secure with a hair / will you maybe succeed in keeping your good name clear.

LALLESWARI (14th century), in Joanna Bankier and Deirdre Lashgari, eds., Women Poets of the World (1983)

See also Honor.

RESEARCH

Research is formalized curiosity. It is poking and prying with a purpose.

ZORA NEALE HURSTON, Dust Tracks on a Road (1942)

The way to do research is to attack the facts at the point of greatest astonishment.

CELIA GREEN, The Decline and Fall of Science (1977)

See also Learning, Science.

RESENTMENT

People don't resent having nothing nearly as much as too little.

IVY COMPTON-BURNETT, *A Family and a Fortune* (1939)

See also Anger, Bitterness.

RESIGNATION

I am not resigned: I am not sure life is long enough to learn that lesson.

GEORGE ELIOT, *The Mill on the Floss* (1860)

I have often observed that resignation is never so perfect as when the blessing denied begins to lose somewhat of its value in our eyes.

JANE AUSTEN, *Pride and Prejudice* (1813)

See also Acceptance.

RESPECT

The respect that is only bought by gold is not worth much.

FRANCES ELLEN WATKINS HARPER, "Our Greatest Want," in *Anglo-African Magazine* (1859)

See also Admiration.

RESPONSIBILITY

Nothing strengthens the judgment and quickens the conscience like individual responsibility.

ELIZABETH CADY STANTON, "Solitude of Self" (1892)

The one with the primary responsibility to the individual's future is that individual.

DORCAS HARDY, in *Christian Science Monitor* (1987)

The first rule in opera is the first rule in life: see to everything yourself.

NELLIE MELBA, *Melodies and Memories* (1925)

No matter how lofty you are in your department, the responsibility for what your lowliest assistant is doing is yours.

BESSIE ROWLAND JAMES, *Adlai's Almanac* (1952)

There's no difference between one's killing and making decisions that will send others to kill. It's exactly the same thing, or even worse.

GOLDA MEIR, quoted by Oriana Fallaci in *L'Europeo* (1973)

I was thinking of my patients, and how the worst moment for them was when they discovered they were masters of their own fate. It was not a matter of bad or good luck. When they could no longer blame fate, they were in despair.

ANAÏS NIN, *The Diary of Anaïs Nin,* vol. 2 (1934–1939)

Parents can only give good advice or put them on the right paths, but the final forming of a person's character lies in their own hands.

ANNE FRANK, *Diary of a Young Girl* (1952)

See also Duty.

RESTLESSNESS

I am a restlessness inside a stillness inside a restlessness.

DODIE SMITH, *I Capture the Castle* (1948)

Now more than ever do I realize that I shall never be content with a sedentary life, and that I shall always be haunted by thoughts of a sun-drenched *elsewhere*.

ISABELLE EBERHARDT (1901), *The Passionate Nomad* (1988)

See also Discontent.

RETIREMENT

Retirement . . . may be looked upon either as a prolonged holiday or as a rejection, a being thrown on to the scrap-heap.

SIMONE DE BEAUVOIR, *The Coming of Age* (1970)

Retirement revives the sorrow of parting, the feeling of abandonment, solitude and uselessness that is caused by the loss of some beloved person.

SIMONE DE BEAUVOIR, *The Coming of Age* (1970)

My voice had a long, nonstop career. It deserves to be put to bed with quiet and dignity, not yanked out every once in a while to see if it can still do what it used to do. It can't.

BEVERLY SILLS, in *Time* (1983)

See also Age, Leisure.

REUNIONS

Reunions are always fraught with awkward tensions—the necessity to account for oneself; the attempt to find, through memories, an ember of the old emotions.

ANITA SHREVE, *Eden Close* (1989)

See also Absence, Meetings.

REVENGE

It would seem that in history it's never a tooth for a tooth, but a thousand, a hundred thousand for one.

SYBILLE BEDFORD, *A Favorite of the Gods* (1963)

Revenge was a very wild kind of justice, and Hewson was a civilized man. He believed in the Good, in the balance of things, and in an eventual, tremendous pay-day.

ELIZABETH BOWEN, "Making Arrangements," *Early Stories* (1951)

See also Vengeance.

REVERIE

Leisure for reverie, gay or somber, does much to enrich life.

MIRIAM BEARD, *Realism in Romantic Japan* (1930)

To make a prairie it takes a clover and one bee, / One clover, and a bee, / And revery. / The revery alone will do, / If bees are few.

EMILY DICKINSON, *Poems, Third Series* (1896)

See also Dreams, Fantasy.

REVOLUTION

Revolution is the festival of the oppressed.

GERMAINE GREER, *The Female Eunuch* (1971)

It is better to die on your feet than to live on your knees.

DOLORES IBÁRRURI, speech (1936)

It is impossible to rise to freedom, from the midst of corruptions, without strong convulsions. They are the salutary crises of a serious disease. We are in want of a terrible political fever, to carry off our foul humors.

MARIE-JEANNE ROLAND (1791), in Lydia Maria Child, *Memoirs of Madame de Staël and of Madame Roland* (1847)

No real social change has ever come about without a revolution.

EMMA GOLDMAN, title essay, *Anarchism* (1910)

The revolution begins at home.

CHERRÍE MORAGA AND GLORIA ANZALDÙA, in Cherríe Moraga and Gloria Anzaldúa, eds., *This Bridge Called My Back* (1983)

By definition, revolutions are not linear, one step at a time, event A leading to event B, and so on. Many causes operate on each other at once. Revolutions shift into place suddenly, like the pattern in a kaleidoscope. They do not so much proceed as crystallize.

MARILYN FERGUSON, *The Aquarian Conspiracy* (1980)

To die for the revolution is a one-shot deal; to live for the revolution means taking on the more difficult commitment of changing our day-to-day life patterns.

FRANCES M. BEAL, "Double Jeopardy: To Be Black and Female," in Robin Morgan, *Sisterhood Is Powerful* (1970)

The classic trap for any revolutionary is always, "What's your alternative?"

SHULAMITH FIRESTONE, *The Dialectic of Sex* (1970)

When you talk of revolution . . . you never talk of the day after.

STORM JAMESON, *The Clash* (1922)

The optimism of politics before a revolution is exceeded only by the pessimism of politics after one.

CATHARINE STIMPSON, "'Thy Neighbor's Wife, Thy Neighbor's Servants': Women's Liberation and Black Civil Rights," in Vivian Gornick and Barbara K. Moran, *Woman in Sexist Society* (1971)

The most radical revolutionary will become a conservative on the day after the revolution.

HANNAH ARENDT, in *New Yorker* (1970)

If misery spelled revolt, we should have had nothing but revolt from the beginning of time. On the contrary, it is quite rare.

CHRISTINA STEAD, *House of All Nations* (1938)

The word "revolution" is a word for which you kill, for which you die, for which you send the laboring masses to their death, but which does not possess any content.

SIMONE WEIL, *Oppression and Liberty* (1955)

See also Change, Social Change, War.

REWARD

Every kind of reward constitutes a degradation of energy.

SIMONE WEIL, *Gravity and Grace* (1947)

RICH

I've been rich and I've been poor. Believe me, honey, rich is better.

SOPHIE TUCKER, *Some of These Days* (1945)

I do want to get rich but I never want to do what there is to do to get rich.

GERTRUDE STEIN, *Everybody's Autobiography* (1937)

If all the rich men in the world divided up their money amongst themselves, there wouldn't be enough to go round.

CHRISTINA STEAD, *House of All Nations* (1938)

When you say fiscal responsibility, it seems to me that you really mean rich people keeping their money.

ALICE ADAMS, *Listening to Billie* (1978)

Rich folks always talks hard times.

LILLIAN SMITH, *Strange Fruit* (1944)

The rich have a passion for bargains as lively as it is pointless.

FRANÇOISE SAGAN, *The Painted Lady* (1983)

The difference between rich and poor is that the poor do everything with their own hands and the rich hire hands to do things.

BETTY SMITH, *A Tree Grows in Brooklyn* (1943)

The rich are never threatened by the poor—they do not notice them.

MARIE DE FRANCE (12th century), in Jeanette Beer, tr., *Medieval Fables of Marie de France* (1981)

To put it quite crudely . . . the poor don't really know how the rich live, and the rich don't know how the poor live, and to find out is really enchanting to both of them.

AGATHA CHRISTIE, *Endless Night* (1968)

It is very much easier for a rich man to invest and grow richer than for the poor man to begin investing at all. And this is also true of nations.

BARBARA WARD, *The Rich Nations and the Poor Nations* (1962)

Now that he was rich he was not thought ignorant any more, but simply eccentric.

MAVIS GALLANT, *The Pegnitz Junction* (1973)

The richer your friends, the more they will cost you.

ELISABETH MARBURY, *My Crystal Ball* (1923)

The old Eskimo hunters she had known in her childhood thought the riches of life were intelligence, fearlessness, and love. A man with these gifts was rich.

JEAN CRAIGHEAD GEORGE, *Julie of the Wolves* (1972)

It is easier to give all your goods to feed the poor, or not to have any goods—only your virtues, to boast of—than it is to judge the rich with charity.

CORRA HARRIS, in Martha Bensley Bruère and Mary Ritter Beard, *Laughing Their Way* (1934)

See also Aristocracy, Luxury, Wealth.

RIGHTS

Individual rights are not subject to a public vote; a majority has no right to vote away the rights of a minority.

AYN RAND, *The Virtue of Selfishness* (1964)

There's no question in my mind but that rights are never won unless people are willing to fight for them.

ELEANOR SMEAL, speech (1985)

A right which goes unrecognized by anybody is not worth very much.

SIMONE WEIL, *The Need for Roots* (1952)

It must become a right of every person to die of old age. And if we secure this right for ourselves, we can, coincidentally, assure it for the planet.

ALICE WALKER, *Living by the Word* (1988)

See also Equality, Justice.

RISK

The human soul has need of security and also of risk. The fear of violence or of hunger or of any other extreme evil is a sickness of the soul. The boredom produced by a complete absence of risk is also a sickness of the soul.

SIMONE WEIL, *Selected Essays 1934–1943* (1962)

The fullness of life is in the hazards of life. And, at the worst, there is that in us which can turn defeat into victory.

EDITH HAMILTON, The Great Age of Greek Literature (1942)

A ship in port is safe, but that's not what ships are built for.

GRACE MURRAY HOPPER, in Ethlie Ann Vare and Greg Ptacek, *Mothers of Invention* (1987)

Our whole way of life today is dedicated to the removal of risk. Cradle to grave we are supported, insulated, and isolated from the risks of life—and if we fall, our government stands ready with Bandaids of every size.

SHIRLEY TEMPLE BLACK, speech (1967)

If you're never scared or embarrassed or hurt, it means you never take any chances.

JULIA SOREL, *See How She Runs* (1978)

Please know that I am aware of the hazards. I want to do it because I want to do it. Women must try to do things as men have tried. When they fail, their failure must be but a challenge to others.

AMELIA EARHART, letter to her husband (1937)

See also Adventure, Courage, Danger, Security.

RITUAL

Ritual and myth are like seed crystals of new patterns that can eventually reshape culture around them.

STARHAWK, *Truth or Dare* (1987)

Ritual is the way we carry the presence of the sacred. Ritual is the spark that must not go out.

CHRISTINA BALDWIN, *Life's Companion, Journal Writing as a Spiritual Quest* (1990)

I believe that we often disguise pain through ritual and it may be the only solace we have.

RITA MAE BROWN, *Starting From Scratch* (1988)

I have elsewhere tried to show that Art is not the handmaid of Religion, but that Art in some sense springs out of Religion, and that between them is a connecting link, a bridge, and that bridge is Ritual.

JANE HARRISON, *Ancient Art and Ritual* (1913)

Ritual is the act of sanctifying action—even ordinary actions—so that it has meaning: I can light a candle because I need the light or because the candle represents the light I need.

CHRISTINA BALDWIN, *Life's Companion, Journal Writing as a Spiritual Quest* (1990)

The preparation for the ritual *is* the ritual.

KATE GREEN, *Shattered Moon* (1986)

See also Habit, Religion, Spirituality, Traditions.

RIVERS

Oh! travelers swift / From secrets to oblivion! Waters wild / That pass in act to bend a flower or lift / The bright limbs of a child!

ALICE MEYNELL, "Rivers Unknown to Song," *The Poems of Alice Meynell* (1923)

When there is a river in your growing up, you probably always hear it.

ANN ZWINGER, *Run, River, Run* (1975)

A river seems a magic thing. A magic, moving, living part of the very earth itself—for it is from the soil, both from its depth and from its surface, that a river has its beginning.

LAURA GILPIN, *The Rio Grande* (1949)

That river—it was full of good and evil together. It would water the fields when it was curbed and checked, but then if an inch were allowed it, it crashed through like a roaring dragon.

PEARL BUCK, *The Old Demon* (1939)

As we were in the midst of the dry season, the river at Vat Thmey was now only a big snake of mud.

MOLYDA SZYMUSIAK, *The Stones Cry Out: A Cambodian Childhood 1975–1980* (1984)

ROME

In Rome people seem to love with more zest, murder with more imagination, submit to creative urges more often, and lose the sense of logic more easily than in any other place.

LETITIA BALDRIGE, Of Diamonds and Diplomats (1968)

In Rome people spend most of their time having lunch. And they do it very well—Rome is unquestionably the lunch capital of the world.

FRAN LEBOWITZ, *Metropolitan Life* (1978)

Night doesn't fall in Rome; it rises from the city's heart, from the gloomy little alleys and courtyards where the sun never gets much more than a brief look-in, and then, like the mist from the Tiber, it creeps over the rooftops and spreads up into the hills.

CAROLINE LLEWELLYN, *The Masks of Rome* (1988)

See also Italy.

ROOMS

A room is a place where you hide from the wolves outside and that's all any room is.

JEAN RHYS, *Good Morning, Midnight* (1939)

A woman must have money and a room of her own if she is to write fiction.

VIRGINIA WOOLF, *A Room of One's Own* (1929)

I have at last got the little room I have wanted so long, and am very happy about it. It does me good to be alone.

LOUISA MAY ALCOTT, *Journals* (1868)

Most women still need a room of their own and the only way to find it may be outside their own homes.

GERMAINE GREER, *The Female Eunuch* (1971)

See also Houses, Space, Walls.

ROOTS

To be rooted is perhaps the most important and least recognized need of the human soul.

SIMONE WEIL, *The Need for Roots* (1949)

I have not seen my birthplace, / where my mother deposited the heavy load of her inside.

TAHEREH SAFFIR ZADEH, "My Birthplace," *Resonance in the Bay* (1971)

Far away from my country I would be like those trees they chop down at Christmastime, those poor rootless pines that last a little while and then die.

ISABEL ALLENDE, *The House of Spirits* (1982)

To separate from my culture (as from my family) I had to feel competent enough on the outside and secure enough inside to live life on my own. Yet in leaving home I did not lose touch with my origins because *lo mexicano* is in my system. I am a turtle, wherever I go I carry "home" on my back.

GLORIA ANZALDÚA, *Borderlands/La Frontera: The New Mestiza* (1987)

If you go away from your own place and people—the place you spent your childhood in, all your life you'll be sick with homesickness and you'll never have a home. You can find a better place, perhaps, a way of life you like better, but the *home* is gone out of your heart, and you'll be hunting it all your life long.

MARY O'HARA, *Thunderhead* (1943)

But there were years when, in search of what I thought was better, nobler things I denied these, my people, and my family. I forgot the songs they sung—and most of those songs are now dead; I erased their dialect from my tongue; I was ashamed of them and their ways of life. But now—yes, I love them; they are a part of my blood; they, with all their virtues and their faults, played a great part in forming my way of looking at life.

AGNES SMEDLEY, *Daughter of Earth* (1929)

The Gringo, locked into the fiction of white superiority, seized complete political power, stripping Indians and Mexicans of their land while their feet were still rooted in it. *Con el destierro y el exilo fuimos desuñados, destroncados, destripados*—we were jerked out by the roots, truncated, disemboweled, dispossessed, and separated from our identity and our history.

GLORIA ANZALDÚA, *Borderlands/La Frontera: The New Mestiza* (1987)

That I can live long enough / To obtain one and only one desire— / That someday I can see again / The mulberry and catalpa trees of home.

TS'AI YEN, "Eighteen Verses Sung to a Tatar Reed Whistle" (c. 200), in Joanna Bankier and Deirdre Lashgari, eds., *Women Poets of the World* (1983)

See also Ancestors, Family, Home.

RUDENESS

Ideological differences are no excuse for rudeness.

JUDITH MARTIN, *Miss Manners' Guide to Excruciatingly Correct Behavior* (1982)

You can't be truly rude until you understand good manners.

RITA MAE BROWN, *Starting From Scratch* (1988)

In point of fact, we are all born rude. No infant has ever appeared yet with the grace to understand how inconsiderate it is to disturb others in the middle of the night.

JUDITH MARTIN, *Common Courtesy* (1985)

See also Etiquette, Manners, Offensiveness, Politeness.

RUMOR

Rumor is untraceable, incalculable, and infectious.

MARGOT ASQUITH, *More or Less About Myself* (1934)

A cruel story runs on wheels, and every hand oils the wheels as they run.

OUIDA, *Wisdom, Wit and Pathos* (1884)

We must be careful what we say. No bird resumes its egg.

EMILY DICKINSON (1874), in Mabel Loomis Todd, *Letters of Emily Dickinson* (1894)

It is harder to kill a whisper than even a shouted calumny.

MARY STEWART, *The Last Enchantment* (1979)

It starts as an inflection of the voice, a question asked in a certain tone and not answered with "no"; a prolonged little silence, a twinkle in the eye, a long-drawn "w-e-e-ell—I don't know." These are the fine roots of the tree whose poisonous fruits are gossip and slander.

MARIA AUGUSTA TRAPP, *The Story of the Trapp Family Singers* (1949)

I thought you were only a rumor.

LOUISE TRACY, widow of Spencer Tracy, to Katharine Hepburn, in Katharine Hepburn, *Me: Stories of My Life* (1991)

See also Calumny, Gossip, "They."

RUSSIA

Keeping your coat on indoors in Russia, no matter how public the place, is far worse than keeping your hat on as the flag goes by. It is worse than going into a Catholic church in Spain with your upper arms bare. It is worse than telling a mother her baby bores you.

ILKA CHASE, *Worlds Apart* (1972)

Moscow seethes and bubbles and gasps for air. It's always thirsting for something new, the newest events, the latest sensation. Everyone wants to be the first to know.

SVETLANA ALLILUYEVA, *Twenty Letters to a Friend* (1967)

You know, our country is on such a low socioeconomic level that at the moment we cannot afford to divide ourselves into "us women" and "us men." We share a common struggle for democracy, a struggle to feed the country.

ELENA BONNER, speech (1990)

S

SACRED

Each being is sacred—meaning that each has inherent value that cannot be ranked in a hierarchy or compared to the value of another being.

STARHAWK, *Truth or Dare* (1987)

There is nothing so secular that it cannot be sacred, and that is one of the deepest messages of the Incarnation.

MADELEINE L'ENGLE, *Walking on Water: Reflections on Faith and Art* (1980)

To survive we must begin to know sacredness
The pace which most of us live prevents this.

CHRYSTOS, "No Rock Scorns Me as Whore," in Cherríe Moraga and Gloria Anzaldúa, eds., *This Bridge Called My Back* (1983)

See also Divinity, God, Holiness.

SACRIFICE

Blessed is the match consumed / in kindling flame.

HANNAH SENESH, "Blessed Is the Match" (1944)

Sacrificers . . . are not the ones to pity. The ones to pity are those that they sacrifice. Oh, the sacrificers, they get it both ways. A person knows themselves that they're able to do without.

ELIZABETH BOWEN, *The Death of the Heart* (1938)

She was a spasmodic selfless torrent like the fizz from her own cider bottles.

KATE CRUISE O'BRIEN, "Trespasses," *A Gift Horse* (1978)

In all proper relationships there is no sacrifice of anyone to anyone.

AYN RAND, *The Fountainhead* (1943)

The capacity to sacrifice, like any skill, always needs some fine tuning. It is one thing to sacrifice briefly one's sleep to comfort a child with a bad dream; it is quite another for a mother to sacrifice her whole career for a child. It is one thing for a father to sacrifice his desire to go fishing today because he needs to go to work to feed the family; it is quite another to work for forty years at a job he hates. . . . Often such massive sacrifice, if not a result of cowardice, comes from an inability to discriminate between giving that is necessary and life-giving and giving that brings death to the Martyr and hence to those around him or her.

CAROL PEARSON, *The Hero Within* (1986)

See also Giving.

SADNESS
See Sorrow, Unhappiness.

SAFETY
See Security.

SAINTS

Saints are non-conformists.

ELEANOR RICE TAYLOR, "Welcome Eumenides" (1972), in Sandra M. Gilbert and Susan Gubar, eds., *The Norton Anthology of Literature by Women* (1985)

I don't believe in God, but I do believe in His Saints.

EDITH WHARTON, in Percy Lubbock, *Portrait of Edith Wharton* (1947)

For the wonderful thing about saints is that they were *human*. They lost their tempers, got hungry, scolded God, were egotistical or testy or impatient in their turns, made mistakes and regretted them. Still they went on doggedly blundering toward heaven.

PHYLLIS MCGINLEY, *Saint-Watching* (1969)

See also Goodness, Holiness.

SANITY

That's the truest sign of insanity—insane people are always sure they're just fine. It's only the sane people who are willing to admit they're crazy.

NORA EPHRON, *Heartburn* (1983)

Sane people did what their neighbors did, so that if any lunatics were at large, one might know and avoid them.

GEORGE ELIOT, *Middlemarch* (1871)

See also Mental Illness.

SATIRE

Satire should, like a polished razor keen, / Wound with a touch that's scarcely felt or seen.

LADY MARY WORTLEY MONTAGU, "Verses Address'd to the Imitator of Horace" (1733), in Robert Halsband and Isobel Grundy, eds., *Lady Mary Wortley Montagu: Essays and Poems* (1977)

A fondness for satire indicates a mind pleased with irritating others; for myself, I never could find amusement in killing flies.

MARIE-JEANNE ROLAND (1776), in Lydia Maria Child, *Memoirs of Madame de Staël and of Madame Roland* (1847)

Oh, life is a glorious cycle of song, / A medley of extemporanea; / And love is a thing that can never go wrong; / and I am Marie of Roumania.

DOROTHY PARKER, "Comment," *Enough Rope* (1926)

See also Humor.

SCHOOL

Neat as a freshly peeled Easter egg, / Just six years old, he sat, *comme il faut,* / In the French Lycée in Berlin.

ELSE LASKER-SCHÜLER, "Hans Jacob," *Hebrew Ballads and Other Poems* (1980)

School was a worry to her. She was not glib or quick in a world where glibness and quickness were easily confused with ability to learn.

TILLIE OLSEN, "I Stand Here Ironing," *Tell Me A Riddle* (1956)

See also Education, Learning, Teaching.

SCIENCE

Science is voiceless; it is the scientists who talk.

SIMONE WEIL, *On Science, Necessity, and the Love of God* (1968)

After all, science is essentially international, and it is only through lack of the historical sense that national qualities have been attributed to it.

MARIE CURIE, "Intellectual Cooperation," *Memorandum* (1926)

Science conducts us, step by step, through the whole range of creation, until we arrive, at length, at God.

MARGUERITE DE VALOIS (1594), *Memoirs* (1910)

A science which does not bring us nearer to God is worthless.

SIMONE WEIL, *Gravity and Grace* (1947)

Real progress in understanding nature is rarely incremental. All important advances are sudden intuitions, new principles, new ways of seeing. We have not fully recognized this process of leaping ahead, however, in part because textbooks tend to tame revolutions, whether cultural or scientific. They describe the advances as if they had been logical in their day, not at all shocking.

MARILYN FERGUSON, *The Aquarian Conspiracy* (1980)

One could count on one's fingers the number of scientists in the entire world who have a general idea of the history and development of their own particular science; there is not one who is really competent as regards sciences other than his own. As science forms an indivisible whole, one may say that there are no longer, strictly speaking, any scientists, but only drudges doing scientific work.

SIMONE WEIL, *Oppression and Liberty* (1955)

Our science is like a store filled with the most subtle intellectual devices for solving the most complex problems, and yet we are almost incapable of applying the elementary principles of rational thought.

SIMONE WEIL, "The Power of Words," *The Simone Weil Reader* (1977)

If you do something once, people will call it an accident. If you do it twice, they call it a coincidence. But do it a third time and you've just proven a natural law.

GRACE MURRAY HOPPER, in Ethlie Ann Vare and Greg Ptacek, *Mothers of Invention* (1987)

The villagers seldom leave the village; many scientists have limited and poorly cultivated minds apart from their specialty.

SIMONE WEIL, *On Science, Necessity, and the Love of God* (1968)

The phrase "popular science" has in itself a touch of absurdity. That knowledge which is popular is not scientific.

MARIA MITCHELL, diary (1866), in Phebe Mitchell Kendall, ed., *Maria Mitchell, Life, Letters, and Journals* (1896)

We especially need imagination in science. It is not all mathematics, nor all logic, but it is somewhat beauty and poetry.

MARIA MITCHELL, diary (1866), in Phebe Mitchell Kendall, ed., *Maria Mitchell, Life, Letters, and Journals* (1896)

Alas! the scientific conscience had got into the debasing company of money obligation and selfish respects.

GEORGE ELIOT, *Middlemarch* (1871)

See also Biology, Research.

SCULPTURE

The sight of such a monument is like a continuous and stationary music.

MADAME DE STAËL, *Corinne* (1807)

It's very inconvenient being a sculptor. It's like playing the double-bass; one's so handicapped by one's baggage.

DOROTHY L. SAYERS, *The Unpleasantness at the Bellona Club* (1928)

The most breadless art of our day.

MARTHA ALBRAND, *The Mask of Alexander* (1955)

He's been a waiten there in th wood you might say since before I was born. I jist brung him out a little—but one a these days, jist you wait an see, we'll find th time an a face fer him an bring him out a that block.

HARRIETTE ARNOW, *The Dollmaker* (1954)

See also Art.

SEA

I was born by the sea and I have noticed that all the great events of my life have taken place by the sea. My first idea of movement, of the dance, certainly came from the rhythm of the waves.

ISADORA DUNCAN, *My Life* (1942)

The voice of the sea speaks to the soul. The touch of the sea is sensuous, enfolding the body in its soft, close embrace.

KATE CHOPIN, *The Awakening* (1899)

It has always been to me, the ocean, overwhelming, monstrous, deep, dark, green and black, so foreign that it requires respect, silence, humility. . . . All of the life in it is menacing, compelling, exquisite, with nothing consoling.

ANDREA DWORKIN, "First Love," in Julia Wolf Mazow, ed., *The Woman Who Lost Her Names* (1980)

The vast Pacific ocean would always remain the islanders' great solace, escape and nourishment, the amniotic fluid that would keep them hedonistic and aloof, guarded, gentle and mysterious.

FRANCINE DU PLESSIX GRAY, *Hawaii: The Sugar-Coated Fortress* (1972)

For all at last return to the sea—to Oceanus, the ocean river, like the ever-flowing stream of time, the beginning and the end.

RACHEL CARSON, *The Sea Around Us* (1950)

It is a curious situation that the sea, from which life first arose, should now be threatened by the activities of one form of that life. But the sea, though changed in a sinister way, will continue to exist; the threat is rather to life itself.

RACHEL CARSON, *The Sea Around Us* (1950)

The mysterious human bond with the great seas that poets write about has a physiological base in our veins and in every living thing, where runs fluid of the same saline proportions as ocean water.

ANNE W. SIMON, *The Thin Edge* (1978)

SEARCH

Often the search proves more profitable than the goal.

E. L. KONIGSBURG, *From the Mixed-Up Files of Mrs. Basil E. Frankweiler* (1967)

We seek him here, we seek him there, / Those Frenchies seek him everywhere. / Is he in heaven?—Is he in hell? / That demmed elusive Pimpernel?

BARONESS ORCZY, *The Scarlet Pimpernel* (1905)

SECRETS

I will have no locked cupboards in my life.

GERTRUDE BELL, in Janet E. Courtney, *An Oxford Portrait Gallery* (1931)

In the mind and nature of a man a secret is an ugly thing, like a hidden physical defect.

ISAK DINESEN, "Of Hidden Thoughts and of Heaven," *Last Tales* (1957)

I don't think secrets agree with me; I feel rumpled up in my mind since you told me that.

LOUISA MAY ALCOTT, *Little Women* (1868)

Sometimes you just gotta trust that your secret's been kept long enough.

ANNE CAMERON, *Daughters of Copper Woman* (1981)

Because after a time having a secret and nobody knowing you have a secret is no fun. And although you don't want others to know what the secret is, you want them to at least know you have one.

E. L. KONIGSBURG, *From the Mixed-Up Files of Mrs. Basil E. Frankweiler* (1967)

Secrets are rarely betrayed or discovered according to any program our fear has sketched out.

GEORGE ELIOT, *The Mill on the Floss* (1860)

A person who has no secrets is a liar. We always fold ourselves away from others just enough to preserve a secret or two, something that we cannot share without destroying our inner landscape.

ANNE ROIPHE, *Lovingkindness* (1987)

One ought to have the right to have a secret and to spring it as a surprise. But if you live inside a family you have neither.

TOVE JANSSON, *Tales from Moominvalley* (1963)

Secrets are kept from children, a lid on top of the soup kettle, so they do not boil over with too much truth.

AMY TAN, *The Joy Luck Club* (1989)

Secrecy is as indispensable to human beings as fire, and as greatly feared.

SISSELA BOK, *Secrets* (1983)

See also Concealment, Hiding, Privacy.

SECURITY

Only in growth, reform, and change, paradoxically enough, is true security to be found.

ANNE MORROW LINDBERGH, *The Wave of the Future* (1940)

Security is when everything is settled, when nothing can happen to you; security is the denial of life.

GERMAINE GREER, *The Female Eunuch* (1971)

Too much safety is abhorrent to the nature of a human being.

AGATHA CHRISTIE, *Curtain* (1975)

No one can build his security on the nobleness of another person.

WILLA CATHER, *Alexander's Bridge* (1912)

Cocooning: The need to protect oneself from the harsh, unpredictable realities of the outside world.

FAITH POPCORN, *The Popcorn Report* (1991)

To multiply the harbors does not reduce the sea.

EMILY DICKINSON, letter (1879), in Mabel Loomis Todd, *Letters of Emily Dickinson* (1894)

See also Danger, Risk.

SEDUCTION

The seduction emanating from a person of uncertain or dissimulated sex is powerful.

COLETTE, *The Pure and the Impure* (1932)

All the delusive seduction of martial music.

FANNY BURNEY, *Diary* (1802)

In Jacqueline's experience, charming out-of-the-way restaurants were frequently attached to out-of-the-way motels.

ELIZABETH PETERS, *Naked Once More* (1989)

See also Flirtation, Sex.

SELF

I am what I am.

ROSARIO MORALES, poem title, in Cherríe Moraga and Gloria Anzaldúa, eds., *This Bridge Called My Back* (1983)

Nothing, nothing am I but a small, loving watercourse.

ROSARIO CASTELLANOS, in Irene Nicholson, *A Guide to Mexican Poetry* (1968)

It was on that road and at that hour that I first became aware of my own self, experienced an inexpressible state of grace, and felt one with the first breath of air that stirred, the first bird, and the sun so newly born that it still looked not quite round.

COLETTE, *Sido* (1930)

Maybe being oneself is always an acquired taste.

PATRICIA HAMPL, in Janet Sternburg, ed., *The Writer on Her Work*, vol. 2 (1991)

Who sees the other half of Self, sees Truth.

ANNE CAMERON, *Daughters of Copper Woman* (1981)

Unless I am what I am and feel what I feel—as hard as I can and as honestly and truly as I can—then I am nothing. Let me feel guilty . . . don't try to educate me . . . don't protect me.

ELIZABETH JANEWAY, *Leaving Home* (1953)

If what I am watching evaporated before my eyes, I would remain.

ANNE TRUITT, *The Journal of an Artist* (1986)

Neither woman nor man lives by work, or love, alone. . . . The human self defines itself and grows through love *and* work: all psychology before and after Freud boils down to that.

BETTY FRIEDAN, *The Second Stage* (1981)

Part of having a strong sense of self is to be accountable for one's actions. No matter how much we explore motives or lack of motives, we are what we do.

JANET GERINGER WOITITZ, *Adult Children of Alcoholics* (1983)

I'll walk where my own nature would be leading— / It vexes me to choose another guide.

EMILY BRONTË, "Stanzas" (1850)

What you have become is the price you paid to get what you used to want.

MIGNON McLAUGHLIN, *The Neurotic's Notebook* (1963)

Everybody must learn this lesson somewhere—that it costs something to be what you are.

SHIRLEY ABBOTT, *Womenfolks: Growing Up Down South* (1983)

I did not lose myself all at once. I rubbed out my face over the years washing away my pain, the same way carvings on stone are worn down by water.

AMY TAN, *The Joy Luck Club* (1989)

But I warn you . . . I am only really myself when I'm somebody else whom I have endowed with these wonderful qualities from my imagination.

ZELDA FITZGERALD, *Save Me the Waltz* (1932)

I am not at all the sort of person you and I took me for.

JANE WELSH CARLYLE, letter to Thomas Carlyle (1822)

She lives on the reflections of herself in the eyes of others.

Anaïs Nin, *The Diary of Anaïs Nin, vol.* 1 (1931–1934)

First, there is the person one thinks he is and the appearance one thinks he has. Then there is the thing one actually is, and there is that which the others think, and here a myriad-faced being arose in her thought, but the second came back as being more difficult to know, for what eyes would see it and where would it stay?

Elizabeth Madox Roberts, *Black Is My Truelove's Hair* (1938)

No sooner do we think we have assembled a comfortable life than we find a piece of ourselves that has no place to fit in.

Gail Sheehy, *Passages* (1976)

"He's not himself at all today," Mr. Somerset told me. People say that about Jeremy quite often, but what they mean is that he is not like other people. He is *always* himself. That's what's wrong with him.

Anne Tyler, *Celestial Navigation* (1974)

When my daughter looks at me, she sees a small old lady. That is because she sees only with her outside eyes. She has no *chuming,* no inside knowing of things. If she had *chuming,* she would see a tiger lady. And she would have careful fear.

Amy Tan, *The Joy Luck Club* (1989)

It so often happens that others are measuring us by our past self while we are looking back on that self with a mixture of disgust and sorrow.

George Eliot, letter (1861), in J. W. Cross, *George Eliot's Life as Related in Her Letters and Journals* (1884)

I change myself, I change the world.

Gloria Anzaldúa, *Borderlands/La Frontera: The New Mestiza* (1987)

It's easier to hide your light under a bushel than to keep your shady side dark.

Helen Rowland, *Reflections of a Bachelor Girl* (1909)

The self is every person's true enemy.

Ding Ling, "Miss Sophia's Diary" (1927), in *I Myself Am a Woman: Selected Writings of Ding Ling* (1989)

See also Identity, Individual, Uniqueness, Wholeness.

SELF-ACTUALIZATION

I do not want to die . . . until I have faithfully made the most of my talent and cultivated the seed that was placed in me until the last small twig has grown.

Käthe Kollwitz (1915), in Hans Kollwitz, ed., *The Diaries and Letters of Käthe Kollwitz* (1955)

One can never consent to creep when one feels an impulse to soar.

Helen Keller, *The Story of My Life* (1902)

If you have got a living force and you're not using it, nature kicks you back. The blood boils just like you put it in a pot.

Louise Nevelson, *Dawns + Dusks* (1976)

So all that is in her will not bloom—but in how many does it?

Tillie Olsen, "I Stand Here Ironing," *Tell Me A Riddle* (1956)

SELF-DESTRUCTION

Give him enough rope and he will hang himself.

Charlotte Brontë, *Shirley* (1849)

It is the loose ends with which men hang themselves.

Zelda Fitzgerald, in *Reader's Digest* (1983)

See also Suicide.

SELF-DETERMINATION

Human beings have an inalienable right to invent themselves; when that right is pre-empted it is called brain-washing.

Germaine Greer, in *The Times* (1986)

I want the freedom to carve and chisel my own face, to staunch the bleeding with ashes, to fashion my own gods out of my entrails.

GLORIA ANZALDÚA, *Borderlands/La Frontera: The New Mestiza* (1987)

You need only claim the events of your life to make yourself yours. When you truly possess all you have been and done, which may take some time, you are fierce with reality.

FLORIDA SCOTT-MAXWELL, *The Measure of My Days* (1968)

Of my own spirit let me be / in sole though feeble mastery.

SARA TEASDALE, "Mastery," *Collected Poems* (1937)

I'm not afraid of storms, for I'm learning how to sail my ship.

LOUISA MAY ALCOTT, *Little Women* (1868)

Such creatures of accident are we, liable to a thousand deaths before we are born. But once we are here, we may create our own world, if we choose.

MARY ANTIN, *The Promised Land* (1912)

We are not born all at once, but by bits. The body first, and the spirit later; and the birth and growth of the spirit, in those who are attentive to their own inner life, are slow and exceedingly painful. Our mothers are racked with the pains of our physical birth; we ourselves suffer the longer pains of our spiritual growth.

MARY ANTIN, *The Promised Land* (1912)

No star is ever lost we once have seen, / We always may be what we might have been.

ADELAIDE A. PROCTOR, "Legend of Provence," *Legends and Lyrics* (1858)

A watermelon that breaks open by itself tastes better than one cut with a knife.

HUALING NIEH, *Mulberry and Peach* (1981)

SELF-ESTEEM

I'm Nobody! Who are you? / Are you—Nobody—Too? / Then there's a pair of us? / Don't tell! they'd advertise—you know!

EMILY DICKINSON (1861), *Poems, Second Series* (1891)

No one can make you feel inferior without your consent.

ELEANOR ROOSEVELT, *This Is My Story* (1937)

You can be pleased with nothing when you are not pleased with yourself.

LADY MARY WORTLEY MONTAGU, letter to her future husband (1712), in Octave Thanet, ed., *The Best Letters of Lady Mary Wortley Montagu* (1901)

We cease loving ourselves if no one loves us.

MADAME DE STAËL, in Charles Augustin Sainte-Beuve, *Portraits of Women* (1845)

He who despises himself esteems himself as a self-despiser.

SUSAN SONTAG, *Death Kit* (1967)

All men seek esteem; the best by lifting themselves, which is hard to do, the rest by shoving others down, which is much easier.

MARY RENAULT, *The Praise Singer* (1978)

She'd been so programmed by Julian to think of herself as inferior material that if a man threw himself at her feet, her immediate reaction would be to call an ambulance.

LUCILLE KALLEN, *Introducing C. B. Greenfield* (1979)

To say something nice about themselves, this is the hardest thing in the world for people to do. They'd rather take their clothes off.

NANCY FRIDAY, *My Mother/My Self* (1977)

Those who believe they are ugly / objectify the rest of us.

JUDY GRAHN, *The Queen of Swords* (1987)

Women who set a low value on themselves make life hard for all women.

NELLIE McCLUNG, *In Times Like These* (1915)

and he said: you pretty full of yourself ain't chu / so she replied: show me someone not full of herself / and i'll show you a hungry person.

NIKKI GIOVANNI, "Poem for a Lady Whose Voice I Like" (1970), *The Women and the Men* (1975)

See also Confidence, Pride.

SELF-IMPORTANCE

He was like a cock who thought the sun had risen to hear him crow.

GEORGE ELIOT, *Adam Bede* (1859)

When someone sings his own praises, he always gets the tune too high.

MARY H. WALDRIP, in *Reader's Digest* (1978)

A pompous woman of his acquaintance, complaining that the head-waiter of a restaurant had not shown her and her husband immediately to a table, said, "We had to tell him who we were." Gerald, interested, inquired, "And who were you?"

EDITH SITWELL, *Taken Care Of* (1965)

Remember to negotiate thickness as well as height on the lettering of your name.

JULIA PHILLIPS, *You'll Never Eat Lunch in This Town Again* (1991)

One trouble: to be a professional anything in the United States is to think of oneself as an expert and one's ideas as semisacred, and to treat others in a certain way—professionally.

MARGE PIERCY, "The Grand Coolie Damn," in Robin Morgan, *Sisterhood Is Powerful* (1970)

She was one of the most unimportantly wicked women of her time—because she could not let her time alone, and yet could never be a part of it. She wanted to be the reason for everything and so was the cause of nothing.

DJUNA BARNES, *Nightwood* (1937)

After us the deluge.

MADAME DE POMPADOUR, to Louis XV (1757)

See also Arrogance, Conceit, Egocentrism, Vanity.

SELF-INDULGENCE

People who are always making allowances for themselves soon go bankrupt.

MARY PETTIBONE POOLE, *A Glass Eye at a Keyhole* (1938)

See also Extravagance.

SELFISHNESS

I have been a selfish being all my life, in practice, though not in principle.

JANE AUSTEN, *Pride and Prejudice* (1813)

But life lived only for oneself does not truly satisfy men or women. There is a hunger in Americans today for larger purposes beyond the self. That is the reason for the religious revival and the new resonance of "family."

BETTY FRIEDAN, *The Second Stage* (1981)

The so-called selfishness of moderns is partly due to the tremendous amount of stimulation received. They are aroused and drawn into experience by theaters, books, automobiles, great cities. The current is quick and strong.

KATHARINE BUTLER HATHAWAY, *The Journals and Letters of the Little Locksmith* (1946)

You are discontented with the world because you can't get just the small things that suit your pleasure, not because it's a world where myriads of men and women are ground by wrong and misery, and tainted with pollution.

GEORGE ELIOT, *Felix Holt, the Radical* (1866)

Do we want laurels for ourselves most, / Or most that no one else shall have any?

AMY LOWELL, "La Ronde du Diable," *What's O'Clock* (1925)

See also Greed.

SELF-KNOWLEDGE

There's a period of life when we swallow a knowledge of ourselves, and it becomes either good or sour inside.

PEARL BAILEY, *The Raw Pearl* (1968)

You can live a lifetime and, at the end of it, know more about other people than you know about yourself.

BERYL MARKHAM, *West With the Night* (1942)

When one is a stranger to oneself then one is estranged from others too. If one is out of touch with oneself, then one cannot touch others.

ANNE MORROW LINDBERGH, *Gift From the Sea* (1955)

It is a fault to wish to be understood before we have made ourselves clear to ourselves.

SIMONE WEIL, *Gravity and Grace* (1947)

I did not know then, as I know now, that people are prone to build a statue of the kind of person that it pleases them to be. And few people want to be forced to ask themselves, "What if there is no me like my statue?"

ZORA NEALE HURSTON, *Dust Tracks on a Road* (1942)

We neither knew nor liked the people we had become.

BARBARA HOWAR, *Laughing All the Way* (1973)

See also Awareness, Knowledge, Understanding.

SELF-PITY

Self-pity in its early stages is as snug as a feather mattress. Only when it hardens does it become uncomfortable.

MAYA ANGELOU, *Gather Together in My Name* (1974)

See also Pity.

SELF-SUFFICIENCY

Let them think I love them more than I do, / Let them think I care, though I go alone, / If it lifts their pride, what is it to me, / Who am self-complete as a flower or a stone?

SARA TEASDALE, "The Solitary," *Collected Poems* (1937)

See also Independence.

SENSES

We live on the leash of our senses.

DIANE ACKERMAN, *A Natural History of the Senses* (1990)

There is no way in which to understand the world without first detecting it through the radar-net of our senses.

DIANE ACKERMAN, *A Natural History of the Senses* (1990)

For all of my patients sensuality is a giving in to "the low side of their nature." Puritanism is powerful and distorts their life with a total anesthesia of the senses. If you atrophy one sense you also atrophy all the others, a sensuous and physical connection with nature, with art, with food, with other human beings.

ANAÏS NIN, *The Diary of Anaïs Nin,* vol. 2 (1934–1939)

The life of sensation is the life of greed; it requires more and more. The life of the spirit requires less and less; time is ample and its passage sweet.

ANNIE DILLARD, *The Writing Life* (1989)

It is immediately apparent . . . that this sense-world, this seemingly real external universe, though it may be useful and valid in other respects, cannot be *the* external world, but only the self's projected picture of it. . . . The evidence of the senses cannot be accepted as evidence of the nature of ultimate reality.

EVELYN UNDERHILL, *Mysticism* (1955)

See also Smell.

SENSITIVITY

I wonder if anyone else has an ear so tuned and sharpened as I have, to detect the music, not of the spheres, but of earth, subtleties of major and minor chord that the wind strikes upon the tree branches. Have you ever heard the earth breathe. . . ?

KATE CHOPIN, "Mrs. Mobry's Reason" (1900), *The Storm* (1974)

If we had a keen vision and feeling of all ordinary human life, it would be like hearing the grass grow and the squirrel's heart beat, and we should die of the roar which lies on the other side of silence. As it is, the quickest of us walk about well wadded with stupidity.

GEORGE ELIOT, *Middlemarch* (1871)

See also Awareness.

SENTIMENTALITY

Sentimentality comes from an inability, for whatever reason, to look reality in the face.

MARILYN SEWELL, *Cries of the Spirit* (1991)

I revolted from sentimentality, less because it was false than because it was cruel.

ELLEN GLASGOW, *The Woman Within* (1954)

See also Nostalgia.

SERIOUSNESS

Seriousness is the refuge of the shallow. There are events and personal experiences that call forth seriousness but they are fewer than most of us think.

RITA MAE BROWN, *Starting From Scratch* (1988)

The one important thing I have learned over the years is the difference between taking one's work seriously and taking one's self seriously. The first is imperative and the second is disastrous.

MARGOT FONTEYN, *Margot Fonteyn: Autobiography* (1975)

Just as we are often moved to merriment for no other reason than that the occasion calls for seriousness, so we are correspondingly serious when invited too freely to be amused.

AGNES REPPLIER, *Under Dispute* (1924)

You're the unfortunate contradiction in terms—a serious good person.

WENDY WASSERSTEIN, *The Heidi Chronicles* (1988)

SERVICE

Service is the rent that you pay for room on this earth.

SHIRLEY CHISHOLM, in Brian Lanker, *I Dream a World* (1989)

There is nothing to make you like other human beings so much as doing things for them.

ZORA NEALE HURSTON, *Dust Tracks on a Road* (1942)

The first small sacrifice of this sort leads the way to others, and a single hand's turn given heartily to the world's great work helps one amazingly with one's own small tasks.

LOUISA M. ALCOTT, *An Old-Fashioned Girl* (1870)

The laws of our being are such that we must perform some degree of use in the world, whether we intend it, or not; but we can deprive ourselves of its indwelling joy, by acting entirely from the love of self.

LYDIA MARIA CHILD, *Letters from New York,* 2nd Series (1845)

Pray for the dead and fight like hell for the living.

MOTHER JONES, in Linda Atkinson, *Mother Jones: The Most Dangerous Woman in America* (1978)

When you cease to make a contribution you begin to die.

ELEANOR ROOSEVELT, letter (1960)

See also Altruism, Giving.

SEX

Sexuality is a sacrament.

STARHAWK, *The Spiral Dance* (1979)

Sexuality is the great field of battle between biology and society.

NANCY FRIDAY, *My Mother/My Self* (1977)

Sex is an emotion in motion.

MAE WEST, in Diane Arbus, "Mae West: Emotion in Motion," *Show* (1965)

Sex is the tabasco sauce which an adolescent national palate sprinkles on every course in the menu.

MARY DAY WINN, *Adam's Rib* (1931)

Sex is never an emergency.

ELAINE PIERSON, book title (1970)

It's pitch, sex is. Once you touch it, it clings to you.

MARGERY ALLINGHAM, *The Fashion in Shrouds* (1938)

The total deprivation of it produces irritability.

ELIZABETH BLACKWELL, *The Human Element in Sex* (1894)

That pathetic short-cut suggested by Nature the supreme joker as a remedy for our loneliness, that ephemeral communion which we persuade ourselves to be of the spirit when it is in fact only of the body—durable not even in memory!

VITA SACKVILLE-WEST, *No Signposts in the Sea* (1961)

All the Freudian system is impregnated with the prejudice which it makes it its mission to fight—the prejudice that everything sexual is vile.

SIMONE WEIL, *Gravity and Grace* (1947)

Sex annihilates identity, and the space given to sex in contemporary novels is an avowal of the absence of character.

MARY MCCARTHY, in George Plimpton, ed., *The Writer's Chapbook* (1989)

Before the child ever gets to school it will have received crucial, almost irrevocable sex education and this will have been taught by the parents, who are not aware of what they are doing.

MARY S. CALDERONE, in *People* (1980)

Most mothers think that to keep young people away from lovemaking it is enough never to speak of it in their presence.

MARIE MADELEINE DE LA FAYETTE, *La Princesse de Clèves* (1678)

As I grew to adolescence, I imagined, from closely observing the boredom and vexations of matrimony, that the act my parents committed and the one I so longed to commit must be two different things.

SHIRLEY ABBOTT, *Womenfolks: Growing Up Down South* (1983)

She knew, even though she was too young to know the reason, that indiscriminate desire and unselective sex were possible only to those who regarded sex and themselves as evil.

AYN RAND, *Atlas Shrugged* (1957)

I do not know, I am only sixty-five.

PRINCESS METTERNICH, when asked at what age a woman ceases to feel the torments of the flesh, in Simone de Beauvoir, *The Second Sex* (1949)

An old body when it is loved becomes a sacred treasure; and sex itself must always, it seems to me, come to us as a sacrament and be so used or it is meaningless. The flesh is suffused by the spirit, and it is forgetting this in the act of lovemaking that creates cynicism and despair.

MAY SARTON, *Recovering: A Journal* (1978)

You mustn't force sex to do the work of love or love to do the work of sex—that's quite a thought, isn't it?

MARY MCCARTHY, *The Group* (1954)

I consider promiscuity immoral. Not because sex is evil, but because sex is too good and too important.

AYN RAND, in *Playboy* (1964)

Aren't women prudes if they don't and prostitutes if they do?

KATE MILLETT, speech (1975)

You think intercourse is a private act; it's not, it's a social act. Men are sexually predatory in life; and women are sexually manipulative. When two individuals come together and leave their gender outside the bedroom door, then they make love. If they take it inside with them, they do something else, because society is in the room with them.

ANDREA DWORKIN, *Intercourse* (1987)

The fact is that heterosexual sex for most people is in no way free of the power relations between men and women.

DEIRDRE ENGLISH AND BARBARA EHRENREICH, in Evelyn Shapiro and Barry M. Shapiro, *The Women Say/The Men Say* (1979)

You cannot decree women to be sexually free when they are not economically free.

SHERE HITE, *The Hite Report* (1976)

I truly feel that there are as many ways of loving as there are people in the world and as there are days in the lives of those people.

MARY S. CALDERONE, in *Ms.* (1979)

It doesn't matter what you do in the bedroom as long as you don't do it in the street and frighten the horses.

MRS. PATRICK CAMPBELL (1910), in Daphne Fielding, *The Duchess of Jermyn Street* (1964)

I don't know what I am, darling. I've tried several varieties of sex. The conventional position makes me claustrophobic. And the others give me either stiff neck or lockjaw.

TALLULAH BANKHEAD, in Lee Israel, *Miss Tallulah Bankhead* (1972)

Really, sex and laughter do go very well together, and I wondered—and still do—which is the more important.

HERMIONE GINGOLD, *How to Grow Old Disgracefully* (1988)

I think that in the sexual act, as delightful as it can be, the very physical part of it is, yes, a hammering away. So it has a certain brutality.

LOUISE NEVELSON, *Dawns + Dusks* (1976)

If sex is a war, I am a conscientious objector: I will not play.

MARGE PIERCY, *Braided Lives* (1982)

See also Eroticism, Love, Passion, Seduction.

SEXISM

Our religion, laws, customs, are all founded on the belief that woman was made for man.

ELIZABETH CADY STANTON, letter to Susan B. Anthony (1860)

Women's chains have been forged by men, not by anatomy.

ESTELLE R. RAMEY, in Francine Klagsbrun, ed., *The First Ms. Reader* (1972)

Our culture thrusts woman into the condition of the lesser, the secondary, the subspecies, the atypical, the abnormal, the adjunct. It subordinates her to the male, who is portrayed as the superior, the species, the typical, the norm, the standard. It reflects the assumption that all people are male until proven female.

BOBBYE D. SORRELS, *The Nonsexist Communicator* (1983)

In our steady insistence on proclaiming sex-distinction we have grown to consider most human attributes as masculine attributes, for the simple reason that they were allowed for men and forbidden to women.

CHARLOTTE PERKINS GILMAN, *Women and Economics* (1900)

It's just as hard for man to break the habit of thinking of himself as central to the species as it was to break the habit of thinking of himself as central to the universe. He sees himself quite unconsciously as the main line of evolution, with a female satellite revolving around him as the moon revolves around the earth. This not only causes him to overlook valuable clues to our ancestry, but sometimes leads him into making statements that are arrant and demonstrable nonsense.

ELAINE MORGAN, *The Descent of Woman* (1972)

Black women, historically, have been doubly victimized by the twin immoralities of Jim Crow and Jane Crow. . . . Black women, faced with these dual barriers, have often found that sex bias is more formidable than racial bias.

PAULI MURRAY, in Mary Lou Thompson, ed., *Voices of the New Feminism* (1970)

Historically our own culture has relied for the creation of rich and contrasting values upon many artificial distinctions, the most striking of which is sex . . . if we are to achieve a richer culture, rich in contrasting values, we must recognize the whole gamut of human potentialities, and so weave a less arbitrary social fabric, one in which each diverse human gift will find a fitting place.

MARGARET MEAD, *Sex and Temperament in Three Primitive Societies* (1963)

Opening the door is a political act. The door-opening ceremony represents a non-obtrusive measure of authority. The hand that holds the door-knob rules the world.

LAUREL RICHARDSON WALUM, in *Observer* (1973)

The world has never yet seen a truly great and virtuous nation, because in the degradation of woman the very fountains of life are poisoned at their source.

LUCRETIA MOTT, speech (1848)

I ask no favors for my sex. . . . All I ask of our brethren is that they will take their feet from off our necks.

SARAH MOORE GRIMKÉ (1838), in Leslie B. Tanner, ed., *Voices From Women's Liberation* (1970)

There is no country in the world where there is so much boasting of the "chivalrous" treatment she enjoys. . . . In short, indulgence is given her as a substitute for justice.

HARRIET MARTINEAU, *Society in America* (1837)

The test for whether or not you can hold a job should not be the arrangement of your chromosomes.

BELLA ABZUG, *Bella!* (1972)

Just as the difference in height between males is no longer a realistic issue, now that lawsuits have been substituted for hand-to-hand encounters, so is the difference in strength between men and women no longer worth elaboration in cultural institutions.

MARGARET MEAD, *Sex and Temperament in Three Primitive Societies* (1963)

People are just not very ambitious for women still. Your son you want to be the best he can be. Your daughter you want to be happy.

ALEXA CANADY, in Brian Lanker, *I Dream a World* (1989)

It is a pity that so often the only way to treat girls like people seems to be to treat them like boys.

KATHARINE WHITEHORN, *Roundabout* (1962)

No one sex can govern alone. I believe that one of the reasons why civilization has failed so lamentably is that it has had one-sided government.

NANCY ASTOR, *My Two Countries* (1923)

Man has always liked to have some woman, especially one about eight feet high and of earnest aspect, to represent his ideas or inventions. At the same time, of course, he anxiously thwarted her attempts to utilize the inventions or pursue the theories he held. Thus, he wanted women to be illiterate, but to represent the Spirit of Education. . . . He wanted some smiling damsel to typify Architecture for him, but never to build his houses. And, much as he insisted on having his women folk meek and shy, he was always portraying them blowing trumpets and leading his armies to war.

MIRIAM BEARD, "Woman Springs From Allegory to Life," in *New York Times* (1927)

Protectiveness has often muffled the sound of doors closing against women.

BETTY FRIEDAN, *The Feminine Mystique* (1963)

We have taken this action, because as women . . . we realize that the condition of our sex is so deplorable that it is our duty even to break the law in order to call attention to the reasons why we do so.

EMMELINE PANKHURST, speech (1908)

You have tampered with women, you have struck a rock.

South African women's protest slogan (1957)

See also Discrimination, Oppression, Sex Roles, Stereotypes, Women and Men.

SEX ROLES

There is no such thing as a sphere for a sex. Every man has a different sphere, and one in which he may shine, and it is the same with every woman; and the same woman may have a different sphere at different times.

ELIZABETH CADY STANTON (1848), in Leslie B. Tanner, ed., *Voices From Women's Liberation* (1970)

See also Men, Women, Women and Men.

SHADOWS

Never fear shadows. They simply mean there's a light shining somewhere nearby.

RUTH E. RENKEL, in *Reader's Digest* (1983)

Marred pleasure's best, shadow makes the sun strong.

STEVIE SMITH, "The Queen and the Young Princess," *Selected Poems* (1964)

There is a time, when passing through a light, that you walk in your own shadow.

KERI HULME, *The Bone People* (1983)

SHAMANS

I am a medicine woman. I live in the beyond and come back.

AGNES WHISTLING ELK, in Lynn V. Andrews, *Medicine Woman* (1981)

True shamans live in a world that is alive with what is to rationalist sight unseen, a world pulsing with intelligence.

PAULA GUNN ALLEN, *Grandmothers of the Light* (1991)

Medicine people are truly citizens of two worlds, and those who continue to walk the path of medicine power learn to keep their balance in both the ordinary and the non-ordinary worlds.

PAULA GUNN ALLEN, *Grandmothers of the Light* (1991)

There are no medicine men, without medicine women. A medicine man is given power by a woman, and it has always been that way. A medicine man stands in the place of the dog. He is merely an instrument of woman. It doesn't look that way anymore, but it is true.

AGNES WHISTLING ELK, in Lynn V. Andrews, *Medicine Woman* (1981)

Sorcerers never kill anybody. They make people kill themselves.

AGNES WHISTLING ELK, in Lynn V. Andrews, *Medicine Woman* (1981)

See also Magic, Spirituality.

SHAPE

I like shape very much. A novel has to have shape, and life doesn't have any.

JEAN RHYS, *Smile Please: An Unfinished Autobiography* (1979)

See also Order.

SHARING

Sharing is sometimes more demanding than giving.

MARY CATHERINE BATESON, *Composing a Life* (1989)

When the animals entered the Ark in pairs, one may imagine that allied species made much private remark on each other, and were tempted to think that so many forms feeding on the same store of fodder were eminently superfluous, as tending to diminish the rations.

GEORGE ELIOT, *Middlemarch* (1871)

Old memories are so empty when they can not be shared.

JEWELLE GOMEZ, "No Day Too Long," in Elly Bulkin, ed., *Lesbian Fiction* (1981)

See also Generosity, Giving.

SHOCKING

Monstrous behavior is the order of the day. I'll tell you when to be shocked. When something human and decent happens!

LUCILLE KALLEN, *Introducing C. B. Greenfield* (1979)

Many people who imagine they are live wires are only shocking.

MARY PETTIBONE POOLE, *A Glass Eye at a Keyhole* (1938)

See also Offensiveness, Unexpected.

SILENCE

Silence is another form of sound.

JANE HOLLISTER WHEELWRIGHT, *The Ranch Papers—A California Memoir* (1988)

Silence may be as variously shaded as speech.

EDITH WHARTON, *The Reef* (1912)

Silences have a climax, when you have got to speak.

ELIZABETH BOWEN, *The House in Paris* (1935)

All artists dream of a silence which they must enter, as some creatures return to the sea to spawn.

IRIS MURDOCH, *The Black Prince* (1973)

God is the friend of silence. Trees, flowers, grass grow in silence. See the stars, moon, and sun, how they move in silence.

MOTHER TERESA, in Kathryn Spink, *For the Brotherhood of Man Under the Fatherhood of God* (1981)

I work out of silence, because silence makes up for my actual lack of working space. Silence substitutes for actual space, for psychological distance, for a sense of privacy and intactness. In this sense silence is absolutely necessary.

RADKA DONNELL, *Quilts as Women's Art: A Quilt Poetic* (1990)

To a poet, silence is an acceptable response, even a flattering one.

Colette, *Paris From My Window* (1944)

Sometimes I feel that every word spoken and every gesture made merely serve to exacerbate misunderstandings. Then what I would really like is to escape into a great silence and impose that silence on everyone else.

Etty Hillesum, *An Interrupted Life: The Diaries of Etty Hillesum 1941–1943* (1983)

When you choose to write using yourself as the source of the story, you are choosing to confront all the silences in which your story has been protectively wrapped. Your job as a writer is to respectfully, determinedly, free the story from the silences and free yourself from both.

Christina Baldwin, lecture (1990)

Silence more musical than any song.

Christina Rossetti, "Rest" (1849), Goblin Market (1862)

An audience of twenty thousand, sitting on its hands, could not have produced such an echoing silence.

Mary Renault, *The Mask of Apollo* (1966)

A small silence came between us, as precise as a picture hanging on the wall.

Jean Stafford, *Boston Adventure* (1944)

But silence is where the victims dwell.

Nelly Sachs, "Glowing Enigma III," *O the Chimneys* (1967)

Every day silence harvests its victims. Silence is a mortal illness.

Natalia Ginzburg, *The Little Virtues* (1962)

Sticks and stones are hard on bones. / Aimed with angry art, / Words can sting like anything. / But silence breaks the heart.

Phyllis McGinley, "Ballade of Lost Objects," *The Love Letters of Phyllis McGinley* (1954)

See also Calm.

SIMPLICITY

Simplicity is the peak of civilization.

Jessie Sampter, *The Emek* (1927)

I am beginning to learn that it is the sweet, simple things of life which are the real ones after all.

Laura Ingalls Wilder (1917), in Lorraine Anderson, ed., *Sisters of the Earth* (1991)

Yes, to become simple and live simply, not only within yourself but also in your everyday dealings. Don't make ripples all around you, don't try so hard to be interesting, keep your distance, be honest, fight the desire to be thought fascinating by the outside world.

Etty Hillesum, *An Interrupted Life: The Diaries of Etty Hillesum 1941–1943* (1983)

I believe we would be happier to have a personal revolution in our individual lives and go back to simpler living and more direct thinking. It is the simple things of life that make living worth while, the sweet fundamental things such as love and duty, work and rest and living close to nature.

Laura Ingalls Wilder (1917), in Lorraine Anderson, ed., *Sisters of the Earth* (1991)

Such words as "God" and "Death" and "Suffering" and "Eternity" are best forgotten. We have to become as simple and as wordless as the growing corn or the falling rain. We must just be.

Etty Hillesum, *An Interrupted Life: The Diaries of Etty Hillesum 1941–1943* (1983)

I like to go to Marshall Field's in Chicago just to see how many things there are in the world that I do not want.

Mother Mary Madeleva, *My First Seventy Years* (1959)

In the end, what affect your life most deeply are things too simple to talk about.

Nell Blaine, in Eleanor Munro, *Originals: American Women Artists* (1979)

See also Small Things.

SIN

Alas, that ever I did sin! It is full merry in Heaven.

Margery Kempe, *The Book of Margery Kempe* (c. 1431)

Sin recognized—but that—may keep us humble, / But oh, it keeps us nasty.

STEVIE SMITH, "Recognition Not Enough," *Selected Poems* (1964)

All sins are attempts to fill voids.

SIMONE WEIL, *Gravity and Grace* (1947)

Sins cut boldly up through every class in society, but mere misdemeanors show a certain level in life.

ELIZABETH BOWEN, *The Death of the Heart* (1938)

Many are saved from sin by being so inept at it.

MIGNON MCLAUGHLIN, *The Neurotic's Notebook* (1963)

The biggest sin is sitting on your ass.

FLORYNCE KENNEDY, in Gloria Steinem, "The Verbal Karate of Florynce Kennedy," *Ms.* (1973)

Fashions in sin change.

LILLIAN HELLMAN, *Watch on the Rhine* (1941)

We don't call it sin today, we call it self-expression.

BARONESS STOCKS, in Jonathon Green, *The Cynic's Lexicon* (1984)

Sin has always been an ugly word, but it has been made so in a new sense over the past half-century. It has been made not only ugly, but passé. People are no longer sinful, they are only immature or underprivileged or frightened, or, more particularly, sick.

PHYLLIS MCGINLEY, "In Defense of Sin," *The Province of the Heart* (1959)

Somewhere, and I can't find where, I read about an Eskimo hunter who asked the local missionary priest, "If I did not know about god and sin, would I go to hell?" "No," said the priest, "not if you did not know." "Then why," asked the Eskimo earnestly, "did you tell me?"

ANNIE DILLARD, *Pilgrim at Tinker Creek* (1974)

See also Crime, Devil, Evil, Mistakes, Slippery Slope, Vice.

SINCERITY

Sincerity is not a spontaneous flower, nor is modesty either.

COLETTE, *The Pure and the Impure* (1932)

The most exhausting thing in life, I have discovered, is being insincere.

ANNE MORROW LINDBERGH, *Gift From the Sea* (1955)

See also Candor, Honesty, Truth.

SINGING

With my singing I can make / A refuge for my spirit's sake, / A house of shining words, to be / My fragile immortality.

SARA TEASDALE, "Interlude," *Love Songs* (1917)

i wanna go see her and ask her if she will teach us how to use our voices like she used hers on that old 78 record.

HATTIE GOSSETT, "billie lives! billie lives!" in Cherríe Moraga and Gloria Anzaldúa, eds., *This Bridge Called My Back* (1983)

Of all musical instruments the human voice is the most beautiful, for it is made by God.

SHUSHA GUPPY, *The Blindfold Horse: Memories of a Persian Childhood* (1988)

All the intelligence and talent in the world can't make a singer. The voice is a wild thing. It can't be bred in captivity.

WILLA CATHER, *The Song of the Lark* (1915)

I have never given all of myself, even vocally, to anyone. I was taught to sing on your interest, not your capital.

LEONTYNE PRICE, in Brian Lanker, *I Dream a World* (1989)

See also Artists, Music, Performance, Song.

SINGLE

But there is a natural tribal hostility between the married and the unmarried. I cannot stand the shows so often quite instinctively put on by married people to insinuate that they are not only more fortunate but in some way more moral than you are.

IRIS MURDOCH, *The Black Prince* (1973)

A bachelor never quite gets over the idea that he is a thing of beauty and a boy forever.

HELEN ROWLAND, *A Guide to Men* (1922)

Being an old maid is like death by drowning, a really delightful sensation after you cease to struggle.

EDNA FERBER, *A Peculiar Treasure* (1939)

See also Alone.

SISTERS

There can be no situation in life in which the conversation of my dear sister will not administer some comfort to me.

LADY MARY WORTLEY MONTAGU, letter (1747), in Octave Thanet, ed., *The Best Letters of Lady Mary Wortley Montagu* (1901)

We are each other's reference point at our turning points.

ELIZABETH FISHEL, *Sisters: Love and Rivalry Inside the Family and Beyond* (1979)

What surprised me was that within a family, the voices of sisters as they're talking are virtually always the same.

ELIZABETH FISHEL, *Sisters: Love and Rivalry Inside the Family and Beyond* (1979)

Often, in old age, they become each other's chosen and most happy companions. In addition to their shared memories of childhood and of their relationship to each other's children, they share memories of the same home, the same homemaking style, and the same small prejudices about housekeeping that carry the echoes of their mother's voice.

MARGARET MEAD, *Blackberry Winter* (1972)

Sisters is probably *the* most competitive relationship within the family, but once the sisters are grown, it becomes the strongest relationship.

MARGARET MEAD, in Elizabeth Fishel, *Sisters: Love and Rivalry Inside the Family and Beyond* (1979)

The desire to be and have a sister is a primitive and profound one that may have everything or nothing to do with the family a woman is born to. It is a desire to know and be known by someone who shares blood and body, history and dreams, common ground and the unknown adventures of the future, darkest secrets and the glassiest beads of truth.

ELIZABETH FISHEL, *Sisters: Love and Rivalry Inside the Family and Beyond* (1979)

Sisters define their rivalry in terms of competition for the gold cup of parental love. It is never perceived as a cup which runneth over, rather a finite vessel from which the more one sister drinks, the less is left for the others.

ELIZABETH FISHEL, *Sisters: Love and Rivalry Inside the Family and Beyond* (1979)

Both within the family and without, our sisters hold up our mirrors: our images of who we are and of who we can dare to become.

ELIZABETH FISHEL, *Sisters: Love and Rivalry Inside the Family and Beyond* (1979)

See also Family.

SIZE

At Stoke Poges, the inn where we stopped was so small, it could have been spelled "in."

MARY ANDERSON, *A Few Memories* (1896)

Big doesn't necessarily mean better. Sunflowers aren't better than violets.

EDNA FERBER, *Giant* (1952)

Too few is as many as too many.

GERTRUDE STEIN, *Everybody's Autobiography* (1937)

See also Quantity.

SKY

Elsewhere the sky is the roof of the world; but here the earth was the floor of the sky.

WILLA CATHER, *Death Comes for the Archbishop* (1927)

Flat country seems to give the sky such a chance.

DODIE SMITH, *I Capture the Castle* (1948)

He wondered whether the peculiar solemnity of looking at the sky comes, not from what one contemplates, but from that uplift of one's head.

AYN RAND, *The Fountainhead* (1943)

See also Moon, Planets, Sun, Sunset.

SLAVERY

No pen can give an adequate description of the all-pervading corruption produced by slavery.

HARRIET A. JACOBS, *Incidents in the Life of a Slave Girl, Written by Herself* (1861)

Oh, was it not strangely inconsistent that men fresh, so fresh, from the baptism of the Revolution should make such concessions to the foul spirit of Despotism! that, when fresh from gaining their own liberty, they could permit the African slave trade—could let their national flag hang a sign of death on Guinea's coast and Congo's shore!

FRANCES ELLEN WATKINS HARPER, letter (1859), in Frances Smith Foster, ed., *A Brighter Coming Day* (1990)

The slave child had no thought for the morrow; but there came that blight, which too surely waits on every human being born to be a chattel.

HARRIET A. JACOBS, *Incidents in the Life of a Slave Girl, Written by Herself* (1861)

Notwithstanding my grandmother's long and faithful service to her owners, not one of her children escaped the auction block. These God-breathing machines are no more, in the sight of their masters, than the cotton they plant, or the horses they tend.

HARRIET A. JACOBS, *Incidents in the Life of a Slave Girl, Written by Herself* (1861)

I was ordered to go for flowers, that my mistress's house might be decorated for an evening party. I spent the day gathering flowers and weaving them into festoons, while the dead body of my father was lying within a mile of me. What cared my owners for that? He was merely a piece of property. Moreover, they thought he had spoiled his children, by teaching them to feel that they were human beings. This was blasphe-

mous doctrine for a slave to teach; presumptuous in him, and dangerous to the masters.

HARRIET A. JACOBS, *Incidents in the Life of a Slave Girl, Written by Herself* (1861)

Could you have seen that mother clinging to her child, when they fastened the irons upon his wrists; could you have heard her heart-rending groans, and seen her bloodshot eyes wander wildly from face to face, vainly pleading for mercy; could you have witnessed that scene as I saw it, you would exclaim, *Slavery is damnable!*

HARRIET A. JACOBS, *Incidents in the Life of a Slave Girl, Written by Herself* (1861)

I can testify, from my own experience and observation, that slavery is a curse to the whites as well as to the blacks. It makes the white fathers cruel and sensual; the sons violent and licentious; it contaminates the daughters, and makes the wives wretched. And as for the colored race, it needs an abler pen than mine to describe the extremity of their sufferings, the depth of their degradation.

HARRIET A. JACOBS, *Incidents in the Life of a Slave Girl, Written by Herself* (1861)

Slavery always has, and always will, produce insurrections wherever it exists, because it is a violation of the natural order of things.

ANGELINA GRIMKÉ, "Appeal to the Christian Women of the South," in *The Anti-Slavery Examiner* (1836)

See also Domination, Oppression.

SLEEP

Rocked in the cradle of the deep, / I lay me down in peace to sleep.

EMMA HART WILLARD, *The Cradle of the Deep* (1831)

No day is so bad it can't be fixed with a nap.

CARRIE SNOW, in *Ms.* (1969)

Then I pillowed myself in goodness and slept righteously.

MAYA ANGELOU, *All God's Children Need Traveling Shoes* (1986)

I did not sleep. I never do when I am over-happy, over-unhappy, or in bed with a strange man.

EDNA O'BRIEN, title story, *The Love Object* (1968)

How do people go to sleep? I'm afraid I've lost the knack. I might try busting myself smartly over the temple with the night-light. I might repeat to myself, slowly and soothingly, a list of quotations beautiful from minds profound; if I can remember any of the damn things.

DOROTHY PARKER, "The Little Hours," *Dorothy Parker* (1944)

His sleep was a sensuous gluttony of oblivion.

P. D. JAMES, *Death of an Expert Witness* (1977)

I reached for sleep and drew it round me like a blanket muffling pain and thought together in the merciful dark.

MARY STEWART, *The Hollow Hills* (1973)

Sleep is death without the responsibility.

FRAN LEBOWITZ, *Metropolitan Life* (1978)

See also Dreams, Fatigue, Insomnia.

SLIPPERY SLOPE

It's darn today, damn tomorrow, and next week it'll be goddamn.

LOUISE MERIWETHER, *Daddy Was a Number Runner* (1970)

I was like many another who starts an intrigue timidly. Once into it, I had to go on, and therefore I had to harden my sensibilities.

ELIZABETH BORTON DE TREVIÑO, *I, Juan de Pareja* (1965)

But I think that sometimes, when one's behaved like a rather second-rate person, the way I did at breakfast, then in a kind of self-destructive shock one goes and does something *really* second-rate. Almost as if to prove it.

ALISON LURIE, *Real People* (1969)

Once you begin being naughty, it is easier to go on and on, and sooner or later something dreadful happens.

LAURA INGALLS WILDER, *On the Banks of Plum Creek* (1937)

When one kicks over a tea table and smashes everything but the sugar bowl, one may as well pick that up and drop it on the bricks, don't you think?

MARGERY ALLINGHAM, *Dancers in Mourning* (1937)

This downhill path is easy, but there's no turning back.

CHRISTINA ROSSETTI, "Amor Mundi" (1865), *The Poetical Works of Christina Georgina Rossetti* (1906)

See also Sin.

SMALL THINGS

One can get just as much exultation in losing oneself in a little thing as in a big thing. It is nice to think how one can be recklessly lost in a daisy!

ANNE MORROW LINDBERGH, *Bring Me a Unicorn* (1971)

I wait for a chance to confer a great favor, and let the small ones slip; but they tell best in the end, I fancy.

LOUISA MAY ALCOTT, *Little Women* (1868)

To be really great in little things, to be truly noble and heroic in the insipid details of everyday life, is a virtue so rare as to be worthy of canonization.

HARRIET BEECHER STOWE (1860), in Mary Alice Warner and Bayna Beilenson, eds., *Women of Faith and Spirit* (1987)

We must not, in trying to think about how we can make a big difference, ignore the small daily differences we can make which, over time, add up to big differences that we often cannot foresee.

MARIAN WRIGHT EDELMAN, *Families in Peril* (1987)

I long to accomplish a great and noble task, but it is my chief duty to accomplish humble tasks as though they were great and noble. The world is moved along, not only by the mighty shoves of its heroes, but also by the aggregate of the tiny pushes of each honest worker.

HELEN KELLER, in Charles L. Wallis, *The Treasure Chest* (1983)

To keep a lamp burning we have to keep putting oil in it.

MOTHER TERESA, in *Time* (1975)

Only those who know the supremacy of the intellectual life—the life which has a seed of ennobling thought and purpose within it—can understand the grief of one who falls from that serene activity into the absorbing soul-wasting struggle with worldly annoyances.

GEORGE ELIOT, *Middlemarch* (1871)

See also Service, Simplicity.

SMELL

Smell is a potent wizard that transports us across thousands of miles and all the years we have lived.

HELEN KELLER, in Diane Ackerman, *A Natural History of the Senses* (1990)

It is almost as hard for us to sense our own species quality as it is to sense our species smell.

LOIS CRISLER, *Arctic Wild* (1958)

For the sense of smell, almost more than any other, has the power to recall memories and it is a pity that we use it so little.

RACHEL CARSON, *The Sense of Wonder* (1965)

Smell is the mute sense, the one without words.

DIANE ACKERMAN, *A Natural History of the Senses* (1990)

See also Senses.

SMILE

Let us always meet each other with a smile, for the smile is the beginning of love.

MOTHER TERESA, in Barbara Shiels, *Women and the Nobel Prize* (1985)

Good-fellowship, unflagging, is the prime requisite for success in our society, and the man or woman who smiles only for reasons of humor or pleasure is a deviate.

MARYA MANNES, *More in Anger* (1958)

She set an attentive smile on her face, like a sentinel, behind which she could cultivate her own thoughts.

DORIS LESSING, *The Summer Before the Dark* (1973)

He stands, smiling encouragement, like a clumsy dentist.

KATHERINE MANSFIELD, "Bank Holiday," *The Garden Party* (1922)

She had long since forgotten the meaning of a smile, but the physical ability to make the gesture remained.

BERYL MARKHAM, *West With the Night* (1942)

People who keep stiff upper lips find that it's damn hard to smile.

JUDITH GUEST, *Ordinary People* (1976)

When she smiled the smile was only in the mouth and a little bitter: the face of an incurable yet to be stricken with its malady.

DJUNA BARNES, *Nightwood* (1937)

Sometimes I not only stand there and take it, I even smile at them and say I'm sorry. When I feel that smile coming onto my face, I wish I could take my face off and stamp on it.

URSULA K. LE GUIN, *Very Far Away From Anywhere Else* (1976)

I really do believe I can accomplish a great deal with a big grin. I know some people find that disconcerting, but that doesn't matter.

BEVERLY SILLS, in *Ms.* (1979)

That grin! She could have taken it off her face and put it on the table.

JEAN STAFFORD, title story, *Bad Characters* (1954)

See also Face, Laughter.

SNOW

In shaping the snow into blossoms— / The north wind is tender after all.

PING HSIN, "The Spring Waters" (1902), in Joanna Bankier and Deirdre Lashgari, eds., *Women Poets of the World* (1983)

You believe it's cold, but if you build yourself a snowhouse it's warm. You think it's white, but at times it looks pink, and another time it's blue. It can be softer than anything, and then again harder than stone. Nothing is certain.

TOVE JANSSON, *Moominland Midwinter* (1958)

See also Weather, Winter.

SOBRIETY

I was rather drunk with what I had done. And I am always one to prefer being sober. I must be sober. It is so much more exciting to be sober, to be exact and concentrated and sober.

GERTRUDE STEIN, in John Malcolm Brinnin, *The Third Rose* (1959)

See also Alcohol.

SOCIAL CHANGE

Use what is dominant in a culture to change it quickly.

JENNY HOLZER, *Truisms* (1977–1979)

The keys to any social reform lie in the acceptance of the need for correction and the commitment to finding ways to make that correction.

BOBBYE D. SORRELS, *The Nonsexist Communicator* (1983)

Thinking about profound social change, conservatives always expect disaster, while revolutionaries confidently anticipate utopia. Both are wrong.

CAROLYN HEILBRUN, *Toward a Recognition of Androgyny* (1973)

Leaders are indispensable, but to produce a major social change many ordinary people must also be involved.

ANNE FIROR SCOTT, "The 'New Woman' in the New South," in *South Atlantic Quarterly* (1962)

Things which matter cost money, and we've got to spend the money if we do not want to have generations of parasites rather than generations of citizens.

BARBARA JORDAN, in Brian Lanker, *I Dream a World* (1989)

If you are trying to transform a brutalized society into one where people can live in dignity and

hope, you begin with the empowering of the most powerless. You build from the ground up.

ADRIENNE RICH, "'Going There' and Being Here," *Blood, Bread, and Poetry* (1986)

The master's tools will never dismantle the master's house.

AUDRE LORDE, speech (1979)

Characteristically, major social movements are spawned in obscurity at the periphery of public awareness, seem to burst suddenly and dramatically into public view, and eventually fade into the landscape not because they have diminished but because they have become a permanent part of our perceptions and experience.

FREDA ADLER, *Sisters in Crime* (1975)

Cultural transformation announces itself in sputtering fits and starts, sparked here and there by minor incidents, warmed by new ideas that may smolder for decades. In many different places, at different times, the kindling is laid for the real conflagration—the one that will consume the old landmarks and alter the landscape forever.

MARILYN FERGUSON, *The Aquarian Conspiracy* (1980)

Under miserable conditions of life, any vision of the possibility of better things makes the present misery more intolerable, and spurs those who suffer to the most energetic struggles to improve their lot, and if these struggles only immediately result in sharper misery, the outcome is sheer desperation.

EMMA GOLDMAN, "The Psychology of Political Violence," *Anarchism* (1910)

Although the connections are not always obvious, personal change is inseparable from social and political change.

HARRIET LERNER, *Dance of Intimacy* (1989)

Those interested in perpetuating present conditions are always in tears about the marvelous past that is about to disappear, without having so much as a smile for the young future.

SIMONE DE BEAUVOIR, *The Second Sex* (1949)

If the shoe doesn't fit, must we change the foot?

GLORIA STEINEM, *Outrageous Acts and Everyday Rebellions* (1983)

See also Change, Revolution.

SOCIETY

Snowflakes, leaves, humans, plants, raindrops, stars, molecules, microscopic entities all come in communities. The singular cannot in reality exist.

PAULA GUNN ALLEN, *Grandmothers of the Light* (1991)

A well ordered society would be one where the State only had a negative action, comparable to that of a rudder: a light pressure at the right moment to counteract the first suggestion of any loss of equilibrium.

SIMONE WEIL, *Gravity and Grace* (1947)

We want a society where people are free to make choices, to make mistakes, to be generous and compassionate. This is what we mean by a moral society; not a society where the state is responsible for everything, and no one is responsible for the state.

MARGARET THATCHER, speech (1977)

We live in a true chaos of contradicting authorities, an age of conformism without community, of proximity without communication.

GERMAINE GREER, *The Female Eunuch* (1971)

Sometimes . . . the world is so much sicker than the inmates of its institutions.

HANNAH GREEN, *I Never Promised You a Rose Garden* (1964)

I'm not interested in pursuing a society that uses analysis, research, and experimentation to concretize their vision of cruel destinies for those who are not bastards of the Pilgrims; a society with arrogance rising, moon in oppression, and sun in destruction.

BARBARA CAMERON, in Cherríe Moraga and Gloria Anzaldúa, eds., *This Bridge Called My Back* (1983)

Societies who do not care for their young people and old people are decadent, decaying societies.

SUZAN SHOWN HARJO, in *Rethinking Schools* (1991)

There are people who eat the earth and eat all the people on it like in the Bible with the locusts. And other people who stand around and watch them eat it.

LILLIAN HELLMAN, *The Little Foxes* (1939)

Man is not made for society, but society is made for man. No institution can be good which does not tend to improve the individual.

MARGARET FULLER, *Memoirs* (1840)

The person and society are yoked, like mind and body. Arguing which is more important is like debating whether oxygen or hydrogen is the more essential property of water.

MARILYN FERGUSON, *The Aquarian Conspiracy* (1980)

Society in its full sense . . . is never an entity separable from the individuals who compose it. No individual can arrive even at the threshold of his potentialities without a culture in which he participates. Conversely, no civilization has in it any element which in the last analysis is not the contribution of an individual.

RUTH BENEDICT, *Patterns of Culture* (1934)

Miss Manners refuses to allow society to seek its own level. Having peered through her lorgnette into the abyss, she can guess how low that level will be.

JUDITH MARTIN, *Miss Manners' Guide for the Turn-of-the-Millennium* (1989)

See also Civilization.

SOLITUDE

Alone, alone, oh! We have been warned about solitary vices. Have solitary pleasures ever been adequately praised? Do many people know that they exist?

JESSAMYN WEST, *Hide and Seek* (1973)

She would not exchange her solitude for anything. *Never again to be forced to move to the rhythms of others.*

TILLIE OLSEN, title story, *Tell Me a Riddle* (1956)

Do not allow yourself to be imprisoned by any affection. Keep your solitude. The day, if it ever comes, when you are given true affection there will be no opposition between interior solitude and friendship, quite the reverse. It is even by this infallible sign that you will recognize it.

SIMONE WEIL, *Gravity and Grace* (1947)

There are days when solitude, for someone my age, is a heady wine that intoxicates you with freedom, others when it is a bitter tonic, and still others when it is a poison that makes you beat your head against the wall.

COLETTE, "Freedom" (1908), *Earthly Paradise* (1966)

The prohibition against solitude is forever. A Carry Nation rises in every person when he thinks he sees someone sneaking off to be alone. It is not easy to be solitary unless you are also born ruthless. Every solitary repudiates someone.

JESSAMYN WEST, *Hide and Seek* (1973)

What a commentary on our civilization, when being alone is considered suspect; when one has to apologize for it, make excuses, hide the fact that one practices it—like a secret vice!

ANNE MORROW LINDBERGH, *Gift From the Sea* (1955)

There is nothing like the bootless solitude of those who are caged together.

IRIS MURDOCH, *The Black Prince* (1973)

For every five well-adjusted and smoothly functioning Americans, there are two who never had the chance to discover themselves. It may well be because they have never been alone with themselves.

MARYA MANNES, in *Vogue* (1964)

If any individual live too much in relations, so that he becomes a stranger to the resources of his own nature, he falls after a while into a distraction, or imbecility, from which he can only be cured by a time of isolation which gives the renovating fountains time to rise up.

MARGARET FULLER, "The Great Lawsuit," in *The Dial* (1843)

She was not accustomed to taste the joys of solitude except in company.

EDITH WHARTON, *The House of Mirth* (1905)

Solitude is un-American.

ERICA JONG, *Fear of Flying* (1973)

See also Alone, Loneliness, Privacy, Self-Sufficiency.

SONG

It is my heart that makes my songs, not I.

SARA TEASDALE, "What Do I Care?" *Flame and Shadow* (1920)

I hang my laundry on the line when I write.

JONI MITCHELL, in Kathleen Kimball, Robin Petersen, Kathleen Johnson, *The Music Lover's Quotation Book* (1990)

The eternal task of song can never be finished in a single lifetime. That is the beauty and fascination of the art. Once you begin to phrase finely, you will feel more joy in the beautiful finish of a beautiful phrase than that caused by the loudest applause of an immense audience. The latter excites for a moment; the former endures forever.

NELLIE MELBA, in Kathleen Kimball, Robin Petersen, Kathleen Johnson, *The Music Lover's Quotation Book* (1990)

See also Music, Singing.

SONS

The tie is stronger than that between father and son and father and daughter. . . . The bond is also more complex than the one between mother and daughter. For a woman, a son offers the best chance to know the mysterious male existence.

CAROLE KLEIN, *Mothers and Sons* (1984)

This is the womb that carried him, / like a stone cave / lived in by a tiger and now abandoned. / It is on the battlefield that you will find him.

AUVAIYAR (3rd century), in Joanna Bankier and Deirdre Lashgari, eds., *Women Poets of the World* (1983)

See also Family.

SORROW

Sorrow was like the wind. It came in gusts.

MARJORIE KINNAN RAWLINGS, *South Moon Under* (1933)

Emptied with weeping / my eyes are / two buckets of the waterman / as he walks among orchard trees.

SAFIYA BINT MUSAFIR, "At the Badr Trench" (7th century), in Joanna Bankier and Deirdre Lashgari, eds., *Women Poets of the World* (1983)

I have been in Sorrow's kitchen and licked out all the pots. Then I have stood on the peaky mountain wrapped in rainbows, with a harp and a sword in my hands.

ZORA NEALE HURSTON, *Dust Tracks on a Road* (1942)

Every sorrow suggests a thousand songs, and every song recalls a thousand sorrows, and so they are infinite in number, and all the same.

MARILYNNE ROBINSON, *Housekeeping* (1980)

The sorrows of humanity are no one's sorrows. . . . A thousand people drowned in floods in China are news: a solitary child drowned in a pond is tragedy.

JOSEPHINE TEY, *The Daughter of Time* (1951)

Words are less needful to sorrow than to joy.

HELEN HUNT JACKSON, *Ramona* (1884)

It was the last night before sorrow touched her life; and no life is ever quite the same again when once that cold, sanctifying touch has been laid upon it.

L. M. MONTGOMERY, *Anne of Green Gables* (1908)

There is no despair so absolute as that which comes with the first moments of our first great sorrow, when we have not yet known what it is to have suffered and be healed, to have despaired and recovered hope.

GEORGE ELIOT, *Adam Bede* (1859)

Sorrow makes us very good or very bad.

GEORGE SAND (1871), in *French Wit and Wisdom* (1950)

It is better to learn early of the inevitable depths, for then sorrow and death take their proper place in life, and one is not afraid.

PEARL BUCK, *My Several Worlds* (1954)

We could never learn to be brave and patient, if there were only joy in the world.

HELEN KELLER, in *Atlantic Monthly* (1890)

Many people misjudge the permanent effect of sorrow and their capacity to live in the past.

IVY COMPTON-BURNETT, *Mother and Son* (1955)

All sorrows can be borne if you put them into a story or tell a story about them.

ISAK DINESEN, in Susan Cahill, ed., *Women and Fiction 2* (1978)

The human heart does not stay away too long from that which hurt it most. There is a return journey to anguish that few of us are released from making.

LILLIAN SMITH, The Journey (1954)

A man's sorrow runs uphill; true it is difficult for him to bear, but it is also difficult for him to keep.

DJUNA BARNES, *Nightwood* (1937)

Sorrow is tranquility remembered in emotion.

DOROTHY PARKER, "Sentiment," *The Portable Dorothy Parker* (1944)

Give your sorrow all the space and shelter in yourself that is its due, for if everyone bears his grief honestly and courageously, the sorrow that now fills the world will abate. But if you do not clear a decent shelter for your sorrow, and instead reserve most of the space inside you for hatred and thoughts of revenge—from which new sorrows will be born for others—then sorrow will never cease in this world and will multiply.

ETTY HILLESUM, *An Interrupted Life: The Diaries of Etty Hillesum 1941–1943* (1983)

I found more joy in sorrow / Than you could find in joy.

SARA TEASDALE, "The Answer," Collected Poems (1937)

A lean sorrow is hardest to bear.

SARAH ORNE JEWETT, *The Life of Nancy* (1895)

See also Grief, Mourning, Pain, Sufferings, Tears, Unhappiness.

SOUL

See there within the flesh / Like a bright wick, englazed / The soul God's finger lit / To give her liberty, / And joy and power and love.

MECHTHILD VON MAGDEBURG, "Love Flows From God" (c. 1250), in Joanna Bankier and Deirdre Lashgari, eds., *Women Poets of the World* (1983)

For what is man's soul but a flame? It flickers in and around the body of a man as does the flame around the rough log.

SELMA LAGERLÖF, *The General's Ring* (1928)

The soul is a breath of living spirit, that with excellent sensitivity, permeates the entire body to give it life. Just so, the breath of the air makes the earth fruitful. Thus the air is the soul of the earth, moistening it, greening it.

HILDEGARDE OF BINGEN, *Scivias* (1141–1150), in Gabriele Uhlein, ed., *Meditations With Hildegarde of Bingen* (1983)

Mystical experiences nearly always lead one to a belief that some aspect of consciousness is imperishable. In a Buddhist metaphor the consciousness of the individual is like a flame that burns through the night. It is not the same flame over time, yet neither is it another flame.

MARILYN FERGUSON, *The Aquarian Conspiracy* (1980)

There is no plummet to sound another's soul.

VIRGILIA PETERSON, *A Matter of Life and Death* (1961)

The soul . . . may have many symbols with which it reaches toward God.

ANYA SETON, *The Turquoise* (1946)

The strongest, surest way to the soul is through the flesh.

MABEL DODGE, *Lorenzo in Taos* (1932)

See also Inner Life, Self, Spirituality.

THE SOUTH

If the production of self-serving folklore qualified as an industry, the South would have been an industrial power since colonial times.

SHIRLEY ABBOTT, *Womenfolks: Growing Up Down South* (1983)

In the South, Sunday morning sex is accompanied by church bells.

FLORENCE KING, *Confessions of a Failed Southern Lady* (1985)

The South may be the last place where dying is still sometimes a community project.

SHIRLEY ABBOTT, *Womenfolks: Growing Up Down South* (1983)

Southerners can never resist a losing cause.

MARGARET MITCHELL, *Gone With the Wind* (1936)

This curious sense of separateness is one of the most stubbornly preserved Southern attitudes. The South, its historians say, stands apart from other American regions because of its peculiar history. History has been cruel to Southerners, has persistently dealt them deuces.

SHIRLEY ABBOTT, *Womenfolks: Growing Up Down South* (1983)

Being Southerners, it was a source of shame to some members of the family that we had no recorded ancestors on either side of the Battle of Hastings.

HARPER LEE, *To Kill a Mockingbird* (1960)

To grow up female in the South is to inherit a set of directives that warp one for life, if they do not actually induce psychosis.

SHIRLEY ABBOTT, *Womenfolks: Growing Up Down South* (1983)

SPACE

We're smart enough to know we need to live in groups to survive, but we're still animals and we needs lots of room. In the case of the male of the species we also probably need that-guy-over-there's space. And his wife and cow, too.

JULIA PHILLIPS, *You'll Never Eat Lunch in This Town Again* (1991)

He [Robert Benchley] and I had an office so tiny that an inch smaller and it would have been adultery.

DOROTHY PARKER, in Malcolm Cowley, ed., *Writers at Work* (1958)

See also Rooms.

SPECIALISTS

The trouble with specialists is that they tend to think in grooves.

ELAINE MORGAN, *The Descent of Woman* (1972)

SPECULATION

Metaphysical speculation is about as pointless as a discussion on the meaning of one's lungs. They're for breathing.

P. D. JAMES, *Death of an Expert Witness* (1977)

SPEECH

You kin tame a bear. You kin tame a wild-cat and you kin tame a panther. . . . You kin tame arything, son, excusin' the human tongue.

MARJORIE KINNAN RAWLINGS, *The Yearling* (1938)

Sweet words are like honey: a little may refresh, but too much gluts the stomach.

ANNE BRADSTREET, "Meditations Divine and Moral" (c. 1655), in John Harvard Ellis, *The Works of Anne Bradstreet in Prose and Verse* (1932)

To know how to say what others only know how to think, is what makes men poets or sages; and to dare to say what others only dare to think, makes men martyrs or reformers, or both.

ELIZABETH RUNDLE CHARLES, *Chronicles of the Schönberg-Cotta Family* (1863)

He went on endlessly, overcome by the facile volubility of a weak nature.

ELLEN GLASGOW, *Barren Ground* (1925)

They . . . talk simply because they think sound is more manageable than silence.

MARGARET HALSEY, *With Malice Toward Some* (1938)

His voice was as intimate as the rustle of sheets.

DOROTHY PARKER, "Dusk Before Fireworks," *The Portable Dorothy Parker* (1944)

Many a pair of curious ears had been lured by that well-timed pause.

LI ANG, *The Butcher's Wife* (1983)

In the heat of a political lifetime, Ronald Reagan innocently squirrels away tidbits of misinformation and then, sometimes years later, casually drops them into his public discourse, like gum balls in a quiche.

LUCY HOWARD, in *Newsweek* (1985)

Women speak because they wish to speak, whereas a man speaks only when driven to speech by something outside himself—like, for instance, he can't find any clean socks.

JEAN KERR, *The Snake Has All the Lines* (1958)

The first duty of a lecturer—to hand you after an hour's discourse a nugget of pure truth to wrap up between the pages of your notebooks and keep on the mantelpiece for ever.

VIRGINIA WOOLF, *A Room of One's Own* (1929)

The best impromptu speeches are the ones written well in advance.

RUTH GORDON, *The Leading Lady* (1948)

He speaks to Me as if I was a public meeting.

QUEEN VICTORIA, in G. W. E. Russell, *Collections and Recollections* (1898)

I very seldom during my whole stay in the country heard a sentence elegantly turned and correctly pronounced from the lips of an American.

FRANCES TROLLOPE, *Domestic Manners of the Americans* (1832)

A nation which does not appreciate that the simple elocution exercise "Merry Mary married hairy Harry" contains not one but *three* vowel sounds.

JESSICA MITFORD, in *Observer* (1979)

He landed on the French word the way a hen lands on the water, skeptical, but hoping for the best.

JESSAMYN WEST, *The Friendly Persuasion* (1940)

Often beauty grows dull or common when speech breaks the mask.

MARY RENAULT, *The Mask of Apollo* (1966)

Blessed is the man who, having nothing to say, abstains from giving us wordy evidence of the fact.

GEORGE ELIOT, *Impressions of Theophrastus Such* (1879)

I like people who refuse to speak until they are ready to speak.

LILLIAN HELLMAN, *An Unfinished Woman* (1969)

Say what you will in two / Words and get through. / Long, frilly / Palaver is silly.

MARIE-FRANÇOISE-CATHERINE DE BEAUVEAU, "Strong Feelings," in Joanna Bankier and Deirdre Lashgari, eds., *Women Poets of the World* (1983)

There are very few people who don't become more interesting when they stop talking.

MARY LOWRY, in *Pacific Sun* (1985)

The commercial class has always mistrusted verbal brilliancy and wit, deeming such qualities, perhaps with some justice, frivolous and unprofitable.

DOROTHY NEVILL, *The Reminiscences of Lady Dorothy Nevill* (1907)

See also Conversation, Discretion, Language, Talking, Words.

SPIRITUALITY

We are not human beings trying to be spiritual. We are spiritual beings trying to be human.

JACQUELYN SMALL, in Anne Wilson Schaef, *Meditations for Women Who Do Too Much* (1990)

In God's sight we do not fall: in our own we do not stand.

JULIAN OF NORWICH, *Revelations of Divine Love* (1373)

The well of Providence is deep. It's the buckets we bring to it that are small.

MARY WEBB, in *Ladies' Home Journal* (1946)

The power to love what is purely abstract is given to few.

MARGOT ASQUITH, *More or Less About Myself* (1934)

Spirituality leaps where science cannot yet follow, because science must always test and measure, and much of reality and human experience is immeasurable.

STARHAWK, *The Spiral Dance* (1979)

One cannot expect to be conscious of God's presence when one has only a bowing acquaintance with Him.

MADAME CHIANG KAI-SHEK, *I Confess My Faith* (1943)

It is not my business to think about myself. My business is to think about God. It is for God to think about me.

SIMONE WEIL, *Waiting for God* (1950)

Spiritual love is a position of standing with one hand extended into the universe and one hand extended into the world, letting ourselves be a conduit for passing energy.

CHRISTINA BALDWIN, *Life's Companion, Journal Writing as a Spiritual Quest* (1990)

Spirituality is the sacred center out of which all life comes, including Mondays and Tuesdays and rainy Saturday afternoons in all their mundane and glorious detail. . . . The spiritual journey is the soul's life commingling with ordinary life.

CHRISTINA BALDWIN, *Life's Companion, Journal Writing as a Spiritual Quest* (1990)

The religious need of the human mind remains alive, never more so, but it demands a teaching which can be *understood*. Slowly an apprehension of the intimate, usable power of God is growing among us, and a growing recognition of the only worth-while application of that power—in the improvement of the world.

CHARLOTTE PERKINS GILMAN, *The Living of Charlotte Perkins Gilman* (1935)

If there be anywhere on earth a lover of God who is always kept safe from falling, I know nothing of it—for it was not shown me. But this was shown—that in falling and rising again we are always kept in the same precious love.

JULIAN OF NORWICH, *Revelations of Divine Love* (1373)

The life of a religious might be compared to the building of a cathedral . . . once a firm foundation has been laid, the building rises slowly.

MARGARET WYVILL ECCLESINE, *A Touch of Radiance* (1966)

The tension between the call to the desert and to the market place arises not from the greater presence of God in one or the other, but from our varying psychological needs to apprehend him in different ways.

SHEILA CASSIDY, "The Peace of God," in *Prayers for Peace* (1962)

Alas, O Lord, to what a state dost Thou bring those who love Thee!

ST. TERESA OF AVILA, *The Interior Castle* (1575)

Oh, to lie upon the rugs of some silent mosque, far from the noise of wanton city life, and, eyes closed, gaze turned heavenwards, listen to Islam's song for ever!

ISABELLE EBERHARDT (1900), *The Passionate Nomad* (1988)

A large part of the popularity and persuasiveness of psychology comes from its being a sublimated spiritualism: a secular, ostensibly scientific way of affirming the primacy of "spirit" over matter.

SUSAN SONTAG, *Illness as Metaphor* (1978)

The liberating encounter with God/ess is always an encounter with our authentic selves resurrected from underneath the alienated self. It is not experienced against, but in and through relationships, healing our broken relations with our bodies, with other people, with nature.

ROSEMARY RUETHER, *Sexism and God-Talk* (1983)

But we are learning from the teaching and example of Jesus that life itself is a religion, that nothing is more sacred than a human being, that the end of all right institutions, whether the home or the church or an educational establishment, or a government, is the development of the human soul.

ANNA HOWARD SHAW (1917), in Aileen S. Kraditor, *The Ideas of the Woman Suffrage Movement 1890–1920* (1965)

We seem to be trapped by a civilization that has accelerated many physical aspects of evolution but has forgotten that other vital part of man—his mind and his psyche.

SYBIL LEEK, ESP—The Magic Within You (1971)

Spirituality promotes passivity when the domain of spirit is defined as outside the world. When this world is the terrain of spirit, we ourselves become actors in the story, and this world becomes the realm in which the sacred must be honored and freedom created.

STARHAWK, *Truth or Dare* (1987)

See also Afterlife, Belief, Christianity, Divinity, Eternity, Faith, God, Holy, Inner Life, Prayer, Religion, Ritual, Sacred, Shamans, Soul, Theology, Visions.

SPORTS

Sport strips away personality, letting the white bone of character shine through. Sport gives players an opportunity to know and test themselves. The great difference between sport and art is that sport, like a sonnet, forces beauty within its own system. Art, on the other hand, cyclically destroys boundaries and breaks free.

RITA MAE BROWN, *Sudden Death* (1983)

[The] third man in the ring makes boxing possible.

JOYCE CAROL OATES, *On Boxing* (1987)

See also Athletes, Tennis.

SPRING

Spring comes: the flowers learn their colored shapes.

MARIA KONOPNICKA, "A Vision" (19th century), in Joanna Bankier and Deirdre Lashgari, eds., *Women Poets of the World* (1983)

Birds that cannot even sing— / Dare to come again in spring!

EDNA ST. VINCENT MILLAY, "Doubt No More That Oberon," *Second April* (1921)

Ye may trace my step o'er the wakening earth, / By the winds which tell of the violet's birth, / By the primrose-stars in the shadowy grass, / By the green leaves opening as I pass.

FELICIA HEMANS, "The Voice of Spring," *Poetical Works* (1836)

A little Madness in the Spring / Is wholesome even for the King.

EMILY DICKINSON (1875), *The Single Hound* (1914)

The air and the earth interpenetrated in the warm gusts of spring; the soil was full of sunlight, and the sunlight full of red dust. The air one breathed was saturated with earthy smells, and the grass under foot had a reflection of blue sky in it.

WILLA CATHER, *Death Comes for the Archbishop* (1927)

In the spring, at the end of the day, you should smell like dirt.

MARGARET ATWOOD, "Unearthing Suite," *Bluebeard's Egg* (1986)

Autumn arrives in the early morning, but spring at the close of a winter day.

ELIZABETH BOWEN, *The Death of the Heart* (1938)

It is in this unearthly first hour of spring twilight that earth's almost agonized livingness is most felt. This hour is so dreadful to some people that they hurry indoors and turn on the lights.

ELIZABETH BOWEN, *The Death of the Heart* (1938)

April's rare capricious loveliness.

JULIA DORR, "November," *Poems* (1913)

STARS

We walk up the beach under the stars. And when we are tired of walking, we lie flat on the sand under a bowl of stars. We feel stretched, expanded to take in their compass. They pour into us until we are filled with stars, up to the brim.

ANNE MORROW LINDBERGH, *Gift From the Sea* (1955)

Myriads with beating / Hearts of fire.

SARA TEASDALE, "Stars," *Flame and Shadow* (1920)

Pegasus and Andromeda faced me brilliantly when I lifted my shade, so I went down and had a friendly reunion with the constellations. . . . I get a wonderful peace and the most exquisite pleasure from my friendship with the stars.

ELLEN GLASGOW, *Letters of Ellen Glasgow* (1958)

When we are chafed and fretted by small cares, a look at the stars will show us the littleness of our own interests.

MARIA MITCHELL (1866), in Phebe Mitchell Kendall, ed., *Maria Mitchell, Life, Letters, and Journals* (1896)

It is strange that there are times when I feel the stars are not at all *solemn;* they are secretly gay.

KATHERINE MANSFIELD (1920), *Journal of Katherine Mansfield* (1927)

See also Moon, Sky.

STATUS QUO

Life is a process of *becoming*, a combination of states we have to go through. Where people fail is that they wish to elect a state and remain in it. This is a kind of death.

ANAÏS NIN, *D.H. Lawrence: An Unprofessional Study* (1932)

We have had, alas, and still have, the doubtful habit of reverence. Above all, we respect things as they are.

CYNTHIA OZICK, "Women and Creativity," *Motive* (1969)

Wasn't that what happened to Lot's Wife? A loyalty to old things, a fear of the new, a fear to change, to look ahead?

TONI CADE BAMBARA, *The Salt Eaters* (1980)

The hardest thing to believe when you're young is that people will fight to stay in a rut, but not to get out of it.

ELLEN GLASGOW, *Barren Ground* (1925)

See also Change, Conventionality, Conventions, Traditions.

STEALTH

When I start huntin' you, I shall be as silent and stealthy as a gas-leak.

DOROTHY L. SAYERS, *The Unpleasantness at the Bellona Club* (1928)

STEREOTYPES

What is repugnant to every human being is to be reckoned always as a member of a class and not as an individual person.

DOROTHY L. SAYERS, "Are Women Human?" speech (1938)

We all know we are unique individuals, but we tend to see others as representatives of groups.

DEBORAH TANNEN, *You Just Don't Understand* (1990)

The new danger is the stereotypes of liberation.

NAOMI THORNTON, in Sara Ruddick and Pamela Daniels, *Working It Out* (1977)

If I had learned to type, I never would have made brigadier general.

ELIZABETH P. HOISINGTON, in *New York Times* (1970)

See also Prejudice, Sexism, Sex Roles.

STORIES

The universe is made of stories, not of atoms.

MURIEL RUKEYSER, title poem, *The Speed of Darkness* (1968)

There are only two or three human stories, and they go on repeating themselves as fiercely as if they had never happened before.

WILLA CATHER, *O Pioneers!* (1913)

The ancient people perceived the world and themselves within that world as part of an ancient continuous story composed of innumerable bundles of other stories.

LESLIE MARMON SILKO, in Lorraine Anderson, ed., *Sisters of the Earth* (1991)

Stories ought not to be just little bits of fantasy that are used to wile away an idle hour; from the beginning of the human race stories have been used—by priests, by bards, by medicine men—as magic instruments of healing, of teaching, as a means of helping people come to terms with the fact that they continually have to face insoluble problems and unbearable realities.

JOAN AIKEN, *The Way to Write for Children* (1982)

The difference between mad people and sane people . . . is that sane people have variety when they talk-story. Mad people have only one story that they talk over and over.

MAXINE HONG KINGSTON, *The Woman Warrior* (1976)

All true histories contain instruction; though, in some, the treasure may be hard to find, and when found, so trivial in quantity, that the dry, shriveled kernel scarcely compensates for the trouble of cracking the nut.

ANNE BRONTË, *Agnes Grey* (1847)

A lie hides the truth. A story tries to find it.

PAULA FOX, *A Servant's Tale* (1984)

There is no agony like bearing an untold story inside you.

ZORA NEALE HURSTON, *Dust Tracks on a Road* (1942)

Writing the short story is essentially an act of grace. It's not a matter of will so much as trust. I try to let the story do some of the work for me. It knows what it wants to do, say, be. I try not to stand in its way.

PAULETTE BATES ALDEN, conference (1990)

Every fine story must leave in the mind of the sensitive reader an intangible residuum of pleasure, a cadence, a quality of voice that is exclusively the writer's own, individual, unique.

WILLA CATHER, "Miss Jewett," *Not Under Forty* (1936)

The short story . . . is the most democratic of all the arts; anyone may tell a story, and if it is an absorbing one someone will listen.

HALLIE BURNETT, *On Writing the Short Story* (1983)

I love the short story for being round, suggestive, insinuating, microcosmic. The story has both the inconvenience and the fascination of new beginnings.

LUISA VALENZUELA, in Janet Sternburg, ed., *The Writer on Her Work*, vol. 2 (1991)

A story has to have muscle as well as meaning, and the meaning has to be in the muscle.

FLANNERY O'CONNOR, in Sally Fitzgerald, ed., *The Habit of Being* (1979)

The story was the important thing and little changes here and there were really part of the story. There were even stories about the different versions of stories and how they imagined the differing versions came to be.

LESLIE MARMON SILKO, *Storyteller* (1981)

See also Fiction, Legends, Myth, Novels, Storytellers, Writing.

STORYTELLERS

The bearers of fables are very welcome.

MONIQUE WITTIG, *Les Guérillères* (1969)

Where the storyteller is loyal, eternally and unswervingly loyal to the story, there, in the end, silence will speak. Where the story has been betrayed, silence is but emptiness.

ISAK DINESEN, "The Blank Page," *Last Tales* (1957)

She was attracted by the art of storytellers more than by any other—those Oriental storytellers who sit in marketplaces and hold beneath their words a group of people who have the faces of nurslings who are suckling. The sand of time flows away and the whole sun lies like a cloak upon the shoulders of the storyteller.

ADRIENNE MONNIER, *Dernières Gazettes et Écrits divers* (1936), in Richard McDougall, tr., *The Very Rich Hours of Adrienne Monnier* (1976)

STRANGERS

I'm a stranger wherever I go, but I'm happy.

HUALING NIEH, *Mulberry and Peach* (1981)

Call no man foe, but never love a stranger.

STELLA BENSON, *This Is the End* (1917)

See also Outsiders, Unknown.

STUBBORNNESS

In the face of an obstacle which is impossible to overcome, stubbornness is stupid.

SIMONE DE BEAUVOIR, *The Ethics of Ambiguity* (1948)

Bulldogs have been known to fall on their swords when confronted by my superior tenacity.

MARGARET HALSEY, *No Laughing Matter* (1977)

See also Determination, Perseverance.

STYLE

Style is the thing that's always a bit phony, and at the same time you cannot write without style.

ELIZABETH BOWEN, *The Death of the Heart* (1938)

Fashion can be bought. Style one must possess.

EDNA WOOLMAN CHASE, *Always in Vogue* (1954)

Styles, like everything else, change. Style doesn't.

LINDA ELLERBEE, *Move On* (1991)

See also Elegance.

SUCCESS

For you to be successful, sacrifices must be made. It's better that they are made by others but failing that, you'll have to make them yourself.

RITA MAE BROWN, *Starting From Scratch* (1988)

I do not know anyone who has got to the top without hard work. That is the recipe. It will not always get you to the top, but it should get you pretty near.

MARGARET THATCHER, in *London Daily Telegraph* (1986)

We all must pay with the current coin of life / For the honey that we taste.

RACHEL [RACHEL BLUMSTEIN], "Jonathan," in Nathan and Marynn Ausubel, *A Treasury of Jewish Poetry* (1957)

To follow, without halt, one aim: There's the secret of success.

ANNA PAVLOVA, in A. H. Franks, ed., *Pavlova: A Biography* (1956)

I must admit that I personally measure success in terms of the contributions an individual makes to her or his fellow human beings.

MARGARET MEAD, in *Redbook* (1978)

The success or failure of a life, as far as posterity goes, seems to lie in the more or less luck of seizing the right moment of escape.

ALICE JAMES, *Journal* (1891)

Success breeds confidence.

BERYL MARKHAM, *West With the Night* (1942)

Success is counted sweetest / By those who ne'er succeed.

EMILY DICKINSON (1859), *Poems, First Series* (1890)

Success has killed more men than bullets.

TEXAS GUINAN, nightclub act (c. 1920)

Even a stopped clock is right twice every day. After some years, it can boast of a long series of successes.

MARIE VON EBNER-ESCHENBACH, *Aphorisms* (1905)

Success can make you go one of two ways. It can make you a prima donna, or it can smooth the edges, take away the insecurities, let the nice things come out.

BARBARA WALTERS, in *Newsweek* (1974)

Success does not implant bad characteristics in people. It merely steps up the growth rate of the bad characteristics they already had.

MARGARET HALSEY, *No Laughing Matter* (1977)

Integrity is so perishable in the summer months of success.

VANESSA REDGRAVE, in David Bailey, *Good-bye Baby and Amen* (1969)

She's the kind of woman who climbed the ladder of success—wrong by wrong.

MAE WEST, *I'm No Angel* (1933)

It was the first operatic mountain I climbed, and the view from it was astounding, exhilarating, stupefying.

LEONTYNE PRICE, in *Life* (1966)

The top is not forever. Either you walk down, or you are going to be kicked down.

JANET COLLINS, in Brian Lanker, *I Dream a World* (1989)

Like most people who have reached the top, I think she finds that the staying is harder than the climb.

ILKA CHASE, *Free Admission* (1948)

I find it's as hard to live down an early triumph as an early indiscretion.

EDNA ST. VINCENT MILLAY (1933), in Liz Rosenberg, "So Young, So Good, So Popular," *New York Times* (1992)

The trouble with being number one in the world—at anything—is that it takes a certain mentality to attain that position in the first place, and that is something of a driving, perfectionist attitude, so that once you do achieve number one, you don't relax and enjoy it.

BILLIE JEAN KING, *Billie Jean* (1982)

"Nothing succeeds as doth succeed Success!" / None who have known Success assent to this.

LAURENCE HOPE, "Happiness," *Stars of the Desert* (1903)

Most successes are unhappy. That's why they are successes—they have to reassure themselves about themselves by achieving something that the world will notice. . . . The happy people are failures because they are on such good terms with themselves that they don't give a damn.

AGATHA CHRISTIE, *Remembered Death* (1945)

I am doomed to an eternity of compulsive work. No set goal achieved satisfies. Success only breeds a new goal. The golden apple devoured has seeds. It is endless.

BETTE DAVIS, *The Lonely Life* (1962)

The penalty of success is to be bored by the attentions of people who formerly snubbed you.

MARY WILSON LITTLE, *A Paragrapher's Reveries* (1904)

Nothing fails like success; nothing is so defeated as yesterday's triumphant Cause.

PHYLLIS MCGINLEY, "How to Get Along with Men," *The Province of the Heart* (1959)

It is a mark of many famous people that they cannot part with their brightest hour: what worked once must always work.

LILLIAN HELLMAN, *Pentimento* (1973)

It's them that take advantage that get advantage i' this world.

GEORGE ELIOT, *Adam Bede* (1859)

To be successful, a woman has to be much better at her job than a man.

GOLDA MEIR, in David Reed, "The Indestructible Golda Meir," *Reader's Digest* (1971)

A tragic irony of life is that we so often achieve success or financial independence after the chief reason for which we sought it has passed away.

ELLEN GLASGOW, *The Woman Within* (1954)

See also Accomplishment, Fame, Prosperity, Winning.

SUFFERING

Suffering belongs to no language.

ADÉLIA PRADO, "Denouement," in Ellen Watson, tr., *The Alphabet in the Park: Selected Poems of Adélia Prado* (1990)

Suffering has always been with us, does it really matter in what form it comes? All that matters is how we bear it and how we fit it into our lives.

ETTY HILLESUM, *An Interrupted Life: The Diaries of Etty Hillesum 1941–1943* (1983)

We do not die of anguish, we live on. We continue to suffer. We drink the cup drop by drop.

GEORGE SAND (1834), in Marie Jenny Howe, The Intimate Journal of George Sand (1929)

His cup is gall, his meat is tears, / His passion lasts a thousand years.

EMMA LAZARUS, "Crowing of the Red Cock" (1881), *Poems* (1888)

Although the world is full of suffering, it is full also of the overcoming of it.

HELEN KELLER, *Optimism* (1903)

The capacity to suffer varies more than anything that I have observed in human nature.

MARGOT ASQUITH, *More or Less About Myself* (1934)

So much that was beautiful and so much that was hard to bear. Yet whenever I showed myself ready to bear it, the hard was directly transformed into the beautiful.

ETTY HILLESUM, *An Interrupted Life: The Diaries of Etty Hillesum 1941–1943* (1983)

True knowledge comes only through suffering.

ELIZABETH BARRETT BROWNING (1844), in Charlotte Porter and Helen A. Clarke, eds., The Complete Works of Elizabeth Barrett Browning (1900)

A *Wounded* deer—leaps highest.

EMILY DICKINSON (1860), *Poems, First Series* (1890)

We desert those who desert us; we cannot afford to suffer; we must live how we can.

ELIZABETH BOWEN, *The Death of the Heart* (1938)

The world has been forced to its knees. Unhappily we seldom find our way there without being beaten to it by suffering.

ANNE MORROW LINDBERGH, *The Wave of the Future* (1940)

So long as one is able to pose one has still much to learn about suffering.

ELLEN GLASGOW, *Letters of Ellen Glasgow* (1958)

The sight or sound of perfect things causes a certain suffering.

ADRIENNE MONNIER, *Les Gazettes d'Adrienne Monnier* (1940), in Richard McDougall, tr., *The Very Rich Hours of Adrienne Monnier* (1976)

See also Grief, Pain, Sorrow.

SUFFRAGE

The single most impressive fact about the attempt by American women to obtain the right to vote is how long it took.

ALICE ROSSI, *The Feminist Papers* (1973)

See also Democracy, Elections.

SUICIDE

People commit suicide for only one reason—to escape torment.

LI ANG, *The Butcher's Wife* (1983)

Human life consists in mutual service. No grief, pain, misfortune, or "broken heart" is excuse for cutting off one's life while any power of service remains. But when all usefulness is over, when one is assured of an unavoidable and imminent death, it is the simplest of human rights to choose a quick and easy death in place of a slow and horrible one.

CHARLOTTE PERKINS GILMAN, from suicide note (1935)

We cannot tear out a single page from our life, but we can throw the whole book into the fire.

GEORGE SAND, *Mauprat* (1837)

Some people say that suicide is a sin, but I have never believed that. I say it's God's way of calling certain folks home early. It's much nicer than an awful accident, where the rest of us are left wondering if the person really wanted to go.

FAITH SULLIVAN, *The Cape Ann* (1988)

Killing herself was the ultimate conversation stopper, the final saying, "No backs."

JANE RULE, "In the Attic of the House," *Christopher Street* (1979)

Razors pain you; / Rivers are damp; / Acids stain you; / And drugs cause cramp. / Guns aren't lawful; / Nooses give; / Gas smells awful; / You might as well live.

DOROTHY PARKER, "Résumé," *Enough Rope* (1926)

See also Death, Dying, Self-Destruction, Self-Determination.

SUMMER

Winter is cold-hearted, / Spring is yea and nay, / Autumn is a weather-cock / Blown every way. / Summer days for me / When every leaf is on its tree.

CHRISTINA ROSSETTI, "Summer" (1845), *Goblin Market* (1862)

August is a wicked month.

EDNA O'BRIEN, book title (1965)

Generally speaking, the poorer person summers where he winters.

FRAN LEBOWITZ, *Social Studies* (1977)

Summer is a verb.

LISA BIRNBACH, *The Official Preppy Handbook* (1980)

SUN

The sun lay like a friendly arm across her shoulder.

MARJORIE KINNAN RAWLINGS, *South Moon Under* (1933)

The sun beating in on me gives my mind a dry feeling. I feel like dust.

EVELYN SCOTT, *Escapade* (1923)

See also Sunset.

SUNDAY

Since her childhood it had seemed to her that the movement of all laws, even natural ones, was either suspended or accelerated on the Sabbath.

ELLEN GLASGOW, *Barren Ground* (1925)

Sundays are terrible because it is clear that there is no one in charge of the world. And this knowledge leaves you drifting around, grappling with unfulfilled expectations and vague yearnings.

SHEILA BALLANTYNE, *Norma Jean the Termite Queen* (1975)

The feeling of Sunday is the same everywhere, heavy, melancholy, standing still. Like when they say "As it was in the beginning, is now, and ever shall be, world without end."

JEAN RHYS, *Voyage in the Dark* (1934)

Sunday afternoons are the longest afternoons of all.

CARSON MCCULLERS, *Clock Without Hands* (1961)

Sunday is sort of like a piece of bright gold brocade lying in a pile of white muslin weekdays.

YOSHIKO UCHIDA, *A Jar of Dreams* (1981)

SUNSET

The pale, cold light of the winter sunset did not beautify—it was like the light of truth itself.

WILLA CATHER, *My Antonia* (1918)

The sunset caught me, turned the brush to copper, / set the clouds / to one great roof of flame / above the earth.

ELIZABETH COATSWORTH, "On the Hills," *Atlas and Beyond* (1924)

Each night the sunset surged with purple pampas-grass plumes, and shot fuchsia rockets into the pink sky, then deepened through folded layers of peacock green to all the blues of India and a black across which clouds sometimes churned like alabaster dolls. The visual opium of the sunset was what I craved.

DIANE ACKERMAN, *A Natural History of the Senses* (1990)

The sky broke like an egg into full sunset and the water caught fire.

PAMELA HANSFORD JOHNSON, *The Unspeakable Skipton* (1981)

See also Sun.

SUPERIORITY

Giving up alcohol or cigarettes is a lead-pipe cinch compared to the renunciation of complacence by a former (self-appointed) elite.

MARGARET HALSEY, *No Laughing Matter* (1977)

Whatever a "superior" group has will be used to justify its superiority, and whatever an "inferior" group has will be used to justify its plight.

GLORIA STEINEM, *Outrageous Acts and Everyday Rebellions* (1983)

When one clings to the myth of innate superiority, one must constantly overlook the virtues and abilities of others.

ANNE WILSON SCHAEF, *Women's Reality* (1981)

Why do people who like to get up early look with disdain on those who like to lie in bed late? And why do people who like to work feel superior to those who prefer to dream?

RUTH STOUT, *How to Have a Green Thumb Without an Aching Back* (1955)

What sense of superiority it gives one to escape reading some book which every one else is reading.

ALICE JAMES, *Journal* (1890)

You know how some people seem to think that their love for classical music makes them spiritual or at least something quite special? And others who think you are a monster if you don't "love children," however obnoxious the children may be? Well, I found out that many people who love flowers look down on those who don't.

RUTH STOUT, *How to Have a Green Thumb Without an Aching Back* (1955)

And where does she find them?

DOROTHY PARKER, on hearing that Clare Boothe Luce was always kind to her inferiors, in Marion Meade, *Dorothy Parker: What Fresh Hell Is This?* (1988)

See also Equality.

SUPERSTITION

There's a rule, I think. You get what you want in life, but not your second choice too.

ALISON LURIE, *Real People* (1969)

The bad times I can handle. It's the good times that drive me crazy. When is the other shoe going to drop?

ERMA BOMBECK, *If Life Is a Bowl of Cherries, What Am I Doing in the Pits?* (1971)

I miss my daily Mass, and have a superstitious feeling that anything may happen on the days I don't go. However, nothing in particular has.

ROSE MACAULAY, *Letters to a Friend 1950–1952* (1962)

No one is so thoroughly superstitious as the godless man.

HARRIET BEECHER STOWE, Uncle Tom's Cabin (1852)

See also Belief, Fear.

SUPPORT

Those whom we support hold us up in life.

MARIE VON EBNER ESCHENBACH, *Aphorisms* (1905)

It was usual for the women of a household to do their own planting; but if a woman was sick, or for some reason was unable to attend to her planting, she sometimes cooked a feast, to which she invited the members of her age society and asked them to plant her field for her.

BUFFALO BIRD WOMAN, *Buffalo Bird Woman's Garden (as told to Gilbert L. Wilson)* (1987)

Sisterhood is powerful.

ROBIN MORGAN, book title (1970)

Proximity was their support; like walls after an earthquake they could fall no further for they had fallen against each other.

ELIZABETH BOWEN, *Friends and Relations* (1931)

SURPLUS

The world has become too full of many things, an overfurnished room.

FREYA STARK, *The Journey's Echo* (1963)

Any surplus is immoral.

JENNY HOLZER, *Truisms* (1977–1979)

See also Profit, Quantity.

SURVIVAL

She endured. And survived. Marginally, perhaps, but it is not required of us that we live well.

ANNE CAMERON, *Daughters of Copper Woman* (1981)

There is often in people to whom "the worst" has happened an almost transcendent freedom, for they have faced "the worst" and survived it.

CAROL PEARSON, *The Hero Within* (1986)

Despite all the evils they wished to crush me with / I remain as steady as the three-legged cauldron.

MONIQUE WITTIG, *Les Guérillères* (1969)

I have not withdrawn into despair, I did not go mad in gathering honey, / I did not go mad, I did not go mad, I did not go mad.

HODA AL-NAMANI, "I Remember I Was a Point, I Was a Circle," in Elizabeth Warnock Fernea, *Women and the Family in the Middle East* (1985)

Surviving meant being born over and over.

ERICA JONG, *Fear of Flying* (1973)

But the guilt of outliving those you love is justly to be borne, she thought. Outliving is something we do to them. The fantasies of dying could be no stranger than the fantasies of living. Surviving is perhaps the strangest fantasy of them all.

EUDORA WELTY, *The Optimist's Daughter* (1968)

Misfortune had made Lily supple instead of hardening her, and a pliable substance is less easy to break than a stiff one.

EDITH WHARTON, *The House of Mirth* (1905)

The question was not how to get a job, but how to live by such jobs as I could get.

DOROTHY RICHARDSON, *The Long Day* (1905)

See also Endurance.

SYMBOLS

Symbols are the imaginative signposts of life.

MARGOT ASQUITH, *More or Less About Myself* (1934)

A vertical line is dignity. The horizontal line is peaceful. The obtuse angle is action. That's universal, it is primary.

JANET COLLINS, in Brian Lanker, *I Dream a World* (1989)

That's the trouble, a sex symbol becomes a thing—I hate to be a thing.

MARILYN MONROE, in *Life* (1962)

Come to think of it, just about every tool was shaped like either a weenie or a pistol, depending on your point of view.

BARBARA KINGSOLVER, *The Bean Trees* (1989)

SYMPATHY

The delicate and infirm go for sympathy, not to the well and buoyant, but to those who have suffered like themselves.

CATHARINE ESTHER BEECHER, "Statistics of Female Health," *Woman Suffrage and Woman's Professions* (1871)

Never does one feel oneself so utterly helpless as in trying to speak comfort for great bereavement.

JANE WELSH CARLYLE, letter to Thomas Carlyle on the death of his mother (1853)

See also Compassion, Consolation, Empathy, Pity, Virtue.

T

TABOOS

The type of figleaf which each culture employs to cover its social taboos offers a twofold description of its morality. It reveals that certain unacknowledged behavior exists and it suggests the form that such behavior takes.

FREDA ADLER, *Sisters in Crime* (1975)

Our chief taboos are no longer conscious. They do not appear as themselves in our laws, and for the most part are not spoken of directly. But when we break them or even think of breaking them, our unconscious knowledge that we are violating sacred rules causes us to feel as if our lives are threatened, as if we may not be allowed to live.

SONIA JOHNSON, *From Housewife to Heretic* (1981)

See also Morality.

TACT

Tact is after all a kind of mind-reading.

SARAH ORNE JEWETT, *The Country of the Pointed Firs* (1896)

Tact is the ability to describe others as they see themselves.

MARY PETTIBONE POOLE, *A Glass Eye at a Keyhole* (1938)

See also Graciousness, Perception, Politeness.

TALENT

Everyone has talent. What is rare is the courage to follow the talent to the dark place where it leads.

ERICA JONG, in William Packard, ed., *The Craft of Poetry* (1974)

We can't take any credit for our talents. It's how we use them that counts.

MADELEINE L'ENGLE, *A Wrinkle in Time* (1962)

The vocation exists, and so does the gift; but vocation and gift are seldom of equal proportions, and I suppose that the struggle to equate them is the true and secret tension.

MAVIS GALLANT, in Susan Cahill, ed., *Women and Fiction 2* (1978)

We do not know and cannot tell when the spirit is with us. Great talent or small, it makes no difference. We are caught within our own skins, our own sensibilities; we never know if our technique has been adequate to the vision.

MADELEINE L'ENGLE, Two-Part Invention (1988)

Talent is helpful in writing, but guts are absolutely necessary.

JESSAMYN WEST, *The Woman Said Yes: Encounters With Life and Death* (1976)

Gift, like genius, I often think only means an infinite capacity for taking pains.

JANE ELLICE HOPKINS, *Work Amongst Working Men* (1870)

Timing and arrogance are decisive factors in the successful use of talent.

MARYA MANNES, *Out of My Time* (1971)

In the first grade, I already knew the pattern of my life. I didn't know the living of it, but I knew the line. . . . From the first day in school until the day I graduated, everyone gave me one hundred plus in art. Well, where do you go in life? You go to the place where you got one hundred plus.

LOUISE NEVELSON, *Dawns + Dusks* (1976)

It all started when I was told that I had a gift. The gods are Yankee traders. There are no gifts. Everything has a price, and in bitter moments I have been tempted to cry "Usury!"

BETTE DAVIS, *The Lonely Life* (1962)

In this world people have to pay an extortionate price for any exceptional gift whatever.

WILLA CATHER, *The Old Beauty and Others* (1948)

Talent, like beauty, to be pardoned, must be obscure and unostentatious.

LADY MARGUERITE BLESSINGTON, *Desultory Thoughts and Reflections* (1839)

Tremendous amounts of talent are being lost to our society just because that talent wears a skirt.

SHIRLEY CHISHOLM, *Unbought and Unbossed* (1970)

But he had all an artist needs, except the spark from the god.

MARY RENAULT, *The Mask of Apollo* (1966)

Nature distributes her favors unequally.

GEORGE SAND (1837), in Marie Jenny Howe, *The Intimate Journal of George Sand* (1929)

I believe talent is like electricity. We don't understand electricity. We use it. Electricity makes no judgment. You can plug into it and light up a lamp, keep a heart pump going, light a cathedral, or you can electrocute a person with it. Electricity will do all that. It makes no judgment. I think talent is like that. I believe every person is born with talent.

MAYA ANGELOU, in Claudia Tate, ed., *Black Women Writers at Work* (1983)

Sell, he can. He can sell last week's bait for tomorrow's halibut.

CHRISTINA STEAD, *House of All Nations* (1938)

See also Genius.

TALKING

She probably labored under the common delusion that you made things better by talking about them.

ROSE MACAULAY, *Crewe Train* (1926)

He talks for the pleasure of his own voice, the way dogs bark and birds sing.

PAULETTE BATES ALDEN, "Blue Mountains," *Feeding the Eagles* (1988)

Why can't they ever let my wanderings alone?! Can't they understand that I'll talk it all to pieces if I have to tell about it.

TOVE JANSSON, *Tales from Moominvalley* (1963)

To mention a loved object, a person, or a place to someone else is to invest that object with reality.

ANNE MORROW LINDBERGH, *North to the Orient* (1935)

There was no way for me to understand it at the time, but the talk that filled the kitchen those afternoons was highly functional. It served as therapy, the cheapest kind available to my mother and her friends. . . . But more than therapy, that freewheeling, wide-ranging, exuberant talk functioned as an outlet for the tremendous creative energy they possessed.

PAULE MARSHALL, "The Making of a Writer: From the Poets in the Kitchen," in *New York Times Book Review* (1983)

See also Conversation, Listening, Speech.

TASTE

Infallible taste is inconceivable; what could it be measured against?

PAULINE KAEL, *I Lost It at the Movies* (1965)

[Good taste] is a nineteenth-century concept. And good taste has never really been defined. The effort of projecting "good taste" is so studied that it offends me. No, I prefer to negate that. We have to put a period to so-called good taste.

LOUISE NEVELSON, *Dawns + Dusks* (1976)

Good taste is the worst vice ever invented.

EDITH SITWELL, in *New York Times* (1962)

In every power, of which taste is the foundation, excellence is pretty fairly divided among the sexes.

JANE AUSTEN, *Northanger Abbey* (1818)

Sex is the great leveler, taste the great divider.

PAULINE KAEL, *I Lost It at the Movies* (1965)

Regrettably, one of the surest signs of the Philistine is his reverence for the superior tastes of those who put him down.

PAULINE KAEL, *I Lost It at the Movies* (1965)

The masses are still ungrateful or ignorant. They prefer murder, poisonings, and crimes generally to a literature possessed of style and feeling.

GEORGE SAND (1863), in Raphaël Ledos de Beaufort, *Letters of George Sand* (1886)

See also Judgment.

TAXES

It has been said that one man's loophole is another man's livelihood. Even if this is true, it certainly is not fair, because the loophole-livelihood of those who are reaping undeserved benefits can be the economic noose of those who are paying more than they should.

MILLICENT FENWICK, newsletter (1975)

TEA

Tea quenches tears and thirst.

JEANINE LARMOTH AND CHARLOTTE TURGEON, *Murder on the Menu* (1972)

Tea to the English is really a picnic indoors.

ALICE WALKER, *The Color Purple* (1982)

Ah, there's nothing like tea in the afternoon. When the British Empire collapses, historians will find that it had made but two invaluable contributions to civilization—this tea ritual and the detective novel.

AYN RAND, *The Fountainhead* (1943)

It was the usual "zoo tea." You know, we eat—the others watch.

PRINCESS MARGARET OF ENGLAND, on public receptions attended by royalty (1954)

TEACHING

Teaching is the royal road to learning.

JESSAMYN WEST, *The Life I Really Lived* (1979)

Good teaching is one-fourth preparation and three-fourths theater.

GAIL GODWIN, *The Odd Woman* (1974)

What was the duty of the teacher if not to inspire?

BHARATI MUKHERJEE, *The Middleman and Other Stories* (1988)

When I teach people, I marry them.

SYLVIA ASHTON-WARNER, *Teacher* (1963)

We teachers can only help the work going on, as servants wait upon a master.

MARIA MONTESSORI, *The Absorbent Mind* (1964)

The only good teachers for you are those friends who love you, who think you are interesting, or very important, or wonderfully funny.

BRENDA UELAND, *If You Want to Write* (1938)

To teach one's self is to be forced to learn twice.

ELLEN GLASGOW, *The Woman Within* (1954)

See also Education, Knowledge, Learning.

TEARS

Rich tears! What power lies in those falling drops.

MARY DELARIVIER MANLEY, *The Royal Mischief* (1696)

How dry eyes can get when they are not allowed to cry!

MARIA AUGUSTA TRAPP, *The Story of the Trapp Family Singers* (1949)

See also Sorrow.

TECHNOLOGY

America's technology has turned in upon itself; its corporate form makes it the servant of profits, not the servant of human needs.

ALICE EMBREE, "Media Images I: Madison Avenue Brainwashing—the Facts," in Robin Morgan, ed., *Sisterhood Is Powerful* (1970)

TELEPHONE

Is this the party to whom I am speaking?

LILY TOMLIN (as "Ernestine"), in Barbara McDowell and Hana Umlauf, *Woman's Almanac* (1977)

E.T. phone home.

MELISSA MATHISON, *E.T.* (1982)

Remember that as a teenager you are at the last stage in your life when you will be happy to hear that the phone is for you.

FRAN LEBOWITZ, *Social Studies* (1977)

It is not rude to turn off your telephone by switching it on to an answering machine, which is cheaper and less disruptive than ripping it out of the wall. Those who are offended because they cannot always get through when they seek, at their own convenience, to barge in on people are suffering from a rude expectation.

JUDITH MARTIN, *Miss Manners' Guide for the Turn-of-the-Millennium* (1989)

All phone calls are obscene.

KAREN ELIZABETH GORDON, *The Well-Tempered Sentence* (1983)

See also Communication.

TELEVISION

Television has proved that people will look at anything rather than each other.

ANN LANDERS, in Bob Chieger, *Was It Good for You, Too?* (1983)

[Television viewing] is a one-way transaction that requires the taking in of particular sensory material in a particular way, no matter what the material might be. There is, indeed, no other experience in a child's life that permits quite so much intake while demanding so little outflow.

MARIE WINN, *The Plug-In Drug* (1977)

I'm always amazed that people will actually choose to sit in front of the television and just be savaged by stuff that belittles their intelligence.

ALICE WALKER, in Brian Lanker, *I Dream a World* (1989)

Even if every program were educational and every advertisement bore the seal of approval of the American Dental Association, we would still have a critical problem. It's not just the programs but the act of watching television hour after hour after hour that's destructive.

ELLEN GOODMAN, *Close to Home* (1979)

TV has created a kind of false collectivity.

ADRIENNE RICH, in *The Hungry Mind Review* (1992)

To a certain extent the child's early television experiences will serve to dehumanize, to mechanize, to make less *real* the realities and relationships he encounters in life. For him, real events will always carry subtle echoes of the television world.

MARIE WINN, *The Plug-In Drug* (1977)

Educational television should be absolutely forbidden. It can only lead to unreasonable expectations and eventual disappointment when your child discovers that the letters of the alphabet do not leap up out of books and dance around the room with royal-blue chickens.

FRAN LEBOWITZ, *Social Studies* (1977)

There are days when any electrical appliance in the house, including the vacuum cleaner, seems to offer more entertainment possibilities than the TV set.

HARRIET VAN HORNE, in *New York World-Telegram & Sun* (1957)

The six and one-fourth hours' television watching (the American average per day) which nonreading children do is what is called alpha-level learning. The mind needn't make any pictures since the pictures are provided, so the mind cuts current as low as it can.

CAROL BLY, *The Passionate, Accurate Story* (1990)

In its effect on family relationships, in its facilitation of parental withdrawal from an active role in the socialization of their children, and in its replacement of family rituals and special events, television has played an important role in the disintegration of the American family.

MARIE WINN, *The Plug-In Drug* (1977)

I asked Mr. Vann which O levels you need to write situation comedy for television. Mr. Vann said that you don't need qualifications at all, you just need to be a moron.

Sue Townsend, *The Secret Diary of Adrian Mole Aged 13-3/4* (1982)

TEMPERAMENT

Mad, bad and dangerous to know.

Lady Caroline Lamb, after meeting Lord Byron, Journal (1812)

Temperament is something that is an integral part of the artist. Not temper, temperament. There is a vast difference.

Bette Davis, *The Lonely Life* (1962)

Artistic temperament . . . sometimes seems a battleground, a dark angel of destruction and a bright angel of creativity wrestling. . . . When the bright angel dominates, out comes a great work of art, a Michelangelo *David* or a Beethoven symphony.

Madeleine L'Engle, *A Severed Wasp* (1982)

She was a woman of mean understanding, little information, and uncertain temper.

Jane Austen, *Pride and Prejudice* (1813)

I have sometimes wondered also whether in people like me who come to the boil fast (*soupe au lait,* the French call this trait, like a milk soup that boils over) the tantrum is not a built-in safety valve against madness or illness.

May Sarton, *Journal of a Solitude* (1973)

See also Behavior, Character, Personality.

TEMPTATION

For to tempt and to be tempted are things very nearly allied, and in spite of the finest maxims of morality impressed upon the mind, whenever feeling has anything to do in the matter, no sooner is it excited than we have already gone vastly farther than we are aware of.

Catherine the Great (c. 1770), in D. Maroger, *The Memoirs of Catherine the Great* (1955)

I generally avoid temptation unless I can't resist it.

Mae West, in *My Little Chickadee* (1940)

TENNIS

In no game played with a ball is concentration a greater virtue than in tennis.

Allison Danzig, *The Racquet Game* (1930)

Good shot, bad luck and hell are the five basic words to be used in a game of tennis.

Virginia Graham, *Say Please* (1949)

See also Sports.

TEXAS

Take Texas the way Texas takes bourbon. Straight. It goes down easier.

Edna Ferber, *Giant* (1952)

I just mean that here in Texas maybe we've got into the habit of confusing bigness with greatness.

Edna Ferber, *Giant* (1952)

THANKSGIVING

Thanksgiving is a typically *American* holiday. In spite of its religious form (giving thanks to God for a good harvest), its essential, secular meaning is a *celebration of successful production.* It is a producers' holiday. The lavish meal is a symbol of the fact that abundant consumption is the result and reward of production.

Ayn Rand, *The Ayn Rand Letter* (1971)

Over the river and through the wood, / To grandfather's house we'll go; / The horse knows the way / To carry the sleigh, / Through the white and drifted snow.

Lydia Maria Child, "Thanksgiving Day," *Flowers for Children* (1844)

THEATER

In the theater lying is looked upon as an occupational disease.

Tallulah Bankhead, *Tallulah* (1952)

Theater is by nature political.

Naomi Thornton, in Sara Ruddick and Pamela Daniels, *Working It Out* (1977)

It is best in the theater to act with confidence no matter how little right you have to it.

LILLIAN HELLMAN, *Pentimento* (1973)

It's one of the tragic ironies of the theater that only one man in it can count on steady work—the night watchman.

TALLULAH BANKHEAD, *Tallulah* (1952)

See also Acting, Audience, Performance.

THEFT

What a shame. If you had stolen a railroad they would have made you a Senator.

MOTHER JONES, to a man imprisoned for stealing a pair of shoes, in Linda Atkinson, *Mother Jones: The Most Dangerous Woman in America* (1978)

See also Crime, Dishonesty.

THEOLOGY

In some not altogether frivolous sense God needs to be liberated from our theology. Theology is not a tabernacle to contain the One who is Ahead, but it is a sign on the way, and thus is provisional. Thus the theologian is not only protester and prophet, if she is lucky, but also pilgrim.

JOAN ARNOLD ROMERO, in Mary Alice Warner and Bayna Beilenson, eds., *Women of Faith and Spirit* (1987)

See also Dogma, God, Religion, Spirituality.

THEORIES

Very dangerous things, theories.

DOROTHY L. SAYERS, *The Unpleasantness at the Bellona Club* (1928)

See also Concepts, Ideas, Thoughts.

"THEY"

Have you heard of the terrible family They, / And the dreadful venomous things They say?

ELLA WHEELER WILCOX, "They Say," *The Collected Poems* (1917)

See also Gossip, Rumor.

THINKING

But lying in bed just before going to sleep is the worst time for *organized* thinking; it is the best time for free thinking. Ideas drift like clouds in an undecided breeze, taking first this direction and then that.

E. L. KONIGSBURG, *From the Mixed-Up Files of Mrs. Basil E. Frankweiler* (1967)

He did not arrive at this conclusion by the decent process of quiet, logical deduction, nor yet by the blinding flash of glorious intuition, but by the shoddy, untidy process halfway between the two by which one usually gets to know things.

MARGERY ALLINGHAM, *Death of a Ghost* (1934)

Readers are plentiful: thinkers are rare.

HARRIET MARTINEAU, *Society in America* (1837)

Never be afraid to sit awhile and think.

LORRAINE HANSBERRY, *A Raisin in the Sun* (1959)

Thinking gets you nowhere. It may be a fine and noble aid in academic studies, but you can't think your way out of emotional difficulties. That takes something altogether different. You have to make yourself passive then, and just listen. Re-establish contact with a slice of eternity.

ETTY HILLESUM, *An Interrupted Life: The Diaries of Etty Hillesum 1941–1943* (1983)

Any positive thinker is compelled to see everything in the light of his own convictions.

ANTOINETTE BROWN BLACKWELL, The Sexes Throughout Nature (1875)

I can't see that she could have found anything nastier to say if she'd thought it out with both hands for a fortnight.

DOROTHY L. SAYERS, *Busman's Honeymoon* (1937)

She had the fluency of tongue and action meted out by divine providence to those who cannot think for themselves.

DJUNA BARNES, *Nightwood* (1937)

She had lost her way in a labyrinth of conjecture.

EDITH WHARTON, "The Angel at the Grave" (1901)

Much of what Mr. [Vice-President Henry A.] Wallace calls his global thinking is, no matter how you slice it, still globaloney.

CLARE BOOTHE LUCE, speech (1943)

See also Ideas, Thoughts.

THOUGHTS

Your energies have wrought / Stout continents of thought.

MARIANNE MOORE, "That Harp You Play So Well," in Burton E. Stevenson, *The Home Book of Modern Verse* (1925)

I have no riches but my thoughts, / Yet these are wealth enough for me.

SARA TEASDALE, "Riches," *Love Songs* (1917)

When one's thoughts are neither frivolous nor flippant, when one's thoughts are neither stiff-necked nor stupid, but rather, are harmonious— they habitually render physical calm and deep insight.

HILDEGARDE OF BINGEN, *Scivias* (1141–1150), in Gabriele Uhlein, ed., *Meditations With Hildegarde of Bingen* (1983)

Thoughts are acrobats, agile and quite often untrustworthy.

BESS STREETER ALDRICH, *Spring Came on Forever* (1935)

We are always in search of the redeeming formula, the crystallizing thought.

ETTY HILLESUM, *An Interrupted Life: The Diaries of Etty Hillesum 1941–1943* (1983)

First thoughts have tremendous energy. It is the way the mind first flashes on something. The internal censor usually squelches them, so we live in the realm of second and third thoughts, thoughts on thought, twice and three times removed from the direct connection of the first fresh flash.

NATALIE GOLDBERG, Writing Down the Bones (1986)

It is sometimes better to slip over thoughts and not go to the bottom of them.

MARIE DE RABUTIN-CHANTAL, MARQUISE DE SÉVIGNÉ, letter to her daughter, *Letters of Madame de Sévigné to Her Daughter and Her Friends* (1811)

Anger and worry are the enemies of clear thought.

MADELEINE BRENT, *The Capricorn Stone* (1979)

There are no evil thoughts except one: the refusal to think.

AYN RAND, *Atlas Shrugged* (1957)

His thoughts swam between us, hidden under rocks, disappearing in weeds, and I was fishing for them, dangling my own words like baits and lures.

LOUISE ERDRICH, *Love Medicine* (1984)

She nibbled away at her thought like a rabbit with a piece of lettuce.

RAE FOLEY, *Death and Mr. Potter* (1955)

Original thought is like original sin: both happened before you were born to people you could not possibly have met.

FRAN LEBOWITZ, *Social Studies* (1977)

See also Concepts, Ideas, Thinking.

TIME

Backward, turn backward, O Time, in your flight, / Make me a child again just for tonight!

ELIZABETH AKERS ALLEN, "Rock Me to Sleep, Mother" (1860)

All my possessions for a moment of time.

ELIZABETH I, last words (1603)

O Time the fatal wrack of mortal things.

ANNE BRADSTREET, "Contemplations" (c. 1655), in John Harvard Ellis, *The Works of Anne Bradstreet in Prose and Verse* (1932)

Time does us violence; it is the only violence.

SIMONE WEIL, *Gravity and Grace* (1947)

Time is a dressmaker specializing in alterations.

FAITH BALDWIN, *Face Toward the Spring* (1956)

In this world we live in a mixture of time and eternity. Hell would be pure time.

SIMONE WEIL, *First and Last Notebooks* (1970)

Time's violence rends the soul; by the rent eternity enters.

SIMONE WEIL, *Gravity and Grace* (1947)

Time was a river, not a log to be sawed into lengths.

MARGARET A. ROBINSON, *A Woman of Her Tribe* (1990)

Time and space are only forms of thought.

EDITH NESBITT, *The Story of the Amulet* (1906)

Duration is not a test of true or false.

ANNE MORROW LINDBERGH, *Gift From the Sea* (1955)

Time is not a line but a dimension, like the dimensions of space. If you can bend space you can bend time also, and if you knew enough and could move faster than light you could travel backwards in time and exist in two places at once.

MARGARET ATWOOD, *Cat's Eye* (1988)

Time is the continuous loop, the snakeskin with scales endlessly overlapping without beginning or end, or time is an ascending spiral if you will, like a child's toy Slinky. Of course we have no idea which arc on the loop is our time, let alone where the loop itself is, so to speak, or down whose lofty flight of stairs the Slinky so uncannily walks.

ANNIE DILLARD, *Pilgrim at Tinker Creek* (1974)

But I began then to think of time as having a shape, something you could see, like a series of liquid transparencies, one laid on top of another. You don't look back along time but down through it, like water. Sometimes this comes to the surface, sometimes that, sometimes nothing. Nothing goes away.

MARGARET ATWOOD, *Cat's Eye* (1988)

Time, when it is left to itself and no definite demands are made on it, cannot be trusted to move at any recognized pace. Usually it loiters; but just when one has come to count upon its slowness, it may suddenly break into a wild irrational gallop.

EDITH WHARTON, *The House of Mirth* (1905)

Neither of them wore watches. On them, watches broke or lost themselves or speeded up to keep some lawless schedule of their own so you could almost see the minute hand racing around the dial.

ANNE TYLER, *Searching for Caleb* (1975)

A woman's sense of time must be quite different from a man's. . . . She connects directly to the source of time, and the moon that pulls the tides around the world also pulls the hormone tide within her; her months are marked off without need of calendar. She carries her months, her years, her spring and winter within her.

ABIGAIL LEWIS, in Margo Culley, ed., *A Day at a Time* (1985)

Time . . . is not a great healer. It is an indifferent and perfunctory one. Sometimes it does not heal at all. And sometimes when it seems to, no healing has been necessary.

IVY COMPTON-BURNETT, *Darkness and Day* (1951)

Time is a great traitor who teaches us to accept loss.

ELIZABETH BORTON DE TREVIÑO, *I, Juan de Pareja* (1965)

Time is a kind friend, he will make us old.

SARA TEASDALE, "Let It Be Forgotten," *Flame and Shadow* (1920)

Just as you began to feel that you could make good use of time, there was no time left to you.

LISA ALTHER, *Kinflicks* (1975)

Time wounds all heels.

JANE ACE, in Goodman Ace, *The Fine Art of Hypochondria* (1966)

Time pulses from the afternoon like blood from a serious wound.

HILMA WOLITZER, *In the Palomar Arms* (1983)

My days ran away so fast. I simply ran after my days.

LEAH MORTON, *I Am a Woman—and a Jew* (1926)

The days slipped down like junket, leaving no taste on the tongue.

BETTY MacDONALD, *The Egg and I* (1945)

The clock talked loud. I threw it away, it scared me what it talked.

TILLIE OLSEN, "I Stand Here Ironing," *Tell Me A Riddle* (1956)

Whiskey and music, I reflected, especially when taken together, made time fly incredibly fast.

JEAN STAFFORD, *Boston Adventure* (1944)

He is invariably in a hurry. Being in a hurry is one of the tributes he pays to life.

ELIZABETH BIBESCO, *Balloons* (1922)

"No hurry, no hurry," said Sir James, with that air of self-denial that conveys the urgent necessity of intense speed.

ADA LEVERSON, *The Twelfth Hour* (1907)

"Twenty-three and a quarter minutes past," Uncle Matthew was saying furiously, "in precisely six and three-quarter minutes the damned fella will be late."

NANCY MITFORD, *Love in a Cold Climate* (1949)

Saving time, it seems, has a primacy that's too rarely examined.

ELLEN GOODMAN, *Close to Home* (1979)

All the clocks were running again. Moomintroll felt less lonely after he had wound them up. As time was lost anyway, he set them at different hours. Perhaps one of them would be right, he thought.

TOVE JANSSON, *Moominland Midwinter* (1958)

I must govern the clock, not be governed by it.

GOLDA MEIR, quoted by Oriana Fallaci in *L'Europeo* (1973)

I've been on a calendar, but never on time.

MARILYN MONROE, in *Look* (1962)

Time spent in a casino is a time given to death, a foretaste of the hour when one's flesh will be diverted to the purposes of the worm and not the will.

REBECCA WEST, in Peter Wolfe, *Rebecca West: Artist and Thinker* (1971)

Time has lost its shoes here / it stood still.

FADWA TUQAN, "From Behind the Bars" (1917), in Joanna Bankier and Deirdre Lashgari, eds., *Women Poets of the World* (1983)

Time is a Test of Trouble— / But not a Remedy— / If such it prove, it prove too / There was no Malady.

EMILY DICKINSON (1863), *Poems, Third Series* (1896)

[Time was] an accordion, all the air squeezed out of it as you grew older.

HELEN HOOVEN SANTMYER, . . . *And Ladies of the Club* (1984)

This is Malaya. Everything takes a long, a very long time in Malaya. Things get done, occasionally, but more often they don't, and the more in a hurry you are, the quicker you break down.

HAN SUYIN, *And the Rain My Drink* (1956)

I shall not tell you in this story about all the days when nothing happened. You will not catch me saying, "thus the sad days passed slowly by"— or "the years rolled on their weary course," or "time went on"—because it is silly; of course time goes on, whether you say so or not.

EDITH NESBITT, *The Bastable Children* (1928)

Killing time takes practice.

KAREN ELIZABETH GORDON, *The Transitive Vampire* (1984)

The one real thing that money buys. Time.

MARITA BONNER, "On Being Young—A Woman—and Colored" (1925), *Frye Street and Environs* (1987)

I am a member of a small, nearly extinct minority group, a kind of urban lost tribe who insist, in the face of all evidence to the contrary, on the sanctity of being on time. Which is to say that we On-timers are compulsively, unfashionably prompt, that there are only handfuls of us in any given city and, unfortunately, we never seem to have appointments with each other.

ELLEN GOODMAN, *Close to Home* (1979)

Time is, as you are probably aware, merely a convenient fiction. There is no such thing as time.

EDITH NESBITT, *The Phoenix and the Carpet* (1903)

See also Busyness, Eras, Eternity, Future, History, Past, Present.

TIMELINESS

Persons who are born too soon, or born too late, seldom achieve the eminence of those who are born at the right time.

KATHARINE ANTHONY, in Helen Hull, *The Writer's Book* (1950)

Things come suitable to the time.

ENID BAGNOLD, *National Velvet* (1935)

The appointed thing comes at the appointed time in the appointed way.

MYRTLE REED, *Master of the Vineyard* (1910)

It ain't no use putting up your umbrella till it rains.

ALICE CALDWELL RICE, *Mrs. Wiggs of the Cabbage Patch* (1901)

Death and taxes and childbirth! There's never any convenient time for any of them!

MARGARET MITCHELL, *Gone With the Wind* (1936)

See also Lateness.

TITLES

I think Hemingway's [book] titles should be awarded first prize in any contest. Each of them is a poem, and their mysterious power over readers contributes to Hemingway's success. His titles have a life of their own, and they have enriched the American vocabulary.

SYLVIA BEACH, *Shakespeare and Company* (1956)

We both [Erdrich and Michael Dorris] have title collections. I think a title is like a magnet. It begins to draw these scraps of experience or conversation or memory to it. Eventually, it collects a book.

LOUISE ERDRICH, in *Writer's Digest* (1991)

See also Books.

TOGETHERNESS

Oh, it's closeness that does you in. Never get too close to people, son—did I tell you that when you were young?

ANNE TYLER, *Dinner at the Homesick Restaurant* (1982)

I don't know why togetherness was ever held up as an ideal of marriage. Away from home for both, then together, that's much *better*.

AMANDA CROSS, *Death in a Tenured Position* (1981)

Love at a distance may be poignant; it is also idealized. Contact, more than separation, is the test of attachment.

ILKA CHASE, *Free Admission* (1948)

See also Friendship, Intimacy, Love, Lovers, Marriage, Relationships.

TOLERANCE

Toleration . . . is the greatest gift of the mind; it requires the same effort of the brain that it takes to balance oneself on a bicycle.

HELEN KELLER, *The Story of My Life* (1902)

Even the word Tolerance is intolerable. No person has a right to tolerate another.

AMALIE TAUBELS, letter (1839)

See also Intolerance.

TOMORROW

After all, tomorrow is another day.

MARGARET MITCHELL, *Gone With the Wind* (1936)

See also Future.

TRADITIONS

Traditions are the guideposts driven deep into our subconscious minds. The most powerful ones are those we can't even describe, aren't even aware of.

ELLEN GOODMAN, *Turning Points* (1979)

See also Conventions, Ritual.

TRAGEDY

Tragedy had its compensations. Once the worst misfortune occurred, one never worried about the minor ones.

MILDRED DAVIS, *The Invisible Boarder* (1974)

Tragedy, no matter how sad, becomes boring to those not caught in its addictive caress.

MAYA ANGELOU, *All God's Children Need Traveling Shoes* (1986)

See also Disaster.

TRAVEL

Traveling is the ruin of all happiness! There's no looking at a building here after seeing Italy.

FANNY BURNEY, *Cecelia* (1782)

To me travel is a triple delight: anticipation, performance, and recollection.

ILKA CHASE, *The Carthaginian Rose* (1961)

My heart is warm with the friends I make, / And better friends I'll not be knowing; / Yet there isn't a train I wouldn't take, / No matter where it's going.

EDNA ST. VINCENT MILLAY, "Travel," *Second April* (1921)

A nomad I will remain for life, in love with distant and uncharted places.

ISABELLE EBERHARDT (1902), *The Passionate Nomad* (1988)

My favorite thing is to go where I've never been.

DIANE ARBUS, in Doon Arbus, ed., *Diane Arbus: An Aperture Monograph* (1972)

The true traveler is he who goes on foot, and even then, he sits down a lot of the time.

COLETTE, *Paris From My Window* (1944)

Certainly, travel is more than the seeing of sights; it is a change that goes on, deep and permanent, in the ideas of living.

MIRIAM BEARD, *Realism in Romantic Japan* (1930)

Through travel I first became aware of the outside world; it was through travel that I found my own introspective way into becoming a part of it.

EUDORA WELTY, *One Writer's Beginnings* (1984)

Traveling is *seeing;* it is the implicity that we travel by.

CYNTHIA OZICK, "Enchanters at First Encounter," in *New York Times* (1985)

This suspension of one's own reality, this being entirely alone in a strange city (at times I wondered if I had lost the power of speech) is an enriching state for a writer. Then the written word . . . takes on an intensity of its own. Nothing gets exteriorized or dissipated; all is concentrated within.

MAY SARTON, *I Knew a Phoenix* (1959)

There is no substitute for the riches gained on a lifetime basis by the young American who studies or works abroad.

LETITIA BALDRIGE, *Of Diamonds and Diplomats* (1968)

I think that to get under the surface and really appreciate the beauty of any country, one has to go there poor.

GRACE MOORE, *You're Only Human Once* (1944)

Writers and travelers are mesmerized alike by knowing of their destinations.

EUDORA WELTY, *One Writer's Beginnings* (1984)

It is such a bewildered, scared feeling to go for the first time to a place and not know where to call out to the driver to stop.

KATHARINE BUTLER HATHAWAY, *Journals and Letters of the Little Locksmith* (1946)

Like building a house, travel always costs more than you estimate.

ILKA CHASE, *Elephants Arrive at Half-Past Five* (1963)

There are few certainties when you travel. One of them is that the moment you arrive in a foreign country, the American dollar will fall like a stone.

ERMA BOMBECK, *When You Look Like Your Passport Photo, It's Time to Go Home* (1991)

The expense of living abroad, I always supposed to be high, but my ideas were nowise adequate to the thing.

ABIGAIL ADAMS, letter to her sister, Mary Smith Cranch (1784)

When traveling abroad if you see something you yearn for if you can afford it at all, buy it. If you don't you'll regret it all your life.

ILKA CHASE, *Second Spring and Two Potatoes* (1965)

Is there *anything* as horrible as *starting* on a trip? Once you're off, that's all right, but the last moments are earthquake and convulsion, and the feeling that you are a snail being pulled off your rock.

ANNE MORROW LINDBERGH, *Hour of Gold, Hour of Lead* (1973)

Whenever I prepare for a journey I prepare as though for death. Should I never return, all is in order. This is what life has taught me.

KATHERINE MANSFIELD (1922), *Journal of Katherine Mansfield* (1927)

While armchair travelers dream of going places, traveling armchairs dream of staying put.

ANNE TYLER, *The Accidental Tourist* (1985)

Traveling is so complicated. There are so many people everywhere. I make my best journeys on my couch.

COCO CHANEL, in Marcel Haedrich, *Coco Chanel: Her Life, Her Secrets* (1972)

O what can be so forlorn in its forlorn parts as this traveling? The ceaseless packing and unpacking, the heartless, uncongenial intercourses, the cheerless hotel, the many hours when you are too tired and your feelings too much dissipated to settle to any pursuit, yet you either have nothing to look at or are weary of looking.

MARGARET FULLER, letter to Ralph Waldo Emerson (1843)

People who travel are always fugitives.

DAPHNE DU MAURIER, *Frenchman's Creek* (1941)

I always think that the most delightful thing about traveling is to always be running into Americans and to always feel at home.

ANITA LOOS, *Gentlemen Prefer Blondes* (1925)

Foreigners can't help living abroad because they were born there, but for an English person to go is ridiculous, especially now that the sun-tan lamps are so readily available.

SUE TOWNSEND, *The Growing Pains of Adrian Mole* (1984)

We of the third sphere are unable to look at Europe or at Asia as they may survey each other.

Wherever we go, across Pacific or Atlantic, we meet, not similarity so much as "the bizarre." Things astonish us, when we travel, that surprise nobody else.

MIRIAM BEARD, *Realism in Romantic Japan* (1930)

Too often travel, instead of broadening the mind, merely lengthens the conversation.

ELIZABETH DREW, *The Literature of Gossip* (1964)

Travel is the most private of pleasures. There is no greater bore than the travel bore. We do not in the least want to hear what he has seen in Hong-Kong.

VITA SACKVILLE-WEST, *Passenger to Teheran* (1926)

How could I go on my travels without that sweet soul waiting at home for my letters?

CARYL CHURCHILL, *Top Girls* (1984)

In the shortest sea voyage there is no sense of time. You have been down in the cabin for hours or days or years. Nobody knows or cares. You know all the people to the point of indifference. You do not believe in dry land any more—you are caught in the pendulum itself, and left there, idly swinging.

KATHERINE MANSFIELD, "The Journey to Bruges" (1910), *Something Childish* (1924)

[The transatlantic crossing was] so rough that the only thing I could keep on my stomach was the first mate.

DOROTHY PARKER (1935), in Marion Meade, *Dorothy Parker: What Fresh Hell Is This?* (1988)

Men travel faster now, but I do not know if they go to better things.

WILLA CATHER, *Death Comes for the Archbishop* (1927)

When you look like your passport photo, it's time to go home.

ERMA BOMBECK, book title (1991)

See also Adventure, Flying, Journeys, Places, Unknown.

TREACHERY

There was no treachery too base for the world to commit; she knew that.

VIRGINIA WOOLF, *To the Lighthouse* (1927)

See also Betrayal, Dishonesty.

TREES

Together with a few human beings, dead and living, and their achievements, trees are what I most love and revere.

HILDEGARD FLANNER, *Brief Cherishing* (1985)

I like trees because they seem more resigned to the way they have to live than other things do.

WILLA CATHER, *O Pioneers!* (1913)

When you look up from your typewriter, look at the trees, not the calendar.

MARY VIRGINIA MICKA, *The Cazenovia Journal* (1990)

Leaves are verbs that conjugate the seasons.

GRETEL EHRLICH, *The Solace of Open Spaces* (1985)

Of the infinite variety of fruits which spring from the bosom of the earth, the trees of the wood are the greatest in dignity.

SUSAN FENIMORE COOPER, *Rural Hours* (1887)

It is the peculiar nature of the forest, that life and death may ever be found within its bounds, in immediate presence of each other; both with ceaseless, noiseless advances, aiming at the mastery; and if the influences of the first be most general, those of the last are the most striking.

SUSAN FENIMORE COOPER, *Rural Hours* (1887)

There is memory in the forest.

MARGARET WIDDEMER, "Not Unto the Forest," *Cross Currents* (1921)

The woods, tall as waves, sang in mixed / tongues that loosened the scalp.

SONIA SANCHEZ, *Under a Soprano Sky* (1987)

I lean against the birch-tree, / My arms around it twine, / It pulses, and leaps, and quivers, / Like a human heart to mine.

AMY LEVY, "The Birch-Tree at Loschwitz," in Nathan and Marynn Ausubel, *A Treasury of Jewish Poetry* (1957)

When I stepped away from the white pine, I had the definite feeling that we had exchanged some form of life energy. . . . Clearly white pines and I are on the same wavelength. What I give back to the trees I cannot imagine. I hope they receive something, because trees are among my closest friends.

ANNE LABASTILLE, *Woodswoman* (1976)

[The] aspen has éclat, a glorious brashness in defiance of the rules, the flapper who does the Charleston in the midst of the grand waltz.

ANN ZWINGER, *Beyond the Aspen Grove* (1970)

The talking oak / To the ancients spoke. / But any tree / Will talk to me.

MARY CAROLYN DAVIES, "Be Deferent to Trees," *The Skyline Trail* (1924)

A stricken tree, a living thing, so beautiful, so dignified, so admirable in its potential longevity, is, next to man, perhaps the most touching of wounded objects.

EDNA FERBER, *A Kind of Magic* (1963)

See also Nature, Plants, Wilderness.

TRENDS

My friend Cassie is the sort of trendsetter they ought to hire over at *People*. . . . She had a Cuisinart and a schefflera when everyone else had a crêpe pan and a philodendron.

ELLEN GOODMAN, *Close to Home* (1979)

See also Fashion.

TROUBLE

Ah, trouble, trouble, there are the two different kinds . . . there's the one you give and the other you take.

KAY BOYLE, *The Crazy Hunter* (1938)

She would take any amount of trouble to avoid trouble.

WILLA CATHER, *The Song of the Lark* (1915)

Women like to sit down with trouble as if it were knitting.

ELLEN GLASGOW, *The Sheltered Life* (1932)

Laugh, and the world laughs with you; / Weep, and you weep alone, / For the sad old earth must borrow its mirth, / But has trouble enough of its own.

ELLA WHEELER WILCOX, "Solitude," *Poems of Passion* (1883)

What fresh hell is this?

DOROTHY PARKER, on the ringing of a doorbell or telephone, in Marion Meade, *Dorothy Parker: What Fresh Hell Is This?* (1988)

Life has this in common with prizefighting: if you've received a belly blow, it's likely to be followed by a right to the jaw.

AMANDA CROSS, *The James Joyce Murder* (1967)

It's a good thing to have all the props pulled out from under us occasionally. It gives us some sense of what is rock under our feet, and what is sand.

MADELEINE L'ENGLE, *The Summer of the Great-Grandmother* (1974)

my trouble / is that I have the spirit of Gertrude Stein / but the personality of Alice B. Toklas.

DIANE WAKOSKI, "My Trouble," *Smudging* (1972)

See also Adversity, Crises, Danger, Disaster, Problems.

TRUST

How desperately we wish to maintain our trust in those we love! In the face of everything, we try to find reasons to trust. Because losing faith is worse than falling out of love.

SONIA JOHNSON, *From Housewife to Heretic* (1981)

Those who trust us, educate us.

GEORGE ELIOT, *Daniel Deronda* (1874)

Foolish are they indeed who trust to fortune!

LADY MURASAKI, *The Tale of Genji* (c. 1008)

Allies never trust each other, but that doesn't spoil their effectiveness.

AYN RAND, *The Fountainhead* (1943)

How can the people trust the harvest, unless they see it sown?

MARY RENAULT, *The King Must Die* (1958)

Where large sums of money are concerned, it is advisable to trust nobody.

AGATHA CHRISTIE, *Endless Night* (1968)

See also Belief, Distrust, Doubt, Faith.

TRUTH

Truth is the only safe ground to stand upon.

ELIZABETH CADY STANTON, *The Woman's Bible* (1895)

Truth, like surgery, may hurt, but it cures.

HAN SUYIN, *A Many-Splendored Thing* (1952)

Truth isn't in accounts but in account books.

JOSEPHINE TEY, *The Daughter of Time* (1951)

What a word is truth. Slippery, tricky, unreliable.

LILLIAN HELLMAN, *Three: An Unfinished Woman, Pentimento, Scoundrel Time* (1979)

Truth—is as old as God.

EMILY DICKINSON (1864), in Mabel Loomis Todd, *Letters of Emily Dickinson* (1894)

Truth is immortal; error is mortal.

MARY BAKER EDDY, *Science and Health* (1875)

Truth is the vital breath of Beauty; Beauty the outward form of Truth.

GRACE AGUILAR, *Amete and Yafeh* (1850)

Let us accept truth, even when it surprises us and alters our views.

GEORGE SAND (1863), in Raphaël Ledos de Beaufort, *Letters of George Sand* (1886)

Any truth creates a scandal.

MARGUERITE YOURCENAR, *Memoirs of Hadrian* (1954)

I tore myself away from the safe comfort of certainties through my love for truth; and truth rewarded me.

SIMONE DE BEAUVOIR, *All Said and Done* (1974)

Not only are there as many conflicting truths as there are people to claim them; there are equally multitudinous and conflicting truths within the individual.

VIRGILIA PETERSON, *A Matter of Life and Death* (1961)

The truth often does sound unconvincing.

AGATHA CHRISTIE, *Ordeal by Innocence* (1959)

Of course it's the same old story. Truth usually is the same old story.

MARGARET THATCHER, in *Time* (1981)

Truth is so impossible. Something has to be done for it.

IVY COMPTON-BURNETT, *Darkness and Day* (1951)

The truth does not change according to our ability to stomach it emotionally.

FLANNERY O'CONNOR, in Sally Fitzgerald, ed., *The Habit of Being* (1979)

Much sheer effort goes into avoiding truth: left to itself, it sweeps in like the tide.

FAY WELDON, *The Rules of Life* (1987)

People do think that if they avoid the truth, it might change to something better before they have to hear it.

MARSHA NORMAN, *The Fortune Teller* (1987)

Truth has as many coats as an onion . . . and each one of them hollow when you peel it off.

HELEN WADDELL, *Peter Abelard* (1933)

Many a truth sprang from an error.

MARIE VON EBNER-ESCHENBACH, *Aphorisms* (1905)

I am the only real truth I know.

JEAN RHYS, in Susan Cahill, ed., *Women and Fiction 2* (1978)

If you do not tell the truth about yourself you cannot tell it about other people.

VIRGINIA WOOLF, The Moment and Other Essays (1947)

You never find yourself until you face the truth.

PEARL BAILEY, *The Raw Pearl* (1968)

I never know how much of what I say is true.

BETTE MIDLER, *A View From a Broad* (1980)

The simplest and commonest truth seems new and wonderful when we experience it the first time in our own life.

MARIE VON EBNER-ESCHENBACH, *Aphorisms* (1905)

There are few nudities so objectionable as the naked truth.

AGNES REPPLIER, *Compromises* (1904)

The naked truth is always better than the best-dressed lie.

ANN LANDERS, advice column (1991)

The truth is balance, but the opposite of truth, which is unbalance, may not be a lie.

SUSAN SONTAG, *Against Interpretation* (1966)

Nobody speaks the truth when there's something they must have.

ELIZABETH BOWEN, *The House in Paris* (1935)

Tell all the Truth but tell it slant— / Success in Circuit lies.

EMILY DICKINSON (1868), *The Poems of Emily Dickinson* (1955)

Truth made you a traitor as it often does in a time of scoundrels.

LILLIAN HELLMAN, *Scoundrel Time* (1976)

I have never seasoned a truth with the sauce of a lie in order to digest it more easily.

MARGUERITE YOURCENAR, in *New York Times* (1980)

You cannot weave truth on a loom of lies.

SUZETTE HADEN ELGIN, *Native Tongue* (1984)

I am not afraid of the pen, or the scaffold, or the sword. I will tell the truth wherever I please.

MOTHER JONES, in Linda Atkinson, *Mother Jones: The Most Dangerous Woman in America* (1978)

What would happen if one woman told the truth about her life? / The world would split open.

MURIEL RUKEYSER, "Käthe Kollwitz," *The Speed of Darkness* (1968)

She died for truth, and she died of it. Some truths are mortal illnesses.

MARILYN FRENCH, *The Women's Room* (1977)

He led a double life. Did that make him a liar? He did not feel a liar. He was a man of two truths.

IRIS MURDOCH, *The Sacred and Profane Love Machine* (1974)

The man who never tells an unpalatable truth "at the wrong time" (the right time has yet to be discovered) is the man whose success in life is fairly well assured.

AGNES REPPLIER, *Under Dispute* (1923)

It is terrible to destroy a person's picture of himself in the interests of truth or some other abstraction.

DORIS LESSING, *The Summer Before the Dark* (1973)

It is always hard to hear the buried truth from another person.

MAY SARTON, *Mrs. Stevens Hears the Mermaids Singing* (1965)

Artistic growth is, more than it is anything else, a refining of the sense of truthfulness. The stupid believe that to be truthful is easy; only the artist, the great artist, knows how difficult it is.

WILLA CATHER, *The Song of the Lark* (1915)

To me the truth is something which cannot be told in a few words, and those who simplify the universe only reduce the expansion of its meaning.

ANAÏS NIN, *The Diary of Anaïs Nin*, vol. 1 (1931–1934)

Truth is the only good and the purest pity. . . . Men lie for profit or for pity. All lies turn to poison, but a lie that is told for pity or shame breeds such a host of ills that no power on earth can compass their redemption.

STORM JAMESON, *The Clash* (1922)

Not everything in church is truth. . . . And not all truth turns up in church.

FAITH SULLIVAN, *The Cape Ann* (1988)

The Truth must dazzle gradually / Or every man be blind.

EMILY DICKINSON (1868), *The Poems of Emily Dickinson* (1955)

Truth is the hardest substance in the world to pin down. But the one certainty is the awesome penalty exacted sooner or later from a society whose reporters stop trying.

FLORA LEWIS, in Julia Edwards, *Women of the World: The Great Foreign Correspondents* (1988)

Truthfulness so often goes with ruthlessness.

DODIE SMITH, *I Capture the Castle* (1948)

There are no new truths, but only truths that have not been recognized by those who have perceived them without noticing.

MARY MCCARTHY, *On the Contrary* (1961)

Everything on our tormented earth that is alive and breathes, that blossoms and bears fruit, lives only by virtue of and in the name of Truth and Good.

SVETLANA ALLILUYEVA, *Twenty Letters to a Friend* (1967)

There are so few truth-speaking traditions in this society in which the myth of "Western civilization" has claimed the allegiance of so many. We have rarely been encouraged and equipped to appreciate the fact that the truth works, that it releases the Spirit and that it is a joyous thing.

TONI CADE BAMBARA, in Claudia Tate, ed., *Black Women Writers at Work* (1983)

Spiritual empowerment is evidenced in our lives by our willingness to tell ourselves the truth, to listen to the truth when it's told to us, and to dispense truth as lovingly as possible, when we feel compelled to talk from the heart.

CHRISTINA BALDWIN, *Life's Companion, Journal Writing as a Spiritual Quest* (1990)

See also Honesty, Lying, Reality, Sincerity.

TYRANNY

Under conditions of tyranny it is far easier to act than to think.

HANNAH ARENDT, in W. H. Auden, *A Certain World* (1970)

Every successful revolution puts on in time the robes of the tyrant it has deposed.

BARBARA TUCHMAN, in *Reader's Digest* (1982)

See also Dictators, Oppression.

U

UNCLES

I have nothing to say against uncles in general. They are usually very excellent people, and very convenient to little boys and girls.

DINAH MULOCK CRAIK, *The Little Lame Prince* (1875)

See also Family.

UNCONSCIOUS

I am always running into people's unconscious.

MARILYN MONROE, in Norman Mailer, *Marilyn* (1973)

UNDERSTANDING

I want, by understanding myself, to understand others. I want to be all that I am capable of becoming.

KATHERINE MANSFIELD (1922), *Journal of Katherine Mansfield* (1927)

The motto should not be: Forgive one another; rather, Understand one another.

EMMA GOLDMAN, "The Tragedy of Woman's Emancipation," *Anarchism* (1910)

Real charity and a real ability never to condemn—the one real virtue—is so often the result of a waking experience that gives a glimpse of what lies beneath things.

IVY COMPTON-BURNETT, letter (1913), in Hilary Spurling, *Ivy* (1984)

People don't want to be understood—I mean not completely. It's too destructive. Then they haven't anything left. They don't want complete sympathy or complete understanding. They want to be treated carelessly and taken for granted lots of times.

ANNE MORROW LINDBERGH, *Bring Me a Unicorn* (1971)

I firmly believe kids don't want your understanding. They want your trust, your compassion, your blinding love and your car keys, but you try to understand them and you're in big trouble.

ERMA BOMBECK, *If Life Is a Bowl of Cherries, What Am I Doing in the Pits?* (1971)

This has been a most wonderful evening. Gertrude has said things tonight it will take her ten years to understand.

ALICE B. TOKLAS, quoted by Mortimer Adler, interview (1976)

If you can keep your head when all about you are losing theirs, it's just possible you haven't grasped the situation.

JEAN KERR, *Please Don't Eat the Daisies* (1957)

For the past several generations we've forgotten what the psychologists call our *archaic understanding,* a willingness to know things in their deepest, most mythic sense. We're all born with archaic understanding, and I'd guess that the loss of it goes directly along with the loss of ourselves as creators.

MADELEINE L'ENGLE, *Walking on Water: Reflections on Faith and Art* (1980)

The growth of understanding follows an ascending spiral rather than a straight line.

JOANNA FIELD, *A Life of One's Own* (1934)

See also Awareness, Empathy, Knowledge, Learning, Self-Knowledge.

UNEXPECTED

Truly nothing is to be expected but the unexpected!

ALICE JAMES, *Journal* (1891)

But the cloud never comes in that quarter of the horizon from which we watch for it.

ELIZABETH GASKELL, *North and South* (1854)

See also Expectations, Shocking.

UNHAPPINESS

Ah! Those strange people who have the courage to be unhappy! Are they unhappy, by the way?

ALICE JAMES, *Journal* (1889)

When you are unhappy or dissatisfied, is there anything in the world more maddening than to be told that you should be contented with your lot?

KATHLEEN NORRIS, *Hands Full of Living* (1931)

See also Bitterness, Depression, Despair, Disappointment, Discontent, Loneliness, Melancholy, Misery, Sorrow, Suffering.

UNIQUENESS

There is a vitality, a life-force, an energy, a quickening that is translated through you into action and because there is only one of you in all of time, this expression is unique. And if you block it, it will never exist through any other medium and be lost.

MARTHA GRAHAM, in Agnes de Mille, *Dance to the Piper* (1952)

Since you are like no other being ever created since the beginning of Time, you are incomparable.

BRENDA UELAND, *If You Want to Write* (1938)

In order to be irreplaceable one must always be different.

COCO CHANEL, in Marcel Haedrich, *Coco Chanel: Her Life, Her Secrets* (1972)

Meeting people unlike oneself does not enlarge one's outlook; it only confirms one's idea that one is unique.

ELIZABETH BOWEN, *The House in Paris* (1935)

Everything about her was at once vigorous and exquisite, at once strong and fine. He had a confused sense that she must have cost a great deal to make, that a great many dull and ugly people must, in some mysterious way, have been sacrificed to produce her.

EDITH WHARTON, *The House of Mirth* (1905)

See also Eccentricity, Human Differences, Individuality.

UNITED STATES

Give me your tired, your poor, / Your huddled masses yearning to breathe free, / The wretched refuse of your teeming shore, / Send these, the homeless, tempest-tossed, to me: / I lift my lamp beside the golden door.

EMMA LAZARUS, "The New Colossus" (1883)

America! America! / God shed His grace on thee / And crown thy good with brotherhood / From sea to shining sea!

KATHERINE LEE BATES, *America the Beautiful* (1895)

What the people want is very simple. They want an America as good as its promise.

BARBARA JORDAN, speech (1977)

America is like an unfaithful lover who promised us more than we got.

CHARLOTTE BUNCH, *Passionate Politics* (1987)

I don't measure America by its achievement, but by its potential.

SHIRLEY CHISHOLM, *Unbought and Unbossed* (1970)

America is God equals America equals Business equals America equals God.

ORIANA FALLACI, *Penelope at War* (1966)

Americans relate all effort, all work, and all of life itself to the dollar. Their talk is of nothing but dollars.

NANCY MITFORD, *Noblesse Oblige* (1956)

Verily what bishops are to the English, bankers are to Americans.

MABEL ULRICH, in *Scribner's Magazine* (1933)

What the Spanish War began the World War accomplished: America became the world's banker and ceased to be the world's pioneer!

ANNA LOUISE STRONG, *I Change Worlds* (1935)

America, which has the most glorious present still existing in the world today, hardly stops to enjoy it, in her insatiable appetite for the future.

Anne Morrow Lindbergh, *Gift From the Sea* (1955)

America has enjoyed the doubtful blessing of a single-track mind.

Ellen Glasgow, *The Woman Within* (1954)

Life for the European is a career; for the American, it is a hazard.

Mary McCarthy, *On the Contrary* (1961)

In the United States there is more space where nobody is than where anybody is. That is what makes America what it is.

Gertrude Stein, *The Geographical History of America* (1936)

We are a nation of twenty million bathrooms, with a humanist in every tub.

Mary McCarthy, *On the Contrary* (1961)

I question whether I want to be integrated into America as it stands now, with its complacency and materialism, its soullessness.

Paule Marshall, title story, *Reena* (1983)

Poor America, of what avail is all her wealth, if the individuals comprising the nation are wretchedly poor? If they live in squalor, in filth, in crime, with hope and joy gone, a homeless, soilless army of human prey.

Emma Goldman, title essay, *Anarchism* (1910)

In America, everybody is, but some are more than others.

Gertrude Stein, *Everybody's Autobiography* (1937)

Most Americans have never seen the ignorance, degradation, hunger, sickness, and futility in which many other Americans live. . . . They won't become involved in economic or political change until something brings the seriousness of the situation home to them.

Shirley Chisholm, *Unbought and Unbossed* (1970)

Memory in America suffers amnesia.

Meridel Le Sueur, in *A Woman's Notebook* (1980)

We are a people who do not want to keep much of the past in our heads. It is considered unhealthy in America to remember mistakes, neu-

rotic to think about them, psychotic to dwell upon them.

Lillian Hellman, *Scoundrel Time* (1976)

The happy ending is our national belief.

Mary McCarthy, *On the Contrary* (1961)

UNIVERSAL

Let me stand in my age with all its waters flowing round me. If they sometimes subdue, they must finally upbear me, for I seek the universal—and that must be the best.

Margaret Fuller, *Summer on the Lakes* (1844)

UNIVERSE

The entire universe is nothing but a great metaphor.

Simone Weil, *First and Last Notebooks* (1970)

Two forces rule the universe: light and gravity.

Simone Weil, *Gravity and Grace* (1947)

UNKNOWN

But settled things were enemies to me and soon lost their newness and color. The unknown called.

Agnes Smedley, *Daughter of Earth* (1929)

There are some people who cannot get onto a train without imagining that they are about to voyage into the significant unknown; as though the notion of movement were inseparably connected with the notion of discovery, as though each displacement of the body were a displacement of the soul.

Margaret Drabble, "A Voyage to Cythera" (1967)

See also Adventure, New, Strangers.

UNSELFISHNESS

A person who can really be called an unselfish person has no place in life.

Ivy Compton-Burnett, *Elders and Betters* (1944)

See also Altruism, Kindness, Virtue.

USELESSNESS

There is no irritant as painful as an ace up your sleeve that you can never use; it's the kind of thing that causes oysters to produce pearls.

SHEILA BALLANTYNE, *Imaginary Crimes* (1982)

See also Futility.

UTILITY

Utility is a metaphysical concept of impregnable circularity; utility is the quality in commodities that makes individuals want to buy them, and the fact that individuals want to buy commodities shows that they have utility.

JOAN ROBINSON, *Economic Philosophy* (1962)

See also Economics.

V

VACATION

One of the fallacies of summer holidays is that you are going to get some serious reading done while you are lying on the beach.

NANCY STAHL, *If It's Raining This Must Be the Weekend* (1979)

Holidays are enticing only for the first week or so. After that, it is no longer such a novelty to rise late and have little to do.

MARGARET LAURENCE, *A Jest of God* (1966)

It has long been my belief that in times of great stress, such as a four-day vacation, the thin veneer of family unity wears off almost at once, and we are revealed in our true personalities.

SHIRLEY JACKSON, *Raising Demons* (1956)

By and large, mothers and housewives are the only workers who do not have regular time off. They are the great vacationless class.

ANNE MORROW LINDBERGH, *Gift From the Sea* (1955)

See also Leisure.

VALUES

Values linger on after the social structures which conceived them.

SHEILA ROWBOTHAM, *Woman's Consciousness, Man's World* (1973)

The essential characteristic of the first half of the twentieth century is the growing weakness, and almost the disappearance, of the idea of value.

SIMONE WEIL, *On Science, Necessity, and the Love of God* (1968)

See also Principles.

VANITY

Vanity, like murder, will out.

HANNAH COWLEY, *The Belle's Stratagem* (1780)

Vanity is the quicksand of reason.

GEORGE SAND, in *French Wit and Wisdom* (1950)

All is vanity, and discovering it—the greatest vanity.

JOHN OLIVER HOBBES, *The Sinner's Comedy* (1893)

We are so vain that we even care for the opinion of those we don't care for.

MARIE VON EBNER-ESCHENBACH, *Aphorisms* (1905)

The inner vanity is generally in proportion to the outer self-deprecation.

EDITH WHARTON, *The House of Mirth* (1905)

He didn't believe she would ever be guilty of those uncatalogued faint treacheries which vanity makes young people commit.

WILLA CATHER, *Lucy Gayheart* (1935)

I never understand how writers can succumb to vanity—what you work the hardest on is usually the worst.

FLANNERY O'CONNOR, in Sally Fitzgerald, ed., *The Habit of Being* (1979)

The passion of vanity has its own depths in the spirit, and is powerfully militant.

ELIZABETH BOWEN, "The Apple Tree," *Look at All Those Roses* (1941)

See also Arrogance, Conceit, Egocentrism, Self-Importance.

VARIETY

Variety is the soul of pleasure.

APHRA BEHN, *The Rover* (1677)

See also Differences, Human Differences.

VENGEANCE

The whole human race loses by every act of personal vengeance.

RAE FOLEY, *Curtain Call* (1961)

Something of vengeance I had tasted for the first time; as aromatic wine it seemed, on swallowing, warm and racy; its afterflavor, metallic and corroding, gave me a sensation as if I had been poisoned.

CHARLOTTE BRONTË, *Jane Eyre* (1847)

See also Revenge.

VENICE

It is the city of mirrors, the city of mirages, at once solid and liquid, at once air and stone.

ERICA JONG, "A City of Love and Death: Venice," in *New York Times* (1986)

The trouble is . . . walking in Venice becomes compulsive once you start. Just over the next bridge, you say, and then the next one beckons.

DAPHNE DU MAURIER, *Don't Look Now* (1970)

A wondrous city of fairest carving, reflected in gleaming waters swirled to new patterning by every passing gondola.

SYLVIA PANKHURST, in Richard Pankhurst, *Sylvia Pankhurst: Artist and Crusader* (1979)

This city, with its weighty past, its small outlines, its strong odor, reveals in essence such wide perspectives that we are outside of time in it. We find here, better than elsewhere, the proof that difficulties are the best artisans of great destinies.

ADRIENNE MONNIER, *Les Gazettes d'Adrienne Monnier* (1936), in Richard McDougall, tr., *The Very Rich Hours of Adrienne Monnier* (1976)

See also Italy.

VERMONT

All in all, Vermont is a jewel state, small but precious.

PEARL BUCK, *Pearl Buck's America* (1971)

VERSE

My verses. I cannot say poems. Like everybody was then, I was following in the exquisite footsteps of Miss Millay, unhappily in my own horrible sneakers.

DOROTHY PARKER, in Malcolm Cowley, ed., *Writers at Work* (1958)

All verse is occasional verse.

ELLEN BRYANT VOIGT, "The Last Class," *The Lotus Flowers* (1987)

See also Poetry.

VICARIOUSNESS

Living by proxy is always a precarious expedient.

SIMONE DE BEAUVOIR, *The Second Sex* (1949)

See also Codependence.

VICE

The vices of the rich and great are mistaken for error; and those of the poor and lowly, for crimes.

LADY MARGUERITE BLESSINGTON, *Desultory Thoughts and Reflections* (1839)

How unjust life is, to make physical charm so immediately apparent or absent, when one can get away with vices untold for ever.

MARGARET DRABBLE, *A Summer Bird-Cage* (1962)

Here's a rule I recommend. Never practice two vices at once.

TALLULAH BANKHEAD, *Tallulah* (1952)

See also Evil, Flaws, Sin.

VILLAINS

As for an authentic villain, the real thing, the absolute, the artist, one rarely meets him even once in a lifetime. The ordinary bad hat is always in part a decent fellow.

COLETTE, *La naissance du jour* (1928)

See also Destroyers, Evil.

VIOLENCE

In violence, we forget who we are.

MARY MCCARTHY, *On the Contrary* (1961)

Violence commands both literature and life, and violence is always crude and distorted.

ELLEN GLASGOW, *Letters of Ellen Glasgow* (1958)

Blows are sarcasms turned stupid.

GEORGE ELIOT, *Felix Holt, The Radical* (1866)

Whipping and abuse are like laudanum: You have to double the dose as the sensibilities decline.

HARRIET BEECHER STOWE, *Uncle Tom's Cabin* (1852)

For you'll ne'er mend your fortunes, nor help the just cause, / By breaking of windows, or breaking of laws.

HANNAH MORE, speech (1817)

Today, together, let us repeat as our slogan that all trace of violence must disappear from this earth, then the sun will be honey-colored and music good to hear.

MONIQUE WITTIG, *Les Guérillères* (1969)

See also Rape.

VIRTUE

I'm part of an old piety that suffers in silence and calls it virtue. And is the very devil to live with.

MARY VIRGINIA MICKA, *The Cazenovia Journal* (1990)

It's queer how it is always one's virtues and not one's vices that precipitate one into disaster.

REBECCA WEST, *There Is No Conversation* (1935)

My virtue's still far too small, I don't trot it out and about yet.

COLETTE, *Claudine at School* (1900)

A man hasn't got a corner on virtue just because his shoes are shined.

ANN PETRY, *The Narrows* (1953)

Slaves learn to fear the master who prefaces his remarks with tributes to his own virtues.

ELIZABETH BORTON DE TREVIÑO, *I, Juan de Pareja* (1965)

As far as the education of children is concerned I think they should be taught not the little virtues but the great ones. Not thrift but generosity and an indifference to money; not caution but courage and a contempt for danger; not shrewdness but frankness and a love of truth; not tact but love for one's neighbor and self-denial; not a desire for success but a desire to be and to know.

NATALIA GINZBURG, *The Little Virtues* (1962)

I am not impressed by external devices for the preservation of virtue in men or women. Marriage laws, the police, armies and navies are the mark of human incompetence.

DORA RUSSELL, *The Right to Be Happy* (1927)

Feminine virtue is nothing but a convenient masculine invention.

NINON DE LENCLOS (c. 1660), *Letters* (1870)

See also Charity, Compassion, Courage, Faithfulness, Generosity, Goodness, Honesty, Humility, Kindness, Love, Mercy, Patience, Purity, Sympathy, Unselfishness.

VISIONS

Any of us can dream, but seeking vision is always done not only to heal and fulfill one's own potential, but also to learn to use that potential to serve all our relations: the two-leggeds, the four-leggeds, the wingeds, those that crawl upon the Earth, and the Mother Earth herself.

BROOKE MEDICINE EAGLE, in Joan Halifax, *Shamanic Voices: A Survey of Visionary Narratives* (1979)

When a vision begins to form everything changes, including the air around me. I seem no longer to be in the same atmosphere. I feel a peacefulness and a love that are indescribable. I stand alone, and nothing worldly can touch me.

JEANE DIXON, in Ruth Montgomery, *A Gift of Prophecy* (1965)

I have gotten back more and more to the ancient ways. This happened as I began to have visions; I was drawn back to the old ways by them. I did not choose it outwardly; it came as I released old ways of being, its irresistible call bringing me home.

BROOKE MEDICINE EAGLE, in Joan Halifax, *Shamanic Voices: A Survey of Visionary Narratives* (1979)

See also Dreams.

VULNERABILITY

All are / naked, none is safe.

MARIANNE MOORE, title poem, *What Are Years?* (1941)

See also Security.

W

WALKING

Walking is also an ambulation of mind.

GRETEL EHRLICH, in William Kittredge, ed., *Montana Spaces* (1988)

WALLS

Constant walls and a roof do something to me at any time and when the aspens turn golden, I seethe inside until finally I revolt and leave everything.

EDITH WARNER, in Peggy Pond Church, *The House at Otowi Bridge* (1959)

But walls have an engrossing quality. If there are many of them they assert themselves and domineer. They insist on the unique importance of the contents of walls and would have you believe that the spaces above them, the slow procession of the seasons and the alternations of sunshine and rain, are accessories, pleasant or unpleasant, of walls,—indeed that they were made, and a bungling job, too, and to be disregarded as a bungling job should be, solely that walls might exist.

EDNA BRUSH PERKINS, *The White Heart of Mojave* (1922)

See also Houses, Rooms.

WAR

You can no more win a war than you can win an earthquake.

JEANNETTE RANKIN, in Hannah Josephson, *Jeannette Rankin: First Lady in Congress* (1947)

No one won the last war, and no one will win the next.

ELEANOR ROOSEVELT, letter to Harry S. Truman (1948)

War will hit you hard / coming at you like lions raging.

HIND BINT UTBA, "Fury Against the Moslems at Uhud" (7th century), in Joanna Bankier and Deirdre Lashgari, eds., *Women Poets of the World* (1983)

All war is insane.

MADELEINE L'ENGLE, *A Wind in the Door* (1973)

No war, not even to punish an aggressor, is a good thing. Today people must learn to take into account each others' interests, if only for the sake of their own survival. I do not believe that, in this system of coordinates, the point where politics and simple human morality intersect is only idealism.

RAISA M. GORBACHEV, *I Hope* (1991)

War is the unfolding of miscalculations.

BARBARA TUCHMAN, *The Guns of August* (1962)

Every war already carries within it the war which will answer it. Every war is answered by a new war, until everything, everything is smashed.

KÄTHE KOLLWITZ, letter (1944), in Hans Kollwitz, ed., *The Diaries and Letters of Käthe Kollwitz* (1955)

I am sure that you will never end war with wars.

NANCY ASTOR, *My Two Countries* (1923)

Everything, everything in war is barbaric. . . . But the worst barbarity of war is that it forces men collectively to commit acts against which individually they would revolt with their whole being.

ELLEN KEY, *War, Peace, and the Future* (1916)

There's a consensus out that it's OK to kill when your government decides who to kill. If you kill inside the country you get in trouble. If you kill outside the country, right time, right season, latest enemy, you get a medal.

JOAN BAEZ, *Daybreak* (1968)

If it's natural to kill, why do men have to go into training to learn how?

JOAN BAEZ, *Daybreak* (1968)

Only very coarse persons wanted wars.

PEARL BUCK, *The Old Demon* (1939)

Our human situation no longer permits us to make armed dichotomies between those who are good and those who are evil, those who are right and those who are wrong. The first blow dealt to the enemy's children will sign the death warrant of our own.

MARGARET MEAD, *Continuities in Cultural Evolution* (1964)

One is left with the horrible feeling now that war settles *nothing;* that to *win* a war is as disastrous as to lose one!

AGATHA CHRISTIE, *An Autobiography* (1977)

Formerly, a nation that broke the peace did not trouble to try and prove to the world that it was done solely from higher motives. . . . *Now war has a bad conscience.* Now every nation assures us that it is bleeding for a human cause, the fate of which hangs in the balance of its victory. . . . No nation dares to admit the guilt of blood before the world.

ELLEN KEY, *War, Peace, and the Future* (1916)

War is the supreme form of prestige.

SIMONE WEIL, *The Notebooks of Simone Weil* (1951)

Since war is a convulsion that occurs when political processes fail to settle disputes among or within nations, the aftermath of war includes an upheaval of the status quo.

JUNE A. WILLENZ, *Women Veterans: America's Forgotten Heroines* (1983)

There never was a war that was / not inward; I must / fight till I have conquered in myself what / causes war, but I would not believe it.

MARIANNE MOORE, "In Distrust of Merits," *Collected Poems* (1951)

All disasters stem from us. . . . Yet we could fight war and all its excrescences by releasing, each day, the love which is shackled inside us, and giving it a chance to live.

ETTY HILLESUM, *An Interrupted Life: The Diaries of Etty Hillesum 1941–1943* (1983)

All wars derive from lack of empathy: the incapacity of one to understand and accept the likeness or difference of another. Whether in nations or the encounters of race and sex, competition then replaces compassion, subjection excludes mutuality.

MARYA MANNES, Out of My Time (1968)

Mine eyes have seen the glory of the coming of the Lord; / He is trampling out the vintage where the grapes of wrath are stored.

JULIA WARD HOWE, "Battle Hymn of the American Republic," in *Atlantic Monthly* (1862)

Arise then, women of this day! Arise, all women who have hearts, whether your baptism be that of water or of tears! Say firmly, "We will not have great questions decided by irrelevant agencies. Our husbands shall not come to us, reeking of carnage, for caresses and applause. Our sons shall not be taken from us to unlearn all that we have been able to teach them of charity, mercy and patience. We women of one country will be too tender of those of another country to allow our sons to be trained to injure theirs." From the bosom of the devastated earth a voice goes up with our own, it says, "Disarm! Disarm!"

JULIA WARD HOWE, "Mother's Day Proclamation" (1870)

The sword of murder is not the balance of justice. Blood does not wipe out dishonor nor violence indicate possession.

JULIA WARD HOWE, "Mother's Day Proclamation" (1870)

Was that what, ultimately, war did to you? It was not the physical dangers—the mines at sea, the bombs from the air, the crisp ping of a rifle bullet as you drove over a desert track. No, it was the spiritual danger of learning how much easier life was if you ceased to think.

AGATHA CHRISTIE, *There Is a Tide* (1948)

Is war perhaps nothing else but a need to face death, to conquer and master it, to come out of it alive—a peculiar form of denial of our own mortality?

ELISABETH KÜBLER-ROSS, *On Death and Dying* (1969)

Modern war, they argued, as it was plain for everyone to see, had become so diabolical, so destructive, so incompatible with ethics, Christian teaching, nineteenth-century thought or mere common sense as to be as unthinkable for men to use against one another as putting one another into a pot to boil and eat. They also saw, being honest men, that very few people anywhere saw anything of the kind.

SYBILLE BEDFORD, *A Favorite of the Gods* (1963)

The worst thing about war is that so many people enjoy it.

ELLEN GLASGOW, *The Woman Within* (1954)

If we justify war, it is because all peoples always justify the traits of which they find themselves possessed, not because war will bear an objective examination of its merits.

RUTH BENEDICT, *Patterns of Culture* (1934)

War is the admission of defeat in the face of conflicting interests: by war the issue is left to chance, and the tacit assumption that the best man will win is not at all justified. It might equally be argued that the worst, the most unscrupulous man will win, although history will continue the absurd game by finding him after all the best man.

GERMAINE GREER, *The Female Eunuch* (1971)

The sky of Beirut rained down missiles and shells and the horror isolated us in shelters and underground vaults where we spent our nights waiting for death, until morning came and then we would start to check on each other and to feel our limbs to see if they were still there.

EMILY NASRALLAH, "Those Memories," in Elizabeth Warnock Fernea, *Women and the Family in the Middle East* (1985)

War and the "war of the sexes" are neither divinely nor biologically ordained.

RIANE EISLER, *The Chalice and the Blade* (1987)

In Europe, war is a disease which has been in the family for generations: no one is surprised when it makes another leap. Even the patient only attends to it with part of his mind.

STORM JAMESON, *Before the Crossing* (1947)

It occurred to me that we live in a lunatic world where the only way to maintain peace is to have an enormous war-making machine.

ILKA CHASE, *Free Admission* (1948)

War, which perpetuates itself under the form of preparation for war, has once and for all given the State an important role in production.

SIMONE WEIL (1933), *Oppression and Liberty* (1955)

The high stage of world-industrial development in capitalistic production finds expression in the extraordinary technical development and destructiveness of the instruments of war.

ROSA LUXEMBURG, *The Crisis in the German Social Democracy* (1919)

A self-respecting nation is ready for anything, including war, except for a renunciation of its option to make war. But why is it so essential to be able to make war? No one knows, any more than the Trojans knew why it was necessary for them to keep Helen.

SIMONE WEIL, "The Power of Words," *The Simone Weil Reader* (1977)

I dream of giving birth to a child who will ask, "Mother, what was war?"

EVE MERRIAM, in *Peacemaking: Day by Day* (1989)

See also Conflict, Militarism, Peace, Revolution.

WASHINGTON, D.C.

There was no other city in the world where rumor fed upon itself so virulently. Whispers wiped out careers just as cholera destroyed its human victims.

EVELYN ANTHONY, *The Avenue of the Dead* (1982)

Washington is, for one thing, the news capital of the world. And for another, it is a company town. Most of the interesting people in Washington either work for the government or write about it.

SALLY QUINN, *We're Going to Make You a Star* (1975)

In Washington it is an honor to be disgraced . . . you have to have *been* somebody to fall.

MEG GREENFIELD, in *Newsweek* (1986)

The cocktail party remains a vital Washington institution, the official intelligence system.

BARBARA HOWAR, *Laughing All the Way* (1973)

I love Washington, but it *is* a self-important town.

LADY BIRD JOHNSON, *A White House Diary* (1970)

WEAKNESS

Our strength is often composed of the weakness that we're damned if we're going to show.

MIGNON MCLAUGHLIN, *The Second Neurotic's Notebook* (1966)

Not to discover weakness is / The Artifice of strength.

EMILY DICKINSON (1865), *The Poems of Emily Dickinson* (1955)

Lack of fairness to an opponent is essentially a sign of weakness.

EMMA GOLDMAN, *Living My Life* (1931)

He [Peter III] did not have a bad heart; but a weak man usually has not.

CATHERINE THE GREAT, in Katharine Anthony, *Catherine the Great* (1926)

In our country everything is weakening. The money is weak. Democracy is weak and the politicians are very weak. Everything that is weak dies one day.

CAROLINA MARIA DE JESUS, *Child of the Dark, The Diary of Carolina Maria de Jesus* (1962)

See also Inadequacy, Limitations.

WEALTH

Wealth means power: the power to subdue, to crush, to exploit, the power to enslave, to outrage, to degrade.

EMMA GOLDMAN, title essay, *Anarchism* (1910)

Great wealth is its own nationality.

VELDA JOHNSTON, *I Came to a Castle* (1969)

Wealth covers sin—the poor / Are naked as a pin.

KASSIA, "Epigrams" (9th century), in Joanna Bankier and Deirdre Lashgari, eds., *Women Poets of the World* (1983)

Wealth is the product of man's capacity to think.

AYN RAND, *Atlas Shrugged* (1957)

The greatest evidence of demoralization is the respect paid to wealth.

GEORGE SAND, in *French Wit and Wisdom* (1950)

Wealth consists not in having possessions but in having few wants.

ESTHER DE WAAL, *Seeking God: The Way of St. Benedict* (1984)

The true defense against wealth is not a fear of wealth—of its fragility and of the vicious consequences that it can bring—the true defense against wealth is an indifference to money.

NATALIA GINZBURG, *The Little Virtues* (1962)

There are many excuses for the persons who made the mistake of confounding money and wealth. Like many others they mistook the sign for the thing signified.

MILLICENT GARRETT FAWCETT, *Political Economy for Beginners* (1870)

No one in the United States has the right to own millions of acres of American land, I don't care how they came by it.

EDNA FERBER, *Giant* (1952)

Why snatch at wealth, and hoard and stock it? / Your shroud, you know, will have no pocket!

BETTY PAOLI, *Neueste Gedichte* (1870)

See also Luxury, Money, Rich.

WEATHER

On the farm the weather was the great fact, and men's affairs went on underneath it, as the streams creep under the ice.

WILLA CATHER, *My Antonia* (1918)

What dreadful hot weather we have! It keeps me in a continual state of inelegance.

JANE AUSTEN, letter to her sister Cassandra (1796)

It is only in sorrow bad weather masters us; in joy we face the storm and defy it.

AMELIA E. BARR, *Jan Vedder's Wife* (1885)

Wild nights are my glory.

MADELEINE L'ENGLE, *A Wrinkle in Time* (1962)

It is impossible, to me at least, to be poetical in cold weather.

GEORGE ELIOT, letter (1840), in J. W. Cross, *George Eliot's Life as Related in Her Letters and Journals* (1884)

See also Rain, Snow, Wind.

WEDDINGS

Our wedding plans please everybody as if we were fertilizing the earth and creating social luck.

MARGE PIERCY, *Braided Lives* (1982)

A wedding invitation is beautiful and formal notification of the desire to share a solemn and joyous occasion, sent by people who have been saying "Do we have to ask them?" to people whose first response is "How much do you think we have to spend on them?"

JUDITH MARTIN, *Miss Manners' Guide to Rearing Perfect Children* (1984)

See also Marriage.

WEIGHT

Give me a dozen heart-breaks like that if you think it would help me lose one pound.

COLETTE, *Cheri* (1920)

There's nothing on earth to do here but look at the view and eat. You can imagine the result since I do not like to look at views.

ZELDA FITZGERALD, letter to her daughter, in Nancy Milford, *Zelda* (1970)

I had no intention of giving her my vital statistics. "Let me put it this way," I said. "According to my girth, I should be a ninety-foot redwood."

ERMA BOMBECK, *If Life Is a Bowl of Cherries, What Am I Doing in the Pits?* (1971)

I am also five three and in the neighborhood of one thirty. It is a neighborhood I would like to get out of.

FLANNERY O'CONNOR, in Sally Fitzgerald, ed., *The Habit of Being* (1979)

His body's taken on the weight his mind still refuses to accept.

TONI CADE BAMBARA, *The Salt Eaters* (1980)

Women should try to increase their size rather than decrease it, because I believe the bigger we are, the more space we'll take up, and the more we'll have to be reckoned with. I think every woman should be fat like me.

ROSEANNE BARR, in *Utne Reader* (1991)

We know that every woman wants to be thin. Our images of womanhood are almost synonymous with thinness.

SUSIE ORBACH, in Kim Chernin, *The Obsession* (1981)

Fat is a feminist issue.

SUSIE ORBACH, book title (1978)

See also Chocolate, Diet, Food.

THE WEST

The West is color. . . . Its colors are animal rather than vegetable, the colors of earth and sunlight and ripeness.

JESSAMYN WEST, in *Woman's Home Companion* (1956)

See also United States.

WHITES

How in the hell could God take the black earth and make himself a white man out of it?

LOUISE MERIWETHER, *Daddy Was a Number Runner* (1970)

Most of the time when "universal" is used, it is just a euphemism for "white": white themes, white significance, white culture.

MERLE WOO, "Letter to Ma," in Cherríe Moraga and Gloria Anzaldúa, eds., *This Bridge Called My Back* (1983)

I know now that once I longed to be white.

NELLIE WONG, "When I Was Growing Up," in Cherríe Moraga and Gloria Anzaldúa, eds., *This Bridge Called My Back* (1983)

The psychological consequences of this spread of white culture have been out of all proportion to the materialistic. This world-wide cultural diffusion has protected us as man had never been protected before from having to take seriously the civilizations of other peoples; it has given to our culture a massive universality that we have long ceased to account for historically, and which we read off rather as necessary and inevitable.

RUTH BENEDICT, *Patterns of Culture* (1934)

The truth is that Mozart, Pascal, Boolean algebra, Shakespeare, parliamentary government, baroque churches, Newton, the emancipation of women, Kant, Marx, Balanchine ballet, *et al.*, don't redeem what this particular civilization has wrought upon the world. The white race *is* the cancer of human history, it is the white race, and it alone—its ideologies and inventions— which eradicates autonomous civilization wherever it spreads, which has upset the ecological balance of the planet, which now threatens the very existence of life itself.

SUSAN SONTAG, in *Partisan Review* (1967)

He had the patient, practical, uninterested tone of the white person willing to help a native with money or authority, so long as he is not expected to listen to any human details of the predicament.

NADINE GORDIMER, *The Lying Days* (1953)

See also Blacks, Blacks and Whites.

WHOLENESS

A person who believes, as she did, that things fit: that there is a whole of which one is a part, and that in being a part one is whole: such a person has no desire whatever, at any time, to play God. Only those who have denied their being yearn to play at it.

URSULA K. LE GUIN, *The Lathe of Heaven* (1971)

African tradition deals with life as an experience to be lived. In many respects, it is much like the Eastern philosophies in that we see ourselves as a part of a life force; we are joined, for instance, to the air, to the earth. We are part of the whole-life process. We live in accordance with, in a kind of correspondence with the rest of the world as a whole. And therefore living becomes an experience, rather than a problem, no matter how bad or how painful it may be.

AUDRE LORDE, in Claudia Tate, ed., *Black Women Writers at Work* (1983)

I knew without a glimmer of doubt that all things in the universe were connected by a living truth that would not relent its continuing search for wholeness until every form of life was united.

LYNN V. ANDREWS, *Crystal Woman* (1987)

I think wholeness comes from living your life consciously during the day and then exploring your inner life or unconscious at night.

MARGERY CUYLER, in Jim Roginski, *Behind the Covers* (1985)

To the extent that either sex is disadvantaged, the whole culture is poorer, and the sex that, superficially, inherits the earth, inherits only a very partial legacy. The more whole the culture, the more whole each member, each man, each woman, each child will be.

MARGARET MEAD, *Male and Female* (1949)

See also Human Family, Inner Life, Interdependence, Self.

WHY

There is really nothing more to say—except why. But since why is difficult to handle, one must take refuge in how.

TONI MORRISON, *The Bluest Eye* (1970)

See also Answers, Explanations, Questions.

WIFE

It is a truth universally acknowledged that a single man in possession of a good fortune, must be in want of a wife.

JANE AUSTEN, *Pride and Prejudice* (1813)

Wife and servant are the same, / But only differ in the name.

LADY MARY CHUDLEIGH, "To the Ladies," *Poems on Several Occasions* (1703)

A successful woman preacher was once asked "what special obstacles have you met as a woman in the ministry?" "Not one," she answered, "except the lack of a minister's wife."

ANNA GARLIN SPENCER, "Woman's Share in Social Culture," *The Family and Its Members* (1923)

See also Family, Husband, Lovers, Marriage.

WILDERNESS

I go into the wilderness and rediscover the home within.

CHINA GALLAND, in Lorraine Anderson, ed., *Sisters of the Earth* (1991)

We use the word "wilderness," but perhaps we mean wildness. Isn't that why I've come here? In wilderness, I seek the wildness in myself—and in so doing, come on the wildness everywhere around me because, after all, being part of nature, I'm cut from the same cloth.

GRETEL EHRLICH, in William Kittredge, ed., *Montana Spaces* (1988)

See also Nature.

WILDLIFE

It is impossible to be among the woods animals on their own ground without a feeling of expanding one's own world, as when any foreign country is visited.

MARJORIE KINNAN RAWLINGS, *Cross Creek* (1942)

If you look close . . . you can see that the wild critters have "No Trespassing" signs tacked up on every pine tree.

MARGUERITE HENRY, *Misty of Chincoteague* (1947)

Probably we never fully credit the interdependence of wild creatures, and their cognizance of the affairs of their own kind.

MARY AUSTIN, *The Land of Little Rain* (1904)

See also Animals.

WIND

Wise guy, he not go against wind. In Chinese we say, Come from South, blow with wind—poom!—North will follow. Strongest wind cannot be seen.

AMY TAN, *The Joy Luck Club* (1989)

And wind moving through grass so that the grass quivers. This moves me with an emotion I don't ever understand.

KATHERINE MANSFIELD (1992), *The Journal of Katherine Mansfield* (1927)

See also Weather.

WINE

Wine is earth's answer to the sun.

MARGARET FULLER, in Lydia Maria Child, *Letters from New York*, 2nd Series (1845)

If you are not proud of your cellar, there is no thrill of satisfaction in seeing your guest hold up his wineglass to the light and look judicial.

GEORGE ELIOT, *Middlemarch* (1871)

Great people talk about ideas, average people talk about things, and small people talk about wine.

FRAN LEBOWITZ, *Social Studies* (1977)

See also Alcohol, Drink.

WINNING

Conquer but don't triumph.

MARIE VON EBNER-ESCHENBACH, *Aphorisms* (1905)

In sports, you simply aren't considered a real champion until you have defended your title successfully. Winning it once can be a fluke; winning it twice proves you are the best.

ALTHEA GIBSON, *I Always Wanted to Be Somebody* (1958)

Winning the prize [1963 Nobel Prize in physics] wasn't half as exciting as doing the work itself.

MARIA GOEPPERT MAYER, in Barbara Shiels, *Women and the Nobel Prize* (1985)

Counting both times I cheated this week / I won at solitaire twice.

Mary Virginia Micka, *Hexameron* (1986)

See also Success.

WINTER

There seems to be so much more winter than we need this year.

Kathleen Norris, *Bread Into Roses* (1937)

The cold was our pride, the snow was our beauty. It fell and fell, lacing day and night together in a milky haze, making everything quieter as it fell, so that winter seemed to partake of religion in a way no other season did, hushed, solemn.

Patricia Hampl, *A Romantic Education* (1981)

That winter, cold settled in the bones as if it would be stored there indefinitely like ice in an icehouse.

Esther Hautzig, *The Endless Steppe* (1968)

Blackberry winter, the time when the hoarfrost lies on the blackberry blossoms; without this frost the berries will not set. It is the forerunner of a rich harvest.

Margaret Mead, *Blackberry Winter* (1972)

In a way winter is the real spring, the time when the inner thing happens, the resurge of nature.

Edna O'Brien, "Clara," *Mrs. Reinhardt* (1978)

There is a privacy about it which no other season gives you. . . . In spring, summer and fall people sort of have an open season on each other; only in the winter, in the country, can you have longer, quiet stretches when you can *savor* belonging to yourself.

Ruth Stout, *How to Have a Green Thumb Without an Aching Back* (1955)

February, when the days of winter seem endless and no amount of recollecting can bring back any air of summer.

Shirley Jackson, *Raising Demons* (1956)

Perhaps I am a bear, or some hibernating animal, underneath, for the instinct to be half asleep all winter is so strong in me.

Anne Morrow Lindbergh, *Bring Me a Unicorn* (1971)

See also Cold, Snow.

WIT

Thou canst not serve both cod and salmon.

Ada Leverson, in *The Times* (1970)

It's not true I had nothing on. I had the radio on.

Marilyn Monroe, in *Time* (1952)

The shortest distance between two points is under construction.

Noelie Alito, in *Omni* (1979)

I fear nothing so much as a man who is witty all day long.

Marie de Rabutin-Chantal, Marquise de Sévigné, *Letters of Madame de Sévigné to Her Daughter and Her Friends* (1811)

See also Humor, Irony, Laughter, Satire.

WOLVES

Wolves . . . are a balance wheel of nature.

Lois Crisler, *Arctic Wild* (1958)

Wolves are brotherly. They love each other, and if you learn to speak to them, they will love you too.

Jean Craighead George, *Julie of the Wolves* (1972)

See also Animals, Wildlife.

WOMEN

And ain't I a woman?

Sojourner Truth, speech (1851)

I am Woman, hear me roar / In numbers too big to ignore.

Helen Reddy, "I Am Woman" (1971)

One is not born, but rather becomes, a woman.

Simone de Beauvoir, *The Second Sex* (1949)

A woman is like a teabag—only in hot water do you realize how strong she is.

NANCY REAGAN, in *Observer* (1981)

Let Greeks be Greeks, and women what they are.

ANNE BRADSTREET, "The Prologue," *The Tenth Muse, Lately Sprung Up in America* (1650)

When will it no longer be necessary to attach special weight to the word "woman" and raise it specially?

DING LING, "Thoughts on March 8" (1942), *I Myself Am a Woman: Selected Writings of Ding Ling* (1989)

Women are not inherently passive or peaceful. We're not inherently anything but human.

ROBIN MORGAN, in Shirley Chisholm, *Unbought and Unbossed* (1970)

Womanhood is the great fact in her life; wifehood and motherhood are but incidental relations.

ELIZABETH CADY STANTON, *The History of Woman Suffrage* (1881)

Women were the slave class that maintained the species in order to free the other half for the business of the world.

SHULAMITH FIRESTONE, *The Dialectic of Sex* (1970)

Women are the true maintenance class. Society is built upon their acquiescence, and upon their small and necessary labors.

SALLY KEMPTON, in *Esquire* (1970)

The economic dependence of women is perhaps the greatest injustice that has been done to us, and has worked the greatest injury to the race.

NELLIE McCLUNG, *In Times Like These* (1915)

The problem that has no name—which is simply the fact that American women are kept from growing to their full human capacities—is taking a far greater toll on the physical and mental health of our country than any known disease.

BETTY FRIEDAN, *The Feminine Mystique* (1963)

The feminine mystique has succeeded in burying millions of American women alive.

BETTY FRIEDAN, *The Feminine Mystique* (1963)

Each suburban wife struggled with it alone. As she made the beds, shopped for groceries, matched slipcover material, ate peanut butter sandwiches with her children, chauffeured Cub Scouts and Brownies, lay beside her husband at night—she was afraid to ask even of herself the silent question—"Is this all?"

BETTY FRIEDAN, *The Feminine Mystique* (1963)

The truth is, we [women] live like bats or owls, labor like beasts, and die like worms.

MARGARET CAVENDISH, DUCHESS OF NEWCASTLE, *Female Orations* (1662)

Woman's normal occupations in general run counter to creative life, or contemplative life, or saintly life.

ANNE MORROW LINDBERGH, *Gift From the Sea* (1955)

Any woman who has a career and a family automatically develops something in the way of two personalities, like two sides of a dollar bill each different in design. . . . Her problem is to keep one from draining the life from the other.

IVY BAKER PRIEST, *Green Grows Ivy* (1958)

I have a brain and a uterus, and I use both.

PATRICIA SCHROEDER, in *New York Times* (1977)

If God had wanted us to think with our wombs, why did he give us a brain?

CLARE BOOTHE LUCE, *Slam the Door Softly* (1970)

The most wasteful "brain drain" in America today is the drain in the kitchen sink.

ELIZABETH GOULD DAVIS, *First Sex* (1971)

This world taught woman nothing skillful and then said her work was valueless. It permitted her no opinions and said she did not know how to think. It forbade her to speak in public, and said the sex had no orators.

CARRIE CHAPMAN CATT, in Susan B. Anthony and Ida H. Harper, *The History of Woman Suffrage*, vol. IV (1902)

Now we are expected to be as wise as men who have had generations of all the help there is, and we scarcely anything.

LOUISA MAY ALCOTT, *Jo's Boys* (1886)

Woman is shut up in a kitchen or in a boudoir, and astonishment is expressed that her horizon is limited. Her wings are clipped, and it is found deplorable that she cannot fly.

SIMONE DE BEAUVOIR, *The Second Sex* (1949)

It is not the inferiority of women that has caused their historical insignificance; it is rather their historical insignificance that has doomed them to inferiority.

SIMONE DE BEAUVOIR, *The Second Sex* (1949)

All women are misfits, I think; we do not fit into this world without amputations.

MARGE PIERCY, *Braided Lives* (1982)

Oh, God, who does not exist, you hate women, otherwise you'd have made them different.

EDNA O'BRIEN, *Girls in Their Married Bliss* (1964)

Women never have young minds. They are born three thousand years old.

SHELAGH DELANEY, *A Taste of Honey* (1958)

This is a time in history when women's voices must be heard, or forever be silenced. It's not because we think better than men, but we think differently. It's not women against men, but women and men. It's not that the world would have been better if women had run it, but that the world will be better when we as women, who bring our own perspective, share in running it.

BETTY BUMPERS, conference speech (1985)

I think being a woman is like being Irish. . . . Everyone says you're important and nice but you take second place all the same.

IRIS MURDOCH, *The Red and the Green* (1965)

If . . . society will not admit of woman's free development, then society must be remodeled.

ELIZABETH BLACKWELL, letter (1848), in Elizabeth Cady Stanton, *The History of Woman Suffrage* (1881)

In education, in marriage, in religion, in every-thing, disappointment is the lot of women. It shall be the business of my life to deepen this disappointment in every woman's heart until she bows down to it no longer.

LUCY STONE, speech (1855), in Elizabeth Cady Stanton, *The History of Woman Suffrage* (1881)

Confusion has seized us, and all things go wrong, / The women have leaped from "their spheres," / And, instead of fixed stars, shoot as comets along, / And are setting the world by the ears!

MARIA CHAPMAN, "The Times That Try Men's Souls," in Elizabeth Cady Stanton, *History of Woman Suffrage* (1881)

There is a hidden fear that somehow, if they are only given a chance, women will suddenly do as they have been done by.

EVA FIGES, *Patriarchal Attitudes* (1970)

That curious social warp which obligates us most to impeach the validity of a woman's opin-ion at the points where it is most supported by experience.

MARY AUSTIN, *A Woman of Genius* (1912)

Whatever women do they must do twice as well as men to be thought half as good. Luckily, this is not difficult.

CHARLOTTE WHITTON, in *Canada Month* (1963)

People call me a feminist whenever I express sen-timents that differentiate me from a doormat or a prostitute.

REBECCA WEST, in *The Clarion* (1913)

Womanist is to feminist as purple to lavender.

ALICE WALKER, *In Search of Our Mothers' Gardens* (1983)

We're half the people; we should be half the Congress.

JEANNETTE RANKIN, in *Newsweek* (1966)

Some of us are becoming the men we wanted to marry.

GLORIA STEINEM, in *Ms.* (1982)

Ginger Rogers did everything that Fred Astaire did. She just did it backwards and in high heels.

Variously attributed to FAITH WHITTLESEY, LINDA ELLERBEE, and ANN RICHARDS (1980s)

It occurred to me when I was thirteen and wear-ing white gloves and Mary Janes and going to dancing school, that no one should have to dance backward all their lives.

JILL RUCKELSHAUS, speech (1973)

I was elected by the women of Ireland, who instead of rocking the cradle, rocked the system.

MARY ROBINSON, news item (1990)

If you sing too often of woe, yours or your sisters', you may be charged with being "too personal," "too autobiographical," too much a woman who cries out, who acknowledges openly, shamelessly, the pain of living and the joy of becoming free.

NELLIE WONG, "In Search of the Self As Hero: Confetti of Voices on New Year's Night," in Cherríe Moraga and Gloria Anzaldúa, eds., *This Bridge Called My Back* (1983)

Women are repeatedly accused of taking things personally. I cannot see any other honest way of taking them.

MARYA MANNES, *More in Anger* (1958)

If you're going to generalize about women, you'll find yourself up to *here* in exceptions.

DOLORES HITCHENS, *In a House Unknown* (1973)

See also Ladies, Wife, Women and Men.

WOMEN AND MEN

I have never in all my various travels seen but two sorts of people, and those very like one another; I mean men and women, who always have been and ever will be the same.

LADY MARY WORTLEY MONTAGU, letter (1747), in Octave Thanet, ed., *The Best Letters of Lady Mary Wortley Montagu* (1901)

The first thing that strikes the careless observer is that women are unlike men. They are "the opposite sex"—(though why "opposite" I do not know; what is the "neighboring sex"?).

DOROTHY L. SAYERS, "The Human-Not-Quite-Human," *Unpopular Opinions* (1947)

The sexes in each species of beings . . . are always true equivalents—equals but not identicals.

ANTOINETTE BROWN BLACKWELL, *The Sexes Throughout Nature* (1875)

What is human and the same about the males and females classified as *Homo sapiens* is much greater than the differences.

ESTELLE R. RAMEY, in Francine Klagsbrun, ed., *The First Ms. Reader* (1972)

There is more difference within the sexes than between them.

IVY COMPTON-BURNETT, *Mother and Son* (1955)

I object to anything that divides the two sexes. My main point is this: human development has now reached a point at which sexual difference has become a thing of altogether minor importance. We make too much of it; we are men and women in the second place, human beings in the first.

OLIVE SCHREINER, *The Letters of Olive Schreiner, 1876–1920* (1976)

Mr. Darwin . . . has failed to hold definitely before his mind the principle that the difference of sex, whatever it may consist in, must itself be subject to natural selection and to evolution.

ANTOINETTE BROWN BLACKWELL, The Sexes Throughout Nature (1875)

The basic discovery about any people is the discovery of the relationship between its men and women.

PEARL BUCK, *Of Men and Women* (1941)

I'm not denyin' the women are foolish: God Almighty made 'em to match the men.

GEORGE ELIOT, *Adam Bede* (1859)

Men and women, women and men. It will never work.

ERICA JONG, *Fear of Flying* (1973)

There should be an end to the bitterness of feeling which has arisen between the sexes in this century.

CHARLOTTE PERKINS GILMAN, *Women and Economics* (1899)

There are only two basic ways of structuring the relations between the female and male halves of humanity. All societies are patterned on either a dominator model—in which human hierarchies are ultimately backed up by force or the threat of force—or a partnership model, with variations in between.

RIANE EISLER, *The Chalice and the Blade* (1987)

A true conception of the relation of the sexes will not admit of conqueror and conquered; it knows of but one great thing; to give of one's self boundlessly, in order to find one's self richer, deeper, better.

EMMA GOLDMAN, *Anarchism* (1910)

So long as women are slaves, men will be knaves.

ELIZABETH CADY STANTON, in Theodore Stanton and Harriot Stanton Blatch, eds., *Elizabeth Cady Stanton as Revealed in Her Letters, Diary and Reminiscences* (1922)

And what is wrong in woman's life / In man's cannot be right.

FRANCES ELLEN WATKINS HARPER, "A Double Standard," *The Sparrow's Fall and Other Poems* (1894)

Of course men play roles, but women play roles too, blanker ones. They have, in the play of life, fewer good lines.

IRIS MURDOCH, *The Black Prince* (1973)

The dogma of woman's complete historical subjection to man must be rated as one of the most fantastic myths ever created by the human mind.

MARY RITTER BEARD, *Woman as Force in History* (1946)

The history of men's opposition to women's emancipation is more interesting perhaps than the story of that emancipation itself.

VIRGINIA WOOLF, *A Room of One's Own* (1929)

Women have served all these centuries as looking-glasses possessing the magic and delicious power of reflecting the figure of man at twice its natural size.

VIRGINIA WOOLF, *A Room of One's Own* (1929)

I long to hear that you have declared an independency—and by the way in the new Code of Laws which I suppose it will be necessary for you to make I desire you would Remember the Ladies, and be more generous and favorable to them than your ancestors. Do not put such unlimited power into the hands of the Husbands. Remember all Men would be tyrants if they could. If particular care and attention is not paid to the Ladies we are determined to foment a Rebellion, and will not hold ourselves bound by any Laws in which we have no voice, or Representation. That your Sex are Naturally Tyrannical is a Truth so thoroughly established as to admit of no dispute, but such of you as wish to be happy willingly give up the harsh title of Master for the more tender and endearing one of Friend.

ABIGAIL ADAMS, letter to her husband, John Adams (1776)

Stupid men, who accuse / women without reason: / you've never noticed, I suppose, / it's you who taught the lesson.

SOR JUANA INÉS DE LA CRUZ, "Hombres Necios" (c. 1690), in Irene Nicholson, *A Guide to Mexican Poetry* (1968)

Women have one great advantage over men. It is commonly thought that if they marry they have done enough, and need career no further. If a man marries, on the other hand, public opinion is all against him if he takes this view.

ROSE MACAULAY, *A Casual Commentary* (1926)

I admit it is better fun to punt than to be punted, and that a desire to have all the fun is nine-tenths of the law of chivalry.

DOROTHY L. SAYERS, *Gaudy Night* (1935)

The most sympathetic of men never fully comprehend woman's concrete situation.

SIMONE DE BEAUVOIR, *The Second Sex* (1949)

The average man is more interested in a woman who is interested in him than he is in a woman—any woman—with beautiful legs.

MARLENE DIETRICH, news item (1954)

When women go wrong, men go right after them.

MAE WEST, in Joseph Weintraub, ed., *The Wit and Wisdom of Mae West* (1967)

See also Androgyny, Gender, Husband, Men, Sexism, Sex Roles, Stereotypes, Wife, Women.

WONDER

Wonder and despair are two sides of a spinning coin. When you open yourself to one, you open yourself to the other. You discover a capacity for joy that wasn't in you before. Wonder is the promise of restoration: as deeply as you dive, so may you rise.

CHRISTINA BALDWIN, *Life's Companion, Journal Writing as a Spiritual Quest* (1990)

Everything has its wonders, even darkness and silence, and I learn, whatever state I may be in, therein to be content.

HELEN KELLER, *The Story of My Life* (1902)

If a child is to keep alive his inborn sense of wonder . . . he needs the companionship of at least one adult who can share it, rediscovering with him the joy, excitement and mystery of the world we live in.

RACHEL CARSON, *The Sense of Wonder* (1965)

If I had influence with the good fairy who is supposed to preside over the christening of all children I should ask that her gift to each child in the world be a sense of wonder so indestructible that it would last throughout life, as an unfailing antidote against the boredom and disenchantments of later years, the sterile preoccupation with things that are artificial, the alienation from the sources of our strength.

RACHEL CARSON, *The Sense of Wonder* (1965)

For the first time in her life she thought, might the same wonders never come again? Was each wonder original and alone like the falling star, and when it fell did it bury itself beyond where you hunted it?

EUDORA WELTY, "The Winds," *The Wide Net* (1943)

See also Curiosity, Miracles.

WORDS

The words! I collected them in all shapes and sizes and hung them like bangles in my mind.

HORTENSE CALISHER, *Extreme Magic* (1964)

Words, once they're printed, have a life of their own.

CAROL BURNETT, in *Reader's Digest* (1982)

Although they are / Only breath, words / which I command / are immortal.

SAPPHO (6th century B.C.), in Mary Barnard, tr., *Sappho: A New Translation* (1958)

We think because we have words, not the other way around. The more words we have, the better able we are to think conceptually.

MADELEINE L'ENGLE, *Walking on Water: Reflections on Faith and Art* (1980)

And now we come to the magic of words. A word, also, just like an idea, a thought, has the effect of reality upon undifferentiated minds.

EMMA JUNG, *Animus and Anima* (1957)

They say that there is no reality before it has been given shape by words rules regulations. They say that in what concerns them everything has to be remade starting from basic principles. They say that in the first place the vocabulary of every language is to be examined, modified, turned upside down, that every word must be screened.

MONIQUE WITTIG, *Les Guérillères* (1969)

For me words still possess their primitive, mystical, incantatory powers. I am inclined to use them as part of an attempt to make my own reality more real for others, as part of an effort to transcend emotional danger. For me, words are a form of action, capable of influencing change. Their articulation represents a complete, lived experience.

INGRID BENGIS, *Combat in the Erogenous Zone* (1972)

A word is dead / When it is said, / Some say. / I say it just / Begins to live / That day.

EMILY DICKINSON, in Mabel Loomis Todd, *Letters of Emily Dickinson* (1894)

Almost all words do have color and nothing is more pleasant than to utter a pink word and see someone's eyes light up and know it is a pink word for him or her too.

GLADYS TABER, *Stillmeadow Daybook* (1955)

I love smooth words, like gold-enameled fish.

ELINOR WYLIE, "Pretty Words," *Nets to Catch the Wind* (1921)

All books are either dreams or swords, / You can cut, or you can drug, with words.

AMY LOWELL, title poem, *Sword Blades and Poppy Seeds* (1914)

Words can destroy. What we call each other ultimately becomes what we think of each other, and it matters.

JEANE J. KIRKPATRICK, speech (1982)

There are worse words than cuss words, there are words that hurt.

TILLIE OLSEN, "Hey Sailor, What Ship?" *Tell Me a Riddle* (1956)

A broken bone can heal, but the wound a word opens can fester forever.

JESSAMYN WEST, *The Life I Really Lived* (1979)

Words set things in motion. I've seen them doing it. Words set up atmospheres, electrical fields, charges.

TONI CADE BAMBARA, in Janet Sternburg, ed., *The Writer on Her Work*, vol. 1 (1980)

Words are sometimes sensitive instruments of precision with which delicate operations may be performed and swift, elusive truths may be touched; often they are clumsy tools with which we grope in the dark toward truths more inaccessible but no less significant.

HELEN MERRELL LYND, *On Shame and the Search for Identity* (1958)

One must be chary of words because they turn into cages.

VIOLA SPOLIN, in *Los Angeles Times* (1974)

Peoples of the earth, / do not destroy the universe of words, / . . . / O that no one mean death when he says life— / and not blood when he speaks cradle.

NELLY SACHS, "Peoples of the Earth," *O the Chimneys* (1967)

We must use words as they are used or stand aside from life.

IVY COMPTON-BURNETT, *Mother and Son* (1955)

Every misused word revenges itself forever upon a writer's reputation.

AGNES REPPLIER, *Points of Friction* (1920)

By men's words we know them.

MARIE DE FRANCE (12th century), in Jeanette Beer, tr., *Medieval Fables of Marie de France* (1981)

in a ward on fire, we must / find words / or burn.

OLGA BROUMAS, "Artemis," *Beginning with O* (1977)

A trite word is an overused word which has lost its identity like an old coat in a second-hand shop. The familiar grows dull and we no longer see, hear, or taste it.

ANAÏS NIN, *The Diary of Anaïs Nin,* vol. 5 (1947–1955)

Nouns and verbs are almost pure metal; adjectives are cheaper ore.

MARIE GILCHRIST, in Leonora Speyer, "On the Teaching of Poetry," in *Saturday Review of Literature* (1946)

Words have their genealogy, their history, their economy, their literature, their art and music, as too they have their weddings and divorces, their successes and defeats, their fevers, their undiagnosable ailments, their sudden deaths. They also have their moral and social distinctions.

VIRGILIA PETERSON, *A Matter of Life and Death* (1961)

If the United Nations is a country unto itself, then the commodity it exports most is words.

ESTHER B. FEIN, in *New York Times* (1985)

Dear me no dears, Sir.

APHRA BEHN, *The Lucky Chance* (1686)

Words of affection, howsoe'er expressed, / The latest spoken still are deem'd the best.

JOANNA BAILLIE, *Dramatic and Poetical Works of Joanna Baillie* (1853)

Just-in-your-own words was Mr. Gilmer's trademark. We often wondered who else's words Mr. Gilmer was afraid his witness might employ.

HARPER LEE, *To Kill a Mockingbird* (1960)

She might struggle like a fly in a web. He wrapped her around and around with beautiful sentences.

MARY CATHERWOOD, "The King of Beaver," *Mackinac and Lake Stories* (1899)

The Greeks had a word for it.

Zoë Akins, play title (1929)

See also Clichés, Euphemisms, Language, Writing.

WORK

A human being *must* have occupation if he or she is not to become a nuisance to the world.

Dorothy L. Sayers, "Are Women Human?" (1947)

The pitcher cries for water to carry / and a person for work that is real.

Marge Piercy, "To be of use," *Circles on the Water* (1982)

Work in some form or other is the appointed lot of all.

Anna Jameson, in Eleanor S. Riemer and John C. Fout, *European Women* (1980)

The simple idea that everyone needs a reasonable amount of challenging work in his or her life, and also a personal life, complete with noncompetitive leisure, has never really taken hold.

Judith Martin, *Common Courtesy* (1985)

Work is creativity accompanied by the comforting realization that one is bringing forth something really good and necessary, with the conviction that a sudden, arbitrary cessation would cause a sensitive void, produce a loss.

Jenny Heynrichs, "Was Ist Arbeit?" in *Neue Bahnen, Organ des Allgemeinen Deutschen Frauenvereins* (1866)

I went back to being an amateur, in the sense of somebody who loves what she is doing. If a professional loses the love of work, routine sets in, and that's the death of work and of life.

Ade Bethune, in Judith Stoughton, *Proud Donkey of Schaerbeek* (1988)

I believe in my work and the joy of it. You have to be with the work and the work has to be with you. It absorbs you totally and you absorb it totally. Everything must fall by the wayside by comparison.

Louise Nevelson, *Dawns + Dusks* (1976)

Know that it is good to work. Work with love and think of liking it when you do it. It is easy and interesting. It is a privilege. There is nothing hard about it but your anxious vanity and fear of failure.

Brenda Ueland, *If You Want to Write* (1938)

The best careers advice given to the young is "Find out what you like doing best and get someone to pay you for doing it."

Katharine Whitehorn, in *Observer* (1975)

To love what you do and feel that it matters—how could anything be more fun?

Katharine Graham, in Jane Howard, "The Power That Didn't Corrupt," *Ms.* (1974)

It has been my experience that one cannot, in any shape or form, depend on human relations for lasting reward. It is only work that truly satisfies.

Bette Davis, *The Lonely Life* (1962)

I've never had a day when I didn't want to work. . . . In my studio I'm as happy as a cow in her stall.

Louise Nevelson, *Dawns + Dusks* (1976)

Workaholics are energized rather than enervated by their work—their energy paradoxically expands as it is expended.

Marilyn Machlowitz, *Workaholics* (1980)

If people are highly successful in their professions they lose their senses. Sight goes. They have no time to look at pictures. Sound goes. They have no time to listen to music. Speech goes. They have no time for conversation. They lose their sense of proportion—the relations between one thing and another. Humanity goes.

Virginia Woolf, *Three Guineas* (1938)

We spend so much time in our work and in work-related activities that our awarenesses and our perceptions become narrower and narrower. We reach a point where we can't talk about anything but our work and, if the truth be known, we don't *want* to talk about anything but our work. . . . We have taken a rainbow and compressed it into a solid, uninteresting beam of light.

Anne Wilson Schaef, *Meditations for Women Who Do Too Much* (1990)

She had worked so hard for so many years that the habit had degenerated into a disease, and thrift had become a tyrant instead of a slave in her life.

ELLEN GLASGOW, *Barren Ground* (1925)

The person who knows "how" will always have a job. The person who knows "why" will always be his boss.

DIANE RAVITCH, speech (1985)

Always be smarter than the people who hire you.

LENA HORNE, interview (1985)

Six months of looking for a job had made me an expert at picking out the people who, like me, were hurrying up to wait—in somebody's outer anything for a chance to make it through their inner doors to prove that you could type two words a minute, or not drool on your blouse while answering difficult questions about your middle initial and date of birth.

GLORIA NAYLOR, *Mama Day* (1988)

There are very few jobs that actually require a penis or vagina. All other jobs should be open to everybody.

FLORYNCE KENNEDY, in *Writer's Digest* (1974)

There are so many ways of earning a living and most of them are failures.

GERTRUDE STEIN, *Ida* (1941)

What's the need of working if it doesn't get you anywhere? What's the use of boring around in the same hole like a worm? Making the hole bigger to stay in?

MARITA BONNER, "The Purple Flower" (1928), *Frye Street and Environs* (1987)

Skilled labor teaches something not to be found in books or in colleges.

HARRIET ROBINSON, *Massachusetts in the Woman Suffrage Movement* (1883)

We need love and creative imagination to do constructive work.

PAULA OLLENDORF, in *Das jahr des jüdisches Frauenbundes* (1928)

Appealing workplaces are to be avoided. One wants a room with no view, so imagination can meet memory in the dark.

ANNIE DILLARD, *The Writing Life* (1989)

I yield to no one in my admiration for the office as a social center, but it's no place actually to get any work done.

KATHARINE WHITEHORN, *Sunday Best* (1976)

See also Business, Housework, Labor.

WORRY

A request not to worry . . . is perhaps the least soothing message capable of human utterance.

MIGNON G. EBERHART, *The House on the Roof* (1934)

A worried man could borrow a lot of trouble with practically no collateral.

HELEN NIELSEN, *Borrow the Night* (1956)

I always feel sorry for people who think more about a rainy day ahead than sunshine today.

RAE FOLEY, *Suffer a Witch* (1965)

That was a snake that would lay eggs in my brain.

FAITH SULLIVAN, *The Cape Ann* (1988)

See also Anxiety, Concern.

WRITERS

A writer is a foreign country.

MARGUERITE DURAS, *Practicalities* (1987)

Writers live twice.

NATALIE GOLDBERG, *Writing Down the Bones* (1986)

The life of a writer is tragic: the more we advance, the farther there is to go and the more there is to say, the less time there is to say it.

GABRIELLE ROY, in Donald Stephens, *Writers of the Prairie* (1973)

Did you ever stop to think that a writer will spend three years, or many more, on a book that the average reader will skim through in a few hours?

ELLEN GLASGOW, *Letters of Ellen Glasgow* (1958)

Miserable is the fate of writers: if they are agreeable, they are offensive; and if dull, they starve.

LADY MARY WORTLEY MONTAGU, letter (1709), in Octave Thanet, ed., *The Best Letters of Lady Mary Wortley Montagu* (1901)

Writers are the moral purifiers of the culture. We may not be pure ourselves but we must tell the truth, which is a purifying act.

RITA MAE BROWN, *Starting From Scratch* (1988)

Writers are given the responsibility of sight. I think that the whole burden, responsibility and beauty of the gift forces us to construct our lives differently so that we are able to become vehicles to transcend, to encompass and articulate not only our own experience but the experiences of others.

ALEXIS DE VEAUX, in Claudia Tate, ed., *Black Women Writers at Work* (1983)

Writers in Latin America live in a reality that is extraordinarily demanding. Surprisingly, our answer to these demands protects and develops our individuality. I feel I am not alone in trying to give their voice to those who don't have it.

ELENA PONIATOWSKA, in Janet Sternburg, ed., *The Writer on Her Work,* vol. 2 (1991)

How can one not speak about war, poverty, and inequality when people who suffer from these afflictions don't have a voice to speak?

ISABEL ALLENDE, in Marie-Lise Gazarian-Gautiez, *Interviews With Latin American Writers* (1989)

I resent people who say writers write from experience. Writers don't write from experience, though many are hesitant to admit that they don't. I want to be clear about this. If you wrote from experience, you'd get maybe one book, maybe three poems. Writers write from empathy.

NIKKI GIOVANNI, in Claudia Tate, ed., *Black Women Writers at Work* (1983)

One of the obligations of the writer is to say or sing *all* that he or she can, to deal with as much of the world as becomes possible to him or her in language.

DENISE LEVERTOV, *The Poet in the World* (1973)

It's an act of faith to be a writer in a postliterate world.

RITA MAE BROWN, *Starting From Scratch* (1988)

There is no denying the fact that writers should be read but not seen. Rarely are they a winsome sight.

EDNA FERBER, *A Kind of Magic* (1963)

Whenever an encounter between a writer of good will and a regular person of good will happens to touch on the subject of writing, each person discovers, dismayed, that good will is of no earthly use. The conversation cannot proceed.

ANNIE DILLARD, *The Writing Life* (1989)

All of a writer that matters is in the book or books. It is idiotic to be curious about the person.

JEAN RHYS, in Carole Angier, *Jean Rhys: Life and Work* (1991)

If I could I would always work in silence and obscurity and let my efforts be known by their results.

EMILY BRONTË (1850), in Bertha W. Smith and Virginia C. Lincoln, eds., *The Writing Art* (1931)

The writer is either a practicing recluse or a delinquent, guilt-ridden one; or both. Usually both.

SUSAN SONTAG, in *New York Times* (1986)

It should surprise no one that the life of the writer—such as it is—is colorless to the point of sensory deprivation. Many writers do little else but sit in small rooms recalling the real world.

ANNIE DILLARD, *The Writing Life* (1989)

The writer of originality, unless dead, is always shocking, scandalous; novelty disturbs and repels.

SIMONE DE BEAUVOIR, *The Second Sex* (1949)

The more original a short-story writer, the odder looking the assortment of things he or she puts together for a story.

CAROL BLY, *The Passionate, Accurate Story* (1990)

But not until I was seven or more, did I begin to pray every night, "O God, let me write books! Please, God, let me write books!"

ELLEN GLASGOW, *The Woman Within* (1954)

Most of the basic material a writer works with is acquired before the age of fifteen.

WILLA CATHER, in René Rapin, *Willa Cather* (1930)

Anyone who is going to be a writer knows enough at fifteen to write several novels.

MAY SARTON, *Mrs. Stevens Hears the Mermaids Singing* (1965)

A young musician plays scales in his room and only bores his family. A beginning writer, on the other hand, sometimes has the misfortune of getting into print.

MARGUERITE YOURCENAR, in *Time* (1981)

To me writing was not a career but a necessity. And so it remains, though I am now, technically, a professional writer. The strength of this inborn desire to write has always baffled me. It is understandable that the really gifted should feel an overwhelming urge to use their gift; but a strong urge with only a slight gift seems almost a genetic mistake.

DERVLA MURPHY, in Susan Cahill, ed., *Mothers: Memories, Dreams and Reflections by Literary Daughters* (1988)

I suppose I am a born novelist, for the things I imagine are more vital and vivid to me than the things I remember.

ELLEN GLASGOW, *Letters of Ellen Glasgow* (1958)

A friend of mine who writes history books said to me that he thought that the two creatures most to be pitied were the spider and the novelist—their lives hanging by a thread spun out of their own guts. But in some ways I think writers of fiction are the creatures most to be envied, because who else besides the spider is allowed to take that fragile thread and weave it into a pattern? What a gift of grace to be able to take the chaos from within and from it to create some semblance of order.

KATHERINE PATERSON, *Gates of Excellence* (1981)

Novelists should never allow themselves to weary of the study of real life.

CHARLOTTE BRONTË, *The Professor* (1846)

I try to live what I consider a "poetic existence." That means I take responsibility for the air I breathe and the space I take up. I try to be immediate, to be totally present for all my work.

MAYA ANGELOU, in Claudia Tate, ed., *Black Women Writers at Work* (1983)

I certainly am glad you like the stories because now I feel it's not bad that I like them so much. The truth is I like them better than anybody and I read them over and over and laugh and laugh, then get embarrassed when I remember I was the one wrote them.

FLANNERY O'CONNOR, in Sally Fitzgerald, ed., *The Habit of Being* (1979)

Show me a writer, any writer, who hasn't suffered and I'll show you someone who writes in pastels as opposed to primary colors.

RITA MAE BROWN, *Starting From Scratch* (1988)

To note an artist's limitations is but to define his talent. A reporter can write equally well about everything that is presented to his view, but a creative writer can do his best only with what lies within the range and character of his deepest sympathies.

WILLA CATHER, "Miss Jewett," *Not Under Forty* (1936)

As a writer you are free. You are about the freest person that ever was. Your freedom is what you have bought with your solitude, your loneliness. You are in the country where *you* make up the rules, the laws. You are both dictator and obedient populace. It is a country nobody has ever explored before. It is up to you to make the maps, to build the cities. Nobody else in the world can do it, or ever could do it, or ever will be able to do it again.

URSULA K. LE GUIN, *Language of the Night* (1979)

Your freedom as a writer is not freedom of expression in the sense of wild blurting; you may not let rip. It is life at its most free, if you are fortunate enough to be able to try it, because you select your materials, invent your task, and pace yourself.

ANNIE DILLARD, *The Writing Life* (1989)

If you are a writer you locate yourself behind a wall of silence and no matter what you are doing, driving a car or walking or doing housework . . . you can still be writing, because you have that space.

JOYCE CAROL OATES, in *New York Times* (1980)

The writer's intention hasn't anything to do with what he achieves. The intent to earn money or the intent to be famous or the intent to be great doesn't matter in the end. Just what comes out.

LILLIAN HELLMAN, in George Plimpton, ed., *Writers at Work,* 3rd Series (1967)

The work reveals the creator—and as our universe in its vastness, its orderliness, its exquisite detail, tells us something of the One who made it, so a work of fiction, for better or worse, will reveal the writer.

KATHERINE PATERSON, *The Spying Heart* (1989)

A person who publishes a book willfully appears before the populace with his pants down. . . . If it is a good book nothing can hurt him. If it is a bad book nothing can help him.

EDNA ST. VINCENT MILLAY, *Letters* (1952)

Could anyone fail to be depressed by a book he or she has published? Don't we always outgrow them the moment the last page has been written?

MARY RITTER BEARD (1943), in Nancy F. Cott, *A Woman Making History* (1991)

Painters work from the ground up. The latest version of a painting overlays earlier versions, and obliterates them. Writers, on the other hand, work from left to right. The discardable chapters are on the left.

ANNIE DILLARD, *The Writing Life* (1989)

The only time I'm pleased with myself is when I'm exhausted and shaking from having written too much.

MABEL SEELEY, in Carmen Nelson Richards and Genevieve Rose Breen, eds., *Minnesota Writes* (1945)

There is no security, no assurance that because we wrote something good two months ago, we will do it again. Actually, every time we begin, we wonder how we ever did it before.

NATALIE GOLDBERG, *Writing Down the Bones* (1986)

The indifference of the world which Keats and Flaubert and other men of genius have found so hard to bear was in her case [the woman writer's] not indifference but hostility. The world did not say to her as it said to them, Write if you choose; it makes no difference to me. The world said with a guffaw, Write? What's the good of your writing?

VIRGINIA WOOLF, *A Room of One's Own* (1929)

Recollect that to a woman who gets her living by her pen, "time is money," as it is to an artist. Therefore, encroaching on her time is lessening her income. And yet how often is this done (either heedlessly or selfishly) by persons professing to be her friends, and who are habitually in the practice of interrupting her in her writing hours.

ELIZA LESLIE, *Miss Leslie's Behavior Book: A Guide and Manual for Ladies* (1859)

They're fancy talkers about themselves, writers. If I had to give young writers advice, I would say don't listen to writers talk about writing or themselves.

LILLIAN HELLMAN, in *New York Times* (1960)

When writers refer to themselves as "we" and to the reader as "you," it's two against one.

JUDITH RASCOE, in *New York Times Book Review* (1984)

For a short-story writer, a story is the combination of what the writer *supposed* the story would likely be about—plus what actually turned up in the course of writing.

CAROL BLY, *The Passionate, Accurate Story* (1990)

Began the second part of "Little Women." . . . Girls write to ask who the little women marry, as if that was the only end and aim of a woman's life. I *won't* marry Jo to Laurie to please any one.

LOUISA MAY ALCOTT, *Journals* (1868)

A writer needs certain conditions in which to work and create art. She needs a piece of time; a peace of mind; a quiet place; and a private life.

MARGARET WALKER, in Janet Sternburg, ed., *The Writer on Her Work,* vol. 1 (1980)

Many a fervid man / Writes books as cold and flat as graveyard stones.

ELIZABETH BARRETT BROWNING, *Aurora Leigh* (1856)

Yes, I learned long ago that the only satisfaction of authorship lies in finding the very few who understand what we mean. As for outside rewards, there is not one that I have ever discovered.

ELLEN GLASGOW, *Letters of Ellen Glasgow* (1958)

Any writer overwhelmingly honest about pleasing himself is almost sure to please others.

MARIANNE MOORE, in *Vogue* (1963)

As I look back on what I have written, I can see that the very persons who have taken away my time are those who have given me something to say.

KATHERINE PATERSON, *The Spying Heart* (1989)

There are enough women to do the childbearing and the childrearing. I know of none who can write my books.

HENRY HANDEL RICHARDSON, in Tillie Olsen, *Silences* (1978)

[The writer] is careful of what he reads, for that is what he will write.

ANNIE DILLARD, *The Writing Life* (1989)

Literature is a place for generosity and affection and hunger for equals—not a prizefight ring. We are increased, confirmed in our medium, roused to do our best, by every good writer, every fine achievement. Would we want one good writer or fine book less?

TILLIE OLSEN, *Silences* (1978)

Writers in a profit making economy are an exploitable commodity whose works are products to be marketed, and are so judged and handled.

TILLIE OLSEN, *Silences* (1978)

It takes years to write a book—between two and ten years. . . . Out of a human population on earth of four and a half billion, perhaps twenty people can write a book in a year. Some people lift cars, too. Some people enter week-long sled-dog races, go over Niagara Falls in barrels, fly planes through the Arc de Triomphe. Some people feel no pain in childbirth. Some people eat cars. There is no call to take human extremes as norms.

ANNIE DILLARD, *The Writing Life* (1989)

Where two people are writing the same book, each believes he gets all the worries and only half the royalties.

AGATHA CHRISTIE, news item (1955)

Many persons erroneously suppose that an author has always on hand an unlimited number of her own books; or that the publisher will kindly give her as many as she can want for herself and friends. This is by no means the case.

ELIZA LESLIE, *Miss Leslie's Behavior Book: A Guide and Manual for Ladies* (1859)

See also Poets, Writing.

WRITING

Writing is thinking. It is more than living, for it is being conscious of living.

ANNE MORROW LINDBERGH, *Locked Rooms and Open Doors* (1974)

Writing, I think, is not apart from living. Writing is a kind of double living. The writer experiences everything twice. Once in reality and once in that mirror which waits always before or behind.

CATHERINE DRINKER BOWEN, in *Atlantic* (1957)

We write to taste life twice, in the moment and in retrospection.

ANAÏS NIN, *The Diary of Anaïs Nin,* vol. 5 (1947–1955)

Writing does not exclude the full life; it demands it.

KATHERINE ANNE PORTER, in Hallie Burnett, *On Writing the Short Story* (1983)

I shall live badly if I do not write, and I shall write badly if I do not live.

FRANÇOISE SAGAN, in *New York Times* (1956)

What a difficult kind of work to choose! But of course one did not choose it. There was no choice.

IVY COMPTON-BURNETT, letter (1962), in Hilary Spurling, *Ivy* (1984)

Looking back, I imagine I was always writing. Twaddle it was, too. But better far write twaddle or anything, anything, than nothing at all.

KATHERINE MANSFIELD (1922), *Journal of Katherine Mansfield* (1927)

There's less skill and more plain hard work to writing than anyone except a writer thinks.

MABEL SEELEY, in Carmen Nelson Richards and Genevieve Rose Breen, eds., *Minnesota Writes* (1945)

Writing is harder than anything else; at least *starting* to write is.

KRISTIN HUNTER, in Claudia Tate, ed., *Black Women Writers at Work* (1983)

Writing is so difficult that I often feel that writers, having had their hell on earth, will escape all punishment hereafter.

JESSAMYN WEST, *To See the Dream* (1957)

Writing is one of the few professions left where you take all the responsibility for what you do. It's really dangerous and ultimately destroys you as a writer if you start thinking about responses to your work or what your audience needs.

ERICA JONG, in William Packard, ed., *The Craft of Poetry* (1974)

Writing is the only thing that . . . when I'm doing it, I don't feel that I should be doing something else instead.

GLORIA STEINEM, *Outrageous Acts and Everyday Rebellions* (1983)

When I say "work" I only mean writing. Everything else is just odd jobs.

MARGARET LAURENCE, in Donald Cameron, ed., *Conversations With Canadian Novelists* (1980)

The most egotistic of occupations, and the most gratifying while it lasts.

VITA SACKVILLE-WEST, *No Signposts in the Sea* (1961)

When I write stories I am like someone who is in her own country, walking along streets that she has known since she was a child, between walls and trees that are hers.

NATALIA GINZBURG, *The Little Virtues* (1962)

If I stop writing my life will have been an abject failure. It is that already to other people. But it could be an abject failure to myself. I will not have earned death.

JEAN RHYS, *Smile Please: An Unfinished Autobiography* (1979)

Writing is a good example of self-abandonment. I never completely forget myself except when I am writing and I am never more completely myself than when I am writing.

FLANNERY O'CONNOR, in Sally Fitzgerald, ed., *The Habit of Being* (1979)

I learned that you should feel when writing, not like Lord Byron on a mountain top, but like a child stringing beads in kindergarten,—happy, absorbed and quietly putting one bead on after another.

BRENDA UELAND, *If You Want to Write* (1938)

But for any writer worthy of the name . . . there are moments during the writing process when the rest of the planet might as well have gone to Venus. And those moments are not for sale.

MARIA LENHART, in *Christian Science Monitor* (1979)

What release to write so that one forgets oneself, forgets one's companion, forgets where one is or what one is going to do next—to be drenched in work as one is drenched in sleep or in the sea. Pencils and pads and curling blue sheets alive with letters heap up on the desk.

ANNE MORROW LINDBERGH, *Gift From the Sea* (1955)

You may write for the joy of it, but the act of writing is not complete in itself. It has its end in its audience.

FLANNERY O'CONNOR, in Sally Fitzgerald, ed., *The Habit of Being* (1979)

I suppose I have written novels to find out what I *thought* about something and poems to find out what I *felt* about something.

MAY SARTON, *Journal of a Solitude* (1973)

It is for this, partly, that I write. How can I know what I think unless I see what I write?

ERICA JONG, *Fear of Flying* (1973)

I write entirely to find out what I'm thinking, what I'm looking at, what I see and what it means. What I want and what I fear.

JOAN DIDION, in Janet Sternburg, ed., *The Writer on Her Work*, vol. 1 (1980)

Writing has been a way of explaining to myself the things I do not understand.

ROSARIO CASTELLANOS, in Irene Nicholson, *A Guide to Mexican Poetry* (1968)

What really annoys me are the ones who write to say, I am doing your book for my final examinations and could you please tell me what the meaning of it is. I find it just so staggering—that you're supposed to explain the meaning of your book to some total stranger! If I knew what the meanings of my books were, I wouldn't have bothered to write them.

MARGARET DRABBLE, in George Plimpton, ed., *The Writer's Chapbook* (1989)

I write in order to belong.

ELENA PONIATOWSKA, in Janet Sternburg, ed., *The Writer on Her Work*, vol. 2 (1991)

I write for myself and strangers. The strangers, dear Readers, are an afterthought.

GERTRUDE STEIN, *The Making of Americans* (1925)

Writers write for themselves and not for their readers. Art has nothing to do with communication between person and person, only with communication between different parts of a person's mind.

REBECCA WEST, "The Art of Skepticism," *Vogue* (1952)

I write because I want more than one life; I insist on a wider selection. It's greed plain and simple. When my characters join the circus, I'm joining the circus. Although I'm happily married, I spend a great deal of my time mentally living with incompatible husbands.

ANNE TYLER, "Because I Want More Than One Life," in *Washington Post* (1976)

As for my next book, I am going to hold myself from writing till I have it impending in me: grown heavy in my mind like a ripe pear; pendant, gravid, asking to be cut or it will fall.

VIRGINIA WOOLF (1928), in Leonard Woolf, ed., *A Writer's Diary* (1954)

For a dyed-in-the-wool author nothing is as dead as a book once it is written. . . . She is rather like a cat whose kittens have grown-up. While they were a-growing she was passionately interested in them but now they seem hardly to belong to her—and probably she is involved

with another batch of kittens as I am involved with other writing.

RUMER GODDEN, in *New York Times* (1963)

When you make a decision to write according to a set schedule and really stick to it, you find yourself writing very fast. At least I do.

FRANÇOISE SAGAN, in Malcolm Cowley, ed., *Writers at Work* (1958)

My muse is a sad cow slowly chewing her cud. And her occasional profound sigh reminds me that hurrying my process comes only to a facile, nearsighted, unrealized writing.

MARY LA CHAPELLE, Minnesota State Arts Board newsletter (1990)

The creative power which bubbles so pleasantly in beginning a new book quiets down after a time, and one goes on more steadily. Doubts creep in. Then one becomes resigned. Determination not to give in, and the sense of an impending shape keep one at it more than anything.

VIRGINIA WOOLF (1920), in Leonard Woolf, ed., *A Writer's Diary* (1954)

The ideal view for daily writing, hour on hour, is the blank brick wall of a cold-storage warehouse. Failing this, a stretch of sky will do, cloudless if possible.

EDNA FERBER, *A Kind of Magic* (1963)

I write in the first person because I have always wanted to make my life more interesting than it was.

DIANE WAKOSKI (1974), in Sandra M. Gilbert and Susan Gubar, eds., *The Norton Anthology of Literature by Women* (1985)

If you don't keep and mature your force and above all have time and quiet to perfect your work, you will be writing things not much better than you did five years ago. . . . Otherwise, what might be strength is only crudeness, and what might be insight is only observation. You will write about life, but never life itself.

SARAH ORNE JEWETT, letter to Willa Cather, *Letters of Sarah Orne Jewett* (1911)

I am dissatisfied with everything I have ever written and regard it all only as a preparation for that one work which probably I don't have it in me to write but which I hope I can go on trying for.

RUTH PRAWER JHABVALA, in Susan Cahill, ed., *Women and Fiction 2* (1978)

Elizabeth Hardwick told me once that all her first drafts sounded as if a chicken had written them. So do mine for the most part.

FLANNERY O'CONNOR, in Sally Fitzgerald, ed., The Habit of Being (1979)

One of the few things I know about writing is this: spend it all, shoot it, play it, lose it, all, right away, every time. . . . Anything you do not give freely and abundantly becomes lost to you. You open your safe and find ashes.

ANNIE DILLARD, *The Writing Life* (1989)

I don't wait for moods. You accomplish nothing if you do that. Your mind must know it has got to get down to work.

PEARL BUCK, in Helen Hull, *The Writer's Book* (1950)

Lunches are just not good. They take the heart out of the day and the spaciousness from the morning's work.

MAY SARTON, *Journal of a Solitude* (1973)

I can't write five words but that I change seven.

DOROTHY PARKER, in Malcolm Cowley, ed., *Writers at Work* (1958)

Volume depends precisely on the writer's having been able to sit in a room every day, year after year, alone.

SUSAN SONTAG, in *New York Times* (1986)

I have the conviction that excessive literary production is a social offense. . . . Everyone who contributes to the "too much" of literature is doing grave social injury.

GEORGE ELIOT (1871), in J. W. Cross, *George Eliot's Life as Related in Her Letters and Journals* (1884)

In any really good subject, one has only to probe deep enough to come to tears.

EDITH WHARTON, *The Writing of Fiction* (1925)

I went for years not finishing anything. Because, of course, when you finish something you can be judged. . . . I had poems which were re-written

so many times I suspect it was just a way of avoiding sending them out.

ERICA JONG, in William Packard, ed., *The Craft of Poetry* (1974)

Writing is like getting married. One should never commit oneself until one is amazed at one's luck.

IRIS MURDOCH, *The Black Prince* (1973)

Read a lot and hit the streets. A writer who doesn't keep up with what's out there ain't gonna be out there.

TONI CADE BAMBARA, in Claudia Tate, ed., *Black Women Writers at Work* (1983)

All is fish that comes to the literary net. Goethe puts his joys and sorrows into poems, I turn my adventures into bread and butter.

LOUISA MAY ALCOTT, *Journals* (1868)

Dislike, displeasure, resentment, fault-finding, indignation, passionate remonstrance, a sense of injustice . . . they make fine fuel.

EDNA FERBER, *A Kind of Magic* (1963)

The only real trouble that writing has ever brought me is an occasional sense of being invaded by the outside world. Why do people imagine that writers, having chosen the most private of professions, should be any good at performing in public, or should have the slightest desire to tell their secrets to interviewers. . . . I will write my books and raise the children. Anything else just fritters me away. I know this makes me seem narrow, but in fact, I *am* narrow. I like routine and rituals and I hate leaving home.

ANNE TYLER, in Janet Sternburg, ed., *The Writer on Her Work,* vol. 1 (1980)

Writing about why you write is a funny business, like scratching what doesn't itch. Impulses are mysterious, and explaining them must be done with mirrors, like certain cunning sleight-of-hand routines.

PATRICIA HAMPL, in Janet Sternburg, ed., *The Writer on Her Work,* vol. 2 (1991)

No matter how true I believe what I am writing to be, if the reader cannot also participate in that truth, then I have failed.

MADELEINE L'ENGLE, *Walking on Water: Reflections on Faith and Art* (1980)

Whatever is clearly expressed is well wrote.

Lady Mary Wortley Montagu, letter (1759), in Robert Halsband, ed., *The Selected Letters of Lady Mary Wortley Montagu* (1970)

A mere chronicle of observed events will produce only journalism; combined with a sensitive memory, it can produce art.

Hallie Burnett, *On Writing the Short Story* (1983)

Love scenes, if genuine, are indescribable; for to those who have enacted them the most elaborate description seems tame, and to those who have not, the simplest picture seems overdone.

Louisa May Alcott, *An Old-Fashioned Girl* (1870)

It is through the [ghost] writer that the great gift of knowledge which the inarticulate have for the world can be made available.

Elizabeth Janeway, in Helen Hull, *The Writer's Book* (1950)

The political writer, then, is the ultimate optimist, believing people are capable of change and using words as one way to try and penetrate the privatism of our lives.

Cherríe Moraga, in Cherríe Moraga and Gloria Anzaldúa, eds., *This Bridge Called My Back* (1983)

There is no "feminine writing" . . . and one makes a mistake in using and giving currency to this expression.

Monique Wittig, "The Point of View: Universal or Particular" (1980), *The Straight Mind* (1992)

As long as mixed grills and combination salads are popular, anthologies will undoubtedly continue in favor.

Elizabeth Janeway, in Helen Hull, *The Writer's Book* (1950)

Having been unpopular in high school is not just cause for book publication.

Fran Lebowitz, *Metropolitan Life* (1978)

But the way to wealth through the quill seems long.

Elizabeth Rundle Charles, *Chronicles of the Schönberg-Cotta Family* (1863)

Money and writing appear to be mutually exclusive.

Rita Mae Brown, *Starting From Scratch* (1988)

Ignorant people always suppose that popular writers are wonderfully well-paid—and must be making rapid fortunes—because they neither starve in garrets, nor wear rags—at least in America.

Eliza Leslie, *Miss Leslie's Behavior Book: A Guide and Manual for Ladies* (1859)

Contrary to what many of you might imagine, a career in letters is not without its drawbacks—chief among them the unpleasant fact that one is frequently called upon to actually sit down and write.

Fran Lebowitz, *Metropolitan Life* (1978)

See also Art, Artists, Autobiography, Biography, Books, Creation, Creativity, Diaries, Essays, Fiction, Fictional Characters, Journalism, Language, Letters, Literature, Magazines, Novels, Poetry, Stories, Words, Writers.

Y

YOUTH

Youth is a mortal wound.

KATHERINE PATERSON, *Jacob Have I Loved* (1980)

My idea of hell is to be young again.

MARGE PIERCY, *Braided Lives* (1982)

All the humiliating, tragicomic, heartbreaking things happened to me in my girlhood, and nothing makes me happier than to realize I cannot possibly relive my youth.

ILKA CHASE, *Past Imperfect* (1942)

Youth is the season of tragedy and despair. Youth is the time when one's whole life is entangled in a web of identity, in a perpetual maze of seeking and of finding, of passion and of disillusion, of vague longings and of nameless griefs, of pity that is a blade in the heart, and of "all the little emptiness of love."

ELLEN GLASGOW, *The Woman Within* (1954)

If youth is the season of hope, it is often so only in the sense that our elders are hopeful about us; for no age is so apt as youth to think its emotions, partings, and resolves are the last of their kind. Each crisis seems final, simply because it is new.

GEORGE ELIOT, *Middlemarch* (1871)

If youth did not matter so much to itself, it would never have the heart to go on.

WILLA CATHER, *The Song of the Lark* (1915)

Who would ever think that so much can go on in the soul of a young girl?

ANNE FRANK, *Diary of a Young Girl* (1952)

A young girl's heart is indestructible.

ESTHER HAUTZIG, *The Endless Steppe* (1968)

Youth is, after all, just a moment, but it is the moment, the spark that you always carry in your heart.

RAISA M. GORBACHEV, *I Hope* (1991)

That's what being young is all about. You have the courage and the daring to think that you can make a difference. You're not prone to measure your energies in time. You're not likely to live by equations.

RUBY DEE, in Brian Lanker, *I Dream a World* (1989)

It is not possible for civilization to flow backward while there is youth in the world. Youth may be headstrong, but it will advance its allotted length.

HELEN KELLER, *Midstream* (1929)

Human nature is so well disposed towards those who are in interesting situations, that a young person, who either marries or dies, is sure to be kindly spoken of.

JANE AUSTEN, *Emma* (1816)

When a man of forty falls in love with a girl of twenty, it isn't her youth he is seeking but his own.

LENORE COFFEE, in John Robert Colombo, *Popcorn in Paradise* (1979)

Young people want to look like peas in a pod, and there is no use trying to make them different.

ILKA CHASE, *Past Imperfect* (1942)

The hatred of the youth culture for adult society is not a disinterested judgment but a terror-ridden refusal to be hooked into the . . . ecological chain of birthing, growing, and dying. It is the demand, in other words, to remain children.

MIDGE DECTER, *The New Chastity and Other Arguments Against Women's Liberation* (1972)

Youth is something very new: twenty years ago no one mentioned it.

COCO CHANEL, in Marcel Haedrich, *Coco Chanel: Her Life, Her Secrets* (1972)

See also Adolescence, Age, Babies, Childhood, Children.

Name Index

Note: Boldfaced page numbers indicate the author is quoted more than once on that page. Pen names are generally set in quotations marks. However, when a quotation is attributed to a pseudonym or self-chosen name, that name is listed in the index followed by the author's name in parentheses.

Abbott, Berenice (1898–1991), U.S. photographer, 245

Abbott, Shirley (1934–), U.S. writer, 14, 55, 72, 117, 205, 250, 283, 289, **303**

Abbott, Sidney (1937–), U.S. writer, **186**, 187

Abouzeid, Leila (20th c.), Moroccan writer, journalist, 158

Abzug, Bella Savitsky (1920–), U.S. lawyer, politician, 63, 134, **141**, 210, 291

Ace, Jane Sherwood (1905–1974), U.S. radio actor, 166, 322

Ackerman, Diane (1948–), U.S. poet, writer, 94, 112, 188, 190, 191, 215, 246, 247, 248, **287**, 298, 312

Adams, Abigail Smith (1744–1818), U.S. letterwriter, activist, 2, 40, 44, 70, 161, 201, 254, 325, 350

Adams, Alice (1926–), U.S. writer, 275

Adams, Sarah Flower (1805–1848), English hymnist, 137

Adamson, Joy (20th c.), Austrian wildlife expert, writer, 15

Addams, Jane (1860–1935), U.S. humanitarian, reformer, settlement house founder, sociologist, Nobel Prize winner, 45, 50

Adler, Freda (1934–), U.S. educator, criminal justice specialist, writer, 70, 88, 91, 179, 184, 267, 299, 315

Adler, Polly (1900–1962), U.S. madam, 154, 189

Adler, Renata (1938–), Italian-born U.S. writer, film critic, philosopher, 36, 123, 193

Adnan, Etel (1925–), Lebanese poet, 82

Aguilar, Grace (1816–1847), English novelist, Jewish scholar, 268, 328

Aidoo, Ama Ata (1940–), Ghanaian poet, playwright, writer, 77

Aiken, Joan (1924–), English writer, 308

Akins, Zoë (Zoë Akins Rumbold, 1886–1958), U.S. playwright, poet, novelist, screenwriter, 75, 353

Albrand, Martha (Heidi Huberta Freybe Lamon, "Katrin Holland," "Heidi Huberta," 1914–1981), German-born U.S. writer, 281

Alcott, Louisa May (1832–1888), U.S. writer, 25, 35, 53, 99, 115, 116, 119, 136, 143, 144, 154, 163, 164, 197, 216, 277, 282, 285, 288, 297, 347, 357, 361, 362

Alden, Paulette Bates (1947–), U.S. writer, 7, 120, 308, 316

Aldrich, Bess Streeter (1881–1954), U.S. writer, 189, 229, 321

Alexander, Mrs. Cecil Frances Humphreys (1818–1895), Irish poet, hymnist, 69

Alexander, Shana Ager (1925–), U.S. writer, editor, journalist, 27, 109, 204, 251

Alito, Noelie (20th c.), U.S., 346

Allen, Elizabeth Anne Chase Akers ("Florence Percy," 1832–1911), U.S. poet, journalist, writer, 321

Allen, Gracie (Grace Ethel Cecile Rosalie Allen, 1905–1964), U.S. comedian, actor, 31, **63**, **99**, 141, 218, 251

Allen, Paula Gunn (1939–), Laguna Pueblo/Sioux writer, scholar, 12, 138, 171, **225**, **292**, 300

Allende, Isabel (1942–), Chilean journalist, novelist, 277, 355

Alliluyeva, Svetlana (1925–), Russian-born writer, 115, 149, 187, 278, 330

Allingham, Margery (Margery Louise Allingham Carter, 1904–1966), English detective story writer, novelist, 14, 111, 118, 169, 172,

198, 220, 234, 235, 241, 288, 297, 320

Alther, Lisa Reed (1944–), U.S. novelist, 4, 13, 67, 78, 79, 92, 102, 106, 238, 322

Americanization Committee, 242

Anderson, Ernestine (1928–), U.S. jazz singer, 167, 222

Anderson, Lorraine (1952–), U.S. editor, writer, 226

Anderson, Margaret Caroline (1886–1973), U.S. writer, musician, 196, 268

Anderson, Marian (1902–1993), U.S. concert singer, U.N. delegate, 214, 257

Anderson, Mary (1859–1940), U.S. actor, 295

Andrews, Lynn V. (20th c.), U.S. writer, spiritual counselor, 69, 344

Angelou, Maya (Marguerite Johnson, 1928–), U.S. poet, writer, entertainer, dancer, producer, 6, 12, 33, 50, 72, 74, 82, 113, 118, 131, 148, 223, 255, 267, 287, 296, 316, 325, 356

Anne (1665–1714), Queen of Great Britain, 213

Anthony, Evelyn (Evelyn Bridget Patricia Stephens Ward-Thomas, "Anthony Evelyn," 1928–), English novelist, 52, 100, 251, 341

Anthony, Katharine Susan (1877–1965), U.S. writer, educator, biographer, 324

Anthony, Susan Brownell (1820–1906), U.S. suffragist, editor, abolitionist, newspaper publisher, 105, 172, 250

Antin, Mary (1881–1949), Russian-born U.S. writer, 163, 164, 176, 240, 241, 258, **285**

Antrim, Minna Thomas (1856–1950), U.S. writer, 61, 110, 114, **147**, 177, 215, 216, 247, 250

Anzaldúa, Gloria Evangelina (20th c.), Tejana Chicana poet, **36**, 70, 155, 163, 212, 234, 274, 277, 278, 284, 285

Arbus, Diane Nemerov (1923–1971), U.S. photographer, 230, **245**, 325

Arden, Elizabeth (Florence Nightingale Graham, 1884–1966), Canadian-born U.S. cosmetician, business executive, 38

Arendt, Hannah (1906–1975), German-born U.S. sociologist, political philosopher, historian, 40, 105, 148, 150, 205, 251, 266, 275, 330

Arnow, Harriette Louisa Simpson (1908–1986), U.S. journalist, writer, 63, 281

Ash, Mary Kay Wagner (1915–), U.S. businesswoman, 62, 103, 114, 185

Ashford, Daisy (Margaret Mary Ashford Devilin, 1881–1972), English child-writer, 145, 195, 196, 198

Ashley, Elizabeth (1939–), U.S. stage actor, 200

Ashton-Warner, Sylvia Constance (1908–1984), New Zealand novelist, teacher, 50, 196, 317

Asian Women United of California, 23

Asquith, Margot (Margaret Emma Alice Tennant, Countess of Oxford and Asquith, 1864–1945), Scottish-born English political figure, writer, 17, 29, 37, 38, 66, 76, 136, 141, 158, 165, 167, 205, 210, 211, 224, 250, 278, 305, 311, 314

Astor, Mary (Lucile Langhanke, 1906–1987), U.S. actor, **3**, **123**, 177, 207, 264

Astor, Nancy Witcher Langhorne Shaw (Lady Astor/Viscountess Astor, 1879–1964), U.S.-born English politician, member of English House of Commons, women's rights worker, 9, 91, 169, 252, 291, 339

Atwood, Margaret Eleanor (1939–), Canadian poet, novelist, **4**, 7, **68**, 86, 120, 133, 307, **322**

Auel, Jean (1936–), U.S. writer, 162

Austen, Jane (1775–1817), English novelist, 5, 29, 43, 61, 66, 73, 83, 89, 118, 124, 130, 200, 204, 212, 220, 232, 239, 240, 246, 251, 273, 286, 316, 319, 342, 344, 363

Austin, Mary Hunter (1868–1934), U.S. writer, suffragist, **16**, 80, 103, 136, 220, 227, 270, 345, 348

Auvaiyar (3rd c.), Indian poet, 301

Axline, Virginia Mae (1911–), U.S. child psychotherapist, writer, 265

Baez, Joan (1941–), U.S. folksinger, civil rights activist, pacifist, 191, 265, **340**

Bagnold, Enid Algerine (Lady Jones, 1889–1981), English playwright, writer, **116**, 177, 324

Bailey, Pearl Mae (Pearl Bailey Bellson, 1918–1990), U.S. singer, entertainer, writer, U.N. special advisor, 158, 171, 191, 286, 329

Baillie, Joanna (1762–1851), Scottish playwright, poet, 352

Bakker, Tammy Faye (1942–), U.S. evangelist, religious figure, 17, 98

Baldrige, Letitia (1927–), U.S. White House social secretary, publicist, 204, 239, 239, 277, 325

Baldwin, Christina (1946–), U.S. writer, educator, 42, 57, 60, 82, 127, 131, 207, **211**, **276**, 293, 305, 330, 351

Baldwin, Faith (Faith Baldwin Cuthrell, 1893–1978), U.S. novelist, 36, 44, 128, 321

Baldwin, Monica (1896–1975), English writer, 216

Ball, Lucille (Lucy Désirée Ball Arnaz Morton, 1911–1989), U.S. comedian, TV personality, 192

Ballantyne, Sheila (1936–), U.S. writer, 40, 95, 118, 119, 163, 188, 215, 219, 312, 334

Bambara, Toni Cade (1939–), U.S. writer, editor, 58, 68, 89, 111, 163, 205, 212, 230, 268, 270, 307, 330, 343, 352, 361

Bankhead, Tallulah Brockman (1902–1968), U.S. actor, **2**, 3, 70, 110, 161, 205, 241, 245, 246, 289, 319, 320, 336

Banning, Margaret Culkin (1891–1982), U.S. novelist, political writer, 122, 254, 269

Barbauld, Anna Letitia Aikin (1743–1825), English poet, essayist, critic, 229

Bardot, Brigitte (1934–), French actor, 115

Baring-Gould, Sabine (1834–1924), Danish hymnist, 229

Barnard, Charlotte Alington ("Claribel," 1830–1869), English songwriter, 240

Barnes, Binnie (Gertrude Maude Barnes, 1905–1983), English actor, 36

Barnes, Djuna Chappell ("Lydia Steptoe," 1892–1982), U.S. novelist, poet, playwright, 48, 56, 57, 100, 101, 110, 148, 158, 161, 162, 163, 166, 178, 188, 189, 197, 286, 298, 302, 320

Barnes, Linda (1949–), U.S. mystery writer, 29

Barr, Amelia Edith Huddleston (1831–1919), English-born U.S. novelist, 75, 197, 343

Barr, Roseanne (Roseanne Barr Arnold, 1952–), U.S. comedian, TV star, 343

Barrows, Sydney Biddle (1952–), U.S. madam, 38

Barry, Lynda (1956–), U.S. cartoonist, writer, 196

Barrymore, Ethel (1879–1959), U.S. actor, 2, 3, 93, 101

Bart, Pauline Bernice (1930–), U.S. sociologist, 74

Bates, Katherine Lee (1850–1929), U.S. poet, educator, editor, writer, 332

Bateson, Mary Catherine (1939–), U.S. anthropologist, writer, 36, 53, 65, 72, 77, 79, 97, 137, 223, 238, 268, 292

Battelle, Phyllis (1922–), U.S. journalist, 31, 37

Baum, Vicki (Hedwig Baum Lerf, 1888–1960), Austrian-born novelist, playwright, screenwriter, 116, 158, 175

Bayles, Martha (1948–), U.S. book/film/TV critic, writer, 35

Beach, Sylvia Woodbridge (1887–1962), U.S. Paris-based publisher and bookstore owner, 35, 262, 324

Beal, Frances M. (20th c.), U.S. civil rights activist, writer, 5, 32, 274

Beard, Mary Ritter (1876–1958), U.S. historian, activist, 79, 105, 150, 177, 180, 350, 357

Beard, Miriam (1901–), U.S. writer, humorist, activist, 53, 59, 175, 244, 274, 291, 325, 326

Beattie, Ann (1947–), U.S. writer, 60

Beattie, Melody Lynn (1948–), U.S. writer, counselor, 57

Beck, Lois (1944–), U.S. anthropologist, educator, writer, 149

Becker, Marion Rombauer (1903–1976), U.S. cook, food writer, **67**

Beckett, Mary (1926–), Irish poet, writer, 152

Bedford, Sybille von Schoenbeck (1911–), German-English novelist, essayist, biographer, 254, 274, 341

Beecher, Catharine Esther (1800–1878), U.S. educator, social reformer, poet, 314

Beeton, Isabella Mary Mayson (1837–1865), English food writer, 234

Begley, Sharon (20th c.), U.S. scientist, researcher, **211**

Behn, Aphra Johnson (1640–1689), English playwright, poet, novelist, 165, 179, 197, 213, 336, 352

Bejar, Heda, 136

Bell, Gertrude Margaret Lowthian (1868–1926), English traveler, political figure, 282

Belmont, Eleanor Elise Robson (1879–1979), English-born U.S. actor, writer, nurse, philanthropist, founder of Metropolitan Opera Guild, 201

Benedict, Agnes Elizabeth (1889–1950), U.S. writer, 257

Benedict, Ruth Fulton (1887–1948), U.S. anthropologist, biographer, philosopher, 57, **72**, 114, **131**, 172, 211, 300, 341, 344

Bengis, Ingrid (1944–), U.S. writer, 351

Benoît, Madame Jehane (1904–1987), Canadian chef, 67

Benson, Stella (1892–1933), English writer, poet, 117, 309

Bentinck, Lady Norah Ida Emily Noel (1881–), English writer, 193

Bentley, Toni (1958–), Australian-born ballet dancer, **27**

Berg, Gertrude Edelstein (1899–1966), U.S. radio/TV/screenwriter, playwright, producer, 16, 34, 244

Bernhardt, Sarah (Henriette Rosine Bernard, 1844–1923), French actor, writer, 102, 147

Bernstein, Paula (1944–), U.S. gynecologist, writer, 38

Berry, Mary Frances (1938–), U.S. history and law professor, 178, 252

Bethune, Ade (1914–), Dutch-born U.S. religious artist, social activist, 28, 139, 353

Bethune, Mary McLeod (1875–1955), U.S. educator, writer, civil rights activist, 33, 115

Bibesco, Princess Elizabeth Asquith (1897–1945), English-born Rumanian poet, writer, 110, 136, 240, 323

Billington-Greig, Teresa (1877–1964), English suffragist, activist, 250

Bingham, Charlotte (1942–), English writer, 34

bint Musafir, Safiya (7th c.), Arabian poet, 302

bint Utba, Hind (7th c.), Arabian poet, 339

Bird, Caroline Mahoney (1915–), U.S. writer, journalist, activist, 98

Birnbach, Lisa (1957–), U.S. writer, editor, **72**, 79, **90**, 192, 312

Bishop, Claire Huchet (1898–1993), French-born U.S. writer, poet, 53

Bishop, Elizabeth (1911–1979), U.S.-born Brazilian poet, **160**

Bishop, Sheila Glencairn (1918–), English writer, 214

Bisset, Jacqueline (1946–), English actor, 28

Bissonette, Susan J. (20th c.), U.S., 234

Black, Shirley Temple (1928–), U.S. actor, diplomat, 276

Blackwell, Antoinette Louisa Brown (1825–1921), U.S. poet, writer, minister, suffragist, abolitionist, 227, 320, **349**

Blackwell, Elizabeth (1821–1910), English-born U.S. physician, 288, 348

Blaine, Nell (1922–), U.S. artist, 21, 293

Blakely, Mary Kay (1948–), U.S. writer, journalist, 86, 167

Blessington, Lady Marguerite Power (1789–1849), Irish writer, salon host, 59, 316, 336

Blum, Arlene (1945–), U.S. mountaineer, 220

Blume, Judy (1938–), U.S. writer, 165, 228

Bly, Carol McLean (1930–), U.S. writer, 57, 80, 106, 144, 193, 318, 355, 357

Bly, Mary (20th c.), U.S. writer, 41

Bogan, Louise (Louise Bogan Holden, 1897–1970), U.S. poet, critic, 177

Bogus, SDiane (1946–), U.S. educator, writer, poet, 217

Bok, Sissela Ann (1934–), U.S. philosopher, 5, 282

Boleyn, Anne (1507–1536), Queen of England, 68, 179

Bombal, Maria-Luisa (1910–1980), Chilean novelist, 146, 222

Bombeck, Erma (1927–), U.S. writer, humorist, 46, 47, 53, 80, 117, 166, 169, 192, 208, 218, 239, 313, 325, 326, 331, 343

Bond, Carrie Jacobs (1862–1946), U.S. composer, poet, publisher, 229

Bonner, Elena (1923–), Russian reformer, 278

Bonner, Marita (1899–1971), U.S. novelist, essayist, playwright, 93, 100, 136, 323, 354

Boston, L.M. (Lucy Maria Boston, 1892–1990), English writer, 29, 55, **140**, 227

Bowen, Catherine Shober Drinker (1897–1973), U.S. historian, biographer, essayist, 30, 130, 222

Bowen, Elizabeth (Elizabeth Dorothea Cole Bowen Cameron, 1899–1973), English/Irish writer, 1, 11, 19, 44, 47, 48, 58, 63, 65, 110, 111, 118, 119, 120, 130, 145, 149, **160**, 163, 165, 168, 169, 175, 201, **206**, 223, 244, 253, 268, 274, 279, 292, 294, 307, 309, 311, 313, 329, 332, 335, 358

Box-Car Bertha (20th c.), U.S. hobo, 116, 217

Boyle, Kay (1903–1992), U.S. writer, poet, 327

Boynton, Sandra Keith (1953–), U.S. artist, greeting card entrepreneur, 51, **52**

Bracken, Peg (1918–), U.S. writer, humorist, 239

Bradstreet, Anne Dudley (1612–1672), U.S. poet, 5, 11, 24, 304, 321, 347

Braiker, Dr. Harriet (1948–), U.S. researcher, writer, 243

Brande, Dorothea Thompson (1893–1948), U.S. writer, critic, 122, 145

Brent, Madeleine (pseud., 20th c.), English writer, 183, 321

Brice, Fanny Borach (1891–1951), U.S. actor, comedian, singer, 59

Brittain, Vera Mary (1893–1970), English writer, poet, pacifist, activist, 251

Brock, Alice May (1941–), U.S. writer, restaurateur, owner "Alice's Restaurant," 125

Brontë, Anne ("Acton Bell," 1820–1849), English writer, poet, 109, 308

Brontë, Charlotte ("Currer Bell," 1816–1855), English writer, poet, 2, 11, 29, 45, 46, 71, 106, 108, 121, 125, 147, 171, 200, 201, 202, 211, 215, 216, 242, 257, 272, 284, 336, 356

Brontë, Emily Jane ("Ellis Bell," 1818–1848), English writer, poet, 68, 89, 195, 283, 355

Brooke, Charlotte (1740–1793), Irish poet, 173

Brooks, Gwendolyn (Gwendolyn Brooks Blakely, 1917–), U.S. poet, educator, writer, 139, 170, 247, 248

Brooks, Louise (1906–1985), U.S. actor, 3

Brothers, Joyce (Diane Brothers Bauer, 1925–), U.S. psychologist, TV/radio personality, columnist, 198

Broumas, Olga (1949–), U.S. poet, 352

Brown, Elsa Barkley (1930–), U.S. history professor, quilter, 265

Brown, Rita Mae (1944–), U.S. writer, poet, activist, 8, 11, 20, 25, 31, **69**, 78, 86, 91, 97, 102, 115, 131, 132, 135, 157, 172, 173, **181,**

182, **193**, 195, 208, 276, 278, 288, 306, 309, **355**, 362

Browning, Elizabeth Barrett (1806–1861), English poet, 62, 82, 110, 136, 137, 143, 144, **195**, **196**, 239, 258, 269, 311, 358

Brownmiller, Susan (1935–), U.S. writer, journalist, activist, **252**, 267

Bry, Adelaide (1920–), U.S. writer, 135, 238

Buck, Pearl Sydenstricker ("John Sedges," 1892–1973), U.S. novelist, Nobel Prize winner, 1, 10, 33, 34, 37, 48, 50, **51**, 56, 60, 78, 88, 92, 108, 109, 115, 121, 126, **128**, 144, **153**, 168, 172, **203**, 213, 221, 230, 234, 255, 262, **266**, 271, 272, 277, 302, 336, 340, 349, 361

Budapest, Zsuzsanna E. (1940–), Hungarian-born U.S. witch, writer, 270

Buffalo Bird Woman (Maxidiwiac, 1839–1918), Hidatsa Indian farmer/gardener, 313

Bumpers, Betty Lou Flanagan (1925–), U.S. political figure, activist, 348

Bunch, Charlotte (1944–), U.S. feminist theorist, writer, 61, 88, 186, 332

Burke, Billie (1885–1970), U.S. actor, comedian, 151

Burnett, Carol (1934–), U.S. actor, comedian, 351

Burnett, Frances Eliza Hodgson (1849–1924), English-born U.S. writer, 164, 169, 202

Burnett, Hallie Southgate (1908–1991), U.S. writer, editor, 308, 362

Burney, Fanny (Frances, Madame d'Arblay, 1752–1840), English novelist, 283, 325

Burton, Gabrielle (1939–), U.S. writer, 64

Buyukmihci, Hope Sawyer (1913–), U.S. naturalist and animal rights activist, 15, 156

Cable, Mary (1920–), U.S. writer, 30

Cachin, Françoise (20th c.), French art museum director, art historian, writer, 237

Caine, Lynn (1925–), U.S. writer, lecturer, 143

Calderone, Mary Steichen (1904–), U.S. physician, public health educator, **289**

Calhoun, Mary (Mary Huiskamp Wilkins, 1926–), U.S. children's writer, 130

Calisher, Hortense (1911–), U.S. novelist, educator, 351

Callas, Maria (Maria Kalogeropoulos, 1923–1977), Greek opera singer, 102, 195, 223

Cameron, Anne (Barbara Anne Cameron, "B.A. Cameron," "Cam Hubert," 1938–), Canadian playwright, writer, 48, 246, 282, 283, 314

Cameron, Barbara M. (1947–), Lakota writer, 226, 300

Campbell, Mrs. Patrick (Beatrice Stella Tanner, 1865–1940), English actor, 84, 183, 203, 289

Canaan, Andrea R. (1950–), U.S. poet, writer, counselor, activist, 187

Canady, Alexa (1950–), U.S. neurosurgeon, 291

Cardozo, Arlene Rossen (1938–), U.S. writer, 220

Carlyle, Jane Baillie Welsh (1801–1866), Scottish poet, letterwriter, 167, 168, 219, 283, 314

Carr, Emily (1871–1945), Canadian artist, writer, 12, 21, 149

Carrighar, Sally (1905–1986), U.S. writer, 224

Carson, Rachel Louise (1907–1964), U.S. environmentalist, marine biologist, writer, 31, 100, 103, **104**, 226, **281**, 298, **351**

Carter, Lillian "Bessie" (1898–1983), U.S. nurse, civil rights worker, peace activist, social service worker, 10

Cary, Lorene (20th c.), U.S. writer, 33, 190, 207

Cassidy, Sheila (1937–), English surgeon, writer, 306

Castellanos, Rosario (1925–), Mexican poet, 114, 258, 283, 360

Cather, Willa Siebert (1873–1947), U.S. novelist, poet, editor, journalist, 10, 20, 21, 43, 50, 55, 80, 117, 118, 130, 135, 145, 146, 150, 156, 168, 179, 185, 200, 207, 213, 225, 228, 246, 262, 264, 282, 294, 295, 307, **308**, 312, 316, 326, **327**, 330, 335, 342, **356**, 363

Catherine II (Catherine the Great, 1729–1796), Empress of Russia, 62, 319, 342

Catherine of Siena, Saint (Caterina Benincasa, 1347–1380), Italian mystic, 101, 201

Catherwood, Mary Hartwell (1847–1902), U.S. writer, 130, 352

Catt, Carrie Clinton Lane Chapman (1859–1947), U.S. suffragist, educator, journalist, 178, 262, 347

Cavell, Edith Louisa (1865–1915), English nurse, patriot, 127

Cavendish, Margaret, Duchess of Newcastle (Margaret Lucas, 1624–1674), English essayist, poet, playwright, 260, 347

Centlivre, Susannah (1669–1723), English playwright, 152, 206

Chafetz, Janet Saltzman (1942–), U.S. sociologist, 186

Chandler, Artie (20th c.), interviewee in *Hillbilly Women*, 38

Chanel, Coco (Gabrielle Bonheur Chanel, 1883–1971), French courturier, 18, 69, 78, 113, 116, **119**, 197, 240, 264, 326, 332, 364

Chaplin, Dora P. (1906–1990), U.S. educator, writer, 54

Chapman, Maria Weston (1806–1885), U.S. abolitionist, women's rights activist, philanthropist, 109, 348

Charles, Elizabeth Rundle (1828–1896), English writer, 9, 82, 85, 256, **271**, 304, 362

Charlotte-Elisabeth, Duchesse d'Orléans ("Elisabeth-Charlotte of Bavaria," "Princess Elizabeth of the Palatinate," 1652–1722), German/French letterwriter, 58

Chase, Edna Woolman (1877–1957), U.S. fashion writer, editor, 309

Chase, Ilka (Ilka Chase Murray Brown, 1905–1978), U.S. writer, actor, radio/TV personality, 5, 24, 35, 79, 102, 108, 203, 212, 246, 271, 278, 310, 324, **325**, 341, **363**

Cheever, Susan (1943–), U.S. writer, 75

Chernin, Kim (1940–), U.S. writer, 200, 218

Chernin, Rose (1903–), Russian-born U.S. activist, 10, 84, 87, 117

Chesler, Phyllis (1940–), U.S. psychiatrist, writer, activist, 226

Chiang Kai-shek, Madame (Mei-ling Soong Chiang, 1899–), Chinese sociologist, educator, reformer, 255, 305

Child, Julia McWilliams (1912–), U.S. chef, cooking consultant, writer, TV personality, 64, 125, 128

Child, Lydia Maria Francis (1802–1880), U.S. abolitionist, suffragist, writer, journalist, editor, 15, 109, 119, 164, 166, 173, 221, 233, 260, 288, 319

Chisholm, Shirley Anita St. Hill (1924–), U.S. politician, member of Congress, educator, 63, **85**, 141, 250, 251, **266**, 288, 316, 332, 333

Chopin, Kate (Katherine O'Flaherty, 1850–1904), U.S. writer, 28, 36, 252, 281, 287

Christie, Agatha (Dame Agatha Mary Clarissa Miller Christie Mallowan, 1891–1976), English detective story writer, 7, 8, 10, 25, **28**, 43, 46, 47, 48, 64, 86, 87, 100, 108, 109, 136, 140, 145, 147, 161, 170, 171, 172, 173, 183, 190, 196, **197**, 207, 214, **215**, 231, 243, 272, 275, 282, 310, 328, 329, **340**, 358

Chrystos (1946–), Menominee-U.S. writer, artist, activist, 103, 104, 171, 186, 225, 227, 279

Chudleigh, Lady Mary (1656–1710), English essayist, 345

Churchill, Caryl (1938–), English playwright, 1, 102, 326

Churchill, Jennie Jerome (1854–1921), U.S.-born English host, writer, 111, 138

Cisneros, Sandra (1954–), Mexican-American writer, poet, educator, 162

Claflin, Tennessee (Lady Cook, 1845–1923), U.S. writer, editor, women's rights worker, 233

Clark, Eleanor (Eleanor Clark Warren, 1913–), U.S. novelist, essayist, 235

Clark, Esther Mary (19th c.), U.S. poet, 129

Clark, Septima Poinsette (1898–1987), U.S. civil rights activist, 44

Clarke, Cheryl (1947–), U.S. poet, writer, **186**, 233

Clarke, Jean Illsley (1925–), U.S. counselor, writer, 117, 196

Clarkson, Lida (19th c.), U.S. artist, 241

Cleghorn, Sarah Norcliffe (1876–1959), U.S. writer, suffragist, civil rights worker, pacifist, antivivisectionist, 168, 209

Clifton, Lucille Sayles (1936–), U.S. poet, children's writer, 226, 250

Coatsworth, Elizabeth (Elizabeth Jane Coatsworth Beston, 1893–1986), U.S. poet, children's writer, 89, 312

Cobb, Jewel Plummer (1924–), U.S. biologist, cancer researcher, educator, 97

Cochran, Jacqueline (Jacqueline Cochran Odlum, 1910–1980), U.S. aviator, war correspondent, business executive, 82

Cody, Liza (1944–), English mystery writer, novelist, 91

Coffee, Lenore J. (1900–1984), U.S. screenwriter, 363

Cohen, Barbara Kauder (1932–1993), U.S. children's writer, 35

Colbert, Claudette (1907–), French actor, 142

Cole, Johnnetta Betsch (1936–), U.S. anthropologist, 219

Colette (Sidonie-Gabrielle Claudine Colette, 1873–1954), French novelist, **1**, 10, 11, 29, 41, 48, 49,

61, 67, 87, 103, 109, 116, 120, 125, 127, **130**, 157, 158, 221, 224, 248, 249, 256, 268, **283**, 293, 294, 301, 325, **337**, 343

Collins, Janet (1917–), U.S. prima ballerina, choreographer, 310, 314

Compton-Burnett, Dame Ivy (1884–1969), English novelist, satirist, 76, 117, 169, 195, 200, 273, 302, 322, 329, 331, 333, 349, 352, 358

Conran, Shirley (1932–), English designer, journalist, novelist, 67, 155

Conway, Jill Ker (Jill Kathryn Ker Conway, 1934–), Australian-born U.S. educator, writer, 240

Cook, Eliza (1818–1889), English poet, 59

Cooper, Anna Julia Haywood (1858–1964), U.S. educator, scholar, writer, 32, 105, 212

Cooper, Jilly (1937–), English writer, humorist, 18, 56, 58, 206

Cooper, Susan Fenimore (1813–1894), U.S. writer, editor, 327

Corcoran, Barbara ("Paige Dixon," "Gail Hamilton," 1911–), U.S. writer, 178

Corelli, Marie (Mary Mackay, 1855–1924), English novelist, 159

Cowley, Hannah Parkhouse (1743–1809), English playwright, 183, 335

Cox, Marcelene Keister (1900–), U.S. writer, 47, 53, 134, 237

Craik, Dinah Maria Mulock (1826–1887), English novelist, poet, 43, 53, 64, 74, 134, 152, 331

Crane, Louise (20th c.), English writer, China scholar, 221

Craven, Margaret (1901–1980), U.S. writer, 55, 219

Crisler, Lois (1896–1971), U.S. wolf expert, writer, 298, 346

Crist, Judith Klein (1922–), U.S. film/drama critic, journalism professor, 50

Cross, Amanda (Carolyn Heilbrun, 1926–), U.S. mystery writer, 42, 209, 324, 328

Cudmore, Lorraine Lee (20th c.), English cell biologist, 31

Curie, Marie (Marja Sklodowska, 1867–1934), Polish-born French physicist, Nobel Prize winner, 2, 226, 280

Curran, Dolores (1932–), U.S. writer, educator, 117

Currie, Edwina (1946–), English politician, 6

Currie, Lady Mary Montgomerie (Violet Lamb Fane, 1843–1905), English poet, writer, 183

Cuyler, Margery Stuyvesant (1948–), U.S. writer, editor, 344

Dacyczyn, Amy (20th c.), U.S. writer, 131

Daly, Mary (1928–), U.S. writer, activist, 14, 69, 138, 139

Danzig, Allison (1898–), U.S. tennis patron, writer, 319

Danziger, Paula (1944–), U.S. writer, 126

Davidson, Laura Lee (1870–1949), U.S. teacher, nature writer, 104

Davies, Mary Carolyn (c. 1892–1941), U.S. poet, songwriter, playwright, 37, 78, 327

Davis, Adelle ("Jane Dunlap," 1904–1974), U.S. nutritionist, writer, **94**, **147**

Davis, Angela Yvonne (1944–), U.S. activist, writer, 86, 154, 259

Davis, Bette (Ruth Elizabeth Davis Farnsworth, 1908–1989), U.S. actor, 2, **3**, 13, 62, 69, 108, 197, 204, 238, 310, 316, 319, 353

Davis, Elizabeth Gould (1925–1974), U.S. writer, librarian, 347

Davis, Mildred B. (1930–), U.S. mystery writer, 324

Davis, Rebecca Blaine Harding (1831–1910), U.S. novelist, children's writer, social critic, 119

Day, Doris (Doris van Kappelhoff, 1924–), U.S. actor, singer, 209

Day, Dorothy (1897–1980), U.S. activist, humanitarian, co-founder of Catholic Worker Movement, 3, 82, 100, 137, **194**, 205, 259, 271

de Beauveau, Marie-Françoise-Catherine (Marquise de Boufflers, 1711–1786), French poet, 305

de Beauvoir, Simone Bertrand, (1908–1986), French writer, philosopher, activist, 8, 11, 25, 53, 76, **88**, 93, 145, 146, 151, 154, 155, 233, 254, 260, **273**, 299, 309, 328, 336, 346, **348**, 350, 355

De Blasis, Celeste N. (1946–), U.S. novelist, 1

de Camp, Catherine Crook (1907–), U.S. writer, 214

de Clue, Charlotte (20th c.), Osage poet, 74

de Cornuel, Anne-Marie Bigot (1605–1694), French society host, 149

DeCrow, Karen (1937–), U.S. lawyer, activist, writer, past president of NOW, 23

Decter, Midge Rosenthal (1927–), U.S. writer, social critic, 364

Dee, Ruby (1923–), U.S. actor, poet, 56, 203, 363

de France, Marie (1155–1190), French poet, 38, 81, 126, 197, 275, 352

de Girardin, Delphine ("Vicomte Charles de Launay," 1804–1855), French writer, 38

de Jesus, Carolina Maria (1923–), Brazilian diarist, lecturer, 56, 249, 342

de la Cruz, Sor Juana Inés (Juana de Asbaje y Góngora, 1651–1695), Mexican poet, scholar, playwright, nun, 32, 108, 234, 259, 350

de la Fayette, Marie Madeleine Pioche de la Vergne (1634–1693), French novelist, 289

Delaney, Shelagh (1939–), English playwright, 74, 102, 199, 348

de la Ramée, Louise (Marie Louise de la Ramée, "Ouida," 1839–1908), English writer, social critic, 88

de Lenclos, Ninon (Anne de Lenclos, 1620–1705), French society figure, 124, 198, 337

de Lespinasse, Julie (1732–1776), French writer, 148

de Lourdes, Sister Mary (20th c.), U.S. educator, 257

de Mille, Agnes George (1908–1993), U.S. dancer, choreographer, 27, **73**, 98, 243

Deming, Barbara (1917–1984), U.S. poet, writer, pacifist, activist, 94

de Poitiers, Diane (Duchesse de Valentinois, 1499–1566), French writer, patron of the arts, 40, 68, 101, 143

de Pompadour, Madame (Jeanne, Marquise de Pompadour), French salon host, mistress/power behind the throne of Louis XV, 286

de Rabutin-Chantal, Marie, Marquise de Sévigné ("Madame de Sévigné," 1626–1696), French letterwriter, 73, 131, 254, 321, 346

Desor, Jeannette Ann (1942–), U.S. scientist, 157

de Staël, Madame (Anne Maria Louise Germaine Necker, Baroness de Staël-Holstein, 1766–1817), Swiss-born French writer, society figure, 128, 197, 221, 281, 285

Deutsch, Babette (Babette Deutsch Yarmolinksy, 1895–1982), U.S. poet, literary historian, critic, 25, 101, 194

de Valois, Marguerite (1553–1615), French letterwriter, 73, 136

de Valois, Dame Ninette (Edrus Stannus, 1898–), Irish-born English dancer, choreographer,

founder/director of Royal Ballet, 136, 280

de Veaux, Alexis (1948–), U.S. writer, journalist, 182, 355

Devi, Indra Petersen (Indra Devi Knauer, 1899–), Russian-U.S. writer, yogini, 211

de Vichy-Chamrond, Marie, Marquise du Deffand (1697–1780), French social, literary leader, 28

Devine, Eleanore (1915–), U.S. writer, 74

Devlin, Josephine Bernadette (1947–), Irish politician, 13, 173

de Waal, Esther (20th c.), U.S. writer, Celtic scholar, 342

Diana, Princess of Wales (1961–), English member of royal family, 46

Dickinson, Emily Elizabeth (1830–1886), U.S. poet, 7, 9, 14, 26, 31, 34, **77**, 89, 92, 93, 100, **115**, 116, 129, 137, **143**, 152, 153, 187, **189**, 195, 199, 201, 220, 236, 239, 248, 256, 274, 278, 283, 285, 306, 309, 311, 323, 328, 329, 330, 342, 351

Didion, Joan (Joan Didion Dunne, 1934–), U.S. writer, 169, 180, 228, 235, 246, 359

Dietrich, Marlene (Maria Magdalene von Losch, 1901–), German-born U.S. actor, 103, **198**, 266, 350

Dillard, Annie Doak (1945–), U.S. writer, poet, naturalist, 15, 16, 54, 58, 65, 69, 92, 139, 150, 168, 173, 191, 192, 234, 287, 294, 322, 354, **355**, 356, 357, **358**, 361

Diller, Phyllis (1917–), U.S. comedian, writer, 10, 154, 155, 232, 264

Dinesen, Isak (Baroness Karen Christence Dinesen Blixen, 1885–1962), Danish writer, 16, 59, 99, 246, 282, 302, 309

Ding Ling (Ting Ling, 1904–1985), Chinese writer, cultural figure, 82, 146, 156, 347

Ditlevsen, Tove (1918–1976), Danish poet, 208

Dix, Dorothy (Elizabeth Meriwether Gilmer, 1861–1951), U.S. journalist, writer, 11, 86, 111, 258

Dixon, Jeane Pinckert (1918–), U.S. psychic, writer, 338

Dizick, Missy (20th c.), U.S. writer, 41

Dodge, Mabel (Mabel Ganson Dodge Luhan, 1879–1962), U.S. writer, patron of the arts, 303

Dodge, Mary Elizabeth Mapes (1838–1905), U.S. writer, editor, 53, **151**, 201

Doerr, Harriet (1910–), U.S. writer, 206

Doherty, Catherine de Hueck (1900–), Russian-born Canadian writer, activist, 242

Donnell, Radka (20th c.), U.S. quilter, 265, 292

Dorr, Julia Caroline Ripley ("Caroline Thomas," 1825–1913), U.S. poet, novelist, essayist, 64, 307

Dostoevsky, Anna (1846–1918), Russian diarist, literary figure, 44

Doubiago, Sharon (1946–), U.S. poet, writer, 217

Douglas, Helen Mary Gahagan (1900–1980), U.S. member of Congress, actor, singer, activist, 60, 228, 242

Drabble, Margaret (1939–), English novelist, critic, 10, 44, 110, 193, 198, 209, 218, 265, 333, 336, 360

Draper, Ruth (1884–1956), U.S. actor, monologuist, 126

Drew, Elizabeth A. (1887–1965), English-born U.S. writer, critic, 187, 192, 262, 326

Dufferin, Lady Helen Selina Sheridan Blackwood (1807–1867), Irish poet, songwriter, 164

Duke, Patty (1946–), U.S. actor, 49

du Maurier, Dame Daphne (1907–1889), English novelist, playwright, 25, 72, 90, 145, 184, 197, 326, 336

Dunbar-Nelson, Alice (Alice Ruth Moore, 1875–1935), U.S. writer, poet, political activist, 124

Duncan, Isadora (1878–1927), U.S. dancer, educator, writer, 43, 50, 98, 190, 281

Dundee, Lora (1902–), English politician, 90

Dundy, Elaine (1927–), U.S. novelist, 2, 190, 229

Duras, Marguerite (Marguerite Donnadieu, 1914–), French writer, filmmaker, 12, **91**, 154, 165, 167, 239, 354

Dworkin, Andrea (1946–), U.S. writer, activist, 36, 161, 198, 259, 281, 289

Earhart, Amelia (Amelia May Earhart Putnam, 1898–1937), U.S. aviation pioneer, 68, 114, 125, 276

Eberhardt, Isabelle (1877–1904), Russian-born traveler, 43, 76, 127, 240, 241, 273, 306, 325

Eberhart, Mignon Good (1899–), U.S. novelist, 212, 354

Ecclesine, Margaret Wyvill (20th c.), U.S. biographer, 305

Eddy, Mary Morse Baker Glover Patterson (1821–1910), U.S. theologian, pastor, writer, founder of Christian Science and *The Christian Science Monitor,* 91, 115, 137, 147, 162, 256, 258, 271, 328

Edelman, Marian Wright (1939–), U.S. lawyer, civil rights activist, founder of Children's Defense Fund, 50, 51, 238, 297

Eden, Dorothy Enid (1912–1982), New Zealand-born English novelist, 70, 78

Eden, Emily (1797–1869), English novelist, 126

Edgeworth, Maria (1767–1849), Irish/English novelist, teacher, 148, 173, 245

Ehrenreich, Barbara (1941–), U.S. journalist, writer, activist, 199, 289

Ehrlich, Carol (20th c.), U.S. women's studies scholar, radio producer, 262, 327

Ehrlich, Gretel (1946–), U.S. writer, 15, **149**, 150, 220, 221, 226, 234, 339, 345

Eisler, Riane Tennenhaus (1931–), Austrian-born U.S. anthropologist, philosopher, writer, 271, 341, 350

Elgin, Patricia Anne Suzette Haden (1936–), U.S. linguist, science fiction writer, 329

Eliot, George (Mary Ann Evans Cross, 1819–1880), English novelist, 2, 13, 15, 17, 19, **25**, 34, 36, 41, **47**, 52, 60, 62, 77, **78**, 84, 85, 86, 91, 98, 99, **100**, 110, 111, **121**, 124, 126, 129, **131**, 139, 140, 144, 155, 158, **162**, **171**, 172, 175, 176, 190, 194, 207, **209**, 211, 212, **219**, 221, 227, **232**, 236, 239, 242, 245, 246, 267, 269, 271, 272, 273, 280, 281, 282, 284, **286**, 287, 292, 298, 302, 304, 310, 328, 337, 343, 345, 349, 361, 363

Elizabeth I (1533–1603), Queen of England, 15, 157, 200, 321

Ellerbee, Linda (1944–), U.S. broadcast journalist, writer, 208, 309, 348

Embree, Alice (20th c.), U.S. writer, activist, 38, 317

England, Jane (Vera Murdock Stuart Jervis, 1899–), English writer, 123

English, Deirdre Elena (1948–), U.S. writer, 199, 289

Ephron, Delia (1944–), U.S. writer, humorist, 4, 64, 243

Ephron, Nora (1941–), U.S. writer, journalist, 15, **67**, 167, 201, 257, 280

Erdrich, Louise (1954–), Chippewa-U.S. writer, poet, 29, 78, 90, 116, 124, 138, 147, 158, 184,

191, 197, 199, 225, 226, 255, 321, 324

Ertz, Susan (1894–1985), U.S. novelist, 164, 271

Evans, Augusta (Augusta C. Jane Evans Wilson, 1835–1909), U.S. novelist, 92, 213

Fairbairn, Ann (Dorothy Tait, 1902–1972), U.S. writer, journalist, editor, 147

Fairbrother, Nan (1913–1971), English writer, landscape architect, 237

Fallaci, Oriana (1930–), Italian writer, journalist, 332

Faraday, Ann (1935–), English psychologist, writer, 89

Farjeon, Eleanor (1881–1965), English writer, 216, 229

Farmer, Fannie Merritt (1857–1915), U.S. chef, cookery writer, 67

Fawcett, Dame Millicent Garrett (1847–1929), English suffragist, 96, 342

Federici, Silvia (20th c.), U.S. writer, 155, 204

Fein, Esther B. (20th c.), U.S. journalist, 352

Fenwick, Millicent Vernon Hammond (1910–1992), U.S. politician, 60, 95, 140, **141**, 167, 251, 317

Ferber, Edna (1885–1968), U.S. novelist, playwright, 19, 36, 44, 83, 110, 126, 154, 198, 208, 210, **295**, **319**, 327, 342, 355, 360, 361

Ferguson, Marilyn (1938–), U.S. writer, social philosopher, 9, 19, 34, 43, 63, 120, 121, 141, 196, 211, 237, 255, 274, 280, 299, 300, 303

Fernea, Elizabeth Warnock (1927–), U.S. writer, ethnographer, 5, 117

Ferris, Jean (1939–), U.S. children's writer, 160

Feuer, Elizabeth (20th c.), U.S. children's writer, 235

Field, Joanna (Marion Blackett Milner, 1905–), English psychologist, diarist, 191, 331

Field, Rachel (Rachel Lyman Field Pederson, 1894–1942), U.S. novelist, poet, 13, 120, 236, 240, **262**

Figes, Eva Unger (1932–), German-born English writer, 61, 348

Firestone, Shulamith (1945–), Canadian/U.S. writer, editor, 47, 226, 237, 254, 274, 347

Fish, Margery Townshend (1892–1969), English gardening writer, **133**, 134, 154

Fishback, Margaret (Margaret Fishback Antolini, 1904–1985),

U.S. poet, humorist, advertising copywriter, 91, 182

Fishel, Elizabeth (1950–), U.S. writer, 118, **295**

Fisher, Dorothy Frances Canfield (1879–1958), U.S. novelist, essayist, 28, 78, 189, 217

Fisher, M.F.K. (Mary Frances Kennedy Fisher Parrish Friede, 1908–1992), U.S. writer, **235**

Fiske, Minnie Maddern (Marie Augusta Davey, 1865–1932), U.S. actor, playwright, director, writer, animal rights activist, 5

Fitzgerald, Ella (1918–), U.S. jazz singer, 222

Fitzgerald, Zelda Sayre (1900–1948), U.S. writer, literary figure, 5, 65, 81, 111, 147, 163, 183, 191, 199, 258, 283, 284, 343

Fitz-Randolph, Jane Currens (1915–), U.S. children's writer, 122

Flanner, Hildegarde (1899–1987), U.S. conservationist, writer, poet, 327

Flanner, Janet ("Genêt," 1892–1978), U.S. journalist, novelist, war correspondent, 18, 151, 213, 239

Foley, Rae (Elinore Denniston, "Dennis Allan," 1900–1978), U.S. writer, 29, 45, 193, 251, 321, 336, 354

Fonteyn, Margot (Margaret "Peggy" Hookham, 1919–1991), English prima ballerina, 10, 22, **188**, 288

Ford, Betty (Elizabeth Bloomer Ford, 1918–), U.S. political figure, 12

Ford, Leslie (Zenith Jones Brown, "Brenda Conrad," "David Frome," 1898–1983), U.S. writer, war correspondent, 32, 215

Fox, Paula (1923–), U.S. children's writer, 308

Frank, Anne (1929–1945), German-Jewish diarist, hero, 13, 28, 35, 176, 273, 363

Frank, Francine Wattman (1931–), U.S. linguist, educator, writer, **182**

Frank, Joan (20th c.), U.S. writer, **58**

Frank, Mary (1933–), U.S. artist, 22

Frankau, Pamela (Pamela Frankau Naylor, 1908–1967), English writer, 103

Fraser, Lady Antonia (1932–), English historian, writer, 178

French, Marilyn (1929–), U.S. writer, scholar, 329

Freud, Anna (1895–1982), Austrian-English psychoanalyst, 70

Friday, Nancy (1937–), U.S. writer, 218, 238, 285, 288

Friedan, Betty Naomi Goldstein (1921–), U.S. activist, writer, founder of NOW, 57, 208, 283, 286, 291, **347**

Fuller, Margaret (Sarah Margaret Fuller, Marchesa d'Ossoli, 1810–1850), U.S. writer, journalist, editor, poet, critic, 1, 14, 20, 48, 49, 64, 71, 83, 89, 106, 128, 136, 152, 190, 256, 270, 300, 301, 326, 333, 345

Gabor, Zsa Zsa (Sari Gabor, 1920–), Hungarian-born U.S. actor, business executive, **159**, 203

Galland, China (1943–), U.S. writer, 345

Gallant, Mavis (1922–), Canadian novelist, 257, 275, 315

Galloway, Terry (20th c.), U.S., 74

Gandhi, Indira (Priyadarshini, 1917–1984), Indian politician, 241, 242

Garbo, Greta (Greta Lovisa Gustafsson, 1905–1990), Swedish-born actor, **12**

Gardner, Jo-Ann Evans (1925–), U.S. psychologist, 267

Garrigue, Jean (1913–1972), U.S. poet, writer, 175, 199

Gaskell, Elizabeth Cleghorn Stevenson (1810–1865), English novelist, biographer, 18, 61, 70, 90, 163, 242, 269, 332

Gearhart, Sally Miller (1931–), U.S. writer, 186

George, Jean Craighead (1919–), U.S. children's writer, 120, 191, 275, 346

Gerould, Katharine Elizabeth Fullerton (1879–1944), U.S. novelist, essayist, 79

Gibson, Althea, (Althea Gibson Darben, 1927–), U.S. tennis pro, golf pro, Olympic champion, 13, 345

Gilbert, Celia (1932–), U.S. poet, 155

Gilchrist, Marie Emilie (1893–), U.S. writer, researcher, 352

Gilligan, Carol (1936–), U.S. writer, researcher, 60

Gilman, Charlotte Anna Perkins Stetson (1860–1935), U.S. writer, lecturer, activist, social critic, poet, 24, 37, 40, 55, 62, 78, 92, **107**, 108, 155, 193, 224, 241, 290, 305, 311, 349

Gilman, Dorothy (Dorothy Gilman Butters, 1923–), U.S. writer, 81, 121, 183, 194

Gilpin, Laura (1891–1979), U.S. photographer, writer, 277

Gingold, Hermione Ferdinanda (1897–1987), English actor, comedian, 102, 159, 208, 290

Ginzburg, Natalia Levi (Alessandra Tornimparte, 1916–1991), Italian novelist, essayist, 4, 90, **102**, 135, 156, 174, 214, 269, 293, 337, 342, 359

Giovanni, Nikki (Yolande Cornelia Giovanniek, Jr., 1943–), U.S. poet, writer, 20, 78, 196, 198, 199, 205, 248, 285, 355

Glasgow, Ellen Anderson Gholson (1873–1945), U.S. novelist, 8, 31, 32, 47, **71**, 88, 93, 107, 128, 157, 158, 165, 170, 173, **180**, 194, 199, 204, 205, 206, 211, 229, 230, 237, **241**, 244, 247, 262, 264, 272, 288, 304, **307**, **311**, 312, 317, 327, 333, 337, 341, **354**, **356**, 358, 363

Glaspell, Susan (1882–1948), U.S. novelist, playwright, 27, 61, 80, 247

Glückel of Hameln (1646–1724), German-born Yiddish diarist, 45, 75, 143, 191, 220

Godden, Rumer (1907–), English novelist, poet, playwright, 360

Godwin, Gail (1937–), U.S. writer, journalist, educator, 48, **89**, 194, 317

Goffstein, M.B. (Marilyn Brooke Goffstein, 1940–), U.S. children's writer, illustrator, 22

Goldberg, Natalie (20th c.), U.S. writer, 12, 321, 354, 357

Goldman, Emma (1869–1940), Lithuanian-born U.S. anarchist, activist, writer, 18, 42, 48, 62, 70, 111, 140, 157, 161, 205, **210**, 211, 251, 261, **262**, 265, 274, 299, 331, 333, **342**, 350

Goldstein, Rebecca (1950–), U.S. writer, 49

Gomez, Jewelle (1948–), U.S. poet, 292

Goodman, Ellen Holtz (1941–), U.S. syndicated columnist, writer, 12, 74, 121, 145, 152, 188, 192, 209, 217, 245, 318, **323**, 324, 327

Goodwin, Doris Helen Kearns (1943–), U.S. political scientist, government official, 150

Gorbachev, Raisa (Rayechka) Maksimovna (1932–), Russian political figure, 71, 103, 159, 339, 363

Gordimer, Nadine (1923–), South African novelist, Nobel Prize winner, 30, 43, 80, 94, 107, 120, 127, 212, 237, 253, 258, 270, 344

Gordon, Karen Elizabeth (1950–), U.S. grammarian, 73, 177, 318, 323

Gordon, Ruth Jones (1896–1985), U.S. actor, scriptwriter, 68, 304

Gordon, Suzanne (1945–), U.S. writer, 12

gosset, hattie (1942–), U.S. writer, 294

Grafton, Sue (1940–), U.S. detective novel writer, 38, 70, 76, 86, 192, 250

Graham, Katherine Meyer (1917–), U.S. newspaper publisher, 264, 353

Graham, Margaret Collier (1850–1910), U.S. writer, 177

Graham, Martha (1894–1991), U.S. dancer, choreographer, educator, 21, 22, **34**, 42, 71, **73**, 166, 205, 212, 246, 332

Graham, Sheilah (Lily Shiel, 1904–1988), English-born U.S. journalist, writer, broadcaster, columnist, 81, 126, 151

Graham, Virginia (1912–), U.S. writer, playwright, radio/TV performer, 66, 91, 102, 108, 206, 222, 319

Grahn, Judy (Judith Grahn, 1940–), U.S. poet, writer, 2, 43, **134**, **135**, 197, 241, 285

Grau, Shirley Ann (Shirley Ann Grau Feibelman, 1929–), U.S. writer, 207, 251

Gray, Francine du Plessix (1930–), French writer, 129, 281

Green, Celia Elizabeth (1935–), English psychphysicist, 79, 272

Green, Hannah (Joanne Goldenberg Greenberg, 1932–), U.S. writer, 147, 178, 300

Green, Kate (1950–), U.S. writer, poet, 258, 276

Greenfield, Meg (1930–), U.S. journalist, 85, 177, 252, 342

Greer, Germaine (1939–), Australian writer, educator, activist, 96, 102, 128, 194, 198, 237, 261, 274, 277, 282, 284, 300, 341

Griffin, Susan (1943–), U.S. poet, writer, educator, 178

Grimes, Martha (1930–), English novelist, 122

Grimké, Angelina Emily (1805–1879), U.S. abolitionist, women's rights advocate, reformer, 296

Grimké, Sarah Moore (1792–1873), U.S. abolitionist, women's rights activist, writer, 290

Gross, Jane (20th c.), U.S. journalist, 11

Grossman, Judith S. (20th c.), English writer, 118

Guest, Judith (1936–), U.S. writer, 95, 163, 217, 298

Guinan, Texas (Mary Louise Cecelia Guinan, 1884–1933), U.S. actor, entertainer, circus performer, 250, 309

Guiney, Louise Imogen (1861–1920), U.S./English poet, essayist, writer, literary scholar, 110

Guppy, Shusha (1938–), Iranian-born writer, editor, singer, songwriter, 117, 196, 294

Gurney, Dorothy Frances (1858–1932), English poet, 134

Gussow, Joan Dye (1928–), U.S. nutritionist, educator, 125

Hale, Sara Josepha Buell (1788–1879), U.S. editor, writer, 231

Hall, Lynn (1937–), U.S. children's writer, 7

Hall, Radclyffe (Marguerite Radclyffe Hall, 1883–1943), English novelist, poet, 63, 110

Halsey, Margaret (Margaret Frances Halsey Stern, 1910–), U.S. writer, 11, 36, 38, 45, 66, 79, 84, 87, 90, 91, **102**, **103**, 107, 120, **125**, 157, 206, 216, 238, 268, 304, 309, 310, 313

Hamilton, Edith (1865–1963), U.S. writer, classical scholar, educator, 20, 96, 98, 128, 211, 223, 276

Hampl, Patricia (1943–), U.S. writer, 57, 95, 125, 206, **207**, 250, 283, 346, 361

Han Suyin (Chou Kuanghu/Elizabeth Comber, 1917–), Chinese physician, writer, 147, 323, 328

Hanff, Helene (1916–1989), U.S. writer, scriptwriter, radio broadcaster, 30, 35, 37

Hansberry, Lorraine Vivian (1930–1965), U.S. playwright, writer, civil rights activist, 37, **166**, 177, 199, 233, 320

Hardwick, Elizabeth (1916–), U.S. critic, novelist, educator, 267

Hardy, Dorcas Ruth (1946–), U.S. government official, 141, 273

Harjo, Joy (1951–), Creek poet, writer, 14, 156, 165, 206, 249

Harjo, Suzan Shown, Cheyenne/Muskogee activist, writer, 300

Harper, Frances Ellen Watkins (1825–1911), U.S. writer, poet, abolitionist, 30, 76, 109, 114, 115, 143, 156, 196, 273, 296, 350

Harper, Ida A. Husted (1851–1931), U.S. political journalist, suffragist, newspaper editor, writer, 250

Harris, Corra May White (1869–1935), U.S. novelist, 275

Harrison, Barbara Grizzuti (1941–), U.S. writer, publicist, 160, 258

Harrison, Jane Ellen (1850–1928), English classical scholar, writer, archaeologist, 276

Haskell, Molly (20th c.), U.S. writer, film critic, 12, 101, 105, 153, 204, 208

Hathaway, Katharine Butler (1890–1942), English novelist, 52, 70, 76, 170, 177, 286, 325

Hautzig, Esther Rudomin (1930–), Polish-born U.S. writer, 25, 121, 346, 363

Hayes, Helen (Helen Brown Hayes MacArthur, 1900–1993), U.S. actor, writer, 5, 66, 196

Hazzard, Shirley (Shirley Hazzard Steegmuller, 1931–), Australian-born U.S. writer, 198

Head, Edith (1898–1981), U.S. costume designer, 3

Heilbrun, Carolyn Gold ("Amanda Cross," 1926–), U.S. writer, social critic, educator, **14**, 65, 160, **203**, 255, 299

Heimel, Cynthia (1947–), U.S. writer, humorist, 126, 261

Hellman, Lillian Florence (1906–1984), U.S. playwright, writer, 28, 43, 47, 59, 64, 72, 114, 128, 151, 219, 228, 244, 252, 294, 300, 305, 310, 320, 328, 329, 333, **357**

Hemans, Felicia Dorothea Browne (1793–1835), English poet, 92, 306

Henderson, Hazel (1933–), U.S. futurist, 96, 132, 170, 210, 232

Hennig, Margaret Marie (1940–), U.S. business executive, writer, 85

Henry, Marguerite (1902–), U.S. writer, 15, 41, 153, 185, 345

Hepburn, Katharine (1907–), U.S. actor, 238, 262

Hepburn, Katharine Houghton (1873–1951), U.S. suffragist, birth control reform leader, 204

Herbst, Josephine Frey (Josephine Herrmann, 1892–1962), U.S. novelist, journalist, 77, 84, 111, 269

Heynrichs, Jenny (19th c.), German editor, 353

Heyward, the Reverend Carter (1946–), U.S. Episcopal priest, writer, 138, 196

Highsmith, Patricia (Mary Patricia Plangman Highsmith, "Claire Morgan," 1921–), U.S. writer, 160

Hildegarde of Bingen (1098–1179), German mystic, theologian, 86, 137, 138, 139, 151, 156, 303, 321

Hill, Patty Smith (1868–1946), U.S. educator, reformer, 32

Hillesum, Etty (Esther Hillesum, 1914–1943), German-Jewish mystic, writer, Auschwitz victim, 62, **69**, 70, **76**, **81**, 82, **109**, 119,

120, 143, **168**, 189, 190, 194, 242, 256, **293**, 302, **311**, 320, 321, 340

Hillis, Margaret Eleanor (1921–), U.S. choral director, conductor, 192

Hinkson, Katharine Tynan (1861–1931), Irish poet, novelist, 67

Hitchens, Dolores (Julia Clara Catherine Dolores Birk Olsen Hitchens, "D.B. Olsen," 1907–1973), U.S. mystery novelist, 349

Hite, Shere (1942–), U.S. writer, researcher, 289

Hobbes, John Oliver (Pearl Mary Teresa Richards Craigie, 1867–1906), U.S. novelist, playwright, essayist, 335

Hobhouse, Penelope (Penelope Hobhouse Malins, 1929–), English horticulturist, writer, 133, **134**

Hodge, Jane Aiken (1917–), U.S. novelist, 5, 45

Hogan, Linda (1947–), Chickasaw poet, novelist, essayist, 77, 152, 171, 192, **225**, 247

Hoisington, Elizabeth Paschel (1918–), U.S. brigadier general, 308

Holmes, Marjorie (1910–), U.S. novelist, inspirational writer, 48

Holzer, Jenny (1950–), U.S. artist, 12, 45, 81, 215, 254, 268, 299, 314

Hooks, Bell (Gloria Watkins, 20th c.), U.S. poet, writer, feminist theorist, cultural critic, 32, 33

Hooper, Ellen Sturgis (1812–1848), U.S. poet, 92

Hoover, Helen (1910–1984), U.S. naturalist, writer, 104, 226

Hope, Laurence (Adela Florence Cory Nicolson, 1865–1904), English poet, 1, 107, 115, 127, 183, 196, 310

Hopkins, Jane Ellice (1836–1904), English social reformer, writer, 315

Hopper, Grace Brewster Murray (1906–1991), U.S. mathematician, naval officer, computer pioneer, 276, 281

Horne, Lena (1917–), U.S. singer, actor, 354

Horney, Karen Clementine Danielson (1885–1952), German-born U.S. psychoanalyst, writer, 62, 261

Houston, Libby (Elizabeth Maynard Houston, 1941–), English poet, broadcaster, 51

Howar, Barbara Dearing (1934–), U.S. TV correspondent, writer, 142, 250, 287, 342

Howard, Jane Temple (1935–), U.S. writer, 116

Howard, Lucy (20th c.), U.S., 304

Howe, Florence (1929–), U.S. writer,
    publisher, activist, 97
Howe, Julia Ward (1819–1910), U.S.
    poet, songwriter, suffragist,
    abolitionist, pacifist, philanthropist,
    340
Howitt, Mary Botham (1799–1888),
    English poet, 31, 230
Hsin, Ping (Hsieh Wan-ying, 1902–),
    Chinese poet, 298
Hubbell, Sue (1935–), U.S. writer,
    beekeeper, 227
Hudson, Virginia Cary (1894–1954),
    U.S. child-writer, 107
Huerta, Dolores Fernandez (1930–),
    Chicana activist, union organizer,
    127
Hufstedler, Shirley Ann Mount (1926–),
    U.S. lawyer, judge, Secretary of
    Education, 182
Hulme, Kathryn (1900–1981), U.S.
    writer, 95
Hulme, Keri (1947–), Maori/New
    Zealand writer, 7, **22**, 76, 77, 83,
    92, 112, 291
Hungerford, Margaret Wolfe Hamilton
    (1855–1897), Irish novelist, 28
Hunter, Kristin (1931–), U.S. writer,
    158, 359
Hurst, Fannie (Fannie Hurst
    Danielson, 1889–1968), U.S.
    novelist, playwright, Zionist,
    women's rights activist, 214
Hurston, Zora Neale (1901–1960),
    U.S. writer, novelist, folklorist,
    cultural anthropologist, 13, 45, 65,
    76, 85, 104, 129, 137, 138, 145,
    196, 243, 244, 253, 266, 272, 287,
    288, 302, 308
Huxley, Elspeth (Josceline Grant,
    1907–), English writer, 6

Ibárruri, Dolores Gomez ("La
    Pasionaria," 1895–1989), Spanish
    political leader, revolutionary,
    journalist, 274
al-'Imarah, Lami'a Abbas (20th c.),
    Iraqi writer, 111
Ingelow, Jean (1820–1897), U.S. poet,
    novelist, 215
Ingram, Kay (20th c.), U.S., 216
Irion, Mary Jean (1922–), U.S. writer,
    114, **115**, 229
Iswolsky, Helene (1896–1975), U.S.
    journalist, activist, 170

Jackson, Helen Maria Fiske Hunt
    ("Saxe Holme," "H.H.,"
    1830–1885), U.S. novelist, poet,
    American Indian rights activist,
    philanthropist, reformer, 75, 259,
    302

Jackson, Mahalia (1911–1972), U.S.
    blues/gospel singer, 165, 222, 223
Jackson, Shirley (Shirley Hardie
    Jackson Hyman, 1919–1965), U.S.
    writer, playwright, screenwriter, 52,
    335, 346
Jacobs, Harriet Ann ("Linda Brent,"
    1813–1897), U.S. diarist, 71, 119,
    296
Jacobs, Jane Butzner (1916–), U.S.
    urbanologist, social critic, writer,
    36, **55**, 95, **96**, 227
James, Alice (1848–1892), U.S. diarist,
    8, 61, 83, 157, 162, 190, 205, 243,
    309, 313, 331, 332
James, Bessie Rowland (1891–1955),
    U.S. journalist, writer, 273
James, P.D. (Baroness Phyllis Dolores
    James, 1920–), English mystery
    writer, 77, 127, 175, 189, 297, 304
Jameson, Anna Brownell Murphy
    (1794–1860),
    English/Canadian/Irish art
    critic/historian, 353
Jameson, Storm (Margaret Storm
    Jameson, 1891–1986), English
    writer, editor, 188, 210, 274, 330,
    341
Janeway, Elizabeth Hall (1913–), U.S.
    novelist, critic, essayist, journalist,
    8, 19, 43, 70, 99, 150, 283, **362**
Jansson, Tove Marika (1914–),
    Finnish painter, writer, 3, 84, 90,
    129, 282, 299, 316, 323
Jardim, Anne (1936–), U.S. business
    executive, writer, 85
Jewett, Sarah Orne (Alice Aliot,
    1849–1909), U.S. writer, 16, 66,
    129, 168, 217, 228, 302, 315, 360
Jhabvala, Ruth Prawer (1927–),
    German-born Indian writer, 112,
    165, 361
Johnson, Carrie (20th c.), U.S.
    government worker, 187
Johnson, Diane (1934–), U.S. writer,
    educator, 230
Johnson, Josephine (1910–1990), U.S.
    writer, 139, 227
Johnson, Lady Bird (Claudia Alta
    Taylor Johnson, 1912–), U.S.
    public figure, wildflower
    conservationist, business executive,
    59, 236, 251, 342
Johnson, Pamela Hansford
    (1912–1981), English novelist, 313
Johnson, Sonia (1936–), U.S. activist,
    Mormon leader, 1, 51, 54, 127,
    181, 229, 271, 315, 328
Johnston, Lynn Beverley (1947–),
    Canadian cartoonist, 64
Johnston, Mary (1870–1936), U.S.
    novelist, pacifist, suffragist,
    internationalist, 134

Johnston, Velda ("Veronica Jason,"
    20th c.), U.S. writer, 342
Jones, Mother (Mary Harris Jones,
    1830–1930), Irish-born U.S. labor
    leader, union organizer,
    humanitarian, 3, 18, 156, 167, 180,
    259, 288, 320, 329
Jong, Erica Mann (1942–), U.S.
    novelist, poet, 13, 29, 118, 121,
    127, 175, 216, 255, 301, 314, 315,
    336, 349, **359**, 361
Joplin, Janis Lyn (1943–1970), U.S.
    rock/blues singer, 61, 223
Jordan, Barbara C. (1936–), U.S.
    lawyer, member of Congress,
    educator, 141, 252, 299, 332
Joseph, Jenny (1932–), English poet, 8
Julian of Norwich (1342–1443),
    English mystic, 52, **64**, 136, 137,
    138, 243, 255, 256, **305**
Jung, Emma (1882–1955), Swiss
    scholar, lecturer, 351

Kael, Pauline (1919–1991), U.S. film
    critic, writer, 5, 19, 20, 23, 69, 71,
    95, **123**, 127, 178, 179, 195, 216,
    261, 268, 316, **317**
Kai-Shek, Madame Chiang. *See*
    Chiang Kai-Shek, Madame
Kallen, Lucille Chernos (1932–), U.S.
    detective story writer, **17**, 29, **44**,
    45, 46, 169, 172, 183, 184, 210,
    260, 285, 292
Kassia (9th c.), Greek poet, 342
Kaufman, Sue (Sue Kaufman
    Barondess, 1926–1977), U.S. writer,
    176
Kaye, M. M. (Mary Margaret Kaye,
    "Mollie Hamilton," "Mollie Kaye,"
    1909–), Indian-born English
    writer, 153
Keddie, Nikki Ragozin (1930–), U.S.
    educator, social historian, writer,
    149
Keller, Helen Adams (1880–1968),
    U.S. activist, educator, writer,
    suffragist, pacifist, 17, 44, 52, 68,
    73, 74, 96, 109, **146**, 148, 188,
    193, 210, 247, 284, 297, 298, 302,
    311, 324, 351, 363
Kempe, Margery (Margery
    Brunham/Burnham, c. 1373–1438),
    English mystic, writer, 293
Kempton, Sally (1943–), U.S. writer,
    101, 347
Kennedy, Florynce R. (1916–), U.S.
    lawyer, activist, 184, 221, **233**, 257,
    294, 354
Kennedy, Rose Fitzgerald (1890–),
    U.S. public figure, philanthropist,
    mental health activist, 177
Kenny, Sister Elizabeth (1886–1952),
    Australian nurse, 68, 210

Kent, Debra (20th c.), U.S., 84

Kenyon, Jane (1947–), U.S. poet, 224

Kerr, Jean Collins (1923–), U.S. playwright, humorist, 3, 27, **28**, 49, 83, 86, 91, 125, 152, 153, 215, 217, 304, 331

Kerr, Judith (Anne-Judith Kerr, 1923–), German-born English writer, 47

Key, Ellen (Karolina Sofia Key, 1849–1926), Swedish writer, activist, 50, 244, 339, 340

Kilgallen, Dorothy Mae (1913–1965), U.S. journalist, columnist, TV/radio personality, 228

Kincaid, Jamaica (1949–), U.S. writer, 7, **218**

King, Billie Jean Moffit (1943–), U.S. tennis pro, 24, 262, 310

King, Florence (1936–), U.S. writer, 49, 116, 118, 154, 216, 267, 303

King, Grace Elizabeth (1852–1932), U.S. historian, 241

Kingsolver, Barbara (1955–), U.S. writer, 314

Kingston, Maxine Hong (1940–), U.S. writer, educator, 17, 18, 158, 237, 238, 246, 308

Kirk, Lisa (1925–), U.S. singer, musical comedy artist, 66

Kirkland, Gelsey (1952–), U.S. prima ballerina, 73

Kirkpatrick, Helen Paull (1909–), U.S. journalist, foreign correspondent, 85

Kirkpatrick, Jeane Jordan (1926–), U.S. diplomat, political scientist, educator, 72, 79, 140, 255, 352

Kirsch, Sarah (1935–), German poet, 124

Kizer, Carolyn (1925–), U.S. poet, critic, 140

Klein, Carole Doreen (1934–), U.S. writer, public relations executive, 301

Knight, Alanna ("Margaret Hope," 1930–), English-born Scottish novelist, playwright, 153

Koller, Alice (1925–), U.S. writer, 2, **199**

Kollwitz, Käthe Schmidt (1867–1945), German sculptor, graphic artist, 7, **10**, 21, 178, 236, 242, 271, 284, 339

Komisar, Lucy (1942–), U.S. journalist, 5

Konecky, Edith (1922–), U.S. writer, poet, 272

Konigsburg, E.L. (Elaine Lobl Konigsburg, 1930–), U.S. children's writer, 101, 146, 185, 270, **282**, 320

Konopnicka, Maria (1842–1910), Polish poet, 306

Kramarae, Cheris (1938–), U.S. linguist, scholar, writer, 16, 252

Krasner, Lee (Lenore Krasner, 1908–1984), U.S. artist, **21**, 240

Kübler-Ross, Elisabeth (1926–), Swiss-born U.S. psychiatrist, thanatologist, writer, 75, 93, 190, 341

Kuhn, Maggie (Margaret E. Kuhn, 1905–), U.S. social activist, writer, founder of Gray Panthers, 153, 254

Kumin, Maxine W. (1925–), U.S. poet, novelist, essayist, 248

Labastille, Anne (1938–), U.S. writer, wildlife ecologist, 327

Labé, Louise (1522–1566), French poet, 200

Laberge, Suzanne (20th c.), U.S. poet, 209

La Chapelle, Mary (1955–), U.S. writer, 360

LaFollette, Suzanne (1893–1983), U.S. politician, editor, writer, activist, **51**, 96, 183

Lagerlöf, Selma Ottiliana Lovisa (1858–1940), Swedish novelist, Nobel Prize winner, 61, 94, 100, 168, 241, 303

Lalleswari (Lalla, 14th c.), Indian poet, 272

Lamb, Lady Caroline Ponsonby (1785–1828), English novelist, 319

Lamb, Mary Ann (1764–1847), English writer, 187

Lanchester, Elsa (1902–1986), English actor, comedian, 59

Landers, Ann (Esther Friedman, 1918–), U.S. advice columnist, 318, 329

Landowska, Wanda Lew (1879–1959), Polish harpsichordist, pianist, composer, musicologist, 170, 222

Lane, Margaret (1907–), English novelist, biographer, 63

Lange, Dorothea (1895–1965), U.S. photographer, 245

Langer, Susanne Katherina Knauth (1895–1985), U.S. philosopher, educator, writer, 19, 244, 264

Larmoth, Jeanine (20th c.), U.S. writer, 317

Lasker-Schüler, Else (1876–1945), German-Swiss poet, 92, 164, 217, 280

Lathbury, Mary Artemisia ("Aunt May," 1841–1913), U.S. writer, hymnist, 132

Laurence, Margaret (Jean Margaret Wemyss Laurence, 1926–1987), Canadian novelist, 118, 335, 359

Lawrence, Hilda (Hildegarde Kronmiller Lawrence, 1906–), U.S. novelist, 44

Lawrence, Kathleen Rockwell (1945–), U.S. writer, 35

Lazarus, Emma (1849–1887), U.S. poet, essayist, playwright, writer, 175, 311, 332

Lebowitz, Fran (1950–), U.S. humorist, essayist, writer, 3, 15, 18, 23, 25, 38, **48**, **49**, **57**, 60, 67, 90, 100, **125**, **126**, 135, 157, 180, 188, 192, 202, 205, 227, 243, 260, 277, 297, **318**, 321, 345, **362**

Lee, Gypsy Rose (Rose Louise Hovick, 1914–1970), U.S. burlesque entertainer, actor, TV personality, 8

Lee, Hannah Farnham Sawyer (1780–1865), U.S. writer on history/art, 231

Lee, Harper (Nelle Lee Harper, 1926–), U.S. writer, 17, 31, 54, 63, 68, 97, 157, 184, 303, 352

Lee, Mary Hope (20th c.), U.S. poet, blues lyricist, 32

Leek, Sybil (1923–1982), English-U.S. journalist, astrologer, writer, 306

Le Gallienne, Eva (1899–1991), U.S. actor, director, producer, translator, 169

Le Guin, Ursula Kroeber (1929–), U.S. science fiction writer, literary critic, 42, 43, 120, 122, 160, 177, 179, 193, 197, 216, **221**, 232, 237, 250, 258, 269, 298, 344, 356

Lehmann, Rosamond Nina (1901–1990), English novelist, 232

Lejeune, Caroline Alice (1897–1973), English film critic, playwright, 123

Lemarchand, Elizabeth Wharton (1906–), English writer, 41

L'Engle, Madeleine (Madeleine Camp L'Engle Franklin, 1918–), U.S. writer, 4, 8, 20, 21, 22, 31, 50, 51, 52, 69, 76, 94, 96, 114, **156**, 162, 170, 173, 185, 200, **203**, 228, **234**, **237**, 241, 258, 279, **315**, 319, 328, 331, 339, 343, 351, 361

Lenhart, Maria (20th c.), U.S. writer, 359

Lerner, Gerda Kronstein (1920–), Austrian-born U.S. historian, writer, screenwriter, educator, 33, 231

Lerner, Harriet Goldhor (20th c.), U.S. therapist, writer, 14, 172, **270**, 299

LeShan, Eda J. (1922–), U.S. family counselor, writer, educator, 238

Leslie, Amy (1860–1939), U.S. actor, light opera singer, drama critic, journalist, 27

Leslie, Eliza (1787–1858), U.S. etiquette maven, cookbook writer, children's writer, humorist, editor, 107, 123, 232, 271, 357, 358, 362

Lessing, Doris May Taylor (1919–), English-Rhodesian writer, playwright, 6, 25, **41**, 42, 51, 65, 109, 127, 183, 184, 185, 200, 266, 298, 330

Le Sueur, Meridel (1900–), U.S. writer, poet, historian, activist, 7, 92, 135, 143, 152, 168, 185, 214, 233, 235, 257, 267, 333

Leverson, Ada Beddington (1862–1933), English novelist, 45, 86, 323

Levertov, Denise (1923–), English-born U.S. poet, writer, 189, 355

Levy, Amy (1861–1889), English poet, 266, 327

Lewald, Fanny (1811–1889), German novelist, 139, 166

Lewis, Abigail (Otis Kidwell Burger, 1923–), U.S. sculptor, writer, 322

Lewis, Flora (1922–), U.S. foreign correspondent, syndicated columnist, writer, 330

Lewis, Janet (1899–), U.S. poet, novelist, 168

Li Ang (Shih Shu-tuan, 1952–), Chinese writer, educator, 17, 106, 304, 311

Liliuokalani, Lydia Kamekeha (1838–1917), Queen of the Hawaiian Islands, songwriter, 223

Lillie, Beatrice Gladys (Lady Peel, 1894–1989), Canadian-born English actor, comedian, writer, 24, 146

Lim, Shirley Geok-lin (1944–), U.S. poet, writer, 23

Lindbergh, Anne Spencer Morrow (1906–), U.S. poet, essayist, aviator, writer, 17, 39, 58, 60, **66**, 75, 82, **124**, 128, 131, **143**, 187, 203, **209**, 220, 227, 236, 258, 260, 282, 286, 294, 297, 301, 307, 311, 316, 322, 326, 331, 333, 335, 346, 347, 358, 359

Lindstrom, Miriam (20th c.), U.S. art educator, 99

Lipman, Maureen (1946–), English actor, writer, 222

Little, Jean Flora (1932–), Canadian children's writer, 88

Little, Mary Wilson (19th c.), U.S. writer, 173, 310

Livermore, Mary Ashton Rice (1820–1905), U.S. health reformer, hospital administrator, suffragist, abolitionist, writer, 87

Livingstone, Belle (1875–1957), U.S. writer, actor, adventurer, 57

Llewellyn, Caroline (Carolyn Llewellyn Champlin, 20th c.), U.S. writer, 223, 277

Lockwood, Belva Ann Bennett McNall (1830–1917), U.S. lawyer, women's rights activist, suffragist, pacifist, politician, 210

Longworth, Alice Roosevelt (1884–1980), U.S. public figure, 131, 140, 245

Loos, Anita (1893–1981), U.S. novelist, screenwriter, humorist, 12, 37, 40, 151, 326

Lorde, Audre Geraldine (1934–1992) West Indian-born U.S. poet, writer, critic, educator, 33, 81, 105, 110, 121, 177, 217, 233, 235, 238, 249, 252, 261, 299, 344

Love, Barbara J. (1937–), U.S. writer, editor, **186**, 187

Lowell, Amy Lawrence (1874–1925), U.S. poet, critic, biographer, 20, 146, 236, 286, 352

Lowry, Edith Belle (1878–1945), U.S. writer, 27

Lowry, Mary (20th c.), U.S., 305

Luce, Clare Boothe (1903–1987), U.S. diplomat, politician, writer, member of Congress, playwright, journalist, 2, 10, 68, 101, 321, 347

Lurie, Alison Bishop (1926–), U.S. writer, 20, 144, 297, 313

Luxemburg, Rosa ("Red Rosa," 1871–1919), Polish-German socialist, revolutionary, writer, activist, pacifist, 128, 341

Lynd, Helen Merrell (1896–1982), U.S. sociologist, writer, educator, 352

Macaulay, Dame Rose (1881–1958), English writer, 4, 35, 49, 105, 117, 122, 125, 155, 176, 249, 269, 313, 316, 350

MacDonald, Betty (Ann Elizabeth Campbell Bard Heskett, 1908–1958), U.S. writer, 58, 219, 322

Machlowitz, Marilyn (1952–), U.S. writer, 353

MacInnes, Helen Clark (Helen Gilbert Highet, 1907–1985), Scottish-born U.S. writer, 56, 98, 189, 207

MacLaine, Shirley Beatty (1934–), U.S. actor, dancer, writer, activist, 86, 244, 261

Madeleva, Mother Mary (Sister Mary Evaline Wolff Madeleva, 1887–1964), U.S. medievalist, writer, college president, 293

Madison, May Anna (c. 1920–), U.S. interviewee in *Drylongso*, 33

Magnus, Lady Katie (1844–1924), English writer, 176

Maio, Kathi (1951–), U.S. film critic, 123, 200

Malcolm, Janet (1935–), Czechoslovakian-born U.S. writer, art critic, 261

Mallet-Joris, Françoise (1930–), French novelist, 52, 130

Malloy, Merrit (20th c.), U.S. writer, 270

Manley, Mary Delarivier, (1663–1724), English novelist, playwright, polemical writer, 68, 119, 258, 317

Mannes, Marya ("Sec," 1904–), U.S. writer, journalist, critic, 104, 124, 171, 182, 224, 260, 269, 298, 301, 315, 340, 349

Manning, Olivia (1915–1980), English writer, 9, 80

Mansfield, Katherine (Kathleen Beauchamp Middleton Murry Mansfield, 1888–1923), New Zealand-born English writer, 1, 29, 48, 93, 106, 114, 120, 123, 126, 127, 129, 131, 187, 191, **198**, 207, 210, 214, 234, 239, 246, 268, 269, 298, 307, **326**, 331, 345, 359

Marbury, Elisabeth (1856–1933), U.S. playwright, theatrical/literary agent, 275

Marcos, Imelda (1931–), Philippine political figure, 143

Margaret, Princess (1930–), English member of royal family, 317

Margrethe II (1940–), Queen of Denmark, 190

Marie Antoinette (1755–1793), Queen of France, 68, 169

Marion, Frances (1886–1973), U.S. novelist, screenwriter, playwright, journalist, 227, 270

Markham, Beryl (1902–1986), Africa-based English writer, aviator, 6, **16**, 106, 170, 240, 266, 286, 298, 309

Marshall, Paule (1929–), U.S. writer, educator, 32, 43, 81, 241, 316, 333

Marshall, Sybil Mary Edwards (1913–), English writer, teacher, 96

Martin, Judith ("Miss Manners," 1938–), U.S. etiquette authority, social philosopher, 4, 49, 55, 90, 94, 107, 144, 152, 180, **202**, 259, **278**, 300, 318, 343, 353

Martineau, Harriet (1802–1876), English writer, journalist, social critic, political economist, 204, 270, 290, 320

Martínez Ten, Carmen (20th c.), Spanish government official, 181

Marvingt, Marie (1875–1963), French pioneer aviator, sportswoman, inventor of ambulance airplane, 125

Mary, Queen (1867–1953), Queen Mother of England, 92

Mary I (1516–1558), Queen of England, 195

Massie, Suzanne Rohrbach (1931–), U.S. writer, 260

Mata Hari (Gertrud Margaretha Zella MacLeod, 1876–1917), Dutch spy, dancer, 188

Mathison, Melissa (1950–), U.S. screenwriter, 318

Matthews, Josephine Riley (1897–), U.S. midwife, 46

Maxwell, Elsa (1883–1963), U.S. host, writer, broadcaster, 36, 37, 101, 147, 188

Mayer, Maria Goeppert (1906–1972), German-born U.S. physicist, Nobel Prize winner, 345

McCabe, Jane, 15

McCabe, Jewell Jackson (1945–), U.S. business leader, activist, 33

McCarthy, Mary Therese (1912–1989), U.S. writer, critic, educator, 38, 63, 70, 78, 98, 99, 113, 167, 188, 216, 230, **289**, 330, 333, 337

McClintock, Barbara (1902–1992), U.S. scientist, Nobel Prize winner, 247

McClung, Nellie Letitia Mooney (1873–1951), Canadian writer, activist, 285, 347

McCormick, Anne Elizabeth O'Hare (1882–1954), U.S. journalist, foreign correspondent, writer, 242

McCrumb, Sharyn (1950–), U.S. mystery novelist, 188

McCullers, Carson (Lulu Carson Smith McCullers, 1917–1967), U.S. novelist, playwright, 12, 48, 53, 122, 161, 211, 240, 253, 259, 312

McGinley, Phyllis (1905–1978), Canadian-born poet, essayist, children's writer, 35, 61, **133**, 146, 150, 212, 239, 259, 280, 293, 294, 310

McIntyre, Joan (1931–), U.S. whale expert, writer, 15, 227

McKechnie, Sheila Marshall (1948–), Scottish-born English activist for homeless, 152

McLaughlin, Mignon (1915–), U.S. writer, editor, humorist, 16, 31, 43, 54, 63, 66, 68, 104, 114, 135, 143, 152, 169, 192, 197, 203, 214, 228, 238, 283, 294, 342

Mead, Margaret (1901–1977), U.S. anthropologist, writer, editor, museum curator, 4, 29, 47, 85, **105,**

135, **142**, 154, 155, 184, 186, 239, 256, 290, 291, **295**, 309, 340, 344, 346

Medicine Eagle, Brooke (1943–), Sioux/Nez Percé poet, writer, ceremonial leader, 225, 337, 338

Meir, Golda (Goldie Mabovitch Myerson, 1898–1978), Russian-born Israeli prime minister, politician, 11, 13, 100, 101, 173, 176, 184, 273, 310, 323

Melba, Dame Nellie (Helen Porter Mitchell, 1861–1931), Australian soprano, 273, 301

Menkes, Suzy Peta (1943–), English fashion editor/writer, 35

Meriwether, Louise (1923–), U.S. writer, 258, 297, 343

Merman, Ethel Agnes Zimmerman (1908–1984), U.S. actor, singer, 24

Merriam, Eve (1916–1992), U.S. poet, writer, 257, 341

Metalious, Grace de Repentigny (1924–1964), English novelist, 146

Metternich, Princess, 289

Meyer, Agnes Elizabeth Ernst (1887–1970), U.S. writer, war correspondent, social worker, activist, 50

Meynell, Alice Christiana Gertrude Thompson (1847–1922), English poet, essayist, critic, 50, 58, 146, 276

Michener, Diana (1940–), U.S. photographer, 202, 245

Micka, C.S.J., Mary Virginia (1922–), U.S. poet, educator, activist, 41, 63, 125, 138, 224, 327, 337, 346

Midler, Bette (1945–), U.S. singer, actor, comedian, 8, 329

Millay, Edna St. Vincent (Edna St. Vincent Millay Boissevain, "Nancy Boyd," 1892–1950), U.S. poet, playwright, activist, 1, 6, 37, 43, 47, 74, 75, 76, 77, 86, 106, 137, 148, 171, 177, 188, 189, 192, 195, 197, 198, 221, 222, 259, 260, 306, 310, 325, 357

Miller, Alice Duer (Alice Miller Wise, 1874–1942), U.S. writer, poet, 198

Miller, Casey (1919–), U.S. nonsexist language pioneer, writer, editor, **181**, 182, 224

Miller, Jean Baker (1927–), U.S. psychiatrist, writer, 62, 85

Millett, Kate (Katherine Murray, 1934–), U.S. writer, critic, sculptor, philosopher, activist, 79, 85, 182, 183, **208**, 233, 289

Minnick, Elizabeth Kamarck (20th c.), U.S. social philosopher, 97, 257

Mitchell, Joni (Roberta Joan Anderson, 1943–), Canadian-born U.S. singer, songwriter, 301

Mitchell, Margaret (Margaret Munnerlyn Mitchell Marsh, 1909–1949), U.S. novelist, 166, 260, 272, 303, **324**

Mitchell, Maria (1818–1889), U.S. astronomer, writer, educator, 35, 101, 179, 185, 271, **281**, 307

Mitchell, Susan Evelyn (1953–), U.S. computer marketing executive, 140

Mitford, Jessica (Jessica Lucy Mitford Treuhaft, 1917–), English-born U.S. journalist, writer, social critic, 90, 93, **131**, 259, 304

Mitford, Nancy Freeman (1904–1973), English wit, biographer, novelist, 18, 139, 255, 268, 323, 332

Mittenthal, Sue (20th c.), U.S., 49

Modersohn-Becker, Paula (1876–1907), German painter, 21

Monnier, Adrienne (1892–1955), French bookseller, 21, 23, 30, 35, 53, 55, 71, 176, 206, 239, **253**, 309, 311, 336

Monroe, Harriet (1861–1936), U.S. poet, editor, 92, 220, 249

Monroe, Marilyn (Norma Jean Baker, 1926–1962), U.S. actor, 314, 323, 331, 346

Montagu, Lady Mary Wortley (Lady Mary Pierrepont, 1689–1762), English traveler, society figure, letterwriter, poet, 6, 9, 61, 66, 101, 160, 166, 171, 196, 201, 249, 250, 267, 280, 285, 295, 349, 355, 362

Montessori, Maria (1870–1952), Italian physician, educator, 97, 317

Montgomery, Charlotte Nichols (1904–), U.S. writer, columnist, 218

Montgomery, L.M. (Lucy Maud Montgomery, 1874–1942), Canadian writer, 26, 68, 84, 124, 128, 172, 302

Moore, Grace (Grace Moore Parera, 1898–1947), U.S. screen/radio actor, musical comedian, opera/popular singer, 325

Moore, Marianne Craig (1887–1972), U.S. poet, critic, 27, 29, 119, 124, 142, 144, 157, 165, 173, 248, 261, 321, 338, 340, 358

Moraga, Cherríe, (1952–), Chicana writer, editor, activist, 73, 156, 158, 233, 249, 274, 362

Morales, Rosario (1930–), U.S. writer, activist, 266, 283

More, Hannah (1745–1835), English poet, playwright, religious writer, philanthropist, 46, 145, 337 ·

Moreau, Jeanne (1928–), French actor, film director, 34

Morgan, Elaine Nevill (1920–), Welsh writer, educator, physical anthropologist, **31**, 181, 290, 304

Morgan, Robin (1941–), U.S. poet, writer, activist, 234, 313, 347

Morris, Jan (James Humphrey Morris, 1926–), English writer, journalist, 14, 135

Morrison, Deane (1950–), U.S. science writer, 104

Morrison, Toni (Chloe Anthony Wofford, 1931–), U.S. writer, editor, 14, **32**, 33, 50, 59, 120, 210, **212**, 233, 344

Morton, Leah (Elisabeth Gertrude Levin Stern, "Eleanor Morton," 1890–1954), Polish-born U.S. writer, journalist, activist, 176, 322

Moses, Grandma (Anna Mary Robertson Moses, 1860–1961), U.S. painter, **23**, 191, 207, 237

Moskowitz, Faye (20th c.), U.S. journalist, radio commentator, educator, 4, 54, 75, 93

Mott, Lucretia Coffin (1793–1880), U.S. women's rights worker, abolitionist, minister, pacifist, social reformer, 188, 290

Moyes, Patricia (Patricia Moyes Haszard, 1923–), Irish-born English detective story writer, 41, 59, 80

Mraz, Barbara (1944–), U.S. minister, teacher, 144

Mukherjee, Bharati (1940–), India-born U.S. novelist, 14, 34, 46, 91, 119, 156, 161, 164, 248, 317

Muller, Marcia (1944–), U.S. mystery writer, 218

Munro, Alice Laidlaw (1931–), Canadian writer, 89, 159, 211

Munro, Eleanor (1929–), U.S. writer, 22

Murasaki, Lady (978–1030), Japanese novelist, diarist, poet, 118, 175, 196, 328

Murdoch, Iris (Iris Jean Murdoch Bayley, 1919–), Irish-born English novelist, philosopher, **19**, 20, 22, 116, 124, 175, 182, 183, 187, 200, 203, 212, 221, 268, 292, 294, 301, 329, 348, 350, 361

Murphy, Dervla (1931–), Irish writer, 111, 269, 356

Murray, Pauli (1910–1985), U.S. lawyer, civil rights activist, writer, educator, 290

Myerson, Bess (1945–), U.S. TV personality, consumer advocate, 165

Myrdal, Alva Reimer (1902–1986), Swedish sociologist, cabinet minister, Nobel Prize winner, 56

Nader, Laura (1930–), U.S. anthropologist, 184

al-Namani, Hoda (20th c.), Syrian-born Lebanese poet, journalist, 314

Nan Shin (Nancy Amphoux, 20th c.), U.S. zen nun, 128, 153

Nasrallah, Emily (20th c.), Lebanese novelist, journalist, children's writer, 341

Nation, Carry Amelia Moore (1846–1911), U.S. prohibitionist, 259

Naylor, Gloria (1950–), U.S. writer, 101, 120, 151, 228, 230, 253, 354

Necker, Madame. *See* de Staël, Madame

Nelson, Paula (1945–), U.S. writer, 213

Nelson, Yvette (1940–), U.S. poet, editor, 11, 92, 215, 267

Nesbitt, Edith (Edith Nesbitt Bland, 1858–1924), English writer, poet, 43, 256, 322, **323**

Nevelson, Louise Berliawsky (1900–1988), Russian-born U.S. sculptor, 9, 34, 58, 69, 74, 106, 194, 268, 270, 284, 290, 315, 316, **353**

Nevill, Dorothy (Lady Dorothy Nevill, 1826–1913), English writer, society figure, 65, 305

Nieh, Hualing (Hualing Nieh Engle, 1925–), Chinese-born writer, educator, 216, 285, 309

Nielsen, Helen Berniece (1918–), U.S. mystery writer, 354

Nightingale, Florence (1820–1910), English nurse, administrator, writer, 2, 7, 39, 65, 84, 153, 231

Nin, Anaïs (1903–1977), French novelist, diarist, 4, 17, 44, 57, 68, 81, 83, 89, 98, 110, 128, 129, 130, **144**, 156, 189, 214, 221, 228, 261, 273, 284, 287, 307, 330, 358

Nixon, Pat (Thelma Catherine Patricia Ryan, 1912–1993), U.S. political figure, 251

Noda, Kesaya E. (20th c.), U.S. educator, 24, 217

Norman, Marsha (1947–), U.S. playwright, 7, 89, 116, 329

Norris, Kathleen (1947–), U.S. poet, essayist, 77, 208

Norris, Kathleen Thompson (1880–1966), U.S. novelist, pacifist, activist, 35, 47, 84, 205, 209, 332, 346

Norton, Eleanor Holmes (1937–), U.S. lawyer, civil rights activist, public official, 33, 203

Norton, Mary (1903–), English children's writer, 37

Oakley, Annie (Phoebe Anne Moses/Mozee Butler, 1860–1926), U.S. sharpshooter, entertainer, 45

Oates, Joyce Carol (1938–), U.S. novelist, poet, educator, 19, 117, 147, 248, 306, 357

O'Brien, Edna (1932–), Irish novelist, playwright, pacifist, 32, 75, 154, 206, 269, 296, 312, 346, 348

O'Brien, Kate (1897–1974), Irish playwright, novelist, journalist, 184, 189

O'Brien, Kate Cruise (1948–), Irish writer, 44, 77, 279

O'Connor, Flannery (Mary Flannery O'Connor, 1925–1964), U.S. writer, 6, 29, 44, 49, 65, 66, **87**, 89, 97, 111, **122**, 123, 162, 173, 229, 230, 251, 263, 308, 329, 335, 343, 356, **359**, 361

Ogilvie, Elisabeth May (1917–), U.S. writer, 60

O'Hara, Mary (Mary Alsop Sture-Vasa, 1885–1980), U.S. novelist, composer, 146, 192, 269, 277

O'Keeffe, Georgia (1887–1986), U.S. artist, 22

Ollendorf, Paula (1860–1928), German writer, women's rights worker, 354

Olsen, Tillie Lerner (1913–), U.S. novelist, critic, essayist, 32, 93, 219, 264, 280, 284, 300, 323, **358**

Orbach, Susie (1946–), English psychotherapist, writer, **283**, **343**

Orczy, Baroness Emmuska (1865–1947), English novelist, playwright, 101, 282

Osborne, Dorothy (Lady Temple, 1627–1695), English letterwriter, 187

Ouida (Marie Louise de la Ramée, 1839–1908), English writer, social critic, 1, 116, 153, **165**, 184, 278

Ozick, Cynthia (1928–), U.S. writer, 96, 113, 160, 181, 214, 307, 325

Paley, Grace Goodside (1922–), U.S. writer, 129, 210, 211, 243

Palma Acosta, Teresa (20th c.), Chicana poet, 265

Pankhurst, Dame Christabel (1880–1958), English suffragist, evangelist, 252

Pankhurst, Emmeline Goulden (1858–1928), English suffragist, founder of Women's Social and Political Union, 141, 178, 291

Pankhurst, Sylvia (Estelle Sylvia Pankhurst, 1882–1960), English artist, suffragist, editor, social reformer, 40, 336

Paoli, Betty (Barbara Elizabeth Glück, 1914–1894), Austrian poet, 342

Papier, Deborah (20th c.), U.S. writer, 54

Pappenheim, Bertha (1849–1938), Austrian-born German poet, dramatist, essayist, activist, 176

Paretsky, Sara (1947–), U.S. mystery writer, 87

Parker, Dorothy Rothschild (1893–1967), U.S. writer, humorist, critic, poet, 17, 37, 40, **46**, 61, **70**, **71**, 72, **77**, 87, 88, 90, 101, 108, 137, 151, 157, 158, 169, 178, 199, 206, **214**, 239, 241, 250, 280, 297, 302, 303, 304, 312, 313, 326, 328, 336, 361

Parton, Dolly (Rebecca Parton, 1946–), U.S. country singer, 17

Paterson, Katherine Womeldorf (1923–), U.S. children's writer, 20, 21, 25, 35, 48, 95, **120**, 123, 183, 189, **224**, 230, 234, **242**, 356, 357, 358, 363

Paulus, Trina (20th c.), U.S. writer, 189

Pavlova, Anna (Anna Pavolvna, 1881–1931), Russian prima ballerina, 136, 146, 309

Pearson, Carol (1944–), U.S. writer, 148, 179, 233, 279, 314

Pepper, Beverly (1924–), U.S. artist, 22

Perkins, Edna Brush (1880–1930), U.S. writer, 339

Perkins, Frances (Frances Perkins Wilson, 1882–1965), U.S. Secretary of Labor, government official, social reformer, 96, 262

Perlman, Mildred (20th c.), U.S. government official, 269

Perón, Eva (Evita Maria Duarte Perón, 1919–1952), Argentine political leader, 45, 118

Perry, Carrie Saxon (1931–), U.S. politician, 253, 254

Peters, Elizabeth (Barbara Louise Gross Mertz, "Barbara Michaels," 1927–), U.S. novelist, 77, 146, 158, 161, 283

Peters, Ellis (Edith Mary Pargeter, 1913–), English writer, 137, 255

Peterson, Virgilia (Virginia Peterson Paulding, 1904–1966), U.S. writer, critic, TV personality, 87, 110, 203, 207, 303, 328

Petry, Ann Lane (1911–), U.S. writer, journalist, literary critic, 59, 101, 235, 337

Peyser, Joan (1931–), U.S. musicologist, writer, 140

Phillips, Baroness (Nora Phillips, 1912–), English politician, activist, 152

Phillips, Julia, (1944–), U.S. film producer, director, 8, 190, 270, 286, 303

Pickford, Mary (Gladys Marie Smith Pickford Fairbanks, 1893–1979), Canadian-born U.S. actor, 114

Pierce, Christine (20th c.), U.S. educator, ethicist, 226

Piercy, Marge (1936–), U.S. writer, poet, 61, 63, 87, 100, 145, 198, 218, 264, 286, 290, 343, 348, 353, 363

Pierson, Elaine Catherine (1925–), U.S. physician, 288

Pines, Ayala Malach (1945–), U.S. writer, 175

Piozzi, Hester Lynch Salusbury Thrale, 1741–1821), English memoirist, 66, 87, 92, 93, 106, 130, 253

Pitzer, Gloria (20th c.), 7

Plain, Belva (1919–), U.S. novelist, 188

Plath, Sylvia (Sylvia Plath Hughes, 1932–1963), U.S. poet, writer, 27, 93, 243

Plenty Chiefs, Ruby (20th c.), North American Indian medicine woman, 16

Pogrebin, Letty Cottin (1939–), U.S. writer, editor, columnist, 155

Pond, Mimi (20th c.), U.S. writer, 252

Poniatowska, Elena (1933–), Mexican journalist, writer, 251, 355, 360

Poole, Mary Pettibone (20th c.), U.S. writer, 8, 11, 36, 37, 72, 110, 130, 180, 183, 213, 265, 286, 292, 315

Popcorn, Faith (1947–), U.S. marketer, trend forecaster, 5, 38, 46, 56, 57, 64, 67, 131, 132, 282

Porter, Eleanor Hodgman (1868–1920), U.S. children's writer, novelist, 15, **137**, 155, 213

Porter, Katherine Anne (Maria Veronica Callista Russell, 1894–1980), U.S. novelist, 93, 172, 358

Porter, Sylvia Field Feldman (1913–1991), U.S. economist, writer, columnist, 214

Post, Emily Price (1873–1960), U.S. etiquette authority, 65

Potter, Beatrix (Helen Beatrix Potter, 1866–1943), English children's book writer, illustrator, 2, 120, 126, 271

Prado, Adélia (1935–), Brazilian poet, 80, 137, 311

Pretty Shield (1858–1935), Crow medicine woman, 103

Price, Leontyne Mary (1927–), U.S. opera singer, 2, 21, 23, 32, 33, 243, 294, 310

Priest, Ivy Maud Baker (1905–1975), U.S. politician, government official, 28, 347

Pritam, Amrita (1919–), Indian poet, 46

Proctor, Adelaide Anne ("Mary Berwick," 1825–1864), English poet, women's rights worker, 222, 285

Pym, Barbara Mary Crampton (1913–1980), English novelist, 163, 199

Quinn, Jane Bryant (1939–), U.S. journalist, columnist, 184

Quinn, Sally (1941–), U.S. journalist, 341

Quintanales, Mirtha (1949–), Cuban-born U.S. writer, 266

Rachel (Rachel Blumstein/Blaustein, 1890–1931), Russian-Jewish poet, lyricist, 309

Rachel (Elizabeth/Elisa Felix, 1821–1856), Swiss-born French actor, 215

Radner, Gilda (1946–1989), U.S. comedian, 59, 69, 87, 119, 162, 165, 190, 192

Raimo, Angela Maria (1939–), U.S. lawyer, educator, 216

Raine, Kathleen Jessie (1908–), English poet, critic, **226**

Ramey, Estelle R. (1917–), U.S. physician, physiologist, endocrinologist, 290, 349

Rand, Ayn (Alissa Rosenbaum O'Connor, 1905–1982), Russian-born U.S. writer, playwright, screenwriter, social critic, 6, 13, 18, 19, 38, 40, 42, 59, 61, 62, 64, 91, 92, 96, 99, **108**, 109, 141, 144, 145, 154, 167, 205, 206, 210, 213, **214**, 232, 244, 261, 267, 275, 279, **289**, 296, 317, 319, 321, 328, 342

Rankin, Jeannette Pickering (1880–1973), U.S. politician, pacifist, suffragist, activist, 79, 184, 339, 348

Rascoe, Judith (1941–), U.S. writer, screenwriter, 357

Raverat, Gwen (Gwendolyn Mary Darwin Raverat, 1885–1957), English wood-engraver, illustrator, writer, 180

Ravitch, Diane Silvers (1938–), U.S. writer, historian, educator, 98, 354

Rawlings, Marjorie Kinnan (1896–1953), U.S. novelist, journalist, 119, 199, 229, 301, 304, 312, 345

Reagan, Nancy Davis (1923–), U.S. actor, political figure, 91, 251, 347

Reben, Martha (Martha Rebentisch, 1911–1964), U.S. writer, 129

Rebeta-Burditt, Joyce (1938–), U.S. programming executive, novelist, 12, 54, 212, 235, 261

Reda, Fatma A. (1944–), Egyptian-born U.S. psychiatrist, activist, 242

Reddy, Helen (Helen Reddy Wald, 1941–), Australian-born U.S. singer, composer, 138, 346

Redgrave, Vanessa (1937–), English actor, 310

Redon, Odilon (1840–1916), French painter, lithographer, etcher, 19, 23

Reed, Myrtle (Myrtle Reed McCullough, 1874–1911), U.S. novelist, essayist, poet, 45, 65, 202, 324

Reese, Lizette Woodworth (1856–1935), U.S. teacher, poet, memoirist, 87

Reibold, Miriam (1917–), U.S. activist, 9

Reid, Coletta (1943–), U.S. writer, 61, 88

Renault, Mary (Eileen Mary Challans, 1905–1983), English novelist, 29, 88, 99, 108, 109, 139, 147, 149, 255, 270, 285, 293, 304, 316, 328

Renkel, Ruth E. (20th c.), U.S., 291

Repplier, Agnes (1855–1950), U.S. essayist, biographer, poet, historian, social critic, 40, 41, 55, 63, 84, 87, 88, 91, 92, 97, 103, 106, 130, 157, 158, 171, 179, 183, 185, 186, 192, 253, 264, 288, 329, 330

Rhys, Jean (Ella Gwendolen Rees Williams, 1890–1979), Dominican-born English novelist, 7, 37, 71, 94, 100, 103, 153, 157, 198, 216, 277, 292, 312, 329, 355, 359

Rice, Alice Hegen Caldwell (1870–1942), U.S. humorist, children's writer, civic worker, 76, 81, 324

Rich, Adrienne Cecile (1929–), U.S. poet, educator, activist, 23, 26, 42, 50, 120, 161, 181, 186, 201, 242, 258, 299, 318

Richards, Ann Willis (1933–), U.S. politician, 348

Richards, Beah (1926–), U.S. actor, poet, playwright, 97, 266

Richards, Dorothy (1894–1985), U.S. naturalist, 15, 156

Richards, Laura Elizabeth Howe (1850–1943), U.S. writer, poet, 99

Richards, Mary Caroline (1916–), U.S. poet, potter, 243

Richardson, Dorothy B. (1882–1955), U.S. writer, journalist, socialist, 314

Richardson, Henry Handel (Ethel Florence Lindesay Richardson, 1870–1946), Australian-born English novelist, 7, 48, 86, 170, 218, 358

Rico, Gabriele Lusser (1937–), U.S. educator, writer, 227

Rinehart, Mary Roberts (1876–1958), U.S. novelist, mystery story writer, journalist, playwright, suffragist, 184, 197, 211, 242

Ristad, Eloise (1925–1985), U.S. musicologist, 114, 185, 243, 260

Rivers, Joan (Joan Molnsky, 1935–), U.S. comedian, entertainer, 59

Robbin, Alexandra (1935–), U.S. writer, editor, 7, 10

Roberts, Elizabeth Madox (1881–1941), U.S. writer, poet, 82, 284

Robinson, Harriet Jane Hanson (1825–1911), U.S. suffragist, abolitionist, women's rights activist, writer, poet, playwright, journalist, merchant, mill worker, 7, 354

Robinson, Joan Violet Maurice (1903–), English economist, 41, 95, 96, 334

Robinson, Margaret Atwood (1937–), U.S. writer, 149, 322

Robinson, Marilynne (1943–), U.S. writer, 45, 74, 113, 116, 191, 194, 302

Robinson, Mary Bourke (1944–), President of Ireland, 349

Rodgers, Carolyn Marie (1945–), U.S. poet, 217

Roe, Anne (1904–), U.S. psychologist, educator, writer, 128

Roiphe, Anne Richardson (1935–), U.S. novelist, 74, 118, 137, 282

Roland, Marie-Jeanne, (Marie-Jeanne Phlipon Roland, "Madame Roland," 1754–1793), French political leader, 36, 167, 186, 187, 206, 274, 280

Roland-Holst, Henriette (1869–1952), Dutch poet, 192

Rollin, Betty (1936–), U.S. writer, editor, actor, TV journalist, 31

Rombauer, Irma S. (Irma Louise von Starkloff Rombauer, 1877–1962), U.S. cookbook writer, 67

Romero, Joan Arnold (20th c.), U.S. theologian, 320

Roosevelt, Eleanor (Anna Eleanor Roosevelt Roosevelt, 1884–1962),

U.S. government official, public figure, writer, reformer, humanitarian, 42, 72, 79, 130, 156, 190, 232, 242, 285, 288, 339

Ros, Amanda McKittrick (Anna Margaret McKittrick Ross, 1860–1939), Irish novelist, poet, 262

Rosenstein, Harriet (1932–), U.S. writer, 257

Ross, Diana (1944–), U.S. singer, actor, entertainer, 103

Ross, Susan C. (1942–), U.S. lawyer, educator, writer, activist, 183

Rossetti, Christina Georgina ("Ellen Alleyne," 1830–1894), English poet, 75, 114, 147, 217, 272, 293, 297, 312

Rossi, Alice Schaerr (1922–), U.S. sociologist, educator, editor, 311

Rossner, Judith Perelman (1935–), U.S. novelist, 68

Rowbotham, Sheila (1943–), English historian, socialist, 88, 169, 181, 233, 254, 335

Rowland, Helen (1876–1950), U.S. writer, journalist, humorist, 151, 204, 213, 284, 295

Roy, Gabrielle (1909–1983), French/Canadian writer, 354

Rubin, Lillian Breslow (1924–), U.S. writer, social scientist, 117, 254

Rubinstein, Helena (1882–1965), Polish-born U.S. cosmetics manufacturer, entrepreneur, art collector, philanthropist, 8

Ruckelshaus, Jill Strickland (1937–), U.S. government official, 348

Rudner, Rita (20th c.), U.S. comedian, 199

Ruether, Rosemary Radford (1936–), U.S. theologian, writer, 306

Rukeyser, Muriel (1913–1980), U.S. poet, biographer, translator, activist, 89, 149, 153, 176, 181, 249, 263, 308, 329

Rule, Jane (1931–), Canadian writer, 123, 160, 312

Rushin, Kate (Donna Kate Rushin), U.S. poet, 36, 142

Russell, Countess Dora Winifred Black (1894–1986), English writer, activist, 31, 337

Russell, Letty Mandeville (1929–), U.S. minister, theologian, 30

Russell, Rosalind (Rosalind Russell Brisson, 1911–1976), U.S. actor, philanthropist, 2, 114

Ruth (8th c. B.C.), Moabite woman in biblical "Book of Ruth," 115

Sabin, Florence Rena (1871–1953), U.S. physician, medical

researcher/educator, public health worker, 159

Sachs, Nelly, (1891–1969), German-born Swedish-Jewish poet, playwright, Nobel Prize winner, 60, 75, 76, 94, **151**, **152**, 178, 229, 247, 293

Sackville-West, Vita (Victoria Sackville-West, 1892–1962), English writer, poet, critic, 13, 52, 62, 67, 203, 204, 288, 326, 359

Saffir-Zadeh, Tahereh (1939–), Iranian poet, 277

Sagan, Françoise (Françoise Quoirez, 1935–), French writer, 19, 46, 104, 175, 193, 275, 358, 360

Sainte-Marie, Buffy (Beverley Sainte-Marie, 1942–), Cree folk singer, songwriter, activist, 221

Sampter, Jessie Ethel (1883–1938), German-born U.S.-Israeli poet, 175, 293

Samuelson, Joan Benoit (1957–), U.S. marathoner, Olympic winner, 49

Sanchez, Sonia (1934–), U.S. writer, poet, professor of English, 247, 327

Sand, George (Amandine Aurore Lucile Dupin, Baronne Dudevant, 1804–1876), French novelist, essayist, 9, 19, 39, 45, 51, 82, 85, 98, 136, 141, 145, 146, 149, 184, 196, 199, 210, 240, 249, 250, 261, 302, **311**, 316, 317, 328, 335, 342

Sanger, Margaret Higgins (Margaret Higgins Sanger Slee, 1883–1966), U.S. nurse, birth control reformer, 31

Santmyer, Helen Hooven (1895–1986), U.S. writer, 323

Sappho (c. 613–580 B.C.), Greek poet, 12, 75, 124, 165, 195, 215, 249, 272, 351

Sarton, Eleanor May (1912–), Belgian-born U.S. writer, poet, 7, 9, **10**, 27, **39**, 42, 53, 62, 70, 75, 79, 81, 95, 110, 114, 116, 117, **121**, 124, 131, 134, 136, 154, 182, 183, 190, 191, **194**, 199, 200, 205, 236, 238, 239, 243, **248**, **249**, 264, 289, 319, 325, 330, 356, 359, 361

Satir, Virginia Mildred (1916–1988), U.S. therapist, writer, 60

Saunders, Margaret Baillie (1873–1949), English writer, 78

Savage, Georgia (20th c.), Australian writer, 51

Sayers, Dorothy L. (Dorothy Leigh Sayers Fleming, 1893–1957), English mystery writer, essayist, **9**, 34, 86, 94, 113, 128, 166, 171, **240**, 265, 281, **307**, **320**, 349, 350, 353

Scarf, Maggie (1932–), U.S. journalist, writer, 11, 256

Schaef, Anne Wilson (1934–), U.S. psychotherapist, addictions pioneer, women's rights activist, 83, 101, 172, 205, 225, 313, 353

Schell, Maria (1926–), Austrian-born U.S. actor, 243

Schinz, Marina (1945–), Swiss-born U.S. photographer, **133**

Schlafly, Phyllis Stewart (1924–), U.S. political activist, anti-ERA campaigner, writer, 141

Schneiders, I.H.M., Sandra Marie (1936–), U.S. theologian, writer, **138**

Schreiner, Olive Emilie Albertina ("Ralph Iron," 1855–1920), South African novelist, activist, pacifist, social critic, 176, 179, 221, 349

Schroeder, Patricia Scott (1940–), U.S. lawyer, member of Congress, 251, 347

Schulder, Diane Blossom (1937–), U.S. lawyer, activist, educator, 184

Schweitzer, Gertrude (1909–), U.S. writer, 142

Schwimmer, Rosika (1877–1948), Hungarian writer, editor, pacifist, suffragist, 156

Scott, Anne Firor (1921–), U.S. history professor, writer, 24, 299

Scott Brown, Denise (1931–), U.S. architect, 18, 202

Scott, Evelyn D. Metcalf (1893–1963), U.S. novelist, poet, traveler, 100, 166, 236, 312

Scott, Hazel Dorothy (1920–1981), West Indian-born U.S. jazz pianist/singer, actor, 32, 51, 104

Scott-Maxwell, Florida Pier (1884–1979), U.S. writer, suffragist, psychologist, playwright, actor, **10**, 13, 83, 93, 142, 188, 189, **218**, 285

Scudder, Vida Dutton (1861–1954), U.S. social reformer, English literature scholar, writer, educator, 69, 223

Seeley, Mabel (Mabel Hodnefield Seeley Ross, 1903–1991), U.S. writer, 357, 359

Senesh, Hannah (Hannah Szenes, 1921–1944), Hungarian-Jewish hero, soldier, political activist, diarist, 148, 228, 279

Seredy, Kate (1899–1975), Hungarian children's writer, illustrator, 114, 214, 236

Seton, Anya (Anya Chase, 1904–1990), U.S. writer, 127, 205, 303

Sévigné, Madame de. *See* de Rabutin-Chantal, Marie, Marquise de Sévigné

Sewell, Anna (1820–1878), English writer, 15, 71, 161, 179, 233, 271

Sewell, Marilyn (20th c.), U.S. minister, writer, 34, 151, 287

Sexton, Anne Grey Harvey (1928–1974), U.S. poet, 8, 120, **137**, 217, 248

Shanahan, Eileen (1924–), U.S. journalist, 206

Shange, Ntozake (Paulette Williams, 1948–), U.S. writer, poet, playwright, 69, 89, 99, 121, 138, 163, 202, 228

Sharp, Margery (1905–), English writer, 133, 249

Sharp, Saundra (1942–), U.S. writer, actor, filmmaker, 217

Shaw, the Reverend Anna Howard (1847–1919), English-born U.S. lecturer, 306

Shaw, Anne (1921–), U.S. writer, 1, 37

Shaw, Elizabeth (20th c.), U.S. art museum official, 23

Shays, Ruth (20th c.), U.S. interviewee in *Drylongso*, 26, 167, 182, 184

Sheehy, Gail (1937–), U.S. writer, social critic, 43, 144, 214, 284

Shelley, Mary Wollstonecraft Godwin (1797–1851), English novelist, 69, 98, 119, 129, 144, 175, 220, 263

Sheppard, Eugenia Benbow (1910–), U.S. journalist, fashion columnist, 17, 119

Sherman, Susan Jean (1939–), U.S. writer, 44

Shinn, Florence Scovel (1877–1940), U.S. illustrator, metaphysicist, 172

Sholl, Betsy (Elizabeth Neary Sholl, 1945–), U.S. poet, writer, 76

Shreve, Anita (20th c.), U.S. writer, 274

Sidransky, Ruth (1929–), U.S. writer, 181

Signoret, Simone (1921–1985), French actor, novelist, 3

Silko, Leslie Marmon (1948–), Laguna Pueblo-U.S. writer, poet, 9, 207, **308**

Sills, Beverly (Belle Miriam Silverman Greenough, "Bubbles," 1929–), U.S. opera singer, administrator, 20, 46, 274, 298

Simon, Anne Wertheim (1914–), U.S. writer, scientist, 282

Simpson, Eileen B. (20th c.), U.S. psychotherapist, writer, 164, 220, 234

Simpson, Mona Elizabeth (1957–), U.S. writer, 113

Sitwell, Dame Edith Louisa (1887–1964), English poet, writer, editor, literary critic, 19, 28, 102, **124**, 152, 157, **222**, **247**, 248, 286, 316

Sklarek, Norma Merrick (1928–), U.S. architect, 18

Slick, Ely (20th c.), U.S., 83

Small, Jacquelyn, 305

Smeal, Eleanor Marie Cutri (1930–), U.S. activist, past president of NOW, 276

Smedley, Agnes (1892–1950), U.S. writer, foreign correspondent, 28, 32, 213, 278, 333

Smiley, Jane Graves (1949–), U.S. writer, 49, 81, 204, 215, 270

Smith, Betty Wehner (1896–1972), U.S. novelist, playwright, 275

Smith, Dodie (Dorothy Gladys Beesley Smith, "C.L. Anthony," 1896–1990), English writer, playwright, 2, 38, 80, **88**, 116, 163, 222, 271, 273, 295, 330

Smith, Elinor Goulding (1917–), U.S. writer, 27

Smith, Hannah Tatum Whitall (1832–1911), U.S. religious writer, evangelist, pacifist, prohibitionist, women's rights activist, 6, 8, 53, 100, 115, 154, 214

Smith, Lillian Eugenia (1897–1966), U.S. novelist, columnist, civil rights worker, social critic, educator, editor, 30, 96, 142, 168, 275, 302

Smith, Liz (1923–), U.S. columnist, writer, 15, 42, 140, 250

Smith, Margaret Chase (1897–), U.S. politician, member of Congress, 42

Smith, Minnie Richard (19th c.), U.S. poet, 244

Smith, Stevie (Florence Margaret Smith, 1902–1971), English poet, novelist, 77, 78, 79, 102, 291, 294

Smith, Willie Mae Ford (1904–), U.S. gospel singer, 92

Snow, Carrie (20th c.), U.S. comedian, 87, 296

Snow, Helen Foster (1907–), U.S. writer, China scholar, 204

Sölle, Dorothee (1929–) German theologian, writer, 136

Sommerfield, Sylvie (20th c.), U.S. writer, 236

Sontag, Susan (1933–), U.S. essayist, writer, critic, filmmaker, 11, 13, 14, 16, **19**, 21, 89, 162, 193, **245**, 252, 285, 306, 329, 344, 355, 361

Sorel, Julia (Rosalyn Drexler, 1926–), U.S. writer, 276

Sorrels, Bobbye D. (20th c.), U.S. writer, activist, 171, 290, 299

South African women, 291

Spacks, Patricia Meyer (1929–), U.S. literature scholar, writer, 42, 140

Spark, Muriel (1918–), Scottish-born English novelist, poet, critic, 8, 65, 97, 170, 209, 237

Spencer, the Reverend Anna Carpenter Garlin (1851–1931), U.S. journalist, suffragist, prohibitionist, pacifist, philanthropist, 345

Spender, Dale (1943–), English writer, sociolinguist, 180, **181**

Spolin, Viola (1911–), U.S. theatrical producer, director, writer, 352

Sproles, Judy (20th c.), U.S., 113

Spyri, Johanna Heusser (1827–1901), Swiss writer, 15, 179, 256

Stafford, Jean (Jean Stafford Lowell Jensen Liebling, 1915–1979), U.S. novelist, 7, 12, 197, 293, 298, 323

Stahl, Nancy (1937–), U.S. writer, illustrator, 238, 335

Stanford, Sally (1903–1982), U.S. madam, civic leader, writer, 261

Stanton, Elizabeth Cady (1815–1902), U.S. suffragist, writer, women's rights activist, editor, social reformer, theologian, abolitionist, 54, **56**, 105, 166, 196, 273, 290, 291, 328, 347, 350

Starhawk (Miriam Simos, 1951–), U.S. leader in feminine spirituality, peace activist, ecofeminist, witch, 69, 96, 202, 223, 224, 276, 279, 288, 305, 306

Stark, Dame Freya Madeline (1893–), French-born English travel writer, photographer, 76, 313

Starkie, Enid (1897–1970), Irish biographer, scholar of French literature, 61

Stead, Christina Ellen (1902–1983), Australian novelist, 38, 46, 56, 86, **139**, 165, **275**, 316

Stein, Gertrude (1874–1946), U.S. ex-patriate writer, literary salon host, 15, 16, 18, 23, 40, 41, 65, 71, 106, 116, **135**, 136, 158, 167, 171, 173, 174, 176, 193, 213, 215, 216, 228, 229, 248, 264, 275, 295, 299, **333**, 354, 360

Steinem, Gloria (1934–), U.S. writer, journalist, founder/editor of *Ms.*, activist, 9, 49, 56, 108, 153, 208, 252, 254, 255, 300, 313, 348, 359

Stewart, Mary Florence Elinor Rainbow (1916–), English novelist, **29**, 121, 143, 190, 254, 278, 297

Stimpson, Catherine Roslyn (1936–), U.S. educator, writer, 254, 274

Stocks, Baroness (Mary Danvers Stocks, Baroness of Kensington and Chelsea, 1895–1975), English economist, broadcaster, educator, 294

Stoll, Clarice Stasz (Clarice Stasz Stoll Orton, 20th c.), U.S. sociologist, writer, 150

Stone, Elizabeth (1946–), U.S. writer, 117, 118, 257

Stone, Judith (20th c.), U.S. science writer, columnist, humorist, 185, 260

Stone, Lucy (Lucy Stone Blackwell, 1818–1893), U.S. suffragist, abolitionist, women's rights activist, social reformer, editor, 85, 348

Storkey, Elaine (20th c.), English writer, activist, 30, 54

Stoughton, C.S.J., Judith (1918–1991), U.S. art historian, activist, writer, 13, 76, 191

Stout, Ruth (1884–1980), U.S. gardener, writer, 67, 107, **133**, **134**, 161, **313**, 346

Stowe, Harriet Elizabeth Beecher (1811–1896), U.S. novelist, abolitionist, social reformer, theologian, 9, 64, 111, 152, 154, 269, 297, 313, 337

Strasberg, Susan Elizabeth (1938–), U.S. actor, writer, 127, 142

Stratton-Porter, Gene (1863–1924), U.S. writer, 177

Stritch, Elaine (1925–), U.S. actor, TV personality, 228

Strobridge, Idah Meacham (1855–1932), U.S. writer, **80**

Strong, Anna Louise (1885–1970), U.S. journalist, writer, socialist, 25, 40, 156, 177, 270, 332

Stuart, Janet Erskine (1857–1914), English poet, letterwriter, 4, 244, 259

Sullivan, Anita T. (1942–), U.S. writer, 222

Sullivan, Faith Scheid Lengas (1933–), U.S. writer, 13, 56, 135, 195, 204, 229, 253, 312, 330, 354

Summerskill, Edith Clara (Baroness Summerskill of Kenwood, 1901–1980), English politician, gynecologist, activist, writer, 95, 224

Swanson, Gloria May Josephine (1899–1983), U.S. actor, producer, business executive, 25

Swetchine, Anne-Sophie (1782–1857), Russian-French writer, 24, 42, 61, 64, 136, 168, 197

Swift, Kate (1923–), U.S. nonsexist language pioneer, writer, editor, **181**, 182, 224

Szold, Henrietta (1860–1945), U.S. writer, Zionist leader, founder of Hadassah, 176

Szymusiak, Molyda (1965–), Cambodian writer, 158, 277

Taber, Gladys (Leonae Bagg, 1899–1980), U.S. archaeologist, writer, 123, 154, 351

Taeko, Tomioko (1935–), Japanese poet, 200

Talbot, Toby (1928–), U.S. translator, writer, 219

TallMountain, Mary Randle (1918–), Koyukan poet, 207

Talmadge, Betty Shingler (1924–), U.S. meat broker, cookbook author, 183

Tan, Amy (1952–), U.S. writer, 29, 84, 107, 201, 207, 218, 219, 254, 282, 283, 284, 345

Tannen, Deborah Frances (1945–), U.S. sociolinguist, writer, 66, 155, 308

Tarbell, Ida Minerva (1857–1944), U.S. journalist, writer, editor, 192

Tate, Claudia C. (1946–), U.S. writer, literature scholar, 22

Taubels, Amalie (19th c.), Czechoslovakian social reformer, 324

Taylor, Ann (1782–1866), English children's writer, 217

Taylor, Eleanor Rice (1920–), U.S. poet, 279

Taylor, Jane (1783–1824), English children's writer, 230

Taylor, Mildred D. (1943–), U.S. children's writer, 33, 150, 172

Teasdale, Sara (Sara Teasdale Filsinger, 1884–1933), U.S. poet, 28, 77, 115, 188, 189, 215, 220, 236, 245, 270, 285, 287, 294, 301, 302, 307, 321, 322

Teresa, Mother (Agnes Gonxha Bejaxhia, 1910–), Yugoslavian missionary in India, 77, 115, 127, 151, 194, 197, 200, 292, 297, 298

Teresa of Avila, Saint (Teresa de Cepeda y Ahumada, 1515–1582), Spanish mystic, poet, 64, 101, 126, 200, 306

Terry, Dame Ellen (Alice Ellen Terry Watts Kelly Carew, 1847–1928), English actor, 83

Tey, Josephine (Elizabeth Mackintosh, "Gordon Daviot," 1896–1952), Scottish playwright, novelist, 86, 153, 302, 328

Thatcher, Margaret Hilda Roberts (1925–), English politician, former prime minister, 182, 213, 232, 241, 262, 300, 309, 329

Thayer, Mary Dixon (1896–), U.S. poet, 148

Therese of Lisieux, Saint (1873–1897), French mystic, diarist, 84

Theroux, Phyllis (1939–), U.S. writer, 133

Thompson, Dorothy (Dorothy Thompson Bad Lewis Kopf, 1894–1961), U.S. journalist, writer, radio commentator, activist, 121, 188, 242

Thorndike, Dame Sybil (1882–1976), English actor, 222

Thornton, Naomi (1935–), U.S. actor, educator, 41, 308, 319

Thrale, Mrs. See Piozzi, Hester Lynch Salusbury Thrale

Thürmer-Rohr, Christina (20th c.), German psychologist, women's studies scholar, 104, 153, 216, 242

Toklas, Alice Babette (1877–1967), U.S.-born French writer, 331

Tomlin, Lily (1939–), U.S. comedian, actor, 317

Tóth, Judit (1936–), Hungarian poet, 27

Toth, Susan Erickson Allen (1940–), U.S. writer, 123, 208

Townsend, Sue (1946–), English writer, 142, 170, 196, 319, 326

Toynbee, Polly (1946–), English activist, 105

Tracy, Louise Treadwell (1896–1983), U.S. actor, educator, humanitarian, 278

Trapp, Maria Augusta (1905–1987), Austrian-born U.S. singer, 83, 143, 219, 256, 278, 317

Treichler, Paula Antonia (1943–), U.S. linguist, scholar, writer, 16, 182, 252

Treviño, Elizabeth Borton de (1904–), U.S. writer, journalist, 28, 34, 112, 297, 322, 337

Trollope, Frances Milton (1780–1863), English/U.S. novelist, 228, 304

Truitt, Anne (1921–), U.S. sculptor, 22, 283

Truman, Margaret (Mary Margaret Truman, 1924–), U.S. singer, writer, 177

Truth, Sojourner (Isabella Van Wagener Baumfree, 1797–1883), U.S. preacher, abolitionist, mystic, women's rights activist, social reformer, 52, 178, 346

Ts'ai Yen (3rd c.), Chinese poet, 278

Tsetsaeyva, Anna Ivanovna (Marina Cvetaeva, 1892–1941), Russian poet, 121

Tsui, Kitty (1952–), Hong Kong-born U.S. writer, 23, 142

Tubman, Harriet (Araminta Ross, 1823–1913), U.S. abolitionist, hero of Underground Railroad, Union spy, nurse, lecturer, 187

Tuchman, Barbara Wertheim (1912–1989), U.S. writer, historian, 34, 60, 149, 150, 152, 210, 330, 339

Tucker, Sophie (Sophie Tucker Abuza, 1884–1966), U.S. singer, comedian, entertainer, 275

Tuqan, Fadwa (1917–), Palestinian poet, 323

Turgeon, Charlotte Snyder (1912–), U.S. cookbook writer, editor, translator, 317

Turnbull, Agnes Sligh (1888–1982), U.S. writer, 86

Tyler, Anne (Anne Tyler Modarressi, 1941–), U.S. novelist, 5, 10, 25, 34, 51, 57, 78, 82, 93, 145, 179, 201, 210, 238, 240, 284, 322, 324, 326, 360, 361

Uchida, Yoshiko (1921–), Japanese-American writer, 164, 312

Ueland, Brenda (1891–1985), U.S. writer, 160, 161, 163, 317, 332, 353, 359

Ulmann, Doris (1882–1934), U.S. photographer, 113, 245

Ulrich, Mabel (1882–), U.S. physician, Red Cross official, 332

Underhill, Evelyn (1875–1941), English mystic, 7, 28, 41, 53, 133, 148, 168, 193, 199, 287

Undset, Sigrid (Sigrid Undset Starsvad, 1881–1949), Norwegian novelist, Nobel Prize winner, 191

Valenzuela, Luisa (1938–), Argentinian novelist, journalist, 308

Van Buren, Abigail (Pauline Friedman, "Dear Abby," 1918–), U.S. advice columnist, 8, 44, 62, 140

Vanderbilt, Amy (Amy Vanderbilt Knopf, 1908–1974), U.S. etiquette authority, 159, 202

Vanderbilt, Gloria (Gloria Morgan Vanderbilt Cooper, 1924–), U.S. artist, writer, designer, 219

Van Horne, Harriet (1920–), U.S. columnist, TV/radio personality, critic, 67, 318

Vermeulen, Martine (20th c.), U.S. potter, sculptor, 21

Victoria, Queen (Alexandrina, 1819–1901), Queen of England, 78, 158, 304

Viguers, Ruth Hill (1903–1971), children's librarian, writer, editor, 50

Villanueva, Alma Luz (1944–), Chicana poet, 31

Viorst, Judith (1931–), U.S. writer, poet, journalist, 203

Voigt, Ellen Bryant (1943–), U.S. poet, 336

von Ebner-Eschenbach, Baroness Marie (Countess Dubsky, 1830–1916), Austrian novelist, 7, 9, 64, 92, 98, 106, 108, 109, 111,

114, 128, 129, 140, 146, 148, 160, 161, 179, 197, 232, 244, 254, 259, **260**, 310, 313, **329**, 335, 345

von Magdeburg, Mechthild (1210–1294), German mystic, poet, 303

von Trapp, Maria. *See* Trapp, Maria Augusta

Vreeland, Diana Dalziel (1903–1989), French-born U.S. fashion editor/journalist, museum consultant, 99

Waddell, Helen Jane (1889–1965), Irish novelist, medieval scholar, translator, poet, 60, 81, 121, 162, 209, 329

Wakoski, Diane (Diane Wakoski Sherbell, 1937–), U.S. poet, 1, 113, 178, **247**, 328, 360

Waldrip, Mary H. (20th c.), U.S. journalist, 206, 286

Walker, Alice Malsenior (1944–), U.S. novelist, essayist, poet, 14, 15, 54, 97, 104, 110, 126, **138**, 139, 180, 189, 190, 217, 223, 235, 236, 260, 270, 276, 317, 318, 348

Walker, Lou Ann (1952–), U.S. writer, 74, 97

Walker, Margaret (Margaret Abigail Walker Alexander, 1915–), U.S. writer, poet, educator, 33, 35, **142**, **147**, 201, 213, 215, 266, 357

Wallace, Lila Bell Acheson (1889–1984), U.S. editor, publisher, 237

Walter, Mildred Pitts (1922–), U.S. children's writer, 52

Walters, Barbara (1931–), U.S. TV commentator, producer, writer, 41, 49, 140, 182, 310

Walum, Laurel Richardson (1938–), U.S. science professor, 290

Walworth, Dorothy Crowell (1900–1953), U.S. novelist, 264

Ward, Dame Barbara Mary (Baroness Jackson of Lodsworth, 1914–1981), English economist, journalist, educator, 3, 254, 260, 275

Warner, Anna Bartlett ("Amy Lothrop," 1820–1915), U.S. writer, poet, 52

Warner, Edith (1892–1951), U.S. tearoom owner, civic figure in Los Alamos, 220, 256, 339

Wasserstein, Wendy (1950–), U.S. playwright, screenwriter, 12, 288

Waters, Maxine (1938–), U.S. politician, 14

Webb, Beatrice Potter (1858–1943), English sociologist, economist, writer, socialist, reformer, 270

Webb, Mary Gladys Meredith (1881–1927), Scottish religious leader, writer, poet, 58, 81, 89, 97, 148, 154, 179, 200, 226, 240, 305

Webster, Jean (Alice Jane Chandler Webster, 1876–1916), U.S. writer, 66, 158, 247

Wedgwood, C.V. (Dame Cicely Veronica Wedgwood, 1910–), English historian, 22, 79, 84, 96, 148, **149**, **150**, 166, 240, 251

Weems, Renita (20th c.), U.S. writer, educator, member of clergy, 217

Weil, Lise (1950–), U.S. editor, translator, 103

Weil, Simone Adolphine (1909–1943), French philosopher, mystic, humanitarian, writer, revolutionary, scholar, 2, **21**, **24**, 54, 56, 60, 71, 72, 78, **82**, 95, 107, 109, 110, 113, 123, 127, 131, 139, 142, 148, **157**, 159, 162, 163, 168, **169**, 178, 185, 193, 213, 227, 240, 253, **255**, 263, 264, 268, 271, **272**, **275**, **276**, 277, **280**, **281**, 287, 289, 294, 300, 301, 305, 321, **322**, **333**, 335, 340, **341**

Weldon, Fay Birkinshaw (1931–), English novelist, playwright, critic, 122, 185, 329

Weller, Frances Ward (20th c.), U.S. children's writer, 129

Wells, Carolyn (Carolyn Wells Houghton, "Rowland Wright," 1869–1942), U.S. writer, humorist, poet, playwright, anthologist, 37, 204

Wells, Ida B. (Ida Bell Wells-Barnett, "Iola," 1862–1931), U.S. journalist, reformer, civil rights activist, publisher, 167

Welty, Eudora Alice (1909–), U.S. writer, 17, 35, 101, 113, 143, 180, **222**, 229, 240, 267, 268, 314, **325**, 351

West, Jessamyn (Mary Jessamyn West McPherson, 1902–1984), U.S. novelist, poet, librettist, screenwriter, 17, 19, 40, 41, 47, 49, 50, 79, 81, 111, 113, **118**, 122, 136, 162, 170, 173, 179, 183, 189, 190, 195, 203, 207, 223, 224, 237, 246, 300, 301, 304, 315, 317, 343, 359

West, Mae (1892–1980), U.S. actor, playwright, screenwriter, comedian, 109, **139**, 149, **208**, 288, 310, 319, 350

West, Dame Rebecca (Cicily Isabel Fairfield Maxwell Andrews, 1893–1983), Scottish/English novelist, journalist, essayist, critic, 20, 21, 30, 31, 45, 67, 87, 130,

156, 176, 207, 222, 240, 323, 337, 348, 360

Weston, Ruth (1911–1955), U.S. actor, 208

Wharton, Edith Newbold Jones (1862–1937), U.S. novelist, critic, 10, 21, 29, 57, 62, **66**, 72, 74, 87, 92, 98, 105, 170, 195, 215, 253, 279, 292, 301, 314, 321, 322, 332, 335, 361

Wheelwright, Jane Hollister (1905–), U.S. Jungian analyst, writer, 292

Whistling Elk, Agnes (20th c.), Cree medicine woman, 73, 175, 291, **292**

Whitehorn, Katharine (Katharine Elizabeth Whitehorn Lyall, 1928–), English journalist, writer, broadcaster, **42**, 60, 123, 148, 155, 162, 215, 219, 234, 238, 242, 243, 291, 353, 354

Whiteman, Roberta Hill (1947–), Oneida poet, 229

Whittlesey, Faith Ryan (1939–), U.S. lawyer, politician, 348

Whitton, Charlotte Elizabeth (1896–1975), Canadian politician, government official, journalist, 348

Widdemer, Margaret (1880–1978), U.S. poet, writer, 327

Wilcox, Ella Wheeler (1850–1919), U.S. writer, poet, journalist, **44**, 46, 106, 261, 320, 328

Wilder, Laura Ingalls (1867–1957), U.S. writer, 25, 82, 267, **293**, 297

Willard, Emma C. Hart (1787–1870), U.S. educator, textbook writer, poet, songwriter, 296

Willard, Frances Elizabeth Caroline (1839–1898), U.S. education philosopher, suffragist, women's rights activist, prohibitionist, philanthropist, 62

Willard, Nancy (1936–), U.S. poet, writer, 70, 253, 256

Willenz, June A. (1924–), U.S. writer, 340

Williams, Joy (1944–), U.S. writer, 144

Williams, Margery (Margery Williams Bianco, 1880–1944), English writer, 268

Williams, Sherley Anne (1944–), U.S. writer, 223

Willour, Margaret (20th c.), U.S., 11

Winfrey, Oprah (1953–), U.S. talk show host, actor, 146

Winn, Marie (1936–), U.S. writer, **318**

Winn, Mary Day (1888–1965), U.S. writer, 96, 171, 288

Winters, Shelley (Shirley Shrift, 1922–), U.S. actor, 3, 102, 244, 270

Wittig, Monique (1944–), French activist, writer, 56, 147, 180, 181, 182, 309, 314, 337, 351, 362

Woititz, Janet Geringer (1938–), U.S. therapist, writer, 283

Wolitzer, Hilma (1930–), U.S. writer, educator, 94, 322

Wollstonecraft, Mary (Mary Wollstonecraft Godwin, 1759–1797), English writer, women's rights worker, activist, 97, 111, 159, 197, 255

Wong, Nellie (1934–), Chinese-American poet, writer, 344, 349

Woo, Merle (20th c.), Chinese/Korean-U.S. writer, teacher, playwright, 343

Wood, Nancy (1936–), U.S. writer, photographer, 219

Wood, Natalie (Natasha Gurdin, 1938–1982), U.S. actor, 208

Woodhull, Victoria Claflin (1838–1927), U.S. writer, editor, reformer, 204

Woodruff, Julia Louisa Matilda Curtiss (1833–1909), U.S. writer, compiler, 2

Woolf, Virginia (Adeline Virginia Stephen Woolf, 1882–1941), English novelist, critic, essayist, 5, 16, 20, 23, 24, 25, 27, 83, 90, 102, **106, 122,** 139, 145, 158, 163, 172, 186, 187, 193, **214, 230,** 241, 249, 258, 262, 268, 277, 304, 327, 329, **350,** 353, 357, **360**

Wordsworth, Elizabeth (1840–1932), U.S. poet, 57

Wylie, Elinor (Elinor Morton Hoyt Wylie Benét, 1885–1928), U.S. poet, novelist, 191, 351

Yalow, Rosalyn Sussman (1921–), U.S. medical physicist, Nobel Prize winner, 185

Yamada, Mitsuye (1923–), Japanese-American teacher, poet, 212

Yamashita, Karen Tei (1951–), Japanese-American writer, poet, 38

Yamauchi, Wakako (1924–), Japanese-American writer, playwright, 236

Yezierska, Anzia (1885–1970), Russian-born U.S. novelist, 11, 28, 30, 81, 90, 98, 104, **164,** 166, 176, 178, 195, 198, 213, 221, 222, 226, 254, 267, 268

Yolen, Jane Hyatt (1939–), U.S. children's writer, editor, 106, 116

Young, Marguerite (1909–), U.S. journalist, novelist, poet, 166

Yourcenar, Marguerite (Marguerite de Crayencour, 1903–1987), French novelist, poet, critic, classical scholar, 35, 122, 328, 329, 356

Zeig, Sande (20th c.), French writer, scholar, 182

Zwinger, Ann Haymond (1925–), U.S. nature writer, 16, 169, 276, 327

Subject Index

Abortion. *See* Birth control,
    Pregnancy
Absence, 1
Absolutes, 1
Acceptance, 1
Accidents, 2
Accomplishment, 2
Acting, 2
Actions, 2–3
Actors, 3
Address, 3
Admiration, 3
Adolescence, 4
Adultery, 4
Adulthood, 4–5
Adventure, 5
Adversity, 5
Advertising, 5
Advice, 5–6
Africa, 6
African Americans. *See*
    Blacks
Afterlife, 7
Age, 7–11
AIDS, 11
Alarm, 11
Alcohol, 11–12
Alienation, 12
Alone, 12–13
Altruism, 13
Alzheimer's, 13
Ambition, 13
Ambivalence, 13
America. *See* United States
Ancestors, 14
Anchorage, 14
Androgyny, 14
Anger, 14–15
Animals, 15–16
Anonymous, 16
Answers, 16
Anticipation, 16
Anxiety, 16–17
Apathy, 17
Appearance, 17–18
Appearances, 18
Approval, 18
Architecture, 18

Aristocracy, 18
Arrogance, 19
Art, 19–21
Artists, 21–23
Asian Americans, 23–24
Association, 24
Athletes, 24
Attention, 24
Audience, 24
Authority, 24–25
Autobiography, 25
Autumn, 25
Awareness, 25–26
Awe. *See* Wonder
Babies, 27
Ballet, 27
Bath, 27
Beauty, 27–28
Beginning, 28
Behavior, 28–29
Belgium, 29
Belief, 29–30
Betrayal, 30
Bible, 30
Biography, 30
Biology, 30–31
Birds, 31
Birth, 31
Birth control, 31
Birthday, 32
Bitterness, 32
Blacks, 32–33
Blacks and whites, 33
Blame, 34
Body, 34
Books, 34–36
Borders, 36
Boredom, 36
Bores, 36–37
Borrowing, 37
Brain, 37
Brevity, 37
Bridge, 37
Broken heart, 37
Bullies, 38
Bureaucracy, 38
Business, 38
Busyness, 39

California, 40
Calm, 40
Calumny, 40
Candor, 40
Capitalism, 40–41
Career. *See* Work
Cats, 41
Causes, 41
Caution, 41
Celebrities, 41–42
Censorship, 42
Certainty, 42
Challenge, 42
Change, 42–43
Chaos, 44
Character, 44–45
Charisma, 45
Charity, 45
Charm, 45–46
Chauvinism, 46
Cheerfulness, 46
Childbirth, 46
Childhood, 47–48
Children, 48–51
China, 51
Chocolate, 51–52
Choice, 52
Christ, 52–53
Christianity, 53
Christmas, 53–54
Church, 54
Circus, 55
Cities, 55
Civilization, 55–56
Class, 56
Cleverness, 56–57
Clichés, 57
Clothes, 57
Codependence, 57
Coffee, 57–58
Cold, 58
Collecting, 58
Colors, 58–59
Comedians, 59
Comfort, 59
Committees, 59
Common sense, 60
Communication, 60

Communism, 60
Compassion, 60–61
Complacency, 61
Complaining, 61
Compromise, 61
Concealment, 61
Conceit, 61–62
Concepts, 62
Concern, 62
Conclusion, 62
Condemnation, 62
Confession, 62
Confidence, 62
Conflict, 62–63
Conformity, 63
Confusion, 63
Congress, 63
Connections, 63
Conscience, 63–64
Consolation, 64
Consumerism, 64
Contentment, 64
Control, 65
Controversy, 65
Conventionality, 65
Conventions, 65
Conversation, 65–67
Cooking, 67
Country, 67
Courage, 68
Creation, 68–69
Creativity, 69–70
Credulity, 70
Crime, 70
Crises, 70
Criticism, 70–71
Critics, 71
Cruelty, 71
Culture, 71–72
Curiosity, 72
Customs. *See* Behavior,
    Conventions, Traditions
Cynicism, 72
Dance, 73
Danger, 73
Darkness, 73–74
Data, 74
Daughters, 74

Dawn, 74
Deafness, 74
Death, 74–78
Debts, 78
Deception, 78
Decision, 78
Deeds, 78
Defeat, 78–79
Delay, 79
Democracy, 79
Depression, 79–80
Deprivation. *See* Privation
Desert, 80
Desertion, 80
Desire, 80–81
Despair, 81
Destiny, 81
Destroyers, 81
Detachment, 81–82
Determination, 82
Devil, 82
Diaries, 82–83
Dictators, 83
Diet, 83
Differences, 83
Dirt, 83
Disabilities, 84
Disappointment, 84
Disapproval, 84
Disaster, 84
Discipline, 84
Discontent, 84
Discouragement, 84–85
Discovery, 85
Discretion, 85
Discrimination, 85–86
Dishonesty, 86
Distrust, 86
Divinity, 86
Divorce, 86–87
Doctors, 87
Dogma, 87
Dogs, 87–88
Domination, 88
Doubt, 89
Dreams, 89–90
Dress, 90
Drink, 90–91
Drivers, 91
Drug abuse, 91
Dualism, 91
Dullness, 91–92
Duty, 92
Dying, 92–93
Earth, 94
Eating, 94–95
Eccentricity, 95
Eclecticism, 95
Economics, 95–96
Education, 96–98
Egocentrism, 98–99
Elections, 99
Elegance, 99

Elephants, 99
Emotions, 99–100
Empathy, 100
End, 101
Endurance, 101
Enemies, 101–102
Energy, 102
England, 102
English, the, 102–103
Enthusiasm, 103
Environment, 103–104
Envy, 104
Equality, 104–105
Eras, 105
Eroticism, 105
Error, 106
Erudition, 106
Essays, 106
Essence, 106–107
Estrangement, 107
Eternity, 107
Ethics, 107
Etiquette, 107–108
Euphemisms, 108
Europe, 108
Euthanasia, 108
Evasion, 108
Evil, 108–109
Excellence, 109
Exceptions, 109
Excess, 109–110
Expectations, 110
Expedience, 110
Experience, 110–111
Explanations, 111
Extravagance, 111
Extremism, 111
Eyes, 112
Face, 113
Facts, 113
Failure, 114
Faith, 114–115
Faithfulness, 115
Fame, 115–116
Familiarity, 116
Family, 116–118
Fanaticism, 118
Fantasy, 118
Farewells, 118–119
Farmers, 119
Fashion, 119
Fastidiousness, 119
Fate, 119
Father, 119–120
Fatigue, 120
Fear, 120–121
Feelings, 121
Fiction, 122
Fictional characters,
    122–123
Films, 123
Fire, 123
Fishing, 123

Flattery, 123–124
Flaws, 124
Flirtation, 124
Flowers, 124–125
Flying, 125
Food, 125–126
Fools, 126–127
Force, 127
Foresight, 127
Forgetting, 127
Forgiveness, 127–128
France, 128
Freedom, 128–129
Free will, 129
Friendliness, 129
Friendship, 129–131
Frugality, 131
Function, 131
Funerals, 131
Futility, 131
Future, 131–132
Gaiety, 133
Gardening, 133
Gardens, 134
Gay, 134–135
Gender, 135
Generations, 135
Generosity, 135
Genius, 136
Ghetto, 136
Giving, 136–137
Gladness, 137
Glamour, 137
Goals, 137
God, 137–139
Gold, 139
Good, 139
Goodness, 139–140
Gorillas, 140
Gossip, 140
Government, 140–142
Grace, 142
Graciousness, 142
Grandparents, 142
Gratitude, 143
Greed, 143
Grief, 143–144
Growth, 144
Guests, 144
Guilt, 144
Habit, 145
Hair, 145
Happiness, 145–146
Hate, 146–147
Health, 147
Heart, 147–148
Heresy, 148
Heroes, 148–149
Hesitation, 149
Hiding, 149
Historians, 149
History, 149–150
Hobbies, 150

Holiday. *See* Vacation
Holiness, 150–151
Holland, 151
Hollywood, 151
Holocaust, 151
Home, 151–152
Homelessness, 152
Honesty, 152
Honor, 152
Hope, 152–153
Horses, 153
Hospital, 153
Houses, 154
Housework, 154–155
Human differences,
    155–156
Human family, 156
Human nature, 157
Humility, 157
Humor, 157–158
Hunger, 158–159
Husband, 159
Hypocrisy, 159
Icebergs, 160
Idealism, 160
Ideas, 160–161
Identity, 161
Idleness, 161
Ignorance, 161–162
Illness, 162–163
Illusion, 163
Images, 163
Imagination, 163
Immigrants, 164
Immortality, 164–165
Impatience, 165
Impermanence, 165
Impossible, 165
Inadequacy, 165
Indecision, 165
Independence, 165
India, 165
Indifference, 165–166
Indignation, 166
Individuality, 166
Indolence, 166
Ineptitude, 167
Infidelity, 167
Influence, 167
Information, 167
Injustice, 167–168
Inner life, 168
Innocence, 168–169
Innovation, 169
Insanity. *See* Mental illness
Insects, 169
Insensitivity, 169
Insight. *See* Cleverness,
    Intuition, Perception,
    Understanding
Insomnia, 169–170
Inspiration, 170
Instinct, 170

Institutions, 170
Intellectuals, 170
Intelligence, 170–171
Intensity, 171
Interdependence, 171
Interesting, 171
Interference, 171–172
Interruption, 172
Intimacy, 172
Intolerance, 172
Introversion, 172
Intuition, 172–173
Invention, 173
Iowa, 173
Ireland, 173
Irony, 173
Irrationality, 173
Israel, 173
Italy, 174
Japan, 175
Jealousy, 175
Jews, 175–176
Journalism, 176–177
Journeys, 177
Joy, 177–178
Judgment, 178
Justice, 178
Kindness, 179
Knowledge, 179
Labor, 180
Ladies, 180
Land, 180
Language, 180–182
Lateness, 183
Laughter, 183
Law, 183–184
Lawyers, 184
Leaders, 184–185
Learning, 185
Legends, 185–186
Leisure, 186
Lesbians, 186–187
Letters, 187
Liberation, 187
Liberty, 187–188
Life, 188–192
Lifestyle, 192
Limitations, 192
Listening, 192
Literature, 192–193
Litigation, 193
Logic, 193
London, 193
Loneliness, 194
Longing, 194
Los Angeles, 195
Loss, 195
Love, 195–200
Lovers, 200
Loyalty, 200
Luck, 201
Luxury, 201
Lying, 201

Magazines, 202
Magic, 202
Manners, 202
Marriage, 202–204
Marxism, 204–205
Materialism, 205
Mathematics, 205
Means, 205
Medication, 205
Mediocrity, 205–206
Meetings, 206
Melancholy, 206
Memory, 206–208
Men, 208
Mental illness, 208
Mercy, 209
Middle age, 209
Middle class, 209–210
Militarism, 210
Mind, 210–211
Mindset, 211
Minorities, 211–212
Miracles, 212
Misanthropy, 212
Mischief, 212
Miserliness, 212
Misery, 212–213
Mistakes, 213
Moderation, 213
Monday, 213
Money, 213–215
Monotony, 215
Moon, 215
Morality, 215–216
Morning, 216–217
Mother, 217–219
Motives, 219
Mountains, 219–220
Mourning, 220
Movements, 220–221
Music, 221–223
Mystery, 223
Mysticism, 223
Myth, 223
Nagging, 224
Naïveté. See Credulity,
    Innocence
Names, 224
Naming, 224
Native Americans, 225–226
"Natural," 226
Nature, 226–227
Necessity, 227
Need, 228
Netherlands, the. See
    Holland
Newness, 228
Newspapers. See Journalism
New York, 228
Night, 229
Normalcy, 229
Nostalgia, 229
Novels, 229–230

Nuclear weapons, 230
Nudists, 230
Numbers. See Quantity
Nursery rhymes, 230–231
Nurses, 231
Objectivity, 232
Obvious, 232
Offensiveness, 232
Opportunities, 232
Opposition, 232
Oppression, 233–234
Optimism, 234
Order, 234
Ordinariness, 234
Orphans, 234–235
Outrage, 235
Outsiders, 235
Oysters, 235
Pacifism, 236
Pain, 236–237
Painting, 237
Paradox, 237
Parenting, 237
Parents, 237–239
Paris, 239
Parties, 239
Parting, 239–240
Passion, 240
Past, 240–241
Pathos, 241
Patience, 241
Patriotism, 241–242
Patronizing, 242
Peace, 242–243
Peace and love, 243
Perception, 243
Perfectionism, 243
Performance, 243–244
Perseverance, 244
Personality, 244
Pessimism, 244
Philanthropy, 244
Philosophy, 244–245
Phobias, 245
Photography, 245–246
Pity, 246
Places, 246
Plagiarism, 246
Planets, 246
Plants, 246–247
Pleasure, 247
Poetry, 247–249
Poets, 249–250
Police, 250
Politeness, 250
Political parties, 250
Politicians, 250–251
Politics, 251–252
Polls, 252
Popularity, 252
Pornography, 252
Possessions, 252–253
Pouting, 253

Poverty, 253–354
Power, 254–255
Powerlessness, 255
Praise, 255
Prayer, 255–256
Precocity, 256
Prefaces, 256
Pregnancy, 256–257
Prejudice, 257
Preparedness, 257–258
Present, 258
Pride, 258–259
Principles, 259
Prison, 259
Privacy, 259
Privation, 259
Privilege, 260
Problems, 260
Profit, 260
Progress, 260
Prosperity, 260
Prostitution, 261
Protest, 261
Prudence. See Caution,
    Common sense
Psychiatry, 261
Public, the, 261–262
Publicity, 262
Public opinion, 262
Publishing, 262
Purity, 263
Purpose, 263
Quantity, 264
Quarreling, 264
Questions, 264–265
Quilts, 265
Quotations, 265
Race, 266
Racism, 266–267
Rain, 267
Rape, 267
Rationality, 267
Reading, 267–268
Real, 268
Reality, 268–269
Reason, 269
Receiving, 269
Refugees, 269
Refusal, 269
Regret, 269
Rejection, 269–270
Relationships, 270
Relatives. See Family
Religion, 270–272
Remedies, 272
Remembrance, 272
Remorse, 272
Renunciation, 272
Reputation, 272
Research, 272
Resentment, 273
Resignation, 273
Respect, 273

Responsibility, 273
Restlessness, 273
Retirement, 273–274
Reunions, 274
Revenge, 274
Reverie, 274
Revolution, 274–275
Reward, 275
Rich, 275
Rights, 275–276
Risk, 276
Ritual, 276
Rivers, 276–277
Rome, 277
Rooms, 277
Roots, 277–278
Rudeness, 278
Rumor, 278
Russia, 278
Sacred, 279
Sacrifice, 279
Sadness. See Sorrow,
     Unhappiness
Safety. See Security
Saints, 279–280
Sanity, 280
Satire, 280
School, 280
Science, 280–281
Sculpture, 281
Sea, 281–282
Search, 282
Seasons. See Autumn,
     Spring, Summer, Winter
Secrets, 282
Security, 282–283
Seduction, 283
Self, 283–284
Self-actualization, 284
Self-destruction, 284
Self-determination, 284–285
Self-esteem, 285
Self-importance, 286
Self-indulgence, 286
Selfishness, 286
Self-knowledge, 286–287
Self-pity, 287
Self-sufficiency, 287
Senses, 287
Sensitivity, 287
Sentimentality, 287–288
Serenity. See Calm,
     Comfort, Contentment,
     Peace, Silence
Seriousness, 288
Service, 288
Sex, 288–290

Sexism, 290–291
Sex roles, 291
Shadows, 291
Shamans, 291–292
Shape, 292
Sharing, 292
Shocking, 292
Silence, 292–293
Simplicity, 293
Sin, 293–294
Sincerity, 294
Singing, 294
Single, 294–295
Sisters, 295
Size, 295
Sky, 295–296
Slavery, 296
Sleep, 296–297
Slippery slope, 297
Small things, 297–298
Smell, 298
Smile, 298
Snow, 298–299
Sobriety, 299
Social change, 299–300
Society, 300
Solitude, 300–301
Song, 301
Sons, 301
Sorrow, 301–302
Soul, 303
South, the, 303
Space, 303
Specialists, 304
Speculation, 304
Speech, 304–305
Spirituality, 305–306
Sports, 306
Spring, 306–307
Stars, 307
Status quo, 307
Stealth, 307
Stereotypes, 307–308
Stories, 308
Storytellers, 309
Strangers, 309
Stubbornness, 309
Style, 309
Success, 309–311
Suffering, 311
Suffrage, 311
Suicide, 311–312
Summer, 312
Sun, 312
Sunday, 312
Sunset, 312–313
Superiority, 313

Superstition, 313
Support, 313
Surplus, 313–314
Survival, 314
Symbols, 314
Sympathy, 314
Taboos, 315
Tact, 315
Talent, 315–316
Talking, 316
Taste, 316–317
Taxes, 317
Tea, 317
Teaching, 317
Tears, 317
Technology, 317
Teenagers. See Adolescence,
     Children, Youth
Telephone, 318
Television, 318–319
Temperament, 319
Temptation, 319
Tennis, 319
Texas, 319
Thanksgiving, 319
Theater, 319–320
Theft, 320
Theology, 320
Theories, 320
"They," 320
Things. See Possessions,
     Small things
Thinking, 320–321
Thoughts, 321
Time, 321–323
Timeliness, 324
Tiredness. See Fatigue
Titles, 324
Togetherness, 324
Tolerance, 324
Tomorrow, 324
Torah, the. See Bible
Traditions, 324
Tragedy, 324–325
Travel, 325–326
Treachery, 327
Trees, 327
Trends, 327
Trouble, 327–328
Trust, 328
Truth, 328–330
Tyranny, 330
Uncles, 331
Unconscious, 331
Understanding, 331
Unexpected, 331–332
Unhappiness, 332

Uniqueness, 332
United States, 332–333
Universal, 333
Universe, 333
Unknown, 333
Unselfishness, 333
Uselessness, 334
Utility, 334
Vacation, 335
Values, 335
Vanity, 335
Variety, 336
Vengeance, 336
Venice, 336
Vermont, 336
Verse, 336
Vicariousness, 336
Vice, 336
Villains, 336–337
Violence, 337
Virtue, 337
Visions, 337–338
Vulnerability, 338
Walking, 339
Walls, 339
War, 339–341
Washington, D.C., 341–342
Weakness, 342
Wealth, 342
Weather, 342–343
Weddings, 343
Weight, 343
West, the, 343
Whites, 343–344
Wholeness, 344
Why, 344
Wife, 344–345
Wilderness, 345
Wildlife, 345
Wind, 345
Wine, 345
Winning, 345–346
Winter, 346
Wisdom. See Common
     sense, Knowledge, Wit
Wit, 346
Wolves, 346
Women, 346–349
Women and men, 349–350
Wonder, 351
Words, 351–353
Work, 353–354
Worry, 354
Writers, 354–358
Writing, 358–362
Youth, 363–364